NATURAL HISTORY

AND

ANTIQUITIES OF SELBORNE.

VIEW OF SELBORNE FROM THE HANGER.

NATURAL HISTORY

ANTIQUITIES OF SELBORNE

BY GILBERT WHITE

WITH

London
MACMILLAN AND CO.
AND NEW YORK
1887

NATURAL HISTORY

AND

ANTIQUITIES OF SELBORNE

By GILBERT WHITE

With Notes by FRANK BUCKLAND

A Chapter on Antiquities by LORD SELBORNE

And New Letters

ILLUSTRATED BY P. H. DELAMOTTE

NEW EDITION

London

MACMILLAN AND CO

AND NEW YORK

1887

RICHARD CLAY AND SONS,
LONDON AND BUNGAY.

PREFACE.

MESSRS. MACMILLAN having requested me to edit White's "Selborne," I accepted the task, feeling assured that the handsome Edition of the works of the founder and pioneer of English Practical Natural History now presented to the public would be the means of attracting many of the present generation—both young and old—to the observation of the living works of the great Creator. They will, moreover, help to counteract the growth of doubt, infidelity, and atheism, which —though regarded at their real worth by a reasoning public —must become bitter weeds in future, of no assistance to science, and sure promoters of a dangerous materialism.

Gilbert White's writings are coloured throughout with that right tone of feeling which recognises the work of a great Creator in everything, both large and small. Gilbert White may, in fact, be said to have planted the acorn which, forty years after his death, grew into a great oak in the form of the Bridgewater Treatises [1] on the "𝔓𝔬𝔴𝔢𝔯, 𝔚𝔦𝔰𝔡𝔬𝔪, 𝔞𝔫𝔡 𝔊𝔬𝔬𝔡𝔫𝔢𝔰𝔰 𝔬𝔣 𝔊𝔬𝔡, 𝔞𝔰 𝔪𝔞𝔫𝔦𝔣𝔢𝔰𝔱𝔢𝔡 𝔦𝔫 𝔱𝔥𝔢 𝔆𝔯𝔢𝔞𝔱𝔦𝔬𝔫."

---

[1] I beg to recommend the readers of White to peruse these Bridgewater Treatises, especially Kirby on the History, Habits and Instinct of Anima's; Dr. Roget on Animal and Vegetable Physiology; Sir Charles Bell on the Hand, and the Rev. Dr. Buckland on Geology and Mineralogy.

In White's time the Bridgewater Treatises were represented
by the writings of Dr. Derham, author of "Physico-Theology,"[1]
the fifth edition of which was published in 1720, the year
White was born.

I have discovered that White had not only deeply studied
Derham and also Ray,[2] but in many cases he illustrates
Derham's arguments by his own observations.

White was a true student of all created things—lynx-eyed,
quick to observe accurately, and patient to interpret the
meaning of facts brought under his notice. The same facts
that White saw and recorded are still going on around us at the
present time. The birds come and go at the same dates as did
their ancestors a century ago. The rabbits, hedgehogs, rats,
bats, snakes, mice, &c., still keep up their old, old customs
unaltered and unchanged. White is the teacher who has shown
four generations how and what to observe—in fact, he taught
them the "Art of Observation." For the above reason,
therefore, White's "Selborne" has held its own as a standard
book for a hundred years, and will probably be as fresh as
ever a hundred years hence.

We live in a beautiful and happy world; the waters teem
with life, the earth is populated by creatures innumerable;
some live on the mountains, some on the plains, some in the
forest, some in the desert; to observe the habits of all living

---

[1] "Physico-Theology; or, A Demonstration of the Being and Attributes of
God—from His Works of Creation; being the Substance of Sixteen Sermons
preached in St. Mary-le-Bow Church, London, at the Honourable Mr. Boyle's
Lectures, in the years 1711 and 1712. With Large Notes and many Curious
Observations." By W. Derham, Canon of Windsor, Rector of Upminster in
Essex, and F.R.S. I have four editions of this work, 1720, 1727, 1732, and
1768. This book is well worthy of a modern edition.

[2] "The Wisdom of God Manifested in the Works of the Creation; in Two
Parts," and "Discourses on Physico-Theology, 1713." By John Ray, late
Fellow of the Royal Society, 1743.

things that came under his notice was White's delight; and
rest assured that if we—like White—love animals (commonly
called dumb because we cannot understand their language), we
shall never experience the feeling of solitude.

It has been more or less the custom to look upon White
as purely an ornithologist; but the attentive reader will find
that he touches upon almost every branch of Natural History.
The plan of this publication allowed me only a certain
amount of space for my notes and observations. I therefore
determined not to write a running commentary, but to give
anecdotes and observations which have principally come under
. my own notice, and which bear more or less on the subjects
mentioned by White. Students of ornithology have now at
their command so many museums, as well as excellent books
on birds, that those who are fond of birds have every
facility for learning all that is known about them up to the
present time.

All I beg on behalf of the wild birds is not to shoot them;
leave the gun at home, and take the opera-glasses and watch
their habits.

Foremost among the works on ornithology is the magnificent
work on "THE BIRDS OF GREAT BRITAIN," by John Gould,
F.R.S. The book that I would recommend as the best and
least expensive handbook for bird-fanciers and those who intend
to begin the study of English wild and cage birds, is Bechstein's
"Cage and Chamber Birds." [1]

In my Notes will be found information about birds, not

---

[1] Bell and Sons, York Street, Covent Garden. Professor Newton is now
bringing out a new edition of Yarrell's "British Birds," Van Voorst, Pater-
noster Row. The Rev. F. O. Morris has published works on British Birds,
Nests and Eggs of Birds, &c., Bickers and Bush, Leicester Square. Nor
must I neglect to recommend the Rev. J. G. Wood's admirable work,
"Illustrated Natural History," Routledge.

copied from any books, but from the experiences of Mr. Davy, for thirty years a practical bird-catcher and dealer.

For the last ten years—from its commencement—I have been editor of the PRACTICAL NATURAL HISTORY and FISHERY columns of *Land and Water*, and have freely quoted from it in this book. I am always anxious to diffuse, by means of this publication, information on the most important national question of the increase of the food of the people by scientific cultivation of the waters, as well as on those subjects of general natural history which White knew and loved so well.

In *Land and Water*, vols. i. and ii., 1866, Mr. Groom Napier published a valuable series of articles on the "Birds Breeding in Great Britain." By his permission I have quoted this gentleman's descriptions of the Nests and Eggs of many birds mentioned by White. I am also under obligations to Colonel Hardy, R.A.; the late Mr. Menzies, of Windsor Park; and to Mr. A. D. Bartlett, of the Zoological Gardens, for assistance; and to my friend, Professor Delamotte, for the pains he has taken in the illustrations for this volume.

In the spring of the year, the London season begins, and large numbers of our fellow-creatures migrate to London. In the fall of the year, these same individuals migrate again from London; this is exactly what happens with the birds, and it would, I am sure, give much pleasure to many of the public if the local, daily, and weekly press throughout the country would take the hint I now give them and record, not only the arrivals and the departures of Lords and Ladies, M.P.'s, and the great people of this our favoured land, but also the arrivals and departures of the birds, who, in most cases, travel much further than we human beings either do or can. If this were done, a new world of pleasurable observation would be opened to thousands.

I trust, moreover, that this book may induce my fellow-countrymen to learn that in this beautiful world there are many other creatures besides themselves, all living and acting with the utmost independence of human aid or advice. They do not consult mankind as to how, when, or where they shall build their nests or make their holes, or how they shall get their daily rations; they do not ask us leave to come, nor do they ask leave to go. They know their own business, and obey what we, for want of a better word, call "instinct," the mysteries of which remain as yet unsolved by human intelligence.

I trust that White's observations may have the effect of showing country proprietors—especially the owners of parks, woodlands, &c.—that they have on their properties a class of tenants to whose existence and good services their attention has possibly never been previously directed. They would do well to stop the destructive hand of the gamekeepers, who are gradually exterminating all our indigenous fauna, for want of knowledge of the way in which the forces of nature are balanced, and the law of "eat and be eaten" carried out. White's "Selborne" again will show clergymen that they have many parishioners inhabiting the woodlands, hedges, and fields, whose welfare they would do well not to neglect. There is hardly a parish in England or Wales where the clergyman has not opportunities more or less favourable for writing a local "White's Selborne," taking White's method of observing and recording as a model for his note-book.

I feel assured that the education of children, both in town and country, might greatly be forwarded if they were taught in the schools what and how to observe. Especially in the country should they be encouraged to make collections of common objects, animal, vegetable, and mineral. They should also be taught to recognise indigenous British birds and beasts, and to send in notes as to what they have observed of their habits. Such studies tend to sharpen the natural faculties, while they humanize the intellect.

The publishers desire in this place to acknowledge the kindness of Lord Selborne in adding some valuable Notes to the chapter on the Antiquities of Selborne, and allowing to be made for its illustration drawings of some curiosities found on his estate.

To Mr. John Webster Edgehill, Culter, Aberdeen, they are indebted, for his courtesy in placing at their disposal a few original letters of Gilbert White never before published, and now printed in the following pages.

It has only to be added, that the whole of the Engravings have been planned and executed under the able superintendence of the artist, Mr. Philip H. Delamotte.

FRANK BUCKLAND.

37, ALBANY STREET, REGENT'S PARK,
    December 17, 1880.

NEW LETTERS.

THE INVITATION : TO SAMUEL BARKER.

NE percuncteris, fundus meus, optime Quincti,
Arvo pascat herum, an baccis opulentet olivæ,
Pomisne et pratis, an amictâ vitibus ulmo :
Scribetur tibi forma loquaciter, et situs agri.

See, Selborne spreads her boldest beauties round,
The vary'd valley, and the mountain-ground·
Wildly majestic : what is all the pride
Of flats, with loads of ornament supply'd ?
Unpleasing, tasteless, impotent expence,
Compar'd with Nature's rude magnificence.
Oft on some evening, sunny, soft, and still,
The Muse shall hand thee to the beech-grown hill,
To spend in tea the cool, refreshful hour,
Where nods in air the pensile, nest-like bower :
Or where the Hermit hangs his straw-clad cell,
Emerging gently from the leafy dell :
Romantic spot ! from whence in prospect lies
Whate'er of landscape charms our feasting eyes ;
The pointed spire, the hall, the pasture-plain,
The russet fallow, and the golden grain ;
The breezy lake that sheds a gleaming light,
'Til all the fading picture fails the sight.

Each to his task : all different ways retire ;
Cull the dry stick ; call forth the seeds of fire ;
Deep fix the nettle's props, a forky row ;
Or give with fanning hat one breeze to blow.
　　Whence is this taste, the furnish'd hall forgot,
To feast in gardens, or th' unhandy grot ?
Or novelty with some new charms surprises ;
Or from our very shifts some joy arises.
　　Hark, while below the village bells ring round,
Echo, sweet Nymph, returns the soften'd sound :
But if gusts rise, the rushing forests roar,
Like the tide tumbling on the pebbly shore.
　　Adown the vale, in lone sequester'd nook,
Where skirting woods imbrown the dimpling brook,
The ruin'd Abbey lies : here wont to dwell (α)
The lazy monk within his cloister'd cell ;
While papal darkness brooded o'er the land ;
Ere Reformation made her glorious stand :
Still oft at eve belated shepherd-swains
See the cowl'd spectre skim the folded plains.
　　To the high Temple would my stranger go, (β)
Whose mountain-brow commands the groves below ?
In Jewry first this order found a name,
When madding Croisades set the world in flame ;
When western climes, urg'd on by Pope and priest,
Pour'd forth their millions o'er the delug'd east :
Luxurious Knights, ill suited to defy
To mortal fight Turcestan chivalry.
　　Nor be the Parsonage by the Muse forgot :
The partial bard admires his native spot ;
Smit with its beauties lov'd, as yet a child,
Unconscious why, its 'scapes grotesque and wild :
High on a mound th' exalted gardens stand ;
Beneath, deep valleys scoop'd by Nature's hand !
　　Now climb the steep, drop now your eye below,
Where round the verdurous village orchards blow ;
There, like a picture, lies my lowly seat
A rural, shelter'd, unobserv'd retreat.

(α.) The ruins of a Priory founded by Peter de Rupibus, Bishop of Winton.
(β.) The remains of a supposed lodge belonging to the Knights Templars.

Me, far above the rest, Selbornian scenes,
The pendent forest, and the mountain-greens,
Strike with delight : . . . there spreads the distant view
That gradual fades, 'til sunk in misty blue :
Here Nature hangs her slopy woods to sight,
Rills purl between, and dart a wavy light.
    When deep'ning shades obscure the face of day,
To yonder bench leaf-shelter'd let us stray,
To hear the drowzy dor come brushing by
With buzzing wing ; or the field-cricket cry ;
To see the feeding bat glance thro' the wood ;
Or catch the distant falling of the flood :
While high in air, and poised upon his wings
Unseen, the soft enamour'd wood-lark sings : (γ)
These, Nature's works, the curious mind employ,
Inspire a soothing, melancholy joy :
As fancy warms a pleasing kind of pain
Steals o'er the cheek, and thrills the creeping vein !
    Each rural sight, each sound, each smell combine ;
The tinkling sheep-bell, or the breath of kine ;
The new-mown hay that scents the swelling breeze,
Or cottage-chimney smoking thro' the trees.
    The chilling night-dews fall : . . . . away, retire,
What time the glow-worm lights her amorous fire. (δ)

                                    Selborne : *Nov :* 3 : 1774.

DEAR SAM,
    When I sat down to write to you in verse, my whole
design was to shew you at once how easy a thing it might be
with a little care for a Nephew to excell his Uncle in the business
of versification : but as you have fully answered that intent by
your late excellent lines ; you must for the future excuse my
replying in the same way, and make some allowance for the
difference of our ages.

(γ.) In hot summer nights woodlarks soar to a prodigious height, and hang
singing in the air.
    (δ.) The light of the glow-worm is a signal to her paramour, a slender
dusky scarab.

However, when at any time you find y^r muse propitious, I shall always rejoice to see a copy of y^r performance; and shall be ready to commend; and what is more rare, yet more sincere, even to object and criticize where there is occasion.

A little turn for English poetry is no doubt a pretty accomplishment for a young Gent: and will not only enable him the better to read and relish our best poets; but will, like dancing to the body, have an happy influence even on his prose compositions. Our best poets have been our best prose-writers: of this assertion Dryden and Pope are notorious instances. It would be in vain to think of saying much here on the art of versification: instead of the narrow limits of a letter such a subject would require a large volume. However, I may say in few words, that the way to excell is to copy only from our best writers. The great grace of poetry consists in a perpetual variation of y^r *cadences*: if possible no two lines following ought to have their pause at the same foot. Another beauty should not be passed over, and that is the use of throwing the sense and pause into the third line, which adds a dignity and freedom to y^r expressions. Dryden introduced this practice, and carryed it to great perfection: but his successor Pope, by his over exactness, corrected away that noble liberty, and almost reduced every sentence within the narrow bounds of a couplet. Alliteration, or the art of introducing words beginning with the same letter in the same or following line, has also a fine effect when managed with discretion. Dryden and Pope practised this art with wonderful success. As, for example, where you say "The polish'd beetle," . . the epithet "burnish'd" would be better for the reason above. But then you must avoid affectation in this case, and let the alliteration slide-in as it were without design: and this secret will make your lines appear bold and nervous.

There are also in poetry allusions, similes, and a thousand nameless graces, the efficacy of which nothing can make you sensible of but the careful reading of our best poets, and a nice and judicious application of their beauties. I need not add that you should be careful to seem not to take any pains about y^r rhimes; they should fall-in as it were of themselves. Our old poets laboured as much formerly to lug-in two chiming words, as a butcher does to drag an ox to be slaughtered: but Mr. Pope has set such a pattern of ease in that way, that few composers now are faulty in the business of rhiming. When I have the pleasure of meeting you we will talk over these and many other

matters too copious for an Epistle. I had like to have forgotten
to add that Jack copied your verses, and sent them to y^r Uncle
John who commended them much : you will be pleased to be
commended by one that is the best performer and the best critic
in that way that I know. With respects to your father and
mother and all the family,

I remain Y^r affect : Uncle, GIL : WHITE.

Nanny White mends apace : she is still at Newton.

(To MRS. BARKER.)

Selborne : Dec : 25 : 78.

DEAR SISTER,

My Nep: Edm^d who is now at Newton, brings a most
sad, account of his mother, whose state of health is very
deplorable, and her infirmities and sufferings very great. As
to our poor brother in Lancashire, I have not heard from
him for some time : the last account was but bad.

Next week we expect at this place a great *navigator*, or rather
navigatress, who within these 20 months has sailed 20,000 miles.
The person alluded to is Miss Shutter, Mrs. Etty's niece, who
set out for Madras in March, 1777 ; and returning to Europe
this autumn in the *Carnatic* India-man, was taken by her own
countrymen near the coast of France and carried to the Downs,
and landed at Deal. This Lady appears in great splendor ; and
is, it is supposed, to be married to a Gent : now on the seas in
his way from India. Bad fevers and sore throats obtain much
in these parts, and many children die. A person at Harkley
buryed three, his whole stock, in one grave last Tuesday. When
I was down at Ringmer I found that district was sickly.
Mrs. Sn : wrote herself some time since, and did not complain of
any particular infirmities. My great parlor turns out a fine
warm winter-room, and affords a pleasant equal warmth. In
blustering weather the chimney smokes a little 'til the shaft
becomes hot. The chief fault that I find is the strong echo,
which, when many people are talking, makes confusion to my
poor dull ears. Your money is disposed of among poor neighbours. I have no doubt but that y^r son will turn out a valuable

young man; and will be far from being injured by a public education. "Omnes omnia bona dicere, et laudare fortunas tuas, qui filium haberes tali ingenio præditum." With respects and the good wishes of the season I remain

Your affect: brother,

GIL: WHITE.

DEAR NIECE ANNE,

After I had experienced the advantage of two agreeable young house-keepers, I was much at a loss when they left me; and have nobody to make whipp'd syllabubs, and grace the upper end of my table. Molly and her father came again, and stayed near a month, during which we made much use of my great room: but they also have left me some time. Whether they carryed-off any *Ladies Traces* I cannot recollect: but it is easy to distinguish them at this season: for soon after they are out of bloom they throw-out *radical leaves*, which abide all the winter. The plant is rare; but happens to abound in the *Long Lithe*, and will be enumerated in the list of more rare plants about Selborne. I wish we could say we had y⁰ *Parnasia*: I have sowed seeds in our bogs several times, but to no purpose. Please to let me know how many inches of rain fell in the late wet fit, which lasted about 5 weeks. The springs from being very low mounted-up to a vast rate; and our *lavants* at Faringdon began to appear last week. My Bar^r is this evening at $30 - 3 - 10_{34}$, the air thick, and warm, and still. Hepaticas and winter-aconites blossom; and *Helleborus fœtidus* in the High-wood, another rare plant. The clouds are all gone; and we may expect frost.

We have here this winter a weekly concert consisting of a first and second fiddle, two repianos, a bassoon, an haut-boy, a violincello, and a German-flute; to the great annoyance of the neighbouring pigs, which complain that their slumbers are interrupted, and their teeth set on edge.

(To Miss Anne Barker.)

Selborne : *Feb :* 5th : 1785.

Dear Niece,

I was just thinking to write to somebody in your family, when your agreeable letter came in.

As the late frost was attended with some unusual circumstances, your father, I trust, will not be displeased to hear the particulars. The first week in Decr was very wet, with the Barom^r very low. On the 7th with the Bar : at 28 – 5 – 10 : there came on a vast snow, which continued all that day and the next, and most part of the following night; so that by the morning of the 9th the works of men were quite overwhelmed, the lanes filled so as to be rendered impassable, and the ground covered 12 or 14 inches where there was no drifting. In the evening of the 9th the air began to be so very sharp that we thought it would be curious to attend to

RAIN AT SELBORNE IN 1784.		
	inc	h
Jan :	— 3	18
Feb :	— 0	77
Mar :	— 3	82
Apr :	— 3	92
May	— 1	52
June	— 3	65
July	— 2	40
Aug :	— 3	88
Sept^r	— 2	51
Oct^r	— 0	39
Nov^r	— 4	70
Dec	— 3	6
Total	33	80

the motions of a Therm^r. We therefore hung out two, one made by Martin and one by Dolland, which soon began to shew us what we were to expect. For by 10 o'clock they fell to 21 :—and at 11^h : to 4, when we went to bed. On the 10th in the morning Dolland's glass was down to *half a degree below zero ;* and Martin's, which absurdly was graduated only to 4 above zero, was quite into the ball : so that when the weather became most interesting, it was quite useless. On the 10th at eleven at night, tho' the air was perfectly still, Dolland's glass went down to 1 *degree below zero !* This strange severity had made my Bro : and me very desirous to know what degree of cold there might be in such an exalted situation as Newton : We had therefore on the morning of the 10th written to Mrs. Yalden, and entreated her to hang-out her Therm^r made by Adams ; and to pay some attention to it morning, and evening, expecting wonderful doings in so elevated a region. But behold on the 10th, at 11 at Night it was down only to 19! and the next morning at 22, when mine was at 10! We were so disturbed at this unexpected reverse of comparative local cold, that we sent one of my glasses up, thinking Mr. Y:'s must, some how be constructed wrong. But when the instruments came to be confronted, they went exactly together. So that for one night at least, the cold at N : was 20 degrees less than at S : and the whole frost thro' ten or twelve. And indeed, when we came to observe consequences, we could readily suppose it. For all my laurustines, bays, Ilexis, and what is much worse my fine sloping laurel-hedge, are all scorched up, and dead! while at Newton the same trees have not lost a leaf! We had steady frost on to the 25th when the therm^r in the morning was down to 10 with us, and at Newton only to 21! Strong frost continued till the 31st when some tendency to thaw was observed : and by Jan : 3rd : 1785 the thaw was confirmed, and some rain fell. There was a circumstance that I must not omit, because it was new to my brother and me; which was that on Friday, Decr 10th, being bright sun-shine, the air was full of icy spiculæ, floating in all directions, like atoms in a sun-beam let into a dark room. We thought at first that they might have been particles of the rime falling from my tall hedges : but were soon convinced to the contrary by making our observations in open places, where no rime could reach us. Were they the watry particles of the air frozen as they floated; or were they the evaporations from the snow frozen as they mounted? We were much obliged to the Therm^r for ye early intimations that they gave us; and hurryed our apples, pears, onions, potatoes, &c., into the cellar, and warm closets : while those, that had not these warnings, lost all their stores, and had their very bread and cheese frozen. For my own part, having a house full of relations, I enjoyed the rigorous season much; and found full employ in shoveling a path round my outlet, and up to Newton; and in observing the Therm^r, &c : and was only sorry for the poor and aged, who suffered much. I must not omit to tell you, that during those two Siberian days my parlor-cat was so electric, when stroked, that had the Stroker been properly *insulated*, he might have given the shock to a whole circle of people. Bro : Tho : and family left us Jan : 5th. The morning before he went away his house at S : Lambeth was assaulted by three villains, one of whom his Gardener shot thro' the body with slugs from the parapet just as they were entering the drawing-room. Mrs. and Miss Etty are well; and Charles just gone to attend his ship in the river, which sails in March. Mr. Richd Chase is released from his 3 years and ½ captivity in India, and is returned to

Madras. Magd : Coll : has just purchased the little life-hold estate on the *Plestor*, in reversion after two lives, intending hereafter to make it glebe to the vicarage. Tell y' Mother I thank her for her gift, which will be very acceptable to the poor : and y' Father, that I should be glad to see *his* account of *rain, frost*, &c. I advise y' Father and Bro' to read S' John Cullun's History of Hawsted, the parish where he is Rector. Mrs. J. White joins in respects.

Y' loving Uncle, GIL : WHITE.

Mr. Yalden, poor man, is in a bad state of health, and is gone to town for advice. Ch : Etty's new ship is named the *Duke of Montrose*, Cap : Elphinstone : all the officers are Scotch except Ch : I have met with Will : *Bercarius*, which name signifies *shepherd :* hence the modern name of *Barker*. Men are cutting the beeches at the top of the hill ; but not those on the hanger this year. We shall lose the beautiful fringe that graces the outline of our prospect that way : but shall gain 60 feet of Horizon. Jupiter wests so fast that at sun-set he is not much above these trees. Snow covers the ground.

(To THOMAS BARKER, ESQ.)

Selborne, *Jan : 1st :* 1791.

DEAR SIR,

As the year 1790 is just at an end, I send you the rain of that period, which, I trust, has been regularly measured. Nov. and Dec. as you see, were very wet, with many storms, that in various places had occasioned much damage. The fall of rain from Nov. 19 to the 22, inclusive, was prodigious ! The thunder storm on Dec. 23 in the morning before day was very aweful : but, I thank God, it did not do us any the least harm. Two millers, in a wind-mill on the Sussex downs near Good-wood, were struck dead by lightning that morning ; and part of the gibbet on Hind-head, on which two murderers were suspended, was beaten down. I am not sure that I was awaked soon enough to hear the whole storm : between the flashes that I saw and the thunder, I counted from 10 to 14 seconds.

RAIN IN 1790.	
Jan :	199
Feb :	49
Mar :	45
Ap :	364
May	438
June	13
July	324
Aug.	230
Sep.	66
Oct.	210
Nov.	695
Dec.	594
	3227

In consequence of my Nat. Hist. I continue to receive various letters from various parts; and in particular from a Mr. Marsham of Stratton near Norwich, an aged Gent: who has published in the R. S. respecting the growth of trees. Do you know any thing about this person? He is an agreeable correspondent. He is such an admirer of oaks, that he has been twice to see the great oak in the Holt.

D\. Chander, and family, who came at first only with an intent to stay with us a few months; have now taken the vicarage house for some time. The Dr. is much busied in writing the life of his founder, William Wainflete: he lives a very studious and domestic life, keeps no horse, and visits few people. We have just received the agreeable news that Mrs. Clement was safely delivered, last Wednesday, of a boy, her 8th child, which are all living. Mr. Churton, who is keeping his Xmas with us as usual, desires his best respects, and many thanks for the hospitable reception and intelligent information which he met with last summer at Lyndon. He is a good antiquary, and much employed in writing the life of Doctor Will. Smith, the founder of Brazenose Coll. of which he is now the senior fellow.

Y' leg, we hope, is recovered from its accident. Mrs. J. White joins in affectionate compliments, and the good wishes of the season. I conclude

Y' most humble servant,

G. WHITE.

CONTENTS.

	PAGE
PREFACE	vii
NEW LETTERS	xiii
NATURAL HISTORY OF SELBORNE	1
NATURALIST'S CALENDAR	263
MEMOIR OF GILBERT WHITE	278
NOTES AND OBSERVATIONS	285
ANTIQUITIES	353
LORD SELBORNE'S APPENDIX	443
INDEX	467

LIST OF ILLUSTRATIONS.

	PAGE
FRONTISPIECE	iv
WELL-HEAD	3
EMSHOT CHURCH	4
PLESTOR, THE	6
GILBERT WHITE'S HOUSE, NOW THE RESIDENCE OF PROFESSOR BELL	9
ROCKY LANE LEADING TO ALTON	11
COTTAGES IN THE VILLAGE	12
OLD COACH ROAD, LEADING INTO THE VILLAGE	15
LYSS CHURCH	16
HEADLEY CHURCH IN GILBERT WHITE'S TIME	18
PATH BY LONG LYTHE, A FAVOURITE WALK OF GILBERT WHITE'S	21
OLD MILL	24
KINGSLEY CHURCH	25
SWALLOW, THE	27
HOOPOE	32
EGG OF HOOPOE	33
THE LYTHE	37
YELLOW WAGTAIL	39
WHEATEAR	41
QUAIL, EGG OF	43
BULLFINCH	45

	PAGE
NUTHATCH	47
EGG OF NUTHATCH	48
EGG OF GOLDEN-CROWNED WREN	48
GOLDEN-CROWNED WREN	50
GREATHAM CHURCH	53
GILBERT WHITE'S HOUSE	55
WILLOW WREN	57
EGG OF WILLOW WREN	58
BUTCHER BIRD	59
EGG OF BUTCHER BIRD	60
EGG OF SANDPIPER	60
BRAMSHOTT CHURCH	62
THE WISHING-STONE	65
CHANCEL DOORWAY, EAST WORLDHAM CHURCH	69
OLD WELL, ELLIS'S FARM	71
EGG OF LANDRAIL	78
EGG OF REED-SPARROW	85
CUCKOO	89
EGG OF CUCKOO	90
HEDGEHOG AND YOUNG	91
EGG OF FIELDFARE	92
RING OUZEL	101
EGG OF RING OUZEL	102
EGG OF CROSSBILL	105
EGG OF CHAFFINCH	109
NIGHTINGALE	113
EGG OF NIGHTINGALE	114
PIED FLYCATCHER	127
EGG OF SPOTTED FLYCATCHER	128

PAGE

HOUSE-MARTIN 135

EGG OF HOUSE-MARTIN 137

EGG OF PHEASANT 153

LONG-TAILED TITMOUSE 154

EGG OF LONG-TAILED TITMOUSE 155

EGG OF REDBREAST 155

WHITETHROAT 156

EGG OF WHITETHROAT 157

EGG OF BLACKCAP 157

REDSTART 158

WRYNECK 160

EGG OF WRYNECK 161

SWIFT 163

EGG OF SWIFT 168

EGG OF MAGPIE 169

EGG OF THRUSH 171

EGG OF GOATSUCKER 186

EGG OF WOODCHAT 196

EGG OF GREENFINCH 202

EGG OF OWL 210

EGG OF RAVEN 211

EGG OF LAPWING OR PLOVER 224

EGG OF SPARROWHAWK 228

EGG OF WOOD-PIGEON 230

HAWFINCH 240

EGG OF STONE-CURLEW 246

PROGRESSIVE GROWTH OF RED DEER HORNS 286

RED DEER, EIGHT YEARS OLD . . . . ·287

MAN TRAPS 289

PAGE

RABBIT WITH DEFORMED TEETH 290

NODULE OF IVORY 291

CAPTAIN SALVIN'S WILD BOAR 293

RAT'S TAIL 294

OLD ENGLISH BLACK RAT 295

MOUSE CAUGHT BY AN OYSTER 297

EGGS OF COMMON SNAKE 305

VERTEBRÆ OF SNAKE 307

NEST OF THE STICKLEBACK 308

SERRATED CLAW OF HERON 311

BLACKBIRD'S NEST ORNAMENTED WITH LACE 315

RABY HEDGEHOG 318

NEST OF WREN BUILT BETWEEN TWO STOATS 321

TAIL OF WOODPECKER 325

FOOT OF WOODPECKER 326

TONGUE OF WOODPECKER 326

MUMMY MONKEY FOUND IN A TREE 331

SECTION OF COW'S HORN 335

DIGGING PAW OF THE MOLE 339

SKIN OF VIPER 341

POISON FANGS OF VIPER 342

RATTLE OF RATTLESNAKE 345

POT OF WOURALI POISON 346

QUIVER OF WOURALI POISON-TIPPED ARROWS 346

AWETO, OR VEGETABLE CATERPILLAR OF NEW ZEALAND 348

GILBERT WHITE'S HOUSE 354

TROTTON CHURCH 355

SELBORNE CHURCH, FROM THE ALTON ROAD 358

SELBORNE CHURCH, SOUTH AISLE 360

PAGE

ORIGINAL BENCHES IN THE SOUTH AISLE OF SELBORNE CHURCH . . 361

SELBORNE CHURCH, VIEW IN CHANCEL 363

AUTOGRAPH OF GILBERT WHITE 364

CERTIFICATE OF GILBERT WHITE'S BURIAL 364

SELBORNE CHURCH, VIEW LOOKING INTO SOUTH PORCH 367

THE YEW-TREE IN THE CHURCHYARD, SELBORNE 369

GILBERT WHITE'S GRAVESTONE 371

ROGATE CHURCH 440

SUN-DIAL IN GILBERT WHITE'S GARDEN 441

MAP 444

LARGE SEPULCHRAL VASE 446

WATER VESSEL 448

DRINKING CUP, BRONZE CELT AND RINGS 449

SPEAR HEADS, &C. 451

SWORDS AND SWORD HANDLES, &C. 455

VASE CONTAINING COINS 456

DITTO, BROKEN 459

ROMAN COINS 461

THE

NATURAL HISTORY OF SELBORNE.

LETTER I.

TO THOMAS PENNANT, ESQ.

THE parish of SELBORNE lies in the extreme eastern corner of
the county of Hampshire, bordering on the county of Sussex,
and not far from the county of Surrey ; it is about fifty miles
south-west of London, in latitude 51°, and near midway between
the towns of Alton and Petersfield. Being very large and extensive, it abuts on twelve parishes, two of which are in Sussex,
viz., Trotton and Rogate. If you begin from the south and proceed
westward the adjacent parishes are Emshot, Newton Valence,
Faringdon, Harteley-Mauduit, Great Wardleham, Kingsley,
Hedleigh, Bramshot, Trotton, Rogate, Lysse, and Greatham.
The soils of this district are almost as various and diversified as
the views and aspects. The high part to the south-west consists
of a vast hill of chalk, rising three hundred feet above the
village, and is divided into a sheep down, the high wood, and a
long hanging wood called the Hanger. The covert of this
eminence is altogether beech, the most lovely of all forest trees,
whether we consider its smooth rind or bark, its glossy foliage,
or graceful pendulous boughs. The down, or sheep-walk, is
a pleasant park-like spot, of about one mile by half that space,
jutting out on the verge of the hill-country, where it begins to
break down into the plains, and commanding a very engaging

view, being an assemblage of hill, dale, woodlands, heath, and water. The prospect is bounded to the south-east and east by the vast range of mountains called the Sussex downs, by Guild-down near Guildford, and by the downs round Dorking, and Ryegate in Surrey, to the north-east, which altogether, with the country beyond Alton and Farnham, form a noble and extensive outline.

At the foot of this hill, one stage or step from the uplands, lies the village, which consists of one single straggling street, three-quarters of a mile in length, in a sheltered vale, and running parallel with the Hanger. The houses are divided from the hill by a vein of stiff clay (good wheat land), yet stand on a rock of white stone, little in appearance removed from chalk; but seems so far from being calcareous, that it endures extreme heat. Yet that the freestone still preserves somewhat that is analogous to chalk, is plain from the beeches which descend as low as those rocks extend, and no farther, and thrive as well on them, where the ground is steep, as on the chalks.

The cart-way of the village divides, in a remarkable manner, two very incongruous soils. To the south-west is a rank clay, that requires the labour of years to render it mellow; while the gardens to the north-east, and small inclosures behind, consist of a warm, forward, crumbling mould, called black malm, which seems highly saturated with vegetable and animal manure; and these may perhaps have been the original site of the town; while the woods and coverts might extend down to the opposite bank.

At each end of the village, which runs from south-east to north west, arises a small rivulet: that at the north-west end frequently fails; but the other is a fine perennial spring, called Well-head, little influenced by drought or wet seasons, inasmuch as it produced on the 14th September, 1781, after a severe hot summer and a preceding dry spring and winter, nine gallons of water in a minute, at a time when many of the wells failed, and all the ponds in the vales were dry.

This spring breaks out of some high grounds joining to Nore Hill, a noble chalk promontory, remarkable for sending forth two streams into two different seas. The one to the south becomes a branch of the Arun, running to Arundel, and so falling into the British Channel: the other to the north. The Selborne stream makes one branch of the Wey; and, meeting the Blackdown stream at Hedleigh, and the Alton and

Farnham stream at Tilford Bridge, swells into a considerable river, navigable at Godalming; from whence it passes to Guildford, and so into the Thames at Weybridge; and thus at the Nore into the German Ocean.

WELL-HEAD.

Our wells, at an average, run to about sixty-three feet, and when sunk to that depth seldom fail; but produce a fine limpid water, soft to the taste, and much commended by those who drink the pure element, but which does not lather well with soap.

To the north-west, north, and east of the village is a range of fair inclosures, consisting of what is called a white malm, a sort of rotten or rubble stone, which, when turned up to the frost and rain, moulders to pieces and becomes manure to itself.

Still on to the north-east, and a step lower, is a kind of white land, neither chalk nor clay, neither fit for pasture nor for the plough, yet kindly for hops, which root deep into the freestone, and have their poles and wood for charcoal growing just at hand. This white soil produces the brightest hops.

As the parish still inclines down towards Wolmer Forest, at the juncture of the clays and sand, the soil becomes a wet, sandy loam, remarkable for its timber and infamous for roads. The oaks of Temple and Blackmoor stand high in the estimation of purveyors, and have furnished much naval timber; while the trees on the freestone grow large, but are what workmen call shaky, and so brittle as often to fall to pieces in sawing. Beyond the sandy loam the soil becomes a hungry lean sand, till it mingles with the forest; and will produce little without the assistance of lime and turnips.

EMSHOT CHURCH.

LETTER II.

TO THOMAS PENNANT, ESQ.

In the court of Norton farmhouse, a manor-farm to the north-west of the village, on the white malm, stood within these twenty years a broad-leaved elm, or wych hazel, *Ulmus folio latissimo scabro*, of Ray, which, though it had lost a considerable leading bough, equal to a moderate tree, in the great storm in the year 1703, yet, when felled, contained eight loads of timber; and being too bulky for carriage, was sawn off at seven feet above the butt, where it measured near eight feet in the diameter. This elm I mention to show to what a bulk planted elms may attain; as this tree must certainly have been such from its situation.

In the centre of the village, and near the church, is a square piece of ground surrounded by houses, and vulgarly called the Plestor. In the midst of this spot stood, in old times, a vast oak, with a short squat body and huge horizontal arms, extending almost to the extremity of the area. This venerable tree, surrounded with stone steps, and seats above them, was the delight of old and young, and a place of much resort in summer evenings; where the former sat in grave debate, while the latter frolicked and danced before them. Long might it have stood, had not the amazing tempest in 1703 overturned it at once, to the infinite regret of the inhabitants and the vicar, who bestowed several pounds in setting it in its place again: but all his care could not avail; the tree sprouted for a time, then withered and died. This oak I mention to show to what a bulk planted oaks also may arrive: and planted this tree must certainly have been, as appears from what is known concerning the antiquities of the village.

On the Blackmoor estate there is a small wood called Losel's, of a few acres, that was lately furnished with a set of oaks of a peculiar growth and great value; they were tall and taper like firs, but standing near together had very small heads, only a little brush without any large limbs. About twenty years ago, the bridge at the Toy, near Hampton Court, being much decayed, some trees were wanted for the repairs that were fifty feet long without bough, and would measure twelve inches diameter at the little end. Twenty such trees did a purveyor find in this little wood, with this advantage, that many of them answered the description at sixty feet. These trees were sold for twenty pounds apiece.

In the centre of this grove there stood an oak, which, though shapely and tall on the whole, bulged out into a large excrescence about the middle of the stem. On this a pair of ravens had fixed their residence for such a series of years, that the oak was distinguished by the title of the Raven Tree. Many were the attempts of the neighbouring youths to get at this eyry : the

THE PLESTOR.

difficulty whetted their inclinations, and each was ambitious of surmounting the arduous task. But when they arrived at the swelling, it jutted out so in their way, and was so far beyond their grasp, that the most daring lads were awed, and acknowledged the undertaking to be too hazardous. So the ravens built on, nest upon nest, in perfect security, till the fatal day arrived in which the wood was to be levelled. It was in the month of February, when those birds usually sit. The saw was applied to the butt, the wedges were inserted into the opening, the woods echoed to the heavy blows of the beetle or mallet, the tree nodded to its fall; but still the dam sat on.   At last, when it gave way, the bird was flung from her nest; and, though her parental affection deserved a better fate, was whipped down by the twigs, which brought her dead to the ground.

LETTER III.

TO THOMAS PENNANT, ESQ.   '

THE fossil-shells of this district, and sorts of stone, such as have fallen within my observation, must not be passed over in silence. And first I must mention, as a great curiosity, a specimen that was ploughed up in the chalky fields, near the side of the down, and given to me for the singularity of its appearance; which, to an incurious eye, seems like a petrified fish of about four inches long, the *cardo* (hinge) passing for a head and mouth.   It is in reality a bivalve of the Linnæan genus of *Mytilus*, and the species of *Crista Galli*; called by Lister, *Rastellum*; by Rumphius, *Ostreum plicatum minus*; by D'Argenville, *Auris porci*, s. *Crista Galli*; and by those who make collections, cock's comb. Though I applied to several such in London, I never could meet with an entire specimen; nor could I ever find in books any engraving from a perfect one.   In the superb museum at Leicester House, permission was given me to examine for this article; and though I was disappointed as to the fossil, I was highly gratified with the sight of several of the shells themselves in high preservation.   This bivalve is only known to inhabit the Indian Ocean, where it fixes itself to a zoophyte known by the name *Gorgonia*.   The curious foldings of the suture, the one into the other, the alternate flutings or grooves, and the curved form of my specimen are much easier expressed by the pencil than by words.

Cornua Ammonis are very common about this village.   As we were cutting an inclining path up the Hanger, the labourers found them frequently on that steep, just under the soil, in the chalk, and of a considerable size.   In the lane above Well-head, in the way to Emshot, they abound in the bank, in a darkish sort of marl, and are usually very small and soft : but in Clay's Pond, a little farther on, at the end of the pit, where the soil is dug out for manure, I have occasionally observed them of large dimensions, perhaps fourteen or sixteen inches in diameter. But as these did not consist of firm stone, but were formed of a kind of *terra lapidosa*, or hardened clay, as soon as they were exposed to the rains and frost they mouldered away. These seemed as if they were of very recent production. In the chalk-pit, at the north-west end of the Hanger, large *nautili* are sometimes observed.

In the very thickest strata of our freestone, and at considerable depths, well-diggers often find large scallops or *pectines*, having both shells deeply striated, and ridged and furrowed alternately. They are highly impregnated with, if not wholly composed of, the stone of the quarry.

LETTER IV.

TO THOMAS PENNANT, ESQ.

As in a former letter the freestone of this place has been only mentioned incidentally, I shall here become more particular. This stone is in great request for hearthstones and the beds of ovens; and in lining of lime-kilns it turns to good account; for the workmen use sandy loam instead of mortar; the sand of which fluxes, and runs by the intense heat, and so cases over the whole face of the kiln with a strong vitrified coat like glass, that it is well preserved from injuries of weather, and endures thirty or forty years. When chiselled smooth, it makes elegant fronts for houses, equal in colour and grain to the Bath stone; and superior in one respect, that, when seasoned, it does not scale. Decent chimney-pieces are worked from it of much closer and finer grain than Portland; and rooms are floored with it; but it proves rather too soft for this purpose. It is a freestone, cutting in all directions; yet has something of a grain parallel with the horizon, and therefore should not be *surbedded* —that is, set edgewise, contrary to its position in the quarry— but laid in the same position that it occupies there. On the ground abroad this fire-stone will not succeed for pavements, because, probably, some degree of saltness prevailing within it, the rain tears the slabs to pieces.[1] Though this stone is too

---

[1] " Fire-stone is full of salts, and has no sulphur: it must be close grained, and have no interstices. Nothing supports fire like salts; saltstone perishes when exposed to wet and frost."—PLOT's *Staff.* p. 152.

hard to be acted on by vinegar, yet both the white part and
even the blue rag ferment strongly in mineral acids.   Though

GILBERT WHITE'S HOUSE, NOW THE RESIDENCE OF PROFESSOR BELL.

the white stone will not bear wet, yet in every quarry at intervals there are thin strata of blue rag, which resist rain and
frost, and are excellent for pitching of stables, paths, and courts,
and for building of dry walls against banks ; a valuable species

of fencing, much in use in this village; and for mending of roads. This rag is rugged and stubborn, and will not hew to a smooth face; but is very durable: yet, as these strata are shallow and lie deep, large quantities cannot be procured but at considerable expense. Among the blue rags turn up some blocks tinged with a stain of yellow or rust colour, which seem to be nearly as lasting as the blue; and every now and then balls of a friable substance, like rust of iron, called rust balls.

In Wolmer Forest, I see but one sort of stone, called by the workmen sand or forest-stone. This is generally of the colour of rusty iron, and might probably be worked as iron ore; is very hard and heavy, and of a firm, compact texture, and composed of a small roundish crystalline grit, cemented together by a brown, terrene, ferruginous matter; will not cut without difficulty, nor easily strike fire with steel. Being often found in broad flat pieces, it makes good pavement for paths about houses, never becoming slippery in frost or rain; is excellent for dry walls, and is sometimes used in buildings. In many parts of that waste it lies scattered on the surface of the ground, but is dug on Weaver's Down, a vast hill on the eastern verge of that forest, where the pits are shallow and the stratum thin. This stone is imperishable.

From a notion of rendering their work the more elegant, and giving it a finish, masons chip this stone into small fragments about the size of the head of a large nail, and then stick the pieces into the wet mortar along the joints of their freestone walls: this embellishment carries an odd appearance, and has occasioned strangers sometimes to ask us pleasantly "whether we fastened our walls together with tenpenny nails."

LETTER V.

TO THOMAS PENNANT, ESQ.

AMONG the singularities of this place the two rocky hollow lanes, the one to Alton, and the other to the forest, deserve our attention. These roads, running through the malm lands, are, by the traffic of ages, and the fretting of water, worn down through the first stratum of our freestone, and partly through the second; so that they look more like water-courses than roads; and are bedded with naked rag for furlongs together. In many places they are reduced sixteen or eighteen feet beneath the level of the fields; and after floods, and in frosts, exhibit very grotesque and wild appearances, from the tangled roots

ROCKY LANE LEADING TO ALTON.

that are twisted among the strata, and from the torrents rushing down their broken sides; and especially when those cascades are frozen into icicles, hanging in all the fanciful shapes of frost-work. These rugged, gloomy scenes affright the ladies when they peep down into them from the paths above, and make timid horsemen shudder while they ride along them; but delight the naturalist with their various botany, and particularly with the curious *filices* with which they abound.

The manor of Selborne, were it strictly looked after, with all its kindly aspects, and all its sloping coverts, would swarm with game; even now hares, partridges, and pheasants abound; and in old days woodcocks were as plentiful.   There are few quails, because they more affect open fields than inclosures; after harvest some few landrails are seen.

COTTAGES IN THE VILLAGE.

The parish of Selborne, by taking in so much of the forest, is a vast district.   Those who tread the bounds are employed part of three days in the business, and are of opinion that the outline, in all its curves and indentings, does not comprise less than thirty miles.

The village stands in a sheltered spot, secured by the Hanger from the strong westerly winds.   The air is soft, but rather moist from the effluvia of so many trees; yet perfectly healthy and free from agues.

The quantity of rain that falls on it is very considerable, as may be supposed in so woody and mountainous a district. As my experience in measuring the water is but of short date, I am not qualified to give the mean quantity, but a very intelligent gentleman assures me (and he speaks from upwards of forty years' experience) that the mean rain of any place cannot be ascertained till a person has measured it for a very long period. I only know that

	Inch.	Hund.
From May 1, 1779, to the end of the year there fell . .	28	37 !
From Jan. 1, 1780, to Jan. 1, 1781	27	32
From Jan. 1, 1781, to Jan. 1, 1782	30	71
From Jan. 1, 1782, to Jan. 1, 1783	50	26 !
From Jan. 1, 1783, to Jan. 1, 1784	33	71
From Jan. 1, 1784, to Jan. 1, 1785	38	80
From Jan. 1, 1785, to Jan. 1, 1786	31	55
From Jan. 1, 1786, to Jan. 1, 1787	39	57

The village of Selborne, and the large hamlet of Oakhanger, with the single farms, and many scattered houses along the verge of the forest, contain upwards of six hundred and seventy inhabitants.

We abound with poor; many of whom are sober and industrious, and live comfortably in good stone or brick cottages, which are glazed, and have chambers above stairs : mud buildings we have none. Besides the employment from husbandry, the men work in hop-gardens, of which we have many; and fell and bark timber. In the spring and summer the women weed the corn; and enjoy a second harvest in September by hop-picking. Formerly, in the dead months they availed themselves greatly by spinning wool, for making of barragons, a genteel corded stuff, much in vogue at that time for summer wear; and chiefly manufactured at Alton, a neighbouring town, by some of the people called Quakers. The inhabitants enjoy a good share of health and longevity, and the parish swarms with children.

LETTER VI.

TO THOMAS PENNANT, ESQ.

SHOULD I omit to describe with some exactness the Forest of Wolmer, of which three-fifths perhaps lie in this parish, my account of Selborne would be very imperfect, as it is a district abounding with many curious productions, both animal and vegetable, and has often afforded me much entertainment both as a sportsman and as a naturalist.

The royal Forest of Wolmer is a tract of land of about seven miles in length by two-and-a-half in breadth, running nearly from north to south, and is abutted on—to begin to the south, and so to proceed eastward—by the parishes of Greatham, Lysse, Rogate, and Trotton, in the county of Sussex; by Bramshot, Hedleigh, and Kingsley. This royalty consists entirely of sand, covered with heath and fern; but is somewhat diversified with hills and dales, without having one standing tree in the whole extent. In the bottoms, where the waters stagnate, are many bogs, which formerly abounded with subterraneous trees; though Dr. Plot says positively [1] that "there never were any fallen trees hidden in the mosses of the southern counties." But he was mistaken: for I myself have seen cottages on the verge of this wild district whose timbers consisted of a black hard wood, looking like oak, which the owners assured me they procured from the bogs by probing the soil with spits, or some such instruments: but the peat is so much cut out, and the moors have been so well examined, that none has been found of late. Old people, however, have assured me that on a winter's morning they have discovered these trees in the bogs by the hoar frost, which lay longer over the space where they were concealed than on the surrounding morass. Nor does this seem to be a fanciful notion, but consistent with true philosophy. Besides the oak, I have also been shown pieces of fossil wood, of a paler colour and softer nature, which the inhabitants called fir: but, upon a nice examination, and trial by fire, I could discover nothing resinous in them; and therefore rather suppose that they were parts of a willow or alder, or some such aquatic tree.

This lonely domain is a very agreeable haunt for many sorts of wild fowls, which not only frequent it in the winter, but breed

[1] See his History of Staffordshire.

there in the summer; such as lapwings, snipes, wild ducks, and, as I have discovered within these few years, teals. Partridges in vast plenty are bred in good seasons on the verge of this forest, into which they love to make excursions: and in particular in the dry summer of 1740 and 1741, and some years after, they swarmed to such a degree that parties of unreasonable sportsmen killed twenty and sometimes thirty brace in a day.

OLD COACH ROAD, LEADING INTO THE VILLAGE.

But there was a nobler species of game in this forest, now extinct, which I have heard old people say abounded much before shooting flying became so common, and that was the heath-cock, or black game. When I was a little boy I recollect one coming now and then to my father's table. The last pack remembered was killed about thirty-five years ago; and within these ten years one solitary grey hen was sprung by some beagles in beating for a hare. The sportsman cried out, "A hen pheasant!" but a gentleman present, who had often seen black game in the north of England, assured me that it was a grey hen.

Nor does the loss of our black game prove the only gap in the *Fauna Selborniensis ;* for another beautiful link in the chain of beings is wanting: I mean the red-deer, which toward the beginning of this century amounted to about five hundred head, and made a stately appearance. There is an old keeper, now alive, named Adams, whose great-grandfather (mentioned in a perambulation taken in 1635), grandfather, father and self, enjoyed the head keepership of Wolmer Forest in succession for more than a hundred years. This person assures me, that his father has often told him, that Queen Anne, as she was journeying on the Portsmouth road, did not think the forest of Wolmer beneath her royal regard. For she came out of the great road at Lippock, which is just by, and, reposing herself on a bank

LYSSE CHURCH.

smoothed for that purpose, lying about half a mile to the east of Wolmer Pond, and still called Queen's Bank, saw with great complacency and satisfaction the whole herd of red-deer brought by the keepers along the vale before her, consisting then of about five hundred head. A sight this worthy the attention of the greatest sovereign! But he farther adds that, by means of the Waltham blacks, or, to use his own expression, as soon as they began blacking, they were reduced to about fifty head, and so continued decreasing till the time of the late Duke of Cumberland. About the year 1737, his highness sent down a huntsman, and six yeomen-prickers, in scarlet jackets laced with gold, attended by the stag-hounds; ordering them to take every deer in this forest alive, and to convey them in carts to Windsor.

In the course of the summer they caught every stag, some of which showed extraordinary diversion : but, in the following winter, when the hinds were also carried off, such fine chases were exhibited as served the country people for matter of talk and wonder for years afterwards. I saw myself one of the yeomen-prickers single out a stag from the herd, and must confess it was the most curious feat of activity I ever beheld. The exertions made by the horse and deer much exceeded all my expectations ; though the former greatly excelled the latter in speed. When the devoted deer was separated from his companions, they gave him, by their watches, law, as they called it, for twenty minutes ; when, sounding their horns, the stop-dogs were permitted to pursue, and a most gallant scene ensued.

LETTER VII.

TO THOMAS PENNANT, ESQ.

THOUGH large herds of deer do much harm to the neighbourhood, yet the injury to the morals of the people is of more moment than the loss of their crops. The temptation is irresistible ; for most men are sportsmen by constitution : and there is such an inherent spirit for hunting in human nature, as scarce any inhibitions can restrain. Hence, towards the beginning of this century, all this country was wild about deer-stealing. Unless he was a hunter, as they affected to call themselves, no young person was allowed to be possessed of manhood or gallantry. The Waltham blacks at length committed such enormities, that Government was forced to interfere with that severe and sanguinary Act called the Black Act (9 Geo. I. c. 22), which comprehends more felonies than any law that ever was framed before. And therefore, Dr. Hoadley, the Bishop of Winchester, when urged to re-stock Waltham-chase, refused, from a motive worthy of a prelate, replying that " it had done mischief enough already."

Our old race of deer-stealers are hardly extinct yet : it was but a little while ago that they used to recount, over their ale, the exploits of their youth ; such as watching the pregnant hind to her lair, and, when the calf was dropped, paring its feet with a penknife to the quick to prevent its escape, till it was large

c

and fat enough to be killed; the shooting at one of their neighbours with a bullet in a turnip-field by moonshine, mistaking him for a deer; and the losing a dog in the following extraordinary manner :—Some fellows, suspecting that a calf new-fallen was deposited in a certain spot of thick fern, went, with a lurcher, to surprise it; when the parent hind rushed out of the brake, and, taking a vast spring with all her feet close

HEADLEY CHURCH IN GILBERT WHITE'S TIME.

together, pitched upon the neck of the dog, and broke it short in two.

Another temptation to idleness and sporting was a number of rabbits, which possessed all the hillocks and dry places; but these being inconvenient to the huntsmen, on account of their burrows, when they came to take away the deer they permitted the country people to destroy them all.

Such forests and wastes, when their allurements to irregularities are removed, are of considerable service to neighbourhoods that verge upon them, by furnishing them with peat and turf for their firing; with fuel for the burning their lime; and with ashes for their grasses; and by maintaining their geese and their stock of young cattle at little or no expense.

The manor-farm of the parish of Greatham has an admitted claim, I see (by an old record taken from the Tower of London), of turning all live stock on the forest, at proper seasons, *bidentibus exceptis.* For this privilege the owner of that estate used to pay to the king annually seven bushels of oats. In the Holt Forest, where a full stock of fallow-deer has been kept up till lately, no sheep are admitted. The reason, I presume, being that sheep are such close grazers, they would pick out all the finest grasses, and hinder the deer from thriving.

Though (by statute 4 and 5 Wm. and Mary, c. 23) "to burn on any waste, between Candlemas and Midsummer, any grig, ling, heath and furze, gorse or fern, is punishable with whipping and confinement in the House of Correction;" yet, in this forest, about March or April, according to the dryness of the season, such vast heath-fires are lighted up, that they often get to a masterless head, and, catching the hedges, have sometimes been communicated to the underwoods, woods, and coppices, where great damage has ensued. The plea for these burnings is, that when the old coat of heath, &c., is consumed, young will sprout up and afford much tender browse for cattle; but, where there is large old furze, the fire, following the roots, consumes the very ground; so that for hundreds of acres nothing is to be seen but smother and desolation, the whole circuit round looking like the cinders of a volcano; and the soil being quite exhausted, no traces of vegetation are to be found for years. These conflagrations, as they take place usually with a northeast or east wind, much annoy this village with their smoke, and often alarm the country; and, once in particular, I remember that a gentleman, who lives beyond Andover, coming to my house, when he got on the downs between that town and Winchester, at twenty-five miles distance was surprised much with smoke and a hot smell of fire; and concluded that Alresford was in flames; but when he came to that town, he then had apprehensions for the next village, and so on to the end of his journey.[1]

---

[1] This description reminds the scholar of the stubble-burning described in Virgil's "Georgics," i. 84, Mitford. There is no better fertilizer for the

On two of the most conspicuous eminences of this forest stand two arbours or bowers made of the boughs of oaks; the one called Waldon Lodge, the other Brimstone Lodge : these the keepers renew annually on the feast of St. Barnabas, taking the old materials for a perquisite. The farm called Blackmoor, in this parish, is obliged to find the posts and brushwood for the former; while the farms at Greatham, in rotation, furnish for the latter; and are all enjoined to cut and deliver the materials at the spot. This custom I mention, because I look upon it to be of very remote antiquity.

LETTER VIII.

TO THOMAS PENNANT, ESQ.

On the verge of the forest, as it is now circumscribed, are three considerable lakes, two in Oakhanger, of which I have nothing particular to say; and one called Bin's, or Bean's Pond, which is worthy the attention of a naturalist or a sportsman. For, being crowded at the upper end with willows, and with the *Carex espitosa ;* the sort which, rising into tall hassocks, is called by the foresters, torrets; a corruption, I suppose, of turrets; it affords such a safe and pleasing shelter to wild ducks, teals, and snipes, that they breed there. In the winter this covert is also frequented by foxes, and sometimes by pheasants; and the bogs produce many curious plants.

By a perambulation of Wolmer Forest and the Holt, made in 1635, and in the eleventh year of Charles the First (which now lies before me), it appears that the limits of the former are much circumscribed. For, to say nothing of the farther side, with which I am not so well acquainted, the bounds on this side, in old times, came into Binswood; and extended to the

soil than the ashes of weeds and other vegetable growths, and this the poet knew.

> " Sæpe etiam steriles incendere profuit agros,
> Atque levem stipulam crepitantibus urere flammis :
> Sive inde occultas vires et pabula terræ
> Pinguia concipiunt."

> " Long practice has a sure improvement found,
> With kindled fires to burn the barren ground ;
> When the light stubble, to the flames resigned,
> Is driven along, and crackles to the wind."—DRYDEN.

ditch of Wardleham Park, in which stands the curious mount called King John's Hill, and Lodge Hill; and to the verge of Hartley Mauduit, called Mauduit Hatch; comprehending also Shortheath, Oakhanger, and Oakwoods; a large district, now private property, though once belonging to the royal domain.

It is remarkable that the term purlieu is never once mentioned in this long roll of parchment. It contains, besides the perambulation, a rough estimate of the value of the timbers, which

PATH BY LONG LYTHE, A FAVOURITE WALK OF GILBERT WHITE'S.

were considerable, growing at that time in the district of the Holt; and enumerates the officers, superior and inferior, of those joint forests, for the time being, and their ostensible fees and perquisites. In those days, as at present, there were hardly any trees in Wolmer Forest.

Within the present limits of the forest are three considerable lakes, Hogmer, Cranmer, and Wolmer; all of which are stocked with carp, tench, eels, and perch; but the fish do not thrive well, because the water is hungry, and the bottoms are a naked sand.

A circumstance respecting these ponds, though by no means peculiar to them, I cannot pass over in silence; and that is, that instinct by which in summer all the kine, whether oxen, cows, calves, or heifers, retire constantly to the water during the hotter hours; where, being more exempt from flies, and inhaling the coolness of that element, some belly deep, and some only to mid-leg, they ruminate and solace themselves from about ten in the morning till four in the afternoon, and then return to their feeding. During this great proportion of the day they drop much dung, in which insects nestle; and so supply food for the fish, which would be poorly subsisted but from this contingency. Thus nature, who is a great economist, converts the recreation of one animal to the support of another! Thomson, who was a nice observer of natural occurrences, did not let this pleasing circumstance escape him. He says, in his "Summer,"

> " A various group the herds and flocks compose :
> ——————— on the grassy bank
> Some ruminating lay ; while others stand
> Half in the flood, and, often bending, sip
> The circling surface. "

Wolmer Pond, so called, I suppose, for eminence sake, is a vast lake for this part of the world, containing, in its whole circumference, 2,646 yards, or very near a mile and a half. The length of the north-west and opposite side is about 704 yards, and the breadth of the south-west end about 456 yards. This measurement, which I caused to be made with good exactness, gives an area of about sixty-six acres, exclusive of a large irregular arm at the north-east corner, which we did not take into the reckoning.

On the face of this expanse of waters, and perfectly secure from fowlers, lie all day long, in the winter season, vast flocks of ducks, teals, and widgeons, of various denominations; where they preen and solace and rest themselves, till towards sunset, when they issue forth in little parties (for in their natural state they are all birds of the night) to feed in the brooks and meadows; returning again with the dawn of the morning. Had this lake an arm or two more, and were it planted round with thick covert (for now it is perfectly naked), it might make a valuable decoy.

Yet neither its extent, nor the clearness of its water, nor the resort of various and curious fowls, nor its picturesque groups of cattle, can render this meer so remarkable as the great quantity of coins that were found in its bed about forty years ago.[1]

LETTER IX.

TO THOMAS PENNANT, ESQ.

BY way of supplement, I shall trouble you once more on this subject, to inform you that Wolmer, with her sister forest Ayles Holt, *alias* Alice Holt,[2] as it is called in old records, is held by grant from the Crown for a term of years.

The grantees that the author remembers are Brigadier-General Emanuel Scroope Howe, and his lady, Ruperta, who was a natural daughter of Prince Rupert by Margaret Hughs ; a Mr. Mordaunt, of the Peterborough family, who married a dowager Lady Pembroke ; Henry Bilson Legge and lady ; and now Lord Stawel, their son.

The lady of General Howe lived to an advanced age, long surviving her husband ; and, at her death, left behind her many curious pieces of mechanism of her father's constructing, who was a distinguished mechanic and artist, as well as warrior; and, among the rest, a very complicated clock, lately in possession of Mr. Elmer, the celebrated game-painter at Farnham, in the county of Surrey.

[1] The circumstances under which these coins were discovered are thus related in the author's "Antiquities of Selborne :"—"In the very dry summers of 1740 and 41, the bed of this lake became as dry and dusty as the surrounding heath ; and some of the forest cottagers, remembering stories of coins found by their fathers and grandfathers, began to search also, and with great success ; they found great heaps of coin, one lying on the other, as shot there out of a bag, many of them in good preservation. They consisted solely of Roman copper coin in hundreds, and some medals of the Lower Empire. The neighbouring gentry and clergy chose what they liked, and some dozens fell to the author, chiefly of Marcus Aurelius and the Empress Faustina. Those of Faustina were in high relief, exhibiting agreeable features, and the medals of a paler colour than the coins."

[2] "In Rot. Inquisit. de statu forest. in Scaccar. 36 Ed. 3, it is called Aisholt." In "Tit. Wolmer and Aisholt Hantisc," we are told "the Lord King had one chapel in his park at Kingesle." "*Dominus Rex habet unam capellam in haiâ suâ de Kingesle.*" "*Haia, sepes, sepimentum, parcus; a Gall. haie and haye.*"—SPELMAN's *Glossary*, p. 272.

Though these two forests are only parted by a narrow range of inclosures, yet no two soils can be more different: for the Holt consists of a strong loam, of a miry nature, carrying a good turf, and abounding with oaks that grow to be large timber; while Wolmer is nothing but a hungry, sandy, barren waste.

The former, being all in the parish of Binsted, is about two miles in extent from north to south, and nearly as much from

THE OLD MILL.

east to west; and contains within it many woodlands and lawns, and the great lodge where the grantees reside; and a smaller lodge called Goose-green; and is abutted on by the parishes of Kingsley, Frinsham, Farnham, and Bentley; all of which have right of common.

One thing is remarkable, that though the Holt has been of old well stocked with fallow-deer, unrestrained by any pales or fences more than a common hedge, yet they were never seen within the limits of Wolmer; nor were the red-deer of Wolmer ever known to haunt the thickets or glades of the Holt.

At present the deer of the Holt are much thinned and reduced by the night-hunters, who perpetually harass them in spite of the efforts of numerous keepers, and the severe penalties that have been put in force against them as often as they have been detected and rendered liable to the lash of the law. Neither fines nor imprisonments can deter them; so impossible is it to extinguish the spirit of sporting, which seems to be inherent in human nature.

KINGSLEY CHURCH.

General Howe turned out some German wild boars and sows in his forests, to the great terror of the neighbourhood; and, at one time, a wild bull or buffalo: but the country rose upon them and destroyed them.[1]

A very large fall of timber, consisting of about one thousand oaks, has been cut this spring (viz. 1784) in the Holt forest; one-fifth of which, it is said, belongs to the grantee, Lord Stawel. He lays claim also to the lop and top; but the poor of the parishes of Binsted and Frinsham, Bentley and Kingsley, assert

[1] German boars and sows were also turned out in the New Forest by Charles the First, which bred and increased: and their stock is supposed to exist still.—MITFORD.

that it belongs to them; and assembling in a riotous manner, have actually taken it all away. One man, who keeps a team, has carried home, for his share, forty stacks of wood. Forty-five of these people his lordship has served with actions. These trees, which were very sound and in high perfection, were winter-cut, viz., in February and March, before the bark would run. In old times, the Holt was estimated to be eighteen miles, computed measure, from water carriage, viz., from the town of Chertsey, on the Thames; but now it is not half that distance, since the Wey is made navigable up to the town of Godalming, in the county of Surrey.

LETTER X.

TO THOMAS PENNANT, ESQ.

IT has been my misfortune never to have had any neighbour whose studies have led him towards the pursuit of natural knowledge; so that, for want of a companion to quicken my industry and sharpen my attention, I have made but slender progress in a kind of information to which I have been attached from my childhood.

As to swallows (*Hirundines rusticæ*) being found in a torpid state during the winter in the Isle of Wight, or any part of this country, I never heard any such account worth attending to. But a clergyman, of an inquisitive turn, assures me that, when he was a great boy, some workmen, in pulling down the battlements of a church tower early in the spring, found two or three swifts (*Hirundines apodes*) among the rubbish, which seemed, at their first appearance, dead; but, on being carried toward the fire, revived. He told me that, out of his great care to preserve them, he put them in a paper bag, and hung them by the kitchen fire, where they were suffocated.

Another intelligent person has informed me that, while he was a schoolboy at Brighthelmstone, in Sussex, a great fragment of the chalk cliff fell down one stormy winter on the beach, and that many people found swallows among the rubbish; but, on my questioning him whether he saw any of those birds himself, to my no small disappointment he answered me in the negative, but that others assured him they did.

Young broods of swallows began to appear this year on July the eleventh, and young martins (*Hirundines urbicæ*) were then fledged in their nests. Both species will breed again once ; for I see by my *fauna* of last year, that young broods came forth so late as September the eighteenth. Are not these late hatchings more in favour of hiding than migration ? Nay, some young martins remained in their nests last year so late as September the twenty-ninth ; and yet they totally disappeared

THE SWALLOW.

with us by the fifth of October. How strange it is that the swift, which seems to live exactly the same life with the swallow and house-martin, should leave us before the middle of August invariably ! while the latter stay often till the middle of October ; once I even saw numbers of house-martins on the seventh of November. The martins, redwings, and fieldfares were flying in sight together ; an uncommon assemblage of summer and winter birds !

[It is not easy to discover whether White really believed in the hybernation of swallows or not; he clings to the idea, and returns to it, although his own arguments seem to refute the notion almost as completely as those of any recent author. Writing twenty years later than the date of this letter, he tells us, in his Observations on Nature, March 23, 1788, that a gentleman who was this week on a visit at Waverly, took the opportunity of examining some of the holes in the sand-bank with which that district abounds. As these are undoubtedly bored by bank martins, and there they avowedly breed, he was in hopes that they might have slept there also, and that he might have surprised them just as they were waking from their winter slumbers. "When we had dug for some time," he says, "we found the holes were horizontal and serpentine, as I had observed before; and that the nests were deposited at the inner end, and had been occupied by broods in former summers, but no torpid birds were to be found. The same search was made many years ago with as little success." March 2, 1793, Mr. White adds, "a single sand-martin was seen hovering and playing round the sandpit at Short-heath, where they abound in summer. April 9, 1793, a sober herd assures me that this day he saw several on West Hanger common, between Hadleigh and Frensham, several sand-martins playing in and out and hanging before some nest-holes where the birds nestle.

"This incident confirms my suspicions, that this species of *hirundo* is to be seen the first of any, and gives reason to suppose that they do not leave their wild haunts at all, but are secreted amidst the clefts and caverns of these abrupt cliffs. The late severe weather considered, it is not very probable that these birds should have migrated so early from a tropical region, through all these cutting winds and pinching frosts; but it is easy to suppose that they may, like bats and flies, have been awakened by the influence of the sun, amidst their secret *latebrœ* where they have spent the uncomfortable foodless months in a torpid state, and in the profoundest slumbers.

"There is a large pond at West Hanger which induces these sand-martins to frequent the district; for I have ever remarked that they haunt near great waters, either rivers or lakes."

A year later, he says, "During the severe winds that often prevail late in the spring, it is not easy to say how the *hirundines* subsist: for they withdraw themselves, and are hardly ever seen,

nor do any insects appear for their support.   That they can retire to rest and sleep away these uncomfortable periods as bats
do, is a matter rather suspected than proved ; or do they not
rather spend their time in deep and sheltered vales near
waters where insects are to be found ?   Certain it is that
hardly any individuals have, at such times, been seen for days
together.

"September 13, 1791, the congregating flocks of *hirundines*
on the church and tower are both beautiful and amusing. When
they fly off together from the roof on any alarm, they quite
swarm in the air. But they soon settle again in heaps, and
pulling their feathers and lifting up their wings to admit the
sun, they seem to enjoy the warm situation. Thus they spend
the heat of the day, preparing for their migration, and, as it
were, consulting when and where they are to go. The flight
about the church seems to consist chiefly of house-martins, about
400 in number ; but there are other places of rendezvous about
the village frequented at the same time. . It is remarkable that,
though most of them sit on the battlements and roof, yet many
of them hang or cling for some time by their claws against the
surface of the walls in a manner not practised by them at other
times of their remaining with us. The swallows seem to delight
more in holding their assemblies on trees.

"November 3, 1789, the swallows were seen this morning, at
Newton Vicarage house, hovering and settling on the roofs and
outbuildings.   None have been observed at Selborne since
October 11. It is very remarkable that after the *hirundines*
have disappeared for some weeks, a few are occasionally seen
again ; sometimes in the first week of November, and that only
for one day. Do they not withdraw and slumber in some hiding-
place during the interval ? for we cannot suppose they had
migrated to warmer climes, and returned again for one day. Is
it not more probable that they are awakened from sleep, and
like the bats are come forth to collect a little food ? These
swallows looked like young ones."]

A little yellow bird (the *Motacilla trochilus*) still continues to
make a sibilous shivering noise in the tops of tall woods. The
stoparola of Ray is called, in your Zoology, the fly-catcher.
There is one circumstance characteristic of this bird, which
seems to have escaped observation, and that is, it takes its stand
on the top of some stake or post, from whence it springs forth
on its prey, catching a fly in the air, and hardly ever touching

the ground, but returning still to the same stand for many times together.

I perceive there are more than one species of the *Motacilla* which visits us. Mr. Derham supposes, in Ray's "Philos. Letters," that he has discovered three. In these there is again an instance of some very common birds that have as yet no English name.

Mr. Stillingfleet makes a question whether the blackcap (*Motacilla atricapilla*) be a bird of passage or not : I think there is no doubt of it : for, in April, in the first fine weather, they come trooping, all at once, into these parts, but are never seen in the winter. They are delicate songsters.

Numbers of snipes breed every summer in some moory ground on the verge of this parish. It is very amusing to see the cock bird on wing at that time, and to hear his piping and humming notes.

I have had no opportunity yet of procuring any of those mice which I mentioned to you in town. The person that brought me the last says they are plentiful in harvest, at which time I will take care to get more ; and will endeavour to put it out of doubt whether it be a nondescript species or not.

I suspect much there may be two species of water-rats. Ray says, and Linnæus after him, that the water-rat is web-footed behind. Now I have discovered a rat on the banks of our little stream that is not web-footed, and yet is an excellent swimmer and diver : it answers exactly to the *Mus amphibius* of Linnæus, which, he says, swims and dives in ditches, "natat in fossis et urinatur." I should be glad to procure "one with the feet feathering out like a palm," "*plantis palmatis.*" Linnæus seems to be in a puzzle about his *Mus amphibius,* and to doubt whether it differs from his *Mus terrestris,* which if it be, as he allows, the " mus agrestis capite grandi brachyurus," a field-mouse, with " a large head and a short tail," is widely different from the water-rat, both in size, make, and manner of life.

As to the *falco,* which I mentioned in town, I shall take the liberty to send it down to you into Wales ; presuming on your candour, that you will excuse me if it should appear as familiar to you as it is strange to me. " Though mutilated, such as you would say it had formerly been, seeing that the remains are what they are," " *qualem dices . . . antehac fuisse, tales cum sint reliquiæ !* "

It haunted a marshy piece of ground in quest of wild ducks

and snipes; but when it was shot, had just knocked down a rook, which it was tearing in pieces. I cannot make it answer to any of our English hawks; neither could I find any like it at the curious exhibition of stuffed birds in Spring Gardens. I found it nailed up at the end of a barn, which is the country-man's museum.

The parish I live in is a very abrupt, uneven country, full of hills and woods, and therefore full of birds.

August 4, 1767.

[In severe weather, fieldfares, redwings, skylarks, and titlarks resort to watered meadows for food; the latter wades up to its belly in pursuit of the pupæ of insects, and runs along upon the floating grass and weeds. Many gnats are on the snow near the water; these support the birds in part.

Birds are much influenced in their choice of food by colour, for though white currants are a much sweeter fruit than red, yet they seldom touch the former till they have devoured every bunch of the latter.

Redstarts, fly-catchers, and blackcaps arrive early in April. If these little delicate beings are birds of passage, how could they, feeble as they seem, bear up against such storms of snow and rain, and make their way through such meteorous turbulences as one should suppose would embarrass and retard the most hardy and resolute of the winged nation? Yet they keep their appointed times and seasons; and in spite of frosts and winds return to their stations periodically, as if they had met with nothing to obstruct them. The withdrawing and reappearance of the short-winged summer birds is a very puzzling circumstance in natural history!

When the boys bring me wasps' nests, my bantam fowls fare deliciously, and when the combs are pulled to pieces, devour the young wasps in their maggot state with the highest glee and delight. Any insect-eating bird would do the same. Birds of prey occasionally feed on insects: thus have I seen a tame kite picking up the female ants full of eggs with much satisfaction.]
—OBSERVATIONS ON NATURE.

LETTER XI.

TO THOMAS PENNANT, ESQ.

It will not be without impatience that I shall wait for your thoughts with regard to the *falco;* as to its weight, breadth, &c. I wish I had set them down at the time ; but, to the best of my remembrance, it weighed two pounds and eight ounces, an

THE HOOPOE.

measured, from wing to wing, thirty-eight inches. Its cere and feet were yellow, and the circle of its eyelids a bright yellow. As it had been killed some days, and the eyes were sunk, I could make no good observation on the colour of the pupils and the irides.[1]

The most unusual birds I ever observed in these parts were a pair of Hoopoes (*upupa*), which came several years ago in the summer, and frequented an ornamented piece of ground, which

[1] The irides are brown in all the British falcons.

joins to my garden, for some weeks. They used to march about in a stately manner, feeding in the walks many times in the day, and seemed disposed to breed in my outlet; but were frighted and persecuted by idle boys, who would never let them be at rest.

Three grosbeaks (*Loxia coccothraustes*) appeared some years ago in my fields, in the winter; one of which I shot; since that, now and then, one is occasionally seen in the same dead season.

[Mr. B. shot a cock grosbeak which he had observed to haunt his garden for more than a fortnight. I began to accuse this bird of making sad havoc among the buds of the cherries, gooseberries, and wall-fruit of all the neighbouring orchards. Upon opening its crop or craw, however, no buds were to be seen, but a mass of kernels of the stones of fruits. Mr. B. observed that

HOOPOE'S EGG.

this bird frequented the spot where plum-trees grow; and that he had seen it with somewhat hard in its mouth, which it broke with difficulty; these were the stones of damsons. The Latin ornithologists call this bird *coccothraustes*, i.e., berry-breaker, because with its large horny beak it cracks and breaks the shells of stone-fruits for the sake of the seed or kernel. Birds of this sort are rarely seen in England, and only in winter.]—OBSERVATIONS ON NATURE.

A cross-bill (*Loxia curvirostra*) was killed last year in this neighbourhood.

Our streams, which are small, and rise only at the end of the village, yield nothing but the bull's head,[1] or miller's thumb (*Gobius fluviatilis capitatus*), the trout (*Trutta fluviatilis*), the eel (*anguilla*), the lampern (*Lampetra parva et fluviatilis*), and the stickleback (*Pisciculus aculeatus*).

We are twenty miles from the sea, and almost as many from

---

[1] *Salmo fario.* Linn.

D

a great river, and therefore see but little of sea-birds. As to wild fowls, we have a few teams of ducks bred in the moors where the snipes breed; and multitudes of widgeons and teals frequent our lakes in the forest in hard weather.

Having some acquaintance with a tame brown owl, I find that it casts up the fur of mice and the feathers of birds in pellets, after the manner of hawks: when full, like a dog, it hides what it cannot eat.

The young of the barn owl are not easily raised, as they want a constant supply of fresh mice: whereas the young of the brown owl will eat indiscriminately all that is brought; snails, rats, kittens, puppies, magpies, and any kind of carrion or offal.

The house-martins have eggs still, and squab-young. The last swift I observed was about the twenty-first of August; it was a straggler.

Redstarts, fly-catchers, white-throats, and gold-crested wrens, *reguli non cristati*, still appear; but I have seen no blackcaps lately.

I forgot to mention that I once saw, in Christ Church college quadrangle in Oxford, on a very sunny, warm morning, a house-martin flying about, and settling on the parapet, so late as the twentieth of November.

At present I know only two species of bats, the common *Vespertilio murinus* and the *Vespertilio auritus*.

I was much entertained last summer with a tame bat, which would take flies out of a person's hand. If you gave it anything to eat, it brought its wings round before the mouth, hovering and hiding its head in the manner of birds of prey when they feed. The adroitness it showed in shearing off the wings of flies, which were always rejected, was worthy of observation, and pleased me much. Insects seemed to be most acceptable, though it did not refuse raw flesh when offered: so that the notion that bats go down chimneys and gnaw men's bacon seems no improbable story. While I amused myself with this wonderful quadruped, I saw it several times confute the vulgar opinion, that bats when down on a flat surface cannot get on the wing again, by rising with great ease from the floor. It ran, I observed, with more despatch than I was aware of; but in a most ridiculous and grotesque manner.

Bats drink on the wing, like swallows, by sipping the surface, as they play over pools and streams. They love to frequent waters, not only for the sake of drinking, but on account of the insects which are found over them in the greatest plenty. As I was going, some years ago, pretty late, in a boat from Richmond to Sunbury, on a warm summer's evening, I think I saw myriads of bats between the two places : the air swarmed with them all along the Thames, so that hundreds were in sight at a time.

SELBORNE, *Sept.* 9, 1767.

LETTER XII.

TO THOMAS PENNANT, ESQ.

IT gave me no small satisfaction to hear that the *falco* turned out an uncommon one. I must confess I should have been better pleased to have heard that I had sent you a bird that you had never seen before ; but that I find would be a difficult task.

I have procured some of the mice mentioned in my former letters, a young one and a female with young, both of which I have preserved in brandy. From the colour, shape, size, and manner of nesting, I make no doubt but that the species is non-descript. They are much smaller, and more slender, than the *Mus domesticus medius* of Ray ; and have more of the squirrel or dormouse colour : their belly is white; a straight line along their sides divides the shades of their back and belly. They never enter into houses ; are carried into ricks and barns with the sheaves; abound in harvest; and build their nests amidst the straws of the corn above the ground, and sometimes in thistles. They breed as many as eight at a litter, in a little round nest, composed of the blades of grass or wheat.

One of these nests I procured this autumn, most artificially platted, and composed of the blades of wheat; perfectly round, and about the size of a cricket-ball ; with the aperture so in-geniously closed, that there was no discovering to what part it belonged. It was so compact and well filled, that it would roll across the table without being discomposed, though it contained eight little mice that were naked and blind. As this nest was perfectly full, how could the dam come at her litter respectively, so as to administer a teat to each ? Perhaps she opens different places for that purpose, adjusting them again when the business is over : but she could not possibly be contained herself in the

D 2

ball with her young, which, moreover, would be daily increasing in bulk. This wonderful procreant cradle, and elegant instance of the efforts of instinct, was found in a wheatfield, suspended in the head of a thistle.

A gentleman curious in birds wrote me word that his servant had shot one last January, in that severe weather, which he believed would puzzle me. I called to see it this summer, not knowing what to expect : but the moment I took it in hand, I pronounced it the male *Garrulus Bohemicus*, or German silk-tail, from the five peculiar crimson tags or points which it carries at the ends of five of the short *remiges*. It cannot, I suppose, with any propriety be called an English bird : and yet I see, by Ray's "Philosophical Letters," that great flocks of them appeared in this kingdom in the winter of 1685, feeding on haws.

The mention of haws puts me in mind that there is a total failure of that wild fruit, so conducive to the support of many of the winged nation. For the same severe weather, late in the spring, which cut off all the produce of the more tender and curious trees, destroyed also that of the more hardy and common.

Some birds, haunting with the missel-thrushes, and feeding on the berries of the yew-tree, which answered to the description of the *Merula torquata*, or ring-ouzel, were lately seen in this neighbourhood. I employed some people to procure me a specimen, but without success.

Query.—Might not Canary-birds be naturalized to this climate, provided their eggs were put, in the spring, into the nests of some of their congeners, as goldfinches, greenfinches, &c. ?   Before winter perhaps they might be hardened, and able to shift for themselves.

About ten years ago I used to spend some weeks yearly at Sunbury, which is one of those pleasant villages lying on the Thames, near Hampton Court.   In the autumn, I could not help being much amused with those myriads of the swallow kind which assemble in those parts.   But what struck me most was, that, from the time they began to congregate, forsaking the chimneys and houses, they roosted every night in the osier-beds of the aits of that river.   Now this resorting towards that element, at that season of the year, seems to give some countenance to the northern opinion (strange as it is) of their retiring under water.   A Swedish naturalist is so much persuaded of that fact, that he talks, in his "Calendar of Flora," as familiarly of the

THE LYTHE.

swallow's going under water in the beginning of September, as he would of his poultry going to roost a little before sunset.

An observing gentleman in London writes me word that he saw a house-martin, on the twenty-third of last October, flying in and out of its nest in the Borough: and I myself, on the twenty-ninth of last October (as I was travelling through Oxford), saw four or five swallows hovering round and settling on the roof of the county hospital.

Now, is it likely that these poor little birds (which perhaps had not been hatched but a few weeks) should, at that late season of the year, and from so midland a county, attempt a voyage to Goree or Senegal, almost as far as the equator? I acquiesce entirely in your opinion—that, though most of the swallow kind may migrate, yet that some do stay behind, and hide with us during the winter.

As to the short-winged soft-billed birds which come trooping in such numbers in the spring, I am at a loss even what to think about them. I watched them narrowly this year, and saw them abound till about Michaelmas, when they appeared no longer. Subsist they cannot openly among us and yet elude the eyes of the inquisitive: and, as to their hiding, no man pretends to have found any of them in a torpid state in winter. But with regard to their migration, what difficulties attend that supposition: that such feeble bad fliers (who the summer long never flit but from hedge to hedge) should be able to traverse vast seas and continents, in order to enjoy milder seasons amidst the regions of Africa!

November 4, 1767.

LETTER XIII.

TO THOMAS PENNANT, ESQ.

As in one of your former letters you expressed the more satisfaction from my correspondence on account of my living in the most southerly county; so now I may return the compliment, and expect to have my curiosity gratified by your living much more to the north.

For many years past I have observed that towards Christmas vast flocks of chaffinches have appeared in the fields; many

more, I used to think, than could be hatched in any one neighbourhood. But, when I came to observe them more narrowly, I
was amazed to find that they seemed to me to be almost all hens.
I communicated my suspicions to some intelligent neighbours,
who, after taking pains about the matter, declared that they also
thought them mostly all females; at least fifty to one. This

THE YELLOW WAGTAIL.

extraordinary occurrence brought to my mind the remark of
Linnæus, that, "before winter all their hen chaffinches migrate
through Holland into Italy." Now I want to know, from some
curious person in the north, whether there are any large flocks
of these finches with them in the winter, and of which sex
they mostly consist? For, from such intelligence, one might be
able to judge whether our female flocks migrate from the

other end of the island, or whether they come over to us from the Continent.

We have, in the winter, vast flocks of the common linnets; more, I think, than can be bred in any one district. These, I observe, when the spring advances, assemble on some tree in the sunshine, and join all in a gentle sort of chirping, as if they were about to break up their winter quarters and betake themselves to their proper summer homes. It is well known, at least, that this is the signal of departure with the swallows and the field-fares, which congregate with a gentle twittering before they take their respective departure.

You may depend on it that the bunting (*Emberiza miliaria*) does not leave this country in the winter. In January, 1767, I saw several dozen of them, in the midst of a severe frost, among the bushes on the downs near Andover: in our woodland inclosed district it is a rare bird.

Wagtails, both white and yellow, are with us all the winter. Quails crowd to our southern coast, and are often killed in numbers by people that go on purpose.

Mr. Stillingfleet, in his Tracts, says that " if the wheatear (*œnanthe*) does not quit England, it certainly shifts places; for about harvest they are not to be found, where there was before great plenty of them." This well accounts for the vast quantities that are caught about that time on the south downs near Lewes, where they are esteemed a delicacy. There have been shepherds, I have been credibly informed, that have made many pounds in a season by catching them in traps. And though such multitudes are taken, I never saw (and I am well acquainted with those parts) above two or three at a time: for they are never gregarious. They may perhaps migrate in general; and, for that purpose, draw towards the coast of Sussex in autumn: but that they do not all withdraw I am sure: because I see a few stragglers in many counties, at all times of the year, especially about warrens and stone-quarries.

I have no acquaintance, at present, among the gentlemen of the navy: but have written to a friend, who was a sea-chaplain in the late war, desiring him to look into his minutes, with respect to birds that settled on their rigging during their voyage up or down the Channel. What Hasselquist says on that subject is remarkable: there were little short-winged birds frequently coming on board his ship all the way from our Channel quite up to the Levant, especially before squally weather.

What you suggest with regard to Spain is highly probable. The winters of Andalusia are so mild, that, in all likelihood, the soft-billed birds that leave us at that season, may find insects sufficient to support them there.

Some young men, possessed of fortune, health, and leisure, should make an autumnal voyage into that kingdom; and should spend a year there, investigating the natural history of that vast

THE WHEATEAR.

country. Mr. Willughby passed through that kingdom on such an errand; but he seems to have skirted along in a superficial manner and an ill-humour, being much disgusted at the rude dissolute manners of the people.

I have no friend left now at Sunbury to apply to about the swallows roosting on the aits of the Thames: nor can I hear any more about those birds which I suspected were *Merulæ torquatæ*.

· As to the small mice, I have further to remark, that though they hang their nests for breeding up amidst the straws of the standing corn, above the ground ; yet I find that, in the winter, they burrow deep in the earth, and make warm beds of grass : but their grand rendezvous seems to be in corn-ricks, into which they are carried at harvest. A neighbour housed an oat-rick lately, under the thatch of which were assembled near an hundred, most of which were taken ; and some I saw. I measured them, and found that from nose to tail, they were just two inches and a quarter, and their tails just two inches long. Two of them, in a scale, weighed down just one copper halfpenny, which is about the third of an ounce avoirdupois : so that I suppose they are the smallest quadrupeds in this island. A full grown *Mus medius domesticus* weighs, I find, one ounce lumping weight, which is more than six times as much as the mouse above ; and measures from nose to rump four inches and a quarter, and the same in its tail. We have had a very severe frost and deep snow this month. My thermometer was one day fourteen degrees and a half below the freezing point, within doors. The tender evergreens were injured pretty much. It was very providential that the air was still, and the ground well covered with snow, else vegetation in general must have suffered prodigiously. There is reason to believe that some days were more severe than any since the year 1739–40.

SELBORNE, *Jan.* 22, 1768.

LETTER XIV.

TO THOMAS PENNANT, ESQ.

IF some curious gentleman would procure the head of a fallow deer, and have it dissected, he would find it furnished with two spiracula, or breathing-places, besides the nostrils ; probably analogous to the *puncta lachrymalia* in the human head. When deer are thirsty they plunge their noses, like some horses, very deep under water while in the act of drinking, and continue them in that situation for a considerable time : but to obviate any inconveniency, they can open two vents, one at the inner corner of each eye, having a communication with the nose. Here seems to be an extraordinary provision of nature worthy our attention; and which has not, that I know of, been noticed by any naturalist. For it looks as if these creatures would not be suffocated though both their mouths and nostrils were stopped. This curious formation of the head may be of singular service to beasts of chase, by affording them free respiration: and no doubt these additional nostrils are thrown open when they are hard run.[1] Mr. Ray observed that at Malta the owners slit up the nostrils of such asses as were hard worked: for they being naturally strait or small, did not admit air sufficient to serve them when they travelled, or laboured, in that hot climate. And we know that grooms, and gentlemen of the turf, think large nostrils necessary, and a perfection in hunters and running horses.

THE EGG OF THE QUAIL.

Oppian, the Greek poet, by the following line, seems to have had some notion that stags have four spiracula :—

"Τετραδύμοί 'ρῖνες, πίσυρες πνοιῇσι δίαυλοι."

"Quadrifidæ nares, quadruplices ad respirationem canales."

Opp. Cyn. Lib. ii. l. 181.

("Nostrils split in four divisions, fourfold passages for breathing.")

Writers, copying from one another, make Aristotle say that goats breathe at their ears; whereas he asserts just the contrary :

"Ἀλκμαίων γὰρ οὐκ ἀληθῆ λέγει, φάμενος ἀναπνεῖν τὰς αἰγὰς κατὰ τὰ

[1] In answer to this account, Mr. Pennant sent me the following curious and pertinent reply :—"I was much surprised to find in the antelope something analogous to what you mention as so remarkable in deer. This animal also has a long slit beneath each eye, which can be opened and shut at pleasure. On holding an orange to one, the creature made as much use of those orifices as of his nostrils, applying them to the fruit, and seeming to smell it through them."—WHITE.

ὦτα." "Alcmæon does not advance what is true, when he avers that goats breathe through their ears."—HISTORY OF ANIMALS, Book i. ch. xi.

SELBORNE, *March* 12, 1768.

LETTER XV.

TO THOMAS PENNANT, ESQ.

SOME intelligent country-people have a notion that we have in these parts a species of the *genus mustelinum*, besides the weasel, stoat, ferret, and polecat; a little reddish beast, not much bigger than a field mouse, but much longer, which they call a cane. This piece of intelligence can be little depended on; but further inquiry may be made.

A gentleman in this neighbourhood had two milk-white rooks in one nest. A booby of a carter, finding them before they were able to fly, threw them down and destroyed them, to the regret of the owner, who would have been glad to have preserved such a curiosity in his rookery. I saw the birds myself nailed against the end of a barn, and was surprised to find that their bills, legs, feet, and claws were milk-white.

[Rooks are continually fighting and pulling each other's nests to pieces: these proceedings are inconsistent with living in such close community. And yet if a pair offer to build on a single tree, the nest is plundered and demolished at once. Some rooks roost on their nest trees. The twigs which the rooks drop in building supply the poor with brushwood to light their fires. Some unhappy pairs are not permitted to finish any nest till the rest have completed their building. As soon as they get a few sticks together, a party comes and demolishes the whole. As soon as rooks have finished their nests, and before they lay, the cocks begin to feed the hens, who receive their bounty with a fondling tremulous voice and fluttering wings, and all the little blandishments that are expressed by the young while in a helpless state. This gallant deportment of the males is continued through the whole season of incubation. These birds do not copulate on trees, nor in their nests, but on the ground in the open fields.][1]

[1] After the first brood of rooks are sufficiently fledged, they all resort to some distant place in search of food, but return regularly every evening, in

A shepherd saw, as he thought, some white larks on a down above my house this winter : were not these the *Emberiza nivalis*, the snow-flake of the Brit. Zool. ? No doubt they were.

THE BULLFINCH.

A few years ago I saw a cock bullfinch in a cage, which had been caught in the fields after it was come to its full colours. In about a year it began to look dingy; and blackening every succeeding year, it became coal-black at the end of four. Its

vast flights, to their nest trees, where, after flying round with much noise and clamour, till they are all assembled together, they take up their abode for the night.—MARKWICK.

chief food was hempseed.   Such influence has food on the colour of animals! The pied and mottled colours of domesticated animals are supposed to be owing to high, various, and unusual food.

I had remarked for years that the root of the cuckoo-pint (*arum*) was frequently scratched out of the dry banks of hedges, and eaten in severe snowy weather. After observing, with some exactness, myself, and getting others to do the same, we found it was the thrush kind that searched it out.   The root of the *arum* is remarkably warm and pungent.

Our flocks of female chaffinches have not yet forsaken us. The blackbirds and thrushes are very much thinned down by that fierce weather in January.

In the middle of February I discovered, in my tall hedges, a little bird that raised my curiosity ; it was of that yellow-green colour that belongs to the *salicaria* kind, and I think was soft-billed.   It was no *parus ;* and was too long and too big for the golden-crowned wren, appearing most like the largest willow-wren.   It hung sometimes with its back downwards, but never continuing one moment in the same place.   I shot at it, but it was so desultory that I missed my aim.

I wonder that the stone-curlew, *Charadrius oedicnemus*, should be mentioned by writers as a rare bird : it abounds in all the campaign parts of Hampshire and Sussex, and breeds, I think, all the summer, having young ones, I know, very late in the autumn.   Already they begin clamouring in the evening.   They cannot, I think, with any propriety be called, as they are by Mr. Ray, dwellers about streams or ponds, *circa aquas versantes ;* for with us, by day at least, they haunt only the most dry, open, upland fields and sheep-walks, far removed from water ; what they may do in the night I cannot say.   Worms are their usual food, but they also eat toads and frogs.

I can show you some good specimens of my new mice.   Linnæus, perhaps, would call the species *Mus minimus*.

LETTER XVI.

TO THOMAS PENNANT, ESQ.

THE history of the stone-curlew, *Charadrius oedicnemus*, is as follows.   It lays its eggs, usually two, never more than three, on the bare ground, without any nest, in the field; so that the countryman, in stirring his fallows, often destroys them. The young run immediately from the egg like partridges, &c., and are withdrawn to some flinty field by the dam, where they skulk among the stones, which are their best security; for their feathers are so exactly of the colour of our grey-spotted flints,

THE NUTHATCH.

that the most exact observer, unless he catches the eye of the young bird, may be eluded. The eggs are short and round; of a dirty white, spotted with dark bloody blotches. Though I might not be able, just when I pleased, to procure you a bird, yet I could show you them almost any day; and any evening you may hear them round the village, for they make a clamour which may be heard a mile. *Oedicnemus* is a most apt and

expressive name for them, since their legs seem swollen like those
,of a gouty man. After harvest I have shot them before the
pointers in turnip-fields.

I make no doubt but there are three species of the willow-
wrens; two I know perfectly: but have not been able yet to
procure the third. No two birds can differ more in their notes,
and that constantly, than those two that I am acquainted with;
for the one has a joyous, easy, laughing note; the other a harsh
loud chirp. The former is every way larger, and three-quarters
of an inch longer, and weighs two drams and a half, while the
latter weighs but two; so the songster is one-fifth heavier than
the chirper. The chirper (being the first summer bird of passage
that is heard, the wryneck sometimes excepted) begins his two
notes in the middle of March, and continues them through the
spring and summer till the end of August, as appears by my
journals. The legs of the larger of these two are flesh-coloured;
of the less, black.

NUTHATCH'S EGG.

GOLDEN-CROWNED WREN'S EGG.

The grasshopper-lark began his sibilous note in my fields last
Saturday. Nothing can be more amusing than the whisper of
this little bird, which seems to be close by though at a hundred
yards distance; and when close at your ear is scarce any louder
than when a great way off. Had I not been a little acquainted
with insects, and known that the grasshopper kind is not yet
hatched, I should have hardly believed but that it had been a
locusta whispering in the bushes. The country people laugh
when you tell them that it is the note of a bird. It is a most
artful creature, skulking in the thickest part of a bush: and
will sing at a yard distance, provided it be concealed. I was
obliged to get a person to go on the other side of the hedge
where it haunted: and then it would run, creeping like a mouse,
before us for a hundred yards together, through the bottom of
the thorns; yet it would not come into fair sight: but in a
morning early, and when undisturbed, it sings on the top of a
twig, gaping and shivering with its wings. Mr. Ray himself
had no knowledge of this bird, but received his account from

Mr. Johnson, who apparently confounds it with the *Reguli non cristati*, from which it is very distinct.

The fly-catcher (*Stoparola*, Ray) has not yet appeared; it usually breeds in my vine. The redstart begins to sing: its note is short and imperfect, but is continued till about the middle of June. The willow-wrens (the smaller sort) are horrid pests in a garden, destroying the peas, cherries, and currants, and are so tame that a gun will not scare them.[1]

My countrymen talk much of a bird that makes a clatter with its bill against a dead bough, or some old pales, calling it a jar-bird. I procured one to be shot in the very fact; it proved to be the nuthatch, (*Sitta Europœa*). Mr. Ray says that the less spotted woodpecker does the same. This noise may be heard a furlong or more off.

Now is the only time to ascertain the short-winged summer birds; for when the leaf is out there is no making any remarks on such a restless tribe: and when once the young begin to appear it is all confusion: there is no distinction of genus, species or sex.

In breeding-times snipes play over the moors, piping and humming: they always hum as they are descending. Is not their hum ventriloquous, like that of the turkey? Some suspect it is made by their wings.

[1] A list of the Summer Birds of Passage discovered in this neighbourhood ranged somewhat in the order in which they appear :—

LINNÆI NOMINA.

Smallest willow-wren,	*Motacilla trochilus.*
Wryneck,	*Junx torquilla.*
House-swallow,	*Hirundo rustica.*
Martin,	*Chelidon urbica.*
Sand-martin,	*Cotile riparia.*
Cuckoo,	*Cuculus canorus.*
Nightingale,	*Lusinia philomela.*
Blackcap,	*Motacilla atricapilla.*
Whitethroat,	*Motacilla sylvia.*
Middle willow-wren,	*Motacilla trochilus.*
Swift,	*Hirundo apus.*
Stone curlew, ?	*Charadrius oedicnemus. ?*
Turtle-dove, ?	*Turtur aldrovandi. ?*
Grasshopper-lark,	*Alauda trivialis.*
Landrail,	*Rallus crex.*
Largest willow-wren,	*Motacilla trochilus.*
Redstart,	*Ruticilla phœnicura.*
Goatsucker, or fern-owl,	*Caprimulgus Europœa.*
Fly-catcher,	*Muscicapa grisola.*

E

This morning I saw the golden-crowned wren, whose crown glitters like burnished gold. It often hangs like a titmouse, with its back downwards.

SELBORNE, *April* 18, 1768.

THE GOLDEN-CROWNED WREN.

LETTER XVII.

TO THOMAS PENNANT, ESQ.

ON Wednesday last arrived your agreeable letter of June the 10th. It gives me great satisfaction to find that you pursue these studies still with such vigour, and are in such forwardness with regard to reptiles and fishes.

The reptiles, few as they are, I am not acquainted with so well as I could wish, with regard to their natural history. There is a degree of dubiousness and obscurity attending the propagation of this class of animals, something analogous to that of the cryptogamia in the sexual system of plants : and the case is the same with regard to some of the fishes ; as the eel, &c.

The method in which toads procreate and bring forth seems to be very much in the dark. Some authors say that they are viviparous : and yet Ray classes them among his oviparous animals ; and is silent with regard to the manner of their bringing forth. Perhaps they may be ἔσω μὲν ὠοτόκοι, ἔξω δὲ ζωοτόκοι, as is known to be the case with the viper. That of frogs is notorious to everybody : because we see them sticking upon each other's backs for a month together in the spring : and yet I never saw or read of toads being observed in the same situation. It is strange that the matter with regard to the venom of toads has not yet been settled. That they are not noxious to some animals is plain : for ducks, buzzards, owls, stone-curlews, and snakes eat them, to my knowledge, with impunity. And I well remember the time, but was not eye-witness to the fact (though numbers of persons were) when a quack at this village ate a toad to make the country-people stare ; afterwards he drank oil.

I have been informed also, from undoubted authority, that some ladies (ladies you will say of peculiar taste) took a fancy to a toad, which they nourished summer after summer, for many years, with the maggots which turn to flesh flies, till he grew to a monstrous size. The reptile used to come forth every evening from a hole under the garden steps ; and was taken up on the table to be fed after supper. But at last a tame raven, kenning him as he put forth his head, gave him such a severe stroke with his horny beak as put out one eye. After this accident the creature languished for some time and died.

I need not remind a gentleman of your extensive reading of the excellent account there is from Mr. Derham, in Ray's "Wisdom of God in the Creation," concerning the migration of frogs from their breeding ponds. In this account he at once subverts that foolish opinion of their dropping from the clouds in rain ; showing that it is from the grateful coolness and moisture of those showers that they are tempted to set out on their travels, which they defer till those fall. Frogs are as yet in their tadpole state; but in a few weeks our lanes, paths, fields, will swarm for a few days with myriads of those emigrants, no larger than my little finger nail. Swammerdam gives a most accurate account of the method and situation in which the male impregnates the spawn of the female. How wonderful is the economy of Providence with regard to the limbs of so vile a reptile! While it is an aquatic, or in a tadpole state, it has a fish-like tail, and no legs: as soon as the legs sprout, the tail drops off as useless, and the animal betakes itself to the land.[1]

Merrit, I trust, is widely mistaken when he advances that the *Rana arborea* is an English reptile; it abounds in Germany and Switzerland.

It is to be remembered that the *Salamandra aquatica* of Ray (the water-newt, or eft) will frequently bite at the angler's bait, and is often caught on his hook. I used to take it for granted that the *Salamandra aquatica* was hatched, lived, and died, in the water. But John Ellis, Esq., F.R.S. (the coralline Ellis), asserts, in a letter to the Royal Society, dated June 5th, 1766, in his account of the *Mud inguana*, an amphibious bipes from South Carolina, that the water-eft, or newt, is only the larva of the land-eft, as tadpoles are of frogs. Lest I should be suspected of misunderstanding his meaning, I shall give it in his own words. Speaking of the opercula or coverings to the gills of the *Mud inguana*, he proceeds to say that "the form of these pennated coverings approaches very near to what I have some time ago observed in the lava or aquatic state of our English *Lacerta*, known by the name of eft or newt: which serve them for coverings to their gills, and for fins to swim with while in this state; and which they lose, as well as the fins of their tails, when they change their state and become land animals, as I have observed, by keeping them alive for some time myself."

Linnæus, in his "Systema Naturæ," hints more than once at what Mr. Ellis advances.

Providence has been so indulgent to us as to allow of but one venomous reptile of the serpent kind in these kingdoms, and that is the viper. As you propose the good of mankind to be an object of your publications, you will not omit to mention common salad-oil as a sovereign remedy against the bite of the viper. As to the blind worm (*Anguis fragilis*, so called because

---

[1] The tale of the tadpole does not drop off; it is absorbed.

it snaps in sunder with a small blow), I have found on examination that it is perfectly innocuous.   A neighbouring yeoman
(to whom I am indebted for some good hints) killed and opened
a female viper about the 27th of May; he found her filled with
a chain of eleven eggs, about the size of those of a blackbird;
but none of them were advanced so far towards a state of maturity as to contain any rudiments of young.   Though they are

GREATHAM CHURCH.

oviparous, yet they are viviparous also, hatching their young
within their bellies, and then bringing them forth.   Whereas
snakes lay chains of eggs every summer in my melon-beds, in
spite of all that my people can do to prevent them; which eggs
do not hatch till the spring following, as I have often expe-

rienced. Several intelligent folks assure me that they have
seen the viper open her mouth and admit her helpless young
down her throat on sudden surprises, just as the female opossum
does her brood into the pouch under her belly, upon the like
emergencies; and yet the London viper-catchers insist on it, to
Mr. Barrington, that no such thing ever happens. The serpent
kind eat, I believe, but once in a year; or, rather, but only just
at one season of the year. Country people talk much of a
water-snake, but, I am pretty sure, without any reason; for the
common snake (*Coluber natrix*) delights much to sport in the
water, perhaps with a view to procure frogs and other food.

I cannot well guess how you are to make out your twelve
species of reptiles, unless it be the various species, or rather
varieties, of our *Lacerti*, of which Ray enumerates five. I have
not had opportunity of ascertaining these; but remember well
to have seen, formerly, several beautiful green *Lacerti* on the
sunny sandbanks near Farnham, in Surrey; and Ray admits
there are such in Ireland.

SELBORNE, *June* 18, 1768.

LETTER XVIII.

TO THOMAS PENNANT, ESQ.

I RECEIVED your obliging and communicative letter of June the
28th, while I was on a visit at a gentleman's house, where I
had neither books to turn to nor leisure to sit down to return
you an answer to many queries, which I wanted to resolve in
the best manner that I am able.

A person, by my order, has searched our brooks, but could
find no such fish as the *Gasterosteus pungitius :* he found the
Gasterosteus aculeatus in plenty. This morning, in a basket, I
packed a little earthen pot full of wet moss, and in it some
sticklebacks, male and female; the females big with spawn :
some lamperns; some bullheads; but I could procure no
minnows. This basket will be in Fleet Street by eight this
evening; so I hope Mazel [1] will have them fresh and fair to-

---

[1] Mr. Peter Mazel was the engraver of Pennant's plates.

morrow morning. I gave some directions in a letter to what particulars the engraver should be attentive.

Finding, while I was on a visit, that I was within a reasonable distance of Ambresbury, I sent a servant over to that town, and procured several living specimens of loaches, which he brought, safe and brisk, in a glass decanter. They were taken in the gullies that were cut for watering the meadows. From these

GILBERT WHITE'S HOUSE FROM THE GARDEN—AS IT APPEARED IN HIS TIME.

fishes (which measured from two to four inches in length) I took the following description :—"The loach, in its general aspect, has a pellucid appearance ; its back is mottled with irregular collections of small black dots, not reaching much below the *linea lateralis,* as are the back and tail fins : a black line runs from each eye down to the nose : its belly is of a silvery white; the upper jaw projects beyond the lower, and is surrounded with six feelers, three on each side; its pectoral fins are large, its ventral much smaller; the fin behind its anus small; its dorsal fin large, containing eight spines; its tail, where it joins to the tail-fin, remarkably broad, without any taperness, so as to be characteristic of this genus: the tail-fin is broad, and square at the end. From the breadth and muscular strength of the tail it appears to be an active nimble fish."

In my visit I was not very far from Hungerford, and did not forget to make some inquiries concerning the wonderful method of curing cancers by means of toads. Several intelligent persons, both gentry and clergy, do, I find, give a great deal of credit to what was asserted in the papers; and I myself dined with a clergyman who seemed to be persuaded that what is related is matter of fact; but when I came to attend to his account, I thought I discerned circumstances which did not a little invalidate the woman's story of the manner in which she came by her skill. She says of herself: "that labouring under a virulent cancer, she went to some church where there was a vast crowd: on going into a pew, she was accosted by a strange clergyman; who, after expressing compassion for her situation, told her that if she would make such an application of living toads as is mentioned she would be well." Now is it likely that this unknown gentleman should express so much tenderness for this single sufferer, and not feel any for the many thousands that daily languish under this terrible disorder? Would he not have made use of this invaluable nostrum for his own emolument; or, at least, by some means of publication or other, have found a method of making it public for the good of mankind? In short, this woman (as it appears to me) having set up for a cancer-doctress, finds it expedient to amuse the country with this dark and mysterious relation.

The water-eft has not, that I can discern, the least appearance of any gills; for want of which it is continually rising to the surface of the water to take in fresh air. I opened a big-bellied one indeed, and found it full of spawn. Not that this circumstance at all invalidates the assertion that they are larvæ; for the larvæ of insects are full of eggs, which they exclude the instant they enter their last state. The water-eft is continually climbing over the brims of the vessel within which we keep it in water, and wandering away; and people every summer see numbers crawling out of the pools where they are hatched, up the dry banks. There are varieties of them, differing in colour; and some have fins up their tail and back, and some have not.

SELBORNE, *July* 27, 1768.

LETTER XIX.

TO THOMAS PENNANT, ESQ.

I HAVE now, past dispute, made out three distinct species of the willow-wrens (*Motacillæ trochili*) which constantly and in-variably use distinct notes; but, at the same time, I am obliged

THE WILLOW-WREN.

to confess that I know nothing of your willow-lark.[1] In my letter of April the 18th, I had told you peremptorily that I knew your willow-lark, but had not seen it then: but when I

[1] Brit. Zool., edit. 1776, octavo, p. 381.

came to procure it, it proved, in all respects, a very *Motacilla trochilus;*[1] only that it is a size larger than the other two, and the yellow-green of the whole upper part of the body is more vivid, and the belly of a clearer white. I have specimens of the three sorts now lying before me, and can discern that there are three gradations of sizes, and that the least has black legs, and the other two flesh-coloured ones. The yellowest bird is considerably the largest, and has its quill feathers and secondary feathers tipped with white, which the others have not. This last haunts only the tops of trees in high beechen woods, and makes a sibilous grasshopper-like noise, now and then, at short intervals, shivering a little with its wings when it sings; and is, I make no doubt now, the *Regulus non cristatus* of Ray ; which he says " cantat voce stridulâ locustæ." Yet this great ornithologist never suspected that there were three species.

SELBORNE, *Aug.* 17, 1768.

WILLOW WREN'S EGG.

LETTER XX.

TO THOMAS PENNANT, ESQ.

IT is, I find, in zoology as it is in botany : all nature is so full, that that district produces the greatest variety which is the most examined. Several birds, which are said to belong to the north only, are, it seems, often in the south. I have discovered this summer three species of birds with us, which writers mention as only to be seen in the northern counties. The first that was brought me (on the 14th of May) was the sandpiper (*Tringa hypoleucus*) : it was a cock bird, and haunted the banks of some ponds near the village ; and as it had a companion, doubtless intended to have bred near that water. Besides, the owner has told me since, that, on recollection, he has seen some of the same birds round his ponds in former summers.

[1] Hedge-warbler (see Letter XXVI.) : *Sylvia loquax*, black legs ; *Sylvia trochilus*, yellowish belly ; *Sylvia sibilatrix*, white belly.

The next bird that I procured (on the 21st of May) was a male red-back butcher bird (*Lanius collurio*). My neighbour who shot it says that it might easily have escaped his notice, had not the outcries and chattering of the white-throats and other small birds drawn his attention to the bush where it was : its craw was filled with legs and wings of beetles.

THE BUTCHER BIRD.

The next rare birds (which were procured for me last week) were some ring-ousels (*Turdus torquatus*).

This week twelve months a gentleman from London being with us, was amusing himself with a gun, and found, he told us, on an old yew hedge where there were berries, some birds like blackbirds, with rings of white round their necks : a neighbouring farmer also at the same time observed the same ; but, as no

specimens were procured, little notice was taken. I mentioned
this circumstance to you in my letter of November the 4th,
1767.   Last week the aforesaid farmer, seeing a large flock,
twenty or thirty, of these birds, shot two cocks and two hens :
and says, on recollection, that he remembers to have observed
these birds last spring, about Lady-day, as it were, on their
return to the north.   If these birds should prove the ousels of
the north of England, then here is a migration disclosed within
our own kingdom never before remarked.   It does not yet appear
whether they retire beyond the bounds of our island to the
south ; but it is most probable that they usually do, or else one
cannot suppose that they would have continued so long unnoticed in the southern counties.   The ousel is larger than a
blackbird, and feeds on haws; but last autumn (when there
were no haws) it fed on yew-berries; in the spring it feeds on
ivy-berries, which ripen only at that season, in March and
April.

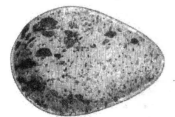

SANDPIPER'S EGG.

BUTCHER BIRD'S EGG.

I must not omit to tell you (as you have been lately on the
study of reptiles) that my people, every now and then of late,
draw up with a bucket of water from my well, which is 63 feet
deep, a large black warty lizard, with a fin-tail and yellow belly.
How they first came down at that depth, and how they were
ever to have got out thence without help, is more than I am able
to say.

My thanks are due to you for your trouble and care in the
examination of a buck's head.   As far as your discoveries reach
at present, they seem much to corroborate my suspicions; and
I hope Mr. Hunt may find reason to give his decision in my
favour; and then, I think, we may advance this extraordinary
provision of nature as a new instance of the wisdom of God in
the creation.

As yet I have not quite done with my history of the *oedicnemus*, or stone-curlew ; for I shall desire a gentleman in Sussex (near whose house these birds congregate in vast flocks in the autumn) to observe nicely when they leave him (if they do leave him), and when they return again in the spring : I was with this gentleman lately, and saw several single birds.

SELBORNE, *Oct.* 8, 1768.

LETTER XXI.

TO THOMAS PENNANT, ESQ.

WITH regard to the *oedicnemus*, or stone-curlew, I intend to write very soon to my friend near Chichester, in whose neighbourhood these birds seem most to abound ; and shall urge him to take particular notice when they begin to congregate, and afterwards to watch them most narrowly, whether they do not withdraw themselves during the dead of the winter. When I have obtained information with respect to this circumstance, I shall have finished my history of the stone-curlew ; which I hope will prove to your satisfaction, as it will be, I trust, very near the truth.

It is very extraordinary, as you observe, that a bird so common with us should never straggle to you.

After a lapse of twenty years, Mr. White adds : [On the 27th of February, 1788, stone-curlews were heard to pipe ; and on March 1st, after it was dark, some were passing over the village, as might be perceived from their quick short note, which they use in their nocturnal excursions by way of watchword, that they may not stray and lose their companions.

Thus, we see, that retire whithersoever they may in the winter, they return again early in the spring, and are, as it now appears, the first summer birds that come back. Perhaps the mildness of the season may have quickened the emigration of the curlews this year.

They spend the day in high elevated fields and sheep-walks ; but seem to descend in the night to streams and meadows, perhaps for water, which their upland haunts do not afford them.]—OBSERVATIONS ON NATURE.

And here will be the properest place to mention, while I think of it, an anecdote which the above-mentioned gentleman told me when I was last at his house; which was that, in a warren joining to his outlet, many daws (*Corvi monedulæ*) build every year in the rabbit-burrows under ground. The way he and his brothers used to take their nests, while they were boys, was by listening at the mouths of the holes; and if they heard the young ones cry, they twisted the nest out with a forked stick. Some water-fowls (viz. the puffins) breed, I know, in that manner; but I should never have suspected the daws of building in holes on the flat ground.

BRAMSHOTT CHURCH.

Another very unlikely spot is made use of by daws as a place to breed in, and that is Stonehenge. These birds deposit their nests in the interstices between the upright and the impost stones of that amazing work of antiquity: which circumstance alone speaks the prodigious height of the upright stones, that they should be tall enough to secure those nests from the annoyance of shepherd boys, who are always idling round that place.

One of my neighbours last Saturday, November the 26th, saw a martin in a sheltered bottom: the sun shone warm, and the bird was hawking briskly after flies. I am now perfectly satisfied that they do not all leave this island in the winter.

You judge very right, I think, in speaking with reserve and caution concerning the cures done by toads; for, let people advance what they will on such subjects, yet there is such a propensity in mankind towards deceiving and being deceived, that one cannot safely relate anything from common report, especially in print, without expressing some degree of doubt and suspicion.

Your approbation, with regard to my new discovery of the migration of the ring-ousel, gives me satisfaction; and I find you concur with me in suspecting that they are foreign birds which visit us. You will be sure, I hope, not to omit to make inquiry whether your ring-ousels leave your rocks in the autumn. What puzzles me most is the very short stay they make with us; for in about three weeks they are all gone. I shall be very curious to remark whether they will call on us at their return in the spring, as they did last year.

I want to be better informed with regard to icthyology. If fortune had settled me near the sea-side, or near some great river, my natural propensity would soon have urged me to have made myself acquainted with their productions: but as I have lived mostly in inland parts, and in an upland district, my knowledge of fishes extends little farther than to those common sorts which our brooks and lakes produce.

SELBORNE, *Nov.* 28, 1768.

LETTER XXII.

TO THOMAS PENNANT, ESQ.

As to the peculiarity of jackdaws building with us under the ground in rabbit-burrows, you have, in part, hit upon the reason; for, in reality, there are hardly any towers or steeples in all this country. And perhaps, Norfolk excepted, Hampshire and Sussex are as meanly furnished with churches as almost any counties in the kingdom. We have many livings of two or three hundred pounds a year whose houses of worship make little better appearance than dove-cots. When I first saw Northamptonshire, Cambridgeshire, and Huntingdonshire, and the fens of Lincolnshire, I was amazed at the number of spires which presented themselves from every point of view. As an admirer of prospects, I have reason to lament this want in my own country ; for such objects are very necessary ingredients in an elegant landscape.

What you mention with respect to reclaimed toads raises my curiosity.   An ancient author, though no naturalist, has well remarked that, "Every kind of beasts, and of birds, and of serpents, and things in the sea, is tamed, and hath been tamed, of mankind" (James iii. 7).

It is a satisfaction to me to find that a green lizard has actually been procured for you in Devonshire; because it corroborates my discovery, which I made many years ago, of the same sort, on a sunny sandbank near Farnham in Surrey.   I am well acquainted with the south hams of Devonshire ; and can suppose that district, from its southerly situation, to be a proper habitation for such animals in their best colours.

Since the ring-ousels of your vast mountains do certainly not forsake them against winter, our suspicions that those which visit this neighbourhood about Michaelmas are not English birds, but are driven from the more northern parts of Europe by the frosts, are still more reasonable ; and it will be worth your pains to endeavour to trace from whence they come, and to inquire why they make so very short a stay.

In the account you gave me of your error with regard to the two species of herons, you incidentally gave me great entertainment in your description of the heronry at Cressi Hall; which is a curiosity I never could manage to see.   Fourscore nests of such a bird on one tree is a rarity which I would ride half as many miles to get a sight of.   Pray tell me in your next whose seat Cressi Hall is, and near what town it lies.[1]   I have often thought that those vast fens have not been sufficiently explored. If half a dozen gentlemen, furnished with a good strength of water-spaniels, were to beat them over for a week, they would certainly find more species.

There is no bird whose manners I have studied more than that of the *caprimulgus* (the goat-sucker) : it is a wonderful and curious creature, but I have always found that though sometimes it may chatter as it flies, as I know it does, yet in general it utters its jarring note sitting on a bough ; and I have for many a half-hour watched it as it sat with its under mandible quivering, and particularly this summer.   It perches usually on

---

[1] Cressi Hall is near Spalding, in Lincolnshire.

a bare twig, with its head lower than its tail, in an attitude well expressed by your draughtsman in the folio "British Zoology." This bird is most punctual in beginning its song exactly at the

THE WISHING STONE.

close of day; so exactly that I have known it strike up more than once or twice just at the report of the Portsmouth evening gun, which we can hear when the weather is still. It appears to me past all doubt that its notes are formed by organic impulse,

F

by the powers of the parts of its windpipe formed for sound, just as cats pur. You will credit me, I hope, when I assure you that as my neighbours were assembled in a hermitage on the side of a steep hill, where we drink tea sometimes, one of these churn-owls came and settled on the cross of that little straw edifice and began to chatter, and continued his note for many minutes; and we were all struck with wonder to find that the organs of the little animal, when put in motion, gave a sensible vibration to the whole building! This bird also sometimes makes a small squeak, repeated four or five times; and I have observed that to happen when the cock has been pursuing the hen in a toying way through the boughs of a tree.

After a lapse of twenty years the author adds the following to his "History of the Fern-owl or Goat-sucker:"—

[The country people have a notion that the fern-owl, or churn-owl, or eve-jarr, which they also call a puckeridge, is very injurious to weanling calves, by inflicting, as it strikes at them, the fatal distemper known to cow-leeches by the name of puckeridge. Thus does this harmless ill-fated bird fall under a double imputation which it by no means deserves—in Italy, of sucking the teats of goats, whence it is called *caprimulgus;* and with us of communicating a deadly disorder to cattle. But the truth of the matter is, the malady above mentioned is occasioned by the *Œstrus bovis*, a dipterous insect, which lays its eggs along the chines of kine, where the maggots, when hatched, eat their way through the hide of the beast into the flesh, and grow to a very large size. I have just talked with a man, who says he has more than once stripped calves who have died of the puckeridge; that the ail or complaint lay along the chine, where the flesh was much swelled, and filled with purulent matter. I myself once saw a large rough maggot of this sort squeezed out of the back of a cow. In Essex these maggots are called wornills.

The least observation and attention would convince men that these birds neither injure the goatherd nor the grazier, but are perfectly harmless, and subsist alone, being night birds, on night insects, such as *scarabœi* and *phalœnœ;* and through the month of July mostly on the *Scarabœus solstitialis*, which in many districts abounds at that season. Those that we have opened have always had their craws stuffed with large night moths and their eggs, and pieces of chafers: nor does it anywise appear how they can, weak and unarmed as they seem, inflict any harm upon kine, unless they possess the powers of animal magnetism, and can affect them by fluttering over them.

A fern-owl this evening (August 27) showed off in a very unusual and entertaining manner, by hawking round and round the circumference of my great spreading oak for twenty times following, keeping mostly close to the grass, but occasionally glancing up amidst the boughs of the tree. This amusing bird was then in pursuit of a brood of some particular *phalæna* belonging to the oak, of which there are several sorts; and exhibited on the occasion a command of wing superior, I think, to that of the swallow itself.

When a person approaches the haunt of fern-owls in an evening, they continue flying round the head of the obtruder; and by striking their wings together above their backs, in the manner that the pigeons called smiters are known to do, make a smart snap: perhaps at that time they are jealous for their young; and their noise and gesture are intended by way of menace.

Fern-owls seem to have an attachment to oaks, no doubt on account of food; for the next evening we saw one again several times among the boughs of the same tree; but it did not skim round its stem over the grass, as on the evening before. In May these birds find the *Scarabæus melolontha* on the oak; and the *Scarabæus solstitialis* at midsummer; but they can only be watched and observed for two hours in the twenty-four; and then in a dubious twilight an hour after sunset and an hour before sunrise.

On this day (July 14, 1789) a woman brought me two eggs of a fern-fowl or eve-jarr, which she found on the verge of the Hanger, to the left of the hermitage, under a beechen shrub. This person, who lives just at the foot of the Hanger, seems well acquainted with these nocturnal swallows, and says she has often found their eggs near that place, and that they lay only two at a time on the bare ground. The eggs were oblong, dusky, and streaked somewhat in the manner of the plumage of the parent bird, and were equal in size at each end. The dam was sitting on the eggs when found, which contained the rudiments of young, and would have been hatched perhaps in a week. From hence we may see the time of their breeding, which corresponds pretty well with that of the swift, as does also the period of their arrival. Each species is usually seen about the beginning of May. Each breeds but once in a summer; and each lays only two eggs.

F 2

July 4, 1790. The woman who brought me two fern-owls' eggs last year on July 14, on this day produced me two more, one of which had been laid this morning, as appears plainly, because there was only one in the nest the evening before. They were found, as last July, on the verge of the down above the hermitage under a beechen shrub, on the naked ground. Last year those eggs were full of young, and just ready to be hatched.

These circumstances point out the exact time when these curious nocturnal migratory birds lay their eggs, and hatch their young. Fern-owls, like snipes, stone-curlews, and some other birds, make no nest. Birds that build on the ground do not make much of their nests.]—OBSERVATIONS ON NATURE.

It would not be at all strange if the bat, which you have procured, should prove a new one, since five species have been found in a neighbouring kingdom. The great sort that I mentioned is certainly a nondescript : I saw but one this summer, and that I had no opportunity of taking.

Your account of the Indian grass was entertaining. I am no angler myself ; but inquiring of those that are what they supposed that part of their tackle to be made of, they replied " of the intestines of a silkworm."

Though I must not pretend to great skill in entomology, yet I cannot say that I am ignorant of that kind of knowledge : I may now and then perhaps be able to furnish you with a little information.

The vast rains ceased with us much about the same time as with you, and since then we have had delicate weather. Mr. Barker, who has measured the rain for more than thirty years, says, in a late letter, that more has fallen this year than in any he ever attended to ; though from July 1763 to January 1764 more fell than in any seven months of this year.

SELBORNE, *Jan.* 2, 1769.

LETTER XXIII.

TO THOMAS PENNANT, ESQ.

IT is not improbable that the Guernsey lizard and our green lizards · may be specifically the same ; all that I know is, that, when some years ago many Guernsey lizards were turned loose in Pembroke College garden, in the university of Oxford, they lived a great while, and seemed to enjoy themselves very well, but never bred. Whether this circumstance will prove anything either way I shall not pretend to say.

I return you thanks for your account of Cressi Hall; but recollect, not without regret, that in June 1746 I was visiting for a week together at Spalding, without ever being told that such a curiosity was just at hand. Pray tell me in your next what sort of tree it is that contains such a quantity of herons'

CHANCEL DOORWAY, EAST WORLDHAM CHURCH.

nests; and whether the heronry consists of a whole grove or wood, or only of a few trees.

It gave me satisfaction to find we accorded so well about the *caprimulgus:* all I contended for was to prove that it often chatters sitting as well as flying; and therefore the noise was voluntary, and from organic impulse, and not from the resistance of the air against the hollow of its mouth and throat.

If ever I saw anything like actual migration, it was last Michaelmas Day. I was travelling, and out early in the morning: at first there was a vast fog; but by the time that I was got seven or eight miles from home towards the coast, the sun broke out into a delicate warm day. We were then on a large heath or common, and I could discern, as the mist began to break away, great numbers of swallows (*Hirundines rusticæ*) clustering on the stunted shrubs and bushes, as if they had roosted there all night. As soon as the air became clear and pleasant they all were on the wing at once; and, by a placid and easy flight, proceeded on southward towards the sea: after this I did not see any more flocks, only now and then a straggler.

I cannot agree with those persons who assert that the swallow kind disappear gradually, as they come, for the bulk of them seem to withdraw at once: only some few stragglers stay behind a long while, and never, there is reason to believe, leave this island. Swallows seem to lay themselves up, and to come forth in a warm day, as bats do continually of a warm evening after they have disappeared for weeks. For a very respectable gentleman assured me that, as he was walking with some friends under Merton wall on a remarkably hot noon, either in the last week in December or the first week in January, he espied three or four swallows huddled together on the moulding of one of the windows of that college. I have frequently remarked that swallows are seen later at Oxford than elsewhere: is this owing to the vast massy buildings of that place, to the many waters round it, or to what else?

When I used to rise in a morning last autumn, and see the swallows and martins clustering on the chimneys and thatch of the neighbouring cottages, I could not help being touched with a secret delight, mixed with some degree of mortification: with delight, to observe with how much ardour and punctuality those poor little birds obeyed the strong impulse towards migration, or hiding, imprinted on their minds by their great Creator; and with some degree of mortification, when I reflected that, after all our pains and inquiries, we are yet not quite certain to what regions they do migrate; and are still farther embarrassed to find that some do not actually migrate at all.

These reflections made so strong an impression on my imagination, that they became productive of a composition that may perhaps amuse you for a quarter of an hour when next I have the honour of writing to you.

SELBORNE, *February* 28, 1769.

OLD WELL, ELLIS'S FARM.

LETTER XXIV.

TO THOMAS PENNANT, ESQ.

THE *Scarabæus fullo* I know very well, having seen it in collections ; but have never been able to discover one wild in its natural state. Mr. Banks told me he thought it might be found on the sea coast.

On the 13th of April I went to the sheep-down, where the ring-ousels have been observed to make their appearance at spring and fall, in their way perhaps to the north or south ; and was much pleased to see three birds about the usual spot. We shot a cock and a hen ; they were plump and in high condition. The hen had but very small rudiments of eggs within her, which proves they are late breeders ; whereas those species of the thrush kind that remain with us the whole year have fledged young before that time. In their crops was nothing very distinguishable, but somewhat that seemed like blades of vegetables nearly digested. In autumn they feed on haws and yew-berries, and in the spring on ivy-berries. I dressed one of these birds, and found it juicy and well-flavoured. It is remarkable that they only stay a few days in their spring visit, but rest nearly a fortnight at Michaelmas. These birds, from the observations of three springs and two autumns, are most punctual in their return; and exhibit a new migration unnoticed by the writers, who supposed they never were to be seen in any of the southern counties.

One of my neighbours lately brought me a new *Salicaria*, which at first I suspected might have proved your willow-lark; [1] but, on a nicer examination, it answered much better to the description of that species which you shot at Revesby, in Lincolnshire. My bird I describe thus:—"It is a size less than the grasshopper-lark; the head, back, and coverts of the wings of a dusky brown, without those dark spots of the grasshopper-lark; over each eye is a milkwhite stroke; the chin and throat are white, and the under parts of a yellowish white: the rump is tawny, and the feathers of the tail sharp-pointed; the bill is dusky and sharp, and the legs are dusky; the hinder claw long and crooked." The person that shot it says that it sung so like a reed-sparrow that he took it for one; and that it sings all night: but this account merits farther inquiry. For my part, I suspect it is a second sort of *locustella*, hinted at by Dr. Derham in "Ray's Letters." He also procured me a grasshopper-lark.

The question that you put with regard to those genera of animals that are peculiar to America, viz. how they came there, and whence? is too puzzling for me to answer; and yet so obvious as often to have struck me with wonder. If one looks into the writers on that subject little satisfaction is to be found. Ingenious men will readily advance plausible arguments to support whatever theory they shall choose to maintain; but then the misfortune is, every one's hypothesis is each as good as another's, since they are all founded on conjecture. The late writers of this sort, in whom may be seen all the arguments of those that have gone before, as I remember, stock America from the western coast of Africa and the south of Europe; and then break down the Isthmus that bridged over the Atlantic. But this is making use of a violent piece of machinery: it is a difficulty worthy of the interposition of a god! "Incredulus odi." "I feel disgusted and disbelieving."

---

[1] For this *Salicaria*, or sedge-warbler, see Letter XXVI. August 30, 1769.

THE NATURALIST'S SUMMER-EVENING WALK.

————"*equidem credo, quia sit divinitus illis
Ingenium.*" [1]—VIRG. *Georg.* i. 415, 416.

WHEN day declining sheds a milder gleam,
What time the May-fly haunts the pool or stream;
When the still owl skims round the grassy mead,
What time the timorous hare limps forth to feed:
Then be the time to steal adown the vale,
And listen to the vagrant cuckoo's tale;
To hear the clamorous curlew [2] call his mate,
Or the soft quail his tender pain relate;
To see the swallow sweep the dark'ning plain
Belated, to support her infant train;
To mark the swift in rapid giddy ring
Dash round the steeple, unsubdued of wing:
Amusive birds! say where your hid retreat
When the frost rages and the tempests beat;
Whence your return, by such nice instinct led,
When spring, soft season, lifts her bloomy head?
Such baffled searches mock man's prying pride,
The GOD of NATURE is your secret guide!
    While deep'ning shades obscure the face of day
To yonder bench leaf-shelter'd let us stray,
'Till blended objects fail the swimming sight,
And all the fading landscape sinks in night;
To hear the drowsy dorr come brushing by
With buzzing wing, or the shrill cricket [3] cry;
To see the feeding bat glance through the wood;
To catch the distant falling of the flood;
While o'er the cliff th' awaken'd churn-owl hung
Through the still gloom protracts his chattering song;
While high in air, and pois'd upon his wings,
Unseen, the soft enamour'd woodlark sings:
These, NATURE's works, the curious mind employ,
Inspire a soothing melancholy joy:
As fancy warms, a pleasing kind of pain
Steals o'er the cheek, and thrills the creeping vein!
    Each rural sight, each sound, each smell combine;
The tinkling sheep-bell, or the breath of kine;
The new-mown hay that scents the swelling breeze,
Or cottage-chimney smoking through the trees.
    The chilling night-dews fall:—away, retire;
For see, the glowworm lights her amorous fire!
Thus, ere night's veil had half obscured the sky,
Th' impatient damsel hung her lamp on high:
True to the signal, by love's meteor led,
Leander hasten'd to his Hero's bed.

SELBORNE, *May* 29, 1769.

---

[1] "I think their instinct is divinely bestowed."
[2] *Charadrius oedicnemus.*   [3] *Gryllus campestris.*

LETTER XXV.

TO THE HONOURABLE DAINES BARRINGTON.

WHEN I was in town last month I partly engaged that I would some time do myself the honour to write to you on the subject of natural history : and I am the more ready to fulfil my promise, because I see you are a gentleman of great candour, and one that will make allowances; especially where the writer professes to be an out-door naturalist, one that takes his observations from the subject itself, and not from the writings of others.

The following is a list of the summer birds of passage which I have discovered in this neighbourhood, ranged somewhat in the order in which they appear :—

	RAII NOMINA.	APPEARS ABOUT
1. Wryneck,	Junx, sive tor-quilla:	The middle of March : harsh note.
2. Smallest willow-wren,	Regulus non cristatus:	March 23 : chirps till September.
3. Swallow,	Hirundo domestica :	April 13.
4. Martin,	Hirundo rustica :	Ditto.
5. Sand-martin,	Hirundo riparia :	Ditto.
6. Blackcap,	Atricapilla:	April 13 : a sweet wild note.
7. Nightingale,	Luscinia :	Beginning of April.
8. Cuckoo,	Cuculus:	Middle of April.
9. Middle willow-wren,	Regulus non cristatus :	Ditto : a sweet plaintive note.
10. White-throat,	Ficedula affinis :.	Ditto : mean note ; sings on till September.
11. Red-start,	Ruticilla :	Ditto : more agreeable song.
12. Stone-curlew,	Oedicnemus :	End of March : loud nocturnal whistle.
13. Turtle-dove,	Turtur.	
14. Grasshopper-lark,	Alauda minima locustæ voce :	Middle of April : a small sibilous note, till the end of July.
15. Swift,	Hirundo apus :	April 27.
16. Less reed-sparrow,	Passer arundinaceus minor :	A sweet polyglot, but hurrying : it has the notes of many birds.
17. Land-rail,	Ortygometra :	A loud harsh note, "crex, crex."
18. Largest willow-wren,	Regulus non cristatus :	"Cantat voce stridulâ locustæ ;" end of April ; on the tops of high beeches.
19. Goat-sucker, or Fern-owl,	Caprimulgus :	Beginning of May : chatters by night with a singular noise.
20. Fly-catcher,	Stoparola :	May 12. A very mute bird. This is the latest summer bird of passage.

This assemblage of curious and amusing birds belongs to ten several genera of the Linnæan system; and are all of the *ordo* of *passeres*, save the *jynx* and *cuculus*, which are *picœ*, and the *charadrius* (*oedicnemus*) and *rallus* (*ortygometra*) which are *grallœ*.

These birds, as they stand numerically, belong to the following Linnæan genera :—

1.	*Jynx* :	13.	*Columba.*
2, 6, 7, 9, 10, 11, 16, 18.	*Motacilla* :	17.	*Rallus.*
3, 4, 5, 15.	*Hirundo* :	19.	*Caprimulgus.*
8.	*Cuculus* :	14.	*Alauda.*
12.	*Charadrius* :	20.	*Muscicapa.*

Most soft-billed birds live on insects, and not on grain and seeds; and therefore at the end of summer they retire : but the following soft-billed birds, though insect-eaters, stay with us the year round :—

RAII NOMINA.

Redbreast,	*Rubecula* :	These frequent houses, and haunt outbuildings in the winter: eat spiders.
Wren,	*Passer troglodytes* :	
Hedge-sparrow,	*Curruca* :	Haunts sinks for crumbs and other sweepings.
White-wagtail,	*Motacilla alba* :	These frequent shallow rivulets near the spring heads, where they never freeze: eat the *aureliæ* of Phryganea. The smallest birds that walk.
Yellow-wagtail,	*Motacilla flava* :	
Grey-wagtail,	*Motacilla cinerea* :	
Wheat-ear,	*Oenanthe* :	Some of these are to be seen with us the winter through.
Whin-chat,	*Ocnanthe secunda.*	
Stone-chatter,	*Oenanthe tertia.*	
Golden - crowned wren,	*Regulus cristatus* :	This is the smallest British bird: haunts the tops of tall trees: stays the winter through.

A List of the Winter Birds of Passage round this neighbourhood, ranged somewhat in the order in which they appear :—

1. Ring-ousel,	*Merula torquata* :	This is a new migration, which I have lately discovered about Michaelmas week, and again about the 14th of March.
2. Redwing,	*Turdus iliacus* :	About old Michaelmas.
3. Fieldfare,	*Turdus pilaris* :	Though a percher by day, roosts on the ground.
4. Royston-crow,	*Cornix cinerea* :	Most frequent on downs.

5. Woodcock,	*Scolopax :*	Appears about old Michaelmas.
6. Snipe,	*Gallinago minor :*	{ Some snipes constantly breed with us.
7. Jack-snipe,	*Gallinago minima.*	
8. Wood-pigeon,	*Oenas :*	{ Seldom appears till late: not in such plenty as formerly.
9. Wild-swan,	*Cygnus ferus :*	On some large waters.
10. Wild-goose,	*Anser ferus.*	
11. Wild-duck,	{ *Anas torquata minor :*	
12. Pochard,	*Anas fera fusca :*	
13. Widgeon,	*Penelope :*	On our lakes and streams.
14. Teal, breeds with us in Wolmer Forest,	*Querquedula :*	
15. Cross-beak,	*Coccothraustes :*	(These are only wanderers that appear occasionally, and are not observant of any regular migration.
16. Cross-bill,	*Loxia :*	
17. Silk-tail,	{ *Garrulus bohemicus :*	

These birds, as they stand numerically, belong to the following
Linnæan genera :—

1, 2, 3,	*Turdus :*	9, 10, 11, 12, 13, 14.	
4,	*Corvus :*		*Anas.*
5, 6, 7,	*Scolopax :*	15, 16,	*Loxia.*
8,	*Columba :*	17,	*Ampelis.*

Birds that sing in the night are but few :—

Nightingale,	*Luscinia :*	{ " In shadiest covert hid."— MILTON.
Woodlark,	*Alauda arborea :*	Suspended in mid air.
Less reed-sparrow,	{ *Passer arundinaceus minor :*	Among reeds and willows.

I should now proceed to such birds as continue to sing after
Midsummer, but, as they are rather numerous, they would exceed
the bounds of this paper; besides, as this is now the season for
remarking on that subject, I am willing to repeat my observations on some birds concerning the continuation of whose song
I seem at present to have some doubt.

SELBORNE, *June* 30, 1769.

[As one of my neighbours was traversing Wolmer Forest from
Bramshot, across the moors, he found a large uncommon bird

fluttering in the heath, but not wounded, which he brought home alive.   On examination it proved to be *Colymbus glacialis*, Linn. the great speckled diver or loon, which is most excellently described in "Willughby's Ornithology."

Every part and proportion of this bird is so incomparably adapted to its mode of life, that in no instance do we see the wisdom of God in the creation to more advantage.   The head is sharp, and smaller than the part of the neck adjoining, in order that it may pierce the water; the wings are placed forward and out of the centre of gravity, for a purpose which shall be noticed hereafter; the thighs quite at the podex, in order to facilitate diving; and the legs are flat, and as sharp backwards almost as the edge of a knife, that in striking they may easily cut the water: while the feet are palmated, and broad for swimming, yet so folded up when advanced forward to take a fresh stroke, as to be full as narrow as the shank.   The two exterior toes of the feet are longest; the nails flat and broad, resembling the human, which give strength and increase the power of swimming.   The foot, when expanded, is not at right angles to the leg or body of the bird; but the exterior part inclining towards the head forms an acute angle with the body; the intention being not to give motion in the line of the legs themselves, but by the combined impulse of both in an intermediate line—the line of the body.

Most people know, that have observed at all, that the swimming of birds is nothing more than a walking in the water, where one foot succeeds the other as on the land; yet no one, as far as I am aware, has remarked that diving fowls, while under water, impel and row themselves forward by a motion of their wings, as well as by the impulse of their feet: but such is really the case, as any person may easily be convinced, who will observe ducks when hunted by dogs in a clear pond.   Nor do I know that any one has given a reason why the wings of diving fowls are placed so forward : doubtless, not for the purpose of promoting their speed in flying, since that position certainly impedes it; but probably for the increase of their motion under water, by the use of four oars instead of two; yet, were the wings and feet nearer together, as in land-birds, they would, when in action, rather hinder than assist one another.

This *colymbus* was of considerable bulk, weighing only three drachms short of three pounds avoirdupois.   It measured in length from the bill to the tail (which was very short) two feet, and to the extremities of the toes four inches more; and the breadth of the wings expanded was forty-two inches. A person attempted to eat the body, but found it very strong and rancid, as is the flesh of all birds living on fish. Divers or loons, though bred in the most northerly parts of Europe, yet are seen with us in very severe winters; and on the Thames are called sprat loons, because they prey much on that sort of fish.

The legs of the *colymbi* and *mergi* are placed so very backward and so out of all centre of gravity, that these birds cannot walk at all. They are called by Linnæus *compedes*, because they move on the ground as if shackled or fettered.

A man brought me a landrail or daker-hen, a bird so rare in this district that we seldom see more than one or two in a season, and those only in autumn. This is deemed a bird of passage by all the writers : yet from its formation seems to

LANDRAIL'S EGG.

be poorly qualified for migration; for its wings are short, and placed so forward and out of the centre of gravity, that it flies in a very heavy and embarrassed manner, with its legs hanging down; and can hardly be sprung a second time, as it runs very fast, and seems to depend more on the swiftness of its feet than on its flying.

When we came to draw it, we found the entrails so soft and tender, that in appearance they might have been dressed like the ropes of a woodcock. The craw or crop was small and lank, containing a mucus; the gizzard thick and strong, and filled with small shell-snails, some whole, and many ground to pieces through the attrition which is occasioned by the muscular force and motion of that intestine. We saw no gravels among the food; perhaps the shell-snails might perform the functions of gravels or pebbles, and might grind one another. Landrails

used to abound formerly, I remember, in the low wet bean-fields
of Christian Malford in North Wilts, and in the meadows near
Paradise Gardens at Oxford, where I have often heard them cry
" crex, crex." The bird mentioned above weighed 7½ oz., was fat
and tender, and in flavour like the flesh of a woodcock. The
liver was very large and delicate.]—OBSERVATIONS ON NATURE.

LETTER XXVI.

TO THOMAS PENNANT, ESQ.

IT gives me satisfaction to find that my account of the ousel
migration pleases you. You put a very shrewd question when
you ask me how I know that their autumnal migration is southward? Was not candour and openness the very life of natural
history, I should pass over this query just as a sly commentator
does over a crabbed passage in a classic; but common ingenuous-
ness obliges me to confess, not without some degree of shame,
that I only reasoned in that case from analogy. For as all other
autumnal birds migrate from the northward to us, to partake of
our milder winters, and return to the northward again when the
rigorous cold abates, so I concluded that the ring-ousels did the
same, as well as their congeners the fieldfares; and especially as
ring-ousels are known to haunt cold mountainous countries: but
I have good reason to suspect since that they may come to us
from the westward; because I hear, from very good authority,
that they breed on Dartmoor, and that they forsake that wild
district about the time that our visitors appear, and do not
return till late in the spring.

I have taken a great deal of pains about your *salicaria* and
mine, with a white stroke over its eye and a tawny rump. I
have surveyed it alive and dead, and have procured several
specimens; and am perfectly persuaded myself (and trust you
will soon be convinced of the same) that it is neither more nor
less than the *Passer arundinaceus minor* of Ray. This bird, by
some means or other, seems to be entirely omitted in the
" British Zoology;" and one reason probably was, because it
is so strangely classed in Ray, who ranges it among his *Pici
affines*. It ought no doubt to have gone among his small birds
with the tail of one colour (*Aviculæ caudâ unicolore*), and among

your slender-billed birds of the same division.   Linnæus might, with great propriety, have put it into his genus of *motacilla*, and the *Motacilla salicaria* of his "Fauna Suecica" seems to come the nearest to it.   It is no uncommon bird, haunting the sides of ponds and rivers where there is covert, and the reeds and sedges of moors.   The country people in some places call it the sedge-bird.   It sings incessantly night and day during the breeding time, imitating the note of a sparrow, a swallow, a skylark, and has a strange hurrying manner in its song.   My specimens correspond must minutely to the description of your fen-*salicaria* shot near Revesby.   Mr. Ray has given an excellent characteristic of it when he says,—"*Rostrum et pedes in hâc aviculâ multò majores sunt quam pro corpóris ratione.*"   "The beak and feet of this little bird are much too large for its body."

I have got you the egg of an *oedicnemus*, or stone-curlew, which was picked up in a fallow on the naked ground : there were two ; but the finder inadvertently crushed one with his foot before he saw them.

When I wrote to you last year on reptiles, I wish I had not forgot to mention the faculty that snakes have of stinking to defend themselves, *se defendendo*.   I knew a gentleman who kept a tame snake, which was in its person as sweet as any animal while in good humour and unalarmed ; but as soon as a stranger, or a dog or cat, came in, it fell to hissing, and filled the room with such nauseous effluvia as rendered it hardly supportable.   Thus the skunck, or stonck, of Ray's Synop. Quadr., is an innocuous and sweet animal ; but, when pressed hard by dogs and men, it can eject such a most pestilent and fetid smell and excrement, than which nothing can be more horrible.

A gentleman sent me lately a fine specimen of the *Lanius minor cinerascens cum maculâ in scapulis alba, Raii ;* which is a bird that, at the time of your publishing your two first volumes of British Zoology, I find you had not seen.   You have described it well from Edwards's drawing.

Selborne, *Aug.* 30, 1769.

LETTER XXVII.

TO THE HONOURABLE DAINES BARRINGTON.

WHEN I did myself the honour to write to you about the end of last June on the subject of natural history, I sent you a list of the summer birds of passage which I have observed in this neighbourhood; and also a list of the winter birds of passage: I mentioned besides those soft-billed birds that stay with us the winter through in the south of England, and those that are remarkable for singing in the night.

According to my proposal, I shall now proceed to such birds (singing birds strictly so called) as continue in full song till after Midsummer; and shall range them somewhat in the order in which they first begin to open as the spring advances.

RAII NOMINA.

1. Woodlark,	*Alauda arborea :*	In January, and continues to sing through all the summer and autumn.
2. Song-thrush,	*Turdus simpliciter dictus :*	In February and on to August, reassume their song in autumn.
3. Wren,	*Passer troglodytes :*	All the year, hard frost excepted.
4. Redbreast,	*Rubecula :*	Ditto.
5. Hedge-sparrow,	*Curruca :*	Early in February to July the 10th.
6. Yellow-hammer,	*Emberiza flava :*	Early in February and on through July to August the 21st.
7. Skylark,	*Alauda vulgaris :*	In February, and on to October.
8. Swallow,	*Hirundo domestica :*	From April to September.
9. Blackcap,	*Atricapilla :*	Beginning of April to July the 13th.
10. Titlark,	*Alauda pratorum :*	From middle of April to July the 16th.
11. Blackbird,	*Merula vulgaris :*	Sometimes in February and March, and so on to July the 23rd ; reassumes in autumn.
12. White-throat,	*Ficedula affinis :*	In April, and on to July the 23rd.
13. Goldfinch,	*Carduelis :*	April, and through to September the 16th.
14. Greenfinch,	*Chloris :*	On to July and August the 2nd.
15. Less reed-sparrow,	*Passer arundinaceus minor :*	May, on to beginning of July.
16. Common linnet,	*Linaria vulgaris :*	Breeds and whistles on till August; reassumes its note when they begin to congregate in October, and again early before the flocks separate.

G

Birds that cease to be in full song, and are usually silent at or before midsummer :—

RAII NOMINA.

17.	Middle wil-low-wren,	*Regulus non cristatus :*	Middle of June : begins in April.
18.	Redstart,	*Ruticilla :*	Ditto : begins in May.
19.	Chaffinch,	*Fringilla :*	Beginning of June : sings first in February.
20.	Nightingale,	*Luscinia :*	Middle of June : sings first in April.

Birds that sing for a short time, and very early in the spring :—

21.	Missel-bird,	*Turdus viscivorus :*	January the 2nd, 1770, in February. Is called in Hampshire and Sussex the storm-cock, because its song is supposed to forbode windy, wet weather : is the largest singing bird we have.
22.	Great Tit-mouse, or Ox-eye,	*Fringillago :*	In February, March, April : reassumes for a short time in September.

Birds that have somewhat of a note or song, and yet are hardly to be called singing birds :—

23.	Golden-crown-ed wren,	*Regulus cristatus :*	Its note as minute as its person ; frequents the tops of high oaks and firs : the smallest British bird.
24.	Marsh - tit-mouse,	*Parus palustris :*	Haunts great woods : two harsh, sharp notes.
25.	Small willow-wren,	*Regulus non cristatus :*	Sings in March, and on to September.
26.	Largest ditto,	*Ditto.*	"Cantat voce stridulâ locustæ ;" from end of April to August.
27.	Grasshopper-lark,	*Alauda minima voce locustæ :*	Chirps all night, from the middle of April to the end of July.
28.	Martin,	*Hirundo agrestis :*	All the breeding time ; from May to September.
29.	Bullfinch,	*Pyrrhula :*	
30.	Bunting,	*Emberiza alba :*	From the end of January to July.

All singing birds, and those that have any pretensions to song, not only in Britain, but perhaps the world through, come under the Linnæan *ordo* of *passeres*.

The above-mentioned birds, as they stand numerically, belong to the following Linnæan genera :—

1, 7, 10, 27.	*Alauda :*	8, 28.	*Hirundo.*
2, 11, 21.	*Turdus :*	13, 16, 19.	*Fringilla.*
3, 4, 5, 9, 12, 15, 17, 18, 20, 23, 25, 26. }	*Motacilla :*	22, 24.	*Parus.*
6, 30.	*Emberiza :*	14, 29.	*Loxia.*

Birds that sing as they fly are but few :—

RAII NOMINA.

Skylark,	*Alauda vulgaris :*	Rising, suspended, and falling.
Titlark,	*Alauda pratorum :*	In its descent ; also sitting on trees, and walking on the ground.
Woodlark,	*Alauda arborea :*	Suspended ; in hot summer nights all night long.
Blackbird,	*Merula :*	Sometimes from bush to bush.
White-throat,	*Ficedula affinis :*	Uses when singing on the wing odd jerks and gesticulations.
Swallow,	*Hirundo domestica :*	In soft sunny weather.
Wren,	*Passer troglodytes :*	Sometimes from bush to bush.

Birds that breed most early in these parts :—

Raven,	*Corvus :*	Hatches in February and March.
Song-thrush,	*Turdus :*	In March.
Blackbird,	*Merula :*	Ditto.
Rook,	*Cornix frugilega :*	Builds the beginning of March.
Woodlark,	*Alauda arborea :*	Hatches in April.
Ring-dove,	*Palumbus torquatus :*	Lays the beginning of April.

All birds that continue in full song till after Midsummer appear to me to breed more than once.

Most kinds of birds seem to me to be wild and shy somewhat in proportion to their bulk; I mean in this island, where they are much pursued and annoyed : but in Ascension Island, and many other desolate places, mariners have found fowls so unacquainted with a human figure, that they would stand still to be taken; as is the case with boobies, &c. As an example of what is advanced, I remark that the golden-crested wren (the smallest British bird) will stand unconcerned till you come within three or four yards of it, while the bustard (*otis*), the largest British land fowl, does not care to admit a person within so many furlongs.

SELBORNE, *Nov.* 2, 1769.

LETTER XXVIII.

TO THOMAS PENNANT, ESQ.

I was much gratified by your communicative letter on your return from Scotland, where you spent, I find, some considerable time, and gave yourself good room to examine the natural curiosities of that extensive kingdom, both those of the islands, as well as those of the highlands. The usual bane of such expeditions is hurry; because men seldom allot themselves half the time they should do: but, fixing on a day for their return, post from place to place, rather as if they were on a journey that required despatch, than as philosophers investigating the works of nature. You must have made, no doubt, many discoveries, and laid up a good fund of materials for a future edition of the British Zoology; and will have no reason to repent that you have bestowed so much pains on a part of Great Britain that perhaps was never so well examined before.

It has always been matter of wonder to me that fieldfares, which are so congenerous to thrushes and blackbirds, should never choose to breed in England : but that they should not think even the highlands cold and northerly, and sequestered enough, is a circumstance still more strange and wonderful. The ring-ousel, you find, stays in Scotland the whole year round; so that we have reason to conclude that those migrators that visit us for a short space every autumn do not come from thence.

And here, I think, will be the proper place to mention that those birds were most punctual again in their migration this autumn, appearing, as before, about the thirtieth of September : but their flocks were larger than common, and their stay protracted somewhat beyond the usual time. If they came to spend the whole winter with us, as some of their congeners do, and then left us, as they do, in spring, I should not be so much struck with the occurrence, since it would be similar to that of the other winter birds of passage; but when I see them for a fortnight at Michaelmas, and again for about a week in the beginning of April, I am seized with wonder, and long to be informed whence these travellers come, and whither they go, since they seem to use our hills merely as an inn or baiting-place.

Your account of the greater brambling, or snow-flock, is very amusing; and strange it is that such a short-winged bird should delight in such perilous voyages over the northern ocean! Some country people in the winter time have every now and then told me that they have seen two or three white larks on our downs; but, on considering the matter, I begin to suspect that these are some stragglers of the birds we are talking of, which sometimes perhaps may rove so far to the southward.

It pleases me to find that white hares are so frequent on the Scottish mountains, and especially as you inform me that it is a distinct species, for the quadrupeds of Britain are so few, that every new species is a great acquisition.

The eagle-owl, could it be proved to belong to us, is so majestic a bird that it would grace our *fauna* much. I never was informed before where wild geese are known to breed.

You admit, I find, that I have proved your fen-*salicaria* to be the lesser reed-sparrow of Ray: and I think you may be secure that I am right; for I took very particular pains to clear up

REED-SPARROW'S EGG.

that matter, and had some fair specimens; but, as they were not well preserved, they are decayed already. You will, no doubt, insert it in its proper place in your next edition. Your additional plates will much improve your work.

De Buffon, I know, has described the water shrew-mouse; but still I am pleased to find you have discovered it in Lincolnshire, for the reason I have given in the article of the white hare.

As a neighbour was lately ploughing in a dry chalky field, far removed from any water, he turned out a water-rat, that was curiously laid up in an hybernaculum artificially formed of grass and leaves. At one end of the burrow lay above a gallon of potatoes regularly stowed, on which it was to have supported itself for the winter. But the difficulty with me is how this *amphibius mus* came to fix its winter station at such a distance from the water. Was it determined in its choice of that place by the mere accident of finding the potatoes which were planted there ? or is it the practice of the aquatic rat to forsake the neighbourhood of the water in the colder months ?

Though I delight very little in analogous reasoning, knowing how fallacious it is with respect to natural history; yet, in the following instance, I cannot help being inclined to think it may conduce towards the explanation of a difficulty that I have mentioned before, with respect to the invariable early retreat of the *Hirundo apus*, or swift, so many weeks before its congeners; and that not only with us, but also in Andalusia, where they also begin to retire about the beginning of August.

The great large bat[1] (which by the by is at present a nondescript in England, and what I have never been able yet to procure) retires or migrates very early in the summer: it also ranges very high for its food, feeding in a different region of the air; and that is the reason I never could procure one. Now this is exactly the case with the swifts, for they take their food in a more exalted region than the other species, and are very seldom seen hawking for flies near the ground, or over the surface of the water. From hence I would conclude that these *hirundines*, and the larger bats, are supported by some sorts of high-flying gnats, scarabs, or *phalœnœ* that are short of continuance; and that the short stay of these strangers is regulated by the defect of their food.

By my journal it appears that curlews clamoured on to October the 31st; since which I have not seen or heard any. Swallows were observed on to November the third.

SELBORNE, *Dec.* 8, 1769.

LETTER XXIX.

TO THE HONOURABLE DAINES BARRINGTON.

IT was no small matter of satisfaction to me to find that you were not displeased with my little *methodus* of birds. If there is any merit in the sketch, it must be in its exactness. For many months I carried a list in my pocket of the birds that were to be remarked on; and, as I rode or walked about, I

---

[1] The little Bat appears almost every month in the year; but I have never seen the large one till the end of April, nor after July. They are most common in June, but never very plentiful.

noted each day the continuance or omission of each bird's song; so that I am as sure of my facts as a man can be of any transaction whatsoever.

I shall now proceed to answer the several queries which you put in your two obliging letters, in the best manner that I am able. Perhaps Eastwick, and its environs, where you heard so very few birds, is not a woodland country, and therefore not stocked with such songsters. If you will cast your eye on my last letter, you will find that many species continued to warble after the beginning of July.

The titlark and yellowhammer breed late, the latter very late; and therefore it is no wonder that they protract their song: for I lay it down as a maxim in ornithology, that as long as there is any incubation going on there is music. As to the redbreast and wren, it is well known to the most incurious observer that they whistle the year round, hard frost excepted; especially the latter.

It was not in my power to procure you a blackcap, or a lesser reed-sparrow, or sedge-bird, alive. As the first is undoubtedly, and the last, as far as I can yet see, a summer bird of passage, they would require more nice and curious management in a cage than I should be able to give them: they are both distinguished songsters. The note of the blackcap has such a wild sweetness that it always brings to my mind those lines in a song in *As You Like It*,—

> "And tune his merry note
> Unto the *wild* bird's throat."
> Shakespeare.

The sedge-bird has a surprising variety of notes resembling the song of several other birds; but then it has also a hurrying manner, not at all to its advantage: it is notwithstanding a delicate polyglot.

It is new to me that titlarks in cages sing in the night; perhaps only caged birds do so. I once knew a tame redbreast in a cage that always sang as long as candles were in the room; but in their wild state no one supposes they sing in the night.

I should be almost ready to doubt the fact, that there are to be seen much fewer birds in July than in any former month, notwithstanding so many young are hatched daily. Sure I am that it is far otherwise with respect to the swallow tribes, which increase prodigiously as the summer advances. I saw, at the

time mentioned, many hundreds of young wagtails on the banks
of the Cherwell, which almost covered the meadows. If the
matter appears as you say in the other species, may it not be
owing to the dams being engaged in incubation, while the young
are concealed by the leaves?

Many times have I had the curiosity to open the stomach of
woodcocks and snipes; but nothing ever occurred that helped
to explain to me what their subsistence might be: all that I
could ever find was a soft mucus, among which lay many
pellucid small gravels.

SELBORNE, *Jan.* 15, 1770.

LETTER XXX.

TO THE HONOURABLE DAINES BARRINGTON.

YOUR observation that "the cuckoo does not deposit its egg
indiscriminately in the nest of the first bird that comes in its
way, but probably looks out a nurse in some degree congenerous,
with whom to intrust its young," is perfectly new to me; and
struck me so forcibly, that I naturally fell into a train of thought
that led me to consider whether the fact was so, and what reason
there was for it. When I came to recollect and inquire, I could
not find that any cuckoo had ever been seen in these parts,
except in the nest of the wagtail, the hedge-sparrow, the titlark,
the whitethroat, and the redbreast, all soft-billed insectivorous
birds. The excellent Mr. Willughby mentions the nest of the
palumbus (ring-dove) and of the *fringilla* (chaffinch), birds that
subsist on acorns and grains, and such hard food: but then he
does not mention them as of his own knowledge, but says
afterwards that he saw himself a wagtail feeding a cuckoo. It
appears hardly possible that a soft-billed bird should subsist on
the same food with the hard-billed; for the former have thin
membranaceous stomachs suited to their soft food, while the
latter, the granivorous tribe, have strong muscular gizzards,
which, like mills, grind, by the help of small gravels and pebbles,
what is swallowed. This proceeding of the cuckoo, of dropping
its eggs as it were by chance, is such a monstrous outrage on
maternal affection, one of the first great dictates of nature, and
such a violence on instinct, that, had it only been related of a

bird in the Brazils, or Peru, it would never have merited our belief. But yet, should it farther appear that this simple bird, when divested of that natural στοργή that seems to raise the kind in general above themselves, and inspire them with extraordinary degrees of cunning and address, may be still endued with a more enlarged faculty of discerning what species are suitable and congenerous nursing mothers for its disregarded eggs and young, and may deposit them only under their care,

THE CUCKOO.

this would be adding wonder to wonder, and instancing, in a fresh manner, that the methods of Providence are not subjected to any mode or rule, but astonish us in new lights, and in various and changeable appearances.

What was said by a very ancient and sublime writer concerning the defect of natural affection in the ostrich may be well applied to the bird we are talking of :—

"*She is hardened against her young ones, as though they were not hers :*

"*Because God hath deprived her of wisdom, neither hath He imparted to her understanding.*" (Job xxxix. 16, 17.)

Does· each female cuckoo lay but one egg in a season, or does she drop several in different nests, according as opportunity offers ?

SELBORNE. *Feb.* 19, 1770.

CUCKOO'S EGG.

LETTER XXXI

TO THOMAS PENNANT, ESQ.

HEDGE-HOGS abound in my gardens and fields. The manner in which they eat the roots of the plantain in the grass-walk is very curious : with their upper mandible, which is much longer than their lower, they bore under the plant, and so eat the root off upwards, leaving the tuft of leaves untouched. In this respect they are serviceable, as they destroy a very troublesome weed ; but they deface the walks in some measure by digging little round holes. It appears, by the dung that they drop upon the turf, that beetles are no inconsiderable part of their food. In June last I procured a litter of five or six young hedge-hogs, which appeared to be about five or six days old ; they, I find, like puppies, are born blind, and could not see when they came to my hands. No doubt their spines are soft and flexible at the time of their birth, or else the poor dam would have but a bad time of it in the critical moment of parturition : but it is plain that they soon harden ; for these little pigs have such stiff prickles on their backs and sides as would easily have fetched blood, had they not been handled with caution. Their spines are quite white at this age ; and they have little hanging ears, which I do not remember to be discernible in the old ones. They can, in part, at this age draw their skin down over their faces ; but are not able to

contract themselves into a ball, as they do, for the sake of
defence, when full grown. The reason, I suppose, is, because the
curious muscle that enables the creature to roll itself up in a ball
was not then arrived at its full tone and firmness. Hedge-hogs
make a deep and warm hybernaculum with leaves and moss,
in which they conceal themselves for the winter: but I never
could find that they stored in any winter provision, as some
quadrupeds certainly do.

I have discovered an anecdote with respect to the fieldfare
(*Turdus pilaris*), which I think is particular enough: this bird,

HEDGE-HOG AND YOUNG.

though it sits on trees in the day-time, and procures the greatest
part of its food from whitethorn hedges; yea, moreover, builds
on very high trees, as may be seen by the "Fauna Suecica," yet
always appears with us to roost on the ground. They are seen
to come in flocks just before it is dark, and to settle and nestle
among the heath on our forest. And besides, the larkers, in
dragging their nets by night, frequently catch them in the wheat
stubbles; while the bat-fowlers, who take many redwings in the
hedges, never entangle any of this species. Why these birds, in
the matter of roosting, should differ from all their congeners, and

from themselves also with respect to their proceedings by day, is a fact for which I am by no means able to account.

I have somewhat to inform you of concerning the moose-deer; but in general foreign animals fall seldom in my way; my little intelligence is confined to the narrow sphere of my own observations at home.

SELBORNE, *Feb.* 22, 1770.

FIELD-FARE'S EGG.

LETTER XXXII.

TO THOMAS PENNANT, ESQ.

ON Michaelmas-day, 1768, I managed to get a sight of the female moose belonging to the Duke of Richmond, at Goodwood; but was greatly disappointed, when I arrived at the spot, to find that it died, after having appeared in a languishing way for some time, on the morning before. However, understanding that it was not stripped, I proceeded to examine this rare quadruped: I found it in an old green-house, slung under the belly and chin by ropes, and in a standing posture; but, though it had been dead for so short a time, it was in so putrid a state that the stench was hardly supportable. The grand distinction between this deer, and any other species that I have ever met with, consisted in the strange length of its legs; on which it was tilted up much in the manner of the birds of the *grallæ* order. I measured it, as they do an horse, and found that, from the ground to the wither, it was just five feet four inches, which height answers exactly to sixteen hands, a growth that few horses arrive at: but then, with this length of legs, its neck was remarkably short, no more than twelve inches; so that, by straddling with one foot forward and the other backward, it grazed on the plain ground,

with the greatest difficulty, between its legs : the ears were vast
and lopping, and as long as the neck ; the head was about twenty
inches long, and ass-like ; and had such a redundancy of upper
lip as I never saw before, with huge nostrils. This lip, travellers
say, is esteemed a dainty dish in North America. It is very
reasonable to suppose that this creature supports itself chiefly by
browsing of trees, and by wading after water plants ; towards
which way of livelihood the length of legs and great lip must
contribute much. I have read somewhere that it delights in
eating the *nymphæa*, or water-lily. From the fore-feet to the
belly behind the shoulder it measured three feet and eight inches :
the length of the legs before and behind consisted a great deal in
the *tibia*, which was strangely long ; but, in my haste to get out
of the stench, I forgot to measure that joint exactly. Its scut
seemed to be about an inch long ; the colour was a grizzly black ;
the mane about four inches long ; the fore-hoofs were upright
and shapely, the hind flat and splayed. The spring before, it was
only two years old, so that most probably it was not then come
to its growth. What a vast tall beast must a full-grown stag be !
I have been told that some arrive at ten feet and a half ! This
poor creature had at first a female companion of the same species,
which died the spring before. In the same garden was a young
stag, or red deer, between whom and this moose it was hoped
that there might have been a breed ; but their inequality of
height must always be a bar. I should have been glad to have
examined the teeth, tongue, lips, hoofs, &c., minutely ; but the
putrefaction precluded all further curiosity. This animal, the
keeper told me, seemed to enjoy itself best in the extreme frost
of the former winter. In the house they showed me the horn of
a male moose, which had no front-antlers, but only a broad palm
with some snags on the edge. The noble owner of the dead moose
proposed to make a skeleton of her bones.

Please to let me hear if my female moose corresponds with that
you saw ; and whether you think still that the American moose
and European elk are the same creature.

SELBORNE, *March*, 1770.

LETTER XXXIII.

TO THE HONOURABLE DAINES BARRINGTON.

I HEARD many birds of several species sing last year after Midsummer; enough to prove that the summer solstice is not the period that puts a stop to the music of the woods. The yellow-hammer, no doubt, persists with more steadiness than any other; but the woodlark, the wren, the redbreast, the swallow, the white-throat, the goldfinch, the common linnet, are all undoubted instances of the truth of what I advance.

If this severe season does not interrupt the regularity of the summer migrations, the blackcap will be here in two or three days. I wish it was in my power to procure you one of those songsters; but I am no birdcatcher; and so little used to birds in a cage, that I fear if I had one it would soon die for want of skill in feeding.

Was your reed-sparrow, which you kept in a cage, the thick-billed reed-sparrow of the "Zoology," p. 30; or was it the less reed-sparrow of Ray, the sedge-bird of Mr. Pennant's "Zoology," p. 16?

As to the matter of long-billed birds growing fatter in moderate frosts, I have doubt within myself what should be the reason. The thriving at those times appears to me to arise altogether from the gentle check with the cold throws upon insensible perspiration. The case is just the same with blackbirds, &c.; and farmers and warreners observe, the first, that their hogs fatten more kindly at such times, and the latter, that their rabbits are never in such good case as in a gentle frost. But when frosts are severe, and of long continuance, the case is soon altered; for then a want of food soon overbalances the repletion occasioned by a checked perspiration. I have observed, moreover, that some human constitutions are more inclined to plumpness in winter than in summer.

When birds come to suffer by severe frost, I find that the first that fail and die are the redwing, fieldfares, and then the song-thrushes.

You wonder, with good reason, that the hedge-sparrows, &c. can be induced at all to sit on the egg of the cuckoo without being scandalized at the vastly disproportioned size of the suppositious egg; but the brute creation, I suppose, have very little idea of size, colour, or number. For the common hen, as I know, when the fury of incubation is on her, will sit on a single shapeless stone instead of a nest full of eggs that have been withdrawn: and, moreover, a hen-turkey, in the same circumstances, would sit on in the empty nest till she perished with hunger.

I think the matter might easily be determined whether a cuckoo lays one or two eggs, or more, in a season, by opening a female during the laying-time. If more than one was come down out of the ovary, and advanced to a good size, doubtless then she would that spring lay more than one. I will endeavour to get a hen, and examine her.

Your supposition that there may be some natural obstruction in singing birds while they are mute, and that when this is removed the song recommences, is new and bold: I wish you could discover some good grounds for this suspicion.

I was glad you were pleased with my specimen of the *caprimulgus*, or fern-owl; you were, I find, acquainted with the bird before.

When we meet, I shall be glad to have some conversation with you concerning the proposal you make of my drawing up an account of the animals in this neighbourhood. Your partiality towards my small abilities persuades you, I fear, that I am able to do more than is in my power: for it is no small undertaking for a man unsupported and alone to begin a natural history from his own autopsia! Though there is endless room for observation in the field of nature, which is boundless, yet investigation (where a man endeavours to be sure of his facts) can make but slow progress; and all that one could collect in many years would go into a very narrow compass.

Some extracts from your ingenious "Investigations of the difference between the present temperature of the air in Italy," &c. have fallen in my way; and gave me great satisfaction; they have removed the objections that always arose in my mind whenever I came to the passages which you quote. Surely the judicious Virgil, when writing a didactic poem for the region of Italy, could never think of describing freezing rivers, unless such severity of weather pretty frequently occurred!

Two swallows have appeared amidst snows and frost.

SELBORNE, *April* 12, 1770.

LETTER XXXIV.

TO THOMAS PENNANT, ESQ.

LAST month we had such a series of cold turbulent weather, such a constant succession of frost, and snow, and hail, and tempest, that the regular migration or appearance of the summer birds was much interrupted. Some, as the blackcap and white-throat, did not show themselves (at least were not heard) till weeks after their usual time; and some, as the grasshopper-lark and largest willow-wren, have not been heard yet. As to the fly-catcher, I have not seen it; it is indeed one of the latest, but should appear about this time: and yet, amidst all this meteorous strife and war of the elements, two swallows discovered them-selves as long ago as the 11th of April, in frost and snow; but they withdrew quickly, and were not visible again for many days. House-martins, which are always more backward than swallows, were not observed till May came in.

Among the monogamous birds several are to be found single after pairing-time, and of each sex: but whether this state of celibacy is matter of choice or necessity, is not so easily discover-able. When the house-sparrows deprive my martins of their nests, as soon as I cause one to be shot, the other, be it cock or hen, presently procures a mate, and so for several times following.

I have known a dove-house infested by a pair of white owls, which made great havoc among the young pigeons: one of the owls was shot as soon as possible; but the survivor readily found a mate, and the mischief went on. After some time the new pair were both destroyed, and the annoyance ceased.

Another instance I remember of a sportsman, whose zeal for the increase of his game being greater than his humanity, after pairing-time he always shot the cockbird of every couple of partridges upon his grounds; supposing that the rivalry of many males interrupted the breed: he used to say, that, though he had widowed the same hen several times, yet he found she was still provided with a fresh paramour, that did not take her away from her usual haunt.

Again: I knew a lover of setting, an old sportsman, who has often told me that soon after harvest he has frequently taken small coveys of partridges, consisting of cock-birds alone; these he pleasantly used to call old bachelors.

There is a propensity belonging to common house-cats that is very remarkable; I mean their violent fondness for fish, which appears to be their most favourite food : and yet nature in this instance seems to have planted in them an appetite that, unassisted, they know not how to gratify : for of all quadrupeds cats are the least disposed towards water; and will not, when they can avoid it, deign to wet a foot, much less to plunge into that element.

Quadrupeds that prey on fish are amphibious : such is the otter, which by nature is so well formed for diving, that it makes great havoc among the inhabitants of the waters. Not supposing that we had any of those beasts in our shallow brooks, I was much pleased to see a male otter brought to me, weighing twenty-one pounds, that had been shot on the bank of our stream below the Priory, where the rivulet divides the parish of Selborne from Harteley-wood.

[One of my neighbours shot a ring-dove on an evening as it was returning from feed and going to roost. When his wife had picked and drawn it, she found its craw stuffed with the most nice and tender tops of turnips. These she washed and boiled, and so sat down to a choice and delicate plate of greens, culled and provided in this extraordinary manner.

Hence we may see that graminivorous birds, when grain fails, can subsist on the leaves of vegetables. There is reason to suppose that they would not long be healthy without ; for turkeys, though corn-fed, delight in a variety of plants, such as cabbage, lettuce, endive, &c. and poultry pick much grass ; while geese live for months together on commons by grazing alone.

> "Nought is useless made ; — — —
> — — — — On the barren heath
> The shepherd tends his flock that daily crop
> Their verdant dinner from the mossy turf
> Sufficient : after them the cackling goose,
> Close-grazer, finds wherewith to ease her want."
> PHILIPS'S *Cyder*.]

—OBSERVATIONS ON NATURE.

SELBORNE, *May* 12, 1770.

LETTER XXXV.

TO THE HONOURABLE DAINES BARRINGTON.

THE severity and turbulence of last month so interrupted the regular process of summer migration, that some of the birds do but just begin to show themselves, and others, as the white-throat, the blackcap, the redstart, the flycatcher, are apparently thinner than usual. I well remember that after the very severe spring in the year 1739–40, summer birds of passage were very scarce. They come hither probably with a south east wind, or when it blows between those points; but in that unfavourable year the winds blowed the whole spring and summer through from the opposite quarters. And yet amidst all these dis-advantages, two swallows, as I mentioned in my last, appeared this year as early as the eleventh of April, amidst frost and snow; but they withdrew again for a time.

I am not pleased to find that some people seem so little satisfied with Scopoli's new publication, "Annus Primus His-torico-Naturalis." There is room to expect great things from the hands of that man, who is a good naturalist : and one would think that an history of the birds of so distant and southern a region as Carniola would be new and interesting. I could wish to see the work, and hope to get it sent down. Dr. Scopoli is physician to the wretches that work in the quicksilver mines of that district.

When you talked of keeping a reed-sparrow, and giving it seeds, I could not help wondering; because the reed-sparrow which I mentioned to you (*Passer arundinaceus minor* Raii)[1] is a soft-billed bird, and most probably migrates hence before winter; whereas the bird you kept (*Passer torquatus* Raii)[2] abides all the year, and is a thick-billed bird. I question whether the latter be much of a songster; but in this matter I want to be better informed. The former has a variety of hurrying notes, and sings all night. Some part of the song of the former, I suspect, is attributed to the latter. We have plenty of the soft-billed sort, which Mr. Pennant had entirely

---

[1] Sedge-warbler, *Salicaria phragmitis*, Selby.
[2] Reed-bunting, *Emberiza schœniclus*, Linn.

left out of his "British Zoology," till I reminded him of his omission.[1]

I have somewhat to advance on the different manners in which different birds fly and walk; but as this is a subject that I have not enough considered, and is of such a nature as not to be contained in a small space, I shall say nothing further about it at present.[2]

No doubt the reason why the sex of birds in their first plumage is so difficult to be distinguished is, as you say, "because they are not to pair and discharge their parental functions till the ensuing spring." As colours seem to be the chief external sexual distinction in many birds, these colours do not take place till sexual attachments commence. The case is the same with quadrupeds, among whom, in their younger days, the sexes differ but little; but, as they advance to maturity, horns and shaggy manes, beards and brawny necks, &c., strongly discriminate the male from the female. We may instance still further in our own species, where a beard and stronger features are usually characteristic of the male sex; but this sexual diversity does not take place in earlier life, for a beautiful youth shall be so like a beautiful girl that the difference shall not be discernible :—

"Quem si puellarum insereres choro,
    Mirè sagaces falleret hospites
Discrimen obscurum, solutis
    Crinibus, ambiguoque vultu."

HOR. (II. v. 21-24.)

"A fellow who, if you put him among a parcel of girls, the difficulty of distinguishing him from them would puzzle a very quick-sighted host, thanks to his long hairs and smooth ambiguous face."

SELBORNE, *May* 21, 1770.

LETTER XXXVI.

TO THOMAS PENNANT, ESQ.

THE French, I think, in general are strangely prolix in their natural history. What Linnæus says with respect to insects holds good in every other branch: "Verbositas præsentis sæculi,

---

[1] See Letter xxvi., to Mr. Pennant, August 30, 1769.
[2] See Letter lxxxiv., to Mr. Barrington, August 7, 1778.

H 2

calamitas artis." "The verbosity of the present generation is the calamity of art."

Pray how do you approve of Scopoli's new work? as I admire his "Entomologia," I long to see it.

I forgot to mention in my last letter (and had not room to insert it in the former) that the male moose, in rutting time, swims from island to island, in the lakes and rivers of North America, in pursuit of the females. My friend, the chaplain, saw one killed in the water as it was on that errand in the river St. Lawrence; it was a monstrous beast, he told me; but he did not take the dimensions.

When I was last in town our friend Mr. Barrington most obligingly carried me to see many curious sights. As you were then writing to him about horns, he carried me to see many strange and wonderful specimens. There is, I remember, at Lord Pembroke's, at Wilton, an horn-room furnished with more than thirty different pairs; but I have not seen that house lately.

Mr. Barrington showed me many astonishing collections of stuffed and living birds from all quarters of the world. After I had studied over the latter for a time, I remarked that every species almost that came from distant regions, such as South America, the coast of Guinea, &c., were thick-billed birds of the *loxia* and *fringilla* genera; and no *motacillæ* or *muscicapæ* were to be met with. When I came to consider, the reason was obvious enough; for the hard-billed birds subsist on seeds which are easily carried on board, while soft-billed birds, which are supported by worms and insects, or, what is a succedaneum for them, fresh raw meat, can meet with neither in long and tedious voyages. It is from this defect of food that our collections (curious as they are) are defective, and we are deprived of some of the most delicate and lively genera.

SELBORNE, *Aug.* 1, 1770.

LETTER XXXVII.

TO THOMAS PENNANT, ESQ.

You saw, I find, the ring-ousels again among their native crags; and are further assured that they continue resident in those cold regions the whole year. From whence then do our ring-ousels migrate so regularly every September, and make their appearance again, as if in their return, every April? They are more early this year than common, for some were seen at the usual hill on the fourth of this month.

An observing Devonshire gentleman tells me that they frequent some parts of Dartmoor, and breed there ; but leave those haunts about the end of September or beginning of October, and return again about the end of March.

THE RING-OUZEL.

Another intelligent person assures me that they breed in great abundance all over the Peak of Derby, and are called there tor-ousels ; withdraw in October and November, and return in spring.   This information seems to throw some light on my new migration.

Scopoli's[1] new work (which I have just procured) has its merit in ascertaining many of the birds of the Tyrol and Carniola. Monographers, come from whence they may, have, I think, fair pretence to challenge some regard and approbation from the

[1] "Annus Primus Historico-Naturalis."

lovers of natural history; for, as no man can alone investigate all the works of nature, these partial writers may, each in their department, be more accurate in their discoveries, and freer from errors, than more general writers; and so by degrees may pave the way to an universal correct natural history. Not that Scopoli is so circumstantial and attentive to the life and conversation of his birds as I could wish: he advances some false facts; as when he says of the *Hirundo urbica* that "it does not feed its young after it leaves the nest:" "pullos extra nidum non nutrit." This assertion I know to be wrong from repeated observation this summer; for house-martins do feed their young flying, though it must be acknowledged not so commonly as the house-swallow; and the feat is done in so quick a manner as not to be perceptible to indifferent observers. He also advances some (I was going to say) improbable facts; as when he says of the woodcock that, "as it flies from its enemies, it carries its young in its beak:" "pullos rostro portat fugiens ab hoste." But candour forbids me to say absolutely that any fact is false because I have never been witness to such a fact. I have only to remark, that the long unwieldy bill of the woodcock is perhaps the worst adapted of any among the winged creation for such a feat of natural affection.

SELBORNE, *Sept.* 14, 1770.

RING-OUZEL'S EGG.

LETTER XXXVIII.

TO THE HONOURABLE DAINES BARRINGTON.

I AM glad to hear that Kuckahn is to furnish you with the birds of Jamaica; a sight of the *hirundines* of that hot and distant island would be a great entertainment to me.

The "Anni" of Scopoli are now in my possession; and I have read the "Annus Primus" with satisfaction; for though some parts of this work are exceptionable, and he may advance some mistaken observations, yet the ornithology of so distant a country as Carniola is very curious.   Men that undertake only one district are much more likely to advance natural knowledge than those that grasp at more than they can possibly be acquainted with: every kingdom, every province should have its own monographer.

The reason perhaps why he mentions nothing of Ray's "Ornithology" is the extreme poverty and distance of his country, into which the works of our great naturalist may never yet have found their way.   You have doubts, I know, whether this "Ornithology" is genuine, and really the work of Scopoli: as to myself, I think I discover strong tokens of authencity; the style corresponds with that of his "Entomologia;" and his characters of the ordines and genera are many of them new, expressive, and masterly.   He has ventured to alter some of the Linnæan genera with sufficient show of reason.

It might perhaps be mere accident that you saw so many swifts and no swallows at Staines; because, in my long observation of those birds, I never could discover the least degree of rivalry or hostility between the species.

Ray remarks that birds of the *Gallinæ* order, as cocks and hens, partridges and pheasants, &c., are *pulveratrices*, such as dust themselves, using that method of cleansing their feathers and ridding themselves of their vermin.   As far as I can observe, many birds that dust themselves never wash: and I once thought that those birds that wash themselves would never dust; but here I find myself mistaken; for common house-sparrows are great *pulveratrices*, being frequently seen grovelling and wallowing in dusty roads; and yet they are great washers.   Does not the skylark dust?

Query.—Might not Mahomet and his followers take one method of purification from these *pulveratrices?* because I find, from travellers of credit, that if a strict Mussulman is journeying in a sandy desert where no water is to be found, at stated hours he strips off his clothes, and most scrupulously rubs his body over with sand or dust.

A countryman told me he had found a young fern-owl in the nest of a small bird on the ground; and that it was fed by the little bird.   I went to see this extraordinary phenomenon, and found that it was a young cuckoo hatched in the nest of a titlark : it was become vastly too big for its nest, appearing " to have its large wings extended beyond the nest,"—

> " — — — — — in tenui re
> Majores pennas nido extendisse — — "

and was very fierce and pugnacious, pursuing my finger, as I teased it, for many feet from the nest, and sparring and buffeting with its wings like a gamecock. The dupe of a dam appeared at a distance, hovering about with meat in its mouth, and expressing the greatest solicitude.

In July I saw several cuckoos skimming over a large pond ; and found, after some observation, that they were feeding on the *libellulæ,* or dragon-flies ; some of which they caught as they settled on the weeds, and some as they were on the wing.   Notwithstanding what Linnæus says, I cannot be induced to believe that they are birds of prey.

This district affords some birds that are hardly ever heard of at Selborne.   In the first place considerable flocks of cross-beaks (*Loxiæ curvirostræ*) have appeared this summer in the pinegroves belonging to this house : the water-ousel is said to haunt the mouth of the Lewes river, near Newhaven ; and the Cornish chough builds, I know, all along the chalky cliffs of the Sussex shore.

I was greatly pleased to see little parties of ring-ousels (my newly discovered migrators) scattered, at intervals, all along the Sussex downs from Chichester to Lewes.   Let them come from whence they will, it looks very suspicious that they are cantoned along the coast, in order to pass the Channel when severe weather advances.   They visit us again in April, as it should seem, in their return ; and are not be found in the dead of winter.   It is remarkable that they are very tame, and seem to have no manner of apprehensions of danger from a person with a gun.

There are bustards on the wide downs near Brighthelmstone. No doubt you are acquainted with the Sussex downs : the prospects and rides round Lewes are most lovely !

As I rode along near the coast I kept a very sharp look-out in the lanes and woods, hoping I might, at this time of the year, have discovered some of the summer short-winged birds of passage crowding towards the coast in order for their departure ; but it was very extraordinary that I never saw a redstart, whitethroat, blackcap, uncrested wren, flycatcher, &c. And I remember to have made the same remark in former years, as I usually come to this place annually about this time. The birds most common along the coast at present are the stone-chatters, whinchats, buntings, linnets, some few wheatears, titlarks, &c. Swallows and house-martins abound yet, induced to prolong their stay by this soft, still, dry season.

A land tortoise, which has been kept for thirty years in a little walled court belonging to the house where I now am visiting, retires under ground about the middle of November, and comes forth again about the middle of April. When it first appears in the spring it discovers very little inclination towards food : but in the height of summer grows voracious : and then as the summer declines its appetite declines also ; so that for the last six weeks in autumn it hardly eats at all. Milky plants, such as lettuces, dandelions, sowthistles, are its favourite dish. In a neighbouring village one was kept till by tradition it was supposed to be a hundred years old. An instance of vast longevity in such a poor reptile !

Ringmer, *near* Lewes, *Oct.* 8, 1770.

CROSSBILL'S EGG.

LETTER XXXIX.

TO THOMAS PENNANT, ESQ.

After an ineffectual search in Linnæus and Brisson, I begin to suspect that I discern my brother's *Hirundo hyberna* in Scopoli's new discovered *Hirundo rupestris.* His description of "Supra murina, subtus albida ; rectrices maculâ ovali albâ in latere interno ; pedes nudi, nigri ; rostrum nigrum ; remiges obscuriores quam plumæ dorsales ; rectrices remigibus concolores, caudâ emarginatâ, nec forcipatâ;"[1] agrees very well with the bird in question; but when he comes to advance that it is "statura hirundinis urbicæ," and that "the definition given of the bank-martin suits this bird also,"—"definitio hirundinis ripariæ Linnæi huic quoque convenit," he in some measure invalidates all he has said; at least he shows at once that he compares them to these species merely from memory: for I have compared the birds themselves, and find they differ widely in every circumstance of shape, size, and colour. However, as you will have a specimen, I shall be glad to hear what your judgment is in the matter.

Whether my brother is forestalled in his nondescript or not, he will have the credit of first discovering that they spend their winters under the warm and sheltery shores of Gibraltar and Barbary.

Scopoli's characters of his ordines and genera are clear, just, and expressive, and much in the spirit of Linnæus. These few remarks are the result of my first perusal of Scopoli's "Annus Primus."

The bane of our science is the comparing one animal to the other by memory: for want of caution in this particular Scopoli falls into errors: he is not so full with regard to the manners of his indigenous birds as might be wished, as you justly observe: his Latin is easy, elegant, and expressive, and very superior to Kramer's "Elenchus Vegetabilium et Animalium per Austriam Inferiorem."

I am pleased to see that my description of the moose corresponds so well with yours.

SELBORNE, *Oct.* 29, 1770.

LETTER XL.

TO THOMAS PENNANT, ESQ.

I was much pleased to see, among the collection of birds from Gibraltar, some of those short-winged English summer birds of passage concerning whose departure we have made so much

---

[1] "Above it is mouse-colour, below whitish, the guiding feathers with an oval white spot on the inner side, the feet bare and black, the beak black, the wing feathers darker than the dorsal ones, the guiders of the same colour as the wings, the tail well defined, not forked."

inquiry. Now, if these birds are found in Andalusia to migrate to and from Barbary, it may easily be supposed that those that come to us may migrate back to the Continent, and spend their winters in some of the warmer parts of Europe. This is certain, that many soft-billed birds that come to Gibraltar appear there only in spring and autumn, seeming to advance in pairs towards the northward, for the sake of breeding during the summer months, and retiring in parties and broods towards the south, at the decline of the year: so that the rock of Gibraltar is the great rendezvous and place of observation from whence they take their departure each way towards Europe or Africa. It is therefore no mean discovery, I think, to find that our small short-winged summer birds of passage are to be seen spring and autumn on the very skirts of Europe; it is a presumptive proof of their emigrations.

Scopoli seems to me to have found the *Hirundo melba*, the great Gibraltar swift, in Tyrol, without knowing it. For what is his *Hirundo alpina* but the afore-mentioned bird in other words? Says he, " It has all the qualities of the preceding, save that the breast is white; it is a little larger than the former;" "Omnia prioris" (meaning the swift); "sed pectus album; paulo major priore." I do not suppose this to be a new species. It is true also of the *melba*, that "it builds on the lofty Alpine cliffs;" "nidificat in excelsis Alpium rupibus." *Vide* "Annum Primum."

My Sussex friend, a man of observation and good sense, but no naturalist, to whom I applied on account of the stone-curlew (*oedicnemus*), sends me the following account:—" In looking over my 'Naturalist's Journal' for the month of April, I find the stone-curlews are first mentioned on the 17th and 18th, which dates seem to me rather late. They live with us all the spring and summer, and at the beginning of autumn prepare to take leave by getting together in flocks. They seem to me a bird of passage that may travel into some dry hilly country south of us, probably Spain, because of the abundance of sheep-walks in that country; for they spend their summers with us in such districts. This conjecture I hazard, as I have never met with any one that has seen them in England in the winter. I believe they are not fond of going near the water, but feed on earthworms, that are common on sheep-walks and downs. They breed on fallows and lay-fields abounding with grey mossy flints, which much resemble their young in colour;

among which they skulk and conceal themselves. They make no nest, but lay their eggs on the bare ground, producing in common but two at a time. There is reason to think their young run soon after they are hatched; and that the old ones do not feed them, but only lead them about at the time of feeding, which, for the most part, is in the night." Thus far my friend.

In the manners of this bird you see there is something very analogous to the bustard, whom it also somewhat resembles in aspect and make, and in the structure of its feet.

For a long time I have desired my relation to look out for these birds in Andalusia; and now he writes me word that, for the first time, he saw one dead in the market on the 3rd of September.

When the stone-curlew (*oedicnemus*) flies, it stretches out its legs straight behind, like a heron.

SELBORNE, *Nov.* 26, 1770.

LETTER XLI.

TO THE HONOURABLE DAINES BARRINGTON.

THE birds that I took for *aberdavines* were reed-sparrows (*Passeres torquati*).

There are doubtless many home internal migrations within this kingdom that want to be better understood: witness those vast flocks of hen chaffinches that appear with us in the winter with hardly any cocks among them. Now, was there a due proportion of each sex, it would seem very improbable that any one district should produce such numbers of these little birds; and much more when only one half of the species appears: therefore we may conclude that the *Fringillæ cœlebes*, for some good purposes, have a peculiar migration of their own in which the sexes part. Nor should it seem so wonderful that the intercourse of sexes in this species of birds should be interrupted in winter; since in many animals, and particularly in bucks and does, the sexes herd separately, except at the season when commerce is necessary for the continuance of the breed. For this matter of the chaffinches see "Fauna Suecica," p. 85, and "Systema Naturæ," p. 318. I see every winter vast flights of hen chaffinches, but none of cocks.

Your method of accounting for the periodical motions of the British singing birds, or birds of flight, is a very probable one; since the matter of food is a great regulator of the actions and proceedings of the brute creation: there is but one that can be set in competition with it, and that is love. But I cannot quite acquiesce with you in one circumstance which you advance— that "when they have thus feasted, they again separate into small parties of five or six, and get the best fare they can within a certain district, having no inducement to go in quest of fresh-turned earth." Now if you mean that the business of congregating is quite at an end from the conclusion of wheat-sowing to the season of barley and oats, it is not the case with us; for larks and chaffinches, and particularly linnets, flock and congregate as much in the very dead of winter as when the husbandman is busy with his ploughs and harrows.

Surely there can be no doubt but that woodcocks and field-fares leave us in the spring, in order to cross the seas, and retire

CHAFFINCH'S EGG.

to some districts more suitable to the purpose of breeding. That the former pair, and that the hens are forward with egg before they retire, I myself, when I was a sportsman, have often experienced. It cannot indeed be denied that now and then we hear of a woodcock's nest, or even young birds, discovered in some part or other of this island: but then they are always mentioned as rarities, and somewhat out of the common course of things; but as to redwings and fieldfares, no sportsman or naturalist has ever yet, that I could hear, pretended to have found the nest or young of those species in any part of these kingdoms. And I the more admire at this instance as extraordinary, since, to all appearance, the same food in summer as well as in winter might support them here which maintains their congeners, the blackbirds and thrushes, did they choose to stay the summer through. Hence it appears that it is not food alone which determines some species of birds with regard to their stay or departure. Fieldfares and redwings disappear sooner or later, according as the warm weather comes on earlier or later, for I

well remember, after that dreadful winter, 1739–40, that cold
north-east winds continued to blow on through April and May,
and that these kinds of birds (what few remained of them)
did not depart as usual, but were seen lingering about till the
beginning of June.

The best authority that we can have for the nidification of the
birds above-mentioned in any district, is the testimony of faunists
that have written professedly the natural history of particular
countries.   Now, as to the fieldfare, Linnæus, in his "Fauna
Suecica," says of it, that "it builds in the largest trees,"—
"maximis in arboribus nidificat;" and of the redwing he says,
in the same place, that "it builds in the middle of shrubs or
hedges, and lays six bluish-green eggs with black spots,"—
"nidificat in mediis arbusculis, sive sepibus: ova sex cæruleo-
viridia maculis nigris variis."   Hence we may be assured that
fieldfares and redwings breed in Sweden.   Scopoli says, in his
"Annus Primus," of the woodcock, that "it comes to us about
the vernal equinox, and, after pairing, it builds its nest in
marshy places, and lays its eggs,"—"nupta ad nos venit circa
æquinoctium vernale;" meaning in Tyrol, of which he is a
native.   And afterwards he adds,—"nidificat in paludibus
alpinis: ova ponit 3—5."   It does not appear from Kramer that
woodcocks breed at all in Austria; but he says:—"This bird
dwells in the northern regions in summer, where, too, it generally
builds its nest. As winter comes on it goes farther south, leaving
this about the October full-moon.   After pairing, it usually
comes back to the north about the full March moon,"—"Avis
hæc septentrionalium provinciarum æstivo tempore incola est;
ubi plerumque nidificat.   Appropinquante hyeme australiores
provincias petit: hinc circa plenilunium mensis Octobris plerumque Austriam transmigrat.   Tunc rursus circa plenilunium
potissimum mensis Martii per Austriam matrimonio juncta ad
septentrionales provincias redit."   For the whole passage (which
I have abridged) see "Elenchus," &c., p. 351.   This seems to
be a full proof of the migration of woodcocks; though little is
proved concerning the place of breeding.

There fell in the county of Rutland, in three weeks of this
present very wet weather, seven inches and a-half of rain, which
is more than has fallen in any three weeks for these thirty year
past in that part of the world.   A mean quantity in that county
for one year is twenty inches and a-half.

SELBORNE, *Dec.* 20, 1770.

LETTER XLII.

TO THE HONOURABLE DAINES BARRINGTON.

You are, I know, no great friend to migration; and the well-attested accounts from various parts of the kingdom seem to justify you in your suspicions, that at least many of the swallow kind do not leave us in the winter, but lay themselves up like insects and bats, in a torpid state, and slumber away the more uncomfortable months till the return of the sun and fine weather awakens them.

But then we must not, I think, deny migration in general; because migration certainly does subsist in some places, as my brother in Andalusia has fully informed me. Of the motions of these birds he has ocular demonstration, for many weeks together, both spring and fall: during which periods myriads of the swallow kind traverse the Straits from north to south, and from south to north, according to the season; and these vast migrations consist not only of *hirundines*, but of bee-birds, hoopoes, *Oro pendolos*, or golden thrushes, &c. &c., and also of many of our soft-billed summer birds of passage; and moreover of birds which never leave us, such as all the various sorts of hawks and kites. Old Belon, two hundred years ago, gives a curious account of the incredible armies of hawks and kites which he saw in the spring-time traversing the Thracian Bosporus from Asia to Europe. Besides the above-mentioned, he remarks that the procession is swelled by whole troops of eagles and vultures.

Now it is no wonder that birds residing in Africa, and especially birds of prey whose blood being heated with hot animal food are more impatient of a sultry climate, should retreat before the sun as it advances, and retire to milder regions; but then I cannot help wondering why kites and hawks, and such hardy birds as are known to defy all the severity of England, and even of Sweden and all north Europe, should want to migrate from the south of Europe, and be dissatisfied with the winters of Andalusia.

It does not appear to me that much stress can be laid on the difficulty and hazard that birds must run in their migrations, by reason of vast oceans, cross winds, &c.; because, if we reflect, a bird, by crossing the water at Dover, and again at

Gibraltar, may travel from England to the equator without launching out and exposing itself to boundless seas. And I advance this obvious remark with the more confidence, because my brother has always found that some of his birds, and particularly the swallow kind, are very sparing of their pains in crossing the Mediterranean; when arrived at Gibraltar, they do not

> "— — — Ranged in figure wedge their way,
> — — — — — and set forth
> Their airy caravan high over seas
> Flying, and over lands with mutual wing
> Easing their flight;" — — — —   MILTON—

but scout and hurry along in little detached parties of six or seven in a company; and, sweeping low, just over the surface of the land and water, direct their course to the opposite continent at the narrowest passage they can find. They usually slope across the bay to the south-west, and so pass over opposite to Tangier, which, it seems, is the narrowest space.

In former letters we have considered whether it was probable that woodcocks in moonshiny nights cross the German ocean from Scandinavia. As a proof that birds of less speed may pass that sea, considerable as it is, I shall relate the following incident, which, though mentioned to have happened so many years ago, was strictly matter of fact:—As some people were shooting in the parish of Trotton, in the county of Sussex, they killed a duck in that dreadful winter of 1708-9, with a silver collar about its neck,[1] on which were engraven the arms of the King of Denmark. This anecdote the rector of Trotton at that time has often told to a near relation of mine; and, to the best of my remembrance, the collar was in the possession of the rector.

At present I do not know anybody near the sea-side that will take the trouble to remark at what time of the moon woodcocks first come: if I lived near the sea myself I would soon tell you more of the matter. One thing I used to observe when I was a sportsman, that there were times in which woodcocks were so sluggish and sleepy, that they would drop again when flushed, just before the spaniels; nay, just at the muzzle of a gun that had been fired at them. Whether this strange laziness

---

[1] White adds in a note, "I have read a like anecdote of a swan."

was the effect of a recent fatiguing journey I shall not presume
to say.

Nightingales not only never reach Northumberland and
Scotland, but also, as I have been always told, Devonshire and

THE NIGHTINGALE.

Cornwall. In those two last counties we cannot attribute the
failure of them to the want of warmth : the defect in the west
is rather a presumptive argument that these birds come over
to us from the Continent at the narrowest passage, and do not
stroll so far westward.

Let me hear from your own observation whether skylarks

I

do not dust. I think they do : and if they do, whether they wash also.

The *Alauda pratensis* of Ray was the poor dupe that was educating the booby of a cuckoo mentioned in Letter XXXVIII. in October last.

Your letter came too late for me to procure a ring-ousel for Mr. Tunstal during their autumnal visit; but I will endeavour to get him one when they call on us again in April. I am glad that you and that gentleman saw my Andalusian birds ; I hope they answered your expectation. Royston, or grey crows, are winter birds that come much about the same time with the woodcock : they, like the fieldfare and redwing, have no apparent reason for migration; for as they fare in the winter like their congeners, so might they in all appearance in the summer. Was not Tenant, when a boy, mistaken? Did he not find a missel-thrush's nest, and take it for the nest of a fieldfare?

NIGHTINGALE'S EGG,

The stock-dove or wood-pigeon, *Ænas Raii*, is the last winter bird of passage which appears with us; and is not seen till towards the end of November; about twenty years ago they abounded in the district of Selborne ; and strings of them were seen, morning and evening, that reached a mile or more ; but since the beechen woods have been greatly thinned they are much decreased in number. The ring-dove, *Palumbus Raii*, stays with us the whole year, and breeds several times through the summer.

Before I received your letter of October last I had just remarked in my journal that the trees were unusually green. This uncommon verdure lasted on late into November; and may be accounted for from a late spring, a cool and moist summer ; but more particularly from vast armies of chafers, or tree-beetles, which, in many places, reduced whole woods to a leafless naked state. These trees shot again at Midsummer, and then retained their foliage till very late in the year.

My musical friend, at whose house I am now visiting, has tried all the owls that are his near neighbours with a pitch-pipe set at concert-pitch, and finds they all hoot in B flat. He will examine the nightingales next spring.

FYFIELD, *near* ANDOVER, *Feb.* 12, 1771.

LETTER XLIII.

TO THOMAS PENNANT, ESQ.

THERE is an insect with us, especially on chalky districts, which is very troublesome and teasing all the latter end of the summer, getting into people's skins, especially those of women and children, and raising tumours which itch intolerably. This animal (which we call a harvest bug) is very minute, scarce discernible to the naked eye; of a bright scarlet colour, and of the genus of *acarus*.[1] They are to be met with in gardens on kidneybeans, or any legumens, but prevail only in the hot months of summer. Warreners, as some have assured me, are much infested by them on chalky-downs, where these insects sometimes swarm to so infinite a degree as to discolour their nets, and to give them a reddish cast, while the men are so bitten as to be thrown into fevers.

There is a small long shining fly in these parts very troublesome to the housewife, by getting into the chimneys, and laying its eggs in the bacon while it is drying: these eggs produce maggots called jumpers, which, harbouring in the gammons and best parts of the hogs, eat down to the bone, and make great waste. This fly I suspect to be a variety of the *Musca putris* of Linnæus: it is to be seen in the summer in farm-kitchens, on the bacon-racks and about the mantelpieces, and on the ceilings.

The insect that infests turnips and many crops in the garden (destroying often whole fields while in their seedling leaves) is an animal that wants to be better known. The country people here call it the turnip-fly and black dolphin; but I know it to be one of the *coleoptera;* the " *Chrysomela oleracea* saltatoria, femoribus posticis crassissimis "—" the vaulting *chrysomela*, with the back part of the thighs very thick." In very hot

---

[1] *Leptus autumnalis* of Latreille.

summers they abound to an amazing degree, and, as you walk in a field or in a garden, make a pattering like rain, by jumping on the leaves of the turnips or cabbages.

There is an *oestrus*, known in these parts to every ploughboy, which, because it is omitted by Linnæus,[1] is also passed over by late writers, and that is the *curvicauda* of old Moufet, mentioned by Derham in his "Physico-Theology," p. 250 : an insect worthy of remark for depositing its eggs as it flies in so dexterous a manner on the single hairs of the legs and flanks of grass-horses. But then Derham is mistaken when he advances that this *oestrus* is the parent of that wonderful star-tailed maggot which he mentions afterwards; for more modern entomologists have discovered that singular production to be derived from the egg of the *Musca chamæleon*.[2]

A full history of noxious insects hurtful in the field, garden, and house, suggesting all the known and likely means of destroying them, would be allowed by the public to be a most useful and important work. What knowledge there is of this sort lies scattered, and wants to be collected; great improvements would soon follow of course. A knowledge of the properties, economy, propagation, and, in short, of the life and conversation of these animals, is a necessary step to lead us to some method of preventing their depredations.

As far as I am a judge, nothing would recommend entomology more than some neat plates that should well express the generic distinctions of insects according to Linnæus; for I am well assured that many people would study insects, could they set out with a more adequate notion of those distinctions than can be conveyed at first by words alone.

SELBORNE, *March* 30, 1771.

LETTER XLIV.

TO THOMAS PENNANT, ESQ.

HAPPENING to make a visit to my neighbour's peacocks, I could not help observing that the trains of those magnificent birds appear by no means to be their tails; those long feathers

[1] This is a mistake on White's part : the Horse Bot-fly, *Gasterophilus equi*, Leach, is described by Linnæus under the name of *Œstrus bovis*.

[2] *Stratiomys chamæleon*, De Geer.

growing not from their *uropygium*, but all up their backs. A range of short, brown, stiff feathers, about six inches long, fixed in the *uropygium*, is the real tail, and serves as the fulcrum to prop the train, which is long and top-heavy when set on end. When the train is up, nothing appears of the bird before but its head and neck; but this would not be the case were those long feathers fixed only in the rump, as may be seen by the turkeycock when in a strutting attitude. By a strong muscular vibration these birds can make the shafts of their long feathers clatter like the swords of a sword-dancer: they then trample very quick with their feet, and run backwards towards the females.

I should tell you that I have got an uncommon *Calculus ægogropila*, taken out of the stomach of a fat ox; it is perfectly round, and about the size of a large Seville orange; such are, I think, usually flat.

SELBORNE, 1771.

LETTER XLV.

TO THE HONOURABLE DAINES BARRINGTON.

FROM what follows, it will appear that neither owls nor cuckoos keep to one note. My musical friend remarks that many (most) of his owls hoot in B flat; but that one went almost half a note below A. The pipe he tried their notes by was a common half-crown pitch-pipe, such as masters use for the tuning of harpsichords; it was the common London pitch.

A neighbour of mine, who is said to have a nice ear, remarks that the owls about this village hoot in three different keys—in G flat, or F sharp, in B flat and A flat. He heard two hooting to each other, the one in A flat, and the other in B flat. Do these different notes proceed from different species, or only from various individuals? The same person finds upon trial that the note of the cuckoo (of which we have but one species) varies in different individuals; for, about Selborne wood, he found they were mostly in D: he heard two sing together, the one in D, the other in D sharp, which made a disagreeable concert; he afterwards heard one in D sharp, and about Wolmer Forest some in

C.[1] As to nightingales, he says that their notes are so short and their transitions so rapid, that he cannot well ascertain their key. Perhaps in a cage, and in a room, their notes may be more distinguishable. This person has tried to settle the notes of a swift, and of several other small birds, but cannot bring them to any criterion.

As I have often remarked that redwings are some of the first birds that suffer with us in severe weather, it is no wonder at all that they retreat from Scandinavian winters: and much more the *ordo* of *grallæ* which, all to a bird, forsake the northern parts of Europe at the approach of winter. "Grallæ tanquam conjuratæ unanimiter in fugam se conjiciunt; ne earum unicam quidem inter nos habitantem invenire possimus; ut enim æstate in australibus degere nequeunt ob defectum lumbricorum, terramque siccam; ita nec in frigidis ob eandem causam," says Ekmarck the Swede, in his ingenious little treatise called "Migrationes Avium," which by all means you ought to read while your thoughts run on the subject of migration.—"The *grallæ*, as though they had conspired, take themselves to flight in an unmannerly fashion; nor can we find even one dwelling amongst us; for as they cannot live in the south during summer because of the dryness of the ground, so neither can they live in the cold countries of the north in winter for the contrary reason."

Birds may be so circumstanced as to be obliged to migrate in one country and not in another: but the *grallæ* (which procure their food from marshes and boggy grounds) must in winter forsake the more northerly parts of Europe, or perish for want of food.

I am glad you are making inquiries from Linnæus concerning the woodcock: it is expected of him that he should be able to account for the motions and manner of life of the animals of his own "Fauna."

[1] The editor of the edition of 1822 remarks that the cuckoo begins early in the season with a tray or third, next to a fourth, then a fifth, after which his voice breaks without attaining a sixth; a very old observation, however, seeing it is the subject of an epigram in the scarce black letter, "Epigrams of John Heywood," dated 1587 :—

> "Use maketh maistry, this hath been said alway ;
> But all is not alway as all men do say.
> In April, the koocoo can sing her song by rote,
> In June of tune she cannot sing a note :
> At first koocoo, koocoo, sing still can she do ;
> At last kooke, kooke, kooke, six kookes to one coo."

Faunists, as you observe, are too apt to acquiesce in bare descriptions and a few synonyms : the reason is plain ; because all that may be done at home in a man's study, but the investigation of the life and conversation of animals is a concern of much more trouble and difficulty, and is not to be attained but by the active and inquisitive, and by those that reside much in the country.

Foreign systematics are, I observe, much too vague in their specific differences ; which are almost universally constituted by one or two particular marks, the rest of the description running in general terms.   But our countryman, the excellent Mr. Ray, is the only describer that conveys some precise idea in every term or word, maintaining his superiority over his followers and imitators in spite of the advantage of fresh discoveries and modern information.

At this distance of years it is not in my power to recollect at what periods woodcocks used to be sluggish or alert when I was a sportsman : but upon my mentioning this circumstance to a friend, he thinks he has observed them to be remarkably listless against snowy foul weather : if this should be the case, then the inaptitude for flying arises only from an eagerness for food ; as sheep are observed to be very intent on grazing against stormy wet evenings.

SELBORNE, *Aug.* 1, 1771.

LETTER XLVI.

TO THOMAS PENNANT, ESQ.

THE summer through I have seen but two of that large species of bat which I call *Vespertilio altivolans*, from its manner of feeding high in the air : I procured one of them, and found it to be a male ; and made no doubt, as they accompanied together that the other was a female ; but happening in an evening or two to procure the other likewise, I was somewhat disappointed when it appeared to be also of the same sex.   This circumstance and the great scarcity of this sort, at least in these parts, occasions some suspicions in my mind whether it is really a species, or whether it may not be the male part of the more known species, one of which may supply many females ; as is known to be the case in sheep, and some other quadrupeds.   But this doubt can only be cleared by a farther examination, and some attention to the sex, of more specimens : all that I know at present is, that my two were amply furnished with the parts of generation much resembling those of a boar.

In the extent of their wings they measured fourteen inches and a half : and four inches and a half from the nose to the tip of the tail : their heads were large, their nostrils bilobated, their shoulders broad and muscular, and their whole bodies fleshy and plump.   Nothing could be more sleek and soft than their fur, which was of a bright chestnut colour; their maws were full of food, but so macerated that the quality could not be distinguished; their livers, kidneys, and hearts, were large, and their bowels covered with fat.   They weighed each, when entire, full one ounce and one drachm.   Within the ear there was somewhat of a peculiar structure that I did not understand perfectly; but refer it to the observation of the curious anatomist.   These creatures sent forth a very rancid and offensive smell.

Sept. 1771.

LETTER XLVII.

TO THOMAS PENNANT, ESQ.

ON the 12th of July I had a fair opportunity of contemplating the motions of the *caprimulgus*, or fern-owl, as it was playing round a large oak that swarmed with *Scarabœi solstitiales*, or fern-chafers.   The powers of its wing were wonderful, exceeding, if possible, the various evolutions and quick turns of the swallow genus.   But the circumstance that pleased me most was, that I saw it distinctly, more than once, put out its short leg while on the wing, and, by a bend of the head, deliver somewhat into its mouth.   If it takes any part of its prey with its foot, as I have now the greatest reason to suppose it does these chafers, I no longer wonder at the use of its middle toe, which is curiously furnished with a serrated claw.

Swallows and martins, the bulk of them I mean, have forsaken us sooner this year than usual; for, on the 22nd of September, they rendezvoused in a neighbour's walnut-tree, where it seemed probable they had taken up their lodgings for the night. At the dawn of the day, which was foggy, they arose all together in infinite numbers, occasioning such a rushing from the strokes of their wings against the hazy air, as might be heard to a considerable distance: since that no flock has appeared, only a few stragglers.

Some swifts staid late, till the 22nd of August—a rare instance! for they usually withdraw within the first week.[1]

On the 24th of September three or four ring-ousels appeared in my fields for the first time this season! how punctual are these visitors in their autumnal and spring migrations!

SELBORNE, 1771.

LETTER XLVIII.

TO THE HONOURABLE DAINES BARRINGTON.

WHEN I ride about in the winter, and see such prodigious flocks of various kinds of birds, I cannot help admiring these congregations, and wishing that it was in my power to account for those appearances almost peculiar to the season. The two great motives which regulate the proceedings of the brute creation are love and hunger; the former incites animals to perpetuate their kind, the latter induces them to preserve individuals; whether either of these should seem to be the ruling passion in the matter of congregating is to be considered. As to love, that is out of the question at a time of the year when that soft passion is not indulged; besides, during the amorous season, such a jealousy prevails between the male birds that they can hardly bear to be together in the same hedge or field. Most of the singing and elation of spirits of that time seem to me to be the effect of rivalry and emulation; and it is to this spirit of jealousy that I chiefly attribute the equal dispersion of birds in the spring over the face of the country.

Now as to the business of food: as these animals are actuated by instinct to hunt for necessary food, they should not, one would suppose, crowd together in pursuit of sustenance at a time when it is most likely to fail; yet such associations do take place in hard

[1] See Letter XCVI. to Mr. Barrington.

weather chiefly, and thicken as the severity increases. As some kind of self-interest and self-defence is no doubt the motive for the proceeding, may it not arise from the helplessness of their state in such rigorous seasons? just as men crowd together when under great calamities, though they know not why. Perhaps approximation may dispel some degree of cold; and a crowd may make each individual appear safer from the ravages of birds of prey and other dangers.

If I admire when I see how much congenerous birds love to congregate, I am the more struck when I see incongenerous ones in such strict amity. If we do not much wonder to see a flock of rooks usually attended by a train of daws, yet it is strange that the former should so frequently have a flight of starlings for their satellites. Is it because rooks have a more discerning scent than their attendants, and can lead them to spots more productive of food? Anatomists say that rooks, by reason of two large nerves which run down between the eyes into the upper mandible, have a more delicate feeling in their beaks than other round-billed birds, and can grope for their meat when out of sight. Perhaps then their associates attend them on the motive of interest, as grey-hounds wait on the motions of their finders; and as lions are said to do on the yelpings of jackals. Lapwings and starlings sometimes associate.

SELBORNE, *Feb.* 8, 1772.

LETTER XLIX.

TO THE HONOURABLE DAINES BARRINGTON.

As a gentleman and myself were walking on the 4th of last November round the sea-banks at Newhaven, near the mouth of the Lewes river, in pursuit of natural knowledge, we were surprised to see three house-swallows gliding very swiftly by us. That morning was rather chilly, with the wind at north-west; but the tenor of the weather for some time before had been delicate, and the noons remarkably warm. From this incident, and from repeated accounts which I meet with, I am more and more induced to believe that many of the swallow kind do not depart from this island; but lay themselves up in holes and caverns; and do, insect-like and bat-like.[1] come forth at mild times, and then retire again to their *latebræ*. Nor make I the least doubt but that, if I lived at Newhaven, Seaford, Bright-helmstone, or any of those towns near the chalk-cliffs of the Sussex coast, I should by proper observations, see swallows stirring at periods of the winter when the noons were soft and inviting and the sun warm and invigorating. And I am the more of this opinion from what I have remarked during some of our late springs, that though some swallows did make their appearance about the usual time, namely, the 13th or 14th of April, yet meeting with a harsh reception, and blustering cold north-east winds, they immediately withdrew, absconding for several days, till the weather gave them better encouragement.

March 9, 1772.

---

[1] Concerning swallows, the reader will see that Mr. White appears to incline more and more in favour of their torpidity, and against their migration. Mr. D. Barrington is still more positive on the same side of the question; yet the ancients generally mention this bird as wintering in Africa. See Anacreon λγ. ed. Brunck. p. 38. The Rhodians had a festival called χελιδόνια, when the boys brought about young swallows; the song which they sang may be seen in the works of Meursius, v. 3, p. 974, fol.

> Ἦλθε, Ἦλθε, χελιδὼν καλὰς,
> Ὥρας ἄγουσα, καὶ καλοὺς Ἐνιαυτοὺς
> Ἐπὶ γάστερα λευκὰ, κ' ἔπι νῶτα μέλαινα.

> "He comes! He comes! who loves to bear
> Soft sunny hours and seasons fair;—
> The swallow hither comes to rest
> His sable wing and snowy breast."

And alluding to this custom, Avienus (who may be considered only as a very bad translator of an excellent poem, the "Periegesis" of Dionysius) thus says, v. 705,—

> "Nam cum vere novo, tellus se dura relaxat,
> Culminibusque cavis, blandum strepit ales hirundo
> Gens devota choros agitat!"

"When in early spring the iron soil relaxes, comes the swallow chirping pleasantly from the hollow eaves, and the pious people begin to dance."

From a passage in the "Birds" of Aristophanes, we learn that among the Greeks the *crane* pointed out the time of *sowing*; the arrival of the *kite*, the time of *sheep-shearing*; and the *swallow*, the time to put on *summer-clothes*. According to the Greek calendar of Flora, kept by Theophrastus at Athens, the Ornithian winds blow, and the swallow comes between the 28th of February and the 12th of March; the kite and nightingale appear between the 11th and 26th of March; the cuckoo appears at the same time the young figs come out, thence his name.—STILLINGFLEET's *Tracts on Natural History.*

LETTER L.

TO THOMAS PENNANT, ESQ.

By my journal for last autumn it appears that the house-
martins bred very late, and staid very late in these parts; for
on the 1st of October I saw young martins in their nest nearly
fledged; and, again, on the 21st of October, we had at the
next house a nest full of young martins just ready to fly; and
the old ones were hawking for insects with great alertness.
The next morning the brood forsook their nest, and were flying
round the village. From this day I never saw one of the
swallow kind till the 3rd of November; when twenty, or
perhaps thirty, house-martins were playing all day long by the
side of the hanging wood, and over my fields. Did these small
weak birds, some of which were nestlings twelve days ago, shift
their quarters at this late season of the year to the other side
of the northern tropic? Or rather, is it not more probable that
the next church, ruin, chalk-cliff, steep covert, or perhaps sand-
bank, lake, or pool, may become their hybernaculum, and afford
them a ready and obvious retreat?

We now begin to expect our vernal migration of ring-ousels
every week. Persons worthy of credit assure me that ring-
ousels were seen at Christmas 1770 in the forest of Bere, on the
southern verge of this county. Hence we may conclude that
their migrations are only internal, and not extended to the continent southward, if they do at first come at all from the
northern parts of this island only, and not from the north of
Europe. Come from whence they will, it is plain, from the
fearless disregard that they show for men or guns, that they
have been little accustomed to places of much resort. Navi-
gators mention that in the Isle of Ascension, and other such
desolate districts, birds are so little acquainted with the human
form that they settle on men's shoulders; and have no more
dread of a sailor than they would have of a goat that was
grazing. A young man at Lewes, in Sussex, assured me that
about seven years ago ring-ousels abounded so about that town
in the autumn that he killed sixteen himself in one afternoon:
he added further, that some had appeared since in every
autumn; but he could not find that any had been observed
before the season in which he shot so many. I myself have

found these birds in little parties in the autumn cantoned all along the Sussex downs, wherever there were shrubs and bushes, from Chichester to Lewes; particularly in the autumn of 1770.

SELBORNE, *March* 15, 1773.

LETTER LI.

TO THE HONOURABLE DAINES BARRINGTON.

WHILE I was in Sussex last autumn my residence was at the village near Lewes, from whence I had formerly the pleasure of writing to you. On the 1st of November I remarked that the old tortoise, formerly mentioned, began first to dig the ground, in order to the forming its hybernaculum, which it had fixed on just beside a great tuft of hepaticas. It scrapes out the ground with its fore-feet, and throws it up over its back with its hind; but the motion of its legs is ridiculously slow, little exceeding the hour-hand of a clock; and suitable to the conposure of an animal said to be a whole month in performing one feat of copulation. Nothing can be more assiduous than this creature night and day in scooping the earth, and forcing its great body into the cavity; but as the noons of that season proved unusually warm and sunny, it was continually interrupted, and called forth by the heat in the middle of the day: and though I continued there till the 13th of November, yet the work remained unfinished. Harsher weather, and frosty mornings, would have quickened its operations. No part of its behaviour ever struck me more than the extreme timidity it always expresses with regard to rain; for though it has a shell that would secure it against the wheel of a loaded cart, yet does it discover as much solicitude about rain as a lady dressed in all her best attire, shuffling away on the first sprinklings, and running its head up in a corner. If attended to it becomes an excellent weather-glass; for as sure as it walks elate, and as it were on tiptoe, feeding with great earnestness in a morning, so sure will it rain before night. It is totally a diurnal animal, and never pretends to stir after it becomes dark. The tortoise, like other reptiles, has an arbitrary stomach as well as lungs; and can refrain from eating as well as breathing for a great part of the year. When first awakened it eats nothing;

nor again in the autumn before it retires : through the height of
the summer it feeds voraciously, devouring all the food that
comes in its way.   I was much taken with its sagacity in
discerning those that do it kind offices ; for as soon as the good
old lady comes in sight who has waited on it for more than thirty
years, it hobbles towards its benefactress with awkward alacrity ;
but remains inattentive to strangers.   Thus not only "the ox
knoweth its owner, and the ass his master's crib,"[1] but the most
abject reptile and torpid of beings distinguishes the hand that
feeds it, and is touched with the feelings of gratitude !

P.S.—In about three days after I left Sussex the tortoise
retired into the ground under the hepatica.

April 12, 1772.

LETTER LII.

TO THE HONOURABLE DAINES BARRINGTON.

THE more I reflect on the στοργή of animals, the more I am
astonished at its effects.   Nor is the violence of this affection
more wonderful than the shortness of its duration.   Thus every
hen is in her turn the virago of the yard, in proportion to the
helplessness of her brood ; and will fly in the face of a dog or a
sow in defence of those chickens, which in a few weeks she will
drive before her with relentless cruelty.

This affection sublimes the passions, quickens the invention,
and sharpens the sagacity of the brute creation.   Thus a hen, just
become a mother, is no longer that placid bird she used to be, but
with feathers standing on end, wings hovering, and clucking note,
she runs about like one possessed.   Dams will throw themselves
in the way of the greatest danger in order to avert it from their
progeny.   Thus a partridge will tumble along before a sportsman
in order to draw away the dogs from her helpless covey.   In the
time of nidification the most feeble birds will assault the most
rapacious.   All the *hirundines* of a village are up in arms at the
sight of a hawk, whom they will persecute till he leaves that
district.   A very exact observer has often remarked that a pair of
ravens nesting in the rock of Gibraltar would suffer no vulture or
eagle to rest near their station, but would drive them from the hill

[1] Isaiah i. 3.

with an amazing fury : even the blue thrush at the season of breeding would dart out from the cliffs of the rocks to chase away the kestrel or the sparrow-hawk.   If you stand near the nest of a bird that has young, she will not be induced to betray them by an inadvertent fondness, but will wait about at a distance with meat in her mouth for an hour together.

Should I further corroborate what I have advanced above by some anecdotes which I probably may have mentioned before in conversation, yet you will, I trust, pardon the repetition for the sake of the illustration.

PIED FLYCATCHER.

The flycatcher of the Zoology (the *Stoparola* of Ray) builds every year in the vines that grow on the walls of my house.

A pair of these little birds had one year inadvertently placed their nest on a naked bough, perhaps in a shady time, not being aware of the inconvenience that followed. But a hot sunny season coming on before the brood was half-fledged, the reflection of the wall became insupportable, and must inevitably have destroyed the tender young, had not affection suggested an expedient, and prompted the parent birds to hover over the nest all the hotter hours, while with wings expanded, and mouths gaping for breath, they screened off the heat from their suffering offspring.

A farther instance I once saw of notable sagacity in a willow-wren, which had built in a bank in my fields. This bird, a friend and myself had observed as she sat in her nest; but were particularly careful not to disturb her, though we saw she eyed us with some degree of jealousy. Some days after, as we passed that way, we were desirous of remarking how this brood went on; but no nest could be found, till I happened to take up a large bundle of long green moss, as it were carelessly thrown over the nest, in order to dodge the eye of any impertinent intruder.

A still more remarkable mixture of sagacity and instinct occurred to me one day as my people were pulling off the lining

SPOTTED FLYCATCHER'S EGG.

of a hotbed in order to add some fresh dung. From out of the side of this bed leaped an animal with great agility that made a most grotesque figure; nor was it without great difficulty that it could be taken; when it proved to be a large white-bellied field-mouse with three or four young clinging to her teats by their mouths and feet. It was amazing that the desultory and rapid motions of this dam should not oblige her litter to quit their hold, especially when it appeared that they were so young as to be both naked and blind!

To these instances of tender attachment, many more of which might be daily discovered by those that are studious of nature, may be opposed that rage of affection, that monstrous perversion of the στοργή, which induces some females of the brute creation to devour their young because their owners have handled them too freely, or removed them from place to place! Swine, and sometimes the more gentle race of dogs and cats, are guilty of this horrid and preposterous murder. When I hear now and then of an abandoned mother that destroys her offspring, I am not so much amazed; since reason perverted, and the bad passions let loose, are capable of any enormity : but why the parental feelings of brutes, that usually flow in one most uniform tenor, should sometimes be so extravagantly diverted, I leave to abler philosophers than myself to determine.

SELBORNE, *March* 26, 1773.

LETTER LIII.

TO THE HONOURABLE DAINES BARRINGTON.

SOME young men went down lately to a pond on the verge of Wolmer Forest to hunt flappers, or young wild-ducks, many of which they caught, and, among the rest, some very minute yet well-fledged wild-fowls alive, which upon examination I found to be teals. I did not know till then that teals ever bred in the south of England, and was much pleased with the discovery : this I look upon as a great stroke in natural history.

We have had, ever since I can remember, a pair of white owls that constantly breed under the eaves of this church. As I have paid good attention to the manner of life of these birds during their season of breeding, which lasts the summer through, the following remarks may not perhaps be unacceptable :—About an hour before sunset (for then the mice begin to run) they sally forth in quest of prey, and hunt all round the hedges of meadows and small inclosures for them, which seem to be their only food. In this irregular country we can stand on an eminence and see them beat the fields over like a setting-dog, often dropping down in the grass or corn. I have minuted these birds with my watch for an hour together, and have found that they return to their nest, the one or the other of them, about once in five minutes ; reflecting at the same time on the adroitness that every animal is possessed of as far as regards the well-being of itself and offspring. But a piece of address which they show when they return loaded should not, I think, be passed over in silence. As they take their prey with their claws, so they carry it in their claws to their nest : but as the feet are necessary in their ascent under the tiles, they constantly perch first on the roof of the chancel, and shift the mouse from their claws to their bill, that the feet may be at liberty to take hold of the plate on the wall as they are rising under the eaves.

K

White owls seem not (but in this I am not positive) to hoot at all : all that clamorous hooting appears to me to come from the wood kinds.   The white owl does indeed snore and hiss in a tremendous manner ; and these menaces will answer the intention of intimidating : for I have known a whole village up in arms on such an occasion, imagining the church-yard to be full of goblins and spectres.   White owls also often scream horribly as they fly along ; from this screaming probably arose the common people's imaginary species of screech-owl, which they super-stitiously think attends the windows of dying persons.   The plumage of the remiges of the wings of every species of owl that I have yet examined is remarkably soft and pliant.   Perhaps it may be necessary that the wings of these birds should not make much resistance or rushing, that they may be enabled to steal through the air unheard upon a nimble and watchful quarry.

While I am talking of owls, it may not be improper to mention what I was told by a gentleman of the county of Wilts.   As they were grubbing a vast hollow pollard-ash that had been the mansion of owls for centuries, he discovered at the bottom, a mass of matter that at first he could not account for.   After some examination, he found that it was the congeries of the bones of mice, and perhaps of birds and bats, that had been heaping together for ages, being cast up in pellets out of the crops of many generations of inhabitants.   For owls cast up the bones, fur, and feathers of what they devour, after the manner of hawks.   He believes, he told me, that there were bushels of this kind of substance.

When brown owls hoot their throats swell as big as a hen's egg. I have known an owl of this species live a full year without any water.   Perhaps the case may be the same with all birds of prey. When owls fly they stretch out their legs behind them as a balance to their large heavy heads : for, as most nocturnal birds have large eyes and ears they must have large heads to contain them.   Large eyes I presume are necessary to collect every ray of light, and large concave ears to command the smallest degree of sound or noise.[1]

The *hirundines* are a most inoffensive, harmless, entertaining, social, and useful tribe of birds ; they touch no fruit in our gardens ; delight, all except one species, in attaching themselves

[1] It will be proper to premise here that the Letters LIII., LV., LVII., and LX., have been published already in the "Philosophical Transactions," but nicer observation has furnished several corrections and additions.

to our houses; amuse us with their migrations, songs, and marvellous agility; and clear our outlets from the annoyances of gnats and other troublesome insects. Some districts in the South Seas, near Guiaquil,[1] are desolated, it seems, by the infinite swarms of venomous mosquitoes, which fill the air, and render those coasts insupportable. It would be worth inquiring whether any species of *hirundines* is found in those regions. Whoever contemplates the myriads of insects that sport in the sunbeams of a summer evening in this country, will soon be convinced to what a degree our atmosphere would be choked with them were it not for the friendly interposition of the swallows.

Many species of birds have their peculiar *lice;* but the *hirundines* alone seem to be annoyed with dipterous insects, which infest every species, and are so large, in proportion to themselves, that they must be extremely irksome and injurious to them. These are the *Hippoboscæ hirundines*, with narrow subulated wings, abounding in every nest; and are hatched by the warmth of the bird's own body during incubation, and crawl about under its feathers.

A species of them is familiar to horsemen in the south of England under the name of forest-fly; and to some of side-fly, from its running sideways like a crab. It creeps under the tails, and about the groins, of horses, which at their first coming out of the north, are rendered half frantic by the tickling sensation; while our own breed little regards them.

The curious Réaumur discovered the large eggs, or rather *pupæ*, of these flies as big as the flies themselves, which he hatched in his own bosom. Any person that will take the trouble to examine the old nests of either species of swallows may find in them the black shining cases or skins of the *pupæ* of these insects: but for other particulars, too long for this place, we refer the reader to "L'Histoire d'Insects" of that admirable entomologist—tom. iv. pl. 11.

SELBORNE, *July* 8, 1773.

---

[1] See Ulloa's "Travels.

LETTER LIV.

TO THOMAS PENNANT, ESQ.

As you desire me to send you such observations as may occur, I take the liberty of making the following remarks, that you may, according as you think me right or wrong, admit or reject what I here advance, in your intended new edition of the "British Zoology."

The osprey was shot about a year ago at Frinsham pond, a great lake, about six miles from hence, while it was sitting on the handle of a plough and devouring a fish: it used to precipitate itself into the water, and so take its prey by surprise.

A great ash-coloured butcher-bird was shot last winter in Tisted Park, and a red-backed butcher-bird at Selborne: they are *raræ aves* in this county.

Crows go in pairs the whole year round.

Cornish choughs abound, and breed on Beachy Head and on all the cliffs of the Sussex coast.

The common wild pigeon, or stock-dove, is a bird of passage in the south of England, seldom appearing till towards the end of November; and is usually the latest winter-bird of passage. Before our beechen woods were so much destroyed, we had myriads of them, reaching in strings for a mile together as they went out in a morning to feed. They leave us early in spring; where do they breed?

The people of Hampshire and Sussex call the missel-bird the storm-cock, because it sings early in the spring in blowing showery weather; its song often commences with the year: with us it builds much in orchards.

A gentleman assures me he has taken the nests of ring-ousels on Dartmoor; they build in banks on the sides of streams.

Titlarks not only sing sweetly as they sit on trees, but also as they play and toy about on the wing; and particularly while they are descending, and sometimes as they stand on the ground.

Adanson's testimony seems to me to be a very poor evidence that European swallows migrate during our winter to Senegal: he does not talk at all like an ornithologist; and probably saw only the swallows of that country, which I know build within Governor O'Hara's hall against the roof. Had he known European swallows, would he not have mentioned the species?

The house-swallow washes by dropping into the water as it flies: this species appears commonly about a week before the house-martin, and about ten or twelve days before the swift.

In 1772 there were young house-martins in their nest till the 23rd of October.

The swift appears about ten or twelve days later than the house-swallow: viz. about the 24th or the 26th of April.

Whin-chats and stone-chatters stay with us the whole year.

Some wheat-ears continue with us the winter through.

Wagtails of all sorts remain with us all the winter.

Bullfinches when fed on hempseed often become wholly black.

We have vast flocks of female chaffinches all the winter, with hardly any males among them.

When you say that in breeding time the cock-snipes make a bleating noise, and I a drumming sound (perhaps I should have rather said a humming), I suspect we mean the same thing. However while they are playing about on the wing they certainly make a loud piping with their mouths: but whether that bleating or humming is ventriloquous, or proceeds from the motion of their wings, I cannot say; but this I know, that when this noise happens, the bird is always descending, and his wings are violently agitated.

Soon after the lapwings have done breeding they congregate, and leaving the moors and marshes, betake themselves to downs and sheep-walks.

Two years ago last spring the little auk was found alive and unhurt, but fluttering and unable to rise, in a lane a few miles from Alresford, where there is a great lake: it was kept a while, but died.

I saw young teals taken alive in the ponds of Wolmer Forest in the beginning of July last, along with flappers, or young wild ducks.

All the swallow kind sip their water as they sweep over the face of pools or rivers: like Virgil's bees they drink flying— "flumina summa libant." In this method of drinking perhaps this genus may be peculiar.

The sedge-bird sings most part of the night; its notes are hurrying, but not unpleasing, and imitative of several birds; as the sparrow, swallow, skylark. When it happens to be silent in the night, by throwing a stone or clod into the bushes where it sits you immediately set it a singing; or in other words, though it slumbers sometimes, yet as soon as it is awakened it reassumes its song.

SELBORNE, *Nov.* 9, 1773.

LETTER LV.

TO THE HONOURABLE DAINES BARRINGTON.

IN obedience to your injunctions I sit down to give you some account of the house-martin or martlet;[1] and, if my monography of this little domestic and familiar bird should happen to meet with your approbation, I may probably soon extend my inquiries to the rest of the British *hirundines*—the swallow, the swift, and the bank-martin.

A few house-martins begin to appear about the 16th of April; usually some few days later than the swallow. For some time after they appear, the *hirundines* in general pay no attention to the business of nidification, but play and sport about, either to recruit from the fatigue of their journey, if they do migrate at all, or else that their blood may recover its true tone and texture after it has been so long benumbed by the severities of winter. About the middle of May, if the weather be fine, the martin begins to think in earnest of providing a mansion for its family. The crust or shell of this nest seems to be formed of such dirt or loam as comes most readily to hand, and is tempered and wrought together with little bits of broken straws to render it tough and tenacious. As this bird often builds against a perpendicular wall without any projecting ledge under, it requires its utmost efforts to get the first foundation firmly fixed, so that it may safely carry the superstructure. On this occasion the bird not only clings with its claws, but partly supports itself by strongly inclining its tail against the wall, making that a fulcrum; and thus steadied, it works and plasters the materials into the face of the brick or stone. But then, that this work may not, while it is soft and green, pull itself down by its own weight, the provident architect has prudence and forbearance enough not to advance her work too fast; but by building only in the morning, and by dedicating the rest of the day to food and amusement, gives it

---

[1] *Hirundo urbica,* Linnæus.

sufficient time to dry and harden.   About half an inch seems to
be a sufficient layer for a day.   Thus careful workmen when
they build mud-walls (informed at first perhaps by this little
bird) raise but a moderate layer at a time, and then desist ; lest
the work should become top-heavy, and so be ruined by its own

THE HOUSE-MARTIN.

weight.   By this method in about ten or twelve days is formed
an hemispheric nest with a small aperture towards the top,
strong, compact, and warm ; and perfectly fitted for all the
purposes for which it was intended.   But then nothing is more
common than for the house-sparrow, as soon as the shell is

finished, to seize on it as its own, to eject the owner, and to line it after its own manner.

After so much labour is bestowed in erecting a mansion, as Nature seldom works in vain, martins will breed on for several years together in the same nest, where it happens to be well sheltered and secured from the injuries of weather. The shell or crust of the nest is a sort of rustic-work full of knobs and protuberances on the outside : nor is the inside of those that I have examined smoothed with any exactness at all ; but is rendered soft and warm, and fit for incubation, by a lining of small straws, grasses, and feathers ; and sometimes by a bed of moss interwoven with wool. In this nest they tread, or engender, frequently during the time of building ; and the hen lays from three to five white eggs.

At first when the young are hatched, and are in a naked and helpless condition, the parent birds, with tender assiduity, carry out what comes away from their young. Were it not for this affectionate cleanliness the nestlings would soon be burnt up, and destroyed in so deep and hollow a nest, by their own caustic excrement. In the quadruped creation the same neat precaution is made use of ; particularly among dogs and cats, where the dams lick away what proceeds from their young. But in birds there seems to be a particular provision, that the dung of nestlings is enveloped in a tough kind of jelly, and therefore is the easier conveyed off without soiling or daubing. Yet, as Nature is cleanly in all her ways, the young perform this office for themselves in a little time by thrusting their tails out at the aperture of their nest. As the young of small birds presently arrive at their ἡλικία, or full growth, they soon become impatient of confinement, and sit all day with their heads out of the orifice, where the dams, by clinging to the nest, supply them with food from morning till night. For a time the young are fed on the wing by their parents ; but the feat is done by so quick and almost imperceptible a slight, that a person must have attended very exactly to their motions before he would be able to perceive it. As soon as the young are able to shift for themselves, the dams immediately turn their thoughts to the business of a second brood, while the first flight, shaken off and rejected by their nurses, congregate in great flocks, and are the birds that are seen clustering and hovering on sunny mornings and evenings round towers and steeples, and on the roofs of churches and houses. These congregatings usually begin to take place about

the first week in August; and therefore we may conclude that
by that time the first flight is pretty well over. The young of
this species do not quit their abodes all together; but the more
forward birds get abroad some days before the rest.   These
approaching the eaves of buildings, and playing about before
them, make people think that several old ones attend one nest.
They are often capricious in fixing on a nesting-place, beginning
many edifices, and leaving them unfinished; but when once a nest
is completed in a sheltered place, it serves for several seasons.
Those which breed in a ready-finished house get the start in
hatching of those that build new by ten days or a fortnight.
These industrious artificers are at their labours in the long days
before four in the morning: when they fix their materials they
plaster them on with their chins, moving their heads with a quick
vibratory motion.   They dip and wash as they fly sometimes in
very hot weather, but not so frequently as swallows. It has been
observed that martins usually build to a north-east or north-west

HOUSE-MARTIN'S EGG.

aspect, that the heat of the sun may not crack and destroy their
nests; but instances are also remembered where they bred for
many years in vast abundance in a hot stifled inn-yard, against
a wall facing to the south.

Birds in general are wise in their choice of situation; but in
this neighbourhood every summer is seen a strong proof to the
contrary at a house without eaves in an exposed district, where
some martins build year by year in the corners of the windows.
But as the corners of these windows (which face to the south-east
and south-west) are too shallow, the nests are washed down every
hard rain; and yet these birds drudge on to no purpose from
summer to summer, without changing their aspect or house.   It
is a piteous sight to see them labouring when half their nest is
washed away, and bringing dirt " to patch the ruins of a fallen
race "—" generis lapsi sarcire ruinas."   Thus is instinct a most
wonderful but unequal faculty; in some instances so much above
reason, in other respects so far below it ! Martins love to frequent
towns, especially if there are great lakes and rivers at hand; nay,

they even affect the close air of London. And I have not only seen them nesting in the Borough, but even in the Strand and Fleet Street; but then it was obvious from the dinginess of their aspect that their feathers partook of the filth of that sooty atmosphere. Martins are by far the least agile of the four species; their wings and tails are short, and therefore they are not capable of such surprising turns and quick and glancing evolutions as the swallow. Accordingly, they make use of a placid easy motion in a middle region of the air, seldom mounting to any great height, and never sweeping long together over the surface of the ground or water. They do not wander far for food, but affect sheltered districts, over some lake, or under some hanging wood, or in some hollow vale, especially in windy weather. They breed the latest of all the swallow kind: in 1772 they had nestlings on to October the 21st, and are never without unfledged young as late as Michaelmas

As the summer declines the congregating flocks increase in numbers daily by the constant accession of the second broods, till at last they swarm in myriads upon myriads round the villages on the Thames, darkening the face of the sky as they frequent the aits of that river, where they roost. They retire, the bulk of them I mean, in vast flocks together about the beginning of October; but have appeared of late years in a considerable flight in this neighbourhood, for one day or two, as late as November the 3rd and 6th, after they were supposed to have been gone for more than a fortnight. They therefore withdraw with us the latest of any species. Unless these birds are very short-lived indeed, or unless they do not return to the district where they are bred, they must undergo vast devastations some-how, and somewhere; for the birds that return yearly bear no manner of proportion to the birds that retire.

House-martins are distinguished from their congeners by having their legs covered with soft, downy feathers down to their toes. They are no songsters; but twitter in a pretty inward soft manner in their nests. During the time of breeding they are often greatly molested with fleas.

SELBORNE, *Nov.* 20, 1773.

LETTER LVI.

TO THE HONOURABLE DAINES BARRINGTON.

I RECEIVED your last favour just as I was setting out for this place; and am pleased to find that my monograph met with your approbation. My remarks are the result of many years observation; and are, I trust, true in the whole: though I do not pretend to say that they are perfectly void of mistake, or that a more nice observer might not make many additions, since subjects of this kind are inexhaustible.

If you think my letter worthy the notice of your respectable society, you are at liberty to lay it before them; and they will consider it, I hope, as it was intended, as a humble attempt to promote a more minute inquiry into natural history; into the life and conversation of animals. Perhaps hereafter I may be induced to take the house-swallow under consideration; and from that proceed to the rest of the British *hirundines*.

Though I have now travelled the Sussex Downs upwards of thirty years, I still investigate that chain of majestic mountains with fresh admiration year by year; and think I see new beauties every time I traverse it. This range, which runs from Chichester eastward as far as Eastbourne, is about sixty miles in length, and is called the South Downs, properly speaking, only round Lewes. As you pass along, it commands a noble view of the wild, or weald, on one hand, and the broad downs and sea on the other. Mr. Ray used to visit a family at Danny, just at the foot of these hills; he was so ravished with the prospect from Plumpton-plain near Lewes, that he mentions those landscapes in his " Wisdom of God in the Works of the Creation" with the utmost satisfaction, and thinks them equal to anything he had seen in the finest parts of Europe.

For my own part, I think there is something peculiarly sweet and pleasing in the shapely figured aspect of chalk-hills in preference to those of stone, which are rugged, broken, abrupt, and shapeless.

Perhaps I may be singular in my opinion, and not so happy as to convey to you the same idea; but I never contemplate these mountains without thinking I perceive somewhat analogous to growth in their gentle swellings and smooth fungus-like pro-tuberances, their fluted sides, and regular hollows and slopes, that

carry at once the air of vegetative dilatation and expansion.   Or
was there ever a time when these immense masses of calcareous
matter were thrown into fermentation by some adventitious
moisture ; were raised and leavened into such shapes by some
plastic power ; and so made to swell and heave their broad
backs into the sky so much above the less animated clay of
the wild below ?

By what I can guess of the admeasurements of the hills that
have been taken round my house, I should suppose that these
hills surmount the wild at an average of about the rate of
five hundred feet.

One thing is very remarkable as to the sheep ; from the westward until you get to the river Adur all the flocks have horns,
and smooth white faces, and white legs ; and a hornless sheep is
rarely to be seen : but as soon as you pass that river eastward,
and mount Beeding Hill, all the flocks at once become hornless,
or, as they call them, poll-sheep ; and have moreover black faces
with a white tuft of wool on their foreheads, and speckled and
spotted legs : so that you would think that the flocks of Laban
were pasturing on one side of the stream, and the variegated
breed of his son-in-law Jacob were cantoned along on the other.
And this diversity holds good respectively on each side from
the valley of Brambler and Beeding to the eastward, and
westward all the whole length of the downs.   If you talk with
the shepherds on this subject, they tell you that the case has
been so from time immemorial ; and smile at your simplicity
if you ask them whether the situation of these two different
breeds might not be reversed ?   However, an intelligent friend of
mine near Chichester is determined to try the experiment, and
has this autumn, at the hazard of being laughed at, introduced
a parcel of black-faced hornless rams among his horned western
ewes.   The black-faced poll-sheep have the shortest legs and
the finest wool.

[The sheep on the downs in the winter of 1769 were very
ragged, and their coats much torn ; the shepherds say they tear
their fleeces with their own mouths and horns, and they are
always in that way in mild wet winters, being teased and tickled
with a kind of lice.

After ewes and lambs are shorn, there is great confusion and
bleating, neither the dams nor the young being able to
distinguish one another as before.   This embarrassment seems
not so much to arise from the loss of the fleece, which may

occasion an alteration in their appearance, as from the defect of that *notus odor*, discriminating each individual personally; which also is confounded by the strong scent of the pitch and tar wherewith they are newly marked; for the brute creation recognize each other more from the smell than the sight; and in matters of identity and diversity appeal much more to their noses than their eyes. After sheep have been washed there is the same confusion, from the reason given above.] —OBSERVATIONS ON NATURE.

As I had hardly ever before travelled these downs at so late a season of the year, I was determined to keep as sharp a look-out as possible so near the southern coast, with respect to the summer short-winged birds of passage. We make great inquiries concerning the withdrawing of the swallow kind, without examining enough into the causes why this tribe is never to be seen in winter; for, *entre nous*, the disappearing of the latter is more marvellous than that of the former, and much more unaccountable. The *hirundines*, if they please, are certainly capable of migration; and yet no doubt are often found in a torpid state: but redstarts, nightingales, whitethroats, blackcaps, which are very ill provided for long flights, have never been once found, as I ever heard of, in a torpid state, and yet can never be supposed in such troops from year to year to dodge and elude the eyes of the curious and inquisitive, which from day to day discern the other small birds that are known to abide our winters. But, notwithstanding all my care, I saw nothing like a summer bird of passage: and, what is more strange, not one wheatear, though they abound so in the autumn as to be a considerable perquisite to the shepherds that take them; and though many are to be seen to my knowledge all the winter through in many parts of the south of England. The most intelligent shepherds tell me that some few of these birds appear on the downs in March, and then withdraw to breed probably in warrens and stone quarries: now and then a nest is ploughed up in a fallow on the downs under a furrow, but it is thought a rarity. At the time of wheat-harvest they begin to be taken in great numbers; are sent for sale in vast quantities to Brighton and Tunbridge; and appear at the tables of all the gentry that entertain with any degree of elegance. About Michaelmas they retire, and are seen no more till March. Though these birds are, when in season, in great plenty on the south downs round Lewes, yet at Eastbourne, which is the eastern extremity of those downs, they abound much more. One thing is very remarkable—that though in the height of the season so many hundreds of dozens are taken, yet they never are seen to flock; and it is a rare thing to see more than three or four at a time: so that there must be a perpetual flitting and constant progressive succession. It does not appear that any wheatears are taken to the westward of Houghton bridge, which stands on the river Arun.

I did not fail to look particularly after my new migration of ring-ousels; and to take notice whether they continued on the downs to this season of the year; as I had formerly remarked them in the month of October all the way from Chichester to Lewes wherever there were any shrubs and coverts: but not one bird of this sort came within my observation. I only saw a few larks and whinchats, some rooks, and several kites and buzzards.

About summer a flight of crossbills comes to the pine-groves about this house, but never makes any long stay.

The old tortoise, that I have mentioned in a former letter, still continues in this garden; and retired under ground about the 20th of November, and came out again for one day on the 30th: it lies now buried in a wet swampy border under a wall facing to the south, and is enveloped at present in mud and mire!

Here is a large rookery round this house, the inhabitants of which seem to get their livelihood very easily; for they spend the greatest part of the day on their nest-trees when the weather is mild. These rooks retire every evening all the winter from this rookery, where they only call by the way, as they are going to roost in deep woods: at the dawn of day they always revisit their nest-trees, and are preceded a few minutes by a flight of daws, that act, as it were, as their harbingers.

RINGMER, *near* LEWES, *Dec.* 9, 1773.

LETTER LVII.

TO THE HONOURABLE DAINES BARRINGTON.

THE house-swallow,[1] or chimney-swallow, is undoubtedly the first comer of all the British *hirundines;* and appears in general on or about the 13th of April, as I have remarked from many

---

[1] Chimney-Swallow, *Hirundo rustica,* Linnæus.

years' observation. Not but now and then a straggler is seen much earlier : and, in particular, when I was a boy I observed a swallow for a whole day together on a sunny warm Shrove Tuesday ; which day could not fall out later than the middle of March, and often happened early in February.

It is worth remarking that these birds are seen first about lakes and mill-ponds ; and it is also very particular, that if these early visitors happen to find frost and snow, as was the case in the two dreadful springs of 1770 and 1771, they immediately withdraw for a time. A circumstance this much more in favour of hiding than migration ; since it is much more probable that a bird should retire to its hybernaculum just at hand, than return for a week or two only to warmer latitudes.

The swallow, though called the chimney-swallow, by no means builds altogether in chimneys, but often within barns and out-houses, against the rafters ; and so she did in Virgil's time :— " Garrula quàm tignis nidos suspendat hirundo." " The twittering swallow hangs its nest from the beams."

In Sweden she builds in barns, and is called *Ladu swala*, the barn-swallow. Besides, in the warmer parts of Europe there are no chimneys to houses, except they are English built : in these countries she constructs her nest in porches, and gateways, and galleries, and open halls.

Here and there a bird may affect some odd, peculiar place ; as we have known a swallow build down the shaft of an old well, through which chalk had been formerly drawn up for the purpose of manure : but in general with us this *hirundo* breeds in chimneys ; and loves to haunt those stacks where there is a constant fire, no doubt for the sake of warmth. Not that it can subsist in the immediate shaft where there is a fire ; but prefers one adjoining to that of the kitchen, and disregards the perpetual smoke of that funnel, as I have often observed with some degree of wonder.

Five or six or more feet down the chimney does this little bird begin to form her nest, about the middle of May, which consists, like that of the house-martin, of a crust or shell composed of dirt or mud, mixed with short pieces of straw to render it tough and permanent : with this difference, that whereas the shell of the martin is nearly hemispheric, that of the swallow is open at the top, and like half a deep dish : this nest is lined with fine grasses, and feathers which are often collected as they float in the air.

Wonderful is the address which this adroit bird shows all day long in ascending and descending with security through so narrow a pass. When hovering over the mouth of the funnel, the vibration of her wings acting on the confined air occasion a rumbling like thunder. It is not improbable that the dam submits to this inconvenient situation so low in the shaft, in order to secure her broods from rapacious birds, and particularly from owls, which frequently fall down chimneys, perhaps in attempting to get at these nestlings.

The swallow lays from four to six white eggs, dotted with red specks; and brings out her first brood about the last week in June, or the first week in July. The progressive method by which the young are introduced into life is very amusing: first, they emerge from the shaft with difficulty enough, and often fall down into the rooms below; for a day or so they are fed on the chimney-top, and then are conducted to the dead leafless bough of some tree, where sitting in a row they are attended with great assiduity, and may then be called perchers. In a day or two more they become flyers, but are still unable to take their own food; therefore they play about near the place where the dams are hawking for flies; and when a mouthful is collected, at a certain signal given the dam and the nestling advance, rising towards each other, and meeting at an angle; the young one all the while uttering such a little quick note of gratitude and complacency, that a person must have paid very little regard to the wonders of nature that has not often remarked this feat.

The dam betakes herself immediately to the business of a second brood as soon as she is disengaged from her first; which at once associates with the first broods of house-martins; and with them congregates, clustering on sunny roofs, towers, and trees. This *hirundo* brings out her second brood towards the middle and end of August.

All the summer long the swallow is a most instructive pattern of unwearied industry and affection; for from morning to night, while there is a family to be supported, she spends the whole day in skimming close to the ground, and exerting the most sudden turns and quick evolutions. Avenues, and long walks under hedges, and pasture-fields, and mown meadows where cattle graze, are her delight, especially if there are trees interspersed; because in such spots insects most abound. When a fly is taken, a smart snap from her bill is heard, resembling the noise at the shutting of a watch-case; but the motion of the mandibles is too quick for the eye.

The swallow, probably the male bird, is the *excubitor* to house-martins, and other little birds, announcing the approach of birds of prey.   For as soon as a hawk appears, with a shrill alarming note he calls all the swallows and martins about him; who pursue in a body, and buffet and strike their enemy till they have driven him from the village, darting down from above on his back, and rising in a perpendicular line in perfect security. This bird will also sound the alarm and strike at cats when they climb on the roofs of houses, or otherwise approach the nests. Each species of *hirundo* drinks as it flies along, sipping the surface of the water; but the swallow alone, in general, washes on the wing, by dropping into a pool for many times together: [1] in very hot weather house-martins and bank-martins also dip and wash a little.

The swallow is a delicate songster, and in soft sunny weather sings both perching and flying; on trees in a kind of concert, and on chimney-tops: it is also a bold flyer, ranging to distant downs and commons even in windy weather, which the other species seem much to dislike; nay, even frequenting exposed sea-port towns and making little excursions over the salt water.   Horse-men on wide downs are often closely attended by a little party of swallows for miles together, which plays before and behind them, sweeping around, and collecting all the skulking insects that are roused by the trampling of the horses' feet: when the wind blows hard, without this expedient, they are often forced to settle to pick up their lurking prey.

This species feeds much on little *coleoptera*, as well as on gnats and flies; and often settles on dug ground, or paths, for gravels to grind and digest its food.   Before they depart, for some weeks they forsake houses and chimneys to a bird, and roost in trees; and usually withdraw about the beginning of October; though some few stragglers may appear at times till the first week in November.

[September 13, 1791.   The congregating flocks of *hirundines* on the church and tower are very beautiful and amusing! When they fly off together from the roof, on any alarm, they

[1] " Now suddenly he skims the glassy pool,
    Now quaintly dips, and with an arrow's speed
    Whisks by.   I love to lie awake, and hear
    His morning song twittered to dawning day."

L

quite swarm in the air. But they soon settle in heaps, and preening their feathers, and lifting up their wings to admit the sun, seem highly to enjoy the warm situation. Thus they spend the heat of the day, preparing for their emigration, and, as it were, consulting when and where they are to go. The flight about the church seems to consist chiefly of house-martins, about 400 in number: but there are other places of rendezvous about the village frequented at the same time.[1]

It is remarkable, that though most of them sit on the battlements and roof, yet many hang or cling for some time by their claws against the surface of the walls, in a manner not practised by them at any other time of their remaining with us.

The swallows seem to delight more in holding their assemblies on trees.

November 3, 1789. Two swallows were seen this morning at Newton vicarage-house hovering and settling on the roofs and out-buildings. None have been observed at Selborne since October 11. It is very remarkable, that after the *hirundines* have disappeared for some weeks, a few are occasionally seen again: sometimes in the first week in November, and that only for one day. Do they not withdraw and slumber in some hiding place during the interval? for we cannot suppose they had migrated to warmer climes, and so returned again for one day. Is it not more probable that they are awakened from sleep, and like the bats are come forth to collect a little food? Bats appear at all seasons through the autumn and spring months, when the thermometer is at 50°, because then *phalænæ* and moths are stirring.

These swallows looked like young ones.]—OBSERVATIONS ON NATURE.

Some few pairs haunt the new and open streets of London, next the fields, but do not enter, like the house-martin, the close and crowded parts of the city.

---

[1] Of their migration the proofs are such as will scarcely admit of a doubt. Sir Charles Wager and Captain Wright saw vast flocks of them at sea, when on their passage from one country to another. Our author, Mr. White, saw what he deemed the actual migration of these birds which he has described at p. 69, and again in the above extract; and I once observed a large flock of house-martins myself on the roof of the church here at Catsfield, which acted exactly in the manner here described by Mr. White, sometimes preening their feathers and spreading their wings to the sun, and then flying off all together, but soon returning to their former situation. The greatest part of these birds seemed to be young ones.—MARKWICK.

Both male and female are distinguished from their congeners by the length and forkedness of their tails. They are undoubtedly the most nimble of all the species; and when the male pursues the female in amorous chase, they then go beyond their usual speed, and exert a rapidity almost too quick for the eye to follow.

After this circumstantial detail of the life and discerning στοργή of the swallow, I shall add, for your further amusement, an anecdote or two not much in favour of their sagacity.

A certain swallow built for two years together on the handles of a pair of garden shears that were stuck up against the boards in an out-house, and therefore must have her nest spoiled whenever that implement was wanted: and, what is stranger still, another bird of the same species built its nest on the wings and body of an owl that happened by accident to hang dead and dry from the rafter of a barn. This owl, with the nest on its wings, and with eggs in the nest, was brought as a curiosity worthy the most elegant private museum in Great Britain. The owner, struck with the oddity of the sight, furnished the bringer with a large shell, or conch, desiring him to fix it just where the owl hung: the person did as he was ordered, and the following year a pair, probably the same pair, built their nest in the conch, and laid their eggs.

The owl and the conch make a strange grotesque appearance, and are not the least curious specimens in that wonderful collection of art and nature.

Thus is instinct in animals, taken the least out of its way, an undistinguishing, limited faculty; and blind to every circumstance that does not immediately respect self-preservation, or lead at once to the propagation or support of their species.

SELBORNE, *Sept.* 9, 1767.

LETTER LVIII.

TO THE HONOURABLE DAINES BARRINGTON.

I RECEIVED your favour of the 8th, and am pleased to find that you read my little history of the swallow with your usual candour: nor was I the less pleased to find that you made objections where you saw reason.

L 2

As to the quotations, it is difficult to say precisely which species of *hirundo* Virgil might intend in the lines in question. since the ancients did not attend to specific differences like modern naturalists; yet somewhat may be gathered, enough to incline me to suppose that in the two passages quoted the poet had his eye on the swallow.

In the first place the epithet *garrula* suits the swallow well, which is a great songster; and not the martin, which is rather a mute bird; and when it sings is so inward as scarce to be heard. Besides, if *tignum* in that place signifies a rafter rather than a beam, as it seems to me to do, then it must be the swallow that is alluded to, and not the martin; since the former does frequently build within the roof against the rafters; while the latter always, as far as I have been able to observe, builds without the roof against eaves and cornices.

As to the simile, too much stress must not be laid on it: yet the epithet *nigra* speaks plainly in favour of the swallow, whose back and wings are very black; while the rump of the martin is milk-white, its back and wings blue, and all its under part white as snow. Nor can the clumsy motions (comparatively clumsy) of the martin well represent the sudden and artful evolutions and quick turns which Juturna gave to her brother's chariot, so as to elude the eager pursuit of the enraged Æneas. The verb *sonat* also seems to imply a bird that is somewhat loquacious.[1]

> " Nigra velut magnas domini cum divitis ædes
> Pervolat, et pennis alta atria lustrat hirundo,
> Pabula parva legens, nidisque loquacibus escas :
> Et nunc porticibus vacuis, nunc humida circum
> Stagna sonat."—(VIRG. *Æn.* xii. 473—477.)

We have had a very wet autumn and winter, so as to raise the springs to a pitch beyond anything since 1764; which was a remarkable year for floods and high waters. The land-springs, which we call levants, break out much on the downs of Sussex, Hampshire, and Wiltshire. The country people say when the levants rise corn will always be dear; meaning that when the earth is so glutted with water as to send forth springs

---

[1] "As when the black swallow flies through the great palace of some wealthy lord, sweeping with its wings through the lofty halls, picking up tiny scraps of food for its chirping nestlings, at one time twittering in the empty porches, and at another round the watery ponds."

on the downs and uplands, the corn-vales must be drowned; and so it has proved for these ten or eleven years past. For land-springs have never obtained more in the memory of man than during that period; nor has there been known a greater scarcity of all sorts of grain, considering the great improvements of modern husbandry. Such a run of wet seasons a century or two ago would, I am persuaded, have occasioned a famine. Therefore pamphlets and newspaper letters, that talk of combinations, tend to inflame and mislead; since we must not expect plenty till Providence sends us more favourable seasons.

The wheat of last year, all round this district, and in the county of Rutland and elsewhere, yields remarkably bad: and our wheat on the ground, by the continual late sudden vicissitudes from fierce frost to pouring rains, looks poorly; and the turnips rot very fast.

SELBORNE, *Feb.* 14, 1774.

LETTER LIX.

TO THE HONOURABLE DAINES BARRINGTON.

THE sand-martin, or bank-martin (*Hirundo riparia,* Linnæus), is by much the least of any of the British *hirundines;* and, as far as we have ever seen, the smallest known *hirundo:* though Biisson asserts that there is one much smaller, and that is the *Hirundo esculenta.*

But it is much to be regretted that it is scarce possible for any observer to be so full and exact as he could wish in reciting the circumstances attending the life and conversation of this little bird, since it is *fera naturâ,* at least in this part of the kingdom, disclaiming all domestic attachments, and haunting wild heaths and commons where there are large lakes; while the other species, especially the swallow and house-martin, are remarkably gentle and domesticated, and never seem to think themselves safe but under the protection of man.   ·

Here are in this parish, in the sand-pits and banks of the lakes of Wolmer Forest, several colonies of these birds; and yet they are never seen in the village; nor do they at all frequent the cottages that are scattered about in that wild district. The only instance I ever remember where this species haunts any building is at the town of Bishop's Waltham, in this county, where many sand-martins nestle and breed in the scaffold holes of the back-wall of William of Wykeham's stables: but then this wall stands in a very sequestered and retired inclosure, and faces upon a large and beautiful lake.   Indeed this species seems so to delight in large waters, that no instance occurs of their abounding but near vast pools or rivers : and in particular it has been remarked that they swarm in the banks of the Thames in some places below London bridge.

It is curious to observe with what different degrees of architectonic skill Providence has endowed birds of the same genus, and so nearly correspondent in their general mode of life![1]   For while the swallow and the house-martin discover the greatest address in raising and securely fixing crusts or shells of loam as *cunabula* for their young, the bank-martin terebrates a round and regular hole in the sand or earth, which is serpentine, horizontal, and about two feet deep.   At the inner end of this burrow does this bird deposit, in a good degree of safety, her rude nest, consisting of fine grasses and feathers, usually goose-feathers, very inartificially laid together.

Perseverance will accomplish anything : though at first one would be disinclined to believe that this weak bird, with her soft and tender bill and claws, should ever be able to bore the stubborn sand-bank without entirely disabling herself; yet with these feeble instruments have I seen a pair of them make great despatch : and could remark how much they had scooped that day by the fresh sand which ran down the bank, and was of a different colour from that which lay loose and bleached in the sun.

In what space of time these little artists are able to mine and finish these cavities I have never been able to discover, for reasons given above ; but it would be a matter worthy of observation, where it falls in the way of any naturalist to make his remarks.   This I have often taken notice of, that several holes of different depths are left unfinished at the end of summer. To imagine that these beginnings were intentionally made in order to be in the greater forwardness for next spring is allowing

---

[1] " Each creature hath a wisdom of its own ;
   The pigeons feed their tender offspring, crying,
   When they are callow, but withdraw their food
   When they are fledged, that they may teach them flying."
                                                    HERBERT.

perhaps too much foresight and *rerum prudentia* to a simple bird. May not the cause of these *latebræ* being left unfinished arise from their meeting in those places with strata too harsh, hard, and solid for their purpose, which they relinquish, and go to a fresh spot that works more freely? Or may they not in other places fall in with a soil as much too loose and mouldering, liable to founder, and threatening to overwhelm them and their labours?

One thing is remarkable—that, after some years, the old holes are forsaken and new ones bored; perhaps because the old habitations grow foul and fetid from long use, or because they may so abound with fleas as to become untenantable. This species of swallow moreover is strangely annoyed with fleas: and we have seen fleas, bed-fleas (*Pulex irritans*), swarming at the mouths of these holes, like bees on the stools of their hives.

The following circumstance should by no means be omitted— that these birds do not make use of their caverns by way of hybernacula, as might be expected; since banks so perforated have been dug out with care in the winter, when nothing was found but empty nests.

The sand-martin arrives much about the same time with the swallow, and lays, as she does, from four to six white eggs. But as this species is *cryptogame*, carrying on the business of nidification, incubation, and the support of its young in the dark, it would not be so easy to ascertain the time of breeding, were it not for the coming forth of the broods, which appear much about the time, or rather somewhat earlier than those of the swallow. The nestlings are supported in common like those of their congeners, with gnats and other small insects; and sometimes they are fed with *libellulæ* (dragon-flies) almost as long as themselves. In the last week in June we have seen a row of these sitting on a rail near a great pool as perchers; and so young and helpless, as easily to be taken by hand: but whether the dams ever feed them on the wing, as swallows and housemartins do, we have never yet been able to determine: nor do we know whether they pursue and attack birds of prey.

When they happen to breed near hedges and inclosures, they are frequently dispossessed of their breeding holes by the house-sparrow, which is on the same account a fell adversary to house-martins.

These *hirundines* are no songsters, but rather mute, making only a little harsh noise when a person approaches their nests.

They seem not to be of a sociable turn, never with us congregating with their congeners in the autumn. Undoubtedly they breed a second time, like the house-martin and swallow, and withdraw about Michaelmas.

Though in some particular districts they may happen to abound, yet in the whole, in the south of England at least, is this much the rarest species. For there are few towns or large villages but what abound with house-martins; few churches, towers, or steeples, but what are haunted by some swifts: scarce a hamlet or a single cottage-chimney that has not its swallow; while the bank-martins, scattered here and there, live a sequestered life among some abrupt sand-hills, and in the precipitous banks of some few rivers.

These birds have a peculiar manner of flying: flitting about with odd jerks, and vacillations, not unlike the motions of a butterfly. Doubtless the flight of all *hirundines* is influenced by, and adapted to, the peculiar sort of insects which furnish their food. Hence it would be worth inquiry to examine what particular genus of insects affords the principal food of each respective species of swallow.

Notwithstanding what has been advanced above, some few sand-martins, I see, haunt the skirts of London, frequenting the dirty pools in Saint George's Fields, and about Whitechapel. The question is where these build, since there are no banks or bold shores in that neighbourhood: perhaps they nestle in the scaffold holes of some old or new deserted building. They dip and wash as they fly sometimes, like the house-martin and swallow.

Sand-martins differ from their congeners in the diminutiveness of their size, and in their colour, which is what is usually called a mouse-colour. Near Valencia in Spain, they are taken, says Willughby, and sold in the markets for the table; and are called by the country people, probably from their desultory jerking manner of flight, *Papilion de Montagna.*

SELBORNE, *Feb.* 26, 1774.

LETTER LX.

TO THOMAS PENNANT, ESQ.

BEFORE your letter arrived, and of my own accord, I had been remarking and comparing the tails of the male and female swallow, and this ere any young broods appeared; so that there was no danger of confounding the dams with their *pulli*: and besides, as they were then always in pairs, and busied in the employ of nidification, there could be no room for mistaking the sexes, nor the individuals of different chimneys the one for the other. From all my observations, it constantly appeared that each sex has the long feathers in its tail that give it that forked shape; with this difference, that they are longer in the tail of the male than in that of the female.

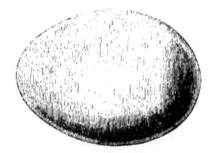

PHEASANT'S EGG.

Nightingales, when their young first come abroad, and are helpless, make a plaintive and a jarring noise; and also a snapping or cracking, pursuing people along the hedges as they walk: these last sounds seem intended for menace and defiance.

The grasshopper-lark chirps all night in the height of summer.

Swans turn white the second year, and breed the third.

Weasels prey on moles, as appears by their being sometimes caught in mole-traps.

Sparrow-hawks sometimes breed in old crows' nests, and the kestril in churches and ruins.

There are supposed to be two sorts of eels in the island of Ely.
The threads sometimes discovered in eels are perhaps their
young: the generation of eels is very dark and mysterious.

Hen-harriers breed on the ground, and seem never to settle on
trees.

THE LONG-TAILED TITMOUSE.

[Of this bold bird White afterwards writes in his "Observations:"—"A gentleman flushed a pheasant in a wheat stubble,
and shot at it; when, notwithstanding the report of the gun, it
was immediately pursued by the blue hawk known by the name
of the hen-harrier, but escaped into some covert. He then
sprung a second and a third in the same field, that got away in

the same manner; the hawk hovering round him all the while that he was beating the field, conscious no doubt of the game that lurked in the stubble. Hence we may conclude that this bird of prey was rendered very daring and bold by hunger, and that hawks cannot always seize their game when they please. We may farther observe, that they cannot pounce on their quarry on the ground, where it might be able to make a stout resistance, since so large a fowl as a pheasant could not but be visible to the piercing eye of a hawk, when hovering over the field. Hence that propensity of cowering and squatting till they are almost trod on, which no doubt was intended as a mode of security; though long rendered destructive to the whole race of *Gallinæ* by the invention of nets and guns.]

When redstarts shake their tails they move them horizontally, as dogs do when they fawn: the tail of a wagtail, when in motion, bobs up and down like that of a jaded horse.

LONG-TAILED TITMOUSE'S EGG.

ROBIN REDBREAST'S EGG.

Hedge-sparrows have a remarkable flirt with their wings in breeding-time; as soon as frosty mornings come they make a very piping plaintive noise.

Many birds which become silent about Midsummer reassume their notes again in September; as the thrush, blackbird, woodlark, willow-wren, &c.; hence August is by much the most mute month, the spring, summer, and autumn through. Are birds induced to sing again because the temperament of autumn resembles that of spring?

Linnæus ranges plants geographically: palms inhabit the tropics, grasses the temperate zones, and mosses and lichens the polar circles; no doubt animals may be classed in the same manner with propriety.

House-sparrows build under eaves in the spring; as the weather becomes hotter they get out for coolness, and nest in plum-trees and apple-trees. These birds have been known sometimes to build in rooks' nests, and sometimes in the forks of boughs under rooks' nests.

As my neighbour was housing a rick he observed that his dogs devoured all the little red mice that they could catch, but rejected the common mice ; and that his cats ate the common mice, refusing the red.

Redbreasts sing all through the spring, summer, and autumn. The reason that they are called autumn songsters is, because in the two first seasons their voices are drowned and lost in the general chorus ; in the latter their song becomes distinguishable. Many songsters of the autumn seem to be the young cock red-

THE WHITETHROAT.

breasts of that year : notwithstanding the prejudices in their favour, they do much mischief in gardens to the summer-fruits. They eat also the berries of the ivy, the honeysuckle, and the *Euonymus Europæus*, or spindle-tree.

The titmouse, which early in February begins to make two quaint notes like the whetting of a saw, is the marsh titmouse ; the great titmouse sings with three cheerful joyous notes, and begins about the same time.

Wrens sing all the winter through, frost excepted.

House-martins came remarkably late this year both in Hampshire and Devonshire. Is this circumstance for or against either hiding or migration?

Most birds drink sipping at intervals; but pigeons take a long-continued draught, like quadrupeds.

Notwithstanding what I have said in a former letter, no gray crows were ever known to breed on Dartmoor: it was my mistake.

The appearance and flying of the *Scarabœus solstitialis*, or fernchafer, commence with the month of July, and cease about the end of it. These scarabs are the constant food of *caprimulgi*, or fern-owls, through that period. They abound on the chalky downs, and in some sandy districts, but not in the clays.

In the garden of the Black-Bear Inn in the town of Reading is a stream or canal running under the stables and out into the fields on the other side of the road : in this water are many

BLACKCAP'S EGG.

WHITETHROAT'S EGG.

carps, which lie rolling about in sight, being fed by travellers, who amuse themselves by tossing them bread; but as soon as the weather grows at all severe these fishes are no longer seen, because they retire under the stables, where they remain till the return of spring. Do they lie in a torpid state? If they do not, how are they supported?

The note of the whitethroat, which is continually repeated, and often attended with odd gesticulations on the wing, is harsh and displeasing. These birds seem of a pugnacious disposition; for they sing with an erected crest and attitudes of rivalry and defiance; are shy and wild in breeding-time, avoiding neighbourhoods, and haunting lonely lanes and commons; nay, even the very tops of the Sussex downs, where there are bushes and covert; but in July and August they bring their broods into gardens and orchards, and make great havoc among the summer fruits.

The blackcap has in common a full, sweet, deep, loud, and

wild pipe; yet that strain is of short continuance, and his motions are desultory; but when that bird sits calmly and engages in song in earnest, he pours forth very sweet, but inward melody, and expresses great variety of soft and gentle modulations, superior perhaps to those of any of our warblers, the nightingale excepted. Blackcaps mostly haunt orchards

THE REDSTART.

and gardens; while they warble, their throats are wonderfully distended.

The song of the redstart is superior, though somewhat like that of the whitethroat: some birds have a few more notes than others. Sitting very placidly on the top of a tall tree in a village, the cock sings from morning till night: he affects neighbourhoods, and avoids solitude, and loves to build in

orchards and about houses; with us he perches on the vane
of a tall maypole.

The flycatcher is of all our summer birds the most mute and
the most familiar; it also appears the last of any. It builds in
a vine, or a sweetbriar, against the wall of a house, or in the
hole of a wall, or on the end of a beam or plate, and often close
to the post of a door where people are going in and out all day
long. This bird does not make the least pretension to song, but
uses a little inward wailing note when it thinks its young in
danger from cats or other annoyances : it breeds but once, and
retires early.

Selborne parish alone can and has exhibited at times more
than half the birds that are ever seen in all Sweden ; the former
has produced more than one hundred and twenty species, the
latter only two hundred and twenty-one. Let me add also, that
it has shown near half the species that were ever known in
Great Britain ; Sweden having two hundred and twenty-one,
Great Britain two hundred and fifty-two species.

On a retrospect, I observe that my long letter carries with it
a quaint and magisterial air, and is very sententious ; but when
I recollect that you requested stricture and anecdote, I hope you
will pardon the didactic manner for the sake of the information
it may happen to contain.

SELBORNE, *Sept.* 2, 1774.

LETTER LXI.

TO THOMAS PENNANT, ESQ.

IT is matter of curious inquiry to trace out how those species
of soft-billed birds, that continue with us the winter through,
subsist during the dead months. The imbecility of birds seems
not to be the only reason why they shun the rigour of our
winters; for the robust wryneck [1] (so much resembling the hardy
race of woodpeckers) migrates, while the feeble little golden-
crowned wren, that shadow of a bird, braves our severest frosts

---

[1] "Wrynecks appear on the grass-plots and walks ; they walk a little as
well as hop, and thrust their bills into the turf, in quest, I conclude, of ants,
which are their food. While they hold their bills in the grass, they draw
out their prey with their tongues, which are so long as to be coiled round
their heads," says White in his " Observations."

without availing himself of houses or villages, to which most of
our winter-birds crowd in distressful seasons, while this keeps
aloof in fields and woods ; but perhaps this may be the reason
why they may often perish, and why they are almost as rare as
any bird we know.

THE WRYNECK.

I have no reason to doubt but that the soft-billed birds,
which winter with us, subsist chiefly on insects in their aurelia
state.   All the species of wagtails in severe weather haunt
shallow streams near their spring heads, where they never
freeze ; and, by wading, pick out the aurelias of the genus
of *Phryganeæ, &c.*[1]

[1] Derham's "Physico Theology."

Hedge-sparrows frequent sinks and gutters in hard weather, where they pick up crumbs and other sweepings : and in mild weather they procure worms, which are stirring every month in the year, as any one may see that will only be at the trouble of taking a candle to a grass-plot on any mild winter's night. Redbreasts and wrens in the winter haunt out-houses, stables, and barns, where they find spiders and flies that have laid themselves up during the cold season. But the grand support of the soft-billed birds in winter is that infinite profusion of *aureliæ* of the *Lepidoptera ordo*, which is fastened to the twigs of trees and their trunks, to the pales and walls of gardens and buildings, and is found in every cranny and cleft of rock or rubbish, and even in the ground itself.

Every species of titmouse winters with us; they have what I call a kind of intermediate bill between the hard and the soft, between the Linnæan genera of *Fringilla* and *Motacilla*. One species alone spends its whole time in the woods and fields, never

WRYNECK'S EGG.

retreating for succour, in the severest seasons, to houses and neighbourhoods ; and that is the delicate long-tailed titmouse, which is almost as minute as the golden-crowned wren : but the blue titmouse, or nun (*Parus cœruleus*), the cole-mouse (*Parus ater*), the great black-headed titmouse (*Parus fringillago*, now *major*), and the marsh titmouse (*Parus palustris*), all resort, at times, to buildings; and in hard weather particularly. The great titmouse, driven by stress of weather, much frequents houses, and, in deep snows, I have seen this bird, while it hung with its back downwards (to my no small delight and admiration), draw straws lengthwise from out the eaves of thatched houses, in order to pull out the flies that were concealed between them, and that in such numbers that they quite defaced the thatch, and gave it a ragged appearance.

The blue titmouse, or nun, is a great frequenter of houses, and a general devourer. Besides insects, it is very fond of flesh; for it frequently picks bones on dunghills : it is a vast admirer of suet,

M

and haunts butchers' shops. When a boy, I have known twenty in a morning caught with snap mouse-traps, baited with tallow or suet. It will also pick holes in apples left on the ground, and will be well entertained with the seeds on the head of a sunflower. The blue, marsh, and great titmice will, in very severe weather, carry away barley and oat straws from the sides of ricks.

How the wheatear and whinchat support themselves in winter cannot be so easily ascertained, since they spend their time on wild heaths and warrens; the former especially, where there are stone quarries: most probably it is that their maintenance arises from the *aureliæ* of the *Lepidoptera ordo*, which furnish them with a plentiful table in the wilderness.

LETTER LXII.

TO THE HONOURABLE DAINES BARRINGTON.

As the swift or black martin is the largest of the Eritish *hirundines*, so is it undoubtedly the latest comer. For I remember but one instance of its appearing before the last week in April; and in some of our late frosty, harsh springs, it has not been seen till the beginning of May. This species usually arrives in pairs.

The swift, like the sand-martin, is very defective in architecture, making no crust, or shell, for its nest; but forming it of dry grasses and feathers, very rudely and inartificially put together. With all my attention to these birds, I have never been able once to discover one in the act of collecting or carrying in materials : so that I have suspected (since their nests are exactly the same) that they sometimes usurp upon the house-sparrows, and expel them, as sparrows do the house and sand-martin; well remembering that I have seen them squabbling together at the entrance of their holes; and the sparrows up in arms, and much disconcerted at these intruders. And yet I am assured by a nice observer in such matters, that they do collect feathers for their nests in Andalusia; and that he has shot them with such materials in their mouths.

Swifts, like sand-martins, carry on the business of nidification quite in the dark, in crannies of castles, and towers, and steeples, and upon the tops of the walls of churches under the roof; and

therefore cannot be so narrowly watched as those species that
build more openly; but, from what I could ever observe, they
begin nesting about the middle of May; and I have remarked,
from eggs taken, that they have sat hard by the 9th of June.
In general they haunt tall buildings, churches, and steeples, and

THE SWIFT.

breed only in such: yet in this village some pairs frequent the
lowest and meanest cottages, and educate their young under those
thatched roofs. I remember but one instance where they bred
out of buildings; and that was in the sides of a deep chalk-pit
near the town of Odiham, in this county, where I have seen many

pairs entering the crevices, and skimming and squeaking round the precipices.

As I have regarded these amusive birds with no small attention, if I should advance something new and peculiar with respect to them, and different from all other birds, I might perhaps be credited; especially as my assertion is the result of many years' exact observation. The fact that I would advance is, that swifts propagate on the wing: and I would wish any nice observer, that is startled at this supposition, to use his own eyes, and I think he will soon be convinced. In another class of animals, viz. the insect, nothing is so common as to see the different species of many genera in conjunction as they fly. The swift is almost continually on the wing; and as it never settles on the ground, on trees, or roofs, would seldom find opportunity for amorous rites, was it not enabled to indulge them in the air. If any person would watch these birds of a fine morning in May, as they are sailing round at a great height from the ground, he would see, every now and then, one drop on the back of another, and both of them sink down together for many fathoms with a loud piercing shriek. This I take to be the juncture when the business of generation is carrying on.

As the swift eats, drinks, collects materials for its nest, and, as it seems, propagates on the wing, it appears to live more in the air than any other bird, and to perform all functions there save those of sleeping and incubation.

This *hirundo* differs widely from its congeners in laying invariably but two eggs at a time, which are milk-white, long, and peaked at the small end; whereas the other species lay at each brood from four to six. It is a most alert bird, rising very early and retiring to roost very late; and is on the wing in the height of summer at least sixteen hours. In the longest days it does not withdraw to rest till a quarter before nine in the evening, being the latest of all day birds. Just before they retire whole groups of them assemble high in the air, and squeak, and shoot about with wonderful rapidity. But this bird is never so much alive as in sultry thundery weather, when it expresses great alacrity, and calls forth all its powers. In hot mornings, several, getting together in little parties, dash round the steeples and churches, squeaking as they go in a very clamorous manner: these, by nice observers, are supposed to be males serenading their sitting hens; and not without reason, since they seldom squeak till they come close to the walls or eaves, and since those within utter at the same time a little inward note of complacency.

When the hen has sat hard all day, she rushes forth for a few minutes, just as it is almost dark, to stretch and relieve her weary limbs, and snatch a scanty meal, and then returns to her duty of incubation. Swifts, when wantonly and cruelly shot while they have young, discover a lump of insects in their mouths, which they pouch and hold under their tongue. In general they feed in a much higher district than the other species; a proof that gnats and other insects do also abound to a considerable height in the air: they also range to vast distances; since locomotion is no labour to them, who are endowed with such wonderful powers of wing. Their powers seem to be in proportion to their levers; and their wings are longer in proportion than those of almost any other bird. When they mute, or ease themselves in flight, they raise their wings, and make them meet over their backs.

At some certain times in the summer I had remarked that swifts were hawking very low for hours together over pools and streams; and could not help inquiring into the object of the pursuit that induced them to descend so much below their usual range. After some trouble, I found that they were taking *phryganeæ*, *ephemeræ* and *libellulæ* (caddis-flies, may-flies, and dragon-flies) that were just emerged from their aurelia state. I then no longer wondered that they should be so willing to stoop for a prey that afforded them such plentiful and succulent nourishment.

They bring out their young about the middle or latter end of July: but as these never become perchers, nor, that ever I could discern, are fed on the wing by their dams, the coming forth of the young is not so notorious as in the other species.

On the 30th of last June I untiled the eaves of a house where many pairs build, and found in each nest only two squab, naked *pulli*: on the 8th of July I repeated the same inquiry, and found they had made very little progress towards a fledged state, but were still naked and helpless. From whence we may conclude that birds whose way of life keeps them perpetually on the wing would not be able to quit their nest till the end of the month. Swallows and martins, that have numerous families, are continually feeding them every two or three minutes; while swifts, that have but two young to maintain, are much at their leisure, and do not attend on their nests for hours together.

Sometimes they pursue and strike at hawks that come in their way; but not with that vehemence and fury that swallows express on the same occasion. They are out all day long in wet days, feeding about, and disregarding still rain: from whence two things may be gathered: first, that many insects abide high in the air, even in rain; and next, that the feathers of these birds must be well preened to resist so much wet. Windy, and particularly windy weather with heavy showers, they dislike; and on such days withdraw, and are scarce ever seen.

There is a circumstance respecting the colour of swifts which seems not to be unworthy our attention. When they arrive in the spring they are all over of a glossy, dark, soot-colour, except their chins, which are white; but, by being all day long in the sun and air, they become quite weather-beaten and bleached before they depart, and yet they return glossy again in the spring. Now, if they pursue the sun into lower latitudes, as some suppose, in order to enjoy a perpetual summer, why do they not return bleached? Do they not rather perhaps retire to rest for a season, and at that juncture moult and change their feathers, since all other birds are known to moult soon after the season of breeding?

Swifts are very anomalous in many particulars, dissenting from all their congeners not only in the number of their young, but in breeding but once in a summer; whereas all the other British *hirundines* breed invariably twice. It is past all doubt that swifts can breed but once, since they withdraw in a short time after the flight of their young, and some time before their congeners bring out their second broods. We may here remark, that, as swifts breed but once in a summer, and only two at a time, and the other *hirundines* twice, the latter, who lay from four to six eggs, increase at an average five times as fast as the former.

But in nothing are swifts more singular than in their early retreat. They retire, as to the main body of them, by the 10th of August, and sometimes a few days sooner: and every straggler invariably withdraws by the 20th, while their congeners, all of them, stay till the beginning of October; many of them all through that month, and some occasionally to the beginning of November. This early retreat is mysterious and wonderful, since that time is often the sweetest season in the year. But, what is more extraordinary, they begin to retire still earlier in the most southerly parts of Andalusia, where they can be no ways influenced by any defect of heat; or, as one might suppose, defect of food. Are they regulated in their motions with us by a failure of food, or by a propensity to moulting, or by a disposition to rest after so rapid a life, or by what? This is one of those incidents in natural history that not only baffles our searches, but almost eludes our guesses!

These *hirundines* never perch on trees or roofs, and so never congregate with their congeners. They are fearless while haunting their nesting-places, and are not to be scared by a gun; and are often beaten down with poles and cudgels as they stoop to go under the eaves. Swifts are much infested with those pests to the genus called *hippoboscæ* (*Anaperæ hirundinis*, Leach), and often wriggle and scratch themselves, in their flight, to get rid of that clinging annoyance.

Swifts are no songsters, and have only one harsh screaming note; yet there are ears to which it is not displeasing, from an agreeable association of ideas, since that note never occurs but in the most lovely summer weather.

They never settle on the ground but through accident; and when down can hardly rise, on account of the shortness of their legs and the length of their wings: neither can they walk, but only crawl; but they have a strong grasp with their feet, by which they cling to walls. Their bodies being flat, they can enter a very narrow crevice; and when they cannot pass on their bellies they will turn up edgewise.

The particular formation of the foot discriminates the swift from all the British *hirundines*; and indeed from all other known birds, the *Hirundo melba*, or great white-bellied swift of Gibraltar, excepted; for it is so disposed as to carry "omnes quatuor digitos anticos"—"all its four toes forward;" besides, the least toe, which should be the back one, consists of one bone only, and the other three of only two apiece: a construction most rare and peculiar, but nicely adapted to the purposes in which their feet are employed. This, and some peculiarities attending the nostrils and under mandible, have induced a discerning naturalist to suppose that this species might constitute a genus by itself.

In London a party of swifts frequent the Tower, playing and feeding over the river just below the bridge: others haunt some of the churches of the Borough next the fields; but do not venture, like the house-martin, into the close, crowded part of the town.

The Swedes have bestowed a very pertinent name on this swallow, calling it " ring swala," from the perpetual rings or circles that it takes round the scene of its nidification.

Swifts feed on *coleoptera*, or small beetles with hard cases over their wings, as well as on the softer insects ; but it does not appear how they can procure gravel to grind their food, as swallows do, since they never settle on the ground. Young ones, overrun with *hippoboscæ*, are sometimes found under their nests, fallen to the ground ; the number of vermin rendering their abode insupportable any longer. They frequent in this village several abject cottages ; yet a succession still haunts the same unlikely roofs : a good proof this that the same birds return to the same spots. As they must stoop very low to get up under these humble eaves, cats lie in wait, and sometimes catch them on the wing.

SWIFT'S EGG.

On the 5th of July, 1775, I again untiled part of a roof over the nest of a swift. The dam sat in the nest ; but so strongly was she affected by her natural στοργή for her brood, which she supposed to be in danger, that, regardless of her own safety, she would not stir, but lay sullenly by them, permitting herself to be taken in hand. The squab young we brought down and placed on the grass-plot, where they tumbled about, and were as helpless as a new-born child. While we contemplated their naked bodies, their unwieldy disproportioned *abdomina*, and their heads too heavy for their necks to support, we could not but wonder when we reflected that these shiftless beings in litttle more than a fortnight would be able to dash through the air almost with the inconceivable swiftness of a meteor ; and perhaps, in their emigration, must traverse vast continents and oceans as distant as the equator. So soon does Nature advance small birds to their ἡλικία, or state of perfection; while the progressive growth of men and large quadrupeds is slow and tedious !

SELBORNE, *Sept.* 28, 1774.

LETTER LXIII.

TO THE HONOURABLE DAINES BARRINGTON.

BY means of a straight-cottage-chimney I had an opportunity this summer of remarking at my leisure how swallows ascend and descend through the shaft; but my pleasure in contemplating the address with which this feat was performed to a considerable depth in the chimney was somewhat interrupted by apprehensions lest my eyes might undergo the same fate with those of Tobit.

Perhaps it may be some amusement to you to hear at what times the different species of *hirundines* arrived this spring in three very distant counties of this kingdom. With us the swallow was seen first on April the 4th, the swift on April the 24th, the

MAGPIE'S EGG.

bank-martin on April the 12th, and the house-martin not till April the 30th. At South Zele, Devonshire, swallows did not arrive till April the 25th; swifts, in plenty, on May the 1st, and house-martins not till the middle of May. At Blackburn, in Lancashire, swifts were seen on April the 28th, swallows April the 29th, house-martins May the 1st. Do these different dates in such distant districts prove anything for or against migration?

A farmer near Weyhill fallows his land with two teams of asses; one of which works till noon, and the other in the afternoon. When these animals have done their work, they are penned all night, like sheep, on the fallow. In the winter they are confined and foddered in a yard, and make plenty of dung.

Linnæus says that hawks "make a truce with other birds as long as the cuckoo is heard:" "paciscuntur inducias cum avibus, quamdiu cuculus cuculat : " but it appears to me that, during that period, many little birds are taken and destroyed by birds of prey, as may be seen by the feathers left in lanes and under hedges.

The missel-thrush is, while breeding, fierce and pugnacious, driving such birds as approach its nest with great fury to a distance. The Welsh call it " pen y llwynn," the head or master of the coppice. He suffers no magpie, jay, or blackbird to enter the garden where he haunts; and is, for the time, a good guard to the new-sown legumens. In general he is very successful in the defence of his family ; but once I observed in my garden, that several magpies came determined to storm the nest of a missel-thrush : the dams defended their mansion with great vigour, and fought resolutely for "their faith and for their homes : " *pro aris et focis;* but numbers at last prevailed, they tore the nest to pieces, and swallowed the young alive.

[Thrushes during long droughts are of great service in hunting out shell-snails,[1] which they pull in pieces for their young, and are thereby very serviceable in gardens. Missel-thrushes do not destroy the fruit in gardens like the other species of *turdi*, but feed on the berries of mistletoe, and in the spring on ivy-berries, which then begin to ripen.[2] In the summer, when their young become fledged, they leave neighbourhoods, and retire to sheep-walks and wild commons. This species of thrush, though wild at other times, delights to build near houses, and in frequented walks and gardens.]

In the season of nidification the wildest birds are comparatively tame. Thus the ring-dove breeds in my fields, though they are continually frequented ; and the missel-thrush, though most shy and wild in the autumn and winter, builds in my garden close to a walk where people are passing all day long.

---

[1] Of the truth of this I have been an eye-witness, having seen the common thrush feeding on the shell-snail.—MARKWICK.

[2] In the very early part of this spring (1797) a bird of this species used to sit every morning on the top of some very high elms close by my windows, and delight me with its charming song, attracted thither, probably, by some ripe ivy-berries that grew near the place.

I have remarked something like the latter fact, for I remember many years ago, seeing a pair of these birds fly up repeatedly and attack some larger bird, which I suppose disturbed their nest in my orchard, uttering at the same time violent shrieks. Since writing the above, I have seen more than once a pair of these birds attack some magpies that had disturbed their nest, with great violence and loud shrieks.—MARKWICK.

Wall-fruit abounds with me this year; but my grapes, that used to be forward and good, are at present backward beyond all precedent: and this is not the worst of the story; for the same ungenial weather, the same black cold solstice, has injured the more necessary fruits of the earth, and discoloured and blighted our wheat. The crop of hops promises to be very large.

Frequent returns of deafness incommode me sadly, and half disqualify me as a naturalist; for, when those fits are upon me, I lose all the pleasing notices and little intimations arising from rural sounds; and May is to me as silent and mute with respect to the notes of birds, &c., as August. My eyesight is, thank God, quick and good ; but with respect to the other sense, I am, at times, disabled :

"And wisdom at one entrance quite shut out."

SELBORNE, *Sept.* 13, 1774.

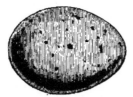

THRUSH'S EGG.

LETTER LXIV.

TO THOMAS PENNANT, ESQ.

SOME future faunist, a man of fortune, will, I hope, extend his visits to the kingdom of Ireland; a new field, and a country little known to the naturalist. He will not, it is to be wished, undertake that tour unaccompanied by a botanist, because the mountains have scarcely been sufficiently examined ; and the southerly counties of so mild an island may possibly afford some plants little to be expected within the British dominions. A person of a thinking turn of mind will draw many just remarks from the modern improvements of that country, both in arts and agriculture, where premiums obtained, long before they were

heard of with us.   The manners of the wild natives, their superstitions, their prejudices, their sordid way of life, will extort
from him many useful reflections.   He should also take with
him an able draughtsman; for he must by no means pass over
the noble castles and seats, the extensive and picturesque lakes
and waterfalls, and the lofty stupendous mountains, so little
known, and so engaging to the imagination when described
and exhibited in a lively manner : such a work would be well
received.

As I have seen no modern map of Scotland, I cannot pretend
to say how accurate or particular any such may be; but this I
know, that the best old maps of that kingdom are very defective.
The great obvious defect that I have remarked in all maps of
Scotland that have fallen in my way is a want of a coloured
line or stroke that shall exactly define the just limits of that
district called the Highlands.   Moreover, all the great avenues
to that mountainous and romantic country want to be well distinguished.   The military roads formed by General Wade are
so great and Roman-like an undertaking that they will merit
attention.   My old map, Moll's map, takes notice of Fort
William ; but could not mention the other forts that have been
erected long since : therefore a good representation of the chain
of forts should not be omitted.

The celebrated zigzag up the Coryarich must not be passed
over.   Moll takes notice of Hamilton and Drumlanrig, and such
capital houses ; but a new survey, no doubt, should represent
every seat and castle remarkable for any great event, or celebrated for its paintings, &c.   Lord Breadalbane's seat and beautiful policy are too curious and extraordinary to be omitted.

The seat of the Earl of Eglintoun, near Glasgow, is worthy of
notice.   The pine-plantations of that nobleman are very grand
and extensive indeed.

SELBORNE, *March* 9, 1775.

LETTER LXV.

TO THE HONOURABLE DAINES BARRINGTON.

ON September the 21st, 1741, being then on a visit, and intent
on field-diversions, I rose before daybreak : when I came into
the inclosures, I found the stubbles and clover-grounds matted

all over with a thick coat of cobweb, in the meshes of which a copious and heavy dew hung so plentifully that the whole face of the country seemed, as it were, covered with two or three setting-nets drawn one over another.   When the dogs attempted to hunt, their eyes were so blinded and hoodwinked that they could not proceed, but were obliged to lie down and scrape the incumbrances from their faces with their fore-feet, so that, finding my sport interrupted, I returned home, musing in my mind on the oddness of the occurrence.

As the morning advanced the sun became bright and warm, and the day turned out one of those most lovely ones which no season but the autumn produces, cloudless, calm, serene, and worthy of the South of France itself.

About nine an appearance very unusual began to demand our attention, a shower of cobwebs falling from very elevated regions, and continuing, without any interruption, till the close of the day.   These webs were not single filmy threads, floating in the air in all directions, but perfect flakes or rags ; some near an inch broad, and five or six long, which fell with a degree of velocity that showed they were considerably heavier than the atmosphere.

On every side, as the observer turned his eyes, might he behold a continual succession of fresh flakes falling into his sight, and twinkling like stars as they turned their sides towards the sun.

How far this wonderful shower extended it would be difficult to say; but we know that it reached Bradley, Selborne, and Alresford, three places which lie in a sort of triangle, the shortest of whose sides is about eight miles in extent.

At the second of those places there was a gentleman (for whose veracity and intelligent turn we have the greatest veneration) who observed it the moment he got abroad ; but concluded that, as soon as he came upon the hill above his house, where he took his morning rides, he should be higher than this meteor, which he imagined might have been blown, like thistledown, from the common above ; but, to his great astonishment, when he rode to the most elevated part of the down, 300 feet above his fields, he found the webs in appearance still as much above him as before ; still descending into sight in a constant succession, and twinkling in the sun, so as to draw the attention of the most incurious.

Neither before nor after was any such fall observed ; but on this day the flakes hung in the trees and hedges so thick, that a diligent person sent out might have gathered baskets full.

The remark that I shall make on these cobweb-like appearances, called gossamer, is, that, strange and superstitious as the notions about them were formerly, nobody in these days doubts but that they are the real production of small spiders, which swarm in the fields in fine weather in autumn, and have a power of shooting out webs from their tails so as to render themselves buoyant, and lighter than air. But why these apterous insects should that day take such a wonderful aërial excursion, and why their webs should at once become so gross and material as to be considerably more weighty than air, and to descend with precipitation, is a matter beyond my skill. If I might be allowed to hazard a supposition, I should imagine that those filmy threads, when first shot, might be entangled in the rising dew, and so drawn up, spiders and all, by a brisk evaporation, into the regions where clouds are formed : and if the spiders have a power of coiling and thickening their webs in the air, as Dr. Lister says they have, then, when they were become heavier than the air, they must fall.[1]

Every day in fine weather, in autumn chiefly, do I see those spiders shooting out their webs and mounting aloft : they will go off from your finger if you will take them into your hand. Last summer one alighted on my book as I was reading in the parlour ; and, running to the top of the page, and shooting out a web, took its departure from thence. But what I most wondered at was, that it went off with considerable velocity in a place where no air was stirring ; and I am sure that I .did not assist it with my breath. So that these little crawlers seem to have, while mounting, some locomotive power without the use of wings, and so move in the air faster than the air itself.

SELBORNE, *June* 8, 1775.

[1] One day when the air was full of such gossamers, Dr. Lister relates that he mounted to the highest part of York Cathedral and found the gossamer webs still far above him.
> "Its sone some wonder at the cause of thunder,
> On ebbe and flode, on gossamer and mist,
> And on all things till that the cause is wist."— CHAUCER.

LETTER LXVI.

TO THE HONOURABLE DAINES BARRINGTON.

THERE is a wonderful spirit of sociality in the brute creation, independent of sexual attachment. Of this the congregating of gregarious birds in the winter is a remarkable instance.

Many horses, though quiet with company, will not stay one minute in a field by themselves : the strongest fences cannot restrain them. My neighbour's horse will not only not stay by himself abroad, but he will not bear to be left alone in a strange stable without discovering the utmost impatience, and endeavouring to break the rack and manger with his fore-feet. He has been known to leap out at a stable-window, through which dung was thrown, after company ; and yet in other respects is remarkably quiet. Oxen and cows will not fatten by themselves : but will neglect the finest pasture that is not recommended by society. It would be needless to add instances in sheep, which constantly flock together.

But this propensity seems not to be confined to animals of the same species ; for we know a doe, still alive, that was brought up from a little fawn with a dairy of cows ; with them it goes a-field, and with them it returns to the yard. The dogs of the house take no notice of this deer, being used to her ; but, if strange dogs come by, a chase ensues ; while the master smiles to see his favourite securely leading her pursuers over hedge, or gate, or stile, till she returns to the cows, who, with fierce lowings and menacing horns, drive the assailants quite out of the pasture.

Even great disparity of kind and size does not always prevent social advances and mutual fellowship. For a very intelligent and observant person has assured me that, in the former part of his life, keeping but one horse, he happened also on a time to have but one solitary hen. These two incongruous animals spent much of their time together in a lonely orchard, where they saw no creature but each other. By degrees an apparent regard began to take place between these two sequestered individuals. The fowl would approach the quadruped with notes of complacency, rubbing herself gently against his legs : while the horse would look down with satisfaction, and move with the greatest caution and circumspection, lest he should trample on his diminutive companion. Thus by mutual good offices, each seemed to console the vacant hours of the other : so that Milton, when he puts the following sentiment in the mouth of Adam, seems to be somewhat mistaken :—

> " Much less can bird with beast, or fish with fowl,
> So well converse, nor with the ox the ape."

SELBORNE, *Aug.* 15, 1775.

LETTER LXVII.

TO THE HONOURABLE DAINES BARRINGTON.

WE have two gangs or hordes of gypsies which infest the south and west of England, and come round in their circuit two or three times in the year. One of these tribes calls itself by the noble name of Stanley, of which I have nothing particular to say; but the other is distinguished by an appellative somewhat remarkable—as far as their harsh gibberish can be understood, they seem to say that the name of their clan is Curleople. Now the termination of this word is apparently Grecian : and as Mezeray and the gravest historians all agree that these vagrants did certainly migrate from Egypt and the East, two or three centuries ago, and so spread by degrees over Europe, may not this family name, a little corrupted, be the very name they brought with them from the Levant? It would be matter of some curiosity, could one meet with an intelligent person among them, to inquire whether, in their jargon, they still retain any Greek words : the Greek radicals will appear in hand, foot, head, water, earth, &c. It is possible that amidst their cant and corrupted dialect many mutilated remains of their native language might still be discovered.

With regard to those peculiar people, the gypsies, one thing is very remarkable, and especially as they came from warmer climates ; and that is, that while other beggars lodge in barns, stables, and cow-houses, these sturdy savages seem to pride themselves in braving the severities of winter, and in living in the open air the whole year round. Last September was as wet a month as ever was known ; and yet during those deluges did a young gypsy-girl lie-in in the midst of one of our hop-gardens, on the cold ground, with nothing over her but a piece of blanket extended on a few hazel-rods bent hoop-fashion, and stuck into the earth at each end, in circumstances too trying for a cow in the same condition: yet within this garden there was a large hop-kiln, into the chambers of which she might have retired had she thought shelter an object worthy her attention.

Europe, itself, it seems, cannot set bounds to the rovings of these vagabonds; for Mr. Bell, in his return from Pekin, met a gang of these people on the confines of Tartary, who were endeavouring to penetrate those deserts and try their fortune in China.[1]

Gypsies are called in French, Bohemians; in Italian and modern Greek, Zingari.

SELBORNE, *Oct.* 2, 1775.

LETTER LXVIII.

TO THE HONOURABLE DAINES BARRINGTON.

"Hic - - - - tædæ pingues, hic plurimus ignis
Semper, et assiduâ postes fuligine nigri."
(VIRG. *Ecl.* vii. 49, 50.)
"Here are fat torches, here abundant fire,
Here constant smoke has black'd each side the door."

I SHALL make no apology for troubling you with the detail of a very simple piece of domestic economy, being satisfied that you think nothing beneath your attention that tends to utility: the matter alluded to is the use of rushes instead of candles, which I am well aware prevails in many districts besides this; but as I know there are countries also where it does not obtain, and as I have considered the subject with some degree of exactness, I shall proceed in my humble story, and leave you to judge of the expediency.

The proper species of rush for this purpose seems to be the *Juncus conglomeratus*, or common soft rush, which is to be found in most moist pastures, by the sides of streams, and under hedges. These rushes are in best condition in the height of

---

[1] See Bell's "Travels in China."

summer; but may be gathered, so as to serve the purpose well, quite on to autumn.   It would be needless to add that the largest and longest are best.   Decayed labourers, women, and children, make it their business to procure and prepare them. As soon as they are cut they must be flung into the water, and kept there; for otherwise they will dry and shrink, and the peel will not run.   At first a person would find it no easy matter to divest a rush of its peel or rind, so as to leave one regular, narrow, even rib from top to bottom that may support the pith : but this, like other feats, soon becomes familiar even to children; and we have seen an old woman, stone-blind, performing this business with great despatch, and seldom failing to strip them with the nicest regularity.   When these *junci* are thus far prepared, they must lie out on the grass to be bleached, and take the dew for some nights, and afterwards be dried in the sun.

Some address is required in dipping these rushes in the scalding fat or grease; but this knack also is to be attained by practice.   The careful wife of an industrious Hampshire labourer obtains all her fat for nothing; for she saves the scummings of her bacon-pot for this use; and, if the grease abounds with salt, she causes the salt to precipitate to the bottom, by setting the scummings in a warm oven.   Where hogs are not much in use, and especially by the sea-side, the coarser animal oils will come very cheap.   A pound of common grease may be procured for fourpence; and about six pounds of grease will dip a pound of rushes; and one pound of rushes may be bought for one shilling; so that a pound of rushes, medicated and ready for use, will cost three shillings.   If men that keep bees will mix a little wax with the grease, it will give it a consistency, and render it more cleanly, and make the rushes burn longer; mutton-suet would have the same effect.

A good rush, which measured in length two feet four inches and a half, being minuted, burnt only three minutes short of an hour : and a rush still of greater length has been known to burn one hour and a quarter.

These rushes give a good clear light.   Watch-lights (coated with tallow), it is true, shed a dismal one, " darkness visible ; " but then the wicks of those have two ribs of the rind, or peel, to support the pith, while the wick of the dipped rush has but one.   The two ribs are intended to impede the progress of the flame and make the candle last.

In a pound of dry rushes, avoirdupois, which I caused to be

weighed and numbered, we found upwards of one thousand six hundred individuals. Now suppose each of these burns, one with another, only half an hour, then a poor man will purchase eight hundred hours of light, a time exceeding thirty-three entire days, for three shillings. According to this account each rush, before dipping, costs $\frac{1}{33}$ of a farthing, and $\frac{1}{11}$ afterwards. Thus a poor family will enjoy $5\frac{1}{2}$ hours of comfortable light for a farthing. An experienced old housekeeper assures me that one pound and a half of rushes completely supplies his family the year round, since working people burn no candle in the long days, because they rise and go to bed by daylight.

Little farmers use rushes much, in the short days, both morning and evening, in the dairy and kitchen; but the very poor, who are always the worst economists, and therefore must continue very poor, buy a halfpenny candle every evening, which, in their blowing open rooms, does not burn much more than two hours. Thus have they only two hours light for their money instead of eleven.

While on the subject of rural economy, it may not be improper to mention a pretty implement of housewifery that I have seen nowhere else; that is, little neat besoms which our foresters make from the stalk of the *Polytricum commune*, or great golden maiden-hair, which they call silk-wood, and find plenty in the bogs. When this moss is well combed and dressed, and divested of its outer skin, it becomes of a beautiful bright chestnut colour; and, being soft and pliant, is very proper for the dusting of beds, curtains, carpets, hangings, &c. If these besoms were known to the brushmakers in town, it is probable they might come much more into use for the purpose above mentioned.[1]

SELBORNE, *Nov.* 1, 1776.

LETTER LXIX.

TO THE HONOURABLE DAINES BARRINGTON.

WE had in this village more than twenty years ago an idiot-boy, whom I well remember, who, from a child, showed a strong propensity to bees; they were his food, his amusement, his sole

---

[1] A besom of this sort is to be seen in Sir Ashton Lever's Museum.

object. And as people of this cast have seldom more than one point in view, so this lad exerted all his few faculties on this one pursuit. In the winter he dozed away his time, within his father's house, by the fireside, in a kind of torpid state, seldom departing from the chimney-corner; but in the summer he was all alert, and in quest of his game in the fields, and on sunny banks. Honey-bees, humble-bees, and wasps, were his prey wherever he found them: he had no apprehensions from their stings, but would seize them *nudis manibus,* and at once disarm them of their weapons, and suck their bodies for the sake of their honey-bags. Sometimes he would fill his bosom between his shirt and his skin with a number of these captives; and sometimes would confine them in bottles. He was a very *Merops apiaster,* or bee-bird; and very injurious to men that kept bees: for he would slide into their bee-gardens, and, sitting down before the stools, would rap with his finger on the hives, and so take the bees as they came out. He has been known to overturn hives for the sake of honey, of which he was passionately fond. Where metheglin was making he would linger round the tubs and vessels, begging a draught of what he called bee-wine. As he ran about he used to make a humming noise with his lips, resembling the buzzing of bees. This lad was lean and sallow, and of a cadaverous complexion; and, except in his favourite pursuit, in which he was wonderfully adroit, discovered no manner of understanding. Had his capacity been better, and directed to the same object, he had perhaps abated much of our wonder at the feats of a more modern exhibiter of bees; and we may justly say of him now,—

> "— — — — — — — — Thou,
> Had thy presiding star propitious shone,
> Shouldst *Wildman* be — — .— —."

When a tall youth he was removed from hence to a distant village, where he died, as I understand, before he arrived at manhood.

SELBORNE, *Dec.* 12, 1775.

LETTER LXX.

TO THE HONOURABLE DAINES BARRINGTON.

It is the hardest thing in the world to shake off superstitious prejudices : they are sucked in, as it were, with our mother's milk ; and, growing up with us at a time when they take the fastest hold and make the most lasting impressions, become so interwoven into our very constitutions, that the strongest good sense is required to disengage ourselves from them.   No wonder therefore, that the lower people retain them their whole lives through, since their minds are not invigorated by a liberal education, and therefore not enabled to make any efforts adequate to the occasion.

Such a preamble seems to be necessary before we enter on the superstitions of this district, lest we should be suspected of exaggeration in a recital of practices too gross for this enlightened age.

But the people of Tring, in Hertfordshire, would do well to remember, that no longer ago than the year 1751, and within twenty miles of the capital, they seized on two superannuated wretches, crazed with age, and overwhelmed with infirmities, on a suspicion of witchcraft ; and, by trying experiments, drowned them in a horse-pond.

In a farm-yard near the middle of this village stands, at this day, a row of pollard-ashes, which, by the seams and long cicatrices down their sides, manifestly show that, in former times, they have been cleft asunder.   These trees, when young and flexible, were severed and held open by wedges, while ruptured children, stripped naked, were pushed through the apertures, under a persuasion that, by such a process, the poor babes would be cured of their infirmity.   As soon as the operation was over, the tree, in the suffering part, was plastered with loam, and carefully swathed up.   If the parts coalesced and soldered together, as usually fell out where the feat was performed with any adroitness at all, the party was cured ; but where the cleft continued to gape, the operation, it was supposed, would prove ineffectual.   Having occasion to enlarge my garden not long since, I cut down two or three such trees, one of which did not grow together.

We have several persons now living in the village, who, in

their childhood, were supposed to be healed by this superstitious ceremony, derived down perhaps from our Saxon ancestors, who practised it before their conversion to Christianity.

At the south corner of the Plestor, or area, near the church, their stood, about twenty years ago, a very old grotesque hollow pollard-ash, which for ages had been looked on with no small veneration as a shrew-ash. Now a shrew-ash is an ash whose twigs or branches, when gently applied to the limbs of cattle, will immediately relieve the pains which a beast suffers from the running of a shrew-mouse over the part affected; for it is supposed that a shrew-mouse is of so baneful and deleterious a nature, that wherever it creeps over a beast, be it horse, cow, or sheep, the suffering animal is afflicted with cruel anguish, and threatened with the loss of the use of the limb. Against this accident, to which they are continually liable, our provident forefathers always kept a shrew-ash at hand, which, when once medicated, would maintain its virtue for ever. A shrew-ash was made thus : [1]—Into the body of the tree a deep hole was bored with an auger, and a poor devoted shrew-mouse was thrust in alive, and plugged in, no doubt, with several quaint incantations long since forgotton. As the ceremonies necessary for such a consecration are no longer understood, all succession is at an end, and no such tree is known to subsist in the manor, or hundred.

As to that on the Plestor, for

> "The late vicar stubb'd and burnt it,"

when he was way-warden, regardless of the remonstrances of the bystanders, who interceded in vain for its preservation, urging its power and effacacy, and alleging that it had been " guarded through many years by the piety of our ancestors ; "

> "Religione patrum multos servata per annos."

SELBORNE, *Jan.* 8, 1776.

---

[1] For a similar practice, White refers us to Plot's "Staffordshire."

LETTER LXXI.

TO THE HONOURABLE DAINES BARRINGTON.

In heavy fogs, on elevated situations especially, trees are perfect alembics : and no one that has not attended to such matters can imagine how much water one tree will distil in a night's time, by condensing the vapour which trickles down the twigs and boughs, so as to make the ground below quite in a float.   In Newton-lane, in October, 1775, on a misty day, a particular oak in leaf dropped so fast that the cartway stood in puddles and the ruts ran with water, though the ground in general was dusty.

In some of our smaller islands in the West Indies, if I mistake not, there are no springs or rivers ; but the people are supplied with that necessary element, water, merely by the dripping of some large tall trees, which, standing in the bosom of a mountain, keep their heads constantly enveloped with fogs and clouds, from which they dispense their kindly, never-ceasing moisture ; and so render those districts habitable by condensation alone.

Trees in leaf have such a vast proportion more of surface than those that are naked, that, in theory, their condensations should greatly exceed those that are stripped of their leaves ; but, as the former imbibe also a great quantity of moisture, it is difficult to say which drip most : but this I know, that deciduous trees that are entwined with much ivy seem to distil the greatest quantity.   Ivy leaves are smooth, and thick, and cold, and therefore condense very fast ; and besides, evergreens imbibe very little.   These facts may furnish the intelligent with hints concerning what sorts of trees they should plant round small ponds that they would wish to be perennial ; and show them how advantageous some trees are in preference to others.

Trees perspire profusely, condense largely, and check evaporation so much, that woods are always moist : no wonder therefore that they contribute much to pools and streams.

That trees are great promoters of lakes and rivers appears from a well known fact in North America ; for, since the woods and forests have been grubbed and cleared, all bodies of water are much diminished ; so that some streams, that were very considerable a century ago, will not now drive a common mill.[1] Besides, most woodlands, forests, and chases, with us abound with pools and morasses; no doubt for the reason given above.

To a thinking mind few phenomena are more strange than the state of little ponds on the summits of chalk-hills, many of which are never dry in the most trying droughts of summer. On chalk-hills I say, because in many rocky and gravelly soils springs usually break out pretty high on the sides of elevated grounds and mountains; but no person acquainted with chalky districts will allow that they ever saw springs in such a soil, but only in valleys and bottoms, since the waters of so pervious a stratum as chalk all lie on one dead level, as well-diggers have assured me again and again.

Now we have many such little round ponds in this district; and one in particular on our sheep-down, three hundred feet above my house; which, though never above three feet deep in the middle, and not more than thirty feet in diameter, and containing perhaps not more than two or three hundred hogsheads of water, yet never is it known to fail, though it affords drink for three hundred or four hundred sheep, and for at least twenty head of large cattle beside. This pond, it is true, is overhung with two moderate-sized beeches, that doubtless at times afford it much supply: but then we have others as small, that, without the aid of trees, and in spite of evaporation from sun and wind, and perpetual consumption by cattle, yet constantly maintain a moderate share of water, without overflowing in the wettest seasons, as they would do if supplied by springs. By my journal of May 1775, it appears that "the small and even considerable ponds in the vales are now dried up, while the small ponds on the very tops of hills are but little affected." Can this difference be accounted for from evaporation alone, which certainly is more prevalent in bottoms? or rather, have not those elevated pools some unnoticed recruits, which in the night time counterbalance the waste of the day, without which the cattle alone must soon exhaust them? And here it will be necessary to enter more minutely into the cause. Dr. Hales, in his Vegetable Statics, advances, from experiment, that "the moister the earth is the more dew falls on it in a night: and more than a double quantity of dew falls on a surface of water than there does on an equal surface of moist earth." Hence we

---

[1] *Vide* Kalm's "Travels in North America."

see that water, by its coolness, is enabled to assimilate to itself
a large quantity of moisture nightly by condensation; and that
the air, when loaded with fogs and vapours, and even with
copious dews, can alone advance a considerable and never-failing
resource.   Persons that are much abroad, and travel early and
late, such as shepherds, fishermen, &c., can tell what prodigious
fogs prevail in the night on elevated downs, even in the hottest
parts of summer; and how much the surfaces of things are
drenched by those swimming vapours, though, to the senses, all
the while, little moisture seems to fall.

SELBORNE, *Feb.* 7, 1776.

LETTER LXXII.

TO THE HONOURABLE DAINES BARRINGTON.

MONSIEUR HERISSANT, a French anatomist, seems persuaded
that he has discovered the reason why cuckoos do not hatch
their own eggs; the impediment, he supposes, arises from the
internal structure of their parts, which incapacitates them for
incubation.   According to this gentleman, the crop or craw of
a cuckoo does not lie before the sternum at the bottom of the
neck, as in the poultry, *gallinæ*, and pigeons, *columbæ*, &c., but
immediately behind it, on and over the bowels, so as to make a
large protuberance in the belly.[1]

Induced by this assertion, we procured a cuckoo; and,
cutting open the breast bone, and exposing the intestines to
sight, found the crop lying as mentioned above.   This stomach
was large and round, and stuffed hard like a pincushion with
food, which, upon nice examination, we found to consist of
various insects; such as small scarabs, spiders, and dragon-
flies; the last of which we have seen cuckoos catching on the
wing as they were just emerging out of the aurelia state.
Among this farrago also were to be seen maggots, and many
seeds, which belonged either to gooseberries, currants, cranberries, or some such fruit; so that these birds apparently
subsist on insects and fruits: nor was there the least appearance
of bones, feathers, or fur to support the idle notion of their
being birds of prey.

[1] Histoire de l'Académie Royale, 1752.

The sternum in this bird seemed to us to be remarkably short, between which and the anus lay the crop, or craw, and immediately behind that the bowels against the back-bone.

It must be allowed, as this anatomist observes, that the crop placed just upon the bowels must, especially when full, be in a very uneasy situation during the business of incubation; yet the test will be to examine whether birds that are actually known to sit for certain are not formed in a similar manner. This inquiry I proposed to myself to make with a fern-owl, or goat-sucker, as soon as opportunity offered: because, if their formation proves the same, the reason for incapacity in the cuckoo will be allowed to have been taken up somewhat hastily.

Not long after a fern-owl was procured, which, from its habit and shape, we suspected might resemble the cuckoo in its internal construction. Nor were our suspicions ill-grounded; for upon dissection, the crop, or craw, also lay behind the

GOAT-SUCKER'S EGG.

sternum, immediately on the viscera, between them and the skin of the belly. It was bulky, and stuffed hard with large *phalænæ*, moths of several sorts, and their eggs, which no doubt had been forced out of those insects by the action of swallowing.

Now as it appears that this bird, which is so well known to practise incubation, is formed in a similar manner with cuckoos, Monsieur Herissant's conjecture, that cuckoos are incapable of incubation from the disposition of their intestines, seems to fall to the ground: and we are still at a loss for the cause of that strange and singular peculiarity in the instance of the *Cuculus canorus*.

We found the case to be the same with the ring-tail hawk, in respect to formation; and, as far as I can recollect, with the swift; and probably it is so with many more sorts of birds that are not granivorous.

SELBORNE, *April* 3, 1776.

LETTER LXXIII.

TO THE HONOURABLE DAINES BARRINGTON.

On August the 4th, 1775, we surprised a large viper, which seemed very heavy and bloated, as it lay in the grass basking in the sun. When we came to cut it up, we found that the abdomen was crowded with young, fifteen in number; the shortest of which measured full seven inches, and were about the size of full-grown earthworms. This little fry issued into the world with the true viper spirit about them, showing great alertness as soon as disengaged from the belly of the dam: they twisted and wriggled about, and set themselves up, and gaped very wide when touched with a stick, showing manifest tokens of menace and defiance, though as yet they had no manner of fangs that we could find, even with the help of our glasses.

To a thinking mind nothing is more wonderful than that early instinct which impresses young animals with the notion of the situation of their natural weapons, and of using them properly in their own defence, even before those weapons subsist or are formed. Thus a young cock will spar at his adversary before his spurs are grown; and a calf or a lamb will push with their heads before their horns are sprouted. In the same manner did these young adders attempt to bite before their fangs were in being. The dam, however, was furnished with very formidable ones, which we lifted up (for they fold down when not used), and cut them off with the point of our scissors.

. There was little room to suppose that this brood had ever been in the open air before; and that they were taken in for refuge, at the mouth of the dam, when she perceived that danger was approaching; because then probably we should have found them somewhere in the neck, and not in the abdomen.

Selborne, *April* 29, 1776.

LETTER LXXIV.

TO THE HONOURABLE DAINES BARRINGTON.

Castration has a strange effect; it emasculates both man, beast, and bird, and brings them to a near resemblance of the other sex. Thus eunuchs have smooth unmuscular arms, thighs, and legs; and broad lips, and beardless chins, and squeaking voices. Gelt stags and bucks have hornless heads, like hinds and does. Thus wethers have small horns, like ewes; and oxen large bent horns, and hoarse voices when they low, like cows : for bulls have short straight horns; and though they mutter and grumble in a deep tremendous tone, yet they low in a shrill high key. Capons have small combs and gills, and look pallid about the head, like pullets; they also walk without any parade, and hover over chickens like hens.[1]   Barrow-hogs have also small tusks like sows.

Thus far it is plain that the deprivation of masculine vigour puts a stop to the growth of those parts or appendages that are looked upon as its insignia.   But the ingenious Mr. Lisle, in his book on husbandry, carries it much farther; for he says that the loss of those insignia alone has sometimes a strange effect on the ability itself; he had a boar so fierce and venereous, that to prevent mischief, orders were given for his tusks to be broken off. No sooner had the beast suffered this injury than his powers forsook him, and he neglected those females to whom before he was passionately attached, and from whom no fences could restrain him.

LETTER LXXV.

TO THE HONOURABLE DAINES BARRINGTON.

THE natural term of a hog's life is little known, and the reason is plain—because it is neither profitable nor convenient to keep that turbulent animal to the full extent of its time : however, my neighbour, a man of substance, who had no occasion to study every little advantage to a nicety, kept a half-bred Bantam sow, who was as thick as she was long, and whose belly swept on the ground, till she was advanced to her seventeenth year, at which period she showed some tokens of age by the decay of her teeth and the decline of her fertility.

For about ten years this prolific mother produced two litters in

---

[1] Réaumur, Mr. Rennie tells us, trained capons to nurse the chickens he hatched by artificial heat. They clucked like hens and proved good nurses.

the year of about ten at a time, and once above twenty at a litter ; but as there were near double the number of pigs to that of teats, many died.   From long experience in the world this female was grown very sagacious and artful ;—when she found occasion to converse with a boar she used to open all the intervening gates, and march, by herself, up to a distant farm where one was kept ; and when her purpose was served would return by the same means.   At the age of about fifteen her litters began to be reduced to four or five ; and such a litter she exhibited when in her fatting-pen.   She proved, when fat, good bacon, juicy, and tender ; the rind, or sward, was remarkably thin.   At a moderate computation she was allowed to have been the fruitful parent of three hundred pigs : a prodigious instance of fecundity in so large a quadruped !   She was killed in spring 1775.

LETTER LXXVI.

TO THE HONOURABLE DAINES BARRINGTON.

"— — — — — — admorunt ubera tigres."
" By tigers suckled."

WE have remarked in a former letter how much incongruous animals, in a lonely state, may be attached to each other from a spirit of sociality ; in this it may not be amiss to recount a different motive which has been known to create as strange a fondness.

My friend had a little helpless leveret brought to him, which the servants fed with milk in a spoon, and about the same time his cat kittened and the young were despatched and buried. The hare was soon lost, and supposed to be gone the way of most fondlings, to be killed by some dog or cat.   However, in about a fortnight, as the master was sitting in his garden in the dusk of the evening, he observed his cat, with tail erect, trotting towards him, and calling with little short inward notes of complacency, such as they use towards their kittens, and something gamboling after, which proved to be the leveret that the cat had supported with her milk, and continued to support with great affection.

Thus was a graminivorous animal nurtured by a carnivorous and predaceous one !

Why so cruel and sanguinary a beast as a cat, of the ferocious genus of *Feles*, the *Murium leo*, as Linnæus calls it, should be affected with any tenderness towards an animal which is its natural prey, is not so easy to determine.

This strange affection probably was occasioned by that desiderium, those tender maternal feelings, which the loss of her kittens had awakened in her breast; and by the complacency and ease she derived to herself from the procuring her teats to be drawn, which were too much distended with milk, till, from habit, she became as much delighted with this fondling as if it had been her real offspring.

This incident is no bad solution of that strange circumstance which grave historians as well as the poets assert, of exposed children being sometimes nurtured by female wild beasts that probably had lost their young. For it is not one whit more marvellous that Romulus and Remus, in their infant state, should be nursed by a she-wolf, than that a poor little suck-ing leveret should be fostered and cherished by a bloody grimalkin.

> "— — — — viridi fœtam Mavortis in antro
> Procubuisse lupam : geminos huic ubera circum
> Ludere pendentes pueros, et lambere matrem
> Impavidos ; illam tereti cervice reflexam
> Mulcere alternos, et corpora fingere linguâ."
> (VIRG. *Æn.* viii. 630-634.)

Or, as Christopher Pitt renders the Roman poet :—

> "Here in a verdant cave's embowering shade,
> The fostering wolf and martial twins were laid ;
> The indulgent mother, half reclined along,
> Look'd fondly back, and formed them with her tongue."

[Again a boy has taken three little squirrels in their nest, or drey, as it is called in these parts. These small creatures he put under the care of a cat who had lately lost her kittens, and finds that she nurses and suckles them with the same assiduity and affection as if they were her own offspring.

So many people went to see the little squirrels suckled by a cat, that the foster-mother became jealous of her charge, and in pain for their safety ; and therefore hid them over the ceiling, where one died. This circumstance shows her affection for these fondlings, and that she supposes the squirrels to be her own young.   Thus hens, when they have hatched ducklings, are equally attached to them, as if they were their own chickens.] —OBSERVATIONS ON NATURE.

SELBORNE, *May* 9, 1776.

LETTER LXXVII.

TO THE HONOURABLE DAINES BARRINGTON.

LANDS that are subject to frequent inundations are always poor ; and probably the reason may be because the worms are drowned.   The most insignificant insects and reptiles are of much more consequence, and have much more influence in the economy of Nature, than the incurious are aware of ; and are mighty in their effect, from their minuteness, which renders them less an object of attention ; and from their numbers and fecundity.   Earth-worms, though in appearance a small and despicable link in the chain of Nature, yet, if lost, would make a lamentable chasm.   For, to say nothing of half the birds, and some quadrupeds which are almost entirely supported by them, worms seem to be great promoters of vegetation, which would proceed but lamely without them ; by boring, perforating, and loosening the soil, and rendering it pervious to rains and the fibres of plants ; by drawing straws and stalks of leaves and twigs into it ; and, most of all, by throwing up such infinite numbers of lumps of earth called worm-casts, which, being their excrement, is a fine manure for grain and grass.   Worms probably provide new soil for hills, and slopes, where the rain washes the earth away ; and they affect slopes, probably to avoid being flooded.   Gardeners and farmers express their detestation of worms ; the farmer because they render their walks unsightly, and make them much work : and the latter because, as they think, worms eat their green corn.   But these men would find that the earth without worms would soon become cold, hard-bound, and void of fermentation ; and consequently sterile : and besides, in favour of worms, it should be hinted that green corn, plants, and flowers are not so much injured by them as by many species of *coleoptera* (scarabs) and *tipulæ* (long-legs) in their larva, or grub-state ; and by unnoticed myriads of small shell-less snails, called slugs, which silently and imperceptibly make amazing havoc in the field and garden.

Farmer Young, of Norton farm, says that this spring (1777) about four acres of his wheat in one field was entirely destroyed by slugs, which swarmed on the blades of corn, and devoured it as it sprang.

These hints we think proper to throw out in order to set the inquisitive and discerning to work.

A good monography of worms would afford much entertainment and information at the same time, and would open a large and new field in natural history. Worms work most in the spring; but by no means lie torpid in the dead months; they are out every mild night in the winter, as any person may satisfy himself. They are hermaphrodites, and are, consequently, very prolific.

SELBORNE, *May* 20, 1777.

LETTER LXXVIII.

TO THE HONOURABLE DAINES BARRINGTON.

You cannot but remember that the 26th and 27th of last March were very hot days; so sultry that everybody complained, and were restless under those sensations to which they had not been reconciled by gradual approaches.

This sudden summer-like heat was attended by many summer coincidences; for on those two days the thermometer rose to sixty-six in the shade; many species of insects revived and came forth; some bees swarmed in this neighbourhood; the old tortoise, near Lewes in Sussex, awakened and came forth out of its dormitory; and, what is most to my present purpose, many house-swallows appeared, and were very alert in many places, and particularly at Cobham, in Surrey.

But as that short warm period was succeeded as well as preceded by harsh severe weather, with frequent frosts and ice, and cutting winds, the insects withdrew, the tortoise returned again into the ground, and the swallows were seen no more until the 10th of April, when the rigour of the spring abating, a softer season began to prevail.

Again, it appears by my journals for many years past, that house-martins retire, to a bird, about the beginning of October; so that a person very observant of such matters would conclude that they had taken their last farewell : but then, it may be seen in my diaries also that considerable flocks have discovered themselves again in the first week of November, and often on the fourth day of that month only for one day ; and that not as if they were in actual migration, but playing about at their leisure and feeding calmly, as if no enterprise of moment at all agitated their spirits. And this was the case in the beginning of this very month ; for, on the 4th of November, more than twenty house-martins, which, in appearance, had all departed about the 7th of October, were seen again, for that one morning only, sporting between my fields and the Hanger, and feasting on insects which swarmed in that sheltered district. The preceding day was wet and blustering, but the 4th was dark and mild, and soft, the wind at south-west, and the thermometer at 58½° ; a pitch not common at that season of the year. Moreover, it may not be amiss to add in this place, that whenever the thermometer is above 50° the bat comes flitting out in every autumnal and winter month.

From all these circumstances laid together, it is obvious that torpid insects, reptiles, and quadrupeds, are awakened from their profoundest slumbers by a little untimely warmth; and therefore that nothing so much promotes this death-like stupor as a defect of heat. And farther, it is reasonable to suppose that two whole species, or at least many individuals of those two species, of British *hirundines*, do never leave this island at all, but partake of the same benumbed state : for we cannot suppose that, after a month's absence, house-martins can return from southern regions to appear for one morning in November, or that house-swallows should leave the districts of Africa to enjoy in March the transient summer of a couple of days.

SELBORNE, *Nov.* 22, 1777.

LETTER LXXIX.

TO THE HONOURABLE DAINES BARRINGTON.

THERE was in this village several years ago a miserable pauper, who, from his birth, was afflicted with a leprosy, as far as we are aware, of a singular kind ; since it affected only the palms of his hands and the soles of his feet. This scaly eruption

o

usually broke out twice in the year, at the spring and fall; and, by peeling away, left the skin so thin and tender that neither his hands nor feet were able to perform their functions; so that the poor object was half his time on crutches, incapable of employ, and languishing in a tiresome state of indolence and inactivity. His habit was lean, lank, and cadaverous. In this sad plight he dragged on a miserable existence, a burden to himself and his parish, which was obliged to support him till he was relieved by death at more than thirty years of age.

The good women, who love to account for every defect in children by the doctrine of longing, said that his mother felt a violent propensity for oysters, which she was unable to gratify; and that the black rough scurf on his hands and feet were the shells of that fish. I knew his parents, neither of whom were lepers; his father in particular lived to be far advanced in years.

In all ages, the leprosy has made dreadful havoc among mankind. The Israelites seem to have been greatly afflicted with it from the most remote times; as appears from the peculiar and repeated injunctions given them in the Levitical law.[1] Nor was the rancour of this foul disorder much abated in the last period of their commonwealth, as may be seen in many passages of the New Testament.

Some centuries ago this horrible distemper prevailed all Europe over; and our forefathers were by no means exempt, as appears by the large provisions made for objects labouring under this calamity. There was a hospital for female lepers in the diocese of Lincoln, a noble one near Durham, three in London and Southwark, and perhaps many more in or near our great towns and cities. Moreover, some crowned heads, and other wealthy and charitable personages, bequeathed large legacies to such poor people as languished under this hopeless infirmity.

It must therefore, in these days, be, to a humane and thinking person, a matter of equal wonder and satisfaction, when he contemplates how nearly this pest is eradicated, and observes that a leper now is a rare sight. He will, moreover, when engaged in such a train of thought, naturally inquire for the reason. This happy change perhaps may have originated and been continued from the much smaller quantity of salted meat and fish now eaten in these kingdoms; from the use of linen next the skin; from

---

[1] See Leviticus xiii. and xiv.

the plenty of better bread; and from the profusion of fruits, roots, legumes, and greens, so common now in every family. Three or four centuries ago, before there were any inclosures, sown-grasses, field-turnips, or field-carrots, or hay, all the cattle which had grown fat in summer, and were not killed for winter use, were turned out soon after Michaelmas to shift as they could through the dead months; so that no fresh meat could be had in winter or spring. Hence the marvellous account of the vast stores of salted flesh found in the larder of the eldest Spencer, viz. six hundred bacons, eighty carcases of beef, and six hundred muttons, in the days of Edward the Second, even so late in the spring as the 3rd of May. It was from magazines like these that the turbulent barons supported in idleness their riotous swarms of retainers ready for any disorder or mischief. But agriculture is now arrived at such a pitch of perfection, that our best and fattest meats are killed in the winter; and no man need eat salted flesh, unless he prefers it.

One cause of this distemper might be, no doubt, the quantity of wretched fresh and salt fish consumed by the commonalty at all seasons as well as in Lent; which our poor now would hardly be persuaded to touch.

The use of linen changes, shirts or shifts, in the room of sordid and filthy woollen, long worn next the skin, is a matter of neatness comparatively modern; but must prove a great means of preventing cutaneous ails. At this very time woollen instead of linen prevails among the poorer Welsh, who are subject to foul eruptions.

The plenty of good wheaten bread that now is found among all ranks of people in the south, instead of that miserable sort which used in old days to be made of barley or beans, may contribute not a little to the sweetening their blood and correcting their juices; for the inhabitants of mountainous districts, to this day, are still liable to the itch and other cutaneous disorders, from poverty of diet.

As to the produce of a garden, every middle-aged person of observation may perceive, within his own memory, both in town and country, how vastly the consumption of vegetables is increased. Green-stalls in cities now support multitudes in a comfortable state, whilst gardeners get fortunes. Every decent labourer has his garden, which is half his support, as well as his delight; and common farmers provide plenty of beans, peas, and greens, for their hinds to eat with their bacon; and those few that do not are despised for their sordid parsimony, and looked upon as regardless of the welfare of their dependants.   Potatoes have prevailed in this little district, by means of premiums, within these twenty years only; and are much esteemed here now by the poor, who would scarce have ventured to taste them in the last reign.

Our Saxon ancestors certainly had some sort of cabbage, because they call the month of February sprout-cale;[1] but, long after their days, the cultivation of gardens was little attended to. The religious, being men of leisure, and keeping up a constant correspondence with Italy, were the first people among us that had gardens and fruit-trees in any perfection, within the walls of their abbeys, priories, and monasteries, where the lamp of knowledge continued to burn, however dimly.   In them men of business were formed for the state: the art of writing was

WOODCHAT'S EGG.

cultivated by the monks; they were the only proficients in mechanics, gardening, and architecture.[2]   The barons neglected every pursuit that did not lead to war or tend to the pleasure of the chase.

It was not till gentlemen took up the study of horticulture themselves that the knowledge of gardening made such hasty advances.   Lord Cobham, Lord Ila, and Mr. Waller of Beaconsfield, were some of the first people of rank that promoted the elegant science of ornamenting without despising the superintendence of the kitchen quarters and fruit walls.

A remark made by the excellent Mr. Ray in his Tour of Europe at once surprises us, and corroborates what has been advanced above; for we find him observing, so late as his days, that "the Italians use several herbs for sallets, which are not yet or have

[1] March was the stormy month with our Saxon ancestors; May, Thromilchi, the cows being then milked three times a-day; June, dig and weed month; September, barley month.—MITFORD.
[2] Dalrymple's "Annals of Scotland."

not been but lately used in England, viz. *selleri* (celery), which
is nothing else but the sweet smallage; the young shoots whereof,
with a little of the head of the root cut off, they eat raw with oil
and pepper." And farther he adds, " curled endive blanched is
much used beyond seas; and, for a raw sallet, seemed to excel
lettuce itself." Now this journey was undertaken no longer ago
than in the year 1663.

SELBORNE, *Jan.* 8, 1778.

LETTER LXXX.

TO THE HONOURABLE DAINES BARRINGTON

> " Fortè puer, comitum seductus ab agmine fido,
> Dixerat, Ecquis adest? et, Adest, responderat Echo.
> Hic stupet; utque aciem partes divisit in omnes;
> Voce, Veni, clamat magnâ. Vocat illa vocantem."
> (OVID, *Met.* iii. 379.)

" The youth being separated by chance from his faithful attendants, calls
aloud, ' Is there any one here?' and echo answers, ' Here.' He is amazed,
he casts his eyes on every side and calls with a loud voice, ' Come!' where-
upon echo calls the youth who calls."

> " She can't begin, but waits for the rebound,
> To catch his voice and then return the sound."
> (DRYDEN.)

IN a district so diversified as this, so full of hollow vales and
hanging woods, it is no wonder that echoes should abound.
Many we have discovered that return the cry of a pack of dogs,
the notes of a hunting-horn, a tunable ring of bells, or the
melody of birds, very agreeably: but we were still at a loss for
a polysyllabical, articulate echo, till a young gentleman, who had
parted from his company in a summer evening walk, and was
calling after them, stumbled upon a very curious one in a spot
where it might least be expected. At first he was much surprised, and could not be persuaded but that he was mocked by
some boy; but, repeating his trials in several languages, and
finding his respondent to be a very adroit polyglot, he then
discerned the deception.

This echo in an evening, before rural noises cease, would

repeat ten syllables most articulately and distinctly, especially if quick dactyls were chosen.   The last syllables of

"Tityre, tu patulæ recubans   —   —   —   —   " [1]

were as audibly and intelligibly returned as the first; and there is no doubt, could trial have been made, but that at midnight, when the air is very elastic, and a dead stillness prevails, one or two syllables more might have been obtained; but the distance rendered so late an experiment very inconvenient.

Quick dactyls, we observed, succeeded best; for when we came to try its powers in slow, heavy, embarrassed spondees of the same number of syllables,

"Monstrum horrendum, informe, ingens   —   —   " [2]

we could perceive a return but of four or five.

All echoes have some one place to which they are returned stronger and more distinct than to any other; and that is always the place that lies at right angles with the object of repercussion, and is not too near, nor too far off.   Buildings, or naked rocks, re-echo much more articulately than hanging wood or vales; because in the latter the voice is as it were entangled, and embarrassed in the covert, and weakened in the rebound.

The true source of this echo, as we found by various experiments, is the stone-built, tiled hop-kiln in Gally-lane, which measures in front 40 feet, and from the ground to the eaves 12 feet.   The true *centrum phonicum*, or just distance, is one particular spot in the King's-field, in the path to Nore-hill, on the very brink of the steep balk above the hollow cart-way.   In this case there is no choice of distance; but the path, by mere contingency, happens to be the lucky, the identical spot, because the ground rises or falls so immediately, if the speaker either retires or advances, that his mouth would at once be above or below the object.

We measured this polysyllabical echo with great exactness, and found the distance to fall very short of Dr. Plot's rule for distinct articulation: for the Doctor, in his history of Oxford-

---

[1] "Beneath the shade which beechen boughs diffuse
You, Tityrus, entertain your sylvan muse."
(DRYDEN's *Virg. Ecl.* i. 1.)

[2] "A monster grim, tremendous, vast and high."
(DRYDEN's *Virg. Æn.* iii. 658.)

shire, allows 120 feet for the return of each syllable distinctly :
hence this echo, which gives ten distinct syllables, ought to
measure 400 yards, or 120 feet to each syllable; whereas our
distance is only 258 yards, or near 75 feet to each syllable. Thus
our measure falls short of the Doctor's, as five to eight: but then
it must be acknowledged that this candid philosopher was convinced afterwards, that some latitude must be admitted of in the
distance of echoes according to time and place.

When experiments of this sort are making, it should always
be remembered that weather and the time of day have a vast
influence on an echo; for a dull, heavy, moist air deadens and
clogs the sound; and hot sunshine renders the air thin and
weak, and deprives it of all its springiness; and a ruffling wind
quite defeats the whole. In a still, clear, dewy evening the air
is most elastic; and perhaps the later the hour the more so.
Echo has always been so amusing to the imagination, that the
poets have personified her; and in their hands she has been the
occasion of many a beautiful fiction. Nor need the gravest man
be ashamed to appear taken with such a phenomenon, since
it may become the subject of philosophical or mathematical
inquiries.

One should have imagined that echoes, if not entertaining,
must at least have been harmless and inoffensive; yet Virgil
advances a strange notion, that they are injurious to bees. After
enumerating some probable and reasonable annoyances, such as
prudent owners would wish far removed from their bee-gardens,
he adds

> "— — — — — — aut ubi concava pulsu
> Saxa sonant, vocisque offensa resultat imago." [1]

[There is a natural occurrence to be met with upon the highest
part of our downs in hot summer days, which always amuses me
much, without giving me any satisfaction with respect to the
cause of it; and that is a loud audible humming as of bees in
the air, though not one insect is to be seen. This sound is to be
heard distinctly the whole common through, from the Money-
dells, to my avenue gate.

[1] " Nor place them where too deep a water flows,
    Or where the yew, their poisonous neighbour, grows ;
    Nor near the steaming stench of muddy ground,
    Nor hollow rocks that render back the sound,
    And double images of voice rebound."
                                (DRYDEN's *Virg. Georg.* iv. 47-50.)

Any person would suppose that a large swarm of bees was in motion, and playing about over his head. This noise was heard last week, on June 28th.

> "Resounds the living surface of the ground,
> Nor undelightful is the ceaseless hum
> To him who muses . . . at noon."
> "Thick in yon stream of light a thousand ways,
> Upward and downward, thwarting and convolved,
> The quivering nations sport."

This wild and fanciful assertion will hardly be admitted by the philosophers of these days; especially as they all now seem agreed that insects are not furnished with any organs of hearing at all. But if it should be urged, that though they cannot hear, yet perhaps they may feel the repercussion of sounds, I grant it is possible they may. Yet that these impressions are distasteful or hurtful, I deny, because bees, in good summers, thrive well in my outlet, where the echoes are very strong: for this village is another Anathoth, a place of responses or echoes. Besides, it does not appear from experiment that bees are in any way capable of being affected by sounds: for I have often tried my own with a large speaking-trumpet held close to their hives, and with such an exertion of voice as would have hailed a ship at the distance of a mile, and still these insects pursued their various employments undisturbed, and without showing the least sensibility or resentment.

Some time since its discovery this echo is become totally silent, though the object, or hop-kiln, remains: nor is there any mystery in this defect; for the field between is planted as a hop-garden, and the voice of the speaker is totally absorbed and lost among the poles and entangled foliage of the hops. And when the poles are removed in autumn the disappointment is the same; because a tall quick-set hedge, nurtured up for the purpose of shelter to the hop-ground, interrupts the repercussion of the voice: so that till those obstructions are removed no more of its garrulity can be expected.

Should any gentleman of fortune think an echo in his park or outlet a pleasing incident, he might build one at little or no expense. For whenever he had occasion for a new barn, stable, dog kennel, or the like structure, it would be only needful to erect this building on the gentle declivity of a hill, with a like rising opposite to it, at a few hundred yards distance; and perhaps success might be the easier insured could some canal, lake, or stream, intervene. From a seat at the *centrum phonicum* he and his friends might amuse themselves sometimes of an evening with the prattle of this loquacious nymph; of whose complacency and decent reserve more may be said than can with truth of every individual of her sex; since she is " always ready with her vocal response, but never intrusive:"—

> "— — — — — — quæ nec reticere loquenti,
> Nec prior ipsa loqui didicit resonabilis echo."

The classsic reader will, I trust, pardon the following lovely quotation, so finely describing echoes, and so poetically accounting for their causes :—

> "Quæ benè quom videas, rationem reddere possis
> Tute tibi atque aliis, quo pacto per loca sola
> Saxa pareis formas verborum ex ordine reddant,
> Palanteis comites quom monteis inter opacos
> Quærimus, et magnâ disperos voce ciemus.
> Sex etiam, aut septem loca vidi reddere voces
> Unam quom jaceres : ita colles collibus ipsis
> Verba repulsantes iterabant dicta referre.
> Hæc loca capripedes Satyros Nymphasque tenere
> Finitimi fingunt, et Faunos esse loquuntur ;
> Quorum noctivago strepitu, ludoque jocanti
> Adfirmant volgo taciturna silentia rumpi,
> Chordarumque sonos fieri, dulceisque querelas,
> Tibia quas fundit digitis pulsata canentum :
> Et genus agricolûm latè sentiscere, quom Pan
> Pinea semiferi capitis velamina quassans,
> Unco sæpe labro calamos percurrit hianteis,
> Fistula silvestrem ne cesset fundere musam."
>
> (LUCRETIUS, lib. iv. l. 576.)

> "This shows thee why, whilst men, through caves and groves
> Call their lost friends, or mourn unhappy loves,
> The pitying rocks, the groaning caves return
> Their sad complaints again, and seem to mourn :
> This all observe, and I myself have known
> Both rocks and hills return six words for one :
> The dancing words from hill to hill rebound,
> They all receive, and all restore the sound :
> The vulgar and the neighbours think, and tell,
> That therè the Nymphs, and Fauns, and Satyrs dwell :
> And that their wanton sport, their loud delight,
> Breaks through the quiet silence of the night :
> Their music's softest airs fill all the plains,
> And mighty Pan delights the list'ning swains :

The goat-faced Pan, whose flocks securely feed ;
With long-hung lip he blows his oaten reed :
The horned, the half-beast god, when brisk and gay,
With pine-leaves crowned, provokes the swains to play."
(CREECH'S *Translation*.)

SELBORNE, *Feb.* 12, 1778.

LETTER LXXXI.

TO THE HONOURABLE DAINES BARRINGTON.

AMONG the many singularities attending those amusing birds
the swifts, I am now confirmed in the opinion that we have every
year the same number of pairs invariably ; at least the result of
my inquiry has been exactly the same for a long time past. The
swallows and martins are so numerous, and so widely distributed
over the village, that it is hardly possible to re-count them ;
while the swifts, though they do not all build in the church, yet

GREENFINCH'S EGG.

so frequently haunt it, and play and rendezvous round it, that
they are easily enumerated. The number that I constantly find
are eight pairs ; about half of which reside in the church, and
the rest build in some of the lowest and meanest thatched cottages.
Now as these eight pairs, allowance being made for accidents,
breed yearly eight pairs more, what becomes of this annual increase ; and what determines every spring which pairs shall visit
us, and reoccupy their ancient haunts ?

Ever since I have attended to the subject of ornithology, I
have always supposed that that sudden reverse of affection, that
strange ἀντιστοργή, or antipathy, which immediately succeeds in
the feathered kind to the most passionate fondness, is the occasion of an equal dispersion of birds over the face of the earth.
Without this provision one favourite district would be crowded
with inhabitants, while others would be destitute and forsaken.

But the parent birds seem to maintain a jealous superiority, and to oblige the young to seek for new abodes : and the rivalry of the males, in many kinds, prevents their crowding the one on the other. Whether the swallows and house-martins return in the same exact number annually is not easy to say, for reasons given above : but it is apparent, as I have remarked before in my Monographies, that the numbers returning bear no manner of proportion to the numbers retiring.

SELBORNE, *May* 13, 1778.

LETTER LXXXII.

TO THE HONOURABLE DAINES BARRINGTON.

THE standing objection to botany has always been, that it is a pursuit that amuses the fancy and exercises the memory, without improving the mind or advancing any real knowledge : and, where the science is carried no farther than a mere systematic classification, the charge is but too true. But the botanist that is desirous of wiping off this aspersion should be by no means content with a list of names ; he should study plants philosophically, should investigate the laws of vegetation, should examine the powers and virtues of efficacious herbs, should promote their cultivation ; and graft the gardener, the planter, and the husbandman, on the phytologist. Not that system is by any means to be thrown aside ; without system the field of Nature would be a pathless wilderness : but system should be subservient to, not the main object of, pursuit.

Vegetation is highly worthy of our attention ; and in itself is of the utmost consequence to mankind, and productive of many of the greatest comforts and elegancies of life. To plants we owe timber, bread, beer, honey, wine, oil, linen, cotton, &c., what not only strengthens our hearts, and exhilarates our spirits, but what secures us from inclemencies of weather and adorns our persons. Man, in his true state of nature, seems to be subsisted by spontaneous vegetation : in middle climes, where grasses prevail, he mixes some animal food with the produce of the field and garden : and it is towards the polar extremes only that, like his kindred bears and wolves, he gorges himself with flesh alone, and is driven to what hunger has never been known to compel the very beasts, to prey on his own species.

The productions of vegetation have had a vast influence on the commerce of nations, and have been the great promoters of navigation, as may be seen in the articles of sugar, tea, tobacco, opium, ginseng, betel, paper, &c. As every climate has its peculiar produce, our natural wants bring on a mutual intercourse; so that by means of trade each distant part is supplied with the growth of every latitude. But without the knowledge of plants and their culture we must have been content with our hips and haws, without enjoying the delicate fruits of India and the salutiferous drugs of Peru.

Instead of examining the minute distinctions of every various species of each obscure genus, the botanist should endeavour to make himself acquainted with those that are useful. You shall see a man readily ascertain every herb of the field, yet hardly know wheat from barley, or at least one sort of wheat or barley from another.

But of all sorts of vegetation the grasses seem to be most neglected; neither the farmer nor the grazier seem to distinguish the annual from the perennial, the hardy from the tender, nor the succulent and nutritive from the dry and juiceless.

The study of grasses would be of great consequence to a northerly and grazing kingdom. The botanist that could improve the sward of the district where he lived would be a useful member of society: to raise a thick turf on a naked soil would be worth volumes of systematic knowledge; and he would be the best commonwealth's man that could occasion the growth of "two blades of grass where only one was seen before."

SELBORNE, *June* 2, 1778.

LETTER LXXXIII.

TO THE HONOURABLE DAINES BARRINGTON.

IN a district so diversified with such a variety of hill and dale, aspects, and soils, it is no wonder that great choice of plants should be found. Chalks, clays, sands, sheep-walks and downs, bogs, heaths, woodlands, and champaign fields, cannot but furnish an ample Flora. The deep rocky lanes abound with *filices*, and the pastures and moist woods with *fungi*. If in any branch of botany we may seem to be wanting, it must be in the large aquatic plants, which are not to be expected on a spot far removed from rivers, and lying up amidst the hill country at the spring-heads. To enumerate all the plants that have been discovered within our limits would be a needless work; but a short list of the more rare, and the spots where they are to be found, may be neither unacceptable nor unentertaining :—

Stinking Hellebore (*Helleborus fœtidus*), Bear's foot or Setterwort, all over the High-wood and Coney-croft-hanger; this continues a great branching plant the winter through, blossoming about January, and is very ornamental in shady walks and shrubberies. The good women give the leaves powdered to children troubled with worms; but it is a violent remedy, and ought to be administered with caution.

Green Hellebore (*Helleborus viridis*), in the deep stony lane on the left hand just before the turning to Norton farm, and at the top of Middle Dorton under the hedge; this plant dies down to the ground early in autumn, and springs again about February, flowering almost as soon as it appears above ground.

Creeping Bilberry, or Cranberries (*Vaccinium oxycoccos*), in the bogs of Bin's-pond.

Whortle, or Bilberries (*Vaccinium myrtillus*), on the dry hillocks of Wolmer Forest.

Round-leaved Sundew (*Drosera rotundiflora*), and Long-leaved Sundew (*Drosera longifolia*), in the bogs of Bin's-pond.

Purple Comarum (*Comarum palustre*), or Marsh Cinquefoil, in the bogs of Bin's-pond.

Tustan, or St. John's Wort (*Hypericum androsæmum*), in the stony, hollow lanes.

Lesser Periwinkle (*Vinca minor*), in Selborne-hanger and Shrub-wood.

Yellow Monotropa (*Monotropa hypopithys*), or Bird's nest, in Selborne-hanger under the shady beeches, to whose roots it seems to be parasitical, at the north-west end of the Hanger.

Perfoliated Yellow - wort (*Chlora perfoliata, Blackstonia perfoliata, Hudsonii*), on the banks in the King's-field.

Herb Paris (*Paris quadrifolia*), True-love, or One-berry, in the Church-litten-coppice.

Opposite Golden Saxifrage (*Chrysosplenium oppositifolium*), in the dark and rocky hollow lanes.

Autumnal Gentian (*Gentiana amarella*), or Fellwort, on the Zig-zag and Hanger.

Tooth-wort (*Lathræa squammaria*), in the Church-litten-coppice under some hazels near the foot-bridge, in Trimming's garden hedge, and on the dry wall opposite Grange-yard.

Small Teasel (*Dipsacus pilosus*), in the Short and Long Lithe.

Narrow-leaved, or Wild Lathyrus (*Lathyrus sylvestris*), in the bushes at the foot of the Short Lithe, near the path.

Ladies' Traces (*Ophrys spiralis*), in the Long Lithe, and towards the south corner of the common.

Birds' Nest Ophrys (*Ophrys nidus avis*), in the Long Lithe, under the shady beeches among the dead leaves; in Great Dorton among the bushes, and on the Hanger plentifully.

Helleborine (*Serapias latifolia*), in the High-wood under the shady beeches.

Spurge Laurel (*Daphne laureola*), in Selborne-hanger and the High-wood.

The Mezereon (*Daphne Mezereum*), in Selborne-hanger, among the shrubs at the south-east end above the cottages.

Truffles (*Lycoperdon tuber*), in the Hanger and the High-wood.

Dwarf Elder, Walwort or Danewort (*Sambucus ebulus*), among the rubbish and ruined foundations of the Priory.

Of all the propensities of plants none seem more strange than their different periods of blossoming. Some produce their flowers in the winter, or very first dawnings of spring; many when the spring is established; some at midsummer, and some not till autumn. When we see the *Helleborus fœtidus* and *Helleborus niger* blowing at Christmas, the *Helleborus hyemalis* in January, and the *Helleborus viridis* as soon as ever it emerges out of the ground, we do not wonder, because they are kindred plants that we expect should keep pace the one with the other. But other congenerous vegetables differ so widely in their time of flowering, that we cannot but admire. I shall only instance at present in the *Crocus sativus*, the vernal and the autumnal crocus, which have such an affinity, that the best botanists only make them varieties of the same genus, of which there is only one species; not being able to discern any difference in the corolla, or in the internal structure. Yet the vernal crocus expands its flowers by the beginning of March at farthest, and often even in very rigorous weather; they cannot be retarded but by some violence offered:—while the autumnal (the Saffron) defies the influence of the spring and summer, and will not blow till most plants begin to fade and run to seed. This circumstance is one of the wonders of the creation, little noticed because a common occurrence: yet it ought not to be overlooked because it is familiar, since it would be as difficult to be explained as the most stupendous phenomenon in nature.

> "Say, what impels, amidst surrounding snow
> Congealed, the crocus' flamy bud to glow?
> Say, what retards, amidst the summer's blaze,
> Th' autumnal bulb, till pale, declining days?
> The GOD of SEASONS; whose pervading power
> Controls the sun, or sheds the fleecy shower:
> He bids each flower His quick'ning word obey;
> Or to each lingering bloom enjoins delay."

SELBORNE, *July* 3, 1778.

LETTER LXXXIV.

TO THE HONOURABLE DAINES BARRINGTON.

" Omnibus animalibus reliquis certus et uniusmodi, et in suo cuique genere incessus est : aves solæ vario meatu feruntur, et in terrâ, et in aëre."—PLIN. *Hist. Nat.* lib. x. cap. 38.

" All animals have a certain definite and peculiar gait ; birds alone move in a *varied* manner both on the ground and in the air."

A GOOD ornithologist should be able to distinguish birds by their air as well as by their colours and shape ; on the ground as well as on the wing, and in the bush as well as in the hand.   For, though it must not be said that every species of birds has a manner peculiar to itself, yet there is somewhat in most genera at least that at first sight discriminates them, and enables a judicious observer to pronounce upon them with some certainty. Put a bird in motion " and it is truly betrayed by its gait."

" — — Et vera incessu patuit — — — —"

Thus kites and buzzards sail round in circles with wings expanded and motionless ; and it is from their gliding manner that the former are still called in the north of England and Scotland "gleds," from the Saxon verb *glidan,* to glide.   The kestrel, or wind-hover, has a peculiar mode of hanging in the air in one place, his wings all the while being briskly agitated. Hen-harriers fly low over heaths or fields of corn, and beat the ground regularly like a pointer or setting-dog.   Owls move in a buoyant manner, as if lighter than the air ; they seem to want ballast.   There is a peculiarity belonging to ravens that must draw the attention even of the most incurious—they spend all their leisure time in striking and cuffing each other on the wing in a kind of playful skirmish ; and, when they move from one place to another, frequently turn on their backs with a loud croak, and seem to be falling to the ground.   When this odd gesture betides them, they are scratching themselves with one foot, and thus lose the centre of gravity.   Rooks sometimes dive and tumble in a frolicsome manner ; crows and daws swagger in their walk ; woodpeckers fly *volatu undoso,* opening and closing their wings at every stroke, and so are always rising or falling in curves. All of this genus use their tails, which incline downward, as a support while they run up trees. Parrots, like all other hooked-clawed birds, walk awkwardly, and make use of their bill as a third foot, climbing and descending with ridiculous caution. All the *gallinæ* parade and walk gracefully, and run nimbly; but fly with difficulty, with an impetuous whirring, and in a straight line. Magpies and jays flutter with powerless wings, and make no despatch; herons seem encumbered with too much sail for their light bodies; but these vast hollow wings are necessary in carrying burdens, such as large fishes, and the like; pigeons, and particularly the sort called smiters, have a way of clashing their wings, the one against the other, over their backs with a loud snap; another variety called tumblers, turn themselves over in the air. Some birds have movements peculiar to the season of love: thus ringdoves, though strong and rapid at other times, yet, in the spring, hang about on the wing in a toying and playful manner; thus the cock-snipe, while breeding, forgetting his former flight, fans the air like the wind-hover; and the greenfinch in particular exhibits such languishing and faltering gestures, as to appear like a wounded and dying bird; the kingfisher darts along like an arrow; fern-owls, or goat-suckers, glance in the dusk over the tops of trees like a meteor; starlings as it were swim along, while missel-thrushes use a wild and desultory flight; swallows sweep over the surface of the ground and water, and distinguish themselves by rapid turns and quick evolutions; swifts dash round in circles; and the bank-martin moves with frequent vacillations like a butterfly. Most of the small birds fly by jerks, rising and falling as they advance; many of them hop; but wagtails and larks walk, moving their legs alternately. Skylarks rise and fall perpendicularly as they sing; woodlarks hang poised in the air; and titlarks rise and fall in large curves, singing in their descent. The white-throat uses odd jerks and gesticulations over the tops of hedges and bushes. All the duck-kind waddle; divers, and auks, walk as if fettered, and stand erect on their tail: these are the *compedes* of Linnæus. Geese and cranes, and most wild-fowl, move in figured flights, often changing their position. The secondary *remiges* of *Tringæ*, wild-ducks, and some others, are very long, and give their wings, when in motion, a hooked appearance. Dab-chicks, moorhens, and coots, fly erect, with their legs hanging down, and hardly make any despatch; the reason is plain, their wings are placed too forward out of the true centre of gravity for rapid progression; as the legs of auks and divers are situated too backward.

Selborne, *Aug.* 7, 1778.

LETTER LXXXV.

TO THE HONOURABLE DAINES BARRINGTON.

From the motion of birds, the transition is natural enough to their notes and language, of which I shall say something. Not that I would pretend to understand their language, like the vizier of the *Spectator*, who, by the recital of a conversation which passed between two owls, reclaimed a sultan, before delighting in conquest and devastation; but I would be thought only to mean that many of the winged tribes have various sounds and voices adapted to express their various passions, wants, and feelings; such as anger, fear, love, hatred, hunger, and the like. All species are not equally eloquent; some are copious and fluent as it were in their utterance, while others are confined to a few important sounds : no bird, like the fish kind, is quite mute, though some are rather silent. The language of birds is very ancient, and, like other ancient modes . of speech, very elliptical; little is said, but much is meant and understood.

The notes of the eagle-kind are shrill and piercing; and about the season of nidification much diversified, as I have been often assured by a curious observer of Nature who long resided at Gibraltar, where eagles abound. The notes of our hawks much resemble those of the king of birds. Owls have very expressive notes; they hoot in a fine vocal sound, much resembling the *vox humana*, and reducible by a pitch-pipe to a musical key. This note seems to express complacency and rivalry among the males : they use also a quick call and a horrible scream; and can snore and hiss when they mean to menace. Ravens, besides their loud croak, can exert a deep and solemn note that makes the woods echo; the amorous sound of a crow is strange and ridiculous; rooks, in the breeding season, attempt sometimes in the gaiety of their hearts to sing, but with no great success; the parrot-kind may have many modulations of voice, as appears by

P

their aptitude to learn human sounds ; doves coo in an amorous
and mournful manner, and are emblems of despairing lovers ; the
woodpecker sets up a sort of loud and hearty laugh ; the fern-owl,
or goat-sucker, from the dusk till daybreak, serenades his mate
with the clattering of castanets. All the tuneful *passeres* express
their complacency by sweet modulations, and a variety of melody.
The swallow, as has been observed in a former letter, by a shrill
alarm bespeaks the attention of the other *hirundines*, and bids
them be aware that the hawk is at hand. Aquatic and gregarious
birds, especially the nocturnal, that shift their quarters in the
dark, are very noisy and loquacious ; as cranes, wild-geese,
wild-ducks, and the like : their perpetual clamour prevents them
from dispersing and losing their companions.

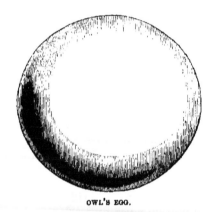

OWL'S EGG.

In so extensive a subject, sketches and outlines are as much as
can be expected ; for it would be endless to instance in all their
infinite variety the notes of the feathered nation. I shall therefore
confine the remainder of this letter to the few domestic fowls of
our yards which are most known, and therefore best understood.
And first the peacock, with his gorgeous train, demands our
attention ; but, like most of the gaudy birds, his notes are grating
and shocking to the ear : the yelling of cats, and the braying of
an ass, are not more disgustful. The voice of the goose is
trumpet-like, and clanking ; and once saved the Capitol at Rome,
as grave historians assert ; the hiss also of the gander is
formidable and full of menace, and "protective of his young."
Among ducks the sexual distinction of voice is remarkable ; for,

while the quack of the female is loud and sonorous, the voice of
the drake is inward and harsh, and feeble, and scarce discernible.
The cock turkey struts and gobbles to his mistress in a most
uncouth manner; he hath also a pert and petulant note when he
attacks his adversary.   When a hen turkey leads forth her
young brood she keeps a watchful eye; and if a bird of prey
appear, though ever so high in the air, the careful mother
announces the enemy with a little inward moan, and watches
him with a steady and attentive look; but, if he approach,
her note becomes earnest and alarming, and her outcries are
redoubled.

No inhabitants of the yard seem possessed of such a variety
of expression and so copious a language as common poultry.
Take a chicken of four or five days old, and hold it up to a
window where there are flies, and it will immediately seize its

RAVEN'S EGG.

prey, with little twitterings of complacency; but if you tender it
a wasp or a bee, at once its note becomes harsh, and expressive
of disapprobation and a sense of danger.   When a pullet is ready
to lay she intimates the event by a joyous soft and easy note.
Of all the occurrences of their life that of laying seems to be the
most important; for no sooner has a hen disburdened herself,
than she rushes forth with a clamorous kind of joy, which the
cock and the rest of his mistresses immediately adopt.   The
tumult is not confined to the family concerned, but catches from
yard to yard, and spreads to every homestead within hearing, till
at last the whole village is in an uproar.   As soon as a hen
becomes a mother her new relation demands a new language; she
then runs clucking and screaming about, and seems agitated,
as if possessed.   The father of the flock has also a considerable

vocabulary; if he finds food, he calls a favourite concubine to partake; and if a bird of prey passes over, with a warning voice he bids his family beware. The gallant chanticleer has, at command, his amorous phrases and his terms of defiance. But the sound by which he is best known is his crowing; by this he has been distinguished in all ages as the countryman's clock or larum, as the watchman that proclaims the divisions of the night. Thus the poet elegantly styles him:

> "— — the crested cock, whose clarion sounds
> The silent hours."

A neighbouring gentleman one summer had lost most of his chickens by a sparrow-hawk, that came gliding down between a faggot pile and the end of his house, to the place where the coops stood. The owner, inwardly vexed to see his flock thus diminishing, hung a setting net adroitly between the pile and the house, into which the caitiff dashed, and was entangled. Resentment suggested the law of retaliation; he therefore clipped the hawk's wings, cut off his talons, and, fixing a cork on his bill, threw him down among the brood-hens. Imagination cannot paint the scene that ensued; the expressions that fear, rage, and revenge inspired were new, or at least such as had been unnoticed before: the exasperated matrons upbraided, they execrated, they insulted, they triumphed. In a word, they never desisted from buffeting their adversary till they had torn him in a hundred pieces.

Selborne, *Sept.* 9, 1778.

LETTER LXXXVI.

TO THE HONOURABLE DAINES BARRINGTON.

> "— — — — — — — monstrent
> — — — — — — —
> Quid tantum oceano properent se tingere soles
> Hyberni: vel quæ tardis mora noctibus obstet."
> (VIRG. Georg. ii. 477–482.)

> "How winter suns in ocean plunge so soon,
> And what belates the tardy nights of June."

GENTLEMEN who have outlets might contrive to make ornament subservient to utility; a pleasing eye-trap might also contribute to promote science : an obelisk in a garden or park might be both an embellishment and a heliotrope.

Any person that is curious, and enjoys the advantage of a good horizon, might, with little trouble, make two heliotropes; the one for the winter, the other for the summer solstice : and these two erections might be constructed with very little expense ; for two pieces of timber framework, about ten or twelve feet high, and four feet broad at the base, close lined with plank, would answer the purpose.

The erection for the former should, if possible, be placed within sight of some window in the common sitting parlour ; because men, at that dead season of the year, are usually within doors at the close of the day ; while that for the latter might be fixed for any given spot in the garden or outlet : whence the owner might contemplate, in a fine summer's evening, the utmost extent that the sun makes to the northward at the season of the longest days. Now nothing would be necessary but to place these two objects with so much exactness, that the westerly limb of the sun, at setting, might but just clear the winter heliotrope to the west of it on the shortest ; the whole disc of the sun clearing the summer heliotrope to the north of it at the longest day.

By this simple expedient it would soon appear that there is no such thing, strictly speaking, as a solstice ; for, from the shortest day, the owner would, every clear evening, see the disc advancing, at its setting, to the westward of the object ; and, from the longest day, observe the sun retiring backwards every evening at its setting, towards the object westward, till, in a few nights, it would set quite behind it, and so by degrees to the west of it : for when the sun comes near the summer solstice, the whole disc of it would at first set behind the object ; after a time the northern limb would first appear, and so every night gradually more, till at length the whole diameter would set northward of it for about three nights ; but on the middle night of the three, sensibly more remote than the former or following. When receding from the summer tropic, it would continue more and more to be hidden every night, till at length it would descend behind the object again ; and so nightly more and more to the westward.

SELBORNE.

LETTER LXXXVII.

TO THE HONOURABLE DAINES BARRINGTON.

" — — — Mugire videbis
Sub pedibus terram, et descendere montibus ornos."
(VIRG. Æn. iv. 490, 491.)

" Earth bellows,
Trees leave their mountains at her potent call ;
Beneath her footsteps groans the trembling ball."
(PITT.)

WHEN I was a boy I used to read, with astonishment and implicit assent, accounts in Baker's " Chronicle " of walking hills and travelling mountains.   John Philips, in his " Cyder," alludes to the credit given to such stories with a delicate but quaint vein of humour peculiar to the author of the " Splendid Shilling : "

"I nor advise, nor reprehend the choice
Of Marcley Hill ; the apple no where finds
A kinder mould ; yet 'tis unsafe to trust
Deceitful ground : who knows but that once more
This mount may journey, and his present site
Forsaken, to thy neighbour's bounds transfer
Thy goodly plants, affording matter strange
For law debates ! "

But, when I came to consider better, I began to suspect that though our hills may never have journeyed far, yet that the ends of many of them have slipped and fallen away at distant periods, leaving the cliffs bare and abrupt.   This seems to have been the case with Nore and Whetham Hills ; and especially with the ridge between Harteley Park and Wardleham, where the ground has slid into vast swellings and furrows ; and lies still in such romantic confusion as cannot be accounted for from any other cause.   A strange event, that happened not long since, justifies our suspicions ; which, though it befell not within the limits of this parish, yet, as it was within the hundred of Selborne, and as the circumstances were singular, may fairly claim a place in this work.

The months of January and February, in the year 1774, were remarkable for great melting snows and vast gluts of rain ; so that by the end of the latter month the land-springs, or lavants, began to prevail, and to be near as high as in the memorable winter of 1764. The beginning of March also went on in the same tenor; when, in the night between the 8th and 9th of that month, a considerable part of the great woody hanger at Hawkley was torn from its place, and fell down, leaving a high free-stone cliff naked and bare, and resembling the steep side of a chalk-pit. It appears that this huge fragment, being perhaps sapped and undermined by waters, foundered, and was ingulfed, going down in a perpendicular direction; for a gate which stood in the field, on the top of the hill, after sinking with its posts for thirty or forty feet, remained in so true and upright a position as to open and shut with great exactness, just as in its first situation. Several oaks also are still standing, and in a state of vegetation, after taking the same desperate leap. That great part of this prodigious mass was absorbed in some gulf below is plain also from the inclining ground at the bottom of the hill, which is free and unincumbered; but would have been buried in heaps of rubbish had the fragment parted and fallen forward. About a hundred yards from the foot of this hanging coppice stood a cottage by the side of a lane; and two hundred yards lower, on the other side of the lane, was a farm-house, in which lived a labourer and his family; and, just by, a stout new barn. The cottage was inhabited by an old woman and her son, and his wife. These people in the evening, which was very dark and tempestuous, observed that the brick floors of their kitchens began to heave and part; and that the walls seemed to open, and the roofs to crack: but they all agree that no tremor of the ground, indicating an earthquake, was ever felt; only that the wind continued to make a most tremendous roaring in the woods and hangers. The miserable inhabitants, not daring to go to bed, remained in the utmost solicitude and confusion, expecting every moment to be buried under the ruins of their shattered edifices. When day-light came they were at leisure to contemplate the devastations of the night: they then found that a deep rift, or chasm, had opened under their houses, and torn them, as it were, in two; and that one end of the barn had suffered in a similar manner; that a pond near the cottage had undergone a strange reverse, becoming deep at the shallow end, and so *vice versâ;* that many large oaks were removed out of their perpendicular, some thrown down, and some fallen into the heads of neighbouring trees; and that a gate was thrust forward, with its hedge, full six feet, so as to require a new track to be made to it. From the foot of the cliff the general course

of the ground, which is pasture, inclines in a moderate descent
for half a mile, and is interspersed with some hillocks, which
were rifted, in every direction, as well towards the great
woody hanger as from it.   In the first pasture the deep clefts
began : and running across the lane, and under the buildings,
made such vast shelves that the road was impassable for some
time; and so over to an arable field on the other side, which
was strangely torn and disordered.   The second pasture field,
being more soft ·and springy, was protruded forward without
many fissures in the turf, which was raised in long ridges
resembling graves, lying at right angles to the motion.   At the
bottom of this inclosure the soil and turf rose many feet against
some oaks that obstructed their farther course, and terminated
this awful commotion.

The perpendicular height of the precipice, in general, is
twenty-three yards; the length of the lapse, or slip, as seen
from the fields below, one hundred and eighty-one; and a
partial fall, concealed in the coppice, extends seventy yards
more : so that the total length of this fragment that fell was
two hundred and fifty-one yards.   About fifty acres of land
suffered from this violent convulsion ; two houses were entirely
destroyed ; one end of a new barn was left in ruins, the walls
being cracked through the very stones that composed them ; a
hanging coppice was changed to a naked rock ; and some grass
grounds and an arable field so broken and rifted by the chasms
as to be rendered, for a time, neither fit for the plough nor safe
for pasturage, till considerable labour and expense had been
bestowed in levelling the surface and filling in the gaping
fissures.

Selborne.

LETTER LXXXVIII.

TO THE HONOURABLE DAINES BARRINGTON.

"— — — resonant arbusta — — —."

(Virg. Ecl. ii. 13.)

" The groves resound."

There is a steep abrupt pasture field interspersed with furze
close to the back of this village, well known by the name of
the Short Lithe, consisting of a rocky dry soil, and inclining to

the afternoon sun.   This spot abounds with *Gryllus campestris*, or field-cricket, which, though frequent in these parts, is by no means a common insect in many other counties.

As their cheerful summer cry cannot but draw the attention of a naturalist, I have often gone down to examine the economy of these *grylli*, and study their mode of life : but they are so shy and cautious, that it is no easy matter to get a sight of them ; for, feeling a person's footsteps as he advances, they stop short in the midst of their song, and retire backward nimbly into their burrows, where they lurk till all suspicion of danger is over.

At first we attempted to dig them out with a spade, but without any great success ; for either we could not get to the bottom of the hole, which often terminated under a great stone ; or else, in breaking up the ground, we inadvertently squeezed the poor insect to death.   Out of one so bruised we took a multitude of eggs, which were long and narrow, of a yellow colour, and covered with a very tough skin.   By this accident we learned to distinguish the male from the female ; the former of which is shining black, with a golden stripe across his shoulders ; the latter is more dusky, more capacious about the abdomen, and carries a long sword-shaped weapon at her tail, which probably is the instrument with which she deposits her eggs in their receptacles.

Where violent methods will not avail, more gentle means will often succeed ; and so it proved in the present case ; for, though a spade be too boisterous and rough an implement, a pliant stock of grass, gently insinuated into the caverns, will probe their windings to the bottom, and quickly bring out the inhabitant ; and thus the humane inquirer may gratify his curiosity without injuring the object of it.   It is remarkable that, though these insects are furnished with long legs behind, and brawny thighs for leaping, like grasshoppers ; yet, when driven from their holes they show no activity, but crawl along in a shiftless manner, so as easily to be taken : and again, though provided with a curious apparatus of wings, yet they never exert them when there seems to be the greatest occasion. The males only make that thrilling noise perhaps out of rivalry and emulation, as is the case with many animals which exert some sprightly note during their breeding time : it is raised by a brisk friction of one wing against the other.   They are solitary beings, living singly male or female, each as it may happen; but there must be a time when the sexes have some intercourse, and then the wings may be useful perhaps during the hours of night. When the males meet they will fight fiercely, as I found by some which I put into the crevices of a dry stone wall, where I should have been glad to have made them settle. For though they seemed distressed by being taken out of their knowledge, yet the first that got possession of the chinks would seize on any that were obtruded upon them with a vast row of serrated fangs. With their strong jaws, toothed like the shears of a lobster's claws, they perforate and round their curious regular cells, having no fore-claws to dig, like the mole-cricket. When taken in hand I could not but wonder that they never offered to defend themselves, though armed with such formidable weapons. Of such herbs as grow before the mouths of their burrows they eat indiscriminately; and on a little platform, which they make just by, they drop their dung; and never, in the day time, seem to stir more than two or three inches from home. Sitting in the entrance of their caverns they chirp all night as well as day, from the middle of the month of May to the middle of July; and in hot weather, when they are most vigorous, they make the hills echo; and, in the stiller hours of darkness, may be heard to a considerable distance. In the beginning of the season their notes are more faint and inward; but become louder as the summer advances, and so die away again by degrees.

Sounds do not always give us pleasure according to their sweetness and melody; nor do harsh sounds always displease. We are more apt to be captivated or disgusted with the associations which they promote, than with the notes themselves. Thus the shrilling of the field-cricket, though sharp and stridulous, yet marvellously delights some hearers, filling their minds with a train of summer ideas of everything that is rural, verdurous and joyous.

About the 10th of March the crickets appear at the mouths of their cells, which they then open and bore, and shape very elegantly. They cast their skins in April which are then seen lying at the mouths of their holes. All that ever I have seen at that season were in their pupa state, and had only the rudiments of wings, lying under a skin or coat, which must be cast before the insect can arrive at its perfect state; from whence I should suppose that the old ones of last year do not always survive the winter. In August their holes begin to be obliterated, and the insects are seen no more till spring.

Not many summers ago I endeavoured to transplant a colony to the terrace in my garden, by boring deep holes in the sloping turf. The new inhabitants stayed some time, and fed and sung; but wandered away by degrees, and were heard at a farther distance every morning; so that it appears that in this emergency they made use of their wings to return to the spot from which they were taken.

One of these crickets, when confined in a paper cage and set in the sun, and supplied with plants moistened with water, will feed and thrive, and become so merry and loud as to be irksome in the same room where a person is sitting : if the plants are not wetted it will die.

SELBORNE.

LETTER LXXXIX.

TO THE HONOURABLE DAINES BARRINGTON.

" Far from all resort of mirth
Save the cricket on the hearth."
MILTON'S *Il Penseroso*.

WHILE many other insects must be sought after in fields, and woods, and waters, the *Gryllus domesticus*, or house-cricket, resides altogether within our dwellings, intruding itself upon our notice whether we will or no. This species delights in new-built houses, being, like the spider, pleased with the moisture of the walls; and besides, the softness of the mortar enables them to burrow and mine between the joints of the bricks or stones, and to open communications from one room to another. They are particularly fond of kitchens and bakers' ovens, on account of their perpetual warmth.

Tender insects that live abroad either enjoy only the short period of one summer, or else doze away the cold uncomfortable months in profound slumbers; but these, residing as it were in a torrid zone, are always alert and merry: a good Christmas fire is to them like the heats of the dog-days. Though they are frequently heard by day, yet is their natural time of motion only in the night. As soon as it grows dusk, the chirping increases, and they come running forth, ranging from the size of a flea to that of their full stature. As one should suppose from the burning atmosphere which they inhabit, they are a thirsty race, and show a great propensity for liquids, being found frequently drowned in pans of water, milk, broth, or the like. Whatever is moist they affect; and therefore often gnaw holes in wet woollen stockings and aprons that are hung to the fire: they are the housewife's barometer, foretelling her when it will rain; and they prognosticate sometimes, she thinks, good or ill luck; the death of near relations, or the approach of an absent lover. By being the constant companions of her solitary hours, they naturally become the objects of her superstition. These crickets are not only very thirsty, but very voracious; for they will eat the scummings of pots, and yeast, salt, and crumbs of bread; and any kitchen offal or sweepings. In the summer we have observed them to fly out of the windows when it became dusk, and over the neighbouring roofs. This feat of activity accounts for the sudden manner in which they often leave their haunts, as it does for the method by which they come to houses where they were not know before. It is remarkable, that many sorts of insects seem never to use their wings but when they have a mind to shift their quarters and settle new colonies. When in the air they move *volatu undoso*, in "waves or curves," like woodpeckers, opening and shutting their wings at every stroke, and so are always rising or sinking.

When they increase to a great degree, as they did once in the house where I am now writing, they become noisome pests, flying into the candles, and dashing into people's faces; but may be blasted and destroyed by gunpowder discharged into their crevices and crannies.

[In November, after the servants are gone to bed, the kitchen hearth swarms with minute crickets not so large as fleas, which must have been lately hatched, so that these domestic insects, cherished by the influence of a constant and large fire, regard not the season of the year, but produce their young at a time when their congeners are either dead or laid up for the winter, passing away the uncomfortable months in a state of torpidity.

When house-crickets are out and running about a room in the night, if surprised by a candle, they utter two or three shrill notes, as if it were a signal to their fellows, that they may escape to their crannies and lurking-places to avoid danger.]

In families, at such times, they are, like Pharaoh's plague of frogs,—in their bedchambers, and upon their beds, and in their ovens, and in their kneading-troughs.[1] Their shrilling noise is occasioned by a brisk attrition of their wings. Cats catch hearth-crickets, and play with them as they do with mice, and then devour them. Crickets may be destroyed, like wasps, by phials half filled with beer, or any other liquid, and set in their haunts; for, being always eager to drink, they will crowd in till the bottles are full.

SELBORNE.

LETTER XC.

TO THE HONOURABLE DAINES BARRINGTON.

How diversified are the modes of life not only of incongruous but even of congenerous animals; and yet their specific distinctions are not more various than their propensities. Thus, while the field-cricket delights in sunny dry banks, and the house-cricket rejoices amidst the glowing heat of the kitchen hearth or oven, the *Gryllus gryllo talpa* (the mole-cricket) haunts moist meadows, and frequents the sides of ponds and banks of streams, performing all its functions in a swampy wet soil. With a pair of fore-feet curiously adapted to the purpose, it burrows and works under ground like the mole, raising a ridge as it proceeds, but seldom throwing up hillocks.

As mole-crickets often infest gardens by the sides of canals, they are unwelcome guests to the gardener, raising up ridges in their subterraneous progress, and rendering the walks unsightly. If they take to the kitchen quarters, they occasion great damage among the plants and roots, by destroying whole beds of cabbages, young legumes, and flowers. When dug out they seem very slow and helpless, and make no use of their wings by day; but at night they come abroad, and make long excursions, as I have been convinced by finding stragglers, in a morning, in improbable places. In fine weather, about the middle of April, and just at the close of day, they begin to solace themselves with a low, dull, jarring note, continued for a long time without interruption, and not unlike the chattering of the fern-owl, or goat-sucker, but more inward.

[1] Exod. viii. 3.

About the beginning of May they lay their eggs, as I was once an eye-witness : for a gardener at a house where I was on a visit, happening to be mowing, on the 6th of that month, by the side of a canal, his scythe struck too deep, pared off a large piece of turf, and laid open to view a curious scene of domestic economy :

> "— — — — ingentem lato dedit ore fenestram :
> Apparet domus intus, et atria longa patescunt :
> Apparent — — — penetralia."
> (VIRG. Æn. ii. 481–483.)

> "A yawning breach of monstrous size he made :
> The inmost house is now to light displayed :
> The admitted light with sudden lustre falls
> On the long galleries and the splendid halls."
> (DRYDEN.)

There were many caverns and winding passages leading to a kind of chamber, neatly smoothed and rounded, and about the size of a moderate snuff-box. Within this secret nursery were deposited near a hundred eggs of a dirty yellow colour, and enveloped in a tough skin, but too lately excluded to contain any rudiments of young, being full of a viscous substance. The eggs lay but shallow, and within the influence of the sun, just under a little heap of fresh-moved mould, like that which is raised by ants.

When mole-crickets fly they move *cursu undoso*, rising and falling in curves, like the other species mentioned before. In different parts of this kingdom people call them fen-crickets, churr-worms, and eve-churrs, all very apposite names.

Anatomists, who have examined the intestines of these insects, astonish me with their accounts ; for they say that, from the structure, position, and number of their stomachs, or maws, there seems to be good reason to suppose that this and the two former species ruminate or chew the cud like many quadrupeds !

SELBORNE.

LETTER XCI.

TO THE HONOURABLE DAINES BARRINGTON.

IT is now more than forty years that I have paid some attention to the ornithology of this district, without being able to exhaust the subject: new occurrences still arise as long as any inquiries are kept alive.

In the last week of last month five of those most rare birds, too uncommon to have obtained an English name, but known to naturalists by the terms of *himantopus*, or *loripes*, and *Charadrius himantopus*, were shot upon the verge of Frinsham pond, a large lake belonging to the Bishop of Winchester, and lying between Wolmer Forest and the town of Farnham, in the county of Surrey. The pond-keeper says there were three brace in the flock; but that, after he had satisfied his curiosity, he suffered the sixth to remain unmolested. One of these specimens I procured, and found the length of the legs to be so extraordinary, that, at first sight, one might have supposed the shanks had been fastened on to impose on the credulity of the beholder: they were legs in *caricatura;* and had we seen such proportions on a Chinese or Japan screen we should have made large allowances for the fancy of the draughtsman. These birds are of the plover family, and might with propriety be called the stilt plovers. Brisson, under that idea, gives them the apposite name of *l'échasse.* My specimen, when drawn and stuffed with pepper, weighed only four ounces and a quarter, though the naked part of the thigh measured three inches and a half, and the legs four inches and a half. Hence we may safely assert that these birds exhibit, weight for inches, incomparably the greatest length of legs of any known bird. The flamingo, for instance, is one of the most long-legged birds, and yet it bears no manner of proportion to the *himantopus;* for a cock flamingo weighs, at an average, about four pounds avoirdupois; and his legs and thighs measure usually about twenty inches. But four pounds are fifteen times and a fraction more than four ounces and one quarter; and if four ounces and a quarter have eight inches of legs, four pounds must have one hundred and twenty inches and a fraction of legs; viz., somewhat more than ten feet; such a monstrous proportion as the world never saw! If you should try the experiment in still larger birds the disparity would still increase. It must be

matter of great curiosity to see the stilt plover move ; to observe
how it can wield such a length of lever with such feeble muscles
as the thighs seem to be furnished with.   At best one should
expect it to be but a bad walker : but what adds to the wonder
is, that it has no back toe.   Now without that steady prop to
support its steps it must be liable, in speculation, to perpetual
vacillations, and seldom able to preserve the true centre of
gravity.

The old name of *himantopus* is taken from Pliny ; and, by an
awkward metaphor, implies that the legs are as slender and
pliant as if cut out of a thong of leather.   Neither Willughby
nor Ray, in all their curious researches, either at home or abroad,
ever saw this bird.   Mr. Pennant never met with it in all Great
Britain, but observed it often in the cabinets of the curious at

LAPWING OR PLOVER'S EGG.

Paris.   Hasselquist says that it migrates to Egypt in the autumn :
and a most accurate observer of nature has assured me that he
has found it on the banks of the streams in Andalusia.

Our writers record it to have been found only twice in Great
Britain.   From all these relations it plainly appears that these
long-legged plovers are birds of South Europe, and rarely visit
our island ; and when they do are wanderers and stragglers, and
impelled to make so distant and northern an excursion from
motives or accidents for which we are not able to account.
One thing may fairly be deduced, that these birds come over to
us from the Continent, since nobody can suppose that a species
not noticed once in an age, and of such a remarkable make, can
constantly breed unobserved in this kingdom.

SELBORNE, *May* 7, 1779.

LETTER XCII.

TO THE HONOURABLE DAINES BARRINGTON.

THE old Sussex tortoise, that I have mentioned to you so often, is become my property. I dug it out of its winter dormitory in March last, when it was enough awakened to express its resentments by hissing; and packing it in a box with earth, carried it eighty miles in post-chaises. The rattle and hurry of the journey so perfectly roused it that, when I turned it out on a border, it walked twice down to the bottom of my garden; however, in the evening, the weather being cold, it buried itself in the loose mould, and continues still concealed.

As it will be under my eye, I shall now have an opportunity of enlarging my observations on its mode of life, and propensities; and perceive already that towards the time of coming forth, it opens a breathing-place in the ground near its head, requiring, I conclude, a freer respiration as it becomes more alive. This creature not only goes under the earth from the middle of November to the middle of April, but sleeps great part of the summer; for it goes to bed in the longest days at four in the afternoon, and often does not stir in the morning till late. Besides, it retires to rest for every shower; and does not move at all in wet days.

When one reflects on the state of this strange being, it is a matter of wonder to find that Providence should bestow such a profusion of days, such a seeming waste of longevity, on a reptile that appears to relish it so little as to squander more than two-thirds of its existence in a joyless stupor, and be lost to all sensation for months together in the profoundest of slumbers.

While I was writing this letter, a moist and warm afternoon, with the thermometer at fifty, brought forth troops of shell-snails, and, at the same juncture, the tortoise heaved up the mould and put out his head; and the next morning came forth, as it were raised from the dead; and walked about till four in the afternoon. This was a curious coincidence! a very amusing occurrence! to see such a similarity of feelings between the two φερεοίκοι! for so the Greeks call both the shell-snail and the tortoise.

Because we call "the old family tortoise" an abject reptile, we

Q

are too apt to undervalue his abilities, and depreciate his powers
of instinct.   Yet he is, as Mr. Pope says of his lord,

" — — — Much too wise to walk into a well : "

and has so much discernment as not to fall down a ha-ha :
but to stop and withdraw from the brink with the readiest
precaution.

Though he loves warm weather, he avoids the hot sun ;
because his thick shell when once heated, would, as the poet says
of solid armour—" scald with safety."   He therefore spends the
more sultry hours under the umbrella of a large cabbage-leaf, or
amidst the waving forests of an asparagus-bed.

But as he avoids heat in the summer, so, in the decline of the
year, he improves the faint autumnal beams by getting within
the reflection of a fruit-wall ; and, though he never has read that
planes inclining to the horizon receive a greater share of warmth,
he inclines his shell, by tilting it against the wall, to collect and
admit every feeble ray.

Pitiable seems the condition of this poor embarrassed reptile :
to be cased in a suit of ponderous armour which he cannot lay
aside ; to be imprisoned, as it were, within his own shell, must
preclude, we should suppose, all activity and disposition for
enterprise.   Yet there is a season of the year (usually the
beginning of June) when his exertions are remarkable.   He then
walks on tiptoe, and is stirring by five in the morning ; and,
traversing the garden, examines every wicket and interstice in
the fences, through which he will escape if possible ; and often has
eluded the care of the gardener, and wandered to some distant
field.   The motives that impel him to undertake these rambles
seem to be of the amorous kind : his fancy then becomes intent
on sexual attachments, which transport him beyond his usual
gravity, and induce him to forget for a time his ordinary solemn
deportment.[1]

[1] "We think we see the worthy pastor," writes the late Mr. Broderip,
"looking down with the air of the melancholy Jaques on his favourite, as
those thoughts occur to him.   It is very possible that Cupid may have been
bestriding the reptile.   White's description looks like the restlessness of
passion : but the love of liberty, and not improbably an annual migratory
impulse to search for fresh pasture, may have been the prevailing motive."
The tenacity of life with which the *testudinata* are gifted is hardly credible.
Rede's operations would have been instant death to any more warm-blooded
animal.   He opened the skull of a land tortoise, and, removing every particle

Summer birds are, this cold and backward spring, unusually late : I have seen but one swallow yet. This conformity with the weather convinces me more and more that they sleep in the winter.

SELBORNE, *April* 21, 1780.

LETTER XCIII.

TO THOMAS PENNANT, ESQ.

A PAIR of honey-buzzards—*Buteo apivorus*, Linn., sive *Vespivorus*, Raii—built them a large shallow nest, composed of twigs, and lined with dead beechen leaves, upon a tall slender beech near the middle of Selborne Hanger, in the summer of 1780. In the middle of the month of June a bold boy climbed this tree, though standing on so steep and dizzy a situation, and brought down an egg, the only one in the nest, which had been sat on for some time, and contained the embryo of a young bird. The egg was smaller, and not so round as those of the common buzzard ; was dotted at each end with small red spots, and surrounded in the middle with a broad bloody zone.

The hen-bird was shot, and answered exactly to Mr. Ray's description of that species ; had a black cere, short thick legs, and a long tail. When on the wing this species may be easily distinguished from the common buzzard by its hawk-like appearance, small head, wings not so blunt, and longer tail. This specimen contained in its craw some limbs of frogs and many grey snails without shells. The irides of the eyes of this bird were of a beautiful bright yellow colour.

About the 10th of July in the same summer a pair of sparrow-hawks bred in an old crow's nest on a low beech in the same hanger ; and as their brood, which was numerous, began to grow up, became so daring and ravenous, that they were a terror

of brain, cleaned the cavity out. It still groped its way about freely, for with the brain its sight departed ; but it lived from November till May. After many other equally cruel experiments, one November he cut off the head of a large tortoise, and it lived for twenty-three days. But, retiring within its shell, it has its privileges.

> "The tortoise securely from danger does well
> When he tucks up his head and his tail in his shell."

Q 2

to all the dames in the village that had chickens or ducklings under their care. A boy climbed the tree, and found the young so fledged that they all escaped from him; but discovered that a good house had been kept: the larder was well stored with provisions; for he brought down a young blackbird, jay, and house-martin, all clean-picked, and some half devoured. The old bird had been observed to make sad havoc for some days among the new-flown swallows and martins, which, being but lately out of their nests, had not acquired those powers and command of wing that enable them when more mature to set such enemies at defiance.

SPARROW-HAWK'S EGG.

LETTER XCIV.

TO THOMAS PENNANT, ESQ.

EVERY incident that occasions a renewal of our correspondence will ever be pleasing and agreeable to me.

As to the wild wood-pigeon, the *œnas*, or *vinago*, of Ray, I am much of your mind; and see no reason for making it the origin of the common house-dove: but suppose those that have advanced that opinion may have been misled by another appellation, often given to the *œnas*, which is that of stock-dove.

Unless the stock-dove in the winter varies greatly in manners from itself in summer, no species seems more unlikely to be domesticated, and to make a house-dove. We very rarely see the latter settle on trees at all, nor does it ever haunt the woods; but the former, as long as it stays with us—from November perhaps to February—lives the same wild life with the ring-dove,

Palumbus torquatus; frequents coppices and groves, supports itself chiefly by mast, and delights to roost in the tallest beeches. Could it be known in what manner stock-doves build, the doubt would be settled with me at once, provided they construct their nests on trees, like the ring-dove, as I much suspect they do.

You received, you say, last spring a stock-dove from Sussex, and are informed that they sometimes breed in that county. But why did not your correspondent determine the place of its nidification, whether on rocks, cliffs, or trees? If he was not an adroit ornithologist I should doubt the fact, because people with us perpetually confound the stock-dove with the ring-dove.

For my own part I readily concur with you in supposing that house-doves are derived from the small blue rock-pigeon, *Columba livia,* for many reasons. In the first place the wild stock-dove is manifestly larger than the common house-dove, against the usual rule of domestication, which generally enlarges the breed. Again, those two remarkable black spots on the *remiges* of each wing of the stock-dove, which are so characteristic of the species, would not, one should think, be totally lost by its being reclaimed; but would often break out among its descendants. But what is worth a hundred arguments is, the instance you give in Sir Roger Mostyn's house-doves in Caernarvonshire; which, though tempted by plenty of food and gentle treatment, can never be prevailed on to inhabit their cote for any time; but as soon as they begin to breed, betake themselves to the fastnesses of Ormshead, and deposit their young in safety amidst the inaccessible caverns and precipices of that stupendous promontory. "You may drive nature out with a pitchfork, but she will always return:"

"Naturam expellas furcâ . . . tamen usque recurret."

I have consulted a sportsman, now in his seventy-eighth year, who tells me that fifty or sixty years back, when the beechen woods were much more extensive than at present, the number of wood-pigeons was astonishing; that he has often killed near twenty in a day; and that with a long wild-fowl piece he has shot seven or eight at a time on the wing as they came wheeling over his head; he moreover adds, which I was not aware of, that often there were among them little parties of small blue doves, which he calls rockiers. The food of these numberless emigrants was beech-mast and some acorns; and particularly barley. which they collected in the stubbles. But of late years,

since the vast increase of turnips, that vegetable has furnished a
great part of their support in hard weather; and the holes they
pick in these roots greatly damage the crop. From this food
their flesh has contracted a rancidness which occasions them to
be rejected by nicer judges of eating, who thought them before
a delicate dish. They were shot not only as they were feeding
in the fields, and especially in snowy weather, but also at the
close of the evening, by men who lay in ambush among the
woods and groves, to kill them as they came in to roost. These
are the principal circumstances relating to this wonderful internal
migration, which with us takes place towards the end of November,
and ceases early in the spring. Last winter we had in Selborne
high-wood about a hundred of these doves; but in former times
the flocks were so vast, not only with us but all the district
round, that on mornings and evenings they traversed the air,

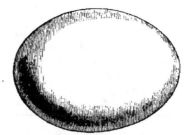

WOOD-PIGEON'S EGG.

like rooks, in strings, reaching for a mile together. When they
thus rendezvoused here by thousands, if they happened to be
suddenly roused from their roost-trees on an evening,

> "Their rising all at once was like the sound
> Of thunder heard remote."

It will by no means be foreign to the present purpose to add,
that I had a relation in this neighbourhood who made it a practice, for a time, whenever he could procure the eggs of a ring-
dove, to place them under a pair of doves that were sitting in his
own pigeon-house; hoping thereby, if he could bring about a
coalition, to enlarge his breed, and teach his own doves to beat
out into the woods and to support themselves by mast; the plan
was plausible, but something always interrupted the success;

for though the birds were usually hatched, and sometimes grew to half their size, yet none ever arrived at maturity. I myself have seen these foundlings in their nest displaying a strange ferocity of nature, so as scarcely to bear to be looked at, and snapping with their bills by way of menace. In short, they always died, perhaps from want of proper sustenance; but the owner thought that by their fierce and wild demeanour they frighted their foster-mothers, and so were starved.

Virgil, as a familiar occurrence, by way of simile, describes a dove haunting the cavern of a rock in such engaging numbers, that I cannot refrain from quoting the passage :—

> "Qualis speluncâ subito commota Columba,
> Cui domus, et dulces latebroso in pumice nidi,
> Fertul in arva volans, plausumque exterrita pennis
> Dat tecto ingentem—mox aere lapsa quieto,
> Radit iter liquidum, celeres neque commovet alas."
>
> (VIRG. *Æn.* v. 213—217.)

> "As when a dove her rocky hold forsakes,
> Roused, in a fright her sounding wings she shakes ;
> The cavern rings with clattering :—out she flies,
> And leaves her callow care, and cleaves the skies ;
> At first she flutters :—but at length she springs
> To smoother flight, and shoots upon her wings."
>
> (DRYDEN's *Translation.*)

SELBORNE, *Nov.* 30, 1780.

LETTER XCV.

TO THE HONOURABLE DAINES BARRINGTON.

I HAVE now read your miscellanies through with much care and satisfaction ; and am to return you my best thanks for the honourable mention made in them of me as a naturalist, which I wish I may deserve.

In some former letters I expressed my suspicions that many of the house-martins do not depart in the winter far from this village. I therefore determined to make some search about the south-east end of the hill, where I imagined they might slumber out the uncomfortable months of winter. But supposing that the examination would be made to the best advantage in the spring, and observing that no martins had appeared by the 11th

of April last, on that day I employed some men to explore the
shrubs and cavities of the suspected spot. The persons took
pains, but without any success; however, a remaikable incident
occurred in the midst of our pursuit—while the labourers were
at work a house-martin, the first that had been seen this year,
came down the village in the sight of several people, and went
at once into a nest, where it stayed a short time, and then flew
over the houses; for some days after no martins were observed,
not till the 16th of April, and then only a pair. Martins in
general were remarkably late this year.

> "— — — — daffodils
> That come before the swallow dares, and take
> The winds of March with beauty."

SELBORNE, *Sept.* 3, .1781.

LETTER XCVI.

TO THE HONOURABLE DAINES BARRINGTON.

I HAVE just met with a circumstance respecting swifts which
furnishes an exception to the whole tenor of my observations
ever since I have bestowed any attention on that species of
hirundines. Our swifts, in general, withdrew this year about
the first day of August, all save one pair, which in two or three
days was reduced to a single bird. The perseverance of this individual made me suspect that the strongest of motives, that of
an attachment to her young, could alone occasion so late a stay.
I watched therefore till the 24th of August, and then discovered
that under the eaves of the church she attended upon two young,
which were fledged, and now put out their white chins from
a crevice. These remained till the 27th, looking more alert
every day, and seeming to long to be on the wing. After
this day they were missing at once; nor could I ever observe
them with their dam coursing round the church in the act of
learning to fly, as the first broods evidently do. On the 31st
I caused the eaves to be searched; but we found in the nest
only two callow, dead, stinking swifts, on which a second nest
had been formed. This double nest was full of the black
shining cases of the *Hippoboscæ hirundinis*.

The following remarks on this unusual incident are obvious. The first is, that though it may be disagreeable to swifts to remain beyond the beginning of August, yet that they can subsist longer is undeniable. The second is, that this uncommon event, as it was owing to the loss of the first brood, so it corroborates my former remark, that swifts breed regularly but once; since, was the contrary the case, the occurrence above could neither be new nor rare.

P.S.—One swift was seen at Lyndon, in the county of Rutland, in 1780, so late as the 3rd of September.

SELBORNE, *Scpt.* 9, 1781.

LETTER XCVII.

TO THE HONOURABLE DAINES BARRINGTON.

As I have sometimes known you make inquiries about several kinds of insects, I shall here send you an account of one sort which I little expected to have found in this kingdom. I have often observed that one particular part of a vine growing on the walls of my house was covered in the autumn with a black dust-like appearance, on which the flies fed eagerly; and that the shoots and leaves thus affected did not thrive; nor did the fruit ripen. To this substance I applied my glasses; but could not discover that it had anything to do with animal life, as I at first expected: but, upon a closer examination behind the larger boughs, we were surprised to find that they were coated over with husky shells, from whose sides proceeded a cotton-like substance, surrounding a multitude of eggs. This curious and uncommon production put me upon recollecting what I have heard and read concerning the *Coccus vitis viniferæ* of Linnæus, which, in the south of Europe, infests many vines, and is a horrid and loathsome pest. As soon as I had turned to the accounts given of this insect, I saw at once that it swarmed on my vine; and did not appear to have been at all checked by the preceding winter, which had been uncommonly severe.

Not being then at all aware that it had anything to do with England, I was much inclined to think that it came from Gibraltar among the many boxes and packages of plants and birds which I had formerly received from thence; and especially as the vine infested grew immediately under my study window, where I usually kept my specimens. True it is that I had received nothing from thence for some years; but as insects are, we know, conveyed from oné country to another in a very unexpected manner, and have a wonderful power of maintaining their existence till they fall into a *nidus* proper for their support and increase, I cannot but suspect still that these *cocci* came to me originally from Andalusia. Yet, all the while, candour obliges me to confess that Mr. Lightfoot has written me word that he once, and but once, saw these insects on a vine at Weymouth in Dorsetshire; which, it is here to be observed, is a sea-port town, to which the *coccus* might be conveyed by shipping.

As many of my readers may possibly never have heard of this strange and unusual insect, I shall here transcribe a passage from a natural history of Gibraltar, written by the Reverend John White, late vicar of Blackburn in Lancashire, but not yet published :—

"In the year 1770 a vine which grew on the east side of my house, and which had produced the finest crops of grapes for years past, was suddenly overspread on all the woody branches with large lumps of a white fibrous substance resembling spiders' webs, or rather raw cotton. It was of a very clammy quality, sticking fast to everything that touched it, and capable of being spun into long threads. At first I suspected it to be the product of spiders, but could find none. Nothing was to be seen connected with it but many brown oval husky shells, which by no means looked like insects, but rather resembled bits of the dry bark of the vine. The tree had a plentiful crop of grapes set, when this pest appeared upon it; but the fruit was manifestly injured by this foul incumbrance. It remained all the summer, still increasing, and loaded the woody and bearing branches to a vast degree. I often pulled off great quantities by handfuls: but it was so slimy and tenacious that it could by no means be cleared. The grapes never filled to their natural perfection, but turned watery and vapid. Upon perusing the works afterwards of M. de Reaumur, I found this matter perfectly described and accounted for. Those husky shells, which I had observed, were no other than the female *coccus*, from whose sides this cotton-like substance exudes, and serves as a covering and security for their eggs."

To this account I think proper to add, that, though the

female *cocci* are stationary, and seldom remove from the place to which they stick, yet the male is a winged insect; and that the black dust which I saw was undoubtedly the excrement of the females, which is eaten by ants as well as flies. Though the utmost severity of our winter did not destroy these insects, yet the attention of the gardener in a summer or two has entirely relieved my vine from this filthy annoyance.

As we have remarked above that insects are often conveyed from one country to another in a very unaccountable manner, I shall here mention an emigration of small *aphides*, which was observed in the village of Selborne no longer ago than August the 1st, 1785.

At about three o'clock in the afternoon of that day, which was very hot, the people of this village were surprised by a shower of *aphides*, or smother-flies, which fell in these parts. Those that were walking in the streets at that juncture found themselves covered with these insects, which settled also on the hedges and gardens, blackening all the vegetables where they alighted. My annuals were discoloured with them, and the stalks of a bed of onions were quite coated over for six days after. These armies were then, no doubt, in a state of emigration, and shifting their quarters; and might have come, as far as we know, from the great hop-plantations of Kent or Sussex, the wind being all that day in the easterly quarter. They were observed at the same time in great clouds about Farnham, and all along the vale from Farnham to Alton.[1]

SELBORNE, *March* 9, 1775.

LETTER XCVIII.[2]

TO THE HONOURABLE DAINES BARRINGTON.

WHEN I happen to visit a family where gold and silver fishes are kept in a glass bowl, I am always pleased with the occurrence, because it offers me an opportunity of observing the actions and propensities of those beings with whom I can be little acquainted

---

[1] For various methods by which several insects shift their quarters, see Derham's "Physico-Theology."

[2] First published in the *Gentleman's Magazine* for 1786, under the signature V.

in their natural state. Not long since I spent a fortnight at the house of a friend where there was such a *vivarium*, to which I paid no small attention, taking every occasion to remark what passed within its narrow limits. It was here that I first observed the manner in which fishes die. As soon as the creature sickens, the head sinks lower and lower, and it stands as it were on its head; till, getting weaker, and losing all poise, the tail turns over, and at last it floats on the surface of the water with its belly uppermost. The reason why fishes, when dead, swim in that manner is very obvious; because, when the body is no longer balanced by the fins of the belly, the broad muscular back preponderates by its own gravity, and turns the belly uppermost, as lighter from its being a cavity, and because it contains the swimming-bladders, which contribute to render it buoyant. Some that delight in gold and silver fishes have adopted a notion that they need no aliment. True it is that they will subsist for a long time without any apparent food but what they can collect from pure water frequently changed; yet they must draw some support from animalcula, and other nourishments supplied by the water; because, though they seem to eat nothing, yet the consequences of eating often drop from them. That they are best pleased with such *jejune* diet may easily be confuted, since if you toss them crumbs they will seize them with great readiness, not to say greediness; however, bread should be given sparingly, lest, turning sour, it corrupt the water. They will also feed on the water-plant called *lemna* (duck's meat), and also on small fry.

When they want to move a little they gently protrude themselves with their *pinnæ pectorales;* but it is with their strong muscular tails only that they and all fishes shoot along with such inconceivable rapidity. It has been said that the eyes of fishes are immovable; but these apparently turn them forward or backward in their sockets as their occasions require. They take little notice of a lighted candle, though applied close to their heads, but flounce and seem much frightened by a sudden stroke of the hand against the support whereon the bowl is hung; especially when they have been motionless, and are perhaps asleep. As fishes have no eyelids, it is not easy to discern when they are sleeping or not, because their eyes are always open. Nothing can be more amusing than a glass bowl containing such fishes : the double refractions of the glass and water represent them, when moving, in a shifting and changeable variety of dimensions, shades, and colours ; while the two mediums, assisted by the concavo-convex shape of the vessel, magnify and distort them vastly ; not to mention that the introduction of another element and its inhabitants into our parlours engages the fancy in a very agreeable manner.

Gold and silver fishes, though originally natives of China and Japan, yet are become so well reconciled to our climate as to thrive and multiply very fast in our ponds and stews. Linnæus ranks this species of fish under the genus of *cyprinus*, or carp, and calls it *Cyprinus auratus.*

Some people exhibit this sort of fish in a very fanciful way ; for they cause a glass bowl to be blown with a large hollow space within, that does not communicate with it. In this cavity they put a bird occasionally ; so that you may see a goldfinch or a linnet hopping as it were in the midst of the water, and the fishes swimming in a circle round it. The simple exhibition of the fishes is agreeable and pleasant ; but in so complicated a way they become whimsical and unnatural, and liable to the objection due to him "who loves to vary every single thing prodigiously "—

"Qui variare cupit rem prodigialitèr unam."
(HOR. *Ars. Poet.* 29.)

LETTER XCIX.

TO THE HONOURABLE DAINES BARRINGTON.

I THINK I have observed before, that much the most considerable part of the house-martins withdraw from hence about the first week in October; but that some, the latter broods I am now convinced, linger on till towards the middle of that month : and that at times, once perhaps in two or three years, a flight, for one day only, has shown itself in the first week in November.

Having taken notice, in October 1780, that the last flight was numerous, amounting perhaps to one hundred and fifty, and that the season was soft and still, I was resolved to pay uncommon attention to those late birds : to find, if possible, where they roosted, and to determine the precise time of their retreat. The mode of life of these latter *hirundines* is very favourable to such a design; for they spend the whole day in the sheltered district between me and the Hanger, sailing about in a placid, easy manner, and feasting on those insects which love to haunt a spot so secure from ruffling winds. As my principal object was to discover the place of their roosting, I took care to wait on them before they retired to rest, and was much pleased to find that, for several evenings together, just at a quarter-past five in the afternoon, they all scudded away in great haste towards the south-east, and darted down among the low shrubs above the cottages at the end of the hill. This spot in many respects seems to be well calculated for their winter residence: for in many parts it is as steep as the roof of any house, and therefore secure from the annoyances of water; and it is moreover clothed with beechen shrubs, which, being stunted and bitten by sheep, make the thickest covert imaginable; they are so entangled as to be impervious to the smallest spaniel: besides, it is the nature of underwood beech never to cast its leaf all the winter; so that, with the leaves on the ground and those on the twigs, no shelter can be more complete. I watched them on to the 13th and 14th of October, and found their evening retreat was exact and uniform; but after this they made no regular appearance. Now and then a straggler was seen; and on the 22nd of October, in the morning, I observed two over the village, and with them my remarks for the season ended.

From all these circumstances put together, it is more than probable that this lingering flight, at so late a season of the year, never departed from the island. Had they indulged me that autumn with a November visit, as I much desired, I presume that, with proper assistants, I should have settled the matter past all doubt; but though the 3rd of November was a sweet day, and in appearance exactly suited to my wishes, yet not a martin was to be seen; and so I was forced reluctantly to give up the pursuit.

I have only to add, that, were the bushes, which cover some acres, and are not my own property, to be grubbed and carefully examined, probably those late broods, and perhaps the whole aggregate body of the house-martins of this district, might be found there, in different secret dormitories; and that, so far from withdrawing into warmer climes, it would appear that they never depart three hundred yards from the village.

October 10, 1781.

LETTER C.

TO THE HONOURABLE DAINES BARRINGTON.

THEY who write on natural history cannot too frequently advert to instinct, that wonderful, but limited faculty, which, in some instances, raises the brute creation as it were above reason, and in others leaves them so far below it. Philosophers have defined instinct to be that secret influence by which every species is impelled naturally to pursue, at all times, the same way or track, without any teaching or example; whereas reason, without instruction, would lead them to do that by many methods which instinct effects by one alone. Now this maxim must be taken in a qualified sense; for there are instances in which instinct does vary and conform to the circumstances of place and convenience.

It has been remarked that every species of bird has a mode of nidification peculiar to itself; so that a schoolboy would at once pronounce on the sort of nest before him. This is the case among fields and woods, and wilds; but in the villages round London, where mosses and gossamer, and cotton from vegetables, are hardly to be found, the nest of the chaffinch has not that elegant finished appearance, nor is it so beautifully studded with lichens, as in a more rural district: and the wren is obliged to construct its house with straws and dry grasses, which do not give it that rotundity and compactness so remarkable in the edifices of that little architect. Again, the regular nest of the house-martin is hemispheric; but where a rafter, or a joist, or a cornice, may happen to stand in the way, the nest is so contrived as to conform to the obstruction, and becomes flat or oval, or compressed.

In the following instances instinct is perfectly uniform and consistent. There are three creatures, the squirrel, the field-mouse, and the bird called the nut-hatch (*Sitta Europœa*), which live much on hazel-nuts; and yet they open them each in a different way. The first, after rasping off the small end, splits the shell in two with his long fore-teeth, as a man does with his knife; the second nibbles a hole with his teeth, as regular as if drilled with a wimble, and yet so small that one would wonder how the kernel can be extracted through it; while the last picks an irregular ragged hole with its bill: but as this artist has no paws to hold the nut firm while he pierces it, like an adroit workman, he fixes it, as it were in a vice, in some cleft of a tree, or in some crevice : when, standing over it, he perforates the stubborn shell.   We have often placed nuts in the chink of a gate-post where nut-hatches have been known to haunt, and have

THE HAWFINCH.

always found that those birds have readily penetrated them. While at work they make a rapping noise, that may be heard at a considerable distance.

You that understand both the theory and practical part of music may best inform us why harmony or melody should so strangely affect some men, as it were by recollection, for days after a concert is over. What I mean the following passage will explain :—

"Præhabebat porrò vocibus humanis, instrumentisque harmonicis musicam illam avium : non quod aliâ quoque non delectaretur ; sed quod ex musicâ humanâ relinqueretur in animo continens quædam, attentionemque et somnum conturbans agitatio ; dum ascensus, exscensus, tenores, ac mutationes illæ sonorum, et consonantiarum euntque, redeuntque per phantasiam : —cum nihil tale relinqui possit ex modulationibus avium, quæ, quod non sunt perinde a nobis imitabiles, non possunt perinde internam facultatem commovere."—*Gassendus.*[1]

This curious quotation strikes me much by so well representing my own case, and by describing what I have so often felt, but never could so well express. When I hear fine music I am haunted with passages therefrom night and day ; and especially at first waking, which, by their importunity, give me more uneasiness than pleasure : elegant lessons still tease my imagination, and recur irresistibly to my recollection at seasons, and even when I am desirous of thinking of more serious matters.

LETTER CI.

TO THE HONOURABLE DAINES BARRINGTON.

A RARE, and I think a new, little bird frequents my garden, which I have great reason to think is the pettichaps :[2] it is common in some parts of the kingdom ; and I have received formerly several dead specimens from Gibraltar. This bird much resembles the white-throat, but has a more white or silvery breast and belly ; is restless and active, like the willow-wrens, and hops

---

[1] "He preferred the music of birds to vocal and instrumental harmony, not that he did not take pleasure in any other, but because the latter left in the mind some constant agitation, disturbing the sleep and the attention ; whilst the several variations of sound and concord go and return through the imagination ; whereas no such effect can be produced by the modulation of birds, because, as they are not equally imitable by us, they cannot equally excite the internal faculty."—*Gassendus in the Life of Peiresc.*

[2] Lesser white-throat (*Sylvia curruca*, Temm.), and not the pettichaps ; the song is very sweet, and more perfect in its notes than that of the whitethroat : it is shy, wary, and even petulant in avoiding intruders.

R

from bough to bough, examining every part for food; it also runs up the stems of the crown-imperials, and putting its head into the bells of those flowers, sips the liquor which stands in the *nectarium* of each petal. Sometimes it feeds on the ground, like the hedge-sparrow, hopping about on the grass-plots and mown walks.

One of my neighbours, an intelligent and observing man, informs me, that, in the beginning of May, and about ten minutes before eight o'clock in the evening, he discovered a great cluster of house-swallows, thirty at least, he supposes, perching on a willow that hung over James Knight's upper-pond. His attention was first drawn by the twittering of these birds, which sat motionless in a row on the bough, with their heads all one way, and, by their weight, pressing down the twig so that it nearly touched the water. In this situation he watched them till he could see no longer. Repeated accounts of this sort, in spring and fall, induce me greatly to suspect that house-swallows have some strong attachment to water, independent of the matter of food; and, though they may not retire into that element, yet they may conceal themselves in the banks of pools and rivers during the uncomfortable months of winter.

One of the keepers of Wolmer Forest sent me a peregrine-falcon, which he shot on the verge of that district, as it was devouring a wood-pigeon. The *Falco peregrinus*, or haggard falcon, is a noble species of hawk seldom seen in the southern counties. In the winter of 1767 one was killed in the neighbouring parish of Farringdon, and sent by me to Mr. Pennant into North Wales.[1] Since that time I have met with none till now. The specimen mentioned above was in fine preservation, and not injured by the shot: it measured forty-two inches from wing to wing, and twenty-one from beak to tail, and weighed two pounds and a half standard weight. This species is very robust, and wonderfully formed for rapine: its breast was plump and muscular; its thighs long, thick, and brawny; and its legs remarkably short and well set: the feet were armed with most formidable sharp, long talons: the eyelids and cere of the bill were yellow; but the irides of the eyes dusky; the beak was thick and hooked, and of a dark colour, and had a jagged process near the end of the upper mandible on each side: its tail, or train, was short in proportion to the bulk of its body: yet the wings, when closed, did not extend to the

---

[1] See my Tenth and Eleventh Letters, pages 30 and 32.

end of the train. From its large and fair proportions it might be supposed to have been a female; but I was not permitted to cut open the specimen. For one of the birds of prey, which are usually lean, this was in high case: in its craw were many barley-corns, which probably came from the crop of the wood-pigeon, on which it was feeding when shot: for voracious birds do not eat grain; but, when devouring their quarry, with un-distinguishing vehemence they swallow bones and feathers, and all matters, indiscriminately. This falcon was probably driven from the mountains of North Wales or Scotland, where they are known to breed, by rigorous weather and the deep snows that had lately fallen.

LETTER CII.

TO THE HONOURABLE DAINES BARRINGTON.

My near neighbour, a young gentleman in the service of the East India Company, has brought home a dog and a bitch of the Chinese breed from Canton; such as are fattened in that country for the purpose of being eaten: they are about the size of a moderate spaniel; of a pale yellow colour, with coarse bristling hairs on their backs; sharp upright ears, and peaked heads, which give them a very fox-like appearance. Their hind legs are unusually straight, without any bend at the hock or ham, to such a degree as to give them an awkward gait when they trot. When they are in motion, their tails are curved high over their backs like those of some hounds; they have a bare place each on the outside from the tip midway, that does not seem to be matter of accident, but is somewhat singular. Their eyes are jet black, small, and piercing; the insides of their lips and mouths of the same colour, and their tongues blue. The bitch has a dew-claw on each hind leg; the dog has none. When taken out into a field, the bitch showed some disposition for hunting, and dwelt on the scent of a covey of partridges, till she sprung them, giving tongue all the time. The dogs in South America are dumb; but these bark much in a short thick manner, like foxes; and have a surly, savage demeanour like their ancestors, which are not domesticated, but bred up in sties, where they are fed for the table, with rice-meal, and other farinaceous food. These dogs having been taken on board as soon as weaned, could not learn much from their dam; yet they did not relish flesh when they came to England. In the islands of the Pacific Ocean the dogs are bred up on vegetables, and would not eat flesh when offered them by our circumnavigators.

We believe that all dogs, in a state of nature, have sharp, upright, fox-like ears; and that hanging ears, which are esteemed so graceful, are the effect of choice breeding and cultivation. Thus, in the travels of Ysbrandt Ides from Muscovy to China, the dogs which draw the Tartars on snow-sledges near the river Obey are engraved with prick-ears, like those from Canton. The Kamschatdales also train the same sort of sharp-eared peaknosed dogs to draw their sledges; as may be seen in an elegant print engraved for Captain Cook's last voyage round the world.

Now we are upon the subject of dogs, it may not be impertinent to add, that spaniels, as all sportsmen know, though they hunt partridges and pheasants as it were by instinct, and with much delight and alacrity, yet will hardly touch their bones when offered as food; nor will a mongrel dog of my own, though he is remarkable for finding that sort of game. But, when we came to offer the bones of partridges to the two Chinese dogs, they devoured them with much greediness, and licked the platter clean.

No sporting dog will flush woodcocks till inured to the scent and trained to the sport, which they then pursue with vehemence and transport; but then they will not touch their bones, but turn from them with abhorrence, even when they are hungry.

Now, that dogs should not be fond of the bones of such birds as they are not disposed to hunt is no wonder; but why they reject, and do not care to eat their natural game, is not so easily accounted for, since the end of hunting seems to be, that the chase pursued should be eaten. Dogs again will not devour the more rancid water-fowls, nor indeed the bones of any wild fowl; nor will they touch the fœtid bodies of birds that feed on offal and garbage: and indeed there may be somewhat of providential instinct in this circumstance of dislike; for vultures,[1] and kites, and ravens, and crows, &c. were intended to be messmates with

---

[1] Hasselquist, in his "Travels to the Levant," observes that the dogs and vultures at Grand Cairo maintain such a friendly intercourse as to bring up their young together in the same place.

dogs over their carrion ; and seem to be appointed by Nature as fellow-scavengers to remove all cadaverous nuisances from the face of the earth.

SELBORNE.

LETTER CIII.

TO THE HONOURABLE DAINES BARRINGTON.

THE fossil wood buried in the bogs of Wolmer Forest is not yet all exhausted, for the peat-cutters now and then stumble upon a log. I have just seen a piece which was sent by a labourer of Oakhanger to a carpenter of this village ; this was the butt-end of a small oak, about five feet long, and about five inches in diameter. It had apparently been severed from the ground by an axe, was very ponderous, and as black as ebony. Upon asking the carpenter for what purpose he had procured it, he told me that it was to be sent to his brother, a joiner, at Farnham, who was to make use of it in cabinet-work, by inlaying it along with whiter woods.

Those that are much abroad on evenings after it is dark, in spring and summer, frequently hear a nocturnal bird passing by on the wing, and repeating often a short quick note. This bird I have remarked myself, but never could make out till lately. I am assured now that it is the stone-curlew (*Charadrius œdicnemus*). Some of them pass over or near my house almost every evening after it is dark : from the uplands of the hill and North field, away down towards Dorton, where, among the streams and meadows, they find a greater plenty of food. Birds that fly by night are obliged to be noisy ; their notes often repeated become signals or watch-words to keep them together, that they may not stray or lose each other in the dark.

The evening proceedings and manœuvres of rooks are curious and amusing in the autumn. Just before dusk they return in long strings from the foraging of the day, and rendezvous by thousands over Selborne-down, where they wheel round in the air, and sport, and dive, in a playful manner, all the while exerting their voices, and making a loud cawing, which, being blended and softened by the distance that we at the village are below them, becomes a confused noise or chiding ; or rather a pleasing murmur, very engaging to the imagination, and not unlike the

cry of a pack of hounds in hollow, echoing woods; or the rushing of the wind in tall trees, or the tumbling of the tide upon a
pebbly shore.   When this ceremony is over, with the last gleam
of day, they retire for the night to the deep beechen woods of
Tisted and Ropley.   We remember a little girl who, as she was
going to bed, used to remark on such an occurrence, in the true
spirit of physico-theology, that the rooks were saying their
prayers; and yet this child was much too young to be aware
that the Scriptures have said of the Deity—that "He feedeth
the ravens who call upon Him."

STONE-CURLEW'S EGG.

LETTER CIV.

TO THE HONOURABLE DAINES BARRINGTON.

IN reading Dr. Huxham's *Observationes de Aëre*, &c., written
at Plymouth, I find by those curious and accurate remarks
which contain an account of the weather from the year 1727
to the year 1748, inclusive, that though there is frequent rain
in that district of Devonshire, yet the quantity falling is not
great; and that some years it has been very small: for in 1731
the rain measured only 17^{inch}.—266^{thou}. and in 1741, 20—354;
and again in 1743 only 20—908.   Places near the sea have
frequent scuds that keep the atmosphere moist, yet do not
reach far up into the country; making thus the maritime

situations appear wet, when the rain is not considerable. In the wettest years at Plymouth, the Doctor measured only once 36; and again once, viz. 1734, 37—114 : a quantity of rain that has twice been exceeded at Selborne in the short period of my observations. Dr. Huxham remarks, that frequent small rains keep the air moist; while heavy ones render it more dry, by beating down the vapours. He is also of opinion that the dingy, smoky appearance in the sky, in very dry seasons, arises from the want of moisture sufficient to let the light through, and render the atmosphere transparent; because he had observed several bodies more diaphanous when wet than dry; and never recollected that the air had that look in rainy seasons.

My friend, who lives just beyond the top of the town, brought his three swivel guns to try them in my outlet, with their muzzles towards the Hanger, supposing that the report would have had a great effect; but the experiment did not answer his expectation. He then removed them to the Alcove on the Hanger; when the sound, rushing along the Lythe and Combwood, was very grand : but it was at the Hermitage that the echoes and repercussions most delighted the hearers; not only filling the Lythe with the roar, as if all the beeches were tearing up by the roots; but, turning to the left, they pervaded the vale above Combwood-ponds; and after a pause seemed to take up the crash again, and to extend round Harteley-hangers, dying away at last among the coppices and coverts of Wardleham. It has been remarked before that this district is an *anathoth*, a place of responses or echoes, and therefore proper for such experiments : we may farther add that the pauses in echoes, when they cease and yet are taken up again, like the pauses in music, surprise the hearers, and have a fine effect on the imagination.

The gentleman above mentioned has just fixed a barometer in his parlour at Newton Valence. The tube was first filled here (at Selborne) twice with care, when the mercury agreed and stood exactly with my own; but, being filled again twice at Newton, the mercury stood, on account of the great elevation of that house, three-tenths of an inch lower than the barometers at this village, and so it continues to do, be the weight of the atmosphere what it may. The plate of the barometer at Newton is figured as low as 27; because in stormy weather the mercury there will sometimes descend below 28. We have

supposed Newton-house to stand two hundred feet higher than
this house : but if the rule holds good, which says that mercury
in a barometer sinks one-tenth of an inch for every hundred
feet elevation, then the Newton barometer, by standing three-
tenths lower than that of Selborne, proves that Newton-house
must be three hundred feet higher than that in which I am
writing, instead of two hundred.

It may not be impertinent to add, that the barometers at
Selborne stand three-tenths of an inch below the barometers at
South Lambeth; whence we may conclude that the former
place is about three hundred feet higher than the latter; and
with good reason, because the streams that rise with us run
into the Thames at Weybridge, and so to London. Of course
therefore there must be lower ground all the way from Selborne
to South Lambeth; the distance between which, all the windings and indentings of the streams considered, cannot be less
than a hundred miles.

LETTER CV.

TO THE HONOURABLE DAINES BARRINGTON.

SINCE the weather of a district is undoubtedly part of its
natural history, I shall make no further apology for the four
following letters, which will contain many particulars concerning some of the great frosts, and a few respecting some very
hot summers, that have distinguished themselves from the rest
during the course of my observations.

As the frost in January 1768 was, for the small time it
lasted, the most severe that we had then known for many
years, and was remarkably injurious to evergreens, some account
of its rigour, and reason of its ravages, may be useful, and not
unacceptable to persons that delight in planting and ornamenting; and may particularly become a work that professes
never to lose sight of utility.

For the last two or three days of the former year there were
considerable falls of snow, which lay deep and uniform on the
ground, without any drifting; wrapping up the more humble
vegetation in perfect security. From the first day to the fifth
of the new year, more snow succeeded; but from that day the

air became entirely clear; and the heat of the sun about noon had considerable influence in sheltered situations.

It was in such an aspect that the snow on the author's evergreens was melted every day, and frozen intensely every night; so that the laurustines, bays, laurels, and arbutuses looked, in three or four days, as if they had been burnt in the fire; while a neighbour's plantation of the same kind, in a high cold situation, where the snow never melted at all, remained uninjured.

From hence I would infer that it is the repeated melting and freezing of the snow that is so fatal to vegetation, rather than the severity of the cold. Therefore it highly behoves every planter, who wishes to escape the cruel mortification of losing in a few days the labour and hopes of years, to bestir himself on such emergencies; and, if his plantations are small, to avail himself of mats, cloths, peasehaum, straw, reeds, or any such covering, for a short time; or, if his shrubberies are extensive, to see that his people go about with prongs and forks, and carefully dislodge the snow from the boughs: since the naked foliage will shift much better for itself than when the snow is partly melted and frozen again.

It may perhaps appear at first like a paradox; but doubtless the more tender trees and shrubs should never be planted in hot aspects; not only for the reason assigned above, but also because, thus circumstanced, they are disposed to shoot earlier in the spring, and to grow on later in the autumn, than they would otherwise do, and so are sufferers by lagging or early frosts. For this reason also, plants from Siberia will hardly endure our climate: because, on the very first advances of spring, they shoot away, and so are cut off by the severe nights of March or April.

Dr. Fothergill and others have experienced the same inconvenience with respect to the more tender shrubs from North America; which they therefore plant under north walls. There should also, perhaps, be a wall to the east, to defend them from the piercing blasts from that quarter.

This observation might without any impropriety be carried into animal life; for discerning bee-masters now find that their hives should not in the winter be exposed to the hot sun, because such unseasonable warmth awakens the inhabitants too early from their slumbers; and, by putting their juices into motion too soon, subjects them afterwards to inconveniences when rigorous weather returns.

The coincidents attending this short but intense frost, were, that the horses fell sick with an epidemic distemper, which injured the wind of many, and killed some; that colds and coughs were general among the human species; that it froze under people's beds for several nights; that meat was frozen so hard that it could not be spitted, and could not be secured but in cellars; that several redwings and thrushes were killed by the frost; and that the large titmouse continued to pull straws lengthwise from the eaves of thatched houses and barns in a most adroit manner, for a purpose that has been explained already.[1]

On the 3rd of January, Benjamin Martin's thermometer within doors, in a close parlour where there was no fire, fell in the night to 20, and on the 4th to 18, and on the 7th to 17½, a degree of cold which the owner never observed in the same situation; and he regrets much that he was not able at that juncture to attend his instrument abroad. All this time the wind continued north and north-east; and yet on the 8th roost-cocks, which had been silent, began to sound their clarions, and crow with clamour, as prognostic of milder weather; moles also began to heave and work, and a manifest thaw took place. From the latter circumstance we may conclude that thaws often originate under ground from warm vapours which arise; else how should subterraneous animals receive such early intimations of their approach. Moreover, we have often observed that cold seems to descend from above; for, when a thermometer hangs abroad in a frosty night, the intervention of a cloud [2] shall immediately raise

---

[1] See Letter LXI. to Mr. Pennant, p. 161.

[2] The cloud of vapour indicates increased radiation of heat and consequent evaporation where it occurs; as the clear sky is indicative of their absence. The following figures represent the temperature in the open air, at one foot and at two feet under ground, the top figures representing the months, those below, the mean average of each during the ten years.

	1	2	3	4	5	6	7	8	9	10	11	12
1 ft.	40·07	39·4	40·90	46·47	53·11	60·02	62·85	61·80	57·54	51·13	46·05	41·13
2 ft.	41·03	40·1	41·59	46·25	52·01	58·47	61·71	61·26	57·89	52·79	47·28	42·83
Air.	88·2	38·1	40·49	46·57	53·34	60·45	63·40	61·28	56·14	49·35	42·89	38·14

It thus appears that the temperature at two feet below the surface is 2° 33′ higher than in the air in January; 1° 70′ in February; 0° 77′ in March;

the mercury ten degrees : and a clear sky shall again compel it to descend to its former gage.

And here it may be proper to observe, on what has been said above, that though frosts advance to their utmost severity by somewhat of a regular gradation, yet thaws do not usually come on by so regular a declension of cold ; but often take place immediately after intense freezing ; as men in sickness often mend at once from a paroxysm.

To the great credit of Portugal laurels and American junipers, be it remembered that they remained untouched amidst the general havoc : hence men should learn to ornament chiefly with such trees as are able to withstand accidental severities, and not subject themselves to the vexation of a loss which may befall them, once, perhaps, in ten years, yet may hardly be recovered through the whole course of their lives.

As it afterwards appeared, the ilexes were much injured, the cypresses were half destroyed, the arbutuses lingered on, but never recovered ; and the bays, laurustines, and laurels were killed to the ground, and the very wild hollies, in hot aspects, were so much affected that they cast all their leaves.

By the 14th of January the snow was entirely gone; the turnips emerged not damaged at all, save in sunny places ; the wheat looked delicate, and the garden-plants were well preserved ; for snow is the most kindly mantle that infant vegetation can be wrapped in ; were it not for that friendly meteor, no vegetable life could exist at all in northerly regions.   Yet in Sweden, the earth in April is not divested of snow for more than a fortnight before the face of the country is covered with flowers.

LETTER CVI.

TO THE HONOURABLE DAINES BARRINGTON.

THERE were some circumstances attending the remarkable frost in January 1776, so singular and striking, that a short detail of them may not be unacceptable.

The most certain way to be exact will be to copy the passages

0° 25′ in August ; 1° 57′ in September ; 2° 80′ in October ; 3° 75′ in November ; and 3° 84′ in December.   On the other hand, the temperature is higher by 0.21′ in the open air in April ; 0·98′ in May ; 1° 21′ in June; and 1° 12′ in July.

from my journal, which were taken from time to time as things occurred. But it may be proper previously to remark, that the first week in January was uncommonly wet, and drowned with vast rains from every quarter : from whence it may be inferred, as there is great reason to believe is the case, that intense frosts seldom take place till the earth is perfectly glutted and chilled with water ;[1] and hence dry autumns are seldom followed by rigorous winters.

January 7th.—Snow driving all the day, which was followed by frost, sleet, and some snow, till the 12th, when a prodigious mass overwhelmed all the works of men, drifting over the tops of the gates, and filling the hollow lanes.

On the 14th the writer was obliged to be much abroad ; and thinks he never, before or since, has encountered such rugged Siberian weather. Many of the narrow roads were now filled above the tops of the hedges ; through which the snow was driven into most romantic and grotesque shapes, so striking to the imagination as not to be seen without wonder and pleasure. The poultry dared not stir out of their roosting-places ; for cocks and hens are so dazzled and confounded by the glare of snow that they would soon perish without assistance. The hares also lay sullenly in their seats, and would not move till compelled by hunger ; being conscious, poor animals, that the drifts and heaps treacherously betray their footsteps, and prove fatal to numbers of them.

From the 14th the snow continued to increase, and began to stop the road-waggons and coaches, which could no longer keep on their regular stages : more especially on the western roads, where the fall appears to have been deeper than in the south. The company at Bath, that wanted to attend the Queen's birthday, were strangely incommoded : the carriages of many persons, who got on their way to town from Bath as far as Marlborough, after strange embarrassments, here met with a *ne plus ultra*. The ladies fretted, and offered large rewards to labourers if they would shovel them a track to London : but the relentless heaps of snow were too bulky to be removed ; and so the 18th passed over, leaving the company in very uncomfortable circumstances at the Castle and other inns.

---

[1] The autumn preceding January 1768 was very wet, and particularly the month of September, during which there fell at Lyndon, in the county of Rutland, six inches and a half of rain. And the terrible long frost in 1739-40 set in after a rainy season, and when the springs were very high.

On the 20th the sun shone out for the first time since the frost began; a circumstance that has been remarked on before as much in favour of vegetation. All this time the cold was not very intense, for the thermometer stood at 29, 28, 25, and thereabout: but on the 21st it descended to 20. The birds now began to be in a very pitiable and starving condition. Tamed by the season, skylarks settled in the streets of towns, because they saw the ground was bare; rooks frequented dunghills close to houses; and crows watched horses as they passed, and greedily devoured what dropped from them; hares now came into the gardens, and, scraping away the snow, devoured such plants as they could find.

On the 22nd the author had occasion to go to London through a sort of Laplandian scene, very wild and grotesque indeed. But the metropolis itself exhibited a still more singular appearance than the country; for, being bedded deep in snow, the pavement of the streets could not be touched by the wheels or the horses' feet, so that the carriages ran about without the least noise. Such an exemption from din and clatter was strange, but not pleasant; it seemed to convey an uncomfortable idea of desolation:

> "— — — — — — ipsa silentia terrent."
> "By silence terrified."

On the 27th much snow fell all day, and in the evening the frost became very intense. At South Lambeth, for the four following nights, the thermometer fell to 11, 7, 6, 6; and at Selborne to 7, 6, 10; and on the 31st of January, just before sunrise, with rime on the trees and on the tube of the glass, the quicksilver sank exactly to zero, being 32 degrees below the freezing point: but by eleven in the morning, though in the shade, it sprang up to $16\frac{1}{2}$ [1]—a most unusual degree of cold this for the south of England! During these four nights the cold was so penetrating, that it occasioned ice in warm chambers, and under beds; and in the day, the wind was so keen, that persons of robust constitutions could scarcely endure to face it. The Thames was at once frozen over both above and below bridge, so that crowds

---

[1] At Selborne, the cold was greater than at any other place that the author could hear of with certainty: though it was reported at the time, that, at a village in Kent, the thermometer fell two degrees below zero, viz. 34 degrees below the freezing-point.

The thermometer used at Selborne was graduated by Benjamin Martin.

ran about on the ice. The streets were now strangely incumbered with snow, which crumbled and trod dusty; and soon turning grey, resembled bay-salt: what had fallen on the roofs was perfectly dry, that, from first to last, it lay twenty-six days on the houses in the city; a longer time than had been remembered by the oldest housekeepers living. According to all appearances, we might now have expected the continuance of this rigorous weather for weeks to come, since every night increased in severity; but behold, without any apparent cause, on the 1st of February a thaw took place, and some rain followed before night, making good the observation above, that frosts often go off as it were at once, without any gradual declension of cold. On the 2nd of February the thaw persisted; and on the 3rd swarms of little insects were frisking and sporting in a courtyard at South Lambeth, as if they had felt no frost. Why the juices in the small bodies, and smaller limbs, of such minute beings are not frozen, is a matter of curious inquiry.

Severe frosts seem to be partial, or to run in currents; for, at the same juncture, as the author was informed by accurate correspondents, at Lyndon, in the county of Rutland, the thermometer stood at 19; at Blackburn, in Lancashire, at 19; and at Manchester at 21, 20 and 18. Thus does some unknown circumstance strangely overbalance latitude, and render the cold sometimes much greater in the southern than the northern parts of this kingdom.

The consequences of this severity were, that in Hampshire, at the melting of the snow, the wheat looked well, and the turnips came forth little injured. The laurels and laurustines were somewhat damaged, but only in hot aspects. No evergreens were quite destroyed; and not half the damage sustained that befell in January 1768. Those laurels that were a little scorched on the south sides were perfectly untouched on their north sides. The care taken to shake the snow day by day from the branches seemed greatly to avail the author's evergreens. A neighbour's laurel-hedge, in a high situation, and facing to the north, was perfectly green and vigorous; and the Portugal laurels remained unhurt.

As to the birds; the thrushes and blackbirds were mostly destroyed; and the partridges were so thinned by the weather and poachers, that few remained to breed the following year.

LETTER CVII.

TO THE HONOURABLE DAINES BARRINGTON.

As the frost in December 1784 was very extraordinary, you, I trust, will not be displeased to hear the particulars; and especially when I promise to say no more about the severities of winter after I have finished this letter.

The first week in December was very wet, with the barometer very low. On the 7th, with the barometer at 28 five-tenths, came on a vast snow, which continued all that day and the next, and most part of the following night; so that by the morning of the 9th the works of men were quite overwhelmed, the lanes filled so as to be impassable, and the ground covered twelve or fifteen inches without any drifting. In the evening of the 9th, the air began to be so very sharp, that we thought it would be curious to attend to the motions of a thermometer: we therefore hung out two; one made by Martin and one by Dollond, which soon began to show us what we were to expect; for, by ten o'clock, they fell to 21, and at eleven, to 4, when we went to bed. On the 10th, in the morning, the quicksilver of Dollond's glass was down to half a degree below zero; and that of Martin's, which was absurdly graduated only to four degrees above zero, sank quite into the brass guard of the ball; so that when the weather became most interesting, this was useless. On the 10th, at eleven at night, though the air was perfectly still, Dollond's glass went down to one degree below zero! This strange severity of the weather made me very desirous to know what degree of cold there might be in such an exalted and near situation as Newton. We had therefore, on the morning of the 10th, written to Mr. ——, and entreated him to hang out his thermometer, made by Adams; and to pay some attention to it, morning and evening; expecting wonderful phenomena, in so elevated a region as two hundred feet or more above my house. But, behold! on the 10th, at eleven at night, it was down only to 17°, and the next morning at 22°, when mine was at 10°! We were so disturbed at this unexpected reverse of comparative local cold, that we sent one of my glasses up, thinking that of Mr. —— must, somehow, be wrongly constructed. But, when the instruments came to be confronted, they went exactly together: so that, for one night at least, the cold at Newton was 18° less than at Selborne; and, through the whole frost, 10° or 12°; indeed, when we came to observe the consequences, we could readily credit this; for all my laurustines, bays, ilexes, arbutuses, cypresses, and even my Portugal laurels, and (which occasions more regret) my fine sloping laurel-hedge, were scorched up; while, at Newton, the same trees had not lost a leaf !

We had steady frost on to the 25th, when the thermometer in the morning was down to 10° with us, and at Newton only to 21°. Strong frost continued till the 31st, when some tendency to thaw was observed; and, by the 3rd of January, 1785, the thaw was confirmed, and some rain fell.

A circumstance that I must not omit, because it was new to us, is, that on Friday, December the 10th, being bright sunshine, the air was full of icy spiculæ, floating in all directions, like atoms in a sunbeam let into a dark room. We thought them, at first, particles of the rime falling from my tall hedges; but were soon convinced to the contrary, by making our observations in open places where no rime could reach us. Were they watery particles of the air frozen as they floated; or were they evaporations from the snow frozen as they mounted ?

We were much obliged to the thermometers for the early information they gave us ; and hurried our apples, pears, onions, &c., into the cellar, and warm closets; while those who had not such warnings, or neglected them, lost all their stores of roots and fruits, and had their very bread and cheese frozen.

I must not omit to tell you, that, during those two Siberian days, my parlour-cat was so electric, that had a person stroked her, and been properly insulated, the shock might have been given to a whole circle of people.

I forgot to mention before, that, during the two severe days, two men, who were tracking hares in the snow, had their feet frozen ; and two others, who were much better employed, had their fingers so affected by the frost, while they were thrashing in a barn, that a mortification followed, from which they did not recover for many weeks.

This frost killed all the furze and most of the ivy, and in many places stripped the hollies of all their leaves. It came at a very early time of the year, before old November ended; and yet may be allowed from its effects to have exceeded any since 1739-40.

LETTER CVIII.

TO THE HONOURABLE DAINES BARRINGTON.

As the effects of heat are seldom very remarkable in the northerly climate of England, where the summers are often so defective in warmth and sunshine as not to ripen the fruits of the earth so well as might be wished, I shall be more concise in my account of the intensity of a summer season, and so make a little amends for the prolix account of the degrees of cold, and the inconveniences that we suffered from some late rigorous winters.

The summers of 1781 and 1783 were unusually hot and dry; to them therefore I shall turn back in my journals, without recurring to any more distant period. In the former of these years my peach and nectarine trees suffered so much from the heat, that the rind on the bodies were scalded and came off; since which the trees have been in a decaying state. This may prove a hint to assiduous gardeners to fence and shelter their wall-trees with mats or boards, as they may easily do, because such annoyance is seldom of long continuance. During that summer, also, I observed that my apples were coddled, as it were, on the trees; so that they had no quickness of flavour, and they did not keep in the winter. This circumstance put me in mind of what I have heard travellers assert, that they never ate a good apple, or apricot, in the south of Europe, where the heats are so great as to render the juices vapid and insipid.

The great pests of a garden are wasps, which destroy all the finer fruits, just as they are coming into perfection. In 1781 we had none; in 1783 there were myriads; which would have devoured all the produce of my garden, had not we set the boys to take the nests; we caught thousands with hazel-twigs tipped with bird-lime: and have since employed the boys to take and destroy the large breeding wasps in the spring. Such expedients have a great effect on these marauders, and will keep them under. Though wasps do not abound but in hot summers, yet they do not prevail then, as I have instanced in the two years above mentioned.

S

In the sultry season of 1783, honey-dews were so frequent as to deface and destroy the beauties of my garden. My honeysuckles, which were one week the most sweet and lovely objects that the eye could behold, became, the next, the most loathsome; being enveloped in a viscous substance, and loaded with black *aphides*, or smother-flies. The occasion of this clammy appearance seems to be this, that, in hot weather, the effluvia of flowers in fields, and meadows, and gardens are drawn up in the day by a brisk evaporation, and then in the night fall down again with the dews, in which they are entangled; that the air is strongly scented, and therefore impregnated with the particles of flowers in summer weather, our senses will inform us; and that this sweet clammy substance is of the vegetable kind we may learn from bees, to whom it is very grateful: we may also be assured that it falls in the night, because it is always first seen in warm still mornings.

On chalky and sandy soils, and in the hot villages about London, the thermometer has been often observed to mount as high as 83 or 84; but with us, in this hilly and woody district, I have hardly ever seen it exceed 80; nor does it often arrive at that pitch. The reason, I conclude, is, that our dense clayey soil, so much shaded by trees, is not so easily heated through as those above mentioned: and besides, our mountains cause currents of air and breezes; and the vast evaporation from our woodlands tempers and moderates our heats.

LETTER CIX.

TO THE HONOURABLE DAINES BARRINGTON.

THE summer of the year 1783 was an amazing and a portentous one, and full of horrible phenomena; for, besides the alarming meteors and tremendous thunderstorms that affrighted and distressed the different counties of this kingdom, the peculiar haze, or smoky fog, that prevailed for many weeks in this island, and in every part of Europe, and even beyond its limits, was a most extraordinary appearance, unlike anything known within the memory of man. By my journal I find that I had noticed this strange occurrence from June 23 to July 20 inclusive, during which period the wind varied to every quarter without making any alteration in the air. The sun, at noon, looked as blank as a clouded moon, and shed a rust-coloured, ferruginous light on the ground, and floors of rooms; but was particularly lurid and blood-coloured at rising and setting. All the time the heat was so intense, that butchers' meat could hardly be eaten on the day after it was killed; and the flies swarmed so in the lanes and hedges that they rendered the horses half frantic, and riding irksome. The country people began to look with a superstitious awe at the red louring aspect of the sun; and indeed there was reason for the most enlightened person to be apprehensive; for, all the while Calabria and part of the isle of Sicily, were torn and convulsed with earthquakes; and about that juncture a volcano sprung out of the sea on the coast of Norway. On this occasion Milton's noble simile of the sun, in his first book of "Paradise Lost," frequently occurred to my mind; and it is indeed particularly applicable, because, towards the end, it alludes to a superstitious kind of dread, with which the minds of men are always impressed by such strange and unusual phenomena.

> "— — — As when the sun, new risen,
> Looks through the horizontal, misty air,
> Shorn of his beams; or from behind the moon,
> In dim eclipse, disastrous twilight sheds
> On half the nations, and with fear of change
> Perplexes monarchs — — — —"

LETTER CX.

TO THE HONOURABLE DAINES BARRINGTON.

WE are very seldom annoyed with thunderstorms; and it is no less remarkable than true, that those which arise in the south have hardly been known to reach this village; for, before they get over us, they take a direction to the east, or to the west, or sometimes divide into two, and go in part to one of those quarters, and in part to the other; as was truly the case in the summer of 1783, when, though the country round was continually harassed with tempests, and often from the south; yet we escaped them all, as appears by my journal of that

s 2

summer.[1] The only way that I can at all account for this fact—for such it is—is that on that quarter between us and the sea there are continual mountains, hill behind hill, such as Nore-hill, the Barnet, Butser-hill, and Ports-down, which somehow divert the storms, and give them a different direction. High promontories and elevated grounds have always been observed to attract clouds, and disarm them of their mischievous contents, which are discharged into the trees and summits as soon as they come in contact with those turbulent meteors; while the humble vales escape, because they are so far beneath them.

But when I say I do not remember a thunderstorm from the south, I do not mean that we never have suffered from thunder-storms at all; for on June 5th, 1784, the thermometer in the morning being at 64°, and at noon at 70°, the barometer at 29°—six-tenths one-half, and the wind north, I observed a blue mist, smelling strongly of sulphur, hanging along our sloping woods, and seeming to indicate that thunder was at hand. I was called in about two in the afternoon, and so missed seeing the gathering of the clouds in the north; which they who were abroad assured me had something uncommon in its appearance. At about a quarter after two, the storm began in the parish of Hartley, moving slowly from north to south; and from thence it came over Norton-farm, and so to Grange-farm, both in this parish. It began with vast drops of rain, which were soon succeeded by round hail, and then by convex pieces of ice, which measured three inches in girth. Had it been as extensive as it was violent, and of any continuance (for it was very short), it must have ravaged all the neighbourhood. In the parish of Hartley it did some damage to one farm; but Norton, which lay in the centre of the storm, was greatly injured; as was Grange, which lay next to it. It did but just reach to the middle of the village, where the hail broke my north windows, and all my garden-lights and hand-glasses, and many of my neighbours' windows. The extent of the storm was about two miles in length and one in breadth. We were just sitting down to dinner; but were soon diverted from our repast by the

---

[1] *Storms.*—To this awful summer of 1783, Cowper also alludes in his "Task," book ii. p. 41 :—

"————————— A world that seems
To toll the death-bell of its own decease ;
And by the voice of all the elements
To preach the general doom."

clattering of tiles and the jingling of glass.   There fell at the same
time prodigious torrents of rain on the farms above mentioned,
which occasioned a flood as violent as it was sudden; doing
great damage to the meadows and fallows, by deluging the one
and washing away the soil of the other.   The hollow lane
towards Alton was so torn and disordered as not to be passable
till mended, rocks being removed that weighed two hundred-
weight.   Those that saw the effect which the great hail had on
ponds and pools, say that the dashing of the water made an
extraordinary appearance, the froth and spray standing up in
the air three feet above the surface.   The rushing and roaring
of the hail as it approached was truly tremendous.

Though the clouds at South Lambeth, near London, were at
that juncture thin and light, and no storm was in sight, nor
within hearing, yet the air was strongly electric; for the bells
of an electric machine at that place rang repeatedly, and fierce
sparks were discharged.

When I first took the present work in hand I proposed to have
added an *Annus Historico-naturalis;* or, The Natural History of
the Twelve Months of the Year; which would have comprised
many incidents and occurrences that have not fallen in my way
to be mentioned in my series of letters; but as Mr. Aikin of
Warrington has published somewhat of this sort, and as the
length of my correspondence has sufficiently put your patience to
the test, I shall here take a respectful leave of you and natural
history together; and am,

With all due deference and regard,

Your most obliged,

And most humble Servant,

GIL. WHITE.

SELBORNE, *June* 25, 1787.

A

COMPARATIVE VIEW

OF THE

NATURALIST'S CALENDAR,

AS KEPT AT

SELBORNE, IN HAMPSHIRE,

BY THE LATE

REV. GILBERT WHITE, M.A.

AND AT

CATSFIELD, NEAR BATTLE, IN SUSSEX,

BY

WILLIAM MARKWICK, ESQ. F.L.S.

FROM THE YEAR 1768, TO THE YEAR 1793.

N.B.—The dates in the following Calendars, when more than one, express the *earliest* and the *latest* times in which the circumstance noted was observed.

A COMPARATIVE VIEW

OF

WHITE'S AND MARKWICK'S CALENDAR.

Of the abbreviations used, *fl.* signifies *flowering; l. leafing;* and *ap.* the first *appearance.*

	WHITE.		MARKWICK.	
REDBREAST (*Sylvia rubecula*) sings	Jan. 1—12		Jan. 8—31, and again Oct.	
Larks (*Alauda arvensis*) congregate	Jan. 1—18		Oct. 16.	Feb. 9 [6
Nuthatch (*Sitta Europœa*) heard	Jan 1—14		Mar. 8.	Apr. 10
Winter aconite (*Helleborus hiemalis*) fl.	Jan. 1.	Feb. 18	Feb. 28.	Apr. 17
Shelless snail or slug (*Limax*) ap.	Jan. 2		Jan. 16.	May 31
Gray wagtail (*Motacilla boarula*) ap. }	Jan. 2—11	{	Jan. 24.	Mar. 23
White wagtail (*Motacilla alba*) ap. }			Dec. 12.	Feb. 28
Missel thrush (*Turdus viscivorus*) sings	Jan. 2—14		Feb. 19.	Apr. 14
Bearsfoot (*Helleborus fœtidus*) fl.	Jan. 2.	Feb. 14	Mar. 1.	May 5
Polyanthus (*Primula Polyantha*) fl.	Jan. 2.	Apr. 12	Jan. 1.	Apr. 9
Double daisy (*Bellis perennis plena*) fl.	Jan. 2.	Feb. 1	Mar. 17.	Apr. 29
Mezereon (*Daphne mezereum*) fl.	Jan. 3.	Feb. 16	Jan. 2.	Apr. 4
Pansie (*Viola tricolor*) fl.	Jan. 3		Jan. 1.	May 10
Red dead-nettle (*Lamium purpureum*) fl.	Jan. 3—21		Jan. 1.	Apr. 5.
Groundsel (*Senecio vulgaris*) fl.	Jan. 3—15		Jan. 1.	Apr. 9
Hazel (*Corylus avelana*) fl.	Jan. 3.	Feb. 28	Jan. 21.	Mar. 11
Hepatica (*Anemone hepatica*) fl.	Jan. 4.	Feb. 18	Jan. 17.	Apr. 9
Hedge sparrow (*Sylvia modularis*) sings	Jan. 5—12		Jan. 16.	Mar. 13
Common flies (*Musca domestica*) seen in numbers	Jan. 5.	Feb. 3	May 15	
Greater titmouse (*Parus major*) sings	Jan. 6.	Feb. 6	Feb. 17.	Mar. 17
Thrush (*Turdus musicus*) sings	Jan. 6—22		Jan. 15.	Apr. 4
Insects swarm under sunny hedges	Jan. 6			
Primrose (*Primula vulgaris*) fl.	Jan. 6.	Apr. 7	Jan. 3.	Mar. 22
Bees (*Apis mellifica*) ap.	Jan. 6.	Mar. 19	Jan. 31.	Apr. 11; last seen
Gnats play about	Jan. 6.	Feb. 3		[Dec. 30
Chaffinches, male and female (*Fringilla cœlebs*), seen in equal numbers	Jan. 6—11		Dec. 2.	Feb. 3
Furze or gorse (*Ulex Europœus*) fl.	Jan. 8.	Feb. 1	Jan. 1.	Mar. 27
Wallflower (*Cheiranthus cheiri; seu fruticulosus* of Smith) fl.	Jan. 8.	Apr. 1	Feb. 21.	May 9
Stock (*Cheiranthus incanus*) fl.	Jan. 8—12		Feb. 1.	June 8
Emberiza alba (bunting) in great flocks	Jan. 9			
Linnets (*Fringilla linota*) congregate	Jan. 9		Jan. 11	
Lambs begin to fall	Jan. 9—11		Jan. 6.	Feb. 21
Rooks (*Corvus frugilegus*) resort to their nest trees	Jan. 10.	Feb. 11	Jan. 23	

	WHITE.		MARKWICK.	
Black hellebore (*Helleborus niger*) fl.	Jan. 10		Apr. 27	
Snowdrop (*Galanthus nivalis*) fl.	Jan. 10.	Feb. 5	Jan. 18.	Mar. 1
White dead nettle (*Lamium album*) fl.	Jan. 18		Mar. 23.	May 10
Trumpet honeysuckle fl.	Jan. 13			
Common creeping crow-foot (*Ranunculus repens*) fl.	Jan. 13		Apr 10.	May 13
House sparrow (*Fringilla domestica*) chirps	Jan. 14		Feb. 17.	May 9
Dandelion (*Leontodon taraxacum*) fl.	Jan. 16.	Mar. 11	Feb. 1	Apr. 17
Bat (*Vespertilio*) ap.	Jan. 16.	Mar. 24	Feb. 6.	June 1, last seen
Spiders shoot their webs	Jan. 16			[Nov. 20
Butterfly ap.	Jan. 16		Feb. 21	May 8, last seen
Brambling (*Fringilla montifringilla*) ap.	Jan. 16		Jan. 10—31	[Dec. 23
Blackbird (*Turdus merula*) whistles	Jan. 17		Feb. 15.	May 18
Wren (*Sylvia troglodytes*) sings	Jan. 17		Feb. 7	June 13
Earthworms lie out	Jan. 18.	Feb. 8		
Crocus (*Crocus vernus*) fl.	Jan. 13.	Mar. 18	Jan. 20	Mar. 19
Skylark (*Alauda arvensis*) sings	Jan. 21		Jan. 12. Feb. 27, sings till	
Ivy casts its leaves	Jan. 22			[Nov. 13
Helleborus hiemalis fl.	Jan. 22—24		Feb. 28. Apr. 17	
Common dor or clock (*Scarabæus stercorarius*)	Jan. 23		Feb. 12. Apr. 19, last seen	
Peziza acetabulum, ap.	Jan. 23			[Nov. 24
Helleborus viridis fl.	Jan. 23.	Mar. 5		
Hazel (*Corylus avellana*) fl.	Jan. 23.	Feb. 1	Jan. 27.	Mar. 11
Woodlark (*Alauda arborea*) sings	Jan. 24.	Feb. 21	Jan. 28.	June 5
Chaffinch (*Fringilla cœlebs*) sings	Jan. 24.	Feb. 15	Jan. 21.	Feb. 20
Jackdaws begin to come to churches	Jan. 25.	Mar. 4		
Yellow wagtail (*Motacilla flava*) ap.	Jan. 25.	Apr. 14	Apr. 13. July 8, last seen	
Honeysuckle (*Lonicera periclymenum*) l.	Jan. 25		Jan. 1. Apr. 9	[Sept. 8
Field or procumbent speedwell (*Veronica agrestis*) fl.	Jan. 27.	Mar. 15	Feb. 12.	Mar 29
Nettle butterfly (*Papilio Urticæ*) ap.	Jan. 27.	Apr. 3	Mar. 5. Apr. 24, last seen	
White wagtail (*Motacilla alba*) chirps	Jan. 18		Mar. 16	[June 6
Shell snail (*Helix nemoralis*) ap.	Jan. 28.	Feb. 24	Apr. 2.	June 11.
Earthworms engender	Jan. 30			
Barren strawberry (*Fragaria sterilis*) fl.	Feb. 1.	Mar. 25	Jan. 13.	Mar. 26
Blue titmouse (*Parus cœruleus*) chirps	Feb. 1		Apr. 27	
Brown wood owls hoot	Feb. 3			
Hen (*Phasianus gallus*) sits	Feb. 3		Mar. 8 hatches	
Marsh titmouse begins his two harsh sharp notes	Feb. 3			
Gossamer floats	Feb. 4.	Apr. 1		
Musca tenax ap.	Feb. 4.	Apr. 8		
Larustine (*Viburnum tinus*) fl.	Feb. 5		Jan. 1.	Apr. 5
Butcher's broom (*Ruscus aculeatus*) fl.	Feb. 5		Jan. 1.	May 10
Fox (*Canis vulpes*) smells rank	Feb. 7		May 19, young brought	
Turkey-cocks strut and gobble	Feb. 10			[forth
Yellowhammer (*Emberiza citrinella*) sings	Feb. 12		Feb. 18.	Apr. 28
Brimstone butterfly (*Papilio Rhamni*) ap.	Feb. 13.	Apr. 2	Feb. 18. Mar. 8, last seen	
Green woodpecker (*Picus viridis*) makes a loud cry	Feb. 13.	Mar. 28	Jan. 1. Apr. 17	[Dec. 24 [June 1
Raven (*Corvus Corax*) builds	Feb. 14—17		Apr. 1. has young ones	
Yew tree (*Taxus baccata*) fl.	Feb. 14.	Mar. 27	Feb. 2.	Apr. 11
Colesfoot (*Tussilago farfara*) fl.	Feb. 15.	Mar. 23	Feb. 18.	Apr. 18
Rooks (*Corvus frugilegus*) build	Feb. 16.	Mar. 6	Feb. 28.	Mar 5.
Partridges (*Perdix cinerea*) pair	Feb. 17		Feb. 16.	Mar. 20
Peas (*Pisum sativum*) sown	Feb. 17.	Mar. 8	Feb. 8.	Mar. 31
House pigeon (*Columba domestica*) has young ones	Feb. 18		Feb. 8	
Field crickets open their holes	Feb. 20.	Mar. 30		
Common flea (*Pulex irritans*) ap.	Feb. 21—26			
Pilewort (*Ficaria verna*) fl.	Feb. 21.	Apr. 13	Jan. 25.	Mar. 26
Goldfinch (*Fringilla carduelis*) sings	Feb. 21.	Apr. 5	Feb. 28.	May 5
Viper (*Coluber berus*) ap.	Feb. 22.	Mar. 23	Feb. 23. May 6, last seen	
				[Oct. 28

	WHITE.		MARKWICK.	
Woodlouse (*Oniscus asellus*) ap.	Feb. 23.	Apr. 1	Apr. 27.	June 17
Missel thrushes pair	Feb. 24			
Daffodil (*Narcissus pseudonarcissus*) fl.	Feb. 24.	Apr. 7	Feb. 26.	Apr. 18
Willow (*Salix alba*) fl.	Feb. 24.	Apr. 2	Feb. 27.	Apr. 11
Frogs (*Rana temporaria*) croak	Feb. 25		Mar. 9.	Apr. 20
Sweet violet (*Viola odurata*) fl.	Feb. 26.	Mar. 31	Feb. 7.	Apr. 5
Phalœna Tinea vestianella ap.	Feb. 26			
Stone curlew (*Otis œdicnemus*) clamours	Feb. 27.	Apr. 24	June 17	
Filbert (*Corylus sativus*) fl.	Feb. 27		Jan. 25.	Mar. 26
Ring-dove coos	Feb. 27.	Apr. 5	Mar. 2.	Aug. 10
Apricot tree (*Prunus armeniaca*) fl.	Feb.		Feb. 28.	Apr. 5
Toad (*Rana bufo*) ap.	Feb. 28.	Mar. 24	Mar. 15.	July 1
Frogs (*Rana temporaria*) spawn	Feb. 28.	Mar. 22	Feb. 9.	Apr. 10, tadpoles [Mar. 19
Ivy-leaved speedwell (*Veronica hederifolia*) fl.	Mar. 1.	Apr. 2	Feb. 16.	Apr. 10
Peach (*Amygdalus Persica*) fl.	Mar. 2.	Apr. 17	Mar. 4.	Apr. 29
Frog (*Rana temporaria*) ap.	Mar. 2.	Apr. 6	Mar. 9	
Shepherd's purse (*Thlaspi bursa pastoris*) fl.	Mar. 3		Jan. 2.	Apr. 16
Pheasant (*Phasianus Colchicus*) crows	Mar. 3—29		Mar. 1.	May 23
Land tortoise comes forth	Mar. 4.	May 8		
Lungwort (*Pulmonoria officinalis*) fl.	Mar. 4.	Apr. 16	Mar. 2.	May 19
Podura fimetaria ap.	Mar. 4			
Aranea scenica saliens ap.	Mar. 4			
Scolopendra forficata ap.	Mar. 5—16			
Wryneck (*Jynx torquilla*) ap.	Mar. 5.	Apr. 25	Mar. 26.	Apr. 23, last seen [Sept. 14
Goose (*Anas anser*) sits on its eggs	Mar. 5		Mar. 21	
Duck (*Anas boschas*) lays	Mar. 5		Mar. 28	
Dog's violet (*Viola canina*) fl.	Mar. 6.	Apr. 18	Feb. 28.	Apr. 22
Peacock butterfly (*Papilio Io*) ap.	Mar. 6		Feb. 13.	Apr. 20, last seen [Dec. 25
Trouts begin to rise	Mar. 7—14			
Field beans (*Vicia faba*) planted	Mar. 8		Apr. 29 emerge	
Bloodworms appear in the water	Mar. 8			
Crow (*Corvus Corone*) builds	Mar. 10		July 1 has young ones	
Oats (*Avena sativa*) sown	Mar. 10—18		Mar. 16.	Apr. 13 [Dec. 23. Jan. 26
Golden crowned wren (*Sylvia regulus*) sings	Mar. 12.	Apr. 30	Apr. 15.	May 22, seen
Asp (*Populus tremula*) fl.	Mar. 12		Feb. 26.	Mar. 28
Common elder (*Sambucus nigra*) l.	Mar. 13—20		Jan. 24.	Apr. 22
Laurel (*Prunus laurocerasus*) fl.	Mar. 15.	May 21	Apr. 2.	May 27
Chrysomela Gotting. ap.	Mar. 15			
Black ants (*Formica nigra*) ap.	Mar. 15.	Apr. 22	Mar. 2.	May 18
Ephemerœ bisetœ ap.	Mar. 16			
Gooseberry (*Ribes grossularia*) l.	Mar. 17.	Apr. 11	Feb. 26.	Apr. 9
Common stitchwort (*Stellaria holostea*) fl.	Mar. 17.	May 19	Mar. 8.	May 7
Wood anemone (*Anemone nemorosa*) fl.	Mar. 17.	Apr. 22	Feb. 27.	Apr. 10
Blackbird (*Turdus Merula*) lays	Mar. 17		Apr. 14, young ones May	
Raven (*Corvus Corax*) sits	Mar. 17		Apr. 1 builds [19	
Wheatear (*Sylvia Œnanthe*) ap.	Mar. 18—30		Mar. 13.	May 23, last seen [Oct. 26.
Musk-wood crowfoot (*Adoxa moschattellina*) fl.	Mar. 18.	Apr. 13	Feb. 23.	Apr. 28
Willow wren [1] (*Sylvia trochilus*) ap.	Mar. 19.	Apr. 13	Mar. 30.	May 16 sits May [27, last seen Oct. 23
Fumaria bulbosa fl.	Mar. 19			
Elm (*Ulmus campestris*) fl.	Mar. 19.	Apr. 4	Feb. 17.	Apr. 25

---

[1] *Willow Wren.*—Mr. White has made strange confusion in the entries respecting the wrens in his calendar. Three sorts were known to him, as he distinctly says in a former passage: the *Sylvia trochilus*, a yellow wren; the *Sylvia sibilatrix*, or wood wren; the *Sylvia hippolais*, or chiff-chaff; but he enters the separate appearance of four such wrens in the Calendar, although there were not four species known in this country, nor did he ever fancy that there were four. By reference to what he has said in other places, it should seem that the chiff-chaff appears the first. Therefore, in the entry, March 19th, we must read, instead of willow wren, *Sylvia trochilus*, chiff-chaff, *Sylvia hippolais*. In page 203, Mr. White states this bird to be the chiff-chaff, and to be usually heard on the 25th of March.—W. H.

	WHITE.		MARKWICK.	
Turkey (*Meleagris gallopavo*) lays	Mar. 19.	Apr. 7	Mar. 18—25, sits Apr. 4, [young ones Apr. 80	
House pigeons (*Columba domestica*) sit	Mar. 20		Mar. 20, young hatched	
Marsh marigold (*Caltha palustris*) fl.	Mar. 20.	Apr. 14	Mar. 22. May 8	
Buzz-fly (*Bombylius medius*) ap.	Mar. 21.	Apr. 28	Mar. 15. Apr. 80	
Sand martin (*Hirundo riparia*) ap.	Mar. 21.	Apr. 12	Apr. 8. May 16, last seen [Sept. 8.	
Snake (*Coluber natrix*) ap.	Mar. 22—80		Mar. 8. Apr. 29, last seen [Oct. 2	
Horse ant (*Formica herculeana*) ap.	Mar. 22.	Apr. 18	Feb. 4. Mar. 26, last seen [Nov. 1	
Greenfinch (*Loxia chloris*) sings	Mar. 22.	Apr. 22	Mar. 6. Apr. 26	
Ivy (*Hedera helix*) berries ripe	Mar. 28.	Apr. 14	Feb. 16. May 19	
Periwinkle (*Vinca minor*) fl.	Mar. 25		Feb. 6. May 7	
Spurge laurel (*Daphne laureola*) fl.	Mar. 25.	Apr. 1	Apr. 12—22 [16	
Swallow (*Hirundo rustica*) ap.	Mar. 26.	Apr. 20	Apr. 7—27, last seen Nov.	
Blackcap (*Sylvia atricapilla*) heard	Mar. 26.	May 4	Apr. 14. May 18, seen Apr. 14. May 20, last seen Sept. 19	
Young ducks hatched	Mar. 27		Apr. 6. May 16	
Golden saxifrage (*Chrysosplenium oppositifolium*) fl.	Mar. 27.	Apr. 9	Feb. 7. Mar. 27	
Martin (*Hirundo urbica*) ap.	Mar. 28.	May 1	Apr. 14. May 8, last seen [Dec. 8	
Double hyacinth (*Hyacinthus orientalis*) fl.	Mar. 29.	Apr. 22	Mar. 13. Apr. 24	
Young geese (*Anas anser*)	Mar. 29		Mar. 29. Apr. 19	
Wood sorrel (*Oxalis acetosella*) fl.	Mar. 80.	Apr. 22	Feb. 26. Apr. 26	
Ring ouzel (*Turdus torquatus*) seen	Mar. 80.	Apr. 17	Oct. 11	
Barley (*Hordeum sativum*) sown	Mar. 81.	Apr. 80	Apr. 12. May 20	
Nightingale (*Sylvia luscinia*) sings	Apr. 1.	May 1	Apr. 5. July 4, last seen	
Ash (*Fraxinus excelsior*) fl.	Apr. 1.	May 4	Mar. 16. May 8 [Aug. 29	
Spiders' webs on the surface of the ground	Apr. 1			
Checquered daffodil (*Fritillaria meleagris*) fl.	Apr. 2—24		Apr. 15. May 1	
Julus terrestris ap.	Apr. 2			
Cowslip (*Primula veris*) fl.	Apr. 8—24		Mar. 8. May 17.	
Ground ivy (*Glecoma hederacea*) fl	Apr. 8—15		Mar. 2. Apr. 16	
Snipe pipes	Apr. 8			
Box tree (*Buxus sempervirens*) fl.	Apr. 8		Mar. 27. May 8.	
Elm (*Ulmus campestris*) l.	Apr. 8		Apr. 2. May 19	
Gooseberry (*Ribes grossularia*) fl.	Apr. 8—14		Mar. 21. May 1	
Currant (*Ribes hortensis*) fl.	Apr. 8—5		Mar. 24. Apr. 28	
Pear tree (*Pyrus communis*) fl.	Apr. 8.	May 21	Mar. 80. Apr. 80	
Lacerta vulgaris (newt or eft) ap.	Apr. 4		Feb. 17. Apr. 15, last seen [Oct. 9	
Dogs' mercury (*Mercurialis perennis*) fl.	Apr. 5—19		Jan. 20. Apr. 16	
Wych elm (*Ulmus glabra* seu *montana* of Smith) fl.	Apr. 5		Apr. 19. May 10, 1	
Ladysmock (*Cardamine pratensis*) fl	Apr. 6—20		Feb. 21. Apr. 26	
Cuckoo (*Cuculus canorus*) heard	Apr. 7—26		Apr. 15. May 8, last heard [June 28	
Blackthorn (*Prunus spinosa*) fl.	Apr. 7.	May 10	Mar. 18. May 8	
Deathwatch (*Termes pulsatorius*) beats	Apr. 7		Mar. 28. May 28	
Gudgeon spawns	Apr. 7			
Redstart (*Sylvia Phœnicurus*) ap.	Apr. 8—28		Apr. 5, sings Apr. 25, last seen Sept. 80	
Crown imperial (*Fritillaria imperialis*) fl.	Apr. 8—24		Apr. 1. May 18	
Titlark (*Alauda pratensis*) sings	Apr. 9—19		Apr. 14—29, sits June 16—	
Beech (*Fagus sylvatica*) l.	Apr. 10.	May 8	Apr. 24. May 25 [27	
Shellsnail (*Helix nemoralis*) comes out in troops	Apr. 11.	May 9	May 17. June 11 ap.	
Middle yellow wren [1] ap.	Apr. 11			

---

[1] Yellow wren (*Sylvia trochilus*).—W. H.　Hay bird (*Trochilus asilus*, RENNIE).—J. R.

	WHITE.		MARKWICK.	
Swift (*Hirundo apus*) ap.	Apr. 13.	May 7	Apr. 28.	May 19
Stinging fly (*Conops calcitrans*) ap.	Apr. 14.	May 17		
Whitlow grass (*Draba verna*) fl.	Apr. 14		Jan. 15.	Mar. 24
Larch tree (*Pinus-larix rubra*) l.	Apr. 14		Apr. 1.	May 9
Whitethroat (*Sylvia cinerea*) ap.	Apr. 14.	May 14	Apr. 14.	May 5, sings May 3—10, last seen Sept. 23
Red ant (*Formica rubra*) ap.	Apr. 14		Apr. 9.	June 26
Mole cricket (*Gryllus gryllotalpa*) churs	Apr. 14			
Second willow or laughing wren[1] ap.	Apr. 14—19—23		Apr. 10.	June 4
Red rattle (*Pedicularis sylvatica*) fl.	Apr. 15—19			
Common flesh-fly (*Musca carnaria*) ap.	Apr. 15			
Ladycow (*Coccinella bipunctata*) ap.	Apr. 16			
Grasshopper lark (*Alauda locustæ roce*) ap.	Apr. 16—80			
Willow wren,[2] its shivering note heard	Apr. 17.	May 7	Apr. 28.	May 1
Middle willow wren[3] (*Regulus non cristatus medius*) ap.	Apr. 17—27			
Wild cherry (*Prunus cerasus*) fl.	Apr. 18.	May 12	Mar. 80.	May 10
Garden cherry (*Prunus cerasus*) fl.	Apr. 18.	May 11	Mar. 25.	May 6
Plum (*Prunus domestica*) fl.	Apr. 18.	May 5	Mar. 24.	May 6
Harebell (*Hyacinthus non-scriptus seu Scilla nutans* of Smith) fl.	Apr. 19—25		Mar. 27.	May 8
Turtle (*Columba turtur*) coos	Apr. 20—27		May 14.	Aug 10, seen
Hawthorn (*Cratægus seu Mespilus oxycantha* of Smith) fl.	Apr. 20.	June 11	Apr. 19.	May 26
Male fool's orchis (*Orchis mascula*) fl.	Apr. 21		Mar. 29.	May 13
Blue flesh fly (*Musca vomitoria*) ap.	Apr. 21.	May 28		
Black snail or slug (*Limax ater*) abounds	Apr. 22		Feb. 1.	Oct. 24. ap.
Apple tree (*Pyrus-malus sativus*) fl.	Apr. 22.	May 25	Apr. 11.	May 26
Large bat ap.	Apr. 22.	June 11		
Strawberry wild wood (*Fragaria vesca sylv.*) fl.	Apr. 23—29		Apr. 8—9	
Sauce alone (*Erysimum alliaria*) fl.	Apr. 23		Mar. 81.	May 8
Wild or bird cherry (*Prunus avium*) fl.	Apr. 24		Mar. 80.	May 10
Apis Hypnorum ap.	Apr. 24			
Musca meridiana ap.	Apr. 24.	May 28		
Wolf fly (*Asilus*) ap.	Apr. 25			
Cabbage butterfly (*Papilio Brassicæ*) ap.	Apr. 28.	May 20	Apr. 29.	June 15
Dragon fly (*Libellula*) ap.	Apr. 80.	May 21	Apr. 18.	May 18, last seen
Sycamore (*Acer pseudoplatanus*) fl.	Apr. 80.	June 6	Apr. 20.	June 4 [Nov. 10
Bombylius minor ap.	May 1			
Glowworm (*Lampyris noctiluca*) shines	May 1.	June 11	June 19.	Sept. 28
Fern owl or goatsucker (*Caprimulgus Europæus*) ap.	May 1—26		May. 16.	Sept. 14
Common bugle (*Ajuga reptans*) fl.	May 1		Mar. 27.	May 10
Field crickets (*Gryllus campestris*) crink	May 2—24			
Chafer or maybug (*Scarabæus melolontha*) ap.	May 2—26		May 2.	July 7
Honeysuckle (*Lonicera periclymenum*) fl.	May 3—30		Apr. 24.	June 21
Toothwort (*Lathræa squamaria*) fl.	May 4—12			
Shell snails copulate	May 4	June 17		
Sedge warbler (*Sylvia salicaria*) sings	May 4		June 2—80	
Mealy tree (*Viburnum lantana*) fl.	May 5—17		Apr. 25.	May 22
Flycatcher (*Stoparola* or *Muscicapa grisola*) ap.	May 10—30		Apr. 29	May 21
Apis longicornis ap.	May 10.	June 9		
Sedge warbler (*Sylvia salicaria*) ap.	May 11—18		Aug. 2	
Oak (*Quercus robur*) fl.	May 13—15		Apr. 29.	June 4
Admiral butterfly (*Papilio Atalanta*) ap.	May 13			
Orange tip (*Papilio cardamines*) ap.	May 14		Mar. 80.	May 19

---

[1] Wood wren (*Sylvia sibilatrix*).—W. H.   (*Trochilus sibillans* RENNIE).—J. R.

[2] Wood wren. W. H.

[3] Yellow wren (*Sylvia trochilus*).—W. H.   Hay bird (*Trochilus asilus* RENNIE).—J. R.

	WHITE.		MARKWICK.	
Beech (*Fagus sylvatica*) fl.	May 15—26		Apr. 23.	May 28
Common maple (*Acer campestre*) fl.	May 16		Apr. 24.	May 27
Barberry tree (*Berberis vulgaris*) fl.	May 17—26		Apr. 28.	June 4
Wood argus butterfly (*Papilio Ægeria*) ap.	May 17			
Orange lily (*Lilium bulbiferum*) fl.	May 18.	June 11	June 14.	July 22
Burnet moth (*Sphinx Filipendulæ*) ap.	May 18.	June 13	May 24.	June 26
Walnut (*Juglans regia*) l.	May 18		Apr. 10.	June 1
Laburnum (*Cytisus laburnum*) fl.	May 18.	June 5	May. 1.	June 28
Forest fly (*Hippobosca equina*) ap.	May 18.	June 9		
Saintfoin (*Hedysarum onobrychis*) fl.	May 19.	June 8	May 21.	July 28
Peony (*Pæonia officinalis*) fl.	May 20.	June 15	Apr. 18.	May 26
Horse chestnut (*Æsculus hippocastanum*) fl.	May 21.	June 9	Apr. 19.	June 7
Lilac (*Syringa vulgaris*) fl.	May 21		Apr. 15.	May 30
Columbine (*Aquilegia vulgaris*) fl.	May 21—27		May 6.	June 13
Medlar (*Mespilus germanica*) fl	May 21.	June 20	Apr. 8.	June 19
Tormentil (*Tormentilla erecta seu officinalis* of Smith) fl.	May 21		Apr. 17.	June 11
Lily of the valley (*Convallaria majalis*) fl.	May 22		Apr. 27.	June 13
Bees (*Apis mellifica*) swarm	May 22.	July 22	May 12.	June 23
Woodroof (*Asperula odorota*) fl.	May 22—25		Apr. 14.	June 4
Wasp, female (*Vespa vulgaris*) ap.	May 23		Apr. 2.	June 4, last seen [Nov. 2
Mountain Ash (*Sorbus seu Pyrus aucuparia* of Smith) fl.	May 23.	June 8	Apr. 20.	June 8
Bird's-nest orchis (*Ophrys nidus avis*) fl.	May 24.	June 11	May 18.	June 12
White-beam tree (*Cratægus seu Pyrus aria* of Smith) fl.	May 24.	June 4	May 8	
Milkwort (*Polygala vulgaris*) fl.	May 24.	June 7	Apr. 18.	June 2
Dwarf cistus (*Cistus helianthemum*) fl.	May 25		May 4.	Aug. 8
Gelder rose (*Viburnum opulus*) fl.	May 26		May 10.	June 8
Common elder (*Sambucus nigra*) fl.	May 26.	June 25	May 6.	June 17
Cantharis noctiluca ap.	May 26			
Apis longicornis bores holes in walks	May 27.	June 9		
Mulberry tree (*Morus nigra*) l.	May 27.	June 18	May 20.	June 11
Wild service tree (*Cratægus seu Pyrus torminalis* of Smith) fl.	May 27		May 13.	June 19
Sanicle (*Sanicula Europœa*) fl.	May 27.	June 18	Apr. 23.	June 4
Avens (*Geum urbanum*) fl.	May 28		May 9.	June 11
Female fool's orchis (*Orchis morio*) fl.	May 28		Apr. 17.	May 20
Ragged Robin (*Lychnis flos cuculi*) fl.	May 29.	June 1	May 12.	June 8
Burnet (*Poterium sanguisorba*) fl.	May 29		Apr. 30.	Aug. 7
Foxglove (*Digitalis purpurea*) fl.	May 30.	June 22	May 23.	June 15
Corn flag (*Gladiolus communis*) fl.	May 30.	June 23	June 9.	July 8
Serapias longifol. fl.	May 30.	June 13		
Raspberry (*Rubus idæus*) fl.	May 30.	June 21	May 10.	June 16
Herb Robert (*Geranium Robertianum*) fl.	May 30		Mar. 7.	May 16
Figwort (*Scrophularia nodosa*) fl.	May 31		May 12.	June 20
Gromwell (*Lithospermum officinale*) fl.	May 31		May 10—24	
Wood spurge (*Euphorbia amygdaloides*) fl.	June 1		Mar. 23.	May 18
Ramsons (*Allium ursinum*) fl.	June 1		Apr. 21.	June 4
Mouse-ear scorpion grass (*Myosotis scorpioides*) fl.	June 1		Apr. 11.	June 1
Grasshopper (*Gryllus grossus*) ap.	June 1—14		Mar. 25.	July 6, last seen
Rose (*Rosa hortensis*) fl.	June 1—21		June 7.	July 1 [Nov. 8
Mouse-ear hawkweed (*Hieracium pilosella*) fl.	June 1.	July 16	Apr. 19.	June 12
Buckbean (*Menyanthes trifoliata*) fl.	June 1		Apr. 20.	June 8
Rose chafer (*Scarabœus auratus*) ap.	June 2—8		Apr. 18.	Aug. 4
Sheep (*Ovis aries*) shorn	June 2—23		May 23.	June 17
Water flag (*Iris pseudo-acorus*) fl.	June 2		May 8.	June 9
Cultivated rye (*Secale cereale*) fl.	June 2		May 27	
Hounds tongue (*Cynoglossum officinale*) fl.	June 2		May 11.	June 7

	WHITE.		MARKWICK.	
Helleborine (*Serapias latifolia*) fl.	June 2.	Aug 6	July 22.	Sept. 6
Green gold fly (*Musca Cæsar*) ap.	June 2			
Argus butterfly (*Papilio moera*) ap.	June 2			
Spearwort (*Ranunculus flammula*) fl.	June 3		Apr. 25.	June 13
Birdsfoot trefoil (*Lotus corniculatus*) fl.	June 3		Apr. 10.	June 3
Fraxinella or white dittany (*Dictamnus albus*) fl.	June 3—11		June 9.	July 24
Phryganea nigra ap.	June 3			
Angler's may-fly (*Ephemera vulg.*) ap.	June 3—14			
Ladies' finger (*Anthyllis vulneraria*) fl.	June 4		June 1.	Aug. 16
Bee orchis (*Ophrys apifera*) fl.	June 4.	July 4		
Pink (*Dianthus deltoides*) fl.	June 5—19		May 26.	July 6
Mock orange (*Philadelphus coronarius*) fl.	June 5		May 16.	June 28
Libellula Virgo ap.	June 5—20			
Vine (*Vitis vinifera*) fl.	June 7.	July 30	June 18.	July 29.
Portugal laurel (*Prunus Lusitanicus*) fl.	June 8.	July 1	June 3.	July 16
Purple spotted martagon (*Lilium martagon*) fl.	June 8—23		June 18.	July 19
Meadow cranes-bill (*Geranium pratense*) fl.	June 8.	Aug. 1		
Black bryony (*Tamus communis*) fl.	June 8		May 15.	June 21
Field pea (*Pisum savitum arvense*) fl.	June 9		May 15.	June 21
Bladder campion (*Cucubalus behen* ceu *Silene inflata* of Smith) fl.	June 9		May 4.	July 13
Bryony (*Bryonia alba*) fl.	June 9		May 18.	Aug. 17
Hedge nettle (*Stachys sylvatica*) fl.	June 10		May 28.	June 24
Bittersweet (*Solanum dulcamara*) fl.	June 11		May 15.	June 20
Walnut (*Juglans regia*) fl.	June 12		Apr. 18.	June 1
Phallus impudicus ap.	June 12.	July 23		
Rosebay willow-herb (*Epilobium angustifolium*) fl.	June 12		June 4.	July 28
Wheat (*Triticum hybernum*) fl.	June 13.	July 22	June 4—30	
Comfrey (*Symphytum officinale*) fl.	June 13		May 4.	June 28
Yellow pimpernel (*Lysimachia nemorum*) fl.	June 13—30		Apr. 10.	June 12
Tremella nostac ap.	June 15.	Aug. 24		
Buckthorn (*Rhamnus catharticus*) l.	June 16		May 25	
Cuckow-spit insect (*Cicada spumaria*) ap.	June 16		June 2—21	
Dog-rose (*Rosa canina*) fl.	June 17, 18		May 24.	June 21
Puff-ball (*Lycoperdon bovista*) ap.	June 17.	Sept. 3	May 6.	Aug. 19
Mullein (*Verbascum thapsus*) fl.	June 18		June 10.	July 22
Viper's bugloss (*Echium anglicum* seu *vulgare* of Smith) fl.	June 19		May 27.	July 3
Meadow hay cut	June 19.	July 20	June 13.	July 7
Stag beetle (*Lucanus cervus*) ap.	June 19		June 14—21	
Borage (*Borago officinalis*) fl.	June 20		Apr. 22.	July 26
Spindle tree (*Evonymus Europæus*) fl.	June 20		May 11.	June 25
Musk thistle (*Carduus nutans*) fl.	June 20.	July 4	June 4.	July 25
Dogwood (*Cornus sanguinea*) fl.	June 21		May 28.	June 27
Field scabious (*Scabiosa arvensis*) fl.	June 21		June 16.	Aug. 14
Marsh thistle (*Carduus palustris*) fl.	June 21—27		May 15.	June 19
Dropwort (*Spiræa filipendula*) fl.	June 22.	July 9	May 8.	Sept. 3
Great wild valerian (*Valeriana officinalis*) fl.	June 22.	July 7	May 22.	July 21
Quail (*Perdix Coturnix*) calls	June 22.	July 4	July 23, seen Sept. 1—18	
Mountain willow herb (*Epilobium montanum*) fl.	June 22		June 5—21	
Thistle upon thistle (*Carduus crispus*) fl.	June 28—29		May 22.	July 22
Cow parsnep (*Heracleum sphondylium*) fl.	June 28		May 27.	July 12
Earth-nut (*Bunium bulbocastanum* seu *flexuosum* of Smith) fl.	June 28		May 4—31	
Young frogs migrate	June 23.	Aug. 2		
Œstrus curvicauda ap.	June 24			
Vervain (*Verbena officionalis*) fl.	June 24		June 10.	July 17
Corn poppy (*Papaver Rhoeas*) fl.	June 24		Apr. 30.	July 15
Self-heal (*Prunella vulgaris*) fl.	June 24		June 7—23	

	WHITE.		MARKWICK.	
Agrimony (*Agrimonia eupatoria*) fl.	June 24—29		June 7.	July 9
Great horse-fly (*Tabanus bovinus*) ap.	June 24	Aug. 2		
Greater knapweed (*Centaurea scabiosa*) fl.	June 25		June 7.	Aug. 14
Mushroom (*Agaricus campestris*) ap.	June 26.	Aug. 30	Apr. 16.	Aug. 16
Common mallow (*Malva sylvestris*) fl.	June 26		May 27.	July 18
Dwarf mallow (*Malva rotundifolia*) fl.	June 26		May 12	July 30
St. John's wort (*Hypericum perforatum*) fl.	June 26		June 15.	July 12
Broom rape (*Orobanche major*) fl.	June 27.	July 4	May 9.	July 25
Henbane (*Hyoscyamus niger*) fl.	June 27		May 13.	June 19
Goats-beard (*Tragopogon pratense*) fl.	June 27		June 5—14	
Deadly nightshade (*Atropa belladonna*) fl.	June 27		May 22.	Aug. 14
Truffles begin to be found	June 28.	July 29		
Young partridges fly	June 28	July 31	July 8—28	
Lime tree (*Tilia Europœa*) fl.	June 28.	July 31	June 12.	July 30
Spear thistle (*Carduus lanceolatus*) fl.	June 28.	July 12	June 27.	July 18
Meadow sweet (*Spiræa ulmaria*) fl.	June 28		June 16.	July 24
Greenweed (*Genista tinctoria*) fl.	June 28		June 4.	July 24
Wild thyme (*Thymus serpyllum*) fl.	June 28		June 6.	July 19
Stachys germanic. fl.	June 29.	July 20		
Day lily (*Hemerocallis flava*) fl.	June 29.	July 4	May 29.	June 9
Jasmine (*Jasminum officinale*) fl.	June 29.	July 30	June 27.	July 21
Holyoak (*Alcea rosea*) fl.	June 29.	Aug. 4	July 4.	Sept. 7
Monotropa hypopithys fl.	June 29.	July 28		
Ladies bedstraw (*Galium verum*) fl.	June 29		June 22.	Aug. 3
Galium palustre fl.	June 29			
Nipplewort (*Lapsana communis*) fl.	June 29		May 30.	July 24
Welted thistle (*Carduus acanthoides*) fl.	June 29			
Sneezewort (*Achillea ptarmica*) fl.	June 30		June 22.	Aug. 3
Musk mallow (*Malva moschata*) fl.	June 30		June 9.	July 14
Pimpernel (*Anagallis arvensis*) fl.	June 30		May 4.	June 22
Hoary beetle (*Scarabæus solstit.*) ap.	June 30.	July 17		
Corn saw-wort (*Serratula arvensis* seu *Carduus arvensis* of Smith) fl.	July 1		June 15.	July 15
Pheasant's eye (*Adonis annua* seu *autumnalis* of Smith) fl.	July 1		April 11.	July 15
Red eyebright (*Euphrasia* seu *Bartsia odontites* of Smith) fl.	July 2		June 20.	Aug. 10
Thorough wax (*Bupleurum rotundifol.*) fl.	June 2			
Cockle (*Agrostemma Githago*) fl.	July 2		May 14.	July 25
Ivy-leaved wild lettuce (*Prenanthes muralis*) fl.	July 2		June 2.	July 25
Feverfew (*Matricaria* seu *Pyrethrum parthenium* of Smith) fl.	July 2		June 19.	July 24
Wall pepper (*Sedum acre*) fl.	July 3		June 8.	July 12
Privet (*Ligustrum vulgare*) fl.	July 3		June 8.	July 13
Common toadflax (*Antirrhinum linaria*) fl.	July 3		June 21.	Aug. 3
Perennial wild flax (*Linum perenne*) fl.	July 4		Apr. 21.	July 6
Whortle-berries ripe (*Vaccinium ulig.*)	July 4—24			
Yellow base rocket (*Reseda lutea*) fl.	July 5		July 19	
Blue-bottle (*Centaurea cyanus*) fl.	July 5		May 15.	Oct. 14
Dwarf carline thistle (*Carduus acaulis*) fl.	July 5—12		June 30.	Aug. 4
Bull-rush or cats-tail (*Typha latifolia*) fl.	July 6		June 29.	July 21
Spiked willow herb (*Lythrum salicaria*) fl	July 6		June 24.	Aug. 17
Black mullein (*Verbascum niger*) fl.	July 6			
Chrysanthemum coronarium fl.	July 6		May 28.	July 28
Marigolds (*Calendula officinalis*) fl.	July 6—9		Apr. 20.	July 16
Little field madder (*Sherardia arvensis*) fl.	July 7		Jan. 11.	June 6
Calamint (*Melissa* seu *Thymus calamintha* of Smith) fl.	July 7		July 21	
Black horehound (*Ballota nigra*) fl.	July 7		June 16.	Sept. 12
Wood betony (*Betonica officinalis*) fl.	July 8—19		June 10.	July 15
Round leaved bell-flower (*Campanula rotundifolia*) fl.	July 8		June 12.	July 20
All-good (*Chenopodium bonus Henricus*) fl.	July 8		Apr. 21.	June 15

	WHITE.		MARKWICK.	
Wild carrot (*Daucus carota*) fl.	July 8		June 7.	July 14
Indian cress (*Epopæolum majus*) fl.	July 8—20		June 11.	July 25
Cat-mint (*Nepeta cataria*) fl.	July 9			
Cow-wheat (*Melampyrum sylvaticum* seu *pratense* of Smith) fl.	July 9		May 2.	June 22
Crosswort (*Valantia cruciata* seu *Galium cruciatum* of Smith) fl.	July 9		Apr. 10.	May 28
Cranberries ripe	July 9—27			
Tufted vetch (*Vicia cracca*) fl.	July 10		May 31.	July 8
Wood vetch (*Vicia sylvat.*) fl.	July 10			
Little throat-wort (*Campanula glomerata*) fl.	July 11		July 28.	Aug. 18
Sheep's scabious (*Jasione montana*) fl.	July 11		June 10.	July 25
Pastinaca sylv. fl.	July 12			
White lily (*Lilium candidum*) fl.	July 12		June 21.	July 22
Hemlock (*Conium maculatum*) fl.	July 13		June 4.	July 20
Caucalis anthriscus fl.	July 13			
Flying ants ap.	July 13.	Aug. 11	Aug. 20.	Sept. 19
Moneywort (*Lysimachia nummularia*) fl.	July 13		June 14.	Aug. 16
Scarlet martagon (*Lilium Chalcedonicum*) fl.	July 14.	Aug. 4	June 21.	Aug. 6
Lesser stitchwort (*Stellaria graminea*) fl.	July 14		May 8.	June 23
Fool's parsley (*Æthusa cynapium*) fl.	July 14		June 9.	Aug. 9
Dwarf elder (*Sambucus Ebulus*) fl.	July 14—29			
Swallows and martins congregate	July 14.	Aug. 29	Aug. 12.	Sept. 8
Potatoe (*Solanum tuberosum*) fl.	July 14		June 3.	July 12
Angelica sylv. fl.	July 15			
Digitalis ferrugin. fl.	July 15—25			
Ragwort (*Senecio jacobæa*) fl.	July 15		June 22.	July 18
Golden rod (*Solidago virgaurea*) fl.	July 15		July 7.	Aug. 29
Star thistle (*Centaurea calcitrapa*) fl.	July 16		July 16.	Aug. 16
Tree primrose (*Oenothera biennis*) fl.	July 16		June 12.	July 18
Peas (*Pisum sativum*) cut	July 17.	Aug. 14	July 13.	Aug. 15
Galega officin. fl.	July 17			
Apricots (*Prunus armeniaca*) ripe	July 17.	Aug. 21	July 5.	Aug. 16
Clown's allheal (*Stachys palustris*) fl.	July 17		June 12.	July 14
Branching Willow-herb (*Epilobium ramos*) fl.	July 17			
Rye harvest begins	July 17.	Aug. 7		
Yellow centaury (*Chlora perfoliata*) fl.	July 18.	Aug. 15	June 15.	Aug. 13
Yellow vetchling (*Lathyrus aphaca*) fl.	July 18			
Enchanter's nightshade (*Circœa lutetiana*) fl.	July 18		June 20.	July 27
Water hemp agrimony (*Eupatorium cannabinum*) fl.	July 18		July 4.	Aug. 6
Giant throatwort (*Campanula trachelium*) fl.	July 19		July 13.	Aug. 14
Eyebright (*Euphrasia officinalis*) fl.	July 19		May 23.	July 19
Hops (*Humulus lupulus*) fl.	July 19.	Aug. 10	July 20.	Aug. 17
Poultry moult	July 19			
Dodder (*Cuscuta europæa* seu *epithymum* of Smith) fl.	July 20		July 9.	Aug. 7
Lesser centaury (*Gentiana* seu *Chironia centaurium* of Smith) fl.	July 20		June 3.	July 19
Creeping water parsnep (*Sium nodiflorum*) fl.	July 20		July 10.	Sept. 11
Common spurrey (*Spergula arvensis*) fl.	July 21		Apr. 10.	July 16
Wild clover (*Trifolium pratense*) fl.	July 21		May 2.	June 7
Buckwheat (*Polygonum fagopyrum*) fl.	July 21		June 27.	July 10
Wheat harvest begins	July 21.	Aug. 28	July 11.	Aug. 26
Great bur-reed (*Sparganium erectum*) fl.	July 22		June 10.	July 23
Marsh St. John's wort (*Hypericum Elodes*) fl.	July 22—31		June 16.	Aug. 10
Sun-dew (*Drosera rotundifolia*) fl.	July 22		Aug. 1	
Marsh cinquefoil (*Comarum palustre*) fl.	July 22		May 27.	July 12
Wild cherries ripe	July 22			

T

	WHITE.		MARKWICK.	
Lancashire asphodel (*Anthericum ossifragum*) fl.	July 22		June 21.	July 29
Hooded willow-herb (*Scutellaria galericulata*) fl.	July 23		June 2.	July 31
Water dropwort (*Œnanthe fistulos*) fl.	July 23			
Horehound (*Marrubium vulg.*) fl.	July 23			
Seseli caruifol. fl.	July 24			
Water plantain (*Alisma plantago*) fl.	July 24		May 31.	July 21
Alopecurus myosuroides fl.	July 25			
Virgin's bower (*Clematis vitalba*) fl.	July 25.	Aug. 9	July 18.	Aug. 14
Bees kill the drones	July 25			
Teasel (*Dypsacus sylvestris*) fl.	July 26		July 16.	Aug. 3
Wild marjoram (*Origanum vulgare*) fl.	July 26		July 17.	Aug. 29
Swifts (*Hirundo apus*) begin to depart	July 27—29		Aug. 5	
Small wild teasel (*Dipsacus pilosus*) fl.	July 28, 29			
Wood sage (*Teucrium scorodonia*) fl.	July 28		June 17.	July 24
Everlasting pea (*Lathyrus latifolius*) fl.	July 28		June 20.	July 30
Trailing St. John's wort (*Hypericum humifusum*) fl.	July 29		May 20.	June 22
White hellebore (*Veratrum album*) fl.	July 30		July 18—22	
Camomile (*Anthemis nobilis*) fl.	July 30		June 21.	Aug. 20
Lesser field Scabious (*Scabiosa columbaria*) fl.	July 30		July 13.	Aug. 9
Sunflower (*Helianthus multiflorus*) fl.	July 31.	Aug. 6	July 4.	Aug. 22
Yellow loosestrife (*Lysimachia vulgaris*) fl.	July 31		July 2.	Aug. 7
Swift (*Hirundo apus*) last seen	July 31.	Aug. 27	Aug. 11	
Oats (*Avena sativa*) cut	Aug. 1—16		July 26.	Aug. 19
Barley (*Hordeum sativum*) cut	Aug. 1—26		July 27.	Sept. 4
Lesser hooded willow-herb (*Scutellaria minor*) fl.	Aug. 1		Aug. 8.	Sept. 7
Middle fleabane (*Inula dysenterica*) fl.	Aug. 2		July 7.	Aug. 3
Apis manicata ap.	Aug. 2			
Swallow-tailed butterfly (*Papalio machaon*) ap.	Aug. 2		Apr. 20.	June 7, last seen [Aug. 28
Whame or burrel fly (*Œstrus bovis*) lays eggs on horses	Aug. 3—19			
Sow thistle (*Sonchus arvensis*) fl.	Aug. 3		June 17.	July 21
Plantain fritillary (*Papilio cinxia*) ap.	Aug. 3			
Yellow succory (*Picris hieracioides*) fl.	Aug. 4		June 6—25	
Musca mystacea ap.				
Canterbury bells (*Campanula medium*) fl.	Aug. 5		June 5.	Aug. 11
Mentha longifol. fl.	Aug. 5			
Carline thistle (*Carlina vulgaris*) fl.	Aug. 7		July 21.	Aug. 18
Venetian sumach (*Rhus cotinus*) fl.	Aug. 7		June 5.	July 20
Ptinus pectinicornus ap.	Aug. 7			
Burdock (*Arctium lappa*) fl.	Aug 8		June 17.	Aug. 4
Fell-wort (*Gentiana amarella*) fl.	Aug. 8.	Sept. 3		
Wormwood (*Artemisia absinthium*) fl.	Aug. 8		July 22.	Aug. 21
Mugwort (*Artemisia vulgaris*) fl.	Aug. 8		July 9.	Aug. 10
St. Barnaby's thistle (*Centaurea solstit.*) fl.	Aug. 10			
Meadow saffron (*Colchicum autumnale*) fl.	Aug. 10.	Sept. 13	Aug. 15.	Sept. 29
Michaelmas daisy (*Aster Tradescanti*) fl.	Aug. 12.	Sept. 27	Aug. 11.	Oct. 8
Meadow rue (*Thalictrum flavum*) fl.	Aug. 14			
Sea holly (*Eryngium marit.*) fl.	Aug. 14			
China aster (*Aster chinensis*) fl.	Aug. 14.	Sept. 28	Aug. 6.	Oct. 2
Boletus albus ap.	Aug. 14		May 10	
Less Venus looking-glass (*Campanula hybrida*) fl.	Aug. 15		May 14	
Carthamus tinctor. fl.	Aug. 15			
Goldfinch (*Fringilla carduelis*) young broods ap.	Aug. 15		June 15	
Lapwings (*Tringa vanellus*) congregate	Aug. 15.	Sept. 12	Sept. 25.	Feb. 4

	WHITE.		MARKWICK.	
Black-eyed marble butterfly (*Papilio semele*) ap.	Aug. 15			
Birds reassume their spring notes	Aug. 16			
Devil's bit (*Scabiosa succisa*) fl.	Aug. 17		June 22.	Aug. 28
Thistle down floats	Aug. 17.	Sept. 10		
Ploughman's spikenard (*Conyza squarrosa*) fl.	Aug. 18			
Autumnal dandelion (*Leontodon autumnale*) fl.	Aug. 18		July 25	
Flies abound in windows	Aug. 18			
Linnets (*Fringilla linota*) congregate	Aug. 18.	Nov. 1	Aug. 22.	Nov. 8
Bulls make their shrill autumnal noise	Aug. 20			
Aster amellus fl.	Aug. 22			
Balsam (*Impatiens balsamina*) fl.	Aug. 23		May 22.	July 26
Milk thistle (*Carduus marianus*) fl.	Aug. 24		Apr. 21.	July 18
Hop-picking begins	Aug. 24.	Sept. 17	Sept. 1—15	
Beech (*Fagus sylvatica*) turns yellow	Aug. 24.	Sept. 22	Sept. 5—29	
Soapwort (*Saponaria officinalis*) fl.	Aug. 25		July 19.	Aug. 23
Ladies' traces (*Ophrys spiralis*) fl.	Aug 27.	Sept. 12	Aug. 18.	Sept. 18
Small golden black-spotted butterfly (*Papilio phlœas*) ap.	Aug. 29			
Swallow (*Hirundo rustica*) sings	Aug. 29		Apr. 11.	Aug. 20
Althœa frutex (*Hibiscus syriacus*) fl.	Aug. 30.	Sept. 2	July 20.	Sept. 28
Great frittilary (*Papilio paphia*) ap.	Aug. 80			
Willow red under-wing moth (*Phalœna pacta*) ap.	Aug. 81			
Stone curlew (*Otis œdicnemus*) clamours	Sept. 1	Nov. 7	June 17	
Phœlana russula ap.	Sept. 1			
Grapes ripen	Sept. 4.	Oct. 24	Aug. 31.	Nov. 4
Wood owls hoot	Sept. 4.	Nov. 9		
Saffron butterfly (*Papilio hyale*) ap.	Sept. 4		Aug. 5.	Sept. 26
Ring ouzel appears on its autumnal visit	Sept. 4—30			
Flycatcher (*Muscicapa grisola*) last seen	Sept. 6—29		Sept. 4—30	
Beans (*Vicia faba*) cut	Sept. 11		Aug. 9.	Oct. 14
Ivy (*Hedera helix*) fl.	Sept. 12.	Oct. 2	Sept. 18.	Oct. 28
Stares congregate	Sept. 12.	Nov. 1	June 4.	Mar. 21
Wild honeysuckles fl. a second time	Sept. 25			
Woodlark sings	Sept. 28.	Oct. 24		
Woodcock (*Scolopax rusticola*) returns	Sept. 29.	Nov. 11	Oct. 1. Nov. 1, young ones Apr. 28, last seen Apr. 11	
Strawberry tree (*Arbutus unedo*) fl.	Oct. 1		May 21.	Dec. 10
Wheat sown	Oct. 3.	Nov. 9	Sept. 28.	Oct. 19
Swallows last seen. (N.B. The house martin the latest)	Oct. 4.	Nov. 5	Nov. 16	
Redwing (*Turdus iliacus*) comes	Oct. 10.	Nov. 10	Oct. 1. Dec. 18, sings Feb. 10, Mar. 21, last seen Apr. 18	
Fieldfare (*Turdus pilaris*) returns	Oct. 12.	Nov. 28	Oct. 18. Nov. 18, last [seen May 1	
Gossamer fills the air	Oct. 15—27			
Chinese holyoak (*Alcea rosea*) fl.	Oct. 19		July 7.	Aug. 21
Hen chaffinches congregate	Oct. 20.	Dec. 81		
Wood pigeons come	Oct. 23.	Dec. 27		
Royston crow (*Corvus cornix*) returns	Oct. 23.	Nov. 29	Oct. 18. Nov. 17, last [seen Apr. 15	
Snipe (*Scolopax gallinago*) returns	Oct. 25.	Nov. 20	Sept. 29. Nov. 11, last [seen Apr. 14	
Tortoise begins to bury himself	Oct. 27.	Nov. 26		
Rooks (*Corvus frugilegus*) return to their nest trees	Oct. 81.	Dec. 25	June 29.	Oct. 20
Bucks grunt	Nov. 1			
Primrose (*Primula vulgaris*) fl.	Nov. 10		Oct. 7.	Dec. 80
Green whistling plover ap.	Nov. 13, 14			
Helvella mitra ap.	Nov. 16			
Greenfinches flock	Nov. 27			
Hepatica fl.	Nov. 80.	Dec. 29	Feb. 19	

T 2

	WHITE.	MARKWICK.
Furze (*Ulex europœus*) fl.	Dec. 4—21	Dec. 16—31
Polyanthus (*Primula polyantha*) fl.	Dec. 7—16	Dec. 31
Young lambs dropped	Dec. 11—27	Dec. 12.　Feb. 21
Moles work in throwing up hillocks	Dec. 12—23	
Helleborus fœtidus fl.	Dec. 14—30	
Daisy (*Bellis perennis*) fl.	Dec. 15	Dec. 26—31
Wallflower (*Cheiranthus cheiri* seu *fruti-culosus* of Smith) fl.	Dec. 15	Nov. 5
Mezereon fl.	Dec. 15	
Snowdrop fl.	Dec. 29	

IN SESE VERTITUR ANNUS.

NOTES, OBSERVATIONS, AND ADDITIONS

BY

FRANK BUCKLAND.

MEMOIR OF GILBERT WHITE.

GILBERT WHITE was born at Selborne, Hants, July 18th, 1720, in the seventh year of the reign of King George I., and died June 26th, 1793, being seventy-two years and eleven months old.

In order fully to appreciate his labours, I will endeavour to throw back the mind of the reader to the prominent events of which Gilbert White might have been witness, or about which he must have heard people talking.

Queen Anne died in 1714, six years before White was born. The year of White's birth (1720) was the year of the South Sea Bubble. When he was one year old, 1721, the great Duke of Marlborough died. When he was three years old, 1723, Atterbury was Dean of Westminster. When he was seven years old, 1727, Sir Isaac Newton died. When he was ten,[1] 1730, the great John Hunter, the anatomist and physiologist, and founder of the Royal College of Surgeons, was born. When he was twenty-five years old, 1745, Prince Charles Edward gained Edinburgh after the victory of Prestonpans. When he was twenty-six, on October 22nd, 1746, he took his degree at Oxford, and was Senior Proctor in 1752. When he was thirty-two, 1752, the new style of computing the almanac was introduced into England. When thirty-seven, 1757, the conquest of India began under Colonel, afterwards Lord, Clive. When thirty-nine, 1759, General Wolfe was killed at Quebec. When he was forty, 1760, George III. ascended the throne. When he was forty-four, 1764, Canada was annexed. When he was fifty-eight, 1778, the Earl of Chatham died. When he was sixty-three, 1783, America was separated from England.

Gilbert White died on June 26th, 1793. The great John Hunter, the anatomist, died also in 1793, viz., on October 16th, aged sixty-four, or nine years younger than Gilbert White.

[1] Gilbert White went to school at Basingstoke, under the Rev. Thomas Warton, Vicar of Basingstoke.

Gilbert White's first letter with a date is Letter X., August 4th, 1767. The preface to the first edition is dated January 1st, 1788. Gilbert White, therefore, must have been writing his letters over twenty years.

If the reader wishes thoroughly to appreciate the great merits of the illustrious author, he must not fail to pay a visit to Selborne itself.[1] The first impression of Selborne, especially when driving in from Alton, is that it is a perfect type of English woodland scenery and country life. The visitor should carry his "White" in his hand and read the great Gilbert's graphic writings on the very spots described ; he should also take a good Ordnance map with him, in order to get a general idea of the neighbouring country.

Under circumstances as above Selborne and its vicinity become most interesting. I do not think the village, a sketch of which is given by Mr. Delamotte, p. 12, can have been much altered since White's time, except that some of the shops now have plate-glass fronts, which would astonish Gilbert White considerably if he could see them.

There is no portrait whatever existing of Gilbert White. In Mr. White's house (see drawing p. 9) the late Professor Bell pointed out to me a portrait of an old gentleman who was White's grandfather as well as godfather ; he has a very intelligent face, strongly-marked furrows ; certainly the face of a man of a well-marked character. White's walking-stick was in one corner of the room : it is a pale Malacca cane ; on the top is a silver plate bearing the figure of an Heraldic creature. A portrait in oil of the hybrid between a black-cock and a pheasant was over the door.

In the edition of 1713 there is a general view of Selborne. The figure standing on the brow of the hill, in the old-fashioned costume of White's time, is supposed to be White himself. He probably wore a clerical wig, knee-breeches and buckles. I tried all I could to get local evidence or stories about White. A villager of the name of Henry Wells told me that "White was thought very little of till he was dead and gone, and then he was thought a great deal of." He then referred me to Mrs. Small.

Mrs. Small is ninety-three years of age, a very shrewd, intelligent old woman. Mrs. Small was eleven years old when White died ; she could not recollect much about him except that "he was a quiet old gentleman with very old-fashioned sayings ;" and that "there was in White's time a butcher's shop opposite his door, and a butcher's shop is there now." "White used to give a number of poor people a goose every Christmas. He was very kind in giving presents to the poor. He used to keep a *locust* which crawled about the garden." When I said "tortoise"[2] she said, "Ah, that's what I mean."

---

[1] Selborne can be reached from London by going from Waterloo Station to Alton, about two hours' journey. Selborne is about five miles from Alton. There is another route from Liss Station on the South Western line.

[2] White's tortoise was named Timothy.

She said that old Dame Terry knew all about White, but Dame Terry had been dead forty-eight years. Dame Terry must have been over eighty, therefore she must have been contemporary with White many years.

Mr. Binnie, gardener to Mr. Bell, said that there was an old man of the name of James Cobb who was nearly ninety, and was eight years old when White died. When Cobb saw White coming he used to run and put stones into the ruts and fill them up. White used to give him a penny and say "Good boy, good boy." Mr. Binnie recollects Butler the thatcher, who was married by White, and who died aged ninety-two. Mr. Binnie said that Hale who died in 1855, aged seventy-eight, described White to him as a "little, thin prim, upright man." Hale must have been sixteen years old when White died.

Gilbert White was a quiet, unassuming, but very observant country parson. The access to Selborne in those days must have been very difficult (*vide* page 11). This worthy man therefore occupied his time in observing and recording the habits of his parishioners, quadruped as well as feathered.

Mr. Bell kindly took me to a room up stairs, where he showed me a large number of White's manuscripts. Having thoroughly inspected White's house and village, I was able to discover why his notes are so disconnected. When he returned home he took a sheet of paper and wrote his observations of the day. I observed the manuscript was very much faded; in those days it is evident that blotting-paper was not invented, or, if so, was little, if at all used, for many of the lines were irridescent, as though the dust used instead of blotting-paper was made of brass filings or some such material.

White's sun-dial still exists at the end of the garden, the lawn of which is covered with the most perfect soft grass carpet.

From page 9 of the book the visitor will at once recognise White's house. It has been little, if at all, altered for many a long year. Out of this very door and through the lattice-gate Gilbert White passed to and fro into the village highway. The Plestor, page 5, is the "Charing Cross" of the village. The word "Plestor" means playing-place :—I suppose it may be freely translated "playground." The oak which White mentions as having been formerly there, and which was said to be 400 years old, is now represented by a sycamore. This must have been a tree of some considerable size thirty-two years ago, and this because Mr. Binnie, Mr. Bell's gardener, tells me that at a fair held in the Plestor, and abolished thirty-two years since, one limb of it fell off and destroyed the booth owned by a black man.

The visitor should examine the magnificent yew-tree in the church-yard; its age is unknown. It is twenty-five feet round. The Vicar, the Rev. Mr. Parsons,[1] kindly lent us the keys of the church. The tablet commemorating White's death is on the wall near the altar on

---

[1] I regret to hear that Mr. Parsons died, Sept. 1875, since the above lines were written.

the right-hand side of the spectator. An inscription on the top reads as follows: "This monument of Gilbert White, M.A., and B. White, Esq., was removed into the chancel MDCCCX." I understand from the Vicar that White was never rector of Selborne, but only curate; he was also curate of Faringdon eighteen years.[1]

The stonework inside the church is completely covered with white-wash, probably the tasteful work of some former churchwarden. The Vicar, I understand, contemplates restoring the inside of his church when sufficient funds are forthcoming. Gilbert White's grave can thus be found:—On coming out of the church door turn to the left and keep to the left, and at a short distance will be found the gravestone with the simple "G. W." cut on it. The tombstones in this churchyard are very much injured by moss and lichens, which have filled up the inscriptions. Over White's grave there ought to be placed a modern monument of some kind.

At page 10 White mentions the " tenpenny nails in the walls," about Selborne. I looked about for these everywhere; at last I found them in abundance, stuck into the walls of the church, and particularly on the wall facing the visitor on his left as he is about to enter the porch.

The visitor should not fail to visit the Zigzag. This is a rough pathway up the side of a very steep hill, which forms part of the hanger or copse which faces the back of Mr. Bell's house. The term hanger is old Saxon for a wood. Holt is also an old Saxon term for wood; we find it in Aldershott, which was formerly Alders-holt, and also in the word Hainhault. The soil of the Zigzag is chalk, easy enough to ascend when dry, but with dew or rain it becomes almost dangerous. At the top there is a splendid view for miles around. At the bottom of the hanger I was fortunate in meeting with Mr. Wells, farmer, of Selborne. He pointed out to me close to the gate a shiver-leaf aspen, which is said to have been planted by Gilbert White. It is eight feet six round and about a hundred feet high.

At and about this place the vegetation is very luxurious. It may be called a "Primæval English forest."

At page 11 will be found Mr. Delamotte's drawing of the rocky lane leading to Alton. White's description of these "hanging lanes" is admirable; but they are now much more wild than in White's time a hundred years since. All traffic has ceased in them, a new road having been made to Alton.

The only road from Alton in White's time was along these dreadful lanes, and it is difficult to conceive how a horse and cart could be got through them. This old lane takes a very circuitous course, and comes out at Alton near the Railway Station. The new road bisects it near Norton Farm, one mile from Selborne: the visitor should get out and examine it at this point. I don't suppose that it has been traversed by human being for many years—it looks like a jungle. There is another

---

[1] The living of Selborne belongs to Magdalen College, Oxford.

very good specimen of these hanging lanes on the road from Selborne to Liss Station : this a terrible-looking place, almost dangerous to walk through.

The only road to Selborne being through these "hanging lanes," it is plain that White could not have had much society. To the existence of these hanging lanes, therefore, I mainly attribute " White's History of Selborne." In these olden times White must have been hemmed in on all sides ; there were few or no human visitors arriving and departing ; the only arrivals and departures that White could notice were those that came through the air, *i.e.* birds'; and of his feathered parishioners he has indeed given us ample reports. The birds, so far as I can ascertain, have not changed their dates of arrival or departure since White's time, one hundred years ago.

For the reason that White was so cut off from populous places his attention was greatly devoted to the manners and habits of birds and their arrival and departure. In fact Selborne was a big birdcage in which White himself was inclosed even more than the birds. It will be observed that White does not go far from home for his descriptions ; his observations were taken within a small radius of his house. He had great opportunities of making observations, as the place was so secluded and quiet.

Shortly afterwards I passed the splendid residence lately erected by Lord Selborne, and all of a sudden I came in view of Wolmer Pond (see page 15). I was amazingly surprised to find this grand pond nearly dried up—a pitiful sight to a fish-culturist. The culture of fish-ponds is a subject to which I have paid great attention. I was just reading the following passage from White :—" This lonely domain is a very agreeable haunt for many sorts of wild fowl, which not only frequent it in the winter, but breed there in the summer,"—when up rose nine wild ducks ; they flew round two or three times and then went straight away. A great portion of what was once the pond is now a mass of different kinds of mosses.

It will be observed that White writes as follows at page 94 : " I wish it was in my power to procure you one of those songsters ; but I am no bird-catcher, and so little used to birds in a cage, that I fear if I had one it would soon die for want of skill in feeding."

When I undertook the task of re-editing this book I was determined, if possible, to do my best to implant upon the original text as much more information as the space afforded would allow. White acknowledged himself that he was no bird-catcher.

I have been, therefore, most fortunate in obtaining the services of Mr. Charles R. Davy, bird-catcher, who for thirty years has largely dealt in all kinds of British birds, both "seed-eating" and "soft-meat." Mr. Davy is thoroughly conversant, from practical observation, with the habits, manners, and treatment of English birds. Mr. Davy, Mr. Searle, my secretary, and myself, have gone through White's remarks two or three times, and I have placed Mr. Davy's observations on record.

NOTES AND OBSERVATIONS

BY

FRANK BUCKLAND.

WYCH HAZEL, OAKS, p. 5.—My late lamented friend Mr. Menzies, Deputy-Surveyor of Windsor Great Park, sends me the following note :—

The Wych Elm referred to at page 5 must have been a remarkably fine one, and, judging by what I know of others, probably 500 years old. The Wych Elm is not nearly so common as the English Elm. The distinguishing feature of the former is its rough serrated leaf. The distinguishing feature of the English Elm, especially under fifty years of age, is the cork-looking excrescences upon the points of the branches.

The finest elms at Windsor and in the Playing Fields of Eton are about 300 years old, and 15 feet in circumference; but the average age of an elm is about 100 years less than this.

The *Vast Oak*, growing in the Plestor, cannot have its age estimated, as no dimensions are given. As a rough rule, there are ten years' growth in every inch of radius of the stem. It is not known to what age or to what dimensions an oak will grow with fair play. In fact, I have never known an oak die of pure old age. Either lightning or neglected wounds have been the cause of death ; you may recover an oak in its last stage by removing the cause of decay.

William the Conqueror's Oak at Windsor is certainly 1,200 to 1,500 years of age, and is about 33 feet round; the King Oak is 35 feet round, and as old ; Queen Elizabeth's Oak, 29 feet round, is probably 1,000 years old ; the age of Shakespeare's Oak it is impossible to estimate, as it is now only a white shell with a few bleached hoary branches.

THE PROGRESSIVE RATE OF GROWTH OF THE HORNS OF RED DEER.—By the kindness of Mr. Durban, curator, and the authorities of the museum at Exeter, I am enabled to give drawings of a series of Red Deer horns. These horns were shed by the same deer, and carefully preserved as they fell off. The following is the account of this most interesting and unique series :—

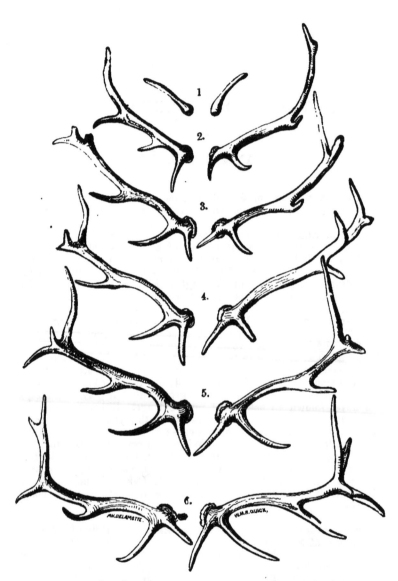

FIGS. 1 TO 6.—PROGRESSIVE GROWTH OF RED DEER HORNS.

"The six pairs of horns belonged to the same animal, reared from a calf by John Clarke, of Lynton, N. Devon, and were shed annually in the spring. The drawings illustrate the mode of growth of the horns or antlers and their annual increase in size from the first to the eighth year of the animal's life. This Red Deer was kept in a dry grass field without water, and was never supplied with any artificial food whatever. Before the animal was one year old the horns began to appear, about the latter end of May. In the following April these were shed, when

FIG. 7.—RED DEER, EIGHT YEARS OLD.

they were nine inches long (Fig. 1). A very short time afterwards, others began to be developed, and in the latter end of April following these were also shed, though not both on the same day. These had 'brow,' 'bay,' and 'tray,' with upright—altogether upwards of two feet in length (Fig. 2). In his fourth year he had the same kind of antlers, with two points on top on one horn, and two and an offer on the other (Fig. 3). In his fifth year, antlers as before, with two points and an offer on each horn (Fig. 4). In his sixth year, antlers the same, with three points on each top. In his seventh year, antlers as before, with four points on each top (Fig. 6). In his eighth year (when he was killed), antlers as before, though on one horn the points were not so perfect as in his seventh year. It will thus be seen that this deer had seven points on each horn, making together fourteen (Fig. 7).

"The age of the stag, or male red deer, which alone bears horns or antlers, may be pretty easily determined by the number of the branches till its seventh or eighth year; but after that period the increase of those parts is not subject to any fixed rule. The oldest have seldom more than ten or twelve branches.

"In England, at the present day, the red deer exists in a state of nature only on Exmoor, a wild tract of country on the borders of Devon and Somerset, from whence came the animal whose head and horns are here exhibited."

The above account is from the pen of Mr. J. Clarke, who has published a "Treatise on the Growth of the Horns of the Red Deer." (A. P. Wood, Bookseller, Barnstaple, 1866.)

Most deer and antelopes have curious depressions called "tear-pits" under the eye. They contain a waxy secretion. The use of this is probably sexual, as they rub the secretion on to the boughs of trees, &c.

MAN-TRAPS AND SPRING-GUNS, p. 17.—In Gilbert White's time man-traps and spring-guns were probably set for the benefit of the Waltham Blacks which he mentions. These instruments were made illegal in 1826. The drawing opposite is taken from a photograph of two man-traps that belonged to my late friend, Sir Robert Clifton, then M.P. for Nottingham; they act upon the principle of a rat-trap, with very strong springs at each end, and inflicted fearful wounds upon the human leg. Their size will be seen from the height of Sir Robert's game-keeper, who has his hand upon the top of the trap. Sir Robert put this man into one of these traps and had a great difficulty to get him out again. In the Ashmolean Museum at Oxford there are three very fine specimens of man-traps, also a spring-gun. The spring-gun is about the size of an old-fashioned navy pistol. It turns upon a pivot; wires were attached to it, which were suspended in all directions among the bushes about the height of a man's knee; by a simple mechanism the gun revolved and went off exactly in the direction of the wire which was touched by the man's leg. Close to these traps in the Ashmolean Museum is the burnt end of a wooden stake, which was, without a doubt, used at the martyrdom of Cranmer, Latimer, and Ridley.

RABBIT WITH DEFORMED TEETH, p. 18.—It often happens that rabbits are shot with teeth deformed in the manner represented in the engraving on page 290. It will be observed that the two lower teeth project upwards and forwards so as to come almost on a level with the top of the rabbit's nose. In order to understand how this deformity came about, the reader should examine the teeth of the next rabbit sent up to table. He will find that the tips are sharp and chisel-like, and that the lower end of the tooth is filled with a gelatinous substance.   The rabbit, by continual gnawing, wears away the tips of these rodent teeth ; as the tooth is continuously growing, the soft pulp at the root gradually hardens itself into true tooth structure.   The four rodent teeth are thus regularly wearing each other down, and, as they all grow at a similar rate, they keep each other level.

MAN TRAPS.

Should any one of the four teeth get injured or knocked out of gear, the opposing tooth still continues to grow.   In the rabbit now before us a shot or some other injury has partially dislocated the lower jaw; the lower teeth, therefore, do not correspond with those in the upper jaw, they have therefore continued to grow unchecked.   Their length is grown to the length of one inch and a quarter.

There is great variey in deformities of rabbits' teeth, and I have in

U

my museum several fine specimens; some teeth are almost in the shape of a ring, others are spiral like a corkscrew.

RABBIT WITH DEFORMED TEETH.

The elephant's tusk grows from a socket in the skull outwards, exactly in the same way as does a rabbit's tooth. Musket-balls are often found inside elephant's tusks, completely grown over with ivory. If we drop a shot into the cavity of the tooth of a boiled rabbit, and imagine the tooth put back again into the rabbit's jaw to grow, it will give some idea how bullets are sometimes imbedded in solid ivory without any apparent hole by means of which they have obtained an entry.

The engraving represents a specimen of a remarkable abnormal growth from the hollow part of the tusk of an elephant. There was nothing in the cavity, but it is evident that nature was attempting to cover up a foreign body which probably was a bullet. The specimen

NODULE OF IVORY.

was presented to me by Messrs. Brooks & Co., of Cumberland Market, who cut up great quantities of ivory in their business.

I now give a note showing a novel use of crabs, viz., a new plan of bolting rabbits from their holes by means of them. Mr. Lambton Young writes me :—

"I have met with a novel way of ferreting for rabbits in Jersey. On the estate of my friend is a rabbit-warren, but lately the rabbits were found to be diminishing in numbers very rapidly. A watch was set, but there were no guns heard, or suspicious persons observed to go on the ground; the only frequenter of the place was an old lame fisherman, who walked with a broomstick to aid his steps. At last suspicion attached to this old fellow, but on being questioned, he said he only passed the warren to go down on the rocks to get his rod to catch grey mullet; but, acting on the advice of one of the workmen in the garden, my friend kept a look-out, and at last saw the lame old rascal, when in the warren, look round first to see if he was observed, and sit down above the most frequented burrow. He then took from his pocket a couple of the small green crabs so common on the sea-shore and put them into the hole, and they at once ran down; soon after, up bolted a fine rabbit, and our infirm friend knocked it over at once with his broomstick and hid it in a furze-bush. He then repeated the trick, and soon killed five fine rabbits."

Mr. Matthias Dunn increases the efficacy of the above prescription thus :—" Allow me to say the crab, to do the work as he ought, when put in the rabbit-hole, must have a lighted end of candle stuck fast to his back, with a little clay or grease to hold it firm, and a formidable creature, thus armed, is he; for neither fox, badger, nor rabbit can withstand his fiery torch. This, then, is the impromptu ferret used in this neighbourhood, and the business is said to be a failure without the candle. Hence I expect the old man had the same machinery at work to get the rabbit."

CARP, p. 21.—Mr. Charles, fishmonger, of Arabella Row, in 1866 sent me two very fine carp. The largest weighed 21½ lbs., was 33 inches long, and 20½ inches in girth. The smaller fish weighed 16½ lbs. being 25 inches in length, and 23 inches in girth. They came from Haarlem Meer, in Holland, and were both females.

I had the opportunity of casting the larger fish, and I also carefully counted her roe, which weighed 3½ lbs. This was done by taking the average of two or three grains, a calculation was then made of the aggregate number of eggs. These amounted to no less than one million three hundred and ten thousand seven hundred and fifty (1,310,750) in this one fish, nearly equal to half the population of London. I also weighed the eggs of the smaller carp, they weighed 5½ lbs., giving their total number, two millions and fifty-nine thousand seven hundred and fifty-nine (2,059,759). I can guarantee the accuracy of the weighing, and also the calculations, which were made for me by Mr. Thomas, a professional accountant.

WILD BOAR, p. 25.—Gilbert White would have been much interested at seeing the wild boar, or rather the wild sow. It is the property of my friend, Captain Salvin, of Whitmoor House, Guildford. Lady Susan—for that is the name of the tame wild sow—is thus described by her kind master :—

" My sow originally came from Syria, and was given to me by H.H. the Mahárajah Duleep Singh. She is a remarkably fine healthy animal, and her instinct and affection can only be equalled by the dog. She follows me almost daily in my walks like a dog, to the great astonishment of strangers. Of course I only take her out before the crops are up, and too low to injure, during the spring and summer months.

" I always have her belled to hear when she is in the woods, &c.;

and the bell, which is a good sheep's bell, is fastened round her neck with a strap and a buckle.

"Her leaping powers are extraordinary either over 'water' or 'timber,' indeed only a few weeks since she cleared some palings (between which she had been purposely placed to secure her for a time) three feet ten inches in height. Knowing my pig's excellent temper, even when she has young pigs, and when domestic sows are always most savage, I was once guilty of a practical joke. I got a blacksmith who was quite ignorant of even the existence of my pig, to 'come and ring a pig.' The stye being under a building, he had to

CAPTAIN SALVIN'S WILD SOW.

enter it at a low door, which was some distance from the sow's yard, where she was feeding. He entered, shutting the door to keep the pig in, and thinking his subject was an ordinary one and that assistants were following him to hold the cord, &c. He had not been gone a minute, before I heard the greatest 'rum-ti-tum' at the door, and cries of 'For goodness' sake, sir, let me out! let me out! I never saw such a beast in my life!' and out came the poor blacksmith, pale with fright, but all the consolation he got was a jolly good laugh at his own expense.

"From the many places called after the wild boar, as Wild Boar Clough in Cheshire, Branspeth and Brandon in the county of Durham,

&c., this animal must have been very common in England some two or three hundred years back. Perhaps I may be forgiven if I explain the connection that Branspeth has with the subject: Bran in the north of England means a boar, and no doubt the 'peth' is a corruption of path, hence Branspeth. Brandon was originally Branden, or the den or lair of the boar, and, curiously enough, tradition says they were very plentiful in the neighbourhood. Clough signifies a wood along the steep sides of two hills close to each other."

RATS AND MICE, p. 30.—In England we have three distinct varieties of rat—the common house or barn rat (originally called the Norway rat), the old black English rat, now almost extinct, and the water rat or water vole. The Norwegian rat is said to have been imported in the holds of ships, and to have successfully invaded the territory of his black brother till he completely dispossessed him. In the spring and summer, the house rat uses the river bank and watercourses in common with the water vole, and as he swims and dives well, though he cannot continue long under water, he gives rise to much confusion and many errors concerning the two species. Apart from many other distinguishing marks, the coat or fur of the house rat is entirely different from that of the water rat—the fur of the water rat being velvety and long. The water rat, save where he bores through water-dams and interferes with drainage, is harmless, living principally on herbage and roots.

OLD BRITISH RAT.—From time to time I receive specimens of the ancient British black rat, which is now gradually becoming extinct. It is disappearing gradually before the common brown or Norway rat. It is probable that the black British rat was introduced into this country from France. In Wales it is called Llygoden Frenzig, or the French mouse. The black rat is much slighter in make, as compared with the brown rat, his upper jaw projects further over the lower jaw than it does in the brown rat, his ears are much larger and his tail very much

RAT'S TAIL.

longer than in his first cousin, and lastly his colour is a jet black, with numerous long hairs projecting out from the lower fur-like coat.

He is a very timid creature, and rarely shows fight; he is in fact not powerful, but his want of strength is made up by his excessive activity. The black rat does not frequent drains, cellars, &c., but rather inhabits the rafters of outhouses: they are said to be still plentiful in the Isle of Dogs, in Jersey, and Bristol. I have described this rat fully in my "Curiosities of Natural History," first series. Bentley, 1874.

Mr. Delamotte has given a very faithful portrait of this interesting little animal; observe the silky appearance of his coat, his delicate attentive ear, his intelligent eye, his long whiskers, by means of which he feels his way about when out feeding at night, and his little pinkish white paws (the rat

always keeps his paws excessively clean. Fear and danger constantly
surround him, yet he looks happy and contented.

To most people a rat's tail is not a very interesting object. If however it be carefully examined it will be found to present a very curious
structure. The skin is arranged in the form of rings, and from between
the rings project rows of fine stiff hairs.

OLD ENGLISH BLACK RAT.

These hairs assist the rat to hold on with his tail as he is climbing
about rafters, &c. ; he also uses his tail as a balancing pole. You will
see all this if you set a tame white rat to climb along a rope.

The following story will illustrate how an elephant can be persecuted
almost to death by rats. There is a very fine elephant at the Zoological
Gardens at Clifton, near Bristol. This elephant was found to be very

sick and sorry; my friend, Mr. Bartlett, of the Zoological Gardens, London, was sent for to prescribe. The animal was paraded on the grass for him to examine. Mr. Bartlett desired the keeper to make the elephant show her feet; when the animal lifted up her feet, they were found to be gnawed into holes by rats. The rats were very abundant in the elephant house, and when the elephant had lain down to sleep they had eaten the gristly portion of her feet away. The rats were of course at once destroyed and the elephant put into a new house, where she is now well and thriving. The poor elephant had been suffering not only from the wounds in her feet, but also from want of sleep, as the rats kept her awake all night by their persecutions. I think it very likely that horses in old stables are often kept awake by rats. All those who are fond of their horses should look to this.

Hoopoe, p. 32.—The "Hoopoe" (from French *huppé*, tufted; or Italian, *bubela,* from its cry "bu bu bu") is not an uncommon bird in Spain, and is abundant in Egypt and Arabia.

Stanley, on Birds, tells us the hoopoe is called the child of Solomon, from the tradition that the hoopoe formed part of the cargo of the ships of Tarshish. The tradition of the people whence the hoopoe was brought was that its crest was at first of gold, but that, owing to man's cupidity for the precious metal, the birds were killed for their crowns; they therefore met and petitioned Solomon to ameliorate their condition, and, as he understood the language of animals, he put up his prayers that the crown of gold might henceforth be changed to a crown of feathers. The change was instantly made to the present lovely crest with which the hoopoe is now adorned.

Mr. Davy informs me that lately two hoopoes were shot on the bank of the Midland Railway, in the neighbourhood of Hampstead, in Gospel Oak field. They are very tame birds, and being very showy are easily detected. They feed on small food on the ground, on caterpillars, worms, and small beetles. Mr. Davy had one in his shop for two years. It was a very ravenous bird, would eat any animal or vegetable matter—prefering animal—it never feeds on trees. It runs and feeds much after the manner of the starling. The hoopoes would probably stay out the summer with us if they were not so persecuted. When tame it is a very funny bird (and when it puts up its crest) a very beautiful bird.

Crossbills, p. 33.—Crossbills are rare in Britain. Their song is very soft. In severe winters they are found sometimes in numbers close to London, and this not unfrequently in Highgate Cemetery; they feed on a species of fir-cones growing in the cemetery. When some fir-trees were cut down near Weybridge, several old nests of crossbills were found in them; it is rare to get the young; they are very fond of the hornbeam seed, which seeds before leafing. *They are remarkably tame birds.*

EELS, p. 33.—HOW TO CATCH EELS.—In the autumn floods the eels descend in vast numbers to the sea. They run best on stormy nights, especially when there is thunder about. I have heard a story of an old fisherman who lived by his eel-trap. The eels would not run freely, so he got a drum and sat up all night tapping upon it. When asked what he was doing, he replied that he was playing the drum to make the eels believe it was thunder.

E. Poole writes me:—"The following dodge may be useful to many gentlemen who own large ponds. A simple way to catch eels is to take a corn-sack, turn down a hem, and run a line round at the mouth. Drop a sheep's paunch into the sack, and fill up with straw as tight as possible. Sink it in the pond or river. The eels work through the straw to the end. By drawing the sack up by the cord, it is closed, and you have your eels bagged."

Another good plan is to put a large barrel under the fall which takes off the overflow from the pond in the autumn-time, when the eels are migrating. Bore plenty of small holes in the tub—these will let the water go out, but not the eels.

MOUSE AND OYSTER.

MOUSE CAUGHT BY AN OYSTER, p. 35.—I have in my museum at South Kensington an excellent specimen of a mouse caught by an oyster. When oysters are exposed to the air any length of time, especially in hot weather, they always "gape their shell;" probably seeking for water. The oyster's beard at this time lies flat upon the shell. In the case portrayed in the engraving the oyster must have gaped his shells.

The mouse hunting about for food put his head in to nibble at the oyster and was trapped. The mouse was killed by the pressure of the oyster's shells. The adductor muscle which works the shells of the oyster is very strong.

The oyster that caught the mouse is very handsome ; the points of a good oyster are, first, a china-like shell, and, second, a deep upper shell to contain the meat.

YEWS, p. 36.—The juice of yew berries is good to eat; the seeds are dangerous. The boughs are fatal to cattle, though it is not often cattle will meddle with them except from mischief or idleness. Cattle and deer seem to prefer the boughs or loppings of yew, laurel, and other evergreens, when they have been cut a few days, and are much more inclined to eat them in that state, than to browse on them as they grow. Gardeners and foresters cannot therefore be too careful as to where they throw refuse of this description.

CANARIES, p. 36.—It is quite possible to breed canaries out of doors ; the eggs should be placed in the nests of chaffinches or greenfinches, those of greenfinches would be preferable.

The cross (artificially produced) between the cock greenfinch and hen canary is common.

Mr. Davy has received from Norwich canaries bred out of doors in aviaries ; but they are, as a rule, of a pale colour to those bred in cages indoors, and consequently are more wild for the first few days.

I learn from Mr. Davy that there is no putting a canary's song into words, but a canary may be taught any bird's song by being brought up from the nest among them. As regards the canary market in England, the great breeding places are Norwich, Yarmouth, Yorkshire, Leicester, and Manchester. These places supply the London market with canaries. Canaries are mostly bred by shoemakers during the summer, and sold to the London trade from October till March. They are sent up in "scores," one score being twenty pairs. If you were to send for a "score" of canaries they would send you forty birds. The breeders prefer sending them in pairs. Three hens are charged as a "pair." The wholesale price in the autumn is 4l. per score. The price rises in the spring, and advances to as much as 7l. per score.

The most valuable and delicate canaries are the Belgian. When undisturbed they sit "all of a lump," but when the cage is taken down they show their beauty by lengthening themselves out like a telescope, and bringing themselves into form. Some will nearly pass through a large wedding ring, and birds of first-class will fetch as much as 10l. per pair. The kind of canary most resembling the Belgian are the Yorkshire birds. These are also very long and graceful. They vary from 7s. 6d. to 30s. per pair. Norwich, as a rule, produces the richest coloured birds. The motto is :—

> Norwich for colour,
> Belgian for shape,
> And German for song.

The best come from the Hartz Mountains. German birds are not much to look at, but command high prices on account of their beautiful song.

CHAFFINCHES, p. 38.—The London bird-catchers take great numbers of cock chaffinches by dummies. A dummy is a stuffed finch, fastened on a peg, which can be placed on a fence or on a tree by means of a small sharpened wire on the end of the peg; bird-lime twigs are placed under and above the dummy. The birds are attracted by the song of a call-bird in a cage, which is placed or hidden in a ditch close by. The wild bird, thinking that the dummy is singing, comes down to attack it by striking at it; the feathers of the wild bird get caught by the bird-lime, and bird and twig fall to the ground. This plan can only be carried out when birds are in full song, when they are "off song" they will not strike at the dummy. The wild bird thinks the dummy is a poacher on his beat.

There are four or five different ways of putting the chaffinch's song into words. Thus one bird sings, "Ring, ring, rattle, chuck wido;" a good "chuck wido" is considered the best song bird; again, another bird sings, "Ring, ring, rattle, Jack white."

The poor Spitalfields weavers will give 3l. or 4l. each for a good chaffinch. These birds are sung in matches for from 1l. to 5l.; many bird-fanciers will come for miles to hear a chaffinch. Most of the matches are sung by gaslight. Two birds are put up at a time in separate cages to sing a match; fifteen minutes is the time allowed for the singing match, and the bird who does the greatest number of complete songs in that time becomes the winner. Some birds are called "Chuck wido" birds, some "Jack white," and some "Kiss me dear," from the finishing words of the chaffinch's song. The best song birds are to be found in Essex. The average price to a shop-keeper is 3s. a dozen. Some turn out good birds, some bad; you are as likely to get a good bird for 6d. as a bad one for 1s.

The greater portion of these finches are "sighted," or, as they call it, "done;" the corner of the eye is slightly touched with a red-hot needle, and the injury is scarcely discernible. They are kept in little square cages till they can find their food and water before they are "done." It is a most cruel practice. The Anti-Cruelty Society should look to this and stop it at once.

Chaffinches remain upon the stubble all the winter till they are ploughed out, and move to other localities for food. When driven by snow they abound about stackyards. They are decidedly migratory; a larger kind and brighter-coloured chaffinch comes from the north and returns in the spring. Mr. Davy has seen the same kind of birds in cages from Germany. London fanciers do not like them; for their song, as a rule, is indifferent.

Large flocks of chaffinches come in the September and October flights. Most bird-catchers catch equal numbers of males and females. They are to be found upon the stubble fields and freshly manured ground, and on long litter, until pairing time in spring.

LINNETS, p. 40.—Linnets come from abroad in immense flocks, and locate themselves on stubble where charlock seed abounds; when spring arrives they go away in flights to their building places. They are taken in·clap-nets by thousands, as are the chaffinches.

The song of the linnet is thus put into words by the London bird-catchers :—

> "Hepe, hepe, hepe, hepe,
> Tollaky, tollaky, quakey, wheet,
> Heep, pipe, chow,
> Heep, tollaky, quakey, wheet,
> Lug, orcher wheet."

The toy-linnet is a bird that has been taught to sing by the titlark, woodlark, or yellow-hammer, and only a very few take the perfect song. The following is the perfect song of the toy-linnet. It begins thus :—

> "Pu poy, tollick, tollick, eky quak,
> E-wheet, tollick, cha eyk, quake, wheet."

This is one stave of the song. The next staves are :—

> "Phillip, cha eke, quake wheet,
> Call up, cha eke, quake, wheet.
>
> Tollick, eke, quake, chow,
> Eke, eke, eke, quak chow.
>
> Cluck, cluck, chay, ter wheet tollick, eke quake, wheet,
> Echup, echup, pipe, chow.
>
> Ah, ah, ah! J-o-e,
> Eke, quake, chow, rattle.
>
> Tuck, tuck, whizzy, ter wheet,
> Tolliky, quake wheet."

This is the finish of the toy-linnet's song. Perfect toy-linnets are worth any sum of money you like to ask—15$l.$ to 20$l.$ would be given readily for a thorough good one. "Broken song" birds are only worth 30$s.$ to 50$s.$ each. A broken song-bird will not make his stops in the song as given above; he will run one into the other. The old song-birds (linnets) are very scarce, as the trainers of them are gradually getting old and dying off. When the above song is put together by a proper bird, he does it just like a flute; it is something splendid. It is said that there is not a perfect bird in London at the present time.

To get these birds to learn the song they must be taken from the nest very young, before they get the call of the parent birds.

SNOW-BUNTING, p. 40.—The common snow-bunting is plentiful in the autumn around the Norfolk coast, particularly at Yarmouth; it is a very hardy bird, feeds freely on oats and any kind of seed. When on flight they are often taken by the ordinary observer to be pied-larks. The old birds are very light, nearly white, and not worth keeping for song, only for aviaries.

"Snow-flakes" are snow-buntings, and arrive in this country in great flocks, about the Norfolk coast particularly. Formerly they were rare, but now the bird-catchers keep call-birds of the same species all the year round, so that the snow-buntings are now very plentiful in the bird-shops in the autumn and early spring. They were taken in abundance at Brighton last year. They are killed and eaten as larks.

WAGTAILS, p. 40.—There are four different kinds of wagtails. 1st. The white wagtail arrives in this country in the beginning of March, and breeds mostly in old barns, and departs in small flights in the middle of September   2nd. The pied wagtail. This bird never leaves this country; it is very common, and breeds near brooks. 3rd. The grey or dun wagtail. This breeds in Scotland, on the moors. They are caught round London from the end of October to the spring. These birds are very rare; they frequent brooks and ditches all the winter, and do not breed here. 4th. The yellow, or Ray's wagtail, breeds on poor land, arrives in April and leaves in the middle of September. The four species are found all over England; they are easily kept in confinement; they have a short song, or rather call; they sing during the breeding-time.

The wagtails have different calls. The call of the black-and-white wagtail is "Physic, physic, physic," quickly repeated: with a whistle Davy can make them come close up. Listen to the first wagtail you hear, and you will find he invokes the aid of the medical profession.

WHEATEAR, p. 41.—The Wheatear arrives very early in the spring, and abounds particularly on the South Downs. After recovering themselves, they make inland to their breeding places. Wiltshire is a favourite locality. They are, without a doubt, a migratory bird, and one of the earliest visitors to this country: they are frequently caught the first week in March. The trap used to catch them is the common nightingale trap. They are very easily caught; the best bait is a meal-worm; they are splendid eating. They are sold in large numbers in Brighton; they are best and fattest in the beginning of April.

STOATS AND WEASELS, p. 44.—Stoats and Weasels are two distinct species and are frequently confounded together, the small female stoat and large male weasel occasion much controversy. There is one distinguishing mark which may always set any question as to species at rest; it is that the stoat always has a black tip to its tail, and the weasel never.

From its size and strength the stoat is far more formidable than the weasel; the latter turns his attention to mice and moles, to which the stoat seldom condescends.

In our islands the stoat retains the same coat winter and summer, except in the north, where it is said occasionally in hard winters to assume a white or ermine garb. In fact the stoat is the true ermine.

Very often stoats and weasels attack the bird-catchers' call and "brace birds." They always seize them by the head.

ROOKS, p. 44.—A few white and cream-coloured starlings are seen every year; if the eye is black, the white starling, after moulting, will come to its proper colour; but if it has a pink eye, it will become white and, as a rule, will have flesh-coloured legs.

BULLFINCHES, p. 45.—Mr. Davy writes :—

"Black bullfinches by some persons are thought a great rarity, but not so with my bird-catchers ; for when a bird moults out of colour, as a rule it loses its natural hoop or call ; it is then, of course, of no use as a call-bird. The reason of its becoming black is overfeeding with hempseed, which causes weakness in moulting. A bird once black, either cock or hen, may, by breaking off this food by degrees, and feeding on summer rape and canary, be brought to its natural colour in the next moult—give plenty of green food also. I know of one cock bullfinch, now in good health, that has been worked out catching, almost daily, nine months in the year ; it is in beautiful plumage, and is kept in a very small cage. This bird has plenty of hemp among its ordinary seed, but by being continually exposed to the fresh air in different parts of the country, and constantly getting a ducking with rain, the seed does not affect the plumage. The above call or decoy-bird has been the means during its career of causing the entrapping by nets and bird-lime of not less than from 300 to 400 birds.

"Too much hempseed will turn the plumage of bullfinches, thrushes, skylarks, and goldfinches black ; it will change the plumage of most birds ; they will get prodigiously fat on it."

The bullfinch is said to be very destructive to buds of fruit-trees. The case ought to be fairly put : he does good also, inasmuch as he prunes the trees ; he knocks off a great many good buds, thereby causing those which remain to be more vigorous and fruitful ; in fact, he is a practical gardener, and by his pruning operations does more good than harm—if he does any harm at all.

LARKS, p. 45.—Immense flights of larks arrive annually in October from the north. The birds that then arrive are much darker in colour and much larger than our native birds. Mr. Davy has had larks, a hundred-weight at a time in hampers, which have been caught on the hills between Newmarket and Cambridge. They are caught in trammel nets, at night, and are killed as they are caught, both males and females, as there is no sale for them as songsters during November and December. As spring advances, the cocks increase in value to bird-fanciers, the hens then are alone sent to the poulterers. The wholesale price obtained by the bird-catchers is about 9s. a gross, or 9d. per dozen ; sometimes they will fetch 2s. a dozen. The lark trammellers cannot work of a bright moonlight night ; and the birds cannot be well caught on rainy nights, as the nets are then too heavy. In times of snow they are caught by springes, *i.e.* horsehair nooses tied on to a string. The best bait is black oats sprinkled along the line of springes; they are generally caught by the head, leg, or wing. The larger larks are called Scotch larks, they are never caught after the end of February.

On one occasion were landed at Folkestone, from Boulogne, a large quantity of larks, weighing about seven hundred-weight, all of which had been snared by the leg with horsehair—a very common practice on the Continent during snowy weather. I find, that twelve larks weigh one pound, therefore, in the seven hundred-weight sent through Folkestone there were no less than 784 dozens, or 9,408 individual larks. At 2*d.* each, the value of these birds amounted to 78*l.* 8*s.* in money.

CHIFF-CHAFF, p. 46.—The bird of the Salicaria kind mentioned by White was probably the chiff-chaff. This bird is the earliest and merriest spring bird we have got. It hangs about leafless trees, arriving often at the end of February; it is very lively.

The chiff-chaff is also called the "chinky-chank;" its only song is chiff-chaff. It is the earliest migratory bird that arrives, and stays very late, even to the end of November. The male bird is brighter in colour than the female. This little bird has been seen by Mr. Bartlett at the Zoological Gardens, Regent's Park, as early as March.

NUT-HATCH, p. 47.—The Nut-hatch makes a very amusing pet if reared from the nest, and becomes perfectly tame; he is always on the move, climbing up the sides of the trees and tapping for insects, &c. The nut-hatch takes possession of an old hole made by the woodpecker, stops up the hole with mud, leaving an aperture just big enough to get in and out. This curious doorway is scarcely perceptible to the eye, as the mud corresponds with the colour of the tree; he builds from four to twelve feet high from the ground; if he cannot find a woodpecker's hole, he will take any other.

The nut-hatch's foot is made for climbing, but he cannot hold anything by the foot. When he cannot get beech-nuts, &c., he will eat all kinds of insect food, he will also eat oleaginous seeds. They make their nests in the old holes which the spotted-woodpecker has dug out. All woodpeckers make holes in the trees and then tunnel downwards about a foot. They carry the chips away as they dig them out.

GRASSHOPPER WARBLER, p. 48.—The grasshopper warbler is a very shy bird, something like the whitethroat; makes its nest on the ground; comes late, about April, and goes away in September. It is entirely an insect-feeder. The song is deceiving, and resembles the croaking of the grasshopper or locust; it shifts about a great deal when singing. Most of the woods round London produce two or three pairs in a season. They prefer quiet woods, and sing on the lowest twigs of bushes. This bird is hard to keep in a cage; the longest time ever known is seven weeks. It requires soft insect food, such as small hairless caterpillars.

None of the bird-catchers have ever seen it migrate; it is here to-day and off to-morrow; but disappears in the beginning of September.

WILLOW-WRENS, p. 49.—No doubt the three willow-wrens mentioned are mistaken for the chiff-chaff, wood-wren, and willow-wren, the wood-wren being very rare; the legs of the willow-wren are flesh-coloured; the chiff-chaff is smaller, and the legs are nearly black.

COLOUR OF YOUNG BIRDS' MOUTHS.—Mr. Bartlett informs me of the curious fact that the mouths of the young of fruit-eating warblers are pink or flesh-coloured; the young of the insect-eating warblers, on the contrary, have the inside of their mouths yellow.

TOADS, FROGS, AND NEWTS, p. 52.—The ponds in the brick-fields about London produce toads and frogs in great quantities. The only sale for frogs and snakes is at the Zoological Gardens, where they are used for feeding purposes. The market price of frogs averages 6d. per dozen.

I do not believe in the "shower of frogs" story.

When frogs get "legged," from being loggerheads or tadpoles, they are wonderfully migratory things, like eels, always on the move.

A very remarkable plague of frogs occurred on the flat lands near Windsor in June, 1875.

I was sent for by H.R.H. Prince Christian to prescribe. I found that they were all migrating from the ornamental lake at "Frogmore," close under Windsor Castle. Hence possibly the name of this Royal Lodge.

Frogs and toads must spawn in water. The ornamental water at Frogmore is certainly the breeding-ground for the frogs and toads from the royal gardens and hothouses.

A hundred years ago people used to make a living by quackery of all sorts, and servants and farm-labourers used to put about that they had been "cured by a toad."

The cancer-doctor of White's time had evidently set up toads as a remedy for this disease. In my own experience a woman gave her child a half-grown frog to suck, as she had been told it would cure the thrush round the child's mouth.

CHRYSALIS DIGGING.—Newts are often dug out at places one mile from water. They are found ten inches down in the ground. They are found by men when chrysalis-digging round roots of trees and along sides of old walls; this is where the best chrysalis hunting-ground is situated. Mr. Davy can discover the haunts of caterpillars where there is clear ground underneath the tree, by looking for the excrement which has fallen from the tree; he then shakes off the caterpillars. Some caterpillars are fetched down by the first sudden jerk; some, on the contrary, will hold the tighter after the first jerk; some "web up" and come into fly the same year; some burrow in the ground till the next spring.

SNAKES' EGGS, p. 53.—The engraving below shows the eggs of the common snake just ready to hatch out. I found them in a dunghill in Aldermaston Park, Reading, when on a visit to my hospitable and kind friend, Higford Burr. I have thus described them in my " Log-Book of a Fisherman and Zoologist : "—" Lifting up the straw most carefully, I was delighted to find first one, then two, then a dozen eggs. The squire and I then proceeded leisurely to dissect out the nest with our pocket-knives and a dung-fork. Snakes' eggs are not quite so large as a blackbird's ; they are round at both ends like a sugar-plum. They have no hard shell like a hen's egg, but the shell is composed of a soft

EGGS OF THE COMMON SNAKE.

elastic substance, like thin wash-leather. Some of the eggs were lying quite separate. The greater part were, however, stuck firmly together, so tightly that it was almost impossible to tear them apart without breaking the skin. The eggs were not held by a ligature, but appeared pasted together by some strong adhesive gum, end to end ; most of the eggs were quite distended ; the shells of some had fallen in, and they looked crumpled. The appearance of the eggs in this dung-heap, just as the parent snake or snakes had placed them, was so striking, that I took them home and cast them in plaster of paris

X

old snake and all.   The cast, coloured to nature, is now in my museum.

" There were sixty-four eggs altogether in this one bunch. I do not know from experience how many eggs the common snake lays, but I should say from twenty to thirty.   It is, therefore, probable that more than one snake had chosen the spot on this dunghill to deposit their eggs, just as one salmon will deposit her eggs in a favourable place without consideration for the other mother-salmon that precedes or follows her.

" The temperature where the eggs were deposited [in the dung-heap] was about 84° in the sun, and the nest was buried about eighteen inches deep on the southern aspect, as though the mother-snake knew that that was the best place for the eggs.   I then proceeded to dissect some of these eggs. A few of them were blanks, containing nothing, but all the rest were good eggs. When the skin was cut through, a quantity of clear albumen came out, just the same as the white of a hen's egg. Floating in this was a yolk of a much yellower colour than that of the hen's egg, and inside this yolk was discoverable the embryo snake. Out of the three embryo baby snakes I examined two of them were quite lively, but gelatinous, and as yet not well enough developed to move more than to give a slight wriggle. The heart, however, could distinctly be seen to beat under the transparent skin for some seconds. The brain also was very prominent. In the drawing two little snakes are represented as just hatched out. My readers should search for snakes' eggs in old dunghills in August and September. My friend Mr. Burr preserves snakes in his park ; he will not allow them to be killed. Vipers, however, are kept down as much as possible."

The drawing (p. 307) shows the wonderful manner in which the vertebræ of snakes are united, so as to combine strength with freedom of motion. This wondrous structure has been so ably described by Dr. Roget, in his Bridgewater Treatise on Animal and Vegetable Physiology, which every one should read, that I quote it as a sample of the Doctor's power of describing evidences of design :—

" It is evident that, in the absence of all external instruments of prehension and of progressive motion, it is necessary that the spine should be rendered extremely flexible, so as to adapt itself to a great variety of movements. This extraordinary flexibility is given, first, by the subdivision of the spinal column into a great number of small pieces ; secondly, by the great freedom of their articulations ; and thirdly, by the peculiar mobility and connection of the ribs.

" Numerous as are the vertebræ of the eel, the spine of which consists of above a hundred, that of a serpent is in general formed of a still greater number.   In the rattle-snake (*Crotalus horridus*) there are about two hundred ; and above three hundred have been counted in the spine of the *Coluber natrix*. These vertebræ are all united by ball-and-socket joints, as in the adult *batrachia ;* the posterior rounded eminence of each vertebra being received into the anterior surface of the next. While provision has thus been made for extent of motion, extraordinary care has at the same time been bestowed upon the security of the joints. Thus we find them effectually protected from dislocation by the locking in above and below of the articular processes, and by the close investment of the capsular ligaments. The direction of the surfaces of these processes, and the shape and length of the spinous processes, are such as to allow of free lateral flexion, but to limit the vertical and longitudinal motions; and whatever degree of freedom of motion may exist between the adjoining vertebræ, that motion being multiplied along the column, the flexibility of the whole becomes very great, and admits of its assuming every degree and variety of curvature. The presence of a sternum, restraining the motions of the ribs, would have impeded all these movements, and would have also been an insurmountable bar to the dilatation of the stomach, which is rendered necessary by the habit of the serpent of gorging its prey entire."

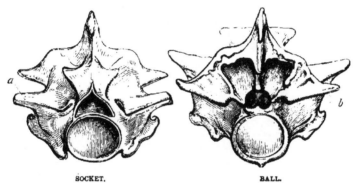

SOCKET.   BALL.

VERTEBRÆ OF SNAKE.

In the Museum of the Royal College of Surgeons, Lincoln's Inn Fields, is a very fine skeleton of the tiger boa, in which the above ball-and-socket apparatus can be examined. It measures eleven feet two inches, and has no less than two hundred and ninety-one vertebræ. The reader can easily examine the structure of snakes' vertebræ for himself; take a snake, the bigger the better (one that has been in spirits will do quite well); cut off his head; run a wire down the spinal column as far as it will go; tie the two ends of the wire together, and boil the snake till the flesh can be easily removed with a knife and brush; the vertebræ will then be found to be strung like the beads of a lady's necklace.

NEST OF STICKLEBACK, p. 54.—There are three well-marked species of sticklebacks in England; two inhabit fresh water, namely, *Gasterosteus aculeatus*, which has three spines, and the *G. pungitus*, which

has ten spines; the third kind, *G. spinachia*, lives in the sea, and has
fifteen spines. The fresh-water stickleback's nest can be found in the
month of May; my readers should look out for them. In October,
1866, I received from Mr. Robert Embleton, of Chathill, Northumberland, a most valuable specimen of the nest of the marine stickleback,
which has been drawn by Mr. Delamotte. The late Mr. Jonathan
Couch thus describes a stickleback's nest which came under his own
observation :—" The situation selected by the fish was the loose end of a
rope, from which the strands hung at about a yard from the surface,
over a depth of four or five fathoms, and to which the material could
only have been brought, of course, in the mouth of the fish from the
distance of about thirty feet. They were formed of the usual aggre-
gation of the finer sorts of green and red ore-weed; but they were so

NEST OF SEA STICKLEBACK.

matted together in the hollow formed by the untwisted strands of the
rope, that the mass constituted an oblong ball of nearly the size of the
fist, in which had been deposited the scattered assemblages of spawn,
and which was bound into shape with the thread of animal substance,
which was passed through and through in various directions, while the
rope itself formed an outside covering to the whole." The threads
formed by the stickleback resemble very much an indiarubber band,
only they are of a white colour. No human being knows how these
threads are formed by this interesting nest-building fish.[1]

[1] In 1879 I received a beautiful specimen of a stickleback's nest found by
Mr. Reid near Wick Harbour, Scotland. This I have fully described in my
" Familiar History of British Fishes." 1880.

BUTCHER-BIRD, p. 59.—The butcher-bird, or shrike, arrives at the end of April, and remains to the end of August. It preys upon beetles, birds, and especially willow-wrens and chiff-chaffs, both young and old, and any young birds from nests. The young of the butcher-bird never comes to its full plumage till it arrives the following season The young are streaky grey. This bird is very common close round London and all over England; he has a quick jerking call, "lack, lack" He is a wonderful plucky bird, and will take the "brace birds"[1] off the "flur sticks" of the bird-catchers. They are easy to keep; they feed on brains of birds, always attacking the bird's skull first, they become wonderfully tame, but are only kept for the sake of curiosity. The great grey shrike comes in winter from Norway and Sweden; it arrives in October and returns in the spring. It is rare. When "hard pushed" the shrike will take almost any bird. It is a wonderful "punisher," and has great power in its beak. The bird generally fixes its dinner on a thorn to hold it while he picks at it. When in a cage he fixes his prey between the bars.

Mr. Gould gives four Shrikes. Genus Lanius: 1. The great grey shrike; *L. excubitor*; 2. Lanius minor, rose-breasted shriket: Genus *Enneoctonus*; 3. Butcher-bird, *E. collurio*; 4. Woodchat shrike, *E. rufus*.

BIRD-CATCHERS' NETS.—In order that the reader may understand the meaning of the terms "flur stick" and "brace birds," I now give an extract from an article I published in *Land and Water*, No. 501, Aug. 28, 1875, describing a day's bird-catching at Mr. Burr's park, at Aldermaston, near Reading, with Mr. Davy, the bird-catcher. The process of laying the nets is as follows :—Two nets, twelve yards long, (and, when open, covering the ground twenty feet wide), are neatly laid down on the ground. It is impossible, without a diagram, to describe the rough yet very excellent machinery by which a pull on the rope held by the bird-catcher[2] will make these harmless-looking nets instantly spring into the air and catch the birds, either on the wing or on the ground. The nets act so quickly that the eye can scarcely follow their spring. Anything on the wing crossing them four feet high will be shut in instantly. It is better to catch the bird before he has time to settle; if he touches the net with his feet he is off instantly.

The next process in bird-catching is to put out the "brace bird." A brace bird is taken from a cage; this bird always wears his brace with a swivel attached, whether at work or not. The brace consists of a piece of string made into a kind of double halter. It is put over the bird's head, and the wings and legs are passed through; in fact when

---

[1] See p. 310.

[2] When catching small birds, the bird-catcher stands eighteen yards from the nets; when catching blackbirds, thrushes, or starlings, position is taken up at twenty-five yards.

I saw Mr. Davy brace a bird I was strongly reminded of a nurse dressing a baby.   When the brace is on the bird, the feathers fall over it and it cannot be seen.   The brace bird is then put on his "flur stick : " this is a straight stick, which by means of a hinge on its lower end is made to rise and fall at the will of the bird-catcher by means of a string.   Then when any bird is seen coming the flur stick is gently pulled up, the brace bird, all the while standing on the stick, is made to hover with his wings and show himself; this, of course, is to attract the wild birds to the place.   The bird-catcher then arranges his call-birds.   These birds when put out begin to sing, especially if they hear another bird of the same kind in the distance.   The wild ones being attracted by the decoys are shown by the brace birds the place where they are wanted to go.   No bait is used for the birds, they simply come to the decoy and imagine from the call that they—the decoys —are feeding there.

The brace bird that Mr. Davy puts on the flur stick has been at work for three years almost daily.   He has been the means of catching thousands of other birds, especially sparrows, ordinarily called "Jims." Mr. Davy says the call-birds get very artful; sometimes they will give a note of warning to the wild birds ; thus a linnet will sometimes set to "hipping," that is, repeating the words, "hip, hip," several times. This note of the call-bird causes the linnets coming in a flight instantly to dash away in all directions.   The goldfinch will oftentimes set to "gidding," that is, saying, "gid," "gid," "gid," several times in succession.   This has the same effect as the "hipping" of the linnet. The birds are off in a moment.

Jackdaws, p. 61.—At Whistley, near Weybridge, the people go in May, when the birds are about a fortnight old, to the ruins of a very old castle.   Men carry long ladders, and with blunt iron hooks take out the young jackdaws, and if there are no buyers they throw them to the ground.   Bird dealers take hampers down to Whistley and bring up all the birds caught, as many as ten dozen of young jackdaws.   They cost on the spot 2s. per dozen.   The reason why they are taken is to stop the increase of jackdaws in the neighbourhood.   If the young jackdaws are taken when about a fortnight old, the old ones will not "go to nest" again that season.   If the eggs only were taken, the birds would lay again immediately.   Mr. Jackdaw is "birdivorous ; " when he has got his young he looks out where there are young sparrows, then "in he pops, and out he pops," with a young sparrow, and so he goes on backwards and forwards till he has taken the lot; he then pulls them to pieces afterwards and feeds his young on them in turn.

Taming Birds, &c., p. 63.—It is very remarkable, that, as a rule, all birds seem to be very timid at the sight of gloves.   If you feed a tame thrush with gloves on he will "chuck, chuck, chuck," and dash about the cage.   This shows fear; the blackbird will do the same thing.

CLAWS OF HERON, p. 64.—The feet of birds afford a field for very great study. Along the sides of the toes of the capercaillie run a series of hard, strong bristles, not at all unlike the teeth of an ordinary comb. I believe the use of these is to act as a snow-shoe to help to support the bird when walking on the snow. The reader should observe for himself the curious serration on one side of the middle toe of the common heron. The same structure is also found in the bittern and cormorant. The use of it is certainly not for prehension, as was formerly supposed, but rather, as its structure indicates, for a comb. Among the feathers of the heron and bittern can always be found a considerable quantity of powder. The bird probably uses this comb to keep the powder and feathers in proper order.

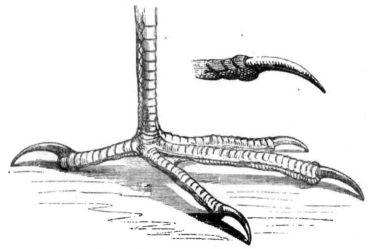

SERRATED CLAW OF THE HERON.

FERN-OWL, p. 66.—The Fern-Owl, or Goat-sucker, arrives here very late in May, the month of cockchafers; the chafers come out with the leaves. The female makes no nest, but lays two eggs on the bare ground. The churring noise is its song; the male bird does it mostly; the male will "churr" when the female is sitting; she can shift her young when danger is near, she probably rolls them away with her wings. Goat-suckers like to have their nest in the hollow made by a horse's or cow's hoof. They devour large quantities of beetles.

It does not seem likely that this bird should use its foot to catch beetles; the mouth is evidently adapted to take any sized beetle. If one of them be shot the beetles may be found alive in the pouch, especially when they are feeding their young. These birds make very fair progress on the boughs of the trees; they shuffle, not walk, along the branches. This is one of the very few birds Mr. Davy has not succeeded in keeping long.

Colonel Leathes kindly sent me in the summer of 1875 two young fern-owls, taken from the nest in his woods near Yarmouth. I fed them on scraped beef and hard-boiled eggs, and they lived some weeks; they were very tame. The bristles round the sides of the mouth to assist in catching insects are very remarkable.

ARRIVAL OF BIRDS, p. 74.—In order to give a comparative table of the arrival of birds at Selborne and in the neighbourhood of London, I give the following list. The London list is given on the authority of Mr. Davy, the bird-catcher:—

| | USUALLY APPEAR ABOUT | |
	SELBORNE.	LONDON.
Wryneck	Middle of March	April 7 or 8
Smallest Willow-wren . .	March 23 . .	March 10
Swallow	April 15 . . .	Middle of April
Martin	„ . .	„
Sand Martin	„ . .	„
Blackcap	April 13 .	End of March
Nightingale	Middle of April .	April 8 to 14
Cuckoo	„ . .	„
Middle Willow-wren .	„ . .	April 12
Whitethroat	„ . .	Middle of April
Redstart	„ . .	Beginning of April
Turtle-dove	. . .	Middle of April
Grasshopper-lark . .	Middle of April .	End of April
Swift	April 27 . .	April 15
Largest Willow-wren . .	End of April . .	Middle of April
Goatsucker	Beginning of May .	End of April
Flycatcher	May 12 . . .	„

When the flycatcher has arrived we anticipate that all the soft meat tribe are here.

When the bird-catchers come home about the 15th or 16th of April, they generally report that the swifts have arrived.

The following birds stay to the end of August:—the cuckoo, the nightingale, the wryneck. This is a great migratory month. The following birds stay to the end of October:—house-swallow, martin, sand-martin. Swallows have been seen in Tottenham Court Road as late as the 5th of November.

Swifts leave about the middle of August; they have been known to stay till the end of September.[1]

MIGRATIONS OF BIRDS FROM ENGLAND.—In September and October the greater portion of our summer visitants are nearly all gone or going,

[1] A correspondent, "J.," thus writes in *Land and Water*:—"The swift, which visits us generally on the 5th of May, retires the earliest, seldom later than the 12th of August, although a few are occasionally later, and in one instance a swift was seen on the 26th of August."

viz.: the nightingale, redstart, wryneck, cuckoo (the old cuckoos are gone, but a few young are still left), flycatchers, warblers, turtle-doves, goatsuckers, tree-pipits, shrikes, grasshopper-larks. A few of the following still remain :—Blackcap, chiff-chaff, meadow pipit, White's wagtail, Ray's wagtail, willow-wren, wheatear, large and lesser white-throat, &c. These are soft-billed or soft-meat birds, which leave England in the autumn.

About the same time that these birds leave us, others arrive, such as goldfinches, woodlarks, skylarks, linnets, redpoles, twites, siskins, and snowbuntings. About the second week in September the flights of these commence, and last for three weeks or a month. The autumn arrivals are seed-eating birds. The London bird-catchers, at this "flight time," go down to the south coast for their harvest, and take large quantities of the arriving birds; many thousands are sent up weekly to London for cage birds, and to be kept for their song. At the end of March the birds which left us in September and October begin to return to this country.

BIRDS OBSERVED AT THE ZOOLOGICAL GARDENS, REGENT'S PARK.—The following is the list of Birds which had been captured or observed in the Zoological Society's Gardens, Regent's Park, by Mr. Edward Bartlett, son of Mr. Bartlett, the Superintendent (see Transactions of Zoological Society, 1863, p. 159) :—

Kestrel.
Barn Owl.
*Spotted Flycatcher.
Missel Thrush.
Fieldfare.
*Song Thrush.
Redwing.
*Blackbird.
Ring-Ousel.
*Hedge Accentor.
Redbreast.
Wheatear.
Blue Tit.
Cole Tit.
Marsh Tit.
Long Tailed Tit.
Pied Wagtail.
Grey Wagtail.
Ray's Wagtail.
Tree Pipet.
Meadow Pipit.
Skylark.
Common Bunting.
Chaffinch.
House Sparrow.

*Reed Warbler.
Sedge Warbler.
Nightingale.
*Blackcap.
Garden Warbler.
Common Whitethroat.
Lesser Whitethroat.
Wood Warbler.
Willow Warbler.
Chiff Chaff.
Golden-crested Regulus.
Great Tit.
Lesser Redpole.
Bullfinch.
Starling.
Carrion Crow.
Rook.
Jackdaw.
Great Spotted Woodpecker.
Common Creeper.
Wren.
*Swallow.
Martin.
Swift.
Nightjar.

Greenfinch.

Hawfinch.

Goldfinch.

Common Linnet.

Wild Duck.

Moorhen.

Coot.

Those marked * have been observed to breed in the Society's Gardens.

BIRDS' CROPS, p. 78.—In his lectures on Geology at Oxford, my father used to tell us that the sellers of antiquities at Rome had a curious and clever way of giving the appearance of antiquity to modern gems. Having cut the device on the stones, they thrust them down the throat of a turkey into his gizzard; after the proper time had passed they killed the bird; the stones in the crop were then found to have assumed the corrugated appearance of antiquity from the grinding action of the hard coats of the turkey's gizzard. In my collection I have some fine specimens of stones found in guano polished by the action of birds' stomachs.

SEDGEBIRD, p. 80.—It is very likely that the bird here mentioned by White was the reed-warbler, or reed-wren. If disturbed by any means during the night it immediately commences its song, which resembles a mixture of other songs of birds—a regular gibberish altogether. In some parts of the country they call it the "thousand songster." These birds partially resemble the reed-sparrow; they are migratory. The young birds do not come to their full plumage till the following spring.

SONG THRUSH, p. 84.—The following is from my description of a day's bird-catching at Aldermaston Park :—As it was very hot we sat down in the shade to rest, while Mr. Davy gave us a yarn about his birds. It was unusual for a thrush to be in song so late, viz., 17th August, as at this time these birds are in full moult. August, in fact, is the dullest month in the year for song. Nearly all the birds, being "sore in moult," hide away in damp, shady places. Mr. Davy has put the song of most birds into words. He repeated the words of a thrush's song, and I found by carefully listening that the bird does actually sing the following words :—

> Knee deep, knee deep, knee deep ;
> Cherry du, cherry du, cherry du, cherry du ;
> White hat, white hat ;
> Pretty Joey, pretty Joey, pretty Joey.

My readers should learn these words by heart, and listen to a thrush singing. They will find the thrush pronounces the above words as nearly as possible. Repeat them all, even when no bird is present, rapidly in a bird-like manner and see the effect.

It is very difficult to "word" a blackbird's song. Mr. Davy can imitate a blackbird's song so well that he can bring Mr. Blackbird up to him to be caught, but he cannot put his song into words.

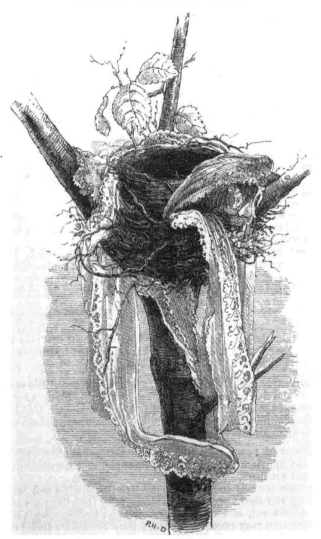

BLACKBIRD'S NEST ORNAMENTED WITH LACE.

BLACKBIRD'S NEST ORNAMENTED WITH LACE.—Mr. Hugh Hamilton, of
Pinmore, Girvan, in Sept. 1875, wrote me as follows :—" In the month
of May some laces were laid out on the washing-green folded all
together. They were left out all night, but when looked for in the

morning were not to be found. As there was a good deal of wind in the
night it was thought they might have been blown over into a neighbour's
garden, but the gardens were searched without success.   About three
weeks after, one of the neighbours' gardeners brought a blackbird's
nest, with five eggs in it, to the owner of the lace, which he had found
in a tree in his garden.   It was festooned with the lace as in the photograph.   There were three different kinds of lace—2¼ yards Lisle, 1 yard
Mechlin, and 1½ yard Valenciennes, besides several pieces of other
lace worked in and out throughout the nest, which were destroyed
in detaching it.   I inclose a photograph which I took myself."
Mr. Hamilton has allowed this photograph to be copied for this book.
The reader will agree with me that it has been most beautifully drawn,
and does great credit to the able pencil of Mr. Delamotte, of King's
College.   My answer was as follows:—"I have no doubt the blackbird used the lace in making its nest.   An interesting question arises
from this as to whether the blackbird had an idea that his nest would
be ornamented with the lace.   The bower-bird certainly uses ornamental substances in making his nest; it is a question if this bird had
the same notions."

The blackbird is a great mimic, or rather a true mocking-bird. If taken
young he may be taught to whistle one or two—not more—tunes perfectly. Davy had a blackbird that would whistle, "Pop goes the weasel,"
and "Hey, jim along, jim along, Josey, hey, jim along, jim along, Joe."
He would sing at any time at command.

If any one wishes to try the experiment of training a blackbird, they
must raise one or two young ones from the nest.   As a rule two out of
three will take the song taught them.   The blackbird is a very pugnacious bird, and this is a drawback to his being kept in an aviary with
other small birds.

LITTLE WATER SHREW (*Sorex fodiens*), p. 85.—These little creatures
eat insects and fish; their teeth are very beautiful.   I find the stomach
and intestines contain some dark fluid pulp-like matter.   This I examined under the microscope, and found to be composed almost entirely
of the horny cases and legs of minute water-insects.

THE SHREW MOUSE, p. 182.—These little things are often found dead
without any apparent mark of injury; some say that the cats kill them,
but will not eat them.

Shrew mice are silly things; they get into dry ditches and cart-ruts,
then run up and down and worry themselves; they have not sense to
get out of the rut, and so they lie down and perish.   Some say that
they die because they cannot get water; they are mostly found dead in
numbers at the approach of autumn in hot, dry weather; they soon
decompose after death.

BLACKCAP, p. 87.—This bird is also called the "mock nightingale"
and the "Norfolk nightingale," and is very easily kept in confinement.
These birds do well upon such food as bread crumbs, bruised hemp-

seed, and a little hard-boiled egg and German paste mixed; they are long lived, and sing freely many months in the year. Numbers are kept in confinement by London fanciers. They are very common in Derbyshire, although there are no nightingales there. Blackcaps do not mind the cold and frosty weather, as they come as early as before the end of March. When they first come they feed on ivy berries. In the autumn they eat quantities of fruit, currants, pears, plums, &c. The Baroness Burdett-Coutts has some large trees close to her residence at Highgate which are covered with ivy. This ivy produces an abundance of berries; as a rule the blackcaps are noticed feeding on the Baroness's ivy earlier than anywhere. They are very close-feathered, hardy birds; when freshly caught, as a rule, few or none are lost in "meating off." The blackcap fattens upon ripe elder berries for the migration.

From August up to the middle of September is the time when all the London bird-catchers take large numbers of "soft meat"[1] birds, as they are then "clean moulted" and "meat off" much easier.

THE YELLOWHAMMER, p. 87.—This is one of our most common birds, and does not migrate. They are not, as a rule, kept as cage-birds, the song not being thought anything of. The song of the yellowhammer is very simple—"Widdle, widdle, widdle, cee, cee, cha." In some part of the country the bird is said to sing thus: "A little bit of bread and no c-h-e-e-s-e."

They have no song during the winter months. They breed late on the ground in banks, and have three nests a year, from April to the end of August.

TITLARK OR TREE PIPIT, p. 87.—This bird, a very common one, arrives at the beginning of April, and begins to migrate in the middle of August. It is very much sought after for its song and for improving the song of nestling linnets. The linnets thus educated have a *mixed* song, and are used for "call-birds." Their song reads thus: "Heep, heep, heep, tollyke, eke, pipe, chow, wheet, fear, lug, orcher, wheet." This is a mixed song of the native linnet improved by the titlark. The words introduced by the titlark into the linnet's song are "fearing" and "chowing." Titlarks are easily kept, and sing well in captivity. They will sing when perched, and also when on the wing.

CUCKOO, p. 89.—I have had several young cuckoos sent me from time to time. The cry is very peculiar. On one occasion Mr. Bartlett chanced to come into my room, where I had a young cuckoo he could not see. I asked him what that cry was; he said "the cry of the young of some soft-billed bird;" this plaintive cry is a wonderful provision to attract soft-billed birds to feed the helpless cuckoo in its foster-mother's nest. The cuckoo almost always picks out the dead branch of

---

[1] "Soft meat" birds are the insect-feeders. "Meating off" means inducing the birds to take artificial food in captivity.

a tree from which to call. It may be attracted by calling and imitating its cry. Mr. Edon reports that when he has decoyed the cuckoo in this way, he finds that, after being deceived and not finding what it expected (say in three visits to the same spot), the bird will not come near again, but will stay at a distance and keep on answering.

Cuckoos are very partial to hedge-sparrows' nests. One pair of hedge-sparrows could not feed such a glutton as a young cuckoo. Its peculiar cry attracts other "soft-meat" birds to help to feed it.

A young cuckoo when well fledged could be easily mistaken for a nightjar when on the wing in the open.

Cuckoos feed upon caterpillars on high trees. They arrive here in April and depart about the end of August.

The places they choose to lay their eggs are the nests of wagtails, titlarks, &c., and other "soft meat" birds. Mr. Davy has never found the cuckoo's egg or young in any other than a "soft meat" bird's nest.

As regards the way in which the young cuckoo turns the young of its foster parents out of the nest, Mr. Gould gives an admirable account in his "Introduction to the Birds of Great Britain."

BABY HEDGEHOG—LIFE SIZE.

HEDGEHOG, p. 91.—In the bristles of the common hedgehog we find a very curious bit of mechanism. The hedgehog has no horny studs, either fastened into the skin, as in the armadillo, nor yet has he a bone-formed dome, covered with horny scales, as in the tortoise. Instead of this his horny covering assumes the form of spines or bristles, each set firmly into the skin at one end, and very sharply pointed at the other end. These bristles the owner can erect in groups with all the points outwards, presenting a most formidable array of weapons; but the hedgehog has also power to lay back all these sharp-pointed spines in one direction, viz., from his head backwards. In this position they form a carpet, which if smoothed the right way with the hand is as soft as velvet. In order to find out how all this mechanism was carried out, I have dissected a hedgehog, and was surprised to find how very slight are the muscles which command the spine. They are fine strings of fibres, very similar to the *Corrugator supercilii*, or frowning muscle in our own forehead; in fact, when a hedgehog curls himself up, he begins work with a tremendous frown as he tucks his head inwards. The muscles that work the spines are attached to prominences which project from the backbone, and especially do they spring from the ribs, which I find to be of unusual strength and abnormal width for so small an animal. The vertebræ are attached to the ribs in a very peculiar manner, and each of the backbones fits on to its neighbour by a wonderful joint, which keeps the chain of bones quite stiff when the animal is walking, but enables him to coil up into a ball at the slightest provocation. I find that the hedgehog has a clavicle, or collar-bone, evidently for the purpose of using his fore-paws for digging. His digging claws are also peculiar, and when curved together assume a shape very like that of the ant-eater, who pulls down the ants' nest with his tremendous claws.

Being anxious to settle the point, mentioned by White, as to whether the spines of the hedgehog at birth are soft, I obtained a hedgehog. I one morning found, among the straw in the box, one baby hedgehog just born. There had been probably a large family born, but the mother had eaten them all but this one. Here is a life-sized picture of him. White was quite correct. The spines were soft and flexible at the birth of the little beast; they were little dumpy spikes, much resembling the incipient feathers of a young bird. Even in the few hours the hedgehog lived these bristles grew considerably. I have made a cast of him, and coloured it to life.

Few people, perhaps, have heard the cry of a hedgehog when caught in a steel trap, and few would imagine that such a cry of pain and agony, somewhat resembling that of a child or a hare, could be produced by it. The flesh of the hedgehog is said to resemble chicken, and is eaten in large quantities by gipsies.

Hedgehogs are popularly said to be able to resist the effects of prussic acid, arsenic, aconite, and wourali. I have tried hedgehogs with vipers. The viper struck the hedgehog two or three times in the face, where there are no bristles; the blows were well aimed, and meant to do business, as at that moment the hedgehog was munching up the attacking viper's tail. The hedgehog did not suffer in the least; on the contrary, he ate up the viper in the course of the night, leaving not a trace of him. Pigs are said to be poison-proof against rattle-snakes' bites.

Mr. Davy has had forty hedgehogs at a time; he sold them chiefly to shopkeepers to sell again; the price, wholesale, was from 8s. to 12s. per dozen. Hedgehogs are very useful in kitchens, bakehouses, and gardens for destroying all kinds of insects, especially blackbeetles; they root in the ground for insects and beetles. He has never known hedgehogs to eat any kind of raw vegetable; they are very fond of bread and milk; they will eat a fresh-killed mouse with avidity, and he believes they take a number of young larks from the nests on the ground. Hedgehogs do a great deal of good on ploughed cultivated land by destroying grubs and other insect pests of the farm. In the natural state they lie torpid in the winter for about four months out of the twelve. They cover themselves with leaves, grass, &c., sometimes three or four feet deep. The hedgehog did not grub about the roots of White's plaintains for the sake of eating the roots, but for the insects and grubs at the root of the plants. He would not go deep enough for "pincher bobs," which are the larvæ of the stag-beetles. Pincher bobs are three years in the larval state.

FIELDFARES, p. 91.—The batfolders about London take numbers of fieldfares, red-wings, and hen blackbirds, which, as a rule, are killed for eating, there being no sale for them as cage-birds. The cock blackbirds are kept alive and sold for songsters. After they have been pressed for animal food and driven to the berries by the snow, in a few days they become very poor and emaciated, and not worth powder and shot.

Fieldfares first arrive in large flocks in October with the redwing and missel-thrush. They feed on the mountain ash and any kind of berry food.

COMMON WREN, p. 94.—"The common wren (*Troglodytes Europæus*)," writes Mr. Napier, "is prolific, but I never saw a well-authenticated instance of its laying more than ten eggs at a sitting. The wren builds a very firm, compact, and comfortable nest, which is made of a great variety of materials. I will describe six in my collection. The first is built of moss and apple-leaves, tightly interwoven. A second, which was placed in a gooseberry-bush, is built of the twigs of that plant, intermixed with moss and apple and ivy leaves : it has a thick lining of feathers. A third is entirely made of green moss, without a lining of feathers. A fourth is made of grass, fern-leaves, and moss, with a scanty lining of feathers. A fifth is made of oak-leaves and moss, and is strengthened at the bottom with clay. A sixth is built on an old swallow's nest, which was placed in the interior of a barn. The swallow's nest is relined with moss and feathers; but it is much more open than is usual with the species. The eggs of the wren vary greatly in size. They are white, spotted with light red and a few dots of lilac. The spots are nearly always small, and are seldom abundant."

Wrens often breed in very queer places. Lord Northwick has been good enough to give me a very good example of this as represented in the drawing opposite. The keeper at Northwick Park is in the habit of nailing the vermin he kills against the side of a barn or outhouse; in this instance a wren had, from some caprice of its own, chosen the interspace between two mummied bodies of stoats to build her nest. It will be observed that the tips of the tails are black, hence it is known that they are stoats or ermines. The nest is about six inches long, and is composed of moss leaves and fine hay, interwoven into the fur of the stoats for support. May we not infer from this that birds do not fear their enemies when dead and dry? I do not think that rooks are scared by the appearance of one of their brethren hung on a stick as a scarecrow.

CITY SPARROWS, p. 96.—In November, 1874, having some fishery business to transact in Billingsgate, I passed by St. Dunstan's Church. Just by the church I heard a most extraordinary noise, which at first I

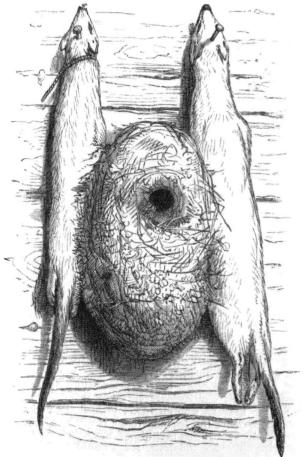

WREN'S NEST BETWEEN TWO STOATS.

imagined to proceed from a steam-pipe with a sore throat. I soon however, found that the noise proceeded from thousands of birds which had settled on two trees in the churchyard. A boy passing by happened to hit a post with a stick; the noise suddenly ceased, but a few

Y

seconds afterwards it began again as loud as ever. The birds were sparrows, and a man who was standing by told me that they generally arrived in large numbers at the end of September and took up their abode for the winter on the trees. They come there every evening at sundown till about the first or second week in February. They go off regularly every morning at daybreak to feed, and he thought that most of them went to Tower-hill and neighbouring streets to pick up the corn dropped from the nosebags of the cab and van horses. Nobody is allowed, luckily, to disturb them. Lovers of birds should not lose the opportunity of hearing this gratuitous concert, which takes place every evening about sundown. I hear there are two trees in Sparrow-passage, close to the Angel, Islington, where the same thing occurs nightly. I cannot think what these city sparrows are talking about; they all talk at once, so the subject of the conversation must be important. I could not make out that they had elected a chairman. They might have been debating who was to be elected " Lord Mayor of all the Sparrows " in November.

Sparrows are much used for shooting-matches. The price is 2s. per dozen. Large numbers of sparrows leave London after harvest and go upon the stubbles to feed; they return again to London during the winter months,[1] when farmers begin to plough in the stubble. In September there are hardly any sparrows in London. After they have been caught at and thinned several times, they become artful, and the moment they see the net they cry, " Jim, jim, jim," and are off. An old Jim is as cunning as an old man, from seeing his friends so often caught in the net.

Sparrows are a great pest to the Zoological Gardens, by entering into the food-houses, and especially the warm houses in winter. Since the establishment of the Zoological Gardens in 1826, more than fifty years ago, the sparrows have been netted, shot, and caught at all seasons; the nests also have been robbed of their young whenever and wherever they could be obtained. In spite of this constant war of extermination —for it is a war—there are probably more sparrows in the gardens at the present time than ever existed since the establishment of the Society. If this constant persecution or destruction of them had not been kept up, it would be utterly impossible to keep a collection of waterfowl, gallinaceous birds, or any grain-eating animal. So tame and impudent is this multitude of sparrows, that they wait in large numbers for the keepers, who go round to feed the various animals, and before he can leave the feeding-trough it will be blackened by the numbers of sparrows. If not caught and destroyed, the poor animals in the gardens, especially the water-fowl, would be starved. Eight-

---

[1] Mr. Bartlett, of the Zoological Gardens, does not think the sparrows go away from London. Sparrows about provincial towns probably do go away into the stubble. Mr. Bartlett's reason for doubting the exodus is that sparrows are of very short flight, and if they did go into the country we should see sparrows with clean feathers on their return : this we never do, the London sparrow being always a smoky, dirty-looking individual.

pence per dozen is paid for sparrows; they are used as food for the serpents, falcons, and small mammalia, and are very useful, as they could not always be bought when required. Many of the smaller animals could not exist without food of this kind.

Mr. Bartlett gives the London sparrow a bad name; they do a vast amount of mischief. In the early spring they collect in the streets and squares every feather and stray straw and other rubbish, with which they build their nests, filling up generally the head of the water-pipe on the top of the house; the first heavy storm washes Mr. Sparrow's nest into the rain-pipe, the consequence is the house becomer flooded.

The Albert Memorial in Hyde Park is being very much disfigured by sparrows building in the recesses of the sculptures.

STRAY HOUSE CATS IN LONDON PARKS.—House cats are great nuisances at the Zoological Gardens. They prowl about the parks at night and easily get over or through the fences into the Gardens, frightening and disturbing the valuable pheasants and other birds by walking on the top of the cages. Mr. Bartlett does his best to catch these cats. They are skinned and given to the eagles to eat. The skinned cats are amazingly like rabbits; when the head and paws are cut off it is difficult to tell a cat from a rabbit. On Saturdays the keepers bring the tails of the cats they have caught to the office and are paid sixpence per tail.

Most of the cats captured in the Gardens are full-grown males, that appear to live in *sheds* and *outhouses*. I have reason to believe the greater part of these poor cats are the result of people allowing their female cats to rear more kittens than they afterwards like to keep, and which, when they grow up, become troublesome, and are then turned adrift in the hope they may find a home. Failing this they turn wild, and become a perfect nuisance by killing and frightening all the birds and small animals they can find.

THE OTTER, p. 97.—In January, 1871, my friend, Dr. Norman, of Yarmouth, sent me a magnificent otter; it weighed 27 lbs., measured 4 feet 3 inches nose to tail, tail 1 foot 3 inches.

When dissecting the body of the beast, I discovered what I believe to be a new fact as regards the œsophagus or gullet. Holding up the pharynx I poured down thin plaster into the stomach, which, of course, hardened, showing its full capacity; it is $9\frac{1}{2}$ inches long and 15 inches round, and would hold rather over three pints of fluid. The œsophagus is 19 inches long, and, strange to say, is a very small tube, the size of a half-inch gas-pipe, or about the size of one's little finger, and only one inch and three-quarters round. I expected to find it a large dilatable tube, as in other fish-eating creatures. The best explanation that I can give of this curiously small œsophagus is that the otter chops up his food very small with his formidable teeth before he eats it.

WEATHER AND MIGRATIONS, p. 98.—Birds have sense and knowledge to keep in the south of England if their food is not ready for them at their breeding-places inland. In fine weather during full moon, and on bright nights, birds, as a rule, come over to their time. Swallows, as a rule, come to their time, although they do not go direct to their breeding-places; they keep under the South Downs, and in protected localities, such as the Devil's Dyke, near Brighton; the weather is always very mild under the Devil's Dyke Hill.

THE WOODPECKER.—FLIGHT AND WALK OF BIRDS, p. 99.[1]—I will now proceed to describe the structure of the woodpecker, as I wish to demonstrate what admirable beauty and design may be found in the commonest objects, if only the student of natural science knows how, when, and where to look. The woodpecker I dissected is the great green woodpecker (*Picus viridis*). It is also called the "rain-bird," the "woodspite," "hewhole," and "woodwall." In Oxfordshire they are called "heccles," or "green aisles." The colouring of the bird is a lovely green. What could be a better dress for a bird who lives in a wood than green? The woodpecker has to run up the sides of trees ; and whereas the tail feathers of a peacock are made to expand, so as to exhibit all the glorious colours of the rainbow, showing that nature intended that this kind of tail should be purely ornamental, so we find, on the contrary, that the tail of the woodpecker is made entirely for utility. The bird has ten feathers on its tail, Fig. A. The two centre feathers are four and a half inches long. They are as stiff as wire, and pointed at the ends somewhat like the head of a spear. The tail-feathers on either side are also spear-headed, so that when the tail is expanded like a lady's fan it forms a most admirable prop, by means of which the bird supports himself as he climbs up the sides of the tree.

Whereas the claws of the fowl are made to scratch in the earth, and the claws of the eagle for seizing its prey, we find that the claws of the woodpecker are so sharply curved that they form half a circle, Fig. B. The points are exceedingly sharp, so as to enable the bird to get a firm hold on the roughness of the bark. The hind claw is very small. The two front claws are of unequal length ; but the middle claw is so situated as almost to turn at right angles with the leg, thus preventing any chance of the bird slipping.

The tongue of the woodpecker, Fig. C., however, is the most remarkable piece of mechanism about his body. If the bill be opened, and the tongue drawn out, it will be observed that it can be protruded nearly four inches from the gape of the beak. It is almost cylindrical, and can be pushed back into a sheath, which fits it just as a pencil can be pushed back into a silver pencil-case. This is very similar to the mechanism that we find in the long worm-like tongue of the great ant-eater of South America ; but the tongue of the woodpecker

[1] This paragraph is quoted from my "Logbook of a Fisherman and Zoologist." Chapman and Hall, Piccadilly.

presents a structure not visible in the ant-eater, for on carefully examining the top of the woodpecker's tongue, we find that it ends in

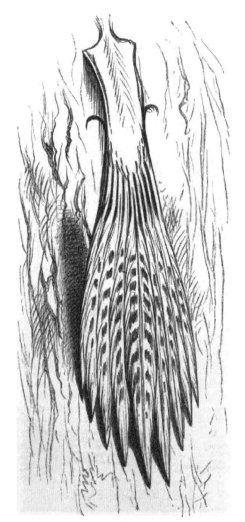

FIG. A.—TAIL OF WOODPECKER.

a sharp horny point, and that on each side of this sharp horny point there are some small barbs directed backwards. Now we find that the hyoid, or tongue-bone, which works this marvellous tongue, extends not only as far back as the base of the head, as is the case with most birds, but is actually prolonged right *over the top of the head*, and is

FIG. B.—FOOT OF WOODPECKER.

firmly fixed into the skull, at the base of the beak, on the right side. The reader can easily realise this curious structure if he imagines the tongue-bone in his own head to be extended backwards on each side of

FIG. C.—TONGUE OF WOODPECKER.

the ears to the poll. These two bones then run parallel with each other in a depression on the top of the skull, and are finally inserted into the bone of the forehead just above the right eye. This tongue of the woodpecker, therefore, may be said to be worked by two highly elastic steel springs, and I have no doubt that in life the bird is enabled to protrude and draw back his tongue with amazing celerity.

The stomach of the woodpecker is simply a fleshy bag, and I was pleased to find it full of food. On opening this bag-like stomach, I discovered a mass of a black-looking substance, which I discerned to be black ants, in number sufficient to fill an egg cup. Here then, we find that the police of nature ordains that the ants should eat decaying vegetable matter, especially in fir woods, where their nests are frequently robbed for the sake of feeding young pheasants with the eggs.

May we not also learn a practical lesson from studying the habits of the woodpecker? I frequently hear complaints that the pine forests of this country and Scotland are seriously injured by a beetle which bores into the sprouting tops of the pine-trees, and thereby does great mischief to woodland property. If the proprietors of the forests are so foolishly ignorant as to allow the woodpecker to be shot, it serves them right that their trees are injured ; when in the pretty harmless woodpeckers they have valuable servants who would, without being paid for their trouble, find out these insect pests on the pine-trees, and very quickly dig them out of their retreat by means of their sharp-pointed bayonet-shaped bills. This pine-boring beetle, *Ligniperda*, is fully described in *Land and Water*, No. 767, *October 2nd*, 1880.

NIGHTINGALE (*P. luscinia*), p. 113.—The earliest place for nightingales is Welwyn in Hertfordshire, where they arrive as early as the 10th of April; in other places they come usually about the 14th. Bird-catchers, when they go out expressly for nightingales, carry with them scraped meat and eggs, and cram the birds about two hours after they are caught, and repeat the cramming several times during the day. The old birds are sometimes very difficult to " meat off," they will put up with any punishment rather than feed. Nightingales are not known in Derby or Yorkshire. Mr. Davy has frequently sent these birds in pairs to both places. The late Sir Charles Slingsby used to take a dozen pairs of nightingales at a time in the hopes of acclimatising them at Knaresborough in Yorkshire. On one occasion nightingales bred there, the keeper found a nest and eggs, but on the whole this experiment has not succeeded. The reason why nightingales are not found in many districts, such as Scotland, Devonshire, Cornwall, is that their proper insect food is not there. The food of the nightingale consists of small beetles and any sort of fleshy caterpillars, not hairy caterpillars. It is stated by some that the nightingale will feed on the glow-worms at night, but this is a mistake; the bird, when once settled down after dark, never moves from his lodging unless disturbed. Any person by starting one or two nightingales singing in a road between coppices, would set the birds all round singing, and they will do their song several times right through.

I now give Mr. Davy's reading of the song of the nightingale. The song is commenced by "wheeting and kurring" which may thus be written :—

"Wheet, wheet, kurr, k-u-u-r-r-r."

. The song after that commences :—

"Sweet, sweet, sweet, sweet,
Jug, jug, jug, jug, jug,
Swot, swot, swot, swotty."

They lie a long time on these notes, finishing up with "swotting and kurring." The song must be pronounced with great inflections (*crescendo-diminuendo*, I think the lady pianists call it), especially modify the "sweet, sweet," and pronounce it in a plaintive manner. The "jug, jug, jug," is quick, like a dog barking.

Bechstein, the German naturalist, has also put the song of the nightingale into words. He writes :—"The song of the nightingale is so articulate that it may very well be written." This is what Bechstein makes of it.

"Tioû, tioû, tioû, tiou,
Spe tiou squa
Tio, tio, tio, tio, tio, tio, tio, tex,
Contio, contio, contio, contio,
Tzu, tzu, tzu, tzu, tzy,"

and so on for twenty more lines. I must prefer Mr. Davy's version of the nightingale's song as given above.

The following is the return of the "soft-meat" birds caught by Mr. Davy's men in April, 1873. This was a very late year for arrivals. "Gales" means nightingales :—

Catchings, April, 1873—
  April 9, 3 Titlarks
  10, 8 „
  12, 7 „
  18, 6 Gales, 5 Titlarks
  19, 5 Gales
  22, 9 Gales, 7 Redstarts
  23, 16 Gales, 9 Whinchats, 11
    Redstarts, 2 Wheatears
  24, 11 Gales
  25, 18 Gales, cocks and hens
    for turning out
  26, 13 Gales
  27, 1 Blackcap
  28, 12 Gales

Catchings, April, 1873
  31, 21 Gales for turning down,
    cocks and hens
  May 2, 15, Gales, 2 Blackcaps
  4, 7 Blackcaps
  6, 8 Gales, 2 Blackcaps
  7, 24 Gales to turn down
Total gales, 158
Lost by deaths, 1873, in "meating off" the above birds :
  64 Gales
  20 Titlarks
  2 Blackcaps
  4 Redstarts
            C. R. DAVY.

The price of nightingales for turning out in copses is thirty shillings a dozen, cocks and hens. When "meated off," and properly caged, a nightingale is worth from five shillings to one guinea, according to the quality of the song.

Mr. Keilich tells me that in Germany there are two kinds of nightingales. The larger is called a "sprossen." In size it is between the nightingale and thrush. These sprossens are common all down the Danube, and the Vistula districts. There is a great number of them about Vienna. These birds are brought to England from Austria by the German bird dealers; they are known to the English bird-catchers as the thrush nightingale. The song is extraordinarily powerful, but its quality is not nearly so good as the British birds. The sprossen is very seldom caught in England, and is not found in France. The noise which White describes as "snapping or cracking" is called by the English bird-catchers "wheeting and kurring," the word sounds, "Kur-r-r, kur-r-r, kur-r," repeated three times, then comes a sharp "wheet, wheet," like a very sharp whistle. Nightingales build their nests about a foot from the ground, in lanes and thick hedgerows. The nests are made principally with dried oakleaves, and lined with fine dried grass. These nests when handled easily fall to pieces. The wheeting and kurring is not intended for menace; this is to delude their enemies, and entice them away from their nest. They will run and fly in front of a man along a low hedgerow. When they have enticed a man away from the nest, they will dart through the hedge and instantly double back to their nest. They are very cunning in building. Like other birds they are not frightened at cattle. They only wheet and kurr to mankind. No bird has any fear or dread of cattle. Nightingales are wonderful birds to run (or rather hop) very quickly. Tie a nightingale's wings and see if you can catch him. Nightingales' wings are always tied by catchers, and kept tied for a week. The cocks are always singing close to their nests, which are often near cottages.

In 1875, two pairs of nightingales built at Highgate; one pair in the Baroness Burdett Coutts' grounds, and another pair bred in the cemetery, on the opposite side of the lane. Numbers of people went there to hear these birds sing. They were both well looked after, and the young and old birds all escaped the bird-catchers. Nightingales return every year to the neighbourhood where they were born, and I hope, therefore, that they will again become abundant at Hampstead. Lord Mansfield's woods at Hampstead have been preserved the last three years, and it is not uncommon of a summer's evening to hear twenty or thirty nightingales singing, especially at early morning and twilight; they do not sing much in the middle of hot days. If the woods had not been preserved there would not have been one nightingale left. Nightingales are caught almost anywhere, within a radius of twenty miles round the suburbs of London, such as Sydenham, Kew, Epping Forest, Edgeware, and Dartford. As a rule, the cocks arrive from eight to ten days before the hens, and when they arrive they take up positions, as the locality suits. They delight in hedgerows, copses, spinneys, &c. As soon as they arrive, if the weather is mild, they commence their song, but if the weather is cold and frosty, they keep very mute. They are caught in this manner: the bird-catcher finds a bush which they frequent, he then makes a "scrape" with a hoe, that is, he turns up the ground to draw the attention of the bird, who comes to look for insects on the fresh turned ground. He then places the trap, baited with a meal-worm. If the birds attempt to ramble away they are driven back by pelting. A round net trap, about a foot across is used; it is baited with maggots or meal-worms placed on a pin. A very enticing bait is a "black-beetle, belly upper-most," which is quickly seen by the bird. A pin is run through the blackbeetle and he is fastened to the cork of the trap, the playing of the legs attracts the nightingale, he "kurrs" when he sights the bait, presently down he comes, and on touching the bait is instantly netted. The "standing net" is better than the "Jack-in-the-box" trap.[1] The bird-catcher wheets and kurrs to the nightingale and does a portion of the song, thus: "Churr, kurr, wheet;" the nightingale answers by singing, as he thinks it is the challenge of another nightingale—a stranger come on his beat. In the autumn nightingales do not sing, they only wheet and kurr. As soon as they get clean moulted they leave this country. It is difficult to "meat off" nightingales, that is, to make them feed. In former times a live meal-worm was put into a glass tube, just large enough to hold him. The following is the plan now adopted. An ordinary watch-glass is placed in a small tin dish; underneath the glass are placed live meal-worms, which of course kept crawling about round the edges of the inside of the glass; well scraped beef and hard-boiled egg are then piled round the outside edge of the glass. The birds seeing the worms moving about, come and peck at them, their beaks glance off the glass, and at almost every peck they get a little of the food. After they have been induced to feed, the glass is taken away and they feed themselves, and there is no further trouble. "Box cages" are most suitable for fresh caught nightingales; they should have thin paper pasted over the front.

TORPIDITY, p. 111. White is continually mentioning torpidity. In this country dormice and hedgehogs become torpid. Here is a portrait of a monkey that in White's time would probably have been said to have laid himself up torpid. This remarkable specimen was given to me by my brother-in-law, the Rev. H. Gordon, of Harting, near Petersfield, with the following history :—

"In 1868 this skeleton was given me by the Rev. H. Mitchell, rector of Bosham, near Chichester. It had been found at Bosham Mill. The owner of the mill had a monkey that disappeared. A birch tree was cut down, and lay for some time in an adjacent carpenter's shop; and when a part of the bark was found to be loose it was detached, and the monkey's sarcophagus was revealed; on showing the bark adjacent to the head, the experienced connoisseurs of English timber pronounced

---

[1] A trap where the net is concealed in a box.

MUMMY MONKEY FOUND IN A TREE.

it to have been living wood when the tree was felled, and added that the said bark was still green, a proof that the tree had lived within two years of 1868.

"This monkey is a Marmozet; his length is—body, six inches; tail, seven inches. The poor little creature is quite dried up into a mummy; the hair on his head and the aspect of the eyes made him look very like a small human baby mummified. The hands rest against the sides of his head as if in pain. I am afraid the poor little fellow must have crawled in and died of starvation.

"It is a very remarkable thing, but there is no mark of his having been touched by any fly or other insect. The body still adheres very tight to the bark; the lower part of the body is very much crushed, but, as Mr. Mitchell remarks, the head remains intact. The appearance of the bark covering the monkey is quite natural."

BLUEBOTTLE FLIES, p. 115.—When I am at work in my dissecting room the pretty little bluebottles and other flies come to help me. It is wonderful how soon they find out what is going on. Though not a bluebottle may be seen about, two or three generally arrive in a minute or two. They help me much to make skeletons.

I once heard of a capital plan to find out the exact *locale* of a rat which had been poisoned and had died under the floor of a sitting-room. A live bluebottle was turned loose; he hunted about the room and at last sat down exactly over the spot where the dead rat was. He found him out by the smell. This fly saved a long carpenter's bill for pulling up the boards and putting them down again.

ELEPHANTS AND FLIES.—Regarding the balance of nature, showing how minute beings might be the destruction of gigantic things, my friend Mr. Bartlett remarks that in the native state flies are great enemies to elephants. If an elephant gets wounded, flies deposit their eggs in the wounds; these eggs turn into maggots, and ultimately cause the death of the animal.

HOUSE-FLY MAGGOTS.—The maggots of the common house-fly (*Musca domestica*) occur abundantly in horse-manure.

Mr. Davy breeds great numbers of maggots every year. He begins to breed them before the arrival of the soft-billed birds, so as to have maggots ready to feed them when first caught. By these means he has been able to rear some of the rarest of the soft-meat birds. He finds that in the early spring the flies will deposit their eggs in dead "birds," in preference to any kind of offal. They commence, as a rule, to "blow" at the nose and eyes first, and on a hot day the eggs will hatch out in fourteen or fifteen hours. The maggot, when ten days old, is ready for the birds. Maggots are used to tempt soft-meat birds to take their artificial food. When the eyes of a dead bird are once filled with fly-blows, another bluebottle coming also to deposit her eggs seems to know that the place has been already taken up; she therefore does not

attempt to lay any more eggs, but takes her departure. To keep
gentles for the winter, Mr. Davy looks out for October fly-blows. He
deposits the mature maggot in damp sand, and buries them in bottles
in the ground. He finds this plan has the effect of preventing them
from changing into the chrysalis state. By this means he is never
without gentles for his birds summer and winter. An immense trade
goes on in gentles for fishing-tackle shops; they are of nominal
value in hot weather, but in early spring they are sometimes worth one
penny a dozen.

Maggots are easier of digestion by soft-meat birds than meal-
worms. The skin of the meal-worms is hard, and contains much
silica. Again, birds find gentles in a state of nature, but they do
not find meal-worms.

PEACOCKS, p. 116.—I hear that peacocks are grand things to kill
snakes and even vipers. My friend, Mr. A. D. Berrington, told me of
an estate in Wales where vipers formerly abounded, and were a great
nuisance till peacocks were turned down. These birds shortly killed
off all the vipers. The peacock runs smartly in upon the viper, hits
him hard with his beak and retires before the viper has a chance of
striking with his fangs.

STARLINGS, p. 122.—Wormwood Scrubs used to be a celebrated place
for bird-catching, especially for starlings. They have been caught
there from two to four dozen starlings at one pull of the net. The
nets must be laid so as to begin catching at dawn. By eleven o'clock
starlings are " fed up " and are off; they go for shelter in the woods,
to get out of the heat of the sun. Five or six dummies—*i.e.*, stuffed
starlings—are placed in the nets to attract the wild birds, and also one
live bird on a "flur stick." The autumn is the best time to catch
starlings. They soon get very artful. It is necessary to "take a cut"
at them—that is, pull the net sharp the moment they get within reach
of it. They will often hover over the net, not making up their minds
to go in. This is the time to "cut them in." The birds about August
being mostly young are not "up to the game"—that is, the net work
—but they will very soon learn it and get artful. The market for
starlings is for shooting matches. Starlings are also extensively used
for trap-shooting. The price varies from 4*s*. to 6*s*. per dozen. Directly
after the breeding season Mr. Davy would take a twenty dozen order
at two days' notice.

STRUCTURE OF A COW'S HORN, p. 125.—It is often the case that in the
commonest objects we may see beautiful examples of engineering
structures. I take the anatomy of the cow's horn as a good example.

I find that over the brain of the cow a strong roof of bone is thrown,
in the shape of an arch, so as to form a substantial foundation for the
horns. This roof is not solid, but is again strengthened below by a
series of bony arches, that are so distributed as to form a series of

hollow chambers, thus forming a structure uniting strength with lightness. The problem now is, how to fasten the horn on each side on to
this buttress. The horn itself must of course be formed of horn
proper, *i.e.*, hardened hair. In the rhinoceros we find a horn composed
entirely of a solid mass of what is really a bunch of hair agglutinated
together; but this kind of horn would have been much too heavy for
the cow's convenient use. What is to be done? Why, hollow out the
centre of the horn, of course; but stay—this will not do, because how
is the horn to be supplied with blood-vessels?—in fact, how is it
to grow? Let us see how it is done by the Great Designer. Cut the
horn right across with a saw, and you will find inside another horn,
only made of bone (see engraving). If the section is made about one-

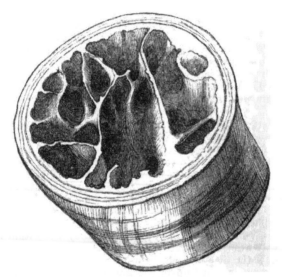

SECTION OF A COW'S HORN.

third of the way down the length of the horn, you will be able to pick
out a piece of bone in the shape of a cone, on which, or rather round
which, the horn proper has shaped itself. This bone fits the cavity
with the greatest accuracy; it is as light as the thinnest paper, and
yet as strong as a cone of tin. It is everywhere perforated with holes
which in life contained the nerves, the veins, and arteries, and we know
a cow has all these in her horns; nerves, proved by the fact that cows
do not like their horns touched, and that they can scratch a fly off
their hides with the tip of the horn; arteries and veins, proved by the
fact that a horn, when broken, will bleed, and that the horn of a living
cow feels quite warm when held in the hand, besides which the nerves

and arteries form a union between the internal core of bone and the external covering of horn proper.

If we now cut the rest of the horn into sections, we shall find that the inside of the bony part is really hollow, but that very strong buttresses of bone are thrown (about every inch or so) across the cavity of the horn in such a manner as to give it the greatest possible support and strength. I have cut a cow's horn and skull into several sections to show these buttresses of bone, and now that the preparation is finished I have another specimen to show that there is design and beauty in all created objects.

Spotted Flycatcher, p. 127.—The spotted flycatcher takes all his food upon the wing. He leaves the branch with a dart, and returns to the same spot. Its brother, the black and white flycatcher, frequents bogs in woods, and places where gnats abound. The latter bird is easily kept in confinement, becomes tame in a few days, and feeds upon eggs and bread and a little scraped beef, and an occasional meal-worm. As a rule he lives round the margins of woods and groves of trees. He is rarely found in the interior of a wood.

Mr. Bartlett informs me that a spotted flycatcher that built in the climbing stalk of a passion flower outside his house in the Zoological Gardens used to throw up little shining pill-like bodies that looked like blue glass. It appears from this that flycatchers disgorge the horn-like and shining bodies of blowflies and other insects in pellets, just as an owl disgorges the pellets containing the bones and skins of the mice and rats. In the case of house-martins, bats, &c., the hard skins of the insects are not disgorged as pellets, but pass through the digestive organs.

White or Barn Owl, p. 129.—This bird is sometimes caught in gins on the tops of posts set for jays in woods. The young ones are taken from holes of trees and barns; both the young and old tame very soon; they are easily raised upon meat, with mouse or bird now and then. They eat moles in dry weather. The old birds throw their pellets outside the nest, the young ones throw them up inside. As a rule they return to the same breeding-place every year. Three lots of young owls from one pair of old ones have been taken out of the same nest in one season. They breed up to the end of October. Young ones are found in May. The boys in Hainault Forest used to collect owls' eggs for sale, as the eggs were of more value than young birds. The old owl kept on laying till she was found dead in the nest with a very small egg, having laid from twelve to fourteen eggs in succession in the space of three weeks. There are from three to five young in a nest, and sometimes there is as much as a week's difference in the age of the young ones, some being in the "white down" and others nearly in "full feather." They fly very light, the wings seem arched out, and "take the wind light." Tawny or brown owls are caught in the trunks of decayed old trees in forests and large woods; they are different in

their habits from the white owl, and prefer solitude. The nest is sometimes five feet deep in the hollow of a tree. The boys find the nests
and get the young birds by taking a woollen stocking and rolling it into
a loose ball; they then by means of a string bob it up and down among
the young owls. The owl chicks turn on their backs and attack it with
their claws; they don't seem to have sense to let go, but keep hold, and
up they must come. The tawny owls are more rare than the white
owls. There is abundance of the tawny owls in the New Forest. Watford
is a noted place for them, especially the old trees in Lord Essex's
park.

These useful birds may be established, if owners of property choose
to do so, and the locality itself is favourable. Seven years ago Mr.
Davy sold to Mr. G. S. Bancroft, M.P. for Leeds, two nests of young
barn owls, this gentleman wishing to establish them amongst the ruins
of Kirkstall Abbey, near Leeds. When the young owls were strong
enough they were turned loose, and being tame, were fed nightly for a
time until they could find their own food and shift for themselves.
Owls from that time to the present can be seen at night time flying about the ruins. The monastery of Kirkstall was built in the
year 1100.

When pressed for food owls will take any kind of small live thing;
they lay up in store mice, &c., round about their nests.

Young ones both of the long and short eared owls are brought from
the neighbourhood of Weybridge. There is always a sale for owls in
London; the common fetch from two shillings; the horned ones, when
matured, average 7s. 6d. each.

Owls will destroy pigeons under a week old, but only when pressed
for food. Stormy and wet evenings keep the mice from moving about;
so owls work very hard in wet weather. A calm, gloomy night is the
time for owls.

At page 115 White says his "owls hoot in B flat." I really wish
that some good musician would go to the Zoological Gardens and put
into writing the various notes sounded by the animals and birds. In
April 1875 I made a splendid cast of an elephant's trunk, also casts of
sections of it. The trunk is used by its owner as a musical instrument.
Visitors at the Zoological Gardens may often have heard a curious
musical trumpeting by the female elephant when she is eating her fresh
hay. As I was anxious to know what this note was in music, my
friend Mr. C. H. Walker, organist of the late Rev. Mr. Stewart's church,
Munster-square, has kindly been up to see what he could make of it; he
has hit it off exactly, and has played it to me on Mr. Stewart's beautiful
organ. He tells me it is the lowest A in the bass on an organ which
goes down to double C. He uses the "Bourdon" stop coupled with the
double open diapason on the great organ. Mr. Walker tells me that
the higher note of the elephant when trumpeting is C sharp. The
musical note of the elephant when eating is almost exactly imitated by
striking gently and continuously and simultaneously the two lowest
A A in the bass on an ordinary piano. Reader, try it.

THE CHOUGH, p. 132.—Numbers of Cornish choughs are sent yearly from Plymouth to London. They are in great demand, buyers for them are at all times to be found; as much as one to two pounds per pair has been paid for young birds. These birds are very much sought after. They are very cunning in building their nests among cliffs and dangerous rocks; the nests are made of small branches or sticks with a lining of wool or soft substance. They are good imitating birds, and may be made to talk like a jackdaw. The choughs are now very rare round Beachy Head, and, like the ravens in the Isle of Wight, are nearly extinct.

SHEEP IN AUSTRALIA, p. 140.—Mr. J. C. Sutherland, who has farmed sheep in Tasmania, tells me that sheep were first introduced into New South Wales not more than one hundred years ago, by a man of the name of McArthur. The sheep originally introduced were the merino of the purest breed. At this present time they have crossed the merino with Leicesters, growing a much heavier sheep and coarser wool. They made this cross because the original breed were getting too small and the wool too fine; the coarse wool now fetches as much in the London markets as did the fine wool formerly.

I am told that when a lamb dies, if the shepherd takes off its skin and sews it on the body of another lamb, the mother recognizing the smell of its own lamb allows the foster-lamb to suck. This confirms White's idea that the animals know each other by the smell more than by sight. When Fortune was travelling in China to collect tea-seeds for the Indian Government he spoke the language so well that he passed muster among them, but the dogs recognized him by the smell and barked at him.

MIGRATORY BIRDS LEAVING THE SOUTH COAST.—Mr. G. D. Rowley, of Brighton, writes in the *Ibis*, No. V. p. 101 :—" Living on the south coast in spring and autumn, I have good opportunities of marking the arrival and departure of some birds. I have seen the swallows (*Hirundo*), over the sea, actually arrive and pass straight inland without a pause or the least show of weariness. Not so the chiff-chaffs and willow-wrens, which stay about the shingle at first till they recover their strength. At least I have seen them at five o'clock on a spring morning within a few yards of the waves. In autumn, on certain days (varying according to the wind), the Gardens about Brighton are full of ring-ouzels, chiff-chaffs, willow-wrens, redstarts; on the Downs are wheatears; in the air goldfinches, greenfinches, swallows, &c. 1 have stood and watched these birds early on a fine morning (for birds of the above kinds do not fly in cloudy, dull days), going in continuous streams down to the sea, following one another as surely in the same direction as if going by a mariner's compass. The Roman augurs were not quite so absurd perhaps as one might at first imagine.; a great many indications may be gathered from the flight of birds. Their motions appear to the common observer to be guided by chance, but the

z

ornithologist knows that each bird he sees is employed on some particular business, and can interpret its actions. Birds always travel by night across the sea, working their way along the coast till a proper wind is blowing, and flying against any light which may appear on the shore. In the days of the old watchmen at Brighton, small birds used frequently to fly against the lanterns which they carried." As a general rule there is no time comparable to the early morning for studying the habits of wild creatures.

MOLES, p. 153.—"After dinner we went round the sweetstuff and toy booths in the street, and the vicar, my brother-in-law, the Rev. H. Gordon, of Harting, Petersfield, Hants, introduced me to a merchant of gingerbread-nuts, who was a great authority on moles. He tends cows for a contractor who keeps a great many of these animals to make concentrated milk for the navy. The moles are of great service; they eat up the worms which eat the grass, and wherever the moles have been afterwards the grass grows there very luxuriantly. When the moles have eaten all the grubs and worms in a certain space, they migrate to another, and repeat their gratuitous work. The grass where the moles have been is always the best for the cows."[1]

In August 1875, when at Mr. Burr's, at Aldermaston Park, Reading, I endeavoured to smoke some moles out of their runs. The Squire had not one of Mr. Bateson's vermin annihilators, by means of which sulphur smoke can be pumped into rat-holes. I had fancied that the smoke I intended to pump in would show me the run of the moles' burrowings. I therefore got from the gardener the apparatus for smoking his plants. I found some fresh molehills, I knocked off the loose earth from the top of a molehill, and then pumped into the run strong smoke made from tobacco and brown-paper. The smoke immediately came out of several of the moles' hillocks, which smoked like young volcanoes. I then traced out Mr. Mole's tunnels by means of a spud, but I had not power enough in the bellows to blow in the smoke a long way so as to start "the little gentleman in black." Mr. Davy informed me that directly the smoke is blown in, Mr. Mole "takes his hook," and while the smoke ascends through the mole-hills he works himself deep into the earth. The Squire's keeper informed me that the moles invariably worked at eight, twelve, and four regularly every day. He took me some little distance to a footpath running across the park, and pointed out how the mole literally had two "diggins," or castles, one on each side of the path, and that he had one tunnel to cross this path, just like the passage in the Houses of Parliament that connects the House of Lords with the House of Commons.

Moles have eyes. Blow the fur backwards, and two very tiny black specks can be seen; these are the eyes. The optic nerves are small, but they exist. A dried mole should be taken off the bushes where

[1] See my "Log Book."

the mole-catchers have hanged moles. If the dry skin is carefully cut off the head, the orifices of the eyes will be easily seen—the anatomy of this most interesting and curious little beast will also be readily made out. Soak one of these dry moles in warm water—cut off the skin with scissors, and a skeleton can be easily made. The skeleton of the mole is one of the most striking instances of structure designedly adapted to habits in the whole animal kingdom. The little lancet-like teeth are specially beautiful. Here is the wonderful digging paw of the mole; it is worked by very powerful muscles.

DIGGING PAW OF THE MOLE.

REDBREAST (*Sylvia rubecula*), p. 155.—Robins are kept by many people in London; they are free singers in cages, and will live for years. In the winter they come to towns and houses. In the spring they entirely disappear to breed in the woods. Like the hedgesparrow, the robins go to nest very early in the spring; the robins pair about the middle of February, no matter how bad the weather may be.

There is much truth in the story of birds pairing at Valentine's Day. About this time the following British birds are to be found in pairs: blackbirds, thrushes, hedge-sparrows, common wrens, long-tail titmouse, &c. In the case of the long-tail titmouse the old birds and the young ones keep together all the winter, but about the middle of February, the happy family party breaks up, and each looks out for its mate.

It is a rule among most canary bird-dealers to "pair up" their birds actually on Valentine's Day.

WRYNECK, p. 160.—This is a migratory bird, arriving here in the middle of April and leaving about the end of August. It breeds in the holes of trees and feeds on banks on ants, and on insects under the bark of trees; they are easily raised from the nest, but "caught birds" will never feed. The young should be fed on scraped beef and hard boiled egg. It is called the cuckoo's mate, because it arrives about the same time as the cuckoo. It is also called the "snake bird," because it has a curious habit of twisting its head right round over its back like a snake. This habit can be easily observed when a live wryneck is held in the hand. The wryneck is an easily caught bird, and is sure to come into the net if the ground is turned up and a fresh "scrape" is made under a hedge, when laying for the summer bird tribe or soft-billed birds.

The toes of the wryneck are very peculiar; there are four on each leg, two long toes outside, the short toes are inside. This is a most peculiar formation, well adapted for climbing a tree. They are wonderful runners on the bark, and will deceive by running round the back of a tree.

HORSES, p. 175.—I am certain that a great many racehorses are made very savage by being shut up in stalls away from other horses; a horse

z 2

is by nature a gregarious animal, and it is pain and misery to him to be shut up alone. Horses have very quick hearing, and at night timid horses are often kept awake by rats moving about. Rats, therefore, should always be exterminated in stables. Goats are often kept in stables; as I am told that goats will face fire. Should the stable take fire, the goats will give the horses the lead out of it, whereas if there were no goat the horses would neither walk nor be led out. It is said that to a horse's eye everything is magnified, and this is the reason why man has such power over him; to a horse a man possibly appears to be of a gigantic size. The molar teeth of horses fastened together with cement form very ornamental mosaic pavement for summer-houses or entrances to hall-doors. They may be also cut and polished to make ornamental tables for the drawing-room.

EFFECTS OF TREES ON RAINFALL, p. 183.—The late Mr. Menzies, Deputy Surveyor of Windsor Forest, writes me thus :—
"Mr. White has entered upon one of the most abstruse questions of forest economy, to which much attention has been given since his time. The only time when trees do truly perspire is in the summer, when some kinds, such as notably the oak and beech, distil a sort of dew from their leaves. It is quite true also that they prevent evaporation from the surface of the ground, and so have a tendency to *prolong* the supply of water that any district may yield; but on the other hand they themselves are great drinkers of the water in the subsoil, and so again they diminish the store. Whether these two tendencies counterbalance one another, or whether trees favour the storage of water most, has by no means been settled. Practically no one would think of surrounding a reservoir of pure drinking-water with trees; because the falling foliage injures the water, and the effects of trees in condensing water which is present in the air, are infinitesimal.
"Any account given by travellers of the diminishing of streams in any country in consequence of the denuding of the district of trees must be received with extreme caution—just as we know that we must be guarded in receiving from people of this country stories of the extremely cold winters and hot summers which used to prevail in their youth. The statistics of rainfall have only been collected in England within the last ten years with anything like scientific accuracy, and in other parts of the world the science is quite unknown. Hence we have no real data to go upon, and without a series of actual gaugings of the streams extending over a number of years, a truly valuable opinion cannot be formed.
"Since Mr. White's time many thousands of acres in England have been cleared, and many thousands have been planted, but no data exist to form any reliable opinion as to the effect, if any, upon the rivers; and such data would become vastly complicated, as it would be necessary at the same time to consider the effect of the agricultural drainage and the formation of canals, &c., that have been done since his time. My own opinion is that in England the trees have had no effect one

way or the other. I have read many accounts of the effect, in other
countries, of large forests in condensing the moisture on the hills, and
the balance of evidence is in favour of their doing so; but at the same
time there was little to support the statement beyond general opinion,
which is subject so much to conjecture. Although, therefore, Mr.
White has given a very charming account of a popular idea, accurate
scientific investigation since his time has not confirmed his views, and
people in England who consider the question of the storage of water
attach no importance whatever to the presence of trees in promoting
that object on any scale in this country.

"Lord Northwick, who for many years past has kept meteorological
records at his seat near Tenbury, informs me that he has ascertained
by experiment that a rain gauge of a given size, without vegetation,
catches three times as much water as a similar gauge planted with
vegetation. The vegetation absorbs the water. His Lordship argues,
from the above observation, that less drainage is required in pasture
lands than where there is no vegetation."

VIPER SWALLOWING ITS YOUNG, p. 187.—It is still believed by many
that a female viper will swallow her young when they are in peril. In
nearly all the cases that have come under my examination, the event
always happened a long time ago. The witness generally begins his
statement thus: "When I was a little boy," "Many years ago," "My
grandmother told me," &c. &c. If vipers swallowed their young "many

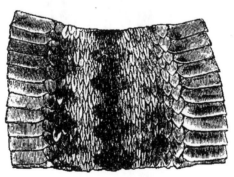

SKIN OF VIPER.

years ago," why should they not do so in our time? A correspondence
on this subject takes place in *Land and Water* almost every year. I
have made many anatomical preparations to show that the young
vipers found inside the mother have never been born. I still continue
my public offer of a reward of £1 for a specimen of a viper which
has been seen to swallow its young, *the young being actually in the*

œsophagus, or in the stomach proper, when it is opened by me in the presence of witnesses.

Holland, the keeper of the snakes, tells me that vipers under his charge at the Zoological Gardens often have young in their glass dens. The vipers that have had young are the Russell viper, black water viper, and the common viper. *In no instance have any of these vipers attempted to swallow their young alive.*

The engraving on the preceding page represents the skin of a viper. Directly the animal is killed, the skin or a portion of it should be stretched on a flat glass. The beautiful pattern of the scales in a skin so treated is much to be admired. Oil-cloth manufacturers should copy it.

Poison Fangs of Viper, p. 187.—Gilbert White does not seem to have been much of an anatomist. He probably therefore never dissected the poison apparatus of the viper or other venomous snakes. I now give a drawing of a dissection I have made of the poison apparatus of the rattlesnake. It is the same, on a larger scale, as the viper. Fig. 1 represents the palate of the snake; the lower jaw is supposed

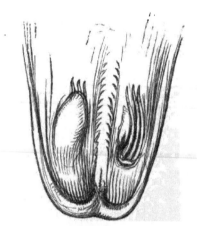

Fig. 1.—PALATE AND POISON FANGS OF THE RATTLESNAKE.

to be removed altogether. The poison fangs, when the snake is not irritated, lie back parallel to the roof of the mouth, so that they will not at all interfere when the snake is swallowing its food. On the left hand of the drawing will be seen the projecting tips of the fangs. The fangs lie in, and are protected by a fold of the gum, which serves two purposes; first of all, it prevents the poison being thrown broadcast when the snake bites, and secondly, it protects the fangs from injury. On the right hand side are seen the fangs from which the bag has been dissected off with the scissors. In this case there are three poison fangs all about the same size.

Fig. 2 shows a further dissection of the fangs as contained in this pouch or bag. One side of the bag being cut away, it will be seen that it envelops more than one poison fang. There are generally five or six in a row, one after the other. On each side of the snake's mouth one fang is fixed firmly on to the bone which works it ; the others are all more or less loose, and by some wonderful process, not yet known to us men, when the front fixed tooth gets broken off or is shed, another immediately comes up as its successor from behind. It will be observed that there is a small bristle running through the largest of the fangs ; the tooth in fact is perforated by a beautiful duct or pipe.

Professor Owen thus writes in his valuable work "Odontography; or, a Treatise on the Comparative Anatomy of the Teeth:"—"A true idea of the structure of a poison-fang will be found by supposing the crown of a simple tooth, as that of a Boa, to be pressed flat and its edges to be then bent towards each other, and soldered together so as to form a hollow cylinder open at both ends. The flattening of the fang and its inflection around the poison duct commences immediately above the base, and the suture of the inflected margins runs along the anterior and convex side of the recurved fang. The poison canal is then in front of the pulp cavity." When a poisonous snake strikes its enemy, it can hardly be said to *bite*. It rather gives a sharp instantaneous stab, knowing instinctively that the poison once injected into the wound will do its work. To enable them to strike so quickly, all poisonous snakes have, about the foremost few inches of their body, very great powers of darting.

FIG. 2.—POISON FANGS DISSECTED.

When experimenting on the poison of living vipers, I found that, when a viper is held tight by the neck, he will erect his two working fangs and move them backward and forward with more or less rapidity, exactly as a man moves his arms when about to fight another. When the viper was thoroughly enraged and had got his steam up, I placed quickly a microscope slide under the fangs. In one moment the fangs came sharply down upon the glass and two drops of poison were emitted, one from each fang. I instantly put these under the microscope, and witnessed a most extraordinary appearance, namely, a crystallization of the poison. Suffice it to say that the poison, when nearly evaporated, very much resembled the crystals of hoar frost on window panes on frosty mornings. This, I believe, has not been observed for about a hundred years. I discovered that Dr. Mead both saw and described it. This learned doctor's account can be found in his book, "A Mechanical Account of Poisons, by Richard Mead, M.D., physician to His Majesty, 1748."

I regret that I have not space to describe here the *Coronella lævis*, a snake exceedingly like a viper, but not poisonous. It is found in the

New Forest, but not at all commonly. It feeds upon lizards. I have had several in my possession.

How to Catch a Viper.—A professional viper-catcher thus describes the *modus operandi* :—"I generally catches him with a forked stick; I pins him to the ground, then I squeezes his mouth sideways, and scrapes or cuts his fangs out with a knife. I then scrapes out his poison bag, and rinses out his mouth in the nearest water; I then puts him in a bag. He will never open his mouth again to bite you any more. I used to find most of these gentlemen round by chalk-pits near Guildford. So long as you gets these vipers short up by neck they cannot harm you, though they start and swish their tails about like mad; they are very dull biters on cold days, but they fly through the grass of a hot day. I puts adders and common snakes in a bag altogether. There is no sale for them in London now—only occasionally a gentleman or two might want them. I know an artist who used to keep four or five in a fern-case to feed with half-grown mice. If they were not doctored well they would dart at the glass. I was once bitten by a viper: I was a beating for larvæ, and did not see my gentleman, who was lying on a chalk bank which I was climbing up from below. I never saw him, so he catches the forefinger of my left hand. The bite was a very sharp prick, like the bite of a mouse. I sucked it for half an hour; I felt pain next morning. It was sore and painful for four or five days."

Mr. Davy's men, as well as himself, have frequently found young adders in lanes in chalky districts in various parts of the country; he has never seen or heard of any one who has seen the viper swallow its young. He says, "I have had men out daily for years in all parts of the country, and none of my practical bird-catchers believe in it. The story of vipers swallowing their young is all *Old Mother Hubbard.*"

My friend, Major Rogers, who has done so much to get tigers destroyed in India, has shown me how to make a noose for handling poisonous snakes or any wild animal; one end of a piece of cord is tied on to the end of a stick, the other end is made to run loose through a turn in the cord; the noose is then slipped over the head of the snake, and thus he can be easily transferred from a box to a cage or other receptacle. Mr. Bartlett informs me that when a poisonous snake arrives at the Zoological Gardens they transfer him to his new residence by unfastening the lid of the box and leaving it on loose; they then put the box into the cage and with a long crooked iron rod push off the lid and hook out the snake; when they wish to remove the snake from the cage into the box, an apparatus like a common twitch, sometimes used by farriers to hold a horse by the nose, is used.

Rattle of Rattlesnake.—Mr. Thomas Hughes, M.P., in January 1871, was kind enough to give me a very fine specimen of the rattle of a rattlesnake. It is about two inches and a half long, and is composed of nine joints. This piece of mechanism is one of the most wonderful in the animal world. It is composed of a horny material, very thin, and is almost as transparent as the sheets of gelatine in which bonbons are wrapped. It is difficult to explain its ultimate structure in words. The rattle before me is formed of nine complete boxes, fitted one into the other in a more ingenious way than any puzzle made by human hands, even those of the Chinese; these boxes fit one into the other so that it is impossible to get them apart without breaking them. See Figure.

The rattle is rather more than half an inch across. The snake does not carry it with its broad side to the ground, but with one edge up and the other down; when shaken with the human hand the noise it makes is very like the noise from a child's rattle; but when the snake plays upon his own instrument its sound is quick and sharp like shot when dropped on a tin plate. I am told that when the snake rattles in the open air the sound appears to come from anywhere but the spot where the snake lies. There can be no doubt that this curious musical instrument (for so it may be called) is given to the snake in order to enable him to get close to his prey. Imagine a blazing hot day on the desolate prairie, no noise, everything is silence itself. We all know what curious noises are heard on occasions like this. The whirr-whirr of a rattlesnake's rattle would, under these circumstances, attract the notice of a bird or small mammal, who could easily escape from his enemy by flight if he knew where his enemy was. He remains perfectly still, however, to listen to the unwonted noise, and gives the snake time to glide noiselessly up to him and strike him with his deadly fangs.

RATTLE OF RATTLE-SNAKE.

I know that rattlesnakes cannot play up their rattles in wet weather. The horn of the rattle becomes more or less saturated with water, and no sound can then be produced from it. By placing a rattle in a glass of water, and letting it soak a while, I find this is the case. When it is dried the sound can again be produced.

WOURALI POISON.—Gilbert White probably never heard of the existence of Wourali poison; it is one of the most fearful poisons known. It is made by the Indians in Demerara, and when made is kept in little gourds, as represented in the engraving. I have two very beautiful specimens of this wourali; it looks like hard pitch or resin. In his "Wanderings," Mr. Waterton gives an interesting account of its manufacture. He says that its principal ingredient is a vine called wourali. The Indian takes the vine and adds to it a root of a very bitter taste, and two kinds of bulbous plants, which contain a green and glutinous juice. To these are added two kinds of ants, one very large and black, and very venomous; the other is a little red ant which stings like a nettle; he then adds the strongest Indian pepper and the pounded fangs of snakes, called Labarri and Conuacouchi. It

POT OF WOURALI POISON.

is then prepared over a fire. Animals killed by wourali are good to eat.

This engraving shows the dart used with the wourali poison. Each dart is about ten inches long, and tipped with the poison. The darts are beautifully fastened together in such a manner that they can be rolled round a centre support. To the top of the quiver in which the arrows are kept is tied a row of sharp teeth of a fish; with these the

DARTS TIPPED WITH WOURALI POISON.

Indian cuts half through the dart just above the poisoned tip. When the animal is struck the dart breaks off short at the point and the little poison-covered end remains in the wound, spreading its lethal influences.

EARTH-WORMS, p. 191, AND SNAILS, p. 225.—My father made several observations on earth-worms. "The digestion of animals is a geological power of greater extent than might at first sight be imagined. In the operations of earth-worms we find an example.

"It is a bad thing to plough up ancient pastures, as a number of years are required to re-form the mould, the result of centuries of digestion by these humble and hitherto unappreciated fellow-labourers with farmers to ameliorate the condition of the earth's surface, and to adapt it to the production of grass, food for the higher animals. Thus the whole of the earth which forms a rind of turf has again and again passed through the entrails of the successive generations of earth-worms. A check upon the too great increase of earth-worms is afforded by their being the food of birds and moles."

The earth-worm is admirably adapted by its structure for tunnelling in the earth, and its wonderful borings are often laid bare in the railway and other cuttings. When we consider the great pressure of earth, besides its solidity, through which these worms have to bore, it seems surprising that their delicate organisms should not be crushed. The body is made of a number of small rings, which are armed with short, stiff, harsh bristles, by means of which they pull themselves along. As the sea-mouse has brilliant hairs, and the Cape mole has lustrous fur, so the earth-worm's cuticle has a shining iridescent lustre, the reason of which I am not in a position to explain. The nervous and vascular system of the earth-worm is very complicated. It lays eggs, for which the reader should look in decayed dung heaps. The mouth consists of two small lips, the superior of which resembles, in some degree, that of the Tapita.

Snails are getting very scarce round London; the collectors have to go long distances in search of them, sometimes as far as Gravesend and Southend, harbours for them being nearly cleaned out round London. The men generally go for them in winter time, when they are collected in great clusters under old ruins, in hollows of trees, &c. The eggs are little white things, and they are deposited in cracks in the ground; eggs and little snails are found in the same crevice. Snails' eggs are found when digging for chrysalis. Snails lay eggs in the middle of August; they lay them often in cages when fresh brought in for market. Mr. Davy has often had many bushels of snails at a time; an ordinary shop would very soon sell a bushel of snails. He used to put snails away in a dry cellar. By so doing they will keep good for twelve mouths.

He once found some snails that must have been in his cellar two years at least. They never had any moisture, nor yet any vegetable matter; they were "cased up" the same as in winter, but the animals were alive inside. As soon as the snails are shut up in any dry place they begin to "case" themselves; they never crawl any more unless they get wet upon them.

They begin to "case" when winter comes on. They creep, half a gallon together, into old pollard trees, and deep into dry banks. If two or three days' hard frost comes, and they have not properly protected themselves, they die in thousands. They get rings on the mouth of the shell every year; some must be very old, seven or eight years at least. They sometimes adhere together, and it is a difficulty to separate them. Snails' eggs are much sought after by thrushes and blackbirds ; they are semi-opaque, quite round, and half the size of a sweet pea or tare.

THE BULRUSH, OR VEGETABLE CATERPILLAR OF NEW ZEALAND.—I now give—apropos to the subject now before us—a drawing of a remarkable

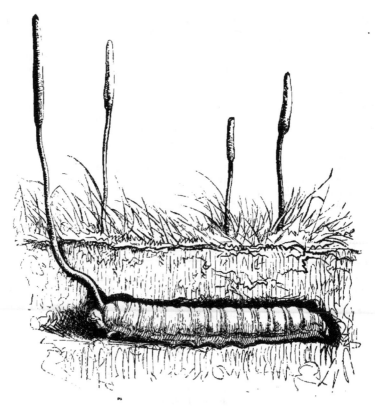

THE AWETO, OR VEGETABLE CATERPILLAR OF NEW ZEALAND.

specimen sent to my father about the year 1844 by the Rev. Henry Hobart, from the Parsonage, Paramatta, New South Wales. In 1873 I received other specimens from Lieut. John Hayes, R.N., H.M.S. *Black Prince*, with the following admirable description by the Rev. R. Taylor, Waimate, New Zealand :—

"The Aweto is only found at the root of one particular tree, the nata (*Metronderos robusta*). The root of the plant, which in every instance exactly fills the body of the caterpillar, attains in the finest specimens a length of three inches and a half, and the stem, which germinates from this metamorphosed body of the caterpillar, is from six to ten inches high. Its apex when in a state of fructification, resembles the club-headed bulrush in miniature, and when examined with a powerful glass, presents the appearance of an ovary. There are no leaves—a solitary stem comprises the entire plant, but if any accident break it off a second stem rises from the same spot. The body is not only always found buried, but the greater portion of the stalk as well, the seed-vessel alone being above ground. When the plant has attained its maturity it soon dies away.

"These curious plants are far from being uncommon. I have examined at least a hundred. The natives eat them when fresh, and likewise use them, when burnt, as colouring matter for their tattooing, rubbing the powder into the wounds, in which state it has a strong animal smell. When newly dug up the substance of the caterpillar is soft, and, when divided longitudinally, the intestinal canal is distinctly seen. Most specimens possess the legs entire, with the horny part of the head, the mandibles and claws. The vegetating process invariably proceeds from the nape of the neck, from which it may be inferred that the insect, in crawling to the place where it inhumes itself prior to its metamorphosis, whilst burrowing in the light vegetable soil, gets some of the minute seeds of this fungus between the scales of its neck, from which in its sickening state it is unable to free itself, and which consequently, being nourished by the warmth and moisture of the insect's body, then lying in a motionless state, vegetate, and not only impede the process of change in the chrysalis, but likewise occasion the death of the insect. That the vegetating process thus commences during the lifetime of the insect appears certain from the fact of the caterpillar when converted into a plant, always preserving its perfect form; in no one instance has decomposition appeared to have commenced, or the skin to have contracted or expanded beyond its natural size. The name of the insect is *Hipialus virescens;* the name of the parasitic fungus is *Sphæria Robertsii.*"

"CHINESE PIGEON-WHISTLES."—My friend, Lady Dorothy Neville, of Dangstein, Petersfield, has in her possession some most ingenious Chinese pigeon-whistles; they are simply light gourds cut so that a whistle is produced when the wind blows into them. These whistles are fastened on to the backs of the pigeons by a very fine wire or string; when the birds pass through the air a very melodious note is produced, reminding me much of the sound of many Æolian harps. The whistles giving different notes are fastened on to the backs of various pigeons, and when many of them are in the air the sound is very striking and most beautiful.

MOLE-CRICKETS, p. 219.—I have had under observation two or three mole-crickets, kindly sent me by Mr. Penny, of Poole. I kept them in a finger-glass on the mantelpiece, but they did not seem to care to bury themselves in the earth unless annoyed; they would feed greedily on worms, which they ate in a peculiar manner, which I have not space here to describe. The thoracic portion of the body is defended by a sort of cuirass, admirably adapted to bear the weight of the superincumbent earth. The anatomy of the mole-cricket has been thoroughly described by Dr. Kidd, late Regius Professor at Oxford, Philos. Trans. 115 (1825), p. 228.

FRANK BUCKLAND.

Nov. 1880.

THE ANTIQUITIES OF SELBORNE

IN THE

COUNTY OF SOUTHAMPTON.

. . . . . . Juvat ire . . . .
Desertosque videre locos . . . . VIRGIL.

THE

ANTIQUITIES OF SELBORNE.

LETTER I.

It is reasonable to suppose that in remote ages this woody
and mountainous district was inhabited only by bears and wolves.
Whether the Britons ever thought it worthy their attention is
not in our power to determine; but we may safely conclude,
from circumstances, that it was not unknown to the Romans.
Old people remember to have heard their fathers and grandfathers say that, in dry summers and in windy weather, pieces
of money were sometimes found round the verge of Wolmer
Pond; and tradition had inspired the foresters with a notion
that the bottom of that lake contained great stores of treasure.
During the spring and summer of 1740 there was little rain;
and the following summer also, 1741, was so uncommonly dry,
that many springs and ponds failed, and this lake in particular,
whose bed became as dusty as the surrounding heaths and
wastes. This favourable juncture induced some of the forest
cottagers to begin a search, which was attended with such success that all the labourers in the neighbourhood flocked to the
spot, and with spades and hoes turned up great part of that
large area. Instead of pots of coins, as they expected, they
found great heaps, the one lying on the other, as if shot out of
a bag; many of which were in good preservation. Silver and
gold these inquirers expected to find; but their discoveries consisted solely of many hundreds of Roman copper coins and some
medallions, all of the lower empire. There was not much *virtù*

A A

stirring at that time in this neighbourhood ; however, some of
the gentry and clergy around bought what pleased them best,
and some dozens fell to the share of the author.

The owners at first held their commodity at a high price,
but, finding that they were not likely to meet with dealers at
such a rate, they soon lowered their terms, and sold the fairest
as they could. The coins that were rejected became current,

GILBERT WHITE'S HOUSE.

and passed for farthings at the petty shops. Of those that we
saw, the greater part were of Marcus Aurelius, and the Empress
Faustina, his wife, the father and mother of Commodus. Some
of Faustina were in high relief, and exhibited a very agreeable
set of features, which probably resembled that lady. The
medallions in general were of a paler colour than the coins.
To pretend to account for the means of their coming to this

place would be spending time in conjecture. The spot, I think, could not be a Roman camp, because it is commanded by hills on two sides; nor does it show the least traces of intrenchments; nor can I suppose that it was a Roman town, because I have too good an opinion of the taste and judgment of those polished conquerors to imagine that they would settle on so barren and dreary a waste.

TROTTON CHURCH.

LETTER II.

THAT Selborne was a place of some distinction and note in the time of the Saxons we can give most undoubted proofs. But as there are few, if any, accounts of villages before Domesday, it will be best to begin with that venerable record. "Ipse rex tenet Selesburne. Eddid regina tenuit, et nunquam geldavit. De isto manerio dono dedit rex Radfredo presbytero dimidiam hidam cum ecclesia. Tempore regis Edwardi et post, valuit duodecim solidos et sex denarios; modo octo solidos et quatuor denarios." Here we see that Selborne was a royal manor; and that Editha, the queen of Edward the Confessor, had been lady

A A 2

of that manor; and was succeeded in it by the Conqueror; and that it had a church. Besides these, many circumstances concur to prove it to have been a Saxon village; such as the name of the place itself,[1] the names of many fields, and some families,[2] with a variety of words in husbandry and common life, still subsisting among the country people.

What probably first drew the attention of the Saxons to this spot was the beautiful spring or fountain called Well-head,[3] which induced them to build by the banks of that perennial current; for ancient settlers loved to reside by brooks and rivulets, where they could dip for their water without the trouble and expense of digging wells and of drawing.

It remains still unsettled among the antiquaries at what time tracts of land were first appropriated to the chase alone for the amusement of the sovereign. Whether our Saxon monarchs had any royal forests does not, I believe, appear on record; but the *Constitutiones de Foresta* of Canute, the Dane, are come down

---

[1] Selesburne, Seleburne, Selburn, Selbourn, Selborne, and Selborn, as it has been variously spelt at different periods, is of Saxon derivation; for *Se* signifies *great*, and *burn* torrents, a brook or rivulet: so that the name seems to be derived from the great perennial stream that breaks out at the upper end of the village. *Sel* also signifies *bonus*, item *fœcundus, fertilis.* "ꝺel-ᵹæꞃꝼ-ꞇun : *fœcunda graminis clausura ; fertile pascuum :* a meadow in the parish of *Godelming* is still called *Sal-gars-ton.*"—LYE's *Saxon Dictionary,* in the Supplement, by Mr. Manning.

[2] Thus the name of *Aldred* signifies *all-reverend,* and that of *Kemp* means a *soldier.* Thus we have a *church-litton,* or inclosure for dead bodies, and not a *church-yard :* there is also a *Culver-craft* near the *Grange-farm,* being the inclosure where the priory pigeon-house stood, from *culver* a pigeon. Again there are three steep pastures in this parish called the *Lithe,* from *Hlithe, clivus.* The wicker-work that binds and fastens down a hedge on the top is called *ether,* from *ether* a hedge. When the good women call their hogs they cry *sic, sic,*[1] not knowing that *sic* is Saxon, or rather Celtic, for a hog. Coppice or brushwood our countrymen call *rise,* from *hris,* frondes ; and talk of a load of *rise.* Within the author's memory the Saxon plurals, *housen* and *peason,* were in common use. But it would be endless to instance in every circumstance : he that wishes for more specimens must frequent a farmer's kitchen. I have therefore selected some words to show how familiar the Saxon dialect was to this district, since in more than seven hundred years it is far from being obliterated.

[3] *Well-head* signifies *spring-head,* and not a deep pit from whence we draw water.—For particulars about which see Letter I. to Mr. Pennant.

---

[1] " Σίκα, porcus, apud, Lacones ; un porceau chez les Lacèdemoniens : ce mot a sans doute esté pris des Celtes, qui discent *sic* pour marquer un porceau. Encore aujour'huy quand les Bretons chassent ces animaux, ils ne disent point autrement que *sic, sic.*"— *Antiquité de la Nation et de la Langue des Celtes,* par PEZRON.

to us. We shall not therefore pretend to say whether Wolmer Forest existed as a royal domain before the Conquest. If it did not, we may suppose it was laid out by some of our earliest Norman kings, who were exceedingly attached to the pleasures of the chase, and resided much at Winchester, which lies at a moderate distance from this district. The Plantagenet princes seem to have been pleased with Wolmer; for tradition says that King John resided just upon the verge, at Wardleham, on a regular and remarkable mount, still called King John's Hill, and Lodge Hill; and Edward III. had a chapel in his park, or inclosure, at Kingsley.[1] Humphrey, Duke of Gloucester, and Richard, Duke of York, say my evidences, were both, in their turns, wardens of Wolmer Forest; which seems to have served for an appointment for the younger princes of the royal family, as it may again.

I have intentionally mentioned Edward III. and the Dukes Humphrey and Richard before King Edward II., because I have reserved for the entertainment of my readers a pleasant anecdote respecting that prince, with which I shall close this letter.

As Edward II. was hunting in Wolmer Forest, Morris Ken, of the kitchen, fell from his horse several times; at which accidents the king laughed immoderately: and, when the chase was over, ordered him twenty shillings;[2] an enormous sum for those days! Proper allowances ought to be made for the youth of this monarch, whose spirits also, we may suppose, were much exhilarated by the sport of the day: but, at the same time, it is reasonable to remark that, whatever might be the occasion of Ken's first fall, the subsequent ones seem to have been designed. The scullion appears to have been an artful fellow, and to have seen the king's foible; which furnishes an early specimen of that easy softness and facility of temper, of which the infamous Gaveston took such advantages as brought innumerable calamities on the nation, and involved the prince at last in misfortunes and sufferings too deplorable to be mentioned without horror and amazement.

---

[1] The parish of Kingsley lies between, and divides Wolmer Forest from Ayles Holt Forest.—See Letter IX. to Mr. Pennant.

[2] "Item, paid at the lodge at Wolmer, when the king was stag-hunting there, to Morris Ken, of the kitchen, because he rode before the king and often fell from his horse, at which the king laughed exceedingly—a gift, by command, of twenty shillings."—A MS. in possession of Thomas Astle, Esq., containing the private expenses of Edward II.

VIEW OF SELBORNE CHURCH FROM THE ALTON ROAD.

LETTER III.

FROM the silence of Domesday respecting churches, it has been supposed that few villages had any at the time when that record was taken; but Selborne, we see, enjoyed the benefit of one: hence we may conclude that this place was in no abject state even at that very distant period. How many fabrics have succeeded each other since the days of Radfredrus the presbyter, we cannot pretend to say; our business leads us to a description of the present edifice, in which we shall be circumstantial.

Our church, which was dedicated to the Virgin Mary, consists of three aisles, and measures fifty-four feet in length by forty-seven in breadth, being almost as broad as it is long. The present building has no pretensions to antiquity; and is, as I suppose, of no earlier date than the beginning of the reign of Henry VII. It is perfectly plain and unadorned, without painted glass, carved work, sculpture, or tracery. But when I say it has no claim to antiquity, I would mean to be understood of the fabric in general; for the pillars which support the roof are undoubtedly old, being of that low, squat, thick order usually called Saxon. These, I should imagine, upheld the roof of a former church, which falling into decay, was rebuilt on those massy props, because their strength had preserved them from the injuries of time.[1] Upon these rest blunt Gothic arches, such as prevailed in the reign above mentioned, and by which, as a criterion, we would prove the date of the building.

At the bottom of the south aisle, between the west and south doors, stands the font, which is deep and capacious, and consists of three massy round stones, piled one on another, without the least ornament or sculpture : the cavity at the top is lined with lead, and has a pipe at bottom to convey off the water after the sacred ceremony is performed.

The east end of the south aisle is called the South Chancel, and, till within these thirty years, was divided off by old carved Gothic frame-work of timber, having been a private chantry. In this opinion we are more confirmed by observing two Gothic niches within the space, the one in the east wall and the other in the south, near which there probably stood images and altars.

In the middle aisle there is nothing remarkable : but I remember when its beams were hung with garlands in honour of young women of the parish, reputed to have died virgins; and recollect to have seen the clerk's wife cutting, in white paper, the resemblances of gloves, and ribbons to be twisted into knots and roses, to decorate these memorials of chastity. In the church of Faringdon, which is the next parish, many garlands of this sort still remain.

The north aisle is narrow and low, with a sloping ceiling,

---

[1] In the same manner, to compare great things with small, did Wykeham, when he new-built the cathedral at Winchester, from the tower westward, apply to his purpose the old piers or pillars of Bishop Walkelin's church, by blending Saxon and Gothic architecture together.—*See* LOWTH's *Life of Wykeham.*

reaching within eight or nine feet of the floor. It had originally
a flat roof covered with lead, till, within a century past, a
churchwarden stripping off the lead, in order, as he said, to
have it mended, sold it to a plumber, and ran away with the
money. This aisle has no door, for an obvious reason; because
the north side of the churchyard, being surrounded by the
vicarage garden, affords no path to that side of the church.

SOUTH AISLE OF THE CHURCH.

Nothing can be more irregular than the pews of this church,
which are of all dimensions and heights, being patched up
according to the fancy of the owners: but whoever nicely
examines them will find that the middle aisle had, on each
side, a regular row of benches of solid oak, all alike, with a
low back-board to each. These we should not hesitate to say
are coeval with the present church: and especially as it is to
be observed that, at their ends, they are ornamented with

carved blunt Gothic niches, exactly correspondent to the arches
of the church, to a niche in the south wall. The south aisle
also has a row of these benches, but some are decayed through
age, and the rest much disguised by modern alterations.

At the supper end of this aisle, and running out to the north,
stands a transept, known by the name of the North Chancel,
measuring twenty-one feet from south to north, and nineteen
feet from east to west : this was intended, no doubt, as a private
chantry ; and was also, till of late, divided off by a Gothic frame-

ORIGINAL BENCHES IN SOUTH AISLE OF THE CHURCH.

work of timber. In its north wall, under a very blunt Gothic arch,
lies perhaps the founder of this edifice, which, from the shape
of its arch, may be deemed no older than the latter end of the
reign of Henry VII. The tomb was examined some years ago,
but contained nothing except the skull and thigh bones of a
large tall man, the bones of a youth or woman, lying in a very
irregular manner, without any escutcheon or other token to
ascertain the names or rank of the deceased. The grave was
very shallow, and lined with stone at the bottom and on
the sides.

From the east wall project four stone brackets, which I conclude supported images and crucifixes. In the great thick pilaster, jutting out between this transept and the chancel, there is a very sharp Gothic niche, of older date than the present chantry or church. But the chief pieces of antiquity are two narrow stone coffin lids, which compose part of the floor, and lie from west to east, with the very narrow ends eastward: these belong to remote times; and, if originally placed here, which I doubt, must have been part of the pavement of an older transept. At present there are no coffins under them, whence I conclude they have been removed to this place from some part of a former church. One of these lids is so eaten by time, that no sculpture can be discovered on it; or, perhaps, it may be the wrong side uppermost: but on the other, which seems to be of stone of a closer and harder texture, is to be discerned a *discus*, with a cross on it, at the end of a staff or rod, the well-known symbol of a Knight Templar.[1]

This order was distinguished by a red cross on the left shoulder of their cloak, and by this attribute in their hand. Now, if these stones belonged to Knights Templars, they must have lain here many centuries; for this order came into England early in the reign of King Stephen in 1113; and was dissolved in the time of Edward II. in 1312, having subsisted only one hundred and ninety-nine years. Why I should suppose that Knights Templars were occasionally buried at this church will appear in some future letter, when we come to treat more particularly concerning the property they possessed here, and the intercourse that subsisted between them and the priors of Selborne.

We must now proceed to the chancel, properly so called, which seems to be coeval with the church, and is in the same plain unadorned style, though neatly kept. This room measures thirty-one feet in length, and sixteen feet and a half in breadth, and is wainscoted all round, as high as to the bottom of the windows. The space for the communion table is raised two steps above the rest of the floor, and railed in with oaken balusters. Here I shall say somewhat of the windows of the chancel in particular, and of the whole fabric in general. They are mostly of that simple and unadorned sort called Lancet, some single, some double, and some in triplets. At the east end of the chancel are two of a moderate size, near each other; and in the north wall

[1] See Dugdale, "Monasticon Anglicanum," vol. ii., where there is a fine engraving of a Knight Templar, by Hollar.

two very distant small ones, unequal in length and height : and
in the south wall are two, one on each side of the chancel door,
that are broad and squat, and of a different order.   At the east
end of the south aisle of the church there is a large lancet-
window in a triplet ; and two very small, narrow single ones in
the south wall, and a broad squat window beside, and a double
lancet one in the west end ; so that the appearance is very
irregular.   In the north aisle are two windows, made shorter

VIEW IN CHANCEL SHOWING GILBERT WHITE'S MONUMENT.

when the roof was sloped; and in the north transept a large
triple window, shortened at the time of a repair in 1721; when
over it was opened a round one of considerable size, which affords
an agreeable light, and renders that chantry the most cheerful
part of the edifice.
     The church and chancels have all coved roofs, ceiled about
the year 1683; before which they were open to the tiles and
shingles, showing the naked rafters, and threatening the

Mary Burby _____ aged 16 of this Parish _____
— — — _____ was buried June 10. _____ 1793
Registered June 10. by me Gil. White Curate.

The Reverend Gilbert White M.A aged 72 of th e Parish
— — — _____ was buried July 1 1793
Registered July 6th _____ by me Ch: Taylor Vicar.

GILBERT WHITE'S AUTOGRAPH. FROM THE PARISH REGISTRY IN SELBORNE CHURCH, SHOWING HE WAS CURATE IN CHARGE.

congregation with the fall of a spar, or a blow from a piece of loose mortar.

On the north wall of the chancel is fixed a large oval white marble monument, with the following inscription; and at the foot of the wall, over the deceased, and inscribed with his name, age, arms, and time of death, lies a large slab of black marble :—

Prope hunc parietem sepelitur
GILBERTUS WHITE, SAMSONIS WHITE, de
Oxon. militis filius tertius, Collegii Magdele-
-nensis ibidem alumnus, & socius. Tandem faven-
-te collegio ad hanc ecclesiam promotus ; ubi primæ-
-vâ morum simplicitate, et diffusâ erga omnes bene-
-volentiâ feliciter consenuit.

Pastor fidelis, comis, affabilis,
Maritus, et pater amantissimus,
A conjuge invicem, et liberis, atque
A parochianis, impensé dilectus.

Pauperibus ita beneficus
ut decimam partem censûs
moribundus
piis usibus consecravit.

Meritis demum juxta et annis plenus
ex hac vitâ migravit Feb. 13.°
anno salutis 127⅘.
Ætatis suæ 77.

Hoc posuit Rebecca
Conjux illius mæstissima,
mox secutura.

On the same wall is newly fixed a small square table monument of white marble, inscribed in the following manner :—

Sacred to the memory
of the Rev.d ANDREW ETTY, B.D.
23 Years Vicar of this parish :
In whose character
The conjugal, the parental, and the sacerdotal virtues
were so happily combined
as to deserve the imitation of mankind.
And if in any particular he followed more invariably
the steps of his blessed Master,
It was in his humility.
His parishioners,
especially the sick and necessitous,
as long as any traces of his memory shall remain,
must lament his death.
To perpetuate such an example, this stone is erected ;
as while living he was a preacher of righteousness,
so, by it, he being dead yet speaketh.
He died April 8.th 1784.   Aged 66 years.

LETTER IV.

WE have now taken leave of the inside of the church, and shall pass by a door at the west end of the middle aisle into the belfry. This room is part of a handsome square embattled tower of forty-five feet in height, and of much more modern date than the church; but old enough to have needed a thorough repair in 1781, when it was neatly stuccoed at a considerable expense, by a set of workmen who were employed on it for the greatest part of the summer. The old bells, three in number, loud and out of tune, were taken down in 1735, and cast into four; to which Sir Simeon Stuart, the grandfather of the present baronet, added a fifth at his own expense: and, bestowing it in the name of his favourite daughter, Mrs. Mary Stuart, caused it to be cast with the following motto round it:—

> " Clara puella dedit, dixitque mihi esto Maria :
> Illius et laudes nomen ad astra sono."

The day of the arrival of this tuneable peal was observed as a high festival by the village, and rendered more joyous by an order from the donor that the treble bell should be fixed bottom upward in the ground and filled with punch, of which all present were permitted to partake.

The porch of the church, to the south, is modern, and would not be worthy attention did it not shelter a fine sharp Gothic doorway. This is undoubtedly much older than the present fabric; and being found in good preservation, was worked into the wall, and is the grand entrance into the church: nor are the folding doors to be passed over in silence; since from their thick and clumsy structure, and the rude flourished work of their hinges, they may possibly be as ancient as the doorway itself.

The whole roof of the south aisle, and the south side of the roof of the middle aisle, is covered with oaken shingles instead of tiles, on account of their lightness, which favours the ancient and crazy timber frame. And indeed, the consideration of accidents by fire excepted, this sort of roofing is much more eligible than tiles. For shingles well seasoned, and cleft from quartered timber, never warp, nor let in drifting snow; nor do they shiver with frost; nor are they liable to be blown off like tiles; but when well nailed down, last for a long period, as

experience has shown us in this place, where those that face to
the north are known to have endured, untouched, by undoubted
tradition for more than a century.

Considering the size of the church, and the extent of the
parish, the churchyard is very scanty; and especially as all

VIEW LOOKING INTO SOUTH PORCH.

wish to be buried on the south side, which is become such a
mass of mortality that no person can be there interred without
disturbing or displacing the bones of his ancestors. There is
reason to suppose that it once was larger, and extended to what

is now the vicarage court and garden; because many human
bones have been dug up in those parts several yards without
the present limits.   At the east end are a few graves; yet
none till very lately on the north side; but, as two or three
families of best repute have begun to bury in that quarter,
prejudice may wear out by degrees, and their example be
followed by the rest of the neighbourhood.

In speaking of the church, I have all along talked of the east
and west end, as if the chancel stood exactly true to those points
of the compass; but this is by no means the case, for the fabric
bears so much to the north of the east, that the four corners
of the tower, and not the four sides, stand to the four cardinal
points.   The best method of accounting for this deviation seems
to be, that the workmen, who probably were employed in
the longest days, endeavoured to set the chancels to the rising
of the sun.

Close by the church, at the west end, stands the vicarage
house; an old but roomy and convenient edifice.   It faces very
agreeably to the morning sun, and is divided from the village by
a neat and cheerful court.   According to the manner of old times,
the hall was open to the roof; and so continued, probably, till the
vicars became family-men, and began to want more conveniences;
when they flung a floor across, and, by partitions, divided the
space into chambers.   In this hall, we remember a date, some
time in the reign of Elizabeth; it was over the door that leads
to the stairs.

Behind the house is a garden of an irregular shape, but well
laid out; whose terrace commands so romantic and picturesque
a prospect, that the first master in landscape might contemplate
it with pleasure, and deem it an object well worthy of his
pencil.

LETTER V.

In the churchyard of this village is a yew-tree, whose aspect
bespeaks it to be of a great age: it seems to have seen several
centuries, and is probably coeval with the church, and therefore
may be deemed an antiquity: the body is squat, short, and thick,
and measures twenty-three feet in the girth, supporting a head

THE YEW-TREE IN THE CHURCHYARD, SELBORNE.

of suitable extent to its bulk.   This is a male tree, which in the spring sheds clouds of dust, and fills the atmosphere around with its farina.

As far as we have been able to observe, the males of this species become much larger than the females; and it has so fallen out that most of the yew-trees in the churchyards of this neighbourhood are males: but this must have been matter of mere accident, since men, when they first planted yews, little dreamed that there were sexes in trees.

In a yard, in the midst of the street, till very lately grew a middle-sized female tree of the same species, which commonly bore great crops of berries.   By the high winds usually prevailing about the autumnal equinox, these berries, then ripe, were blown down into the road, where the hogs ate them.   And it was very remarkable, that, though barrow-hogs and young sows found no inconvenience from this food, yet milch-cows often died after such a repast: a circumstance that can be accounted for only by supposing that the latter, being much exhausted and hungry, devoured a larger quantity.

While mention is making of the bad effects of yew-berries, it may be proper to remind the unwary, that the twigs and leaves of yew, though eaten in a very small quantity, are certain death to horses and cows, and that in a few minutes.   A horse tied to a yew hedge, or to a faggot stack of dead yew, shall be found dead before the owner can be aware that any danger is at hand: and the writer has been several times a sorrowful witness to losses of this kind among his friends; and in the island of Ely had once the mortification to see nine young steers or bullocks of his own all lying dead in a heap from browzing a little on a hedge of yew in an old garden into which they had broken in snowy weather.   Even the clippings of a yew hedge have destroyed a whole dairy of cows when thrown inadvertently into a yard. And yet sheep and turkeys, and, as park-keepers say, deer will crop these trees with impunity.

Some intelligent persons assert that the branches of yew, while green, are not noxious; and that they will kill only when dead and withered, by lacerating the stomach: but to this assertion we cannot by any means assent, because, among the number of cattle that we have known fall victims to this deadly food, not one has been found, when it was opened, but had a lump of green yew in its paunch.   True it is, that yew-trees stand for twenty years or more in a field, and no bad consequences ensue: but

at some time or other cattle, either from wantonness when full,
or from hunger when empty (from both which circumstances
we have seen them perish), will be meddling, to their certain
destruction; the yew seems to be a very improper tree for a
pasture field.

Antiquaries seem much at a loss to determine at what period
this tree first obtained a place in churchyards. A statute passed
A.D. 1307, and 35 Edward I., the title of which is "Ne rector
arbores in cemeterio prosternat." Now if it is recollected that we

GRAVESTONE TO GILBERT WHITE, EAST END OF CHURCHYARD.

seldom see any other very large or ancient tree in a churchyard
but yews, this statute must have principally related to this
species of tree; and consequently their being planted in churchyards is of much more ancient date than the year 1307.

As to the use of these trees, possibly the more respectable
parishioners were buried under their shade before the improper
custom was introduced of burying within the body of the church,
where the living are to assemble. Deborah, Rebekah's nurse,[1]

----

[1] Gen. xxxv. 8.

was buried under an oak ; the most honourable place of interment probably next to the cave of Machpelah,[1] which seems to have been appropriated to the remains of the patriarchal family alone.

The further use of yew trees might be as a screen to churches, by their thick foliage, from the violence of winds; perhaps also for the purpose of archery, the best long bows being made of that material : and we do not hear that they are planted in the churchyards of other parts of Europe, where long bows were not so much in use.   They might also be placed as a shelter to the congregation assembling before the church doors were opened, and as an emblem of mortality by their funereal appearance.   In the south of England every churchyard almost has its tree, and some two ; but in the north, we understand few are to be found.

The idea of R. C., that the yew tree afforded its branches instead of palms for the processions on Palm Sunday, is a good one, and deserves attention.—See *Gent. Mag.*, vol. i. p. 128.

LETTER VI.

The living of Selborne was a very small vicarage ; but, being in the patronage of Magdalen College, in the University of Oxford, that society endowed it with the great tithes of Selborne, more than a century ago : and since the year 1758 again with the great tithes of Oakhanger, called Bene's Parsonage : so that, together, it is become a respectable piece of preferment, to which one of the fellows is always presented.   The vicar holds the great tithes, by lease, under the college.   The great disadvantage of this living is, that it has not one foot of glebe near home.[2]

ITS PAYMENTS ARE,

	£	s.	d.
King's books	8	2	1
Yearly tenths	0	16	2½
Yearly procurations for Blackmore and Oakhanger Chap : with acquit :	0	1	7
Selborne procurations and acquit :	0	9	0

[1] Gen. xxiii. 9.

[2] At Bene's, or Bin's, parsonage there is a house and stout barn, and seven acres of glebe.   Bene's parsonage is three miles from the church.

I am unable to give a complete list of the vicars of this parish till towards the end of the reign of Queen Elizabeth; from which period the registers furnish a regular series.

In Domesday we find thus—"De isto manerio dono dedit Rex Radfredo presbytero dimidiam hidam cum ecclesia." So that before Domesday, which was compiled between the years 1081 and 1086, there was an officiating minister at this place.

After this, among my documents, I find occasional mention of a vicar here and there : the first is

Roger, instituted in 1254.

In 1410 John Lynne was vicar of Selborne.

In 1411 Hugo Tybbe was vicar.

The presentations to the vicarage of Selborne generally ran in the name of the prior and the convent; but Tybbe was presented by prior John Wynechestre only.

June 29, 1528, William Fisher, vicar of Selborne, resigned to Miles Peyrson.

1594, William White appears to have been vicar to this time. Of this person there is nothing remarkable, but that he hath made a regular entry twice in the register of Selborne of the funeral of Thomas Cowper, Bishop of Winchester, as if he had been buried at Selborne; yet this learned prelate, who died 1594, was buried at Winchester, in the cathedral, near the episcopal throne.[1]

1595, Richard Boughton, vicar.

1596, William Inkforbye, vicar.

May 1606, Thomas Phippes, vicar.

June 1631, Ralph Austine, vicar.

July 1632, John Longworth. This unfortunate gentleman, living in the time of Cromwell's usurpation, was deprived of his preferment for many years, probably because he would not take the league and covenant : for I observe that his father-in-law, the Reverend Jethro Beal, rector of Faringdon, which is the next parish, enjoyed his benefice during the whole of that unhappy period. Longworth, after he was dispossessed, retired to a little tenement about one hundred and fifty yards from the church, where he earned a small pittance by the practice of physic. During those dismal times it was not uncommon for the deposed clergy to take up a medical character; as was the case in particular, I know, with the Reverend Mr. Yalden, rector of Compton, near Guildford, in the county of Surrey. Vicar Longworth used

---

[1] See Godwin, "De Præsulibus," folio, Cant. 1743, p. 239.

frequently to mention to his sons, who told it to my relations, that, the Sunday after his deprivation, his puritanical successor stepped into the pulpit with no small petulance and exultation; and began his sermon from Psalm xx. 8, "They are brought down and fallen; but we are risen, and stand upright." This person lived to be restored in 1660, and continued vicar for eighteen years; but was so impoverished by his misfortunes, that he left the vicarage house and premises in a very abject and dilapidated state.

July 1678. Richard Byfield, who left eighty pounds by will, the interest to be applied to apprentice out poor children: but this money, lent on private security, was in danger of being lost, and the bequest remained in an unsettled state for near twenty years, till 1700; so that little or no advantage was derived from it. About the year 1759 it was again in the utmost danger by the failure of a borrower; but by prudent management, has since been raised to one hundred pounds stock in the three per cents. reduced. The trustees are the vicar and the renters or owners of Temple, Priory, Grange, Blackmore, and Oakhanger House, for the time being. This gentleman seemed inclined to have put the vicarial premises in a comfortable state; and began by building a solid stone wall round the front court, and another in the lower yard, between that and the neighbouring garden; but was interrupted by death from fulfilling his laudable intentions.

April 1680, Barnabas Long became vicar.

June 1681. This living was now in such low estimation in Magdalen College, that it descended to a junior fellow, Gilbert White, M.A., who was instituted to it in the thirty-first year of his age. At his first coming he ceiled the chancel, and also floored and wainscoted the parlour and hall, which before were paved with stone, and had naked walls; he enlarged the kitchen and brewhouse, and dug a cellar and well: he also built a large new barn in the lower yard, removed the hovels in the front court, which he laid out in walks and borders; and entirely planned the back garden, before a rude field with a stone-pit in the midst of it. By his will he gave and bequeathed "the sum of forty pounds to be laid out in the most necessary repairs of the church; that is, in strengthening and securing such parts as seem decaying and dangerous." With this sum two large buttresses were erected to support the east end of the south wall of the church; and the gable end wall of the west end of the south aisle was new built from the ground.

By his will also he gave " One hundred pounds to be laid out on lands; the yearly rents whereof shall be employed in teaching the poor children of Selbourn parish to read and write, and say their prayers and catechism, and to sew and knit :— and be under the direction of his executrix as long as she lives; and, after her, under the direction of such of his children and their issue, as shall live in or within five miles of the said parish : and on failure of any such, then under the direction of the vicar of Selbourn for the time being; but still to the uses above-named." With this sum was purchased, of Thomas Turville, of Hawkeley, in the county of Southampton, yeoman, and Hannah his wife, two closes of freehold land, commonly called Collier's, containing, by estimation, eleven acres, lying in Hawkeley aforesaid. These closes are let at this time, 1785, on lease, at the rate of three pounds by the year.

This vicar also gave by will two hundred pounds towards the repairs of the highways [1] in the parish of Selborne. That sum was carefully and judiciously laid out in the summer of the year 1730, by his son John White, who made a solid and firm causey from Rood Green all down Honey Lane, to a farm called Oak Woods, where the sandy soil begins. This miry and gulfy lane was chosen as worthy of repair, because it leads to the forest, and thence through the Holt to the town of Farnham in Surrey, the only market in those days for men who had wheat to sell in this neighbourhood. This causey was so deeply bedded with stone, so properly raised above the level of the soil, and so well drained, that it has, in some degree, withstood fifty-four years of neglect and abuse; and might, with moderate attention, be rendered a solid and comfortable road. The space from Rood Green to Oak Woods measures about three quarters of a mile.

In 1727 William Henry Cane, B.D., became vicar; and, among several alterations and repairs, new built the back front of the vicarage house.

On February 1, 1740, Duncombe Bristowe, D.D., was instituted to this living. What benefactions this vicar bestowed on the parish will be best explained by the following passages from his will :—" Item, I hereby give and bequeath to the minister and churchwardens of the parish of Selbourn, in the county of

---

[1] " Such legacies were very common in former times, before any effectual laws were made for the repairs of highways."—Sir JOHN CULLUM's *Hawsted*, p. 15.

Southampton, a mahogany table, which I have ordered to be made for the celebration of the Holy Communion; and also the sum of thirty pounds, in trust, to be applied in manner following; that is, ten pounds towards the charge of erecting a gallery at the west end of the church; and ten pounds to be laid out for clothing, and such like necessaries, among the poor (and especially among the ancient and infirm) of the said parish; and the remaining ten pounds to be distributed in bread, at twenty shillings a week, at the discretion of John White, Esq., or any of his family who shall be resident in the said parish."

On November 12, 1758, Andrew Etty, B.D., became vicar. Among many useful repairs he new roofed the body of the vicarage house; and wainscoted up to the bottom of the windows, the whole of the chancel; to the neatness and decency of which he always paid the most exact attention.

On September 25, 1784, Christopher Taylor, B.D., was inducted into the vicarage of Selborne.

LETTER VII.

I SHALL now proceed to the Priory, which is undoubtedly the most interesting part of our history.

The Priory of Selborne was founded by Peter de la Roche, or de Rupibus,[1] one of those accomplished foreigners that resorted to the court of King John, where they were usually caressed, and met with a more favourable reception than ought, in prudence, to have been shown by any monarch to strangers. This adventurer was a Poictevin by birth, had been bred to arms in his youth, and distinguished by knighthood. Historians all agree not to speak very favourably of this remarkable man; they allow that he was possessed of courage and fine abilities, but then they charge him with arbitrary principles, and violent conduct. By his insinuating manners he soon rose high in the favour of John; and in 1205, early in the reign of that prince, was appointed Bishop of Winchester. In 1214 he became Lord Chief Justiciary of England, the first magistrate in the state, and a kind of viceroy, on whom depended all the

---

[1] See Godwin, "De Præsulibus Angliæ," folio, London, 1743, p. 217.

civil affairs in the kingdom. After the death of John, and during the minority of his son Henry, this prelate took upon him the entire management of the realm, and was soon appointed protector of the king and kingdom.

The barons saw with indignation a stranger possessed of all the power and influence, to part of which they thought they had a claim; they therefore entered into an association against him, and determined to wrest some of that authority from him which he had so unreasonably usurped. The bishop discerned the storm at a distance; and, prudently resolving to give way to that torrent of envy which he knew not how to withstand, withdrew quietly to the Holy Land, where he resided some time.

At this juncture a very small part of Palestine remained in the hands of the Christians: they had been by Saladin dispossessed of Jerusalem, and all the internal parts, near forty years before; and with difficulty maintained some maritime towns and garrisons; yet the busy and enterprising spirit of de Rupibus could not be at rest; he distinguished himself by the splendour and magnificence of his expenses, and amused his mind by strengthening fortresses and castles, and by the improving and endowing of churches. Before his expedition to the East he had signalised himself as a founder of convents, and as a benefactor to hospitals and monasteries.

In the year 1231 he returned again to England; and the very next year, in 1232, began to build and endow the PRIORY of SELBORNE. As this great work followed so close upon his return, it is not improbable that it was the result of a vow made during his voyage; and especially as it was dedicated to the Virgin Mary. Why the bishop made choice of Selborne for the scene of his munificence can never be determined now: it can only be said that the parish was in his diocese, and lay almost midway between Winchester and Farnham, or South Waltham and Farnham; from either of which places he could without much trouble overlook his workmen, and observe what progress they made; and that the situation was retired, with a stream running by it, and sequestered from the world, amidst woods and meadows, and so far proper for the site of a religious house.[1]

[1] The institution at Selborne was a priory of Black Canons of the order of St. Augustine, called also Canons Regular. Regular Canons were such as lived in a conventual manner, under one roof, had a common refectory and

The first person with whom the founder treated about the purchase of land was Jacobus de Achangre, or Ochangre, a gentleman of property who resided at that hamlet; and, as appears, at the house now called Oakhanger House. With him he agreed for a croft, or little close of land, known by the name of La Liega, or La Lyge, which was to be the immediate site of the Priory.

De Achangre also accommodated the bishop at the same instant with three more adjoining crofts, which for a time was all the footing that this institution obtained in the parish. The seller in the conveyance says "Warantizabimus, defendemus, et æquietabimus *contra omnes gentes;*" viz. "We will warrant the thing sold against all claims from any quarter." In modern conveyancing this would be termed a covenant for *further assurance.* Afterwards is added—"Pro hac autem donacione, &c., dedit mihi pred. Episcopus sexdecem marcas argenti in Gersumam:" *i.e.* "The bishop gave me sixteen silver marks as a consideration for the thing purchased."

As the grant from Jac. de Achangre was without date,[1] and the next is circumstanced in the same manner, we cannot say exactly what interval there was between the two purchases; but we find that Jacobus de Nortun, a neighbouring gentleman, also soon sold to the Bishop of Winchester some adjoining grounds, through which our stream passes, that the priory might be accommodated with a mill, which was a common necessary appendage to every manor: he also allowed access to these lands by a road for carts and waggons.—" Jacobus de Nortun concedit Petro Winton episcopo totum cursum aque que descèndit de Molendino de Durton, usq; ad boscum Will. Mauduit, et croftam terre vocat: Edriche croft, cum extensione ejusdem et abuttamentis; ad fundandam domum religiosam de ordine Sti.

dormitory, and were bound by vows to observe the rules and statutes of their order: in fine, they were a kind of religious, whose discipline was less rigid than the monks. The chief rule of these canons was that of St. Augustine, who was constituted Bishop of Hippo, A.D. 395: but they were not brought into England till after the conquest; and seem not to have obtained the appellation of *Augustine canons* till some years after. Their habit was a long black cassock, with a white rochet over it; and over that a black cloak and hood. The monks were always shaved: but these canons wore their hair and beards, and caps on their heads. There were of these canons, and women of the same order called Canonesses, about one hundred and seventy-five houses.

[1] The custom of affixing dates to deeds had not become general in the reign of Henry III.

Augustini. Concedit etiam viam ad carros, et caretas," &c. This vale, down which runs the brook, is now called the Long Lithe, or Lythe. Bating the following particular expression, this grant runs much in the style of the former: "Dedit mihi episcopus predictus triginta quinque marcas argenti *ad me acquietandum versus Judæos.*"—That is, "The bishop advanced me thirty-five marks of silver to pay my debts to the Jews," who were then the only lenders of money.

Finding himself still straitened for room, the founder applied to his royal master, Henry, who was graciously pleased to bestow certain lands in the manor at Selborne on the new priory of his favourite minister. These grounds had been the property of Stephen de Lucy; and, abutting upon the narrow limits of the convent, became a very commodious and agreeable acquisition. This grant, I find, was made on March the 9th, in the eighteenth year of Henry, viz. 1234, being two years after the foundation of the monastery. The royal donor bestowed his favour with a good grace, by adding to it almost every immunity and privilege that could have been specified in the law-language of the times.—"Quare volumus prior, &c., habeant totam terram, &c., cum omnibus libertatibus in bosco et plano, in viis et semitis, pratis et pascuis; aquis et piscariis; infra burgum, et extra burgum cum soka et saca, Thol et Them, Infangenethef et Utfangenethef, et hamsocne et blodwite, et pecunia que dari solet pro murdro et forstal, et flemenestrick, et cum quietancia de omni scotto et geldo, et de omnibus auxiliis regum, vice comitum, et omn: ministralium suorum; et hidagio et exercitibus, et scutagiis, et tallagiis, et shiris et hundredis, et placitis et querelis, et warda et wardpeny, et opibus castellorum et pontium, et clausuris parcorum, et omni carcio et sumagio, et domor: regal: edificatione, et omnimoda reparatione, et cum omnibus aliis libertatibus." This grant was made out by Richard, Bishop of Chichester, then Chancellor, at the town of Northampton, before the Lord Chief Justiciary, who was the founder himself.

The charter of foundation of the Priory, dated 1233, comes next in order to be considered; but being of some length, I shall not interrupt my narrative by placing it here. My copy, taken from the original, I have compared with Dugdale's copy, and find that they perfectly agree; except that in the latter the preamble and the names of the witnesses are omitted. Yet I think it proper to quote a passage from this charter—"Et ipsa

domus religiosa *a cujuslibet alterius domûs religiosæ subjectione
libera* permaneat, et in omnibus *absoluta* "—to show how much
Dugdale was mistaken when he inserted Selborne among the
alien priories; forgetting that this disposition of the convent
contradicted the grant that he had published. In the "Monasticon Anglicanum," in English, p. 119, is part of his catalogue
of alien priories, suppressed 2 Henry V. viz. 1414, where may
be seen as follows :—

8.

Sele, Sussex.
SELEBURN.
Shirburn.

This appeared to me from the first to have been an oversight,
before I had seen my authentic evidences. For priories alien, a
few conventual ones excepted, were little better than granges to
foreign abbeys; and their priors little more than bailiffs, re-
movable at will : whereas the priory of Selborne possessed the
valuable estates and manors of Selborne, Achangre, Norton,
Brompden, Bassinges, Basingstoke, and Natele; and the prior
challenged the right of Pillory, Thurcet, and Furcas, and every
manorial privilege.

I find next a grant from Jo. de Venur, or Venuz, to the prior
of Selborne—"de tota mora [a moor or bog] ubi Beme oritur
usque ad campum vivarii, et de prato voc. Sydenmeade cum
abutt : et de cursu aque Molendini." And also a grant in reversion " unius virgate terre " [a yard land], in Achangre at the
death of Richard Actedene, his sister's husband, who had no
child. He was to present a pair of gloves of one penny value
to the prior and canons, to be given annually by the said
Richard; and to quit all claim to the said lands in reversion,
provided the prior and canons would engage annually to pay
to the king through the hands of his bailiffs of Aulton, ten
shillings at four quarterly payments, " pro omnibus serviciis,
consuetudinibus, exactionibus, et demandis."

This Jo. de Venur was a man of property at Oakhanger, and
lived probably at the spot now called Chapel Farm. The grant
bears date the seventeenth year of the reign of Henry III.
[viz. 1233.]

It would be tedious to enumerate every little grant for lands
or tenements that might be produced from my vouchers. I shall

therefore pass over all such for the present, and conclude this letter with a remark that must strike every thinking person with some degree of wonder. No sooner had a monastic institution got a footing, but the neighbourhood began to be touched with a secret and religious awe. Every person round was desirous to promote so good a work; and either by sale, by grant, or by gift in reversion, was ambitious of appearing a benefactor. They who had not lands to spare gave roads to accommodate the infant foundation. The religious were not backward in keeping up this pious propensity, which they observed so readily influenced the breasts of men. Thus did the more opulent monasteries add house to house, and field to field; and by degrees manor to manor : till at last " there was no place left ; " but every district around became appropriated to the purposes of their founders, and every precinct was drawn into the vortex.

LETTER VIII.

Our forefathers in this village were no doubt as busy and bustling, and as important, as ourselves : yet have their names and transactions been forgotten from century to century, and have sunk into oblivion ; nor has this happened only to the vulgar, but even to men remarkable and famous in their generation. I was led into this train of thinking by finding in my vouchers that Sir Adam Gurdon was an inhabitant of Selborne, and a man of the first rank and property in the parish. By Sir Adam Gurdon I would be understood to mean that leading and accomplished malcontent in the Mountfort faction who distinguished himself by his daring conduct in the reign of Henry III. The first that we hear of this person in my papers is, that with two others he was bailiff of Alton before the sixteenth of Henry III. viz. about 1231, and then not knighted. Who Gurdon was, and whence he came, does not appear : yet there is reason to suspect that he was originally a mere soldier of fortune, who had raised himself by marrying women of property. The name of Gurdon does not seem to be known in the south ; but there is a name so like it in an adjoining kingdom, and which belongs to two or three noble families, that it is probable this remarkable person was a North Briton; and the more so, since the Christian name of Adam is a distinguished one to this day among the family of the Gordons. But, be this as it may, Sir Adam Gurdon has been noticed by all the writers of English history for his bold disposition and disaffected spirit, in that he not only figured during the successful rebellion of Leicester, but kept up the war after the defeat and death of that baron, intrenching himself in the woods of Hampshire, towards the town of Farnham. After the battle of Evesham, in which Mountfort fell, in the year 1265, Gurdon might not think it safe to return to his house for fear of a surprise; but cautiously fortified himself amidst the forests and woodlands with which he was so well acquainted. Prince Edward, desirous of putting an end to the troubles which had so long harassed the kingdom, pursued the arch-rebel into his fastnesses; attacked his camp; leaped over the intrenchments; and, singling out Gurdon, ran him down, wounded him, and took him prisoner.[1]

There is not perhaps in all history a more remarkable instance of command of temper and magnanimity, than this before us: that a young prince, in the moment of victory, when he had the fell adversary of the crown and royal family at his mercy, should be able to withhold his hand from that vengeance which the vanquished so well deserved. A cowardly disposition would have been blinded by resentment: but this gallant heir-apparent saw at once a method of converting a most desperate foe into a lasting friend. He raised the fallen veteran from the ground, he pardoned him, he admitted him into his confidence, and introduced him to the queen, then lying at Guildford, that very evening.[1] This unmerited and unexpected lenity melted the heart of the rugged Gurdon at once; he became in an instant a loyal and useful subject, trusted and employed in matters of moment by Edward when king, and confided in till the day of his death.

LETTER IX.

It has been hinted in a former letter that Sir Adam Gurdon had availed himself by marrying women of property. By my evidences it appears that he had three wives, and probably in

---

[1] M. Paris, p. 675, and Triveti Annale.

the following order: Constantia, Ameria, and Agnes. The first of these ladies, who was the companion of his middle life, seems to have been a person of considerable fortune, which she inherited from Thomas Makerel, a gentleman of Selborne, who was either her father or uncle. Tha second, Ameria, calls herself the quondam wife of Sir Adam, "quæ fui uxor," &c., and talks of her sons under age. Now Gurdon had no son: and beside Agnes in another document says, "Ego Agnes, quondam uxor Domini Adæ Gurdon, in pura et ligea viduitate mea:" but Gurdon could not leave two widows; and therefore it seems probable that he had been divorced from Ameria, who afterwards married, and had sons. By Agnes Sir Adam had a daughter Johanna, who was his heiress, to whom Agnes in her lifetime surrendered part of her jointure:—he had also a bastard son.

Sir Adam seems to have inhabited the house now called Temple, lying about two miles east of the church, which had been the property of Thomas Makerel.

In the year 1262 he petitioned the prior of Selborne in his own name, and that of his wife Constantia only, for leave to build him an oratory in his manor house, "in curia sua." Licenses of this sort were frequently obtained by men of fortune and rank from the bishop of the diocese, the archbishop, and sometimes, as I have seen instances, from the pope; not only for convenience' sake, and on account of distance, and the badness of the roads, but as a matter of state and distinction. Why the owner should apply to the prior, in preference to the bishop of the diocese, and how the former became competent to such a grant, I cannot say; but that the priors of Selborne did take that privilege is plain, because some years afterward, in 1280, Prior Richard granted to Henry Waterford and his wife Nichola a license to build an oratory in their courthouse, "curia sua de Waterford," in which they might celebrate divine service, saving the rights of the mother church of Basynges. Yet all the while the prior of Selborne grants with such reserve and caution, as if in doubt of his power, and leaves Gurdon and his lady answerable in future to the bishop, or his ordinary, or to the vicar for the time being, in case they should infringe the rights of the mother church of Selborne.

The manor house called Temple is at present a single building, running in length from south to north, and has been occupied as a common farmhouse from time immemorial. The south end is modern, and consists of a brewhouse, and then a kitchen. The middle part is a hall twenty-seven feèt in length, and nineteen feet in breadth; and has been formerly open to the top; but there is now a floor above it, and also a chimney in the western wall. The roofing consists of strong massive rafter-work ornamented with carved roses. I have often looked for the lamb and flag, the arms of the Knights Templars, without success; but in one corner found a fox with a goose on his back, so coarsely executed, that it required some attention to make out the device.

Beyond the hall to the north is a small parlour with a vast heavy stone chimney-piece; and, at the end of all, the chapel or oratory, whose massive thick walls and narrow windows at once bespeak great antiquity. This room is only sixteen feet by sixteen feet eight inches; and full seventeen feet nine inches in height. The ceiling is formed of vast joists, placed only five or six inches apart. Modern delicacy would not much approve of such a place of worship: for it has at present much more the appearance of a dungeon than of a room fit for the reception of people of condition. The field on which this oratory abuts is still called Chapel Field. The situation of this house is very particular, for it stands upon the immediate verge of a steep abrupt hill.

Not many years since, this place was used for a hop-kiln, and was divided into two stories by a loft, part of which remains at present, and makes it convenient for peat and turf, with which it is stowed.

LETTER X.

THE Priory at times was much obliged to Gurdon and his family. As Sir Adam began to advance in years he found his mind influenced by the prevailing opinion of the reasonableness and efficacy of prayers for the dead; and therefore, in conjunction with his wife Constantia, in the year 1271, granted to the prior and convent of Selborne all his right and claim to a certain place, *placea*, called La Pleystow, in the village aforesaid, "in *liberam, puram,* et *perpetuam elemosinam.*" This Pleystow,[1]

---

[1] In Saxon 𝔓𝔩𝔢𝔤𝔰𝔱𝔬𝔴, or 𝔓𝔩𝔢𝔤𝔰𝔱𝔬𝔴; viz. Plegestow, or Plegstow.

locus ludorum, or play-place, is a level area near the church of about forty-four yards by thirty-six, and is known now by the name of the Plestor.[1]

It continues still, as it was in old times, to be the scene of recreation for the youths and children of the neighbourhood; and impresses an idea on the mind that this village, even in Saxon times, could not be the most abject of places, when the inhabitants thought proper to assign so spacious a spot for the sports and amusements of its young people.[2]

As soon as the prior became possessed of this piece of ground, he procured a charter for a market[3] from King Henry III. and began to erect houses and stalls, "*seldas,*" around it. From this period Selborne became a market town: but how long it enjoyed that privilege does not appear. At the same time Gurdon reserved to himself and his heirs a way through the said Plestor to a tenement and some crofts at the upper end, abutting on the south corner of the churchyard. This was, in old days, the manorial house of the street manor, though now a poor cottage; and is known at present by the modern name of Elliot's. Sir Adam also did, for the health of his own soul, and that of his wife Constantia, their predecessors and successors, grant to the prior and canons quiet possession of all the tenements and gardens, "*curtillagia,*" which they had built and laid out on the lands in Selborne, on which he and his vassals, "*homines,*" had undoubted right of common: and moreover did grant to the convent the full privilege of that right of common; and empowered the religious to build tenements and make gardens along the king's highway in the village of Selborne.

From circumstances put together it appears that the above were the first grants obtained by the Priory in the village of

[1] At this juncture probably the vast oak, mentioned p. 5, was planted by the prior, as an ornament to his new acquired market-place. According to this supposition the oak was aged four hundred and thirty-two years when blown down.

[2] For more circumstances respecting the Plestor, see Letter II. to Mr. Pennant.

[3] Bishop Tanner, in his "Notitia Monastica," has made a mistake respecting the market and fair at Selborne: for in his references to Dodsworth, cart. 54 Hen. III. m. 3, he says, "*De mercatu, et feria de Seleburn.*" But this reference is wrong; for instead of Seleburn, it proves that the place there meant was Lekeborne, or Legeborn, in the county of Lincoln. This error was copied from the index of the Cat. MSS. Angl. It does not appear that there ever was a chartered fair at Selborne.—For several particulars respecting the present fair at Selborne see Letter XXVI. of these Antiquities.

Selborne, after it had subsisted about thirty-nine years : moreover, they explain the nature of the mixed manor still remaining in and about the village, where one field or tenement shall belong to Magdalen College in the University of Oxford, and the next to Norton Powlet, Esq., of Rotherfield House; and so down the whole street.   The case was, that the whole was once the property of Gurdon, till he made his grants to the convent ; since which some belongs to the successors of Gurdon in the manor, and some to the college ; and this is the occasion of the strange jumble of property.   It is remarkable that the tenement and crofts which Sir Adam reserved at the time of granting the Plestor should still remain a part of the Gurdon manor, though so desirable an addition to the vicarage that is not as yet possessed of one inch of glebe at home : but of late, viz. in January, 1785, Magdalen College purchased that little estate, which is life-holding, in reversion, for the generous purpose of bestowing it, and its lands, being twelve acres (three of which abut on the churchyard and vicarage garden) as an improvement hereafter to the living, and an eligible advantage to future incumbents.

The year after Gurdon had bestowed the Plestor on the Priory, viz. in 1272, Henry III. King of England died, and was succeeded by his son Edward.   This magnanimous prince continued his regard for Sir Adam, whom he esteemed as a brave man, and made him warden, " *custos*," of the forest of Wolmer.[1]   Though

---

[1] Since the letters respecting Wolmer Forest and Ayles Holt, from p. 15 to p. 26, were printed, the author has been favoured with the following extracts :—

In the "Act of Resumption, 1 Hen. VII." it was provided, that it be not prejudicial to "Harry at Lode, ranger of our forest of Wolmere, to him by oure letters patents before tyme gevyn."—Rolls of Parl. vol. vi. p. 370.

In the 11 Hen. VII. 1495.—"Warlham [Wardleham] and the office of forest [forester] of Wolmere" were held by Edmund, Duke of Suffolk.—Rolls, ib. 474.

Act of general pardon, 14 Hen. VIII. 1523, not to extend to "Rich. Bp. of Wynton [Bishop Fox] for any seizure or forfeiture of liberties, &c. within the forest of Wolmer, Alysholt, and Newe Forest ; nor to any person for waste, &c. within the manor of Wardlam, or parish of Wardlam [Wardleham ;] nor to abusing, &c. of any office or fee, within the said forests of Wolmer or Alysholt, or the said park of Wardlam."—County Suth't.——Rolls prefixed to first vol. of Journals of the Lords, p. xciii. b.

To these may be added some other particulars, taken from a book lately published, entitled "An Account of all the Manors, Messuages, Lands, &c., in the Different Counties of England and Wales, held by Lease from the Crown ; as contained in the Report of the Commissioners appointed to

little emolument might hang to the appointment, yet are there reasons why it might be highly acceptable; and, in a few reigns after, it was given to princes of the blood.[1] In old days gentry resided more at home on their estates, and having fewer resources of elegant in-door amusement, spent most of their leisure hours in the field and the pleasures of the chase. A large domain, therefore, at little more than a mile distance, and well stocked with game, must have been a very eligible acquisition, affording him influence as well as entertainment; and especially as the manorial house of Temple, by its exalted situation, could command a view of near two-thirds of the forest.

That Gurdon, who had lived some years the life of an outlaw and at the head of an army of insurgents, was, for a considerable time, in high rebellion against his sovereign, should have been guilty of some outrages, and should have committed some depredations, is by no means matter of wonder. Accordingly we find a *distringas* against him, ordering him to restore to the Bishop of Winchester some of the temporalities of that see, which he had taken by violence and detained; viz. some lands in Hocheleye, and a mill.[2] By a breve, or writ, from the king he is also enjoined to readmit the Bishop of Winchester, and

---

inquire into the State and Condition of the Royal Forests," &c.—London, 1787.
"Southampton."

P. 64. "A fee-farm rent of 34*l*. 2*s*. 11*d*. out of the manors of East and West Wardleham; and also the office of lieutenant or keeper of the forest or chase of Aliceholt and Wolmer, with all offices, fees, commodities, and privileges thereto belonging.

"Names of lessees, William, Earl of Dartmouth and others (in trust).

"Date of the last lease, March 23, 1780; granted for such term as would fill up the subsisting term to thirty-one years.

"Expiration, March 23, 1811."
"Appendix, No. III."
"Southampton."
"Hundreds—Selborne and Finchdeane."
"Honours and manors," &c.

"Aliceholt Forest, three parks there.

"Bensted and Kingsley; a petition of the parishioners concerning the three parks in Aliceholt Forest."

William, first Earl of Dartmouth, and paternal grandfather to the present Lord Stawel, was a lessee of the forests of Aliceholt and Wolmer before Brigadier-General Emanuel Scroope Howe.

[1] See Letter II. of these Antiquities.

[2] Hocheleye, now spelt Hawkley, is in the hundred of Selborne, and has a mill at this day.

his tenants of the parish and town of Farnham, to pasture their horses, and other larger cattle "*averia*," in the Forest of Wolmer, as had been the usage from time immemorial. This writ is dated in the tenth year of the reign of Edward, viz. 1282.

All the king's writs directed to Gurdon are addressed in the following manner : " Edwardus, Dei gratia, &c., dilecto et fideli suo Ade Gurdon salutem ; " and again, " Custodi foreste sue de Wolvemere."

In the year 1293 a quarrel between the crews of an English and a Norman ship, about some trifle, brought on by degrees such serious consequences, that in 1295 a war broke out between the two nations. The French king, Philip the Hardy, gained some advantages in Gascony ; and, not content with those, threatened England with an invasion, and, by a sudden attempt, took and burnt Dover.

Upon this emergency Edward sent a writ to Gurdon, ordering him and four others to enlist three thousand soldiers in the counties of Surrey, Dorset, and Wiltshire, able-bodied men, " tam sagittare quam balistare potentes : " and to see that they were marched, by the feast of All Saints, to Winchelsea, there to be embarked aboard the king's transports.

The occasion of this armament appears also from a summons to the Bishop of Winchester to parliament, part of which I shall transcribe on account of the insolent menace which is said therein to have been denounced against the English language :— " qualiter rex Franciæ de terra nostra Gascon nos fraudulenter et cautelose decepit, eam nobis nequiter detenendo . . . vero predictis fraude et nequitia non contentus, ad expugnationem regni nostri classe maxima et bellatorum copiosa multitudine congregatis, cum quibus regnum nostrum et regni ejusdem incolas hostiliter jam invasurus, *linguam Anglicam,* si concepte iniquitatis proposito detestabili potestas correspondeat, quod Deus avertat, *omnino de terra delere proponit.*" Dated 30th September, in the year of King Edward's reign xxiii.[1]

The above are the last traces that I can discover of Gurdon's appearing and acting in public. The first notice that my evidences give of him is, that, in 1232, being the sixteenth of Henry III. he was the king's bailiff, with others, for the town of Alton. Now, from 1232 to 1295 is a space of sixty-three

---

[1] Reg. Wynton, Stratford, but query Stratford ; for Stratford was not Bishop of Winton till 1323, near thirty years afterwards.

years; a long period for one man to be employed in active life!
Should any one doubt whether all these particulars can relate
to one and the same person, I should wish him to attend to
the following reasons why they might. In the first place, the
documents from the Priory mention but one Sir Adam Gurdon,
who had no son lawfully begotten: and in the next, we are to
recollect that he must have probably been a man of uncommon
vigour both of mind and body; since no one, unsupported by
such accomplishments, could have engaged in such adventures,
or could have borne up against the difficulties which he sometimes must have encountered: and, moreover, we have modern
instances of persons that have maintained their abilities for near
that period.

Were we to suppose Gurdon to be only twenty years of age
in 1232, in 1295 he would be eighty three; after which advanced
period it could not be expected that he should live long. From
the silence, therefore, of my evidences it seems probable that
this extraordinary person finished his life in peace, not long
after, at his mansion of Temple. Gurdon's seal had for its device
—a man with a helmet on his head, drawing a cross-bow; the
legend, "Sigillum Ade de Gurdon;" his arms were, "Goulis, iii
floures argent issant de testes de leopards."[1]

If the stout and unsubmitting spirit of Gurdon could be so
much influenced by the belief and superstition of the times,
much more might the hearts of his ladies and daughter. And
accordingly we find that Ameria, by the consent and advice
of her sons, though said to be all under age, makes a grant for
ever of some lands down by the stream at Durton; and also
of her right of the common of Durton itself.[2] Johanna, the
daughter and heiress of Sir Adam, was married, I find, to
Richard Achard; she also grants to the prior and convent lands
and tenements in the village of Selborne, which her father
obtained from Thomas Makerel; and also her goods and chattels
in Selborne for the consideration of two hundred pounds sterling.
This last business was transacted in the first year of Edward II.
viz. 1307. It has been observed before that Gurdon had a
natural son: this person was called by the name of John
Dastard, alias Wastard, but more probably Bastard; since

---

[1] From the collection of Thomas Martin, Esq., in the "Antiquarian Reper-
tory," p. 109, No. XXXI.
[2] Durton, now called Dorton, is still a common for the copyholders of
Selborne manor.

bastardy in those days was not deemed any disgrace, though dastardy was esteemed the greatest. He was married to Gunnorie Duncun; and had a tenement and some land granted him in Selborne by his sister Johanna.

LETTER XI.

THE Knights Templars,[1] who have been mentioned in a former letter, had considerable property in Selborne; and also a preceptory at Sudington; now called Southington, a hamlet lying one mile to the east of the village. Bishop Tanner mentions only two such houses of the Templars in all the county of Southampton, viz. Godesfield, founded by Henry de Blois, Bishop

[1] *The Military Orders of the Religious :—*
The Knights Hospitalars of St. John of Jerusalem, afterwards called Knights of Rhodes, now of Malta, came into England about the year 1100, 1 Hen. I.
The Knights Templars came into England pretty early in Stephen's reign, which commenced 1135. The order was dissolved in 1312, and their estates given by act of Parliament to the Hospitalars in 1323 (all in Edw. II.) though many of their estates were never actually enjoyed by the said Hospitalars.—Vid. Tanner, p. xxiv. x.
The commandries of the Hospitalars, and preceptories of Templars, were each subordinate to the principal house of their respective religion in London. Although these are the different denominations which Tanner at p. xxviii. assigns to the cells of these different orders, yet throughout the work very frequent instances occur of preceptories attributed to the Hospitalars; and if in some passages of *Notitia Monast.* commandries are attributed to the Templars, it is only where the place afterwards became the property of the Hospitalars, and so is there indifferently styled preceptory or commandry; see pp. 243, 263, 276, 577, 678. But, to account for the first observed inaccuracy, it is probable the preceptories of the Templars, when given to the Hospitalars, were still vulgarly, however, called by their old name of preceptories; whereas in propriety the societies of the Hospitalars were indeed (as has been said) commandries. And such deviation from the strictness of expression in this case might occasion these societies of Hospitalars also to be indifferently called preceptories, which had originally been vested in them, having never belonged to the Templars at all.—See in Archer, p. 609. Tanner, p. 300, col. 1, 720, note *e*.
It is observable that the very statute for the dissolution of the Hospitalars holds the same language; for there in the enumeration of particulars, occur " commandries, preceptories." Codex, p. 1190. Now this intercommunity of names, and that in an act of parliament too, made some of our ablest

of Winchester, and South Badeisley, a preceptory of the Knights
Templars, and afterwards of St. John of Jerusalem, valued at
one hundred and eighteen pounds sixteen shillings and seven-
pence per annum.   Here then was a preceptory unnoticed by
antiquaries, between the village and Temple.   Whatever the
edifice of the preceptory might have been, it has long since been
dilapidated; and the whole hamlet contains now only one mean
farmhouse, though there were two in the memory of man.

It has been usual for the religious of different orders to fall
into great dissensions, and especially when they were near
neighbours.   Instances of this sort we have heard of between
the monks of Canterbury; and again between the old abbey
of St. Swythun, and the comparatively new minster of Hyde in
the city of Winchester.[1]   These feuds arose probably from
different orders being crowded within the narrow limits of a

antiquaries look upon a preceptory and commandry as strictly synonymous;
accordingly we find Camden, in his "Britannia," explaining *præceptoria* in
the text by a commandry in the margin, pp. 356, 510.—J. L.

Commandry, a manor or chief messuage with lands, &c. belonging to the
priory of St. John of Jerusalem; and he who had the government of such
house was called the commander, who could not dispose of it but to the use
of the priory, only taking thence his own sustenance, according to his degree,
who was usually a brother of the same priory.—Cowell.   He adds (confounding these with preceptories) they are in many places termed Temples, as
Temple Bruere in Lincolnshire, &c.   Preceptories were possessed by the more
eminent sort of Templars, whom the chief master created and called *Præ-
ceptores Templi.*   Cowell, who refers to Stephen's De Jurisd. lib. 4, c. 10,
num. 27.

Placita de juratis et assis coram Salom. de Roff et sociis suis justic. Itiner.
apud, Wynton, &c. anno regni R. Edwardi fil. Reg. Hen. octavo.—"et Magr.
Milicie Templi in Angl. ht emendasse panis, & suis [cerevisiæ] in Sodington,
& nescint q". war. et—et magist. Milicie Templi nōn vēn iō distr.—Chapter
House, Westminster.

[1] *Notitia Monastica,* p. 155.

"Winchester, Newminster.   King Alfred founded here first only a house
and chapel for the learned monk Grimbald, whom he had brought out of
Flanders: but afterwards projected, and by his will ordered, a noble church
or religious house to be built in the cemetery on the north side of the old
minster or cathedral; and designed that Grimbald should preside over it.
This was begun A.D. 901, and finished to the honour of the Holy Trinity,
Virgin Mary, and St. Peter, by his son King Edward, who placed therein
secular canons: but A.D. 963, they were expelled, and an abbot and monks
put in possession by Bishop Ethelwold.

"Now the churches and habitations of these two societies being so very
near together, the differences which were occasioned by their singing, bells,
and other matters, arose to so great a height, that the religious of the new
monastery thought fit, about A.D. 1119, to remove to a better and more quiet

city, or garrison-town, where every inch of ground was precious, and an object of contention. But with us, as far as my evidences extend, and while Robert Saunford was master,[1] and Richard Carpenter was preceptor, the Templars and the Priors lived in an intercourse of mutual good offices.

My papers mention three transactions, the exact time of which cannot be ascertained, because they fell out before dates were usually inserted; though probably they happened about the middle of the thirteenth century; not long after Saunford became master. The first of these is that the Templars shall pay to the priory of Selborne, annually, the sum of ten shillings at two half-yearly payments from their chamber, "*camera*," at Sudington, "per manum *preceptoris*, vel *ballivi* nostri, qui pro tempore fuerit ibidem," till they can provide the prior and canons with an equivalent in lands or rents within four or five miles of the said convent. It is also further agreed that, if the Templars shall be in arrears for one year, that then the prior shall be empowered to distrain upon their live stock in Bradeseth. The next matter was a grant from Robert de Saunford to the Priory for ever, of a good and sufficient road, " *cheminum*," capable of admitting carriages, and proper for the drift of their larger cattle, from the way which extends from Sudington towards Blakemere, on to the lands which the convent possesses in Bradeseth.

The third transaction (though for want of dates we cannot say which happened first and which last) was a grant from Robert Samford to the Priory of a tenement and its appurtenances in the village of Selborne, given to the Templars by Americus de Vasci.[2] This property, by the manner of describing it,—"totum tenementum cum omnibus pertinentiis suis, scilicet in terris,

situation without the walls, on the north part of the city called HYDE, where King Henry I. at the instance of Will. Gifford, Bishop of Winton, founded a stately abbey for them. St. Peter was generally accounted patron; though it is sometimes called the monastery of St. Grimbald, and sometimes of St. Barnabas," &c.

Note. A few years since a county bridewell, or house of correction, has been built on the immediate site of Hyde Abbey. In digging up the old foundations the workmen found the head of a crosier in good preservation.

[1] Robert Saunforde was master of the Temple in 1241; Guido de Foresta was the next in 1292. The former is fifth in a list of the masters in a MS. Bib. Cotton. Nero. E. VI.

[2] Americus de Vasci, by his name, must have been an Italian, and had been probably a soldier of fortune, and one of Gurdon's captains. Americus Vespucio, the person who gave name to the new world, was a Florentine.

& *hominibus*, in pratis & pascuis, & nemoribus," '&c., seems to have been no inconsiderable purchase, and was sold for two hundred marks sterling, to be applied for the buying of more land for the support of the holy war.

Prior John is mentioned as the person to whom Vasci's land is conveyed. But in Willis's list there is no Prior John till 1339, several years after the dissolution of the order of the Templars in 1312; so that unless Willis is wrong, and has omitted a Prior John since 1262 (that being the date of his first prior), these transactions must have fallen out before that date.

I find not the least traces of any concerns between Gurdon and the Knights Templars; but probably after his death his daughter Johanna might have, and might bestow, Temple on that order in support of the Holy Land : and, moreover, she seems to have been moving from Selborne when she sold her goods and chattels to the Priory, as mentioned above.

Temple no doubt did belong to the knights, as may be asserted, not only from its name, but also from another corroborating circumstance of its being still a manor tithe-free; "for, by virtue of their order," says Dr. Blackstone, "the lands of the Knights Templars were privileged by the pope with a discharge from tithes."

Antiquaries have been much puzzled about the terms *preceptores* and *preceptorium*, not being able to determine what officer or edifice was meant. But perhaps all the while the passage quoted above from one of my papers "per   ıum *preceptoris* vel *ballivi* nostri, qui pro tempore fuerit ibidem," may help to explain the difficulty. For if it be allowed here that *preceptor* and *ballivus* are synonymous words, then the brother who took on him that office resided in the house of the Templars at Sudington, a *preceptory;* where he was their *preceptor*, superintended their affairs, received their money; and, as in the instance there mentioned, paid from their chamber, "*camera*," as directed : so that, according to this explanation, a *preceptor* was no other than a steward, and a *preceptorium* was his residence. I am well aware that, according to strict Latin, the *vel* should have been *seu* or *sive*, and the order of the words "*preceptoris nostri*, vel ballivi, qui"—et "*ibidem*" should have been *ibi; ibidem* necessarily having reference to *two* or more persons : but it will hardly be thought fair to apply the niceties of classic rules to the Latinity of the thirteenth century, the

writers of which seem to have aimed at nothing farther than to
render themselves intelligible.

There is another remark that we have made, which, I think,
corroborates what has been advanced; and that is, that Richard
Carpenter, preceptor of Sudington, at the time of the transactions
between the Templars and Selborne Priory, did always sign *last*
as a witness in the three deeds: he calls himself *frater*, it is
true, among many other brothers, but subscribes with a kind
of difference, as if, for the time being, his office rendered him
an inferior in the community.[1]

LETTER XII.

THE ladies and daughters of Sir Adam Gurdon were not the
only benefactresses to the Priory of Selborne; for, in the year
1281, Ela Longspee obtained masses to be performed for her
soul's health; and the prior entered into an engagement that one
of the convent should every day say a special mass for ever for
the said benefactress, whether living or dead. She also engaged
within five years to pay to the said convent one hundred marks
of silver for the support of a chantry and chantry-chaplain, who
should perform his masses daily in the parish church of Selborne.[2]

---

[1] In two or three ancient records relating to St. Oswald's Hospital in the
city of Worcester, printed by Dr. Nash, pp. 227 and 228, of his Collections
for the History of Worcestershire, the words *preceptorium* and *preceptoria*
signify the *mastership* of the said hospital : "ad *preceptorium* sive *magisterium* presentavit—*preceptorii* sive *magisterii* patronus. Vacavit dicta *preceptoria* seu *magisterium*—ad *preceptoriam* et regimen dicti hospitalis—Te
preceptorem sive magistrum prefecimus."

Where *preceptorium* denotes a building or apartment it may probably mean
the master's lodgings, or at least the preceptor's apartment, whatsoever may
have been the office or employment of the said preceptor.

A preceptor is mentioned in Thoresby's "Ducatus Leodinensis," or History
of Leeds, p. 225, and a deed witnessed by the preceptor and chaplain before
dates were inserted.—Du Fresne's Supplement : "*Preceptoriæ*, prædia *pre-
ceptoribus* assignata."—Cowell, in his Law Dictionary, enumerates sixteen
preceptoriæ, or *preceptorics*, in England ; but Sudington is not among them.—
It is remarkable that Gurtelerus, in his "Historia Templariorum Amstel."
1691, never once mentions the words *preceptor* or *preceptorium*.

[2] A chantry was a chapel joined to some cathedral or parish church, and
endowed with annual revenues for the maintenance of one or more priests to
sing mass daily for the soul of the founder, and others.

In the east end of the south aisle there there are two sharp-pointed Gothic niches; one of these probably was the place under which these masses were performed; and there is the more reason to suppose as much, because till within these thirty years, this place was fenced off with Gothic wooden railing, and was known by the name of the south chancel.[1]

The solicitude expressed by the donor plainly shows her piety and firm persuasion of the efficacy of prayers for the dead; for she seems to have made every provision for the payment of the sum stipulated within the appointed time; and to have felt much anxiety lest her death, or the neglect of her executors or assigns, might frustrate her intentions.—" Et si contingat me in solucione predicte pecunie annis predictis in parte aut in toto deficere, quod absit; concedo et obligo pro me et assignatis meis, quod Vice-Comes... Oxon et ..... qui pro tempore fuerint, per omnes terras et tenementa, et omnia bona mea mobilia et immobilia ubicunque in balliva sua fuerint inventa ad solucionem predictam faciendam possent nos compellere." And again—" Et si contingat dictos religiosos labores seu expensas facere circa predictam pecuniam, seu circa partem dicte pecunie; volo quod dictorum religiosorum impense et labores levantur ita quod predicto priori vel uni canonicorum suorum super hiis simplici verbo credatur sine alterius honere probacionis; et quod utrique predictorum virorum in unam marcam argenti pro cujuslibet distrincione super me facienda tenear.—Dat. apud Wareborn *die sabati* proxima ante festum St. Marci evangeliste, anno regni regis Edwardi tertio decimo." [2]

But the reader perhaps would wish to be better informed respecting this benefactress, of whom as yet he has heard no particulars.

The Ela Longspee therefore above mentioned was a lady of high birth and rank, and became countess to Thomas de Newburgh, the sixth Earl of Warwick: she was the second daughter of the famous Ela Longspee, Countess of Salisbury, by William Longspee, natural son of King Henry II. by Rosamond.

---

[1] For what is said more respecting this chantry see Letter III. of these Antiquities.—Mention is made of a Nicholas Langrish, capellanus de Selborne, in the time of Henry VIII. Was he chantry-chaplain to Ela Longspee, whose masses were probably continued to the time of the Reformation? More will be said of this person hereafter.

[2] Ancient deeds are often dated on a Sunday, having been executed in churches and churchyards for the sake of notoriety, and for the conveniency of procuring several witnesses to attest.

Our lady, following the steps of her illustrious mother,[1] "was a great benefactress to the University of Oxford, to the canons of Oseney, the nuns of Godstow, and other religious houses in Oxfordshire.   She died very aged in the year 1300,[2] and was buried before the high altar in the abbey church of Oseney, at the head of the tomb of Henry D'Oily, under a flat marble, on which was inlaid her portraiture, in the habit of a vowess, engraved on a copper-plate."—EDMONSON'S *History and Genealogical Account of the Grevilles*, p. 23.

LETTER XIII.

THE reader is here presented with the titles of five forms respecting the choosing of a prior : No. 108. "Charta petens licentiam elegendi *prelatum* a Domino episcopo Wintoniensi :" —"Forma licentie concesse : "—"Forma decreti post electionem conficiendi :"—108.   "Modus procendendi ad electionem per formam scrutinii : "—et "Forma ricte presentandi electum." Such evidences are rare and curious, and throw great light upon the general *monastico-ecclesiastical* history of this kingdom, not yet sufficiently understood.

In the year 1324 there was an election for a prior at Selborne ; when some difficulties occurring, and a devolution taking place, application was made to Stratford, who was Bishop of Winchester at that time, and of course the visitor and patron of the convent at the spot above mentioned.[3]

AN EXTRACT FROM REG. STRATFORD. WINTON.

P. 4.   "Commissio facta sub-priori de Selebourne " by the bishop enjoining him to preserve the discipline of the order

---

[1] Ela Longspee, Countess of Salisbury, in 1232, founded a monastery at Lacock, in the county of Wilts, and also another at Hendon, in the county of Somerset, in her widowhood, to the honour of the Blessed Virgin and St. Bernard.—CAMDEN.

[2] Thus she survived the foundation of her chantry at Selborne fifteen years. About this lady and her mother consult Dugdale's Baronage, i. 72, 175, 177. —Dugdale's Warwickshire, i. 383.—Leland's Itin. ii. 45.

[3] Stratford was Bishop of Winchester from 1323 to 1333, when he was translated to Canterbury.

in the convent during the vacancy made by the late death of
the prior, ("super pastoris solatio destituta,") dated 4th. kal.
Maii. ann. 2do sc. of his consecration. [sc. 1324.]

P. 6. "Custodia Prioratus de Selebourne vacantis," committed
by the bishop to Nicholas de la . . ., a layman, it belonging
to the bishop "ratione vacationis ejusdem," in July, 1324,
ibid. "negotium electionis de Selebourne. Acta coram Johanne
Episcopo, &c. 1324 in negotio electionis de fratre Waltero de
Insula concanonico prioratus de Selebourne," lately elected by
the sub-prior and convent, by way of scrutiny : that it appeared
to the bishop, by certificate from the Dean of Alton, that solemn
citation and proclamation had been made in the church of the
convent where the election was held, that any who opposed the
said election or elected should appear. Some difficulties were
started, which the bishop overruled, and confirmed the election,
and admitted the new prior *sub hac forma :*—

"In Dei nomine Amen. Ego Johannes permissione divina,
&c. te Walterum de Insula ecclesie de Selebourne nostre dioceseos
nostrique patronatus vacantis, canonicum et cantorem, virum
utique providum, et discretum, literarum scientia preditum,
vita moribus et conversatione merito commendatum, in ordine
sacerdotali et etate legitima constitutum, de legitimo matrimonio
procreatum, in ordine et religione Sancti Augustini de Selebourne
expresse professum, in spiritualibus et temporalibus circum-
spectum, *jure* nobis hac vice *devoluto* in hac parte, in dicte ecclesie
de Selebourne perfectum priorem ; curam et administrationem
ejusdem tibi in spiritualibus et temporalibus committentes. Dat.
apud Selebourne XIII kalend. Augusti anno supradicto."

There follows an order to the sub-prior and convent pro
obedientia :

A mandate to Nicholas above-named to release the Priory
to the new prior :

A mandate for the induction of the new prior.

LETTER XIV.

"In the year 1373 Wykeham, Bishop of Winchester, held a
visitation of his whole diocese; not only of the secular clergy
through the several deaneries, but also of the monasteries, and
religious houses of all sorts, which he visited in person. The

next year he sent his commissioners with power to correct and reform the several irregularities and abuses which he had discovered in the course of his visitation.

" Some years afterward, the bishop having visited *three several times* all the religious houses throughout his diocese, and being well informed of the state and condition of each, and of the particular abuses which required correction and reformation, besides the orders which he had already given, and the remedies which he had occasionally applied by his commissioners, now issued his injunctions to each of them. They were accommodated to their several exigencies, and intended to correct the abuses introduced, and to recall them all to a strict observation of the rules of their respective orders. Many of these injunctions are still extant, and are evident monuments of the care and attention with which he discharged this part of his episcopal duty." [1]

Some of these injunctions I shall here produce ; and they are such as will not fail, I think, to give satisfaction to the antiquary, both as never having been published before, and as they are a curious picture of monastic irregularities at that time.

The documents that I allude to are contained in the Notabilis Visitatio de Selebourne, held at the Priory of that place, by Wykeham in person, in the year 1387.

This evidence, in the original, is written on two skins of parchment ; the one large, and the other smaller, and consists of a preamble, thirty-six items, and a conclusion, which altogether evince the patient investigation of the visitor, for which he had always been so remarkable in all matters of moment, and how much he had at heart the regularity of those institutions, of whose efficacy in their prayers for the dead he was so firmly persuaded. As the bishop was so much in earnest, we may be assured that he had nothing in view but to correct and reform what he found amiss ; and was under no bias to blacken, or misrepresent, as the commissioners of Thomas Lord Cromwell seem in part to have done at the time of the Reformation.[2] We may therefore with reason suppose that the bishop gives us an exact delineation of the morals and manners of the canons of Selborne at that juncture ; and that what he found they had omitted he enjoins them ; and for what they had done amiss, and

---

[1] See Lowth's " Life of Wykeham."
[2] Letters of this sort from Dr. Layton to Thomas Lord Cromwell are still extant.

contrary to their rules and statutes, he reproves them; and threatens them with punishment suitable to their irregularities.

This *visitatio* is of considerable length, and cannot be introduced into the body of this work; we shall therefore take some notice, and make some remarks, on the most singular items as they occur.

In the preamble the visitor says—"Considering the charge lying upon us, that your blood may not be required at our hands, we came down to visit your Priory, as our office required: and every time we repeated our visitation we found something still not only contrary to regular rules, but also repugnant to religion and good reputation."

In the first article after the preamble—"he commands them on their obedience, and on pain of the greater excommunication, to see that the canonical hours by night and by day be sung in their choir, and the masses of the Blessed Mary, and other accustomed masses, be celebrated at the proper hours with devotion and at moderate pauses; and that it be not allowed to any to absent themselves from the hours and masses, or to withdraw before they are finished."

Item 2d. He enjoins them to observe that silence to which they are so strictly bound by the rule of St. Augustine at stated times, and wholly to abstain from frivolous conversation.

Item 4th. "Not to permit such frequent passing of secular people of both sexes through their convent, as if a thoroughfare, from whence many disorders may and have arisen."

Item 5th. "To take care that the doors of their church and Priory be so attended that no suspected and disorderly females, 'suspectæ et aliæ inhonestæ,' pass through their choir and cloister in the dark;" and to see that the doors of their church between the nave and the choir, and the gates of their cloister opening into the fields, be constantly kept shut until their first choir-service is over in the morning, at dinner time, and when they meet at their evening collation.[1]

Item 6th mentions that several of the canons are found to be very ignorant and illiterate, and enjoins the prior to see that they be better instructed by a proper master.

Item 8th. The canons are here accused of refusing to accept of their statutable clothing year by year, and of demanding a certain specified sum of money, as if it were their annual rent

---

[1] A collation was a meal or repast on a fast day in lieu of a supper.

and due. This the bishop forbids, and orders that the canons
shall be clothed out of the revenue of the Priory, and the old
garments be laid by in a chamber and given to the poor, according to the rule of St. Augustine.

In Item 9th is a complaint that some of the canons are given
to wander out of the precincts of the convent without leave ; and
that others ride to their manors and farms, under pretence of
inspecting the concerns of the society, when they please, and
stay as long as they please. But they are enjoined never to stir
either about their own private concerns or the business of the
convent without leave from the prior : and no canon is to go
alone, but to have a grave brother to accompany him.

The injunction in Item 10th, at this distance of time, appears
rather ludicrous ; but the visitor seems to be very serious on the
occasion, and says that it has been evidently proved to him that
some of the canons, living dissolutely after the flesh, and not
after the spirit, sleep naked in their beds without their breeches
and shirts, " absque femoralibus et camisiis." [1]   He enjoins that
these culprits shall be punished by severe fasting, especially if
they shall be found to be faulty a third time ; and threatens the
prior and sub-prior with suspension if they do not correct this
enormity.

In Item 11th the good bishop is very wroth with some of the
canons, whom he finds to be professed hunters and sportsmen,
keeping hounds, and publicly attending hunting matches. These
pursuits, he says, occasion much dissipation, danger to the soul
and body, and frequent expense ; he, therefore, wishing to
extirpate this vice wholly from the convent, "radicibus extir-
pare," does absolutely enjoin the canons never intentionally to
be present at any public noisy tumultuous huntings ; or to keep
any hounds, by themselves or by others, openly or by stealth,
within the convent, or without. [2]

In Item 12th he forbids the canons in office to make their

---

[1] The rule alluded to in Item 10th, of not sleeping naked, was enjoined the
Knights Templars, who also were subject to the rules of St. Augustine. —See
GURTLERI *Hist. Templariorum.*

[2] Considering the strong propensity in human nature towards the pleasures
of the chase, it is not to be wondered that the canons of Selborne should
languish after hunting, when, from their situation so near the precincts of
Wolmer Forest, the king's hounds must have often been in hearing, and
sometimes in sight from their windows. If the bishop was so offended at
these sporting canons, what would he have said to our modern fox-hunting
divines ?

business a plea for not attending the service of the choir; since by these means either divine worship is neglected or their brother canons are overburdened.

By Item 14th we are informed that the original number of canons at the Priory of Selborne was fourteen; but that at this visitation they were found to be let down to eleven. The visitor therefore strongly and earnestly enjoins them that, with all due speed and diligence, they should proceed to the election of proper persons to fill up the vacancies, under pain of the greater excommunication.

In Item 17th, the prior and canons are accused of suffering, through neglect, notorious dilapidations to take place among their manorial houses and tenements, and in the walls and inclosures of the convent itself, to the shame and scandal of the institution: they are therefore enjoined, under pain of suspension, to repair all defects within the space of six months.

Item 18th. Charges them with grievously burdening the said Priory by means of sales, and grants of liveries[1] and corrodies.[2]

The bishop, in Item 19th, accuses the canons of neglect and omission with respect to their perpetual chantry-services.

Item 20th. The visitor here conjures the prior and canons not to withhold their original alms, " *eleemosynas*; " nor those that they were enjoined to distribute for the good of the souls of founders and benefactors: he also strictly orders that the fragments and broken victuals, both from the hall of their prior and their common refectory, should be carefully collected together by their *eleemosynarius*, and given to the poor without any diminution; the officer to be suspended for neglect or omission.

Item 23rd. He bids them distribute their pittances, " *pitancias*, "[3] regularly on obits, anniversaries, festivals, &c.

---

[1] " *Liberationes*, or *liberaturæ*, allowances of corn, &c. to servants, delivered at certain times, and certain quantities, as clothes were among the allowances from religious houses to their dependants."--See the corrodies granted by Croyland Abbey.—*Hist. of Croyland*, Appendix, No. xxxiv.

" It is not improbable that the word in after ages came to be confined to the uniform of the retainers or servants of the great, who were hence called livery servants."—SIR JOHN CULLUM'S *Hist. of Hawsted*.

[2] A *corrody* is an allowance to a servant living in an abbey or priory.

[3] " *Pitancia*, an allowance of bread and beer, or other provision to any pious use, especially to the religious in a monastery, &c. for augmentation of their commons."—*Gloss. to Kennet's Par. Antiq.*

D D

Item 25th. All and every one of the canons are hereby in-
hibited from standing godfather to *any boy* for the future, " ne
compatres alicujus pueri de cetero fieri presumatis," unless by
express license from the bishop obtained ; because from . such
relationship favour and affection, nepotism, and undue influence
arise, to the injury and detriment of religious institutions.[1]

Item 26th. The visitor herein severely reprimands the canons
for appearing publicly in what would be called in the universities an *unstatutable manner*, and for wearing of boots, " caligæ
de Burneto, et *sotularium*——in ocrearum loco, ad modum
sotularium." [2]

It is remarkable that the bishop expresses more warmth
against this than any other irregularity ; and strictly enjoins
them, under pain of ecclesiastical censures, and even imprison-
ment if necessary (a threat not made use of before) for the
future to wear boots, " ocreis seu botis," according to the regular
usage of their ancient order.

Item 29th. He here again, but with less earnestness, forbids
them foppish ornaments, and the affectation of appearing like
beaux with garments edged with costly furs, with fringed gloves,
and silken girdles trimmed with gold and silver. It is remarkable that no punishment is annexed to this injunction.

Item 31st. He here singly and severally forbids each canon
not admitted to a cure of souls to administer extreme unction,

---

[1] " The relationship between sponsors and their god-children, who were
called spiritual sons and daughters, was formerly esteemed much more sacred
than at present. The presents at christenings were sometimes very considerable : the connection lasted through life, and was closed with a legacy. This
last mark of attention seems to have been thought almost indispensable :
for, in a will, from whence no extracts have been given, the testator left every
one of his god-children a bushel of barley."—SIR JOHN CULLUM'S *Hist. of
Hawsted.*

" D. Margaretæ filiæ Regis primogenitæ, quam *filiolam*, quia ejus in bap-
tismo *compater* fuit, appellat, cyphum aureum et quadraginta libras, legavit."
—ARCHBISHOP PARKER, *De Antiquitate Eccles. Brit.* speaking of Archbishop
Morton.

[2] Du Fresne is copious on *caligæ* of several sorts. " Hoc item de Clericis,
presertim beneficiatis : *caligis* scacatis (chequered) rubeis, et viridibus publice
utentibus dicimis esse censendum."—*Statut. Eccles. Tutel.* The chequered
boots seem to be the. Highland plaid stockings.—" Burnetum, *i.e.* Brunetum,
pannus non ex lanâ nativi coloris confectus."—" Sotularium, *i.e.* subtalaris,
quia sub talo est. Peculium genus, quibus maxime Monachi nocte utebantur
in æstate ; in hyeme vero Soccis."

This writer gives many quotations concerning Sotularia, which were not to
be made too shapely ; nor were the *caligæ* to be laced on too nicely.

or the sacrament, to clergy or laity; or to perform the service of matrimony, till he has taken out the license of the parish priest.

Item 32nd. The bishop says in this item that he had observed and found, in his several visitations, that the sacramental plate and cloths of the altar, surplices, &c., were sometimes left in such an uncleanly and disgusting condition as to make the beholders shudder with horror;—"quod aliquibus sunt horrori;"[1] he therefore enjoins them for the future to see that the plate, cloths, and vestments, be kept bright, clean, and in decent order: and, what must surprise the reader, adds—that he expects for the future that the sacrist should provide for the sacrament good wine, pure and unadulterated; and not, as had often been the practice, that which was sour, and tending to decay:—he says farther, that it seems quite preposterous to omit in sacred matters that attention to decent cleanliness, the neglect of which would disgrace a common convivial meeting.[2]

Item 33rd says that, though the relics of saints, the plate, holy vestments, and books of religious houses, are forbidden by canonical institutes to be pledged or lent out upon pawn; yet, as the visitor finds this to be the case in his several visitations, he therefore strictly enjoins the prior forthwith to recall those pledges, and to restore them to the convent; and orders that all the papers and title deeds thereto belonging should be safely deposited, and kept under three locks and keys.

In the course of the Visitatio Notabilis the constitutions of Legate Ottobonus are frequently referred to. Ottobonus was afterwards Pope Adrian V. and died in 1276. His constitutions are in Lyndewood's Provinciale, and were drawn up in the 52nd of Henry III.

---

[1] "Men abhorred the offering of the Lord."—1 Sam. chap. ii. v. 17. Strange as this account may appear to modern delicacy, the author, when first in orders, twice met with similar circumstances attending the sacrament at two churches belonging to two obscure villages. In the first he found the inside of the chalice covered with birds' dung; and in the other the communion-cloth soiled with cabbage and the greasy drippings of a gammon of bacon. The good dame at the great farm-house, who was to furnish the cloth, being a notable woman, thought it best to save her clean linen, and so sent a foul cloth that had covered her own table for two or three Sundays before.

[2] " . . . . ne turpe toral, ne sordida mappa
Corruget nares; ne non et cantharus, et lanx
Ostendat tibi te . . . ."

In the Visitatio Notabilis the usual punishment is fasting on bread and beer; and in cases of repeated delinquency on bread and water. On these occasions *quarta feria*, et *sexta feria*, are mentioned often, and are to be understood of the days of the week numerically on which such punishment is to be inflicted.

LETTER XV.

THOUGH Bishop Wykeham appears somewhat stern and rigid in his visitatorial character towards the Priory of Selborne, yet he was on the whole a liberal friend and benefactor to that convent, which, like every society or individual that fell in his way, partook of the generosity and benevolence of that munificent prelate.

"In the year 1377, William of Wykeham, out of his mere good will and liberality, discharged the whole debts of the prior and convent of Selborne, to the amount of one hundred and ten marks eleven shillings and sixpence;[1] and, a few years before he died, he made a free gift of one hundred marks to the same Priory: on which account the prior and convent voluntarily engaged for the celebration of two masses a day by two canons of the convent for ten years, for the bishop's welfare, if he should live so long; and for his soul if he should die before the expiration of this term."[2]

At this distance of time it seems matter of great wonder to us how these societies, so nobly endowed, and whose members were exempt by their very institutions from every means of personal and family expense, could possibly run in debt without squandering their revenues in a manner incompatible with their function.

Religious houses might sometimes be distressed in their revenues by fires among their buildings, or large dilapidations from storms, &c.; but no such accident appears to have befallen the Priory of Selborne. Those situate on public roads, or in great towns, where there were shrines of saints, were liable to

[1] Yet in ten years' time we find, by the Notabilis Visitatio, that all their relics, plate, vestments, title deeds, &c. were in pawn.
[2] Lowth's Life of Wykeham.

be intruded on by travellers, devotees, and pilgrims ; and were subject to the importunity of the poor, who swarmed at their gates to partake of doles and broken victuals.   Of these disadvantages some convents used to complain, and especially those of Canterbury ; but this Priory, from its sequestered situation, could seldom be subject to either of these inconveniences, and therefore we must attribute its frequent debts and embarrassments, well endowed as it was, to the bad conduct of its members, and a general inattention to the interests of the institution.

LETTER XVI.

BEAUFORT was Bishop of Winchester from 1405 to 1447 ; and yet, notwithstanding this long episcopate, only tom. i. of Beaufort's Register is to be found.   This loss is much to be regretted, as it must unavoidably make a gap in the History of Selborne Priory, and perhaps in the list of its priors.

In 1410 there was an election for a prior, and again in 1411.

In vol. i. p. 24, of Beaufort's Register, is the instrument of the election of John Wynchestre to be prior—the substance as follows :

Richard Elstede, senior canon, signifies to the bishop that brother Thomas Weston, the late prior, died October 18th, 1410, and was buried November 11th.   That the bishop's license to elect having been obtained, he and the whole convent met in the chapter-house, on the same day, about the hour of vespers, to consider of the election :—that brother John Wynchestre, then sub-prior, with the general consent, appointed the 12th of November, *ad horam ejusdem diei capitularem,* for the business :—when they met in the chapter-house, *post missam de Sancto Spiritu,* solemnly celebrated in the church ;—to wit, Richard Elstede ; Thomas Halyborne ; John Lemyngton, sacrista ; John Stepe, cantor ; Walter Ffarnham ; Richard Putworth, celerarius ; Hugh London ; Henry Brampton *alias* Brompton ; John Wynchestre, senior ; John Wynchestre, junior ;—then " Proposito primitus verbo Dei," and then ympno " Veni Creator Spiritus " being solemnly sung, cum " versiculo et oratione," as

usual, and his letter of license, with the appointment of the
hour and place of election, being read, *alta voce*, in valvis of the
chapter-house ;—John Wynchestre, senior, the sub-prior, in his
own behalf and that of all the canons, and by their mandate,
" quasdam monicionem et protestacionem in scriptis redactas
fecit, legit, et interposuit "—that all persons disqualified, or not
having right to be present, should immediately withdraw ; and
protesting against their voting, &c.—that then having read the
constitution of the general council " Quia propter," and explained
the modes of proceeding to election, they agreed unanimously to
proceed " per viam seu formam *simplicis compromissi;* " when
John Wynchestre, sub-prior, and all the others (the commissaries
undernamed excepted) named and chose brothers Richard Elstede, Thomas Halyborne, John Lemyngton the sacrist, John
Stepe, chantor, and Richard Putworth, canons, to be commissaries, who were sworn each to nominate and elect a fit person
to be prior : and empowered by letters patent under the common
seal, to be in force only until the darkness of the night of the
same day ;—that they, or the greater part of them, should elect
for the whole convent, within the limited time, from their own
number, or from the rest of the convent ;—that one of them
should publish their consent in common before the clergy and
people :—they then all promised to receive as prior the person
these five canons should fix on.   These commissaries seceded
from the chapter-house to the refectory of the Priory, and were
shut in with master John Penkester, bachelor of laws ; and John
Couke and John Lynne, perpetual vicars of the parish churches
of Newton and Selborne ; and with Sampson Maycock, a public
notary ; where they treated of the election ; when they unanimously agreed on John Wynchestre, and appointed Thomas
Halyborne, to choose him in common for all, and to publish the
election, as customary ; and returned long before it was dark to
the chapter-house, where Thomas Halyborne read publicly the
instrument of election ; when all the brothers, the new prior
excepted, singing solemnly the hymn "Te Deum laudamus,"
fecerunt deportari novum electum, by some of the brothers, from
the chapter-house to the high altar of the church ;[1] and the
hymn being sung, *dictisque versiculo et oratione consuetis in hac*

---

[1] It seems here as if the canons used to chair their new elected prior from
the chapter-house to the high altar of their convent-church.   In Letter XXI.
on the same occasion, it is said—" et sic canentes dictum electum ad majus
altare ecclesie *deduximus,* ut apud nos moris est."

parte, Thomas Halyborne, *mox tunc ibidem*, before the clergy and people of both sexes solemnly published the election *in vulgari*. Then Richard Elstede, and the whole convent by their proctors and nuncios appointed for the purposes, Thomas Halyborne and John Stepe required several times the assent of the elected; "et tandem post diutinas interpellationes, et deliberationem providam penes se habitam, in hac parte divine nolens, ut asseruit, resistere voluntati," within the limited time he signified his acceptance in the usual written form of words. The bishop is then supplicated to confirm their election, and do the needful, under common seal, in the chapter-house. November 14, 1410.

The bishop, January 6, 1410, *apud* Esher *in camera inferiori*, declared the election duly made, and ordered the new prior to be inducted—for this the Archdeacon of Winchester was written to; "stallumque in choro, et locum in capitulo juxto morem preteriti temporis," to be assigned him; and every thing beside necessary to be done.

BEAUFORT'S REGISTER, Vol. I.

P. 2. Taxatio spiritualis Decanatus de Aulton, Ecclesia de Selebourn, cum Capella,—xxx marc. decima x lib. iii. sol. Vicaria de Selebourn non taxatur propter exilitatem.

P. 9. Taxatio bonorum temporalium religiosorum in Archidiac. Wynton.

Prior de Selebourn habet maneria de

Bromdene taxat. ad	xxx s. ii d.
Apud Schete ad	xvii s.
P. Selebourn ad	vi lib.
In civitate Wynton de reddit . .	vi lib. viii ob.
Tannaria sua taxat. ad	x lib. s.

Summa tax. xxxviii lib. xiiii d. ob. Inde decima vi lib. s. q. ob.

LETTER XVII.

INFORMATION being sent to Rome respecting the havoc and spoil that was carrying on among the revenues and lands of the Priory of Selborne, as we may suppose by the Bishop of Winchester, its visitor, Pope Martin,[1] as soon as the news of these proceedings came before him, issued forth a bull, in which he enjoins his commissary immediately to revoke all the property that had been alienated.

In this instrument his holiness accuses the prior and canons of having granted away (they themselves and their predecessors) to certain clerks and laymen their tithes, lands, rents, tenements, and possessions, to some of them for their lives, to others for an undue term of years, and to some again for a perpetuity, to the great and heavy detriment of the monastery : and these leases were granted, he continues to add, under their own hands, with the sanction of an oath and the renunciation of all rights and claims, and under penalties, if the right was not made good. But it will be best to give an abstract from the bull.

N. 298. Pope Martin's bull, touching the revoking of certain things alienated from the Priory of Seleburne. Pontif. sui ann. 1.

"Martinus Eps. servus servorum Dei. Dilecto filio Priori de Suthvale[2] Wyntonien. dioc. Salutem & apostolicam ben. Ad audientiam nostram pervenit quam tam dilecti filii prior et conventus monasterii de Seleburn per Priorem soliti gubernari ordinis S[ti]. Augustini Winton. dioc. quam de predecessores eorum decimas, terras, redditus, domos, possessiones, *vineas,*[3] et quedam alia bona ad monasterium ipsum spectantia, datis super hoc litteris, interpositis juramentis, factis renunciationibus, et penis adjectis, in gravem ipsius monasterii lesionem nonnullis clericis et laicis, aliquibus eorum ad vitam, quibusdam vero ad non modi-

---

[1] Pope Martin V. chosen about 1417. He attempted to reform the Church, but died in 1431, just as he had summoned the council of Basil.

[2] Should have been no doubt Southwick, a priory under Portsdown.

[3] Mr. Barrington is of opinion that anciently the English *vinea* was in almost every instance an orchard ; not perhaps always of apples merely, but of other fruits ; as cherries, plums, and currants. We still say a plum or cherry-orchard.—See Vol. iii. of Archæologia.

In the instance above the pope's secretary might insert *vineas* merely because they were a species of cultivation familiar to him in Italy.

cum tempus, & aliis perpetuo ad firmam, vel sub censu annuo concesserunt ; quorum aliqui dicunt super hiis a sede aplica in communi forma confirmationis litteris impetrasse.   Quia vero nostra interest lesis monasteriis subvenire—[He the Pope here commands] — ea ad jus et proprietatem monasterii studeas legitime revocare," &c.

The conduct of the religious had now for some time been generally bad.   Many of the monastic societies, being very opulent, were become very voluptuous and licentious, and had deviated entirely from their original institutions.   The laity saw with indignation the wealth and possessions of their pious ancestors perverted to the service of sensuality and indulgence ; and spent in gratifications highly unbecoming the purposes for which they were given.   A total disregard of their respective rules and discipline drew on the monks and canons a heavy load of popular odium.   Some good men there were who endeavoured to oppose the general delinquency ; but their efforts were too feeble to stem the torrent of monastic luxury.   As far back as the year 1381 Wickliffe's principles and doctrines had made some progress, were well received by men who wished for a reformation, and were defended and maintained by them as long as they dared ; till the bishops and clergy began to be so greatly alarmed, that they procured an act to be passed by which the secular arm was empowered to support the corrupt doctrines of the Church ; but the first Lollard was not burnt until the year 1401.

The wits also of those times did not spare the gross morals of the clergy, but boldly ridiculed their ignorance and profligacy. The most remarkable of these were Chaucer, and his contemporary, Robert Langelande, better known by the name of Piers Plowman.   The laughable tales of the former are familiar to almost every reader ; while the visions of the latter are but in few hands.   With a quotation from the " Passus Decimus " of this writer I shall conclude my letter ; not only on account of the remarkable prediction therein contained, which carries with it somewhat of the air of a prophecy ; but also as it seems to have been a striking picture of monastic insolence and dissipation ; and a specimen of one of the keenest pieces of satire now perhaps subsisting in any language, ancient or modern.

> " Now is religion a rider, a romer by streate ;
> A leader of love-days, and a loud begger ;
> A pricker on a palfrey from maner to maner,

A heape of hounds at his arse, as he a lord were.
And but if his knave kneel, that shall his cope bring,
He loureth at him, and asketh him who taught him curtesie.
Little had lords to done, to give lands from her heirs,
To religious that have no ruth if it rain on her altars.
In many places ther they persons be, by himself at ease :
Of the poor have they no pity, and that is her charitie ;
And they letten hem as lords, her lands lie so broad.
And *there shal come a king*,[1] and confess you religious ;
And beate you, as the bible telleth, for breaking your rule,
And amend monials, and monks, and chanons,
And put hem in her penaunce *ad pristinum statum ire.*"

LETTER XVIII.

WILLIAM OF WAYNFLETE became Bishop of Winchester in
the year 1447, and seems to have pursued the generous
plan of Wykeham, in endeavouring to reform the Priory of
Selborne.

When Waynflete came to the see he found Prior Stype
alias Stepe, still living, who had been elected as long ago
as the year 1411.

Among my documents I find a curious paper of the things put
into the custody of Peter Bernes the sacrist, and especially some
relics : the title of this evidence is "No. 50. Indentura prioris
de Selborne quorundam tradit. Petro Bernes sacristæ, ibidem,
ann. Hen. VI. . . . una cum confiss. ejusdem Petri script." The
occasion of this catalogue, or list of effects, being drawn between
the prior and sacrist does not appear, nor the date when; only
that ·it happened in the reign of Henry VI. This transaction
probably took place when Bernes entered on his office; and

---

[1] F. l. a. "This prediction, although a probable conclusion concerning a
king who after a time would suppress the religious houses, is remarkable. I
imagined it might have been foisted into the copies in the reign of king
Henry VIII., but it is to be found in MSS. of this poem older than the year
1400." Fol. l. a. b.

"Again, where he, Piers Plowman, alludes to the Knight Templars, lately
suppressed, he says,
' . . . . Men of holie kirk
    Shall turn as Templars did ; the tyme approacheth nere.'
"This, I suppose, was a favourite doctrine in Wickliffe's discourses."—
WARTON'S *Hist. of English Poetry*, vol. i. p. 282.

there is the more reason to suppose that to be the case, because the list consists of vestments and implements, and relics such as belonged to the church of the Priory, and fell under the care of the sacrist. I shall just mention the relics, although they are not all specified; and the state of the live stock of the monastery at that juncture.

"Item 2. *osculator*. argent.

"Item 1. *osculatorium* cum *osse digiti auricular*,—S[tt]. Johannis Baptistæ.[1]

"Item 1. parvam *crucem* cum V. *reliquiis*.

"Item 1. *anulum* argent. et deauratum St. Edmundi.[2]

"Item 2. *osculat*. de coper.

"Item 1. *junctorium* St. Ricardi.[3]

"Item 1. *pecten* St. Ricardi."[4]

The *staurum*, or live stock, is quite ridiculous, consisting only of "2 vacce, 1 sus, 4 hoggett. et 4 porcell." viz. two cows, one sow, four porkers, and four pigs.

LETTER XIX.

STEPE died towards the end of the year 1453, as we may suppose pretty far advanced in life, having been prior forty-four years.

---

[1] How the convent came by the bone of the little finger of St. John the Baptist does not appear; probably the founder, while in Palestine, purchased it among the Asiatics, who were at that time great traders in relics. We know from the best authority that as soon as Herod had cruelly beheaded that holy man, "his disciples came and took up the body and buried it, and went and told Jesus."—Matt. iv. 12.—Farther it would be difficult to say.

[2] November 20, in the calendar, Edmund, king and martyr, in the ninth century.—See also a Sanctus Edmundus in Godwin, among the archbishops of Canterbury, in the thirteenth century; his surname Rich, in 1234.

[3] April 3, ibid. Richard, Bishop of Chicester, in the thirteenth century; his surname De la Wich, in 1245.

Junctorium, perhaps a joint or limb of St. Richard; but what particular joint the religious were not such osteologists as to specify. This barbarous word was not to be found in any dictionary consulted by the author.

[4] " *Pecten* inter ministeria sacra recensetur, quo scil. sacerdotes ac clerici, antequam in ecclesiam procederent, crines pecterent. E quibus colligitur monachos, tunc temporis, non omnino tonsos fuisse."—Du Fresne.

The author remembers to have seen in great farm houses a family comb chained to a post for the use of the hinds when they came in to their meals.

On the very day that the vacancy happened, viz. January 26, 1453-4, the sub-prior and convent petitioned the visitor—"vos unicum levamen nostrum, et spem unanimiter rogamus, quatinus eligendum ex nobis unum confratrem de gremio nostro, in nostra religione probatum et expertem, licenciam vestram paternalem cum plena libertate nobis concedere dignemini graciose."—Reg. Waynflete, tom. i.

Instead of the license requested we find next a commission "custodie prioratus de Selebourne durante vacatione," addressed to brother Peter Berne, canon-regular of the Priory of Selebourne, and of the order of St. Augustine, appointing him keeper of the said Priory, and empowering him to collect and receive the profits and revenues, and "alia bona" of the said Priory; and to exercise in every respect the full power and authority of a prior; but to be responsible to the visitor finally, and to maintain this superiority during the bishop's pleasure only. This instrument is dated from the bishop's manor-house in Southwark, March 1, 1453-4, and the seventh of his consecration.

After this transaction it does not appear that the chapter of the Priory proceeded to any election: on the contrary, we find that at six months' end from the vacancy the visitor declared that a lapse had taken place; and that therefore he did confer the priorship on Peter Berne.—"Prioratum vacantem et ad nostram collationem, seu provisionem jure ad nos in hac parte *per lapsum* temporis legitime devoluntu spectantem, tibi (sc. P. Berne) de legitimo matrimonio procreato, &c.—conferimus," &c. This deed bears date, July 28, 1454.—Reg. Waynflete, tom. i. p. 69.

On February 8, 1462, the visitor issued out a power of sequestration against the Priory of Selborne on account of notorious dilapidations which threatened manifest ruin to the roofs, walls, and edifices of the said convent; and appointing John Hammond, B.D., rector of the parish church of Hetlegh, John Hylling, vicar of the parish church of Newton Valence, and Walter Gorfin, inhabitant of the parish of Selborne, his sequestrators, to exact, collect, levy, and receive, all the profits and revenues of the said convent: he adds, "ac ea sub areto, et tuto custodiatis, custodirive faciatis;" as they would answer it to the bishop at their peril.

In consequence of these proceedings Prior Berne, on the last day of February, and the next year, produced a state of the revenues of the Priory, No. 381, called "A paper conteyning the value of the manors and lands pertayning to the Priory of Selborne. 4 Edward III. with a note of charges yssuing out of it."

This is a curious document. From circumstances in this paper it is plain that the sequestration produced good effects; for in it are to be found bills of repairs to a considerable amount.

By this evidence also it appears that there were at that juncture only four canons at the Priory;[1] and that these, and their four household servants, during this sequestration, for their clothing, wages, and diet, were allowed *per ann.* xxx lib.; and that the annual pension of the lord prior, reside where he would, was to be x lib.

In the year 1468, Prior Berne, probably wearied out by the dissensions and want of order that prevailed in the convent, resigned his priorship into the hands of the bishop.—Reg. Waynflete, tom. i. pars. i^{ma}, fol. 157.

March 28, A.D. 1468. "In quadam alta camera juxta magnam portam marnerii of the Bishop of Wynton de Waltham coram eodem rev. patre ibidem tunc sedente, Peter Berne, prior of Selborne, ipsum prioratum in sacras, et venerabiles manus of the bishop, viva voce libere resignavit: and his resignation was admitted before two witnesses and a notary-public. In consequence, March 29th, before the bishop, in capella manerii sui ante dicti pro tribunali sedente, comparuerunt fratres" Peter Berne, Thomas London, William Wyndesor, and William Paynell, *alias* Stretford, canons regular of the Priory, "capitulem, et conventum ejusdem ecclesie facientes; ac jus et voces in electione futura prioris dicti prioratus solum et in solidum, ut asseruerunt, habentes;" and after the bishop had notified to them the vacancy of a prior, with his free license to elect, deliberated a while, and then, by way of compromise, as they affirmed, unanimously transferred their right of election to the bishop before witnesses. In consequence of this the bishop, after full deliberation, proceeded, April 7th, "in capella manerii sui de Waltham," to the election of a prior; "et fratrem Johannem Morton, priorem ecclesie conventualis de Reygate dicti ordinis S^{ti} Augustini Wynton. dioc. in priorem vice et nomine omnium et singulorum canonicorum predictorum elegit, in ordine

---

[1] If Bishop Wykeham was so disturbed (see Notab. Visitatio) to find the number of canons reduced from fourteen to eleven, what would he have said to have seen it diminished below one-third of that number !

sacerdotali, et etate licita constitutum, &c." And on the same day, in the same place, and before the same witnesses, John Morton resigned to the bishop the priorship of Reygate *viva voce*. The bishop then required his consent to his own election; "qui licet in parte renitens tanti reverendi patris se confirmans," obeyed, and signified his consent *oraculo vive vocis*. Then was there a mandate citing any one who would gainsay the said election to appear before the bishop or his commissary in his chapel at Farnham on the 2nd day of May next. The dean of the deanery of Aulton then appeared before the chancellor, his commissary, and returned the citation or mandate dated April 22nd, 1468, with signification, in writing, of his having published it as required, dated Newton Valence, May 1st, 1468. This certificate being read, the four canons of Selborne appeared and required the election to be confirmed; *et ex super abundanti* appointed William Long their proctor to solicit in their name that he might be canonically confirmed. John Morton also appeared, and proclamation was made; and no one appearing against him, the commissary pronounced all absentees contumacious, and precluded them from objecting at any other time; and, at the instance of John Morton and the proctor, confirmed the election by his decree, and directed his mandate to the rector of Hedley and the vicar of Newton Valence to install him in the usual form.

Thus, for the first time, was a person, a stranger to the convent of Selborne, and never canon of that monastery, elected prior; though the style of the petitions in former elections used to run thus,—"Vos . . . rogamus quatinus eligendum ex *nobis* unum *confratrem* de *gremio nostro*,—licentiam vestram—nobis concedere dignemini."

LETTER XX.

PRIOR MORTON dying in 1471, two canons, by themselves proceeded to election, and chose a prior; but two more (one of them Berne) complaining of not being summoned, objected to the proceedings as informal; till at last the matter was compromised that the bishop should again, for that turn, nominate as he had before. But the circumstances of this election will be best explained by the following extract:

Reg. Waynflete, tom. ii. pars i^{ma}, fol. 7.

William Wyndesor, a canon-regular of the Priory of Selborne, having been elected prior on the death of Brother John, appeared in person before the bishop in his chapel at South Waltham. He was attended on this occasion by Thomas London and John Bromesgrove, canons, who elected him. Peter Berne and William Stratfield, canons, also presented themselves at the same time, complaining that in this business they had been overlooked, and not summoned; and that therefore the validity of the election might with reason be called in question, and quarrels and dissensions might probably arise between the newly chosen prior and the parties thus neglected.

After some altercation and dispute they all came to an agreement with the new prior, that what had been done should be rejected and annulled; and that they would again, for this turn, transfer to the bishop their power to elect, order, and provide them another prior, whom they promised unanimously to admit.

The bishop accepted of this offer before witnesses; and on September 27th, in an inner chamber near the chapel above-mentioned, after full deliberation, chose brother Thomas Fairwise, vicar of Somborne, a canon-regular of St. Augustine in the Priory of Bruscough, in the diocese of Coventry and Lichfield, to be prior of Selborne. The form is nearly as above in the last election. The canons are again enumerated; W. Wyndesor, sub-prior, P. Berne, T. London, W. Stratfield, J. Bromesgrove, who had formed the chapter, and had requested and obtained licence to elect, but had unanimously conferred their power on the bishop. In consequence of this proceeding, the bishop taking the business upon himself, that the Priory might not suffer detriment for want of a governor, appoints the aforesaid T. Fairwise to be prior. A citation was ordered as above for gainsayers to appear October 4th, before the bishop or his commissaries at South Waltham; but none appearing, the commissaries admitted the said Thomas, ordered him to be installed, and sent the usual letter to the convent to render him due obedience.

Thus did the Bishop of Winchester a second time appoint a stranger to be prior of Selborne, instead of one chosen out of the chapter. For this seeming irregularity the visitor had no doubt good and sufficient reasons, as probably may appear hereafter.

LETTER XXI.

WHATEVER might have been the abilities and disposition of Prior Fairwise, it could not have been in his power to have brought about any material reformation in the Priory of Selborne, because he departed this life in the month of August, 1472, before he had presided one twelvemonth.

As soon as their governor was buried, the chapter applied to their visitor for leave to choose a new prior, which being granted, after deliberating for a time, they proceeded to an election by a scrutiny. But as this mode of voting has not been described, an extract from the bishop's register, representing the manner more fully, may not be disagreeable to several readers :—

WAYNFLETE REG. tom. ii. pars 1ᵐᵃ, fol. 15.

"Reverendo, &c., ac nostro patrono graciosissimo vestri humiles, et devote obedientie filii," &c.

To the right reverend Father in God, and our most gracious patron, we, your obedient and devoted sons, William Wyndesor, president of the chapter of the Priory of Selborne, and the convent of that place, do make known to your lordship, that our priorship being lately vacant by the death of Thomas Fairwise, our late prior, who died August 11th, 1472, having committed his body to decent sepulture, and having requested, according to custom, leave to elect another, and having obtained it under your seal, we William Wyndesor, president of the convent, on the 29th of August, in our chapter-house assembled, and making a chapter, taking to us in this business Richard ap Jenkyn, and Galfrid Bryan, chaplains, that our said Priory might not by means of this vacancy incur harm or loss, unanimously agreed on August the last for the day of election; on which day, having first celebrated mass, "De sancto spiritu," at the high altar, and having called a chapter by tolling a bell about ten o' the clock, we, William Wyndesor, president, Peter Berne, Thomas London, and William Stratfeld, canons, who alone had voices, being the only canons, about ten o' the clock, first sung " Veni Creator," the letters and license being read in the presence of many persons there.   Then William Wyndesor, in his own name, and that of all the canons, made solemn proclamation, enjoining all who had no right to vote to depart out of the chapter-house. When all were withdrawn except Guyllery de Lacuna, in decretis Baccalarius, and Robert Peverell, notary-public, and also the two chaplains, the first was requested to stay, that he might direct and'inform us in the mode of election ; the other, that he might record and attest the transactions ; and the two last that they might be witnesses to them.

Then, having read the constitution of the general council " Quia propter," and the forms of elections contained in it being sufficiently explained to them by De Lacuna, as well in Latin as the vulgar tongue, and having deliberated in what mode to proceed in this election, they resolved on that of scrutiny. Three of the canons, Wyndesor, Berne, and London, were made scrutators: Berne, London, and Stratfeld, choosing Wyndesor; Wyndesor, London, and Stratfeld, choosing Berne ; Wyndesor, Berne, and Stratfeld, choosing London.

They were empowered to take each other's vote, and then that of Stratfeld ; " et ad inferiorem partem angularem " of the chapter-house, " juxta ostium ejusdem declinentes," with the other persons (except Stratfeld, who stayed behind), proceeded to voting, two swearing, and taking the voice of the third, in succession, privately.   Wyndesor voted first : " Ego credo Petrum Berne meliorem et utiliorem ad regimen istius ecclesie, et in ipsum consentio, ac eum nomino," &c.   Berne was next sworn, and in like manner nominated Wyndesor ; London nominated Berne : Stratfeld was then called and sworn, and nominated Berne.

" Quibus in scriptis redactis," by the notary-public, they returned to the upper part of the chapter-house, where by Wyndesor " sic purecta fecerunt in communi," and then solemnly, in form written, declared the election of Berne : when all, " antedicto nostro electo excepto, approbantes et ratificantes, cepimus decantare solemniter ' Te Deum Laudamus,' et sic canentes dictum electum ad majus altare ecclesie deduximus, ut apud nos est moris."   Then Wyndesor " electionem clero et populo

E E

infra chorum dicte ecclesie congregatis publicavit, et personam electi publice et personaliter ostendit." We then returned to the chapter-house, except our prior; and Wyndesor was appointed by the other two their proctor, to desire the assent of the elected, and to notify what had been done, to the bishop; and to desire him to confirm the election, and do whatever else was necessary. Then their proctor, before the witnesses, required Berne's assent in the chapter-house: "qui quidem instanciis et precibus multiplicatis devictus," consented "licet indignus electus," in writing. They therefore requested the bishop's confirmation of their election, " sic canonice et solemniter celebrata," &c. &c. Sealed with their common seal, and subscribed and attested by the notary. Dat. in the chapter-house, September 5th, 1472.

In consequence, September 11th, 1472, in the bishop's chapel at Esher, and before the bishop's commissary, appeared W. Wyndesor, and exhibited the above instrument, and a mandate from the bishop for the appearance of gainsayers of the election there on that day:—and no one appearing, the absentees were declared contumacious, and the election confirmed; and the vicar of Aulton was directed to induct and install the prior in the usual manner.

Thus did Canon Berne, though advanced in years, reassume his abdicated priorship for the second time, to the no small satisfaction, as it may seem, of the Bishop of Winchester, who professed, as will be shown not long hence, a high opinion of his abilities and integrity.

LETTER XXII.

As Prior Berne, when chosen in 1454, held his priorship only to 1468, and then made a voluntary resignation, wearied and disgusted, as we may conclude, by the disorder that prevailed in his convent; it is no matter of wonder that, when re-chosen in 1472, he should not long maintain his station; as old age was then coming fast upon him, and the increasing anarchy and misrule of that declining institution required unusual vigour and resolution to stem that torrent of profligacy which was hurrying it on to its dissolution. We find, accordingly, that in 1478 he resigned his dignity again into the hands of the bishop.

WAYNFLETE REG. Fol. 55.

Resignatio Prioris de Seleborne.

May 14, 1478. Peter Berne resigned the priorship. May 16, the bishop admitted his resignation "in manerio suo de Waltham," and declared the priorship void; "et priorat. solacio destitutum esse;" and granted his letters for proceeding to a new election: when all the religious, assembled in the chapter-house, did transfer their power under their seal to the bishop by the following public instrument :

"In Dei nomine Amen," &c. A.D. 1478, Maii 19. In the chapter-house for the election of a prior for that day, on the free resignation of Peter Berne, having celebrated in the first place mass at the high altar "De spiritu sancto," and having called a chapter by tolling a bell, *ut moris est ;* in the presence of a notary and witnesses appeared personally Peter Berne, Thomas Ashford, Stephen Clydgrove, and John Ashton, presbyters, and Henry Canwood,[1] in chapter assembled; and after singing the hymn "Veni Creator Spiritus," "cum versiculo et oratione '*Deus qui corda ;*' declarataque licentia Fundatoris et patroni; futurum priorem eligendi concessa, et constitutione consilii generalis que incipit '*Quia propter*' declaratis; viisque per quas possent ad hanc electionem procedere," by the *decretorum doctorem,* whom the canons had taken to direct them—they all and every one "dixerunt et affirmarunt se nolle ad aliquam viam procedere :"— but, for this turn only, renounced their right, and unanimously transferred their power to the bishop, the ordinary of the place, promising to receive whom he should provide; and appointed a proctor to present the instrument to the bishop under their seal; and required their notary to draw it up in due form, &c. subscribed by the notary.

---

[1] Here we see that all the canons were changed in six years; and that there was quite a new chapter, Berne excepted, between 1472 and 1478; for, instead of Wyndesor, London, and Stratfeld, we find Ashford, Clydgrove, Ashton, and Canwood, all new men, who were soon gone in their turn off the stage, and are heard of no more. For, in six years after, there seem to have been no canons at all.

After the visitor had fully deliberated on the matter, he proceeded to the choice of a prior, and elected, by the following instrument, John Sharp, *alias* Glastonbury.

Fol. 56. Provisio Prioris per Epm.

Willmus, &c. to our beloved brother in CHRIST, John Sharp, *alias* Glastonbury, Ecclesie conventualis de Bruton, of the order of St. Austin, in the diocese of Bath and Wells, canon-regular—*salutem*, &c. " De tue circumspectionis industria plurimum confidentes, te virum providum et discretum, literarum scientia, et moribus merito commendandum," &c.—do appoint you prior—under our seal. " Dat. in manerio nostro de Suthwaltham, May 20, 1478, et nostre Consec. 31."

Thus did the bishop, three times out of the four that he was at liberty to nominate, appoint a prior from a distance, a stranger to the place, to govern the convent of Selborne, hoping by this method to have broken the cabal, and to have interrupted that habit of mismanagement that had pervaded the society; but he acknowledges, in an evidence lying before us, that he never did succeed to his wishes with respect to those late governors,— " quos tamen male se habuisse, et inutiliter administrare, et administrasse usque ad presentia tempora post debitam investigationem, &c. invenit." The only time that he appointed from among the canons, he made choice of Peter Berne, for whom he had conceived the greatest esteem and regard.

When Prior Berne first relinquished his priorship, he returned again to his former condition of canon, in which he continued for some years: but when he was rechosen, and had abdicated a second time, we find him in a forlorn state, and in danger of being reduced to beggary, had not the Bishop of Winchester interposed in his favour, and with great humanity insisted on a provision for him for life. The reason for this difference seems to have been, that, in the first case, though in years, he might have been hale and capable of taking his share in the duty of the convent; in the second, he was broken with age, and no longer equal to the functions of a canon.

Impressed with this idea the bishop very benevolently interceded in his favour, and laid his injunctions on the new elected prior in the following manner.

Fol. 56. " In Dei nomine Amen. Nos Willmus, &c. consider-

antes Petrum Berne," late prior "in administratione spiritualium
et temporalium prioratus laudabiliter vixisse et rexisse: ipsum-
que senio et corporis debilitate confractum; ne in opprobrium
religionis *mendicari cogatur;*—eidem annuam pensionem a
Domino Johanne Sharp, *alias* Glastonbury, priore moderno,"
and his successors, and, from the Priory or church, to be paid
every year during his life, "de voluntate et ex consensu ex-
pressis" of the said John Sharp, "sub ea que sequitur forma
verborum—assignamus:"

1st. That the said prior and his successors, for the time being,
honeste exhibebunt of the fruits and profits of the priorship,
"eidem esculenta et poculenta," while he remained in the Priory,
"sub consimili portione eorundem prout convenienter priori,"
for the time being, *ministrari contigerit;* and in like manner *uni
famulo*, whom he should choose to wait on him, as to the
servientibus of the prior.

Item. "Invenient seu exhibebunt eidem unam honestam
cameram" in the Priory, "cum focalibus necessariis seu oppor-
tunis ad eundem."

Item. We will, ordain, &c. to the said P. Berne an annual
pension of ten marks, from the revenue of the Priory, to be paid
by the hands of the prior quarterly.

The bishop decrees farther, that John Sharp, and his successors,
shall take an oath to observe this injunction, and that before
their installation.

"Lecta et facta sunt hæc in quondam alto oratorio," belonging
to the bishop at Suthwaltham, May 25, 1478, in the presence of
John Sharp, who gave his assent, and then took the oath before
witnesses, with the other oaths before the chancellor, who de-
creed he should be inducted and installed; as was done that
same day.

How John Sharp, *alias* Glastonbury, acquitted himself in his
priorship, and in what manner he made a vacancy, whether by
resignation, or death, or whether he was removed by the visitor,
does not appear: we only find that some time in the year 1484
there was no prior, and that the bishop nominated canon
Ashford to fill the vacancy.

LETTER XXIII.

THIS Thomas Ashford was most undoubtedly the last prior of Selborne; and therefore here will be the proper place to say something concerning a list of the priors, and to endeavour to improve that already given by others.

At the end of Bishop Tanner's "Notitia Monastica," the folio edition, among Brown Willis's Principals of Religious Houses, occur the names of eleven of the priors of Selborne, with dates. But this list is imperfect, and particularly at the beginning; for though the Priory was founded in 1232, yet it commences with Nich. de Cantia, elected in 1262; so that for the first thirty years no prior is mentioned; yet there must have been one or more. We were in hopes that the register of Peter de Rupibus would have rectified this omission; but, when it was examined, no information of the sort was to be found. From the year 1410 the list is much corrected and improved: and the reader may depend on its being thenceforward very exact.

A List of the Priors of Selborne Priory, from Brown Willis's Principals of Religious Houses, with additions within [ ] by the Author.

[John ⸺ was prior, *sine dat.*[1]]
Nich. de Cantia el. . . . . 1262.
[Peter ⸺ was prior in . . . . 1271.]
[Richard ⸺ was prior in . . . . 1280.]
Will. Basing was prior in . . . . 1299.
Walter de Insula el. in . . . . 1324.
   [Some difficulties, and a devolution; but the election
     confirmed by Bishop Stratford.]
John de Winton . . . . 1339.
Thomas Weston . . . . 1377.
John Winchester [Wynchestre] . . . . 1410.
   [Elected by Bishop Beaufort "per viam vel formam
     simplicis compromissi."]
[John Stype, alias Stepe, in . . . . 1411.]

---

[1] See, in Letter XI. of these Antiquities, the reason why prior John ⸺, who had transactions with the Knight Templars, is placed in the list before the year 1262.

Peter Bene [*alias* Berne or Bernes, appointed keeper,
and, by lapse to Bishop Wayneflete, prior] in . . . 1454.
[He resigns in 1468.]
John Morton [Prior of Reygate] in . . . . 1468.
[The canons by compromise transfer the power of
election to the bishop.]
Will. Winsor [Wyndesor, prior for a few days] . . . 1471.
[but removed on account of an irregular election.]
Thomas Farwill [Fairwise, vicar of Somborne] . . . 1471.
[by compromise again elected by the bishop.]
[Peter Berne, re-elected by scrutiny in . . . . . . 1472.]
[resigns again in 1478.]
John Sharper [Sharp] *alias* Glastonbury . . . . . 1478.
[Canon-reg. of Bruton, elected by the bishop by compromise.]
[Thomas Ashford, canon of Selborne, last prior elected
by the Bishop of Winchester, some time in the year 1484.
and deposed at the dissolution.]

LETTER XXIV.

BISHOP WAINFLEET'S efforts to continue the Priory still
proved unsuccessful; and the convent, without any canons, and
for some time without a prior, was tending swiftly to its
dissolution.

When Sharp's *alias* Glastonbury's priorship ended does not
appear. The bishop says that he had been obliged to remove
some priors for mal-administration : but it is not well explained
how that could be the case with any, unless with Sharp ; because
all the others, chosen during his episcopate, died in their office,
viz. Morton and Fairwise ; Berne only excepted, who relinquished
twice voluntarily, and was moreover approved of by Wainfleet
as a person of integrity. But the way to show what ineffectual
pains the bishop took, and what difficulties he met with, will be
to quote the words of the libel of his proctor, Radulphus
Langley, who appeared for the bishop in the process of the
impropriation of the Priory of Selborne. The extract is taken
from an attested copy.

"Item—that the said bishop—dicto prioratui et personis ejusdem pie compatiens, sollicitudines pastorales, labores, et diligentias gravissimas quam plurimas, tam per se quam per suos, pro reformatione premissorum impendebat : et aliquando illius loci prioribus, propter malam et inutilem administrationem, et dispensationem bonorum predicti prioratus, suis demeritis exigentibus, amotis ; alios priores in quorum circumspectione et diligentia confidebat, prefecit : quos tamen male se habuisse ac inutiliter administrare, et administrasse, usque ad presentia tempora post debitam investigationem, &c. invenit." So that he despaired, with all his care,—"statum ejusdem reparare vel restaurare : et considerata temporis malicia, et preteritis timendo, et conjecturando futura, de aliqua bona et sancta religione ejusdem ordinis, &c. juxta piam intentionem primevi fundatoris ibidem habend. desperatur."

William Wainfleet, Bishop of Winchester, founded his college of St. Mary Magdalen, in the university of Oxford, in or about the year 1459 ; but the revenues proving insufficient for so large and noble an establishment, the college supplicated the founder to augment its income by putting it in possession of the estates belonging to the Priory of Selborne, now become a deserted convent, without canons or prior. The president and fellows state the circumstances of their numerous institution and scanty provision, and the ruinous and perverted condition of the Priory. The bishop appoints commissaries to inquire into the state of the said monastery; and, if found expedient, to confirm the appropriation of it to the college, which soon after appoints attorneys to take possession, September 24, 1484. But the way to give the reader a thorough insight respecting this transaction, will be to transcribe a farther proportion of the process of the impropriation from the beginning, which will lay open the manner of proceeding, and show the consent of the parties.

IMPROPRIATIO SELBORNE, 1485.

"Universis sancte matris ecclesie filiis, &c. Ricardus Dei gratia prior ecclesie conventualis de Novo Loco, &c.[1] ad univer-

---

[1] Ecclesia Conventualis de Novo Loco was the monastery afterwards called the New Minster, or Abbey of Hyde, in the city of Winchester. Should any intelligent reader wonder to see that the prior of Hyde Abbey was commissary to the Bishop of Winton, and should conclude that there was a

sitatem vestre notitie deducimus, &c. quod coram nobis commissario predicto in ecclesia parochiali S^{ti}. Georgii de Essher, dict. Winton. dioc. 3°. die Augusti, A.D. 1485. Indictione tertia pontificat. Innocentii 8^{vi}. ann. 1mo. judicialiter comparuit venerabilis vir Jacobus Preston, S. T. P. infrascriptus, et exhibuit literas commissionis—quas quidem per magistrum Thomam Somercotes notarium publicum, &c. legi fecimus, tenorem sequentem in se continentes." The same as No. 103, but dated— "In manerio nostro de Essher, Augusti, 1mo. A.D. 1485, et nostre consec. anno 39." [No. 103 is repeated in a book containing the like process in the preceding year by the same commissary, in the parish church of St. Andrew the apostle, at Farnham, Sept. 6th, anno 1484.] "Post quarum literarum lecturam—: dictus magister Jacobus Preston, quasdam procuratorias literas mag. Richardi Mayewe presidentis, ut asseruit, collegii beate Marie Magdalene, &c. sigillo rotundo communi, &c. in cera rubea impresso sigillatas realiter exhibuit, &c. et pro eisdem dnis suis, &c. fecit se partem, ac nobis supplicavit ut juxta formam in eisdem traditam procedere dignaremur, &c." After these proclamations no contradictor or abjector appearing—" ad instantem petitionem ipsius mag. Jac. Preston, procuratoris, &c. procedendum fore decrevimus vocatis jure vocandis; nec non mag. Tho. Somercotes, &c. in actorum nostrorum scribam nominavimus. Consequenter et ibidem tunc comparuit magister Michael Clyff, &c. et exhibuit in ea parte procuratorium suum," for the prior and convent of the cathedral of Winton, "et fecit se partem pro eisdem.—Deinde comperuit coram nobis, &c. honestus vir Willmus Cowper," proctor for the bishop as patron of the Priory of Selborne, and exhibited his "procuratorium," &c. After these were read in the presence of Clyff and Cowper, "Preston, viva voce," petitioned the commissary to annex and appropriate the Priory of Selborne to the college—"propter quod fructus, redditus, et proventus ejusdem coll. adeo tenues sunt, et exiles, quod ad sustentationem ejus, &c. non sufficiunt."—The commissary, "ad libellandum et articulandum in scriptis "—adjourned the court to the 5th of August, then to be held again in the parish church of Essher.

mistake in titles, and that the abbot must have been here meant, he will be pleased to recollect that this person was the second in rank; for "next under the abbot, in every abbey, was the prior."—Pref. to Notit. Monast. p. xxix. Besides, abbots were great personages, and too high in station to submit to any office under the bishop.

W. Cowper being then absent, Radulphus Langley appeared for the bishop, and was admitted his proctor. Preston produced his libel or article in scriptis for the union, &c. "et admitti petiit eundem cum effectu; cujus libelli tenor sequitur.—In Dei nomine, Amen. Coram nobis venerabili in Christo patre Richardo, priore, &c. de Novo Loco, &c. commissario, &c." Part of the college of Magd. dicit. allegat. and in his "scriptis proponit," &c.

"Imprimis"—that said college consists of a president and eighty scholars, besides sixteen choristers, thirteen "servientes inibi altissimo famulantibus, et in scientiis plerisque liberalibus, presertim in sacra theologia studentibus, nedum ad ipsorum presidentis et scholarium pro presenti et imposterum, annuente deo, incorporandorum in eodem relevamen; verum etiam ad omnium et singulorum tam scholarium quam religiosorum cujuscunque ordinis undequaque illuc confluere pro salubri doctrina volentium utilitatem multiplicem ad incrementa virtutis fideique catholice stabilimentum. Ita videlicet quod omnes et singuli absque personarum seu nationum delectu illuc accedere volentes, lecturas publicas et doctrinas tam in grammatica loco ad collegium contiguo, ac philosophiis morali et naturali, quam in sacra theologia in eodem collegio perpetuis temporibus continuandas libere atque gratis audire valeant et possint ad laudem gloriam et honorem Dei, &c. extitit fundatum et stabilitum."

For the first item in this process see the beginning of this letter. Then follows item the second—"that the revenues of the college non sufficiunt his diebus." "Item—that the premisses are true, &c. et super eisdem laborarunt, et laborant publica vox et fama. Unde facta fide petit pars eorundem that the Priory be annexed to the college: ita quod dicto prioratu vacante liceat iis ex tunc to take possession," &c. This libel, with the express consent of the other proctors, we, the commissary, admitted, and appointed the 6th of August for proctor Preston to prove the premisses.

Preston produced witnesses, W. Gyfford, S. T. P., John Nele, A.M., John Chapman, chaplain, and Robert Baron, literatus, who were admitted and sworn, when the court was prorogued to the 6th of August; and the witnesses, on the same 5th of August, were examined by the commissary, "in capella infra manerium de Essher situata, secrete et singillatim." Then follow the "literæ procuratoriæ:" first that of the college, appointing Preston and Langport their proctors, dated August

30th, 1484; then that of the prior and convent of the cathedral
of Winton, appointing David Husband and Michael Cleve,
dated September 4th, 1484 : then that of the bishop, appointing
W. Gyfford, Radulphus Langley, and Will. Cowper, dated
September 3rd, 1484. Consec. 38°.—"Quo die adveniente in
dicta ecclesia parochiali," appeared "coram nobis" James
Preston to prove the contents of his libel, and exhibited some
letters testimonial with the seal of the bishop, and these were
admitted ; and consequenter Preston produced two witnesses,
viz. Dominum Thomam Ashforde *nuper priorem dicti prioratus*,
et Willm. Rabbys literatum, who were admitted and sworn, and
examined as the others, by the commissary ; "tunc & ibidem
assistente scriba secrete & singillatim;" and their depositions
were read and made public, as follows :

Mr. W. Gyfford, S. T. P. aged 57, of the state of Magd. Coll.
&c. &c. as before :

Mr. John Nele, aged 57, proves the articles also :

Robert Baron, aged 56 :

Johannes Chapman, aged 35, also affirmed all the five articles :

Dompnus Thomas Ashforde, aged 72 years—"dicit 2^{dum} 3um
4um articulos in eodem libello contentos, concernentes statum
dicti prioratus de Selebourne, fuisse et esse veros."

W. Rabbys, ætat. 40 ann. agrees with Gyfford, &c.

Then follows the letter from the bishop, "in subsidium pro-
bationis," above mentioned—"Willmus, &c. salutem, &c. noverint
universitas vestra, quod licet nos prioratui de Selebourne, &c.
pie compacientes sollicitudines pastorales, labores, diligentias
quamplurimas per nos & commissarios nostros pro reformatione
status ejus impenderimus, justicia id poscente; nihilominus
tamen," &c. as in the article—to "desperatur," dated "in manerio nostro de Essher, Aug. 3d. 1485, & consec. 39." Then, on
the 6th of August, Preston; in the presence of the other proctors,
required that they should be compelled to answer; when they
all allowed the articles "fuisse & esse vera;" and the commissary, at the request of Preston, concluded the business, and
appointed Monday, Aug. 8th, for giving his decree in the same
church of Essher ; and it was that day read, and contains a
recapitulation, with the sentence of union, &c. witnessed and
attested.

As soon as the president and fellows of Magdalen College had
obtained the decision of the commissary in their favour, they
proceeded to supplicate the pope, and to entreat his holiness that

he would give his sanction to the sentence of union. Some difficulties were started at Rome; but they were surmounted by the college agent, as appears by his letters from that city. At length Pope Innocent VIII. by a bull [1] bearing date the 8th day of June, in the year of our Lord 1486, and in the second year of his pontificate, confirmed what had been done, and suppressed the convent.

Thus fell the considerable and well endowed Priory of Selborne after it had subsisted about two hundred and fifty-four years; about seventy-four years after the suppression of Priories alien by Henry V., and about fifty years before the general dissolution of monasteries by Henry VIII. The founder, it is probable, had fondly imagined that the sacredness of the institution, and the pious motives on which it was established, might have preserved it inviolate to the end of time—yet it fell,

> "To teach us that God attributes to *place*
> No sanctity, if none be thither brought
> By men who there frequent, or therein dwell."
> MILTON's "Paradise Lost."

LETTER XXV.

WAINFLEET did not long enjoy the satisfaction arising from this new acquisition; but departed this life in a few months after he had effected the union of the Priory with his late founded college; and was succeeded in the see of Winchester by Peter Courtney, some time towards the end of the year 1486.

In the beginning of the following year the new bishop released the president and fellows of Magdalen College from all actions respecting the Priory of Selborne; and the prior and convent of St. Swithin, as the chapter of Winchester cathedral, confirmed the release.[2]

[1] There is nothing remarkable in this bull of Pope Innocent except the statement of the annual revenue of the Priory of Selborne, which is therein estimated at 160 *flor. auri*; whereas Bishop Godwin sets it at 337*l.* 15*s.* 6¼*d.* Now a floren, so named, says Camden, because made by Florentines, was a gold coin of King Edward III. in value 6*s.* whereof 160 is not one-seventh part of 337*l.* 15*s.* 6¼*d.*

[2] The bishops of Winchester were patrons of the Priory.

N. 293. "Relaxatio Petri ēpi Wintōn Ricardo Mayew, Presidenti omnium actionum occasione indempnitatis sibi debite pro unione Prioratus de Selborne dicto collegio. Jan. 2. 1487. et translat. anno 1°."

N. 374. "Relaxatio *prioris* et *conventus* S^u Swithini Wintōn confirmans relaxationem Petri ep. Winton." 1487. Jan. 13.

Ashforde, the deposed prior, who had appeared as an evidence for the impropriation of the Priory at the age of seventy-two years, that he might not be destitute of a maintenance, was pensioned by the college to the day of his death ; and was living on till 1490, as appears by his acquittances.

Reg. A. ff. 46.

"Omnibus Christi fidelibus ad quos presens scriptum pervenerit, Richardus Mayew, presidens, &c. et scolares, salutem in Domino.

"Noveritis nos prefatos presidentem et scolares dedisse, concessisse, et hoc presenti scripto confermasse Thome Ashforde, *capellano*, quendam annualem redditum sex librarum tresdecim solidorum et quatuor denariorum bone et legalis monete Anglie —ad terminum vite prefati Thome"—to be paid from the possessions of the college in Basingstoke.—"In cujus rei testimonium sigillum nostrum commune presentibus apponimus. Dat. Oxon. in coll. nostro supra dicto primo die mensis Junii anno regis Ricardi tertii secundo, viz. 1484." The college, in their grant to Ashforde, style him only *capellanus ;* but the annuitant very naturally, and with a becoming dignity, asserts his late title in his acquittances, and identifies himself by the addition of *nuper priorem,* or late prior.

As, according to the persuasion of the times, the depriving the founder and benefactors of the Priory of their masses and services would have been deemed the most impious of frauds, Bishop Wainfleet, having by statute ordained four obits for himself to be celebrated in the chapel of Magdalen College, enjoined in one of them a special collect for the anniversary of Peter de Rupibus, with a particular prayer—"*Deus Indulgentiarum.*"

The college also sent Nicholas Langrish, who had been a chantry priest at Selborne, to celebrate mass for the souls of all that had been benefactors to the said Priory and college, and for all the faithful who had departed this life.

N. 356. Thomas Knowles, presidens, &c.—"damus et concedimus Nicholao Langrish quandum capellaniam, vel salarium, sive alio quocunque nomine censeatur, in prioratu *quondam* de Selborne pro termino 40 annorum, si tam diu vixerit. Ubi dictis mag^r. Nicholaus celebrabit pro animabus omnium benefactorum. Insuper nos, &c. concedimus eidem ibidem celebranti in sustentationem suam quandam annualem pensionem sive annuitatem octo librarum, &c.—in dicta capella dicti prioratus —concedimus duas cameras contiguas ex parte boreali dicte capelle, cum *una coquina*, et cum uno stabulo conveniente pro tribus equis, cum pomerio eidem adjacente voc. le Orcheyard— Preterea 26*s*. 8*d*. per ann. ad inveniendum unum clericum ad serviendum sibi ad altare, et aliis negotiis necessariis ejus."— His wood to be granted him by the president on the progress.— He was not to absent himself beyond a certain time; and was to superintend the coppices, wood, and hedges.—"Dat. 5to. die Julii, an°, Hen. VIII^{vi}. 36°." [viz. 1546.]

Here we see the Priory in a new light, reduced as it were to the state of a chantry, without prior and without canons, and attended only by a priest, who was also a sort of bailiff or woodman, his assistant clerk, and his female cook. Owen Oglethorpe, president, and Magd. Coll. in the fourth year of Edward VI. viz. 1551, granted an annuity of ten pounds a year for life to Nich. Langrish, who, from the preamble, appears then to have been fellow of that society: but, being now superannuated for business, this pension is granted him for thirty years, if he should live so long. It is said of him—"cum jam sit provectioris etatis quam ut," &c.

Laurence Stubb, president of Madg. Coll., leased out the Priory lands to John Sharp, husbandman, for the term of twenty years, as early as the seventeenth year of Henry VIII.—viz. 1526; and it appears that Henry Newlyn had been in possession of a lease before, probably towards the end of the reign of Henry VII. Sharp's rent was vi^{li}. per annum.—Regist. B. p. 43.

By an abstract from a lease lying before me, it appears that Sharp found a house, two barns, a stable, and a duf-house [dove-house], built, and standing on the south side of the old Priory, and late in the occupation of Newlyn. In this abstract also are to be seen the names of all the fields, many of which

continue the same to this day.[1] Of some of them I shall take
notice where anything singular occurs.

And here first we meet with Paradyss [Paradise] Mede.
Every convent had its Paradise; which probably was an enclosed orchard, pleasantly laid out, and planted with fruit trees.
Tylehouse Grove, so distinguished from having a tiled house
near it.[2] Butt-wood close; here the servants of the Priory
and the village swains exercised themselves with their long
bows, and shot at a mark against a butt, or bank.[3] Cundyth
[conduit] Wood : the engrosser of the lease not understanding
this name has made a strange barbarous word of it. Conduit
Wood was and is a steep rough cow-pasture, lying above the
Priory, at about a quarter of a mile to the south-west. In the
side of this field there is a spring of water that never fails ; at
the head of which a cistern was built which communicated with
leaden pipes that conveyed water to the monastery. When
this reservoir was first constructed does not appear, we only
know that it underwent a repair in the episcopate of Bishop
Wainfleet, about the year 1462.[4] Whether these pipes only
conveyed the water to the Priory for common and culinary
purposes, or contributed to any matters of ornament and
elegance, we shall not pretend to say ; nor when artists and
mechanics first understood anything of hydraulics, and that
water confined in tubes would rise to its original level. There
is a person now living who had been employed formerly in
digging for these pipes, and once discovered several yards,
which they sold for old lead.

[1] It may not be amiss to mention here that various names of tithings,
farms, fields, woods, &c. which appear in the ancient deeds, and evidences of
several centuries standing, are still preserved in common use with little or no
variation :—as Norton, Southington, Durton, Achangre, Blackmore, Bradshot,
Rood, Plestor, &c., &c. At the same time it should be acknowledged that
other places have entirely lost their original titles, as Le Buri and Trucstede
in this village ; and La Liega, or Lo Lyge, which was the name of the original
site of the Priory, &c.

[2] Men at first heaped sods, or fern, or heath, on their roofs to keep off the
inclemencies of the weather; and then by degrees laid straw or haum. The
first refinements on roofing were shingles, which are very ancient. Tiles are
a very late and imperfect covering, and were not much in use till the beginning of the sixteenth century. The first tiled house at Nottingham was in
1503.

[3] There is also a Butt-close just at the back of the village.

[4] V. 381. "Clausure terre abbatie ecclesie parochiali de Seleburne, ixs.
iiii*d*. Reparacionibus demorum predicti prioratus iiii. *lib.* xi*s.* *Aque conduct.*
ibidem. xxiii*d.*

There was also a plot of ground called Tan House Garden: and "*Tannaria sua,*" a tan-yard of their own, has been mentioned in Letter XVI. This circumstance I just take notice of, as an instance that monasteries had trades and occupations carried on within themselves.[1]

Registr. B. pag. 112. Here we find a lease of the parsonage of Selborne to Thomas Sylvester and Miles Arnold, husbandmen —of the tythes of all manner of corne pertaining to the personage—with the offerings at the chapel of Whaddon, belonging to the said parsonage. Dat. June 1. 27th. Hen. 8th. [viz. 1536.]

As the chapel at Whaddon has never been mentioned till now, and as it is not noticed by Bishop Tanner in his "Notitia Monastica," some more particular account of it will be proper in this place. Whaddon was a chapel of ease to the mother church of Selborne, and was situated in the tithing of Oakhanger, at about two miles distance from the village. The farm and field whereon it stood are still called Chapel Farm and Field :[2] but there are no remains or traces of the building itself, the very foundations having been destroyed before the memory of man. In a farm yard at Oakhanger we remember a large hollow stone of a close substance, which had been used as a hog-trough, but was then broken. This stone, tradition said, had been the baptismal font of Whaddon chapel. The chapel had been in a very ruinous state in old days; but was new-built at the instance of Bishop Wainfleet, about the year 1463, during the first priorship of Berne, in consequence of a sequestration issued forth by that visitor against the Priory on account of notorious and shameful dilapidations.[3]

The Selborne rivulet becomes of some bread that Oakhanger, and, in very wet seasons, swells to a large flood. There is a bridge over the stream at this hamlet of considerable antiquity and peculiar shape, known by the name of Tunbridge: it consists of one single blunt Gothic arch, so high and sharp as to render the passage not very convenient or safe. Here was also,

---

[1] There is still a wood near the Priory, called Tanner's Wood.

[2] This is a manor-farm, at present the property of Lord Stawell; and belonged probably in ancient times to Jo. de Venur, or Venuz, one of the first benefactors to the Priory.

[3] See Letter XIX. of these Antiquities.—"Summa total. solut. de novis edificationibus, et reparacionibus per idem tempus, ut pates per comput."

"Videlicet de nova edificat. Capelle Marie de Wadden. xiiii. *lib.* v. *s.* viii. *d.*—Reparacionibus ecclesie Prioratus, cancellor. et capellar. ecclesiarum et capellarum de Selborne, et Estwarhlam."—&c. &c.

we find, a bridge in very early times; for Jacobus de Hochangre, the first benefactor to the Priory of Selborne, held his estate at Hochangre by the service of providing the king one foot soldier for forty days, and by building the bridge. "Jacobus de Hochangre tenet Hochangre in com. Southampton, *per Serjantiam*,[1] inveniendi unum valectum in exercitu Domini regis [scil. Henrici III^{tii}] per 40 dies; et ad faciendum *pontem* de Hochangre: et valet per ann. C. s."—BLOUNT's *Ancient Tenures*, p. 84.

A dove-house was a constant appendant to a manorial dwelling: of this convenience more will be said hereafter.

A corn-mill was also esteemed a necessary appendage of every manor; and therefore was to be expected of course at the Priory of Selborne.

The prior had *secta molendini*, or *ad molendinum*:[2] a power of compelling his vassals to bring their corn to be ground at his mill, according to old custom. He had also, according to Bishop Tanner, *secta molondini de* Strete: but the purport of Strete, we must confess, we do not understand. Strete, in old English, signifies a road or highway, as Watling Strete, &c. therefore the prior might have some mill on a high road. The Priory had only one mill originally at Selborne; but, by grants of lands, it became possessed of one at Durton, and one at Oakhanger, and probably some on its other several manors.[3] The mill at the Priory was in use within the memory of man, and the ruins of the mill-house were standing within these thirty years: the pond and dam, and miller's dwelling, still remain. As the stream was apt to fail in very dry summers, the tenants found their situation very distressing, for want of water, and so were forced to abandon the spot. This inconvenience was probably never felt in old times, when the whole district was nothing but woodlands: and yet several centuries ago there seem to have been two or three mills between Well-head and the Priory. For the reason of this assertion, see Letter XXIX. to Mr. Barrington.

---

[1] *Sargentia*, a sort of tenure of doing something for the king.
[2] "Servitium, quo feudatorii grana sua ad Domini molendinum, ibi molenda perferre, ex consuetudine, astringuntur."
[3] Thomas Knowles, president, &c. ann. Hen. 8vi. xxiii.° [viz. 1532.] demised to J. Whitelie their mills, &c. for twenty years. Rent xxiiis. iiid.— Accepted Frewen, president, &c. ann. Caroli xv. [viz. 1640] demised to Jo. Hook and Elizabeth, his wife, the said mills. Rent as above.

Occasional mention has been made of the many privileges and immunities enjoyed by the convent and its priors ; but a more particular statement seems to be necessary.   The author therefore thinks this the proper place, and before he concludes these antiquities, to introduce all that has been collected by the judicious Bishop Tanner, respecting the Priory and its advantages, in his "Notitia Monastica," a book now seldom seen, on account of the extravagance of its price ; and being but in a few hands cannot be easily consulted.[1]   He also adds a few of its many privileges from other authorities :—the account is as follows (Tanner, page 166) :—

SELEBURNE.

A Priory of black canons, founded by the often-mentioned Peter de Rupibus, Bishop of Winchester, A.D. 1233, and dedicated to the Blessed Virgin Mary : but was suppressed—and granted to William Wainfleet, Bishop of Winchester, who made it part of the endowment of St. Mary Magdalen College in Oxford.   The Bishops of Winchester were patrons of it.   [Pat. 17. Edw. II.]—Vide in Mon.   Angl. tom. ii. p. 343.   "Cartan fundationis ex ipso autographo in archivis Coll. Magd. Oxōn. ubietiam conservata sunt registra, cartæ, rentalia et alia munimenta ad hunc prioratum spectantia.

"Extracta quædam e registro MSS. in Bibl. Bodl.—Dodsworth, vol. 89. f. 140."

"Cart. antiq. N. N. n. 33. P. P. n. 48. et 71. Q. Q. n. 40. plac. coram justit. itin. [Southampton] 20 Hen. rot. 25.   De eccl. de Basing, & Basingstoke.   Plac. de juratis apud Winton. 40 Hen. III. rot.—Prosecta molendini de Strete. Cart. 54. Hen. III. m. 3. [*De mercatu, & feria apud* Selborne, a mistake.]   Pat. 9. Edw. I. m.—Pat. 30. Edw. 1. m.   Pat. 33. Edw. 1. p. 1. m.— Pat. 35. Edw. I. m.—Pat. 1. Edw. II. p. 1. m. 9.   Pat. 5. Edw. II. p. 1. m. 21.   De terris in Achanger.   Pat. 6. Edw. II. p. 1. m. 7. de eisdem. Brev. in Scacc. 6 Edw. II. Pasch. rot. 8.   Pat. 17. Edw. II. p. 1. m.—Cart. 10. Edw. III. n. 24.   Quod terræ suæ in Seleburn, Achangre, Norton, Basings, Basingstoke, and Nately, sint de afforestatæ, and pro aliis libertatibus.   Pat. 12.

---

[1] A few days after this was written a new edition of this valuable work was announced, in the month of April of the year 1787, as published by Mr. Nasmith.

Edw. III. p. 3. m. 3.—Pat. 13. Edw. III. p. 1. m.—Cart. 18. Edw. III. n. 24."

" N. N. 33. Rex concessit quod prior, et canonici de Seleburn habeant per terras suas de Seleburne, Achangre, Norton, Brompden, Basinges, Basingstoke, & Nately, diversas libertates.

" P. P. 48.   Quod prior de Selburne, habeat terras suas quietas de vasto, et regardo."—Extracts from Ayloffe's Calendars of Ancient Charters.

" Placita de juratis & assis coram Salōm   Roff, & sociis suis justic. itiner. apud Wynton in comitatu Sutht.—anno regni R. Edvardi filii reg. Henr. octavo.—Et Por de Seleborn ht in Selebr. *fure. thurset. pillory, emendasse pants, & suis.*" [cerevisiæ.] —Chapter House, Westminster.

" Placita Foreste apud Wyntōn in com. Sutham.—Anno reg. Edwardi octavo coram Rog. de Clifford.—&c. Justic. ad eadem placita audienda et tminand. assigtis.

" Carta Pror de Seleburn, H. Dei gra. rex. angl. &c.   Concessim. prior. sce. Marie de Seleburn. et canonicis ibidem Deo servient. . . . . q ipi et oes hoies sui in pdcis terri suis et tenementis manentes sint in ppetum quieti de sectis Swanemotor. et omnium alior. placitor. for. et de *espeltamentis* canum. et de omnibus submonitoibz placitis querelis et exaccoibus et occoibz. ad for. et for. et viridar. et eor. ministros ptinentibz."— Chapter House, Westminster.

" Plita Forestarum in com. Sutht. apud Suthamton . . . . . . anno regni regis Edwardi tcii post conquestum quarto coram Johe Mantvers. &c. justic. itinand &c.

" De hiis qui clamant libtates infra Forestas in com Sutht.

" Prior de Selebourne clamat esse quietus erga dnm regem de omnibus finibus et amerciamentis p tnsgr. et omnibus exaccoibz ad Dom. regem vel hered. suos ptinent, pret. plita corone reg.

" Item clamat q^d si aliquis hominum suorum de terris. et ten. p. delicto suo vitam aut membrum debeat amittere vel fugiat, & judico stare noluerit vel aliud delictum fecit pro quo debeat catella sua amittere, ubicunq ; justitia fieri debeat omnia catella illa sint ptci Prioris et successor. suor.   Et liceat eidem priori et ballis suis ponere se in seisinam in hujusmodi catall. in casibus pdcis sine disturbacone ballivor. dni reg. quorumcunque.

" Item clam. quod licet aliqua libtatum p dnm regem con-
cessar. pcessu temporis quocunq ; casu contingente usi non
fuerint, nlominus postea eadm libtate uti possit. Et pdcus prior
quesitus p justic. quo waranto clamat omn. terr. et. ten. sua
in Seleburne, Norton, Basynges, Basyngestoke, & Nattele, que
prior domus pdte huit & tenuit X^{mo}. die April anno regni dni
Hen. reg. pavi dni reg. nue XVIII. imppm esse quieta de
vastro et regardo, et visu forestarior. et viridarior regardator.
et omnium ministrorum foreste." &c. &c.—Chapter House,
Westminster.

LETTER XXVI.

THOUGH the evidences and documents of the Priory and parish
of Selborne are now at an end, yet, as the author has still
several things to say respecting the present state of that convent
and its Grange, and other matters, he does not see how he
can acquit himself of the subject without trespassing again
on the patience of the reader by adding one supplementary
letter.

No sooner did the Priory (perhaps much out of repair at the
time) become an appendage to the college, but it must at once
have tended to swift decay. Magdalen College wanted now
only two chambers for the chantry priest and his assistant ; and
therefore had no occasion for the hall, dormitory, and other
spacious apartments belonging to so large a foundation. The
roofs, neglected, would soon become the possession of daws and
owls ; and, being rotted and decayed by the weather, would fall
in upon the floors ; so that all parts must have hastened to
speedy dilapidation and a scene of broken ruins. Three full
centuries have now passed since the dissolution ; a series of
years that would craze the stoutest edifices. But, besides the
slow hand of time, many circumstances have contributed to
level this venerable structure with the ground ; of which nothing
now remains but one piece of a wall about ten feet long, and
as many feet high, which probably was part of an out-house.
As early as the latter end of the reign of Hen. VII. we find

that a farm-house and two barns were built to the south of the
Priory, and undoubtedly out of its materials. Avarice, again,
has much contributed to the overthrow of this stately pile, as
long as the tenants could make money of its stones or timbers.
Wantonness, no doubt, has had a share in the demolition; for
boys love to destroy what men venerate and admire. A remarkable instance of this propensity the writer can give from
his own knowledge. When a schoolboy, more than fifty years
ago, he was eyewitness, perhaps a party concerned, in the un-
dermining a portion of that fine old ruin at the north end of
Basingstoke town, well known by the name of Holy Ghost
Chapel. Very providentially the vast fragment, which these
thoughtless little engineers endeavoured to sap did not give
way so soon as might have been expected; but it fell the night
following, and with such violence that it shook the very ground,
and, awakening the inhabitants of the neighbouring cottages,
made them start up in their beds as if they had felt an earthquake. The motive for this dangerous attempt does not so
readily appear: perhaps the more danger the more honour,
thought the boys; and the notion of doing some mischief
gave a zest to the enterprise. As Dryden says upon another
occasion—

"It look'd so like a sin it pleased the more."

Had the Priory been only levelled to the surface of the
ground, the discerning eye of an antiquary might have ascertained its ichnography, and some judicious hand might have
developed its dimensions. But, beside other ravages, the very
foundations have been torn up for the repair of the highways:
so that the site of this convent is now become a rough, rugged
pasture-field, full of hillocks and pits, choked with nettles and
dwarf-elder, and trampled by the feet of the ox and the heifer.
As the tenant at the Priory was lately digging among the
foundations, for materials to mend the highways, his labourers
discovered two large stones, with which the farmer was so
pleased that he ordered them to be taken out whole. One of
these proved to be a large Doric capital, worked in good taste;
and the other a base of a pillar; both formed out of the soft
freestone of this district. These ornaments, from their dimensions,
seem to have belonged to massive columns; and show that the
church of this convent was a large and costly edifice. They

were found in the space which has always been supposed to have
contained the south transept of the Priory church.   Some
fragments of large pilasters were also found at the same time.
The diameter of the capital was two feet three inches and a half;
and of the column, where it had stood on the base, eighteen
inches and three quarters.

Two years ago some labourers digging again among the ruins
found a sort of rude thick vase or urn of soft stone, containing
about two gallons in measure, on the verge of the brook, in the
very spot which tradition has always pointed out as having been
the site of the convent kitchen.   This clumsy utensil,[1] whether
intended for holy water, or whatever purpose, we were going to
procure, but found that the labourers had just broken it in pieces,
and carried it out on the highways.

The Priory of Selbourne had possessed in this village a Grange,
a usual appendage to manorial estates, where the fruits of their
lands were stowed and laid up for use, at a time when men took
the natural produce of their estates in kind.   The mansion of
this spot is still called the Grange, and is the manor-house of
the convent possessions in this place.   The author has conversed
with very ancient people who remembered the old original
Grange; but it has long given place to a modern farm-house.
Magdalen College holds a court-leet and court-baron[2] in the great
wheat-barn of the said Grange, annually, where the president
usually superintends, attended by the bursar and steward of the
college.[3]

The following uncommon presentment at the court is not
unworthy of notice.   There is on the south side of the king's
field (a large common field so called) a considerable tumulus, or
hillock, now covered with thorns and bushes, and known by the
name of Kite's Hill, which is presented, year by year, in court
as not ploughed.   Why this injunction is still kept up respecting

---

[1] A judicious antiquary, who saw this vase, observed, that it possibly
might have been a standard measure between the monastery and its
tenants.   The Priory we have mentioned claimed the assize of bread and
beer in Selborne manor: and probably the adjustment of dry measures
for grain, &c.

[2] The time when this court is held is the mid-week between Easter and
Whitsuntide.

[3] Owen Oglethorp, president, &c. an. Edw. Sexti, primo [viz. 1547] demised
to Robert Arden, Selborne Orange, for twenty years.   Rent v^{li}.—Index of
Leases.

this spot, which is surrounded on all sides by arable land, may be a question not easily solved, since the usage has long survived the knowledge of the intention thereof. We can only suppose that as the prior, besides *thurset* and *pillory*, had also *furcas*, a power of life and death, that he might have reserved this little eminence as the place of execution for delinquents. And there is the more reason to suppose so, since a spot just by is called Galley [Gallows] Hill.

The lower part of the village next the Grange, in which is a pond and a stream, is well known by the name of Gracious Street, an appellation not at all understood. There is a lake in Surrey, near Chobham, called also Gracious Pond; and another, if we mistake not, near Hedleigh, in the county of Hants. This strange denomination we do not at all comprehend, and conclude that it may be a corruption from some Saxon word, itself perhaps forgotten.

It has been observed already, that Bishop Tanner was mistaken when he refers to an evidence of Dodsworth, "*De mercatu et* FERIA *de* Seleburne." Selborne never had a chartered fair; the present fair was set up since the year 1681, by a set of jovial fellows, who had found in an old almanack that there had been a fair here in former days on the 1st of August; and were desirous to revive so joyous a festival. Against this innovation the vicar set his face, and persisted in crying it down, as the probable occasion of much intemperance. However the fair prevailed; but was altered to the 29th of May, because the former day often interfered with wheat harvest. On that day it still continues to be held, and is become a useful mart for cows and calves. Most of the lower housekeepers brew beer against this holiday, which is dutied by the exciseman; and their becoming victuallers for the day without a licence is overlooked.

Monasteries enjoyed all sorts of conveniences within themselves. Thus at the Priory, a low and moist situation, there were ponds and stews for their fish: at the same place also, and at the Grange in Culver Croft,[1] there were dove-houses; and on the hill opposite to the Grange the prior had a warren, as the names of the Coney Crofts and Coney Croft Hanger plainly testify.[2]

Nothing has been said as yet respecting the tenure or holding

---

[1] Culver, as has been observed before, is Saxon for a pigeon.
[2] A warren was a usual appendage to a manor.

of the Selborne estates.   Temple and Norton are manor farms
and freehold ; as is the manor of Chapel near Oakhanger, and
also the estate at Oakhanger House and Blackmoor.   The
Priory and Grange are leasehold under Magdalen College, for
twenty-one years, renewable every seven: all the smaller
estates in and round the village are copyhold of inheritance
under the college, except the little remains of the Gurdon
manor, which had been of old leased out upon lives, but have
been freed of late by their present lord, as fast as those lives
have dropped.

ROGATE CHURCH.

Selborne seems to have derived much of its prosperity from
the near neighbourhood of the Priory.   For monasteries were of
considerable advantage to places where they had their sites and
estates, by causing great resort, by procuring markets and fairs,
by freeing them from the cruel oppression of forest-laws, and by
letting their lands at easy rates.   But, as soon as the convent
was suppressed, the town which it had occasioned began to
decline, and the market was less frequented ; the rough and
sequestered situation gave a check to resort, and the neglected
roads rendered it less and less accessible.

That it had been a considerable place for size formerly
appears from the largeness of the church, which much exceeds
those of the neighbouring villages ; by the ancient extent of the
burying ground, which, from human bones occasionally dug up,
is found to have been much encroached upon ; by giving a name
to the hundred : by the old foundations and ornamented stones
and tracery of windows that have been discovered on the
north-east side of the village ; and by the many vestiges of
disused fish-ponds still to be seen around it.   For ponds and
stews were multiplied in the times of popery, that the affluent
might enjoy some variety at their tables on fast days ; therefore
the more they abounded the better probably was the condition of
the inhabitants.

SUN-DIAL IN GILBERT WHITE'S GARDEN.

APPENDIX

ON THE

ROMAN-BRITISH ANTIQUITIES OF SELBORNE.

MAP OF SELBORNE PARISH.

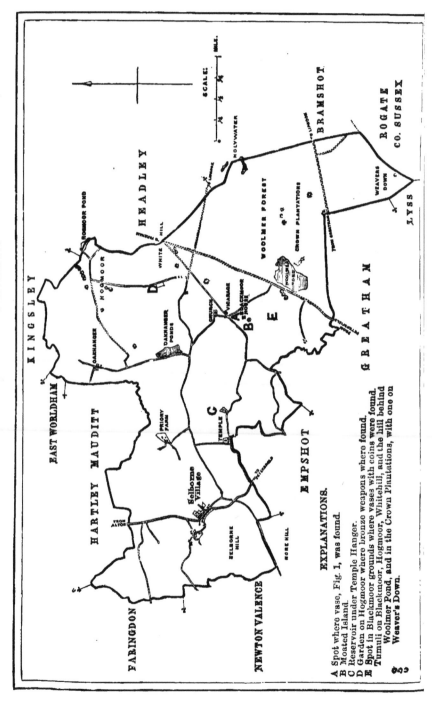

EXPLANATIONS.

A Spot where vase, Fig. 1, was found.
B Moated Island.
C Reservoir under Temple Hanger.
D Garden on Hogmoor where bronze weapons where found.
E Spot in Blackmoor grounds where vases with coins were found.
Tumuli on Blackmoor, Hogmoor, Whitehill, and the hill behind Woolmer Pond, and in the Crown Plantations, with one on Weaver's Down.

APPENDIX.

By LORD SELBORNE.

THE conclusion, drawn by White from the discovery of Roman coins during the first half of the last century in the bed of Woolmer pond, that Selborne was not unknown to the Romans ("Antiquities," p. 1), has been abundantly confirmed by other and more recent discoveries.

About the year 1774 (as appears by a letter dated in August, 1777, from Mr. Sewell, then residing at Headley, to Mr. White, for the communication of which I am indebted to the kindness of Professor Bell), a large pot of coins or medals was also found in Woolmer Pond, from which Mr. Sewell obtained a complete series of all the Roman Emperors, from Claudius the First to Commodus (both inclusive), and the two Faustinas, and Crispina, the wife of Commodus, extending over nearly 150 years, from A.D. 43 to A.D. 194. There were none, he says, later than Commodus. And I learn from Mr. Prettejohn (now residing at Yanston in Devonshire), who lived for more than thirty years near Woolmer Pond, and was "foreman" of the Forest for a period including the reign of George the Fourth, that in his time Roman coins were occasionally found in the gravel and sand of Woolmer Pond, on the Blackmoor side, and sometimes also in the old roads and paths in the open Forest, and within the present grounds of Blackmoor House. He himself, and other members of his family, have found more than twenty, among the siftings of gravel, dug to repair the turnpike road by the side of the pond; four of which (being all that he has retained) he has had the goodness to show me. They are much defaced, and the legends are wholly obliterated : but one can be recognized as of the younger Faustina, and one as of Crispina, the Empress of Commodus.

In 1865, having purchased the Temple and Blackmoor estates, I chose for my residence the spot then occupied by Blackmoor

FIG. 1.—LARGE SEPULCHRAL VASE. (*Blackmoor.*)

Farm House, the position of which is shown by the words "Blackmoor House," on the accompanying map. The name "Blackmoor" properly belongs to the western and northern parts of the sandy ridges (raised considerably above the lower level of Woolmer Forest, and themselves overlooked from the

west by the escarpments of the upper green-sand and the still
loftier chalk summits behind them) by which the basin of
Woolmer Forest, where it is crossed by the main road between
Petersfield and Farnham, is enclosed.   To the north-east and
east, the ridges of Blackmoor connect themselves with those of
Hogmoor, Whitehill, and Wall-Down; between which and the
south-eastern and southern ridges, dividing this forest basin from
the valley traversed by the road between Greatham and Liphook
(on which stand fir plantations belonging to the crown), rises the
conspicuous landmark of Holy-Water (or Holly-Water) Clump.
The intermediate low ground, covered with rough heather, and
interspersed here and there with pools of water at certain
seasons, is in breadth about a mile and a half from north to
south, by about two miles in length from east to west.   In a
depression, at the narrowest point between the government
plantations to the south-east and the most southerly part of the
Blackmoor ridges, lies Woolmer Pond ; a shallow lake, nearly
always fordable by man or horse in every part, and varying
with the seasons from a large and broad sheet of water
to a bed of sand, almost entirely dry in times of prolonged
drought.

.All these ridges, and the basin below them, are upon the
formation called by geologists the lower green-sand, which is
naturally barren, or covered only with furze and heath, though
now planted in many places, chiefly with Scotch fir.   But the
westerly ridge of Blackmoor extends back as far as the gault clay,
on which there is abundance of oak and other wood.   At the
exact point of junction between these two formations, at the east
end of Blackmoor Wood, and within the limits of the present
gardens of Blackmoor House, is a small square island, surrounded
by a moat of water ; and behind, and higher than Blackmoor
House, to the north (also included within the present gardens),
is a piece of land formerly called the "Chapel Field."   Here, at
the spot marked A on the map, while the foundations were being
dug in 1867 for a kitchen-garden wall, the first discovery of
Roman, or Roman-British, remains was made.   A large sepulchral
earthenware vase (Fig. 1) was dug up, much broken in the
upper part ; in which were contained a small bronze cup,
enamelled in various colours, nearly perfect ; and the remains
of a bronze patera of extreme thinness, of which what seems
to have been a handle is figured (Fig. 15); also one large
bronze coin, much worn, which is pronounced by competent

authority to be of Lucius Verus.   There were in this vase
some small remains of bones.

In other parts of the gardens and grounds and in digging the
foundations for the house and offices, there were found many
fragments of various articles of Roman pottery, including some
of Samian or imitated from Samian ware; some Roman tiles,

FIG. 2.—WATER VESSEL.—(*Blackmoor.*)

many of which were in the island already mentioned, and
seem to have belonged to flues for the passage of hot water or
air; a bronze Celt or axe-head (Figure 4); a large leaden
ring, such as might have been run through a staple fixed into
a post or wall; and two iron axe-heads: an iron socket for

FIG. 3.—DRINKING CUP.

FIG. 4.—BRONZE CELT.

FIG. 5.—BRONZE RINGS.

FIGS. 3 TO 5.—(*Blackmoor.*)

G G

receiving the head of an axe or other weapon; a large iron
cattle-bell; and fragments of iron nails, &c.   The dates of these
leaden and iron articles (all which were much oxidated) I do not
profess to determine.

In 1868, the moat round the small island (marked B on
the map) was cleaned out; and at the bottom of it were found
a large earthenware water-vessel (Fig. 2, p. 448) and a small
earthenware drinking-cup (Fig. 3, p. 449), both in excellent
preservation.

A reservoir, for the storage of water, was constructed under
the Temple "hanger," at the spot marked C on the map, in
1869–1870; and in digging out this reservoir some further
fragments of Roman pottery were found.

In the spring of 1870, in the garden of a cottage on the
western side of the road ascending from Eveley corner to
Hogmoor, at the spot marked D on the map, a number of bronze
weapons, or parts of weapons (Roman or Roman-British), were
found under peat, free from rust or oxidation. They consisted of
twenty-seven fragments of sword blades, some of which, when
put together, made complete swords; two fragments of sword
sheaths; one grooved socket for connecting a spear-head with
the shaft; eighteen large, and six small, spear-heads; two spear
points; three rings; and two fragments of uncertain use. Most
of the sword handles had bronze nails, evidently intended to
fasten the iron port of the handle to some covering material,
remaining perfect in their holes; and in the cavities of several
of the spear-heads the wooden points, which had been inserted to
fix them in sockets connecting the head with the shaft of the
spear, were still remaining. Some of the edges of these weapons
were hacked and notched, in a manner which could hardly have
resulted from use; and of the sword blades, some had been
forcibly bent, before being broken; proving that those who
buried them had first taken pains to render them useless.
Some of these fragments of swords are figured (Figs. 10, 11,
12, 13, p. 455 with the section); two of the larger and one
of the smaller spear-heads, are figured (Figs. 6, 7, p. 451);
the grooved socket is figured (Fig. 9, p. 451) with a
section; the bronze rings are figured (Fig. 5, p. 449); and
one of the fragments of uncertain use is figured (Fig. 14,
p. 455.)

In the same cottage garden, there have also since been found,
in a fragment of a small earthenware pot, nearly 100 copper

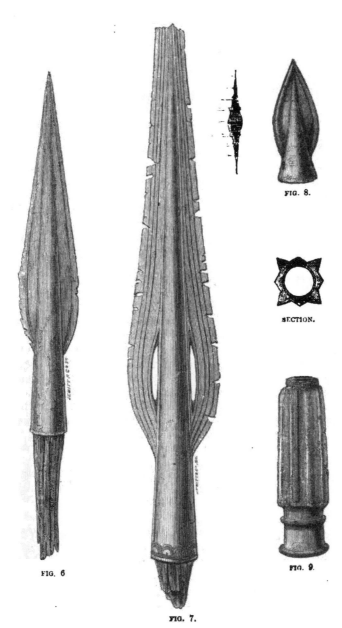

FIG. 8.

SECTION.

FIG. 9.

FIG. 6

FIG. 7.

FIGS. 6 TO 9. - SPEAR HEADS, ETC. —(Blackmoor.)

coins, much defaced, chiefly of the elder Tetricus, but including
a few of his son and of Gallienus and Victorinus.

The next discovery was that of two large earthenware
vases (Figs. 16, 17), which, when perfect, must have
contained considerably more than 30,000 Roman and Roman-
British coins, the number of those which still remained in
them when found, or which were recovered by myself from the
surrounding earth, having been counted at 29,773. They were
buried at the spot marked E on the map, rather less than
half-way between Blackmoor House and Woolmer Pond, where
they were found, covered by about two feet of soil, on the 30th
of October, 1873, by some workmen employed in trenching
ground for a plantation. The upper parts of both vases were
much broken, probably by agricultural operations. The coins
in them were closely caked together (see Fig. 17, showing
part of those in one vase, after many had been removed),
and completely filled what was left of the vases. They were
all coated, more or less, with green oxide of copper. Some
fragments of the broken parts of the vases, and a small piece of
the bottom of a Roman mortar, were soon afterwards found near
the same spot; but nothing else was there discovered.

The coins, on examination, were found to be chiefly bronze
varying from a size rather larger than a shilling to less than
sixpence, those of the same size being often of very unequal
thickness and weight. There were also a large number, principally *denarii*, of or plated with the base metal called by
numismatologists " billon." Of the whole quantity, about one-
third only have been cleaned; 24,985, having been sorted, prove
to be as follows :—

Gordian the younger (emperor A.D. 238—244)	2
Philip the Arabian (emperor A.D. 244—249)	1
Otacilia (wife of Philip)	1
Volusian (son and associate of Gallus, who was emperor A.D. 252—254).	1
Valerian (emperor A.D. 254—260)	25
Gallienus (son and associate of Valerian, and sole emperor from A.D. 260—268	3,209
Salonina (wife of Gallienus)	265
Saloninus (son of Gallienus)	6
Postumus (Tyrant in Britain and Gaul, A.D. 258—265)	294
Lælianus (ditto, A.D. 265)	8
Marius (ditto, A.D. 265)	56
Victorinus (ditto, A.D. 265—268)	4,305[1]

---

[1] There may be some of Postumus (uncleaned) among those of Victorinus.

Tetricus Augustus (ditto, A.D. 268—271) . . . . }	11,254[1]
Tetricus Cæsar (son of Tetricus Augustus) . . . . . . }	
Claudius Gothicus (emperor A.D. 268—270)	3,787[2]
Quintillus (brother of Claudius, emperor A.D. 270)	691
Aurelian (emperor A.D. 270—275)	164
Severina (wife of Aurelian)	14
Tacitus (emperor A.D. 275, 276)	206
Florian (brother of Tacitus, emperor A.D. 276)	22
Probus (emperor A.D. 276—282)	430
Carus (emperor A.D. 282, 283)	12
Carinus (Cæsar A.D. 282 ; emperor 283—285).	24
Numerian (brother and colleague of Carinus)	14
Magnia Urbica (wife of Carinus)	2
Diocletian (emperor A.D. 285—305)	76
Maximian (colleague of Diocletian, A.D. 286—305)	53
Constantius Chlorus (Cæsar A.D. 292 ; became emperor A.D. 305)	1
Carausius (emperor in Britain A.D. 286—294).	502
Allectus (ditto, A.D. 294—296)	82

Total 24,985

Among the coins which have been examined there are 110 (and doubtless there are many more among the rest) which must have come from the mint in an imperfect state, some of them having either no heads or no reverses; some having a reverse on both sides; some twice struck, either with the head of the same prince or with the head of one prince on a coin previously bearing that of another. A large number (4,767 on the whole, most of them, apparently, of the commoner sorts) have been laid aside, as too much defaced to be capable of any satisfactory identification. In Figs. 18–19 two specimens of the coins of Carausius, one of Tacitus, and one of Diocletian, are engraved.

With respect to the condition of these coins, it is worth observation that those of Valerian, Gallienus, Salonina, Claudius, Victorinus, the two Tetrici, and Carausius are generally the most worn and defaced—a fact which as to those of Carausius (almost the latest in the whole series) seems remarkable. All the imperial coins of later date than Aurelian (as also those of Severina, and many of Aurelian himself), and all the coins of Allectus, are comparatively unworn and in fine condition,

[1] The uncleaned coins of the younger Tetricus have not been separated from those of the elder. Of those which have been cleaned, the coins of the elder are to those of the younger in the proportion of 27 to 11.

[2] Some coins of Quintillus may be among the uncleaned coins of Claudius.

except when (as has happened in a few cases) they have sustained accidental damage, from excessive oxidation or adhesion while underground, or in the processes of separation and cleaning. In the legends and reverses, there is great variety, and some specimens are rare, some may perhaps be unique.

This is understood to be the largest deposit of Roman or Roman-British coins ever yet found in Great Britain; and it is rendered still more remarkable by the fact (already referred to), that, in the last century, other large quantities (the number has not been recorded) were found within a quarter of a mile of the same spot, in the bed of Woolmer Pond; some in a large pot, probably similar to the vases above mentioned, and others (being those mentioned by White) not inclosed in any vessel, but appearing to have been hastily thrown or poured into the water in a large heap or heaps. These appear to have been, if not wholly, in part at all events, of earlier date: and they were probably (at least in part) of greater size and value than those found at Blackmoor: for Mr. Sewell speaks of medals, and White speaks of medallions as well as coins; and describes those which he saw as having been in very good condition.

This account of the antiquities discovered in the parish of Selborne would be imperfect without adding that, on the ridges surrounding the forest basin, of which a description has been given, there are (as I reckon them) thirty-five circular tumuli, or sepulchral mounds, some larger than others, but none of very large size; of which eleven are on or near Hogmoor, to the north-east (seven together in one place, three near together in another, and one by itself apart); four are on Whitehill, to the east (three together, close to the high road, and one a little distance apart); one is by itself on the south-easterly projection of the northern Blackmoor Ridge (the ridge on which the church and vicarage-house now stand); five are in a line together at the southern extremity of the western Blackmoor Ridge (close by the high road, overlooking Woolmer Pond); six, close together, are at the top of the opposite hill, on the other side of Woolmer Pond; four, close together, are in the government fir plantations, about a quarter of a mile eastward from the east end of Woolmer Pond; three are in the highest part of the same plantations, to the north-west of the high road from Greatham to Liphook (one apart from the others, to the south-west; the other two close together); and one, remote from all the rest, is on the summit ridge of Weaver's Down, close to the extreme southern boundary

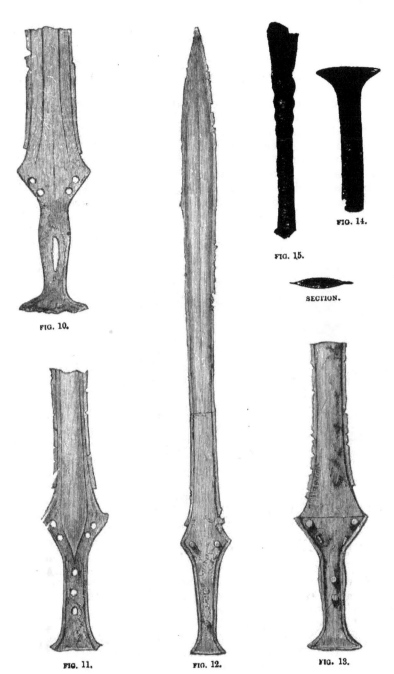

FIG. 10.

FIG. 11.

FIG. 12.

FIG. 13.

FIG. 14.

FIG. 15.

SECTION.

FIGS. 10 TO 15 —SWORD AND SWORD HANDLES, ETC. —'*Blackmoor.*'

of Selborne parish. The positions of these tumuli are marked on the map. Some of them appear to have been much, and all, or almost all of them, more or less disturbed : with what results I have no information, except what I have obtained from Mr. Prettejohn, who was present at the opening of five of them in 1829. He states that Mrs. Barlow, a lady then residing at Midhurst, by the permission of the proper authorities, caused that examination to be made. The first four mounds appeared

FIG. 16.—VASE CONTAINING COINS.—(*Blackmoor.*)

to have been previously explored ; and nothing was found in them, except pieces of charcoal, ashes, calcined bones, and (in one of them within the Brimstone Lodge inclosure) some small fragments of an urn, " old, rotten, decayed, crookey," and seeming to have been sun-dried, and not regularly burnt in a potter's kiln. In the fifth (being the smaller of two upon "Cold-down Hill, not far from Hogmoor Pond and Binn's Pond ") an urn was found, placed on the original level of the ground, covered by a flat stone, and containing (as I infer) calcined human bones or ashes.   Mr. Prettejohn describes it as " of a bilged shape, something between a pitcher and a flower-pot ; " about eleven or twelve inches high, and capable of containing two or three quarts.   It was " in appearance, weak ; " but it was, with care, sent off " by two men to Midhurst " (a distance of twelve miles), " carrying it on a sling on a pole." Mrs. Barstow supposed it to be not only a relic of much interest and value, but of antiquity far greater than Roman-British times : but a friend, learned in these subjects, whom I have consulted, is led, by the description given, to doubt the soundness of that opinion.   No coins were found in any of the tumuli thus examined.

With respect to earlier explorations, all that I can gather, through the recollections of old inhabitants, is, that some of the tumuli on the Forest were opened by a gentleman named Butler, certainly not less than sixty years ago.   I have myself lately opened the largest of those not covered by plantations on my own property ; nothing, however, was found there, except traces of former disturbance of the ground down to the natural level, and a cavity, which might, not improbably, have once contained a sepulchral urn.

It occurs to me also to mention in this place (though their origin, nature, and purpose are obscure) that, immediately, to the south-west of the five tumuli on the Blackmoor Ridge, over-looking Woolmer Pond, are a series of ancient parallel trenches (six or seven in number), of some depth, running nearly north and south from the top of the ridge down to the present high road.   They are certainly not the result of natural or aitificial drainage : and from their number and proximity to each other, they can hardly represent ancient tracks or ways.   Whether they could, under any circumstances, have been intended for military defence, I do not know.

From the pottery and other remains found at and near Black-moor House, it may be concluded with certainty that, on or close to that site, there once stood Roman or Roman-British buildings of some importance ; and the name of the adjoining parish, Greatham, may perhaps indicate the situation (at least as early as Saxon times) of a hamlet or village more consider-able than others in that neighbourhood.   Mr. Sewell, in his letter of 1777 already referred to, speaks of Roman and British entrenchments, as visible at that time on Headley Heath and

Common; and he also describes, as a known historical event (I know not on what authority), a march by Vespasian, as General under Claudius, about A.D. 47, from the neighbourhood of London towards Porchester, Southampton, and the Isle of Wight, by way of Headley and Woolmer; adding, that he (Vespasian) then fixed, at or near Woolmer Pond, "an abiding station or city, which remained near 150 years; when they seem to have been expelled thence by the Britons, or perhaps by an earthquake or some other cause." I have not myself met with any mention of what Mr. Sewell calls "the Roman city or station of Wulmere in Hants," in any writer, ancient or modern, with whose works I am acquainted; and it is possible (as the end of the period of "near 150 years," which he assigns for its continuance, coincides with the time of Commodus, whose coins were the latest which had been found in Woolmer Pond) that his statements, however historical in form, may have been founded upon conjecture.

From the condition of the fragments of weapons found at Hogmoor, and from the circular tumuli on the ridges surrounding the forest basin, it seems, further, to be a probable conjecture that this part of the parish of Selborne was a battle-field in Roman-British times; and the burial of so large a quantity of money in one spot, and the burying and casting away of another quantity (perhaps more valuable) in the water within a quarter of a mile of the same spot (on both sides of which water tumuli now appear), seem to tell a tale of panic and flight. If we ask how so large a number and variety of coins, thus hidden and cast away, came to be brought together (including, as they do, some so imperfectly minted, that they can hardly have been issued for circulation), it occurs to me, as a not improbable supposition, that they may have been hastily collected and carried off from some station in which there was a military chest, and perhaps also a mint, either to provide for the pay of a retreating army, or to prevent them from falling into the hands of an approaching enemy. The Roman Clausentum (now Bittern, near Southampton) was a garrison town, in which there was also a mint, in the times of Carausius and Allectus; some of whose coins, found at Blackmoor, bear the mint-marks of that place. The latest in date of all the coins found are eighty-two of Allectus and a single coin of Constantius Chlorus:—of which the legend is, "FL. VAL. CONSTANTIUS NOB. C." (Flavius Valerius Constantius Nobilis Cæsar); and,

on the reverse, "VIRTUS AUGG." (Virtus Augustorum); with
the device of Hercules leaning on his club, and holding a bow,
with the lion's skin over his arm:—plainly, one of his early
coins, before his accession to the empire.   The date, therefore,
of their deposit cannot have been earlier than the reign of
Allectus; and if it had been later than the re-conquest of
Britain by Constantius, it is not probable that only one coin
of that prince would have been found.

FIG. 17.—VASE CONTAINING COINS.—(*Blackmoor.*)

On the other hand, there would be nothing in the occurrence
among this treasure even of several coins of Constantius, while
only Cæsar, inconsistent with the hypothesis that it may have
belonged to Allectus himself, and may have been buried and cast
away at the time when his retreat from the coast was inter-
cepted by Asclepiodotus, the Prætorian prefect of Constantius,
and when the engagement took place in which Allectus lost his
life.   Constantius was made Cæsar by the Emperor Diocletian,
A.D. 292, four years before his invasion of Britain, while
Carausius was living: and nothing is more probable than that

during the interval coins struck with the effigy of Constantius might obtain currency in Britain.

My own conclusion is, that in the basin of Woolmer Forest, and in the neighbouring ridges and hills, we have probably the scene of important events, of which a narrative, strictly contemporaneous, has been preserved to us, in the panegyric of the orator Eumenius, pronounced in honour of Constantius Cæsar, on his recovery of Britain.

Carausius, a native of the country between the Meuse and the Scheldt, of the same Belgic race by which, as early as the time of Julius Cæsar, Hampshire and the adjoining maritime parts of England were peopled, and a man of high reputation in naval warfare, was intrusted by Diocletian, soon after his succession to the empire, with the defence of the northern coast of Gaul from the incursions, then already frequent, of Saxon and Scandinavian corsairs. This he did successfully; but, being accused of permitting the corsairs to commit depredations, with the view of appropriating the spoil, when recaptured, to his own use, Maximian ordered him to be put to death. Carausius then (A.D. 286) declared himself independent, and established an empire of his own in Britain; retaining also Boulogne and other neighbouring places in Gaul. To Britain he carried over with him the fleet under his command, which had been equipped for the defence of the opposite coast; and he built other ships of war in British ports, manning them with merchant seamen from various parts of Gaul, and with fighting men, attracted to his service from different barbarous nations, whom he instructed in naval as well as military warfare. The Roman legion, or legions, stationed in Britain, acknowledged his sovereignty; which seems, from traces still remaining in various parts of the island, north as well as south, to have extended throughout Great Britain. The condition of this island, improved by two centuries and a half of Roman civilization, was at that time highly prosperous. "Non mediocris" (says Eumenius), "jactura erat reipublicæ terra, tanto frugum ubere, tanto læta munere pastionum, tot metallorum fluens rivis, tot vectigalibus quæstuosa, tot accincta portubus, tanto immensa circuitu." Carausius became a considerable potentate—in naval power, especially, superior to the Romans; who, since their conquest of all the countries bordering on the Mediterranean, had neglected maritime warfare. Maximian in vain attempted an expedition against him; and in A.D. 289 terms of peace were agreed to, by

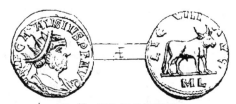

FIG. 18.—COIN OF CARAUSIUS.

FIG. 19.—COIN OF CARAUSIUS.

FIG. 20.—COIN OF TACITUS.

FIG. 21.—COIN OF DIOCLETIAN.

FIGS. 18 TO 21.—COINS.—(*Blackmoor.*)

which that prince and Diocletian recognised him as (in Britain) their partner in the empire.

When, however (A.D. 292), Constantius and Galerius were created "Cæsars" (or presumptive successors to the empire), Constantius, to whom the government of Gaul, Spain, and Britain was assigned, lost no time in attacking Boulogne and reuniting to the empire that and the other continental possessions which Carausius still held. But no invasion of Britain appears to have been then apprehended.

In A.D. 294 Carausius was assassinated by his friend and minister, Allectus, who himself assumed the purple in Britain. Preparations were now made by the Roman emperors for an invasion; and in the third year of Allectus (A.D. 296) Constantius, having collected two fleets of transports, one at Boulogne and the other at the mouth of the Seine, set sail with a considerable force from both ports simultaneously (himself embarking at Boulogne), with contrary winds, and in thick, foggy weather. Part of the expedition lost its way, and eventually sailed up the Thames to London; the main body, with Constantius himself and his Prætorian prefect Asclepiodotus, made for the British coast opposite the Isle of Wight, near which the navy of Allectus was on the look-out for them. Under cover of the fog, that part of the force which was under the command of Asclepiodotus passed unseen by the British fleet, and effected a landing, setting fire, immediately afterwards, to their ships. Allectus, who was in possession of the neighbouring port (doubtless Portsmouth), and encamped upon the shore, hastily abandoned his position, and retreated inland, as soon as the sails of the ships which followed with Constantius came in sight. His retreat was cut off, and his army surprised, after it had advanced some distance into the interior, by the force under Asclepiodotus. The British troops were totally routed, and Allectus and many of his followers were slain; whose bodies, distinguished by their long, fair hair, and gay, barbaric apparel, were found dispersed over hill and plain in various directions—while scarcely one Roman soldier perished. The remnant of the British army made its way to London, intending first to pillage, and then to abandon that city; but, meeting there with those troops of Constantius who had sailed up the Thames, it was put to the sword. And thus Britain was recovered to the Roman empire.

Such (supplying only, from other sources, some of the intro-

ductory facts, with the names of Asclepiodotus and of Carausius,
whom the orator calls the "arch pirate," and Allectus, whom he
styles a "satellite" of Carausius, and the "standard-bearer" of
the rebel party) is the substance of what we learn from Eumenius.
The passages most material to the question of the identity of
the battle-field with Woolmer Forest are subjoined, in the
original Latin.

"Ad tempus ipsum tantæ se dorso maris nebulæ miscuerunt,
"ut inimica classis, apud Vectam insulam in speculis atque
"insidiis collocata, ignorantibus omnino hostibus præteriretur. . .
"Jam vero idem ille vestro auspicio invictus exercitus, statim
"atque Britanniæ litus invaserat, universis navibus suis injecit
"ignes. . . . Ipse autem Signifer nefariæ factionis, cur ab eo
"litore, quod tenebat, abscessit, cur classem portumque deseruit,
"nisi quod te, Cæsar invicte, cujus imminentia vela conspexerat,
"timuit jam jamque venturum? . . . Te tamen ille fugiens,
"incidit in tuorum manus; a te victus, a tuis exercitibus op-
"pressus est.   Denique adeo trepidus, et te post terga respiciens,
"et in modum amentis attoniti properavit in mortem, ut nec
"explicaret aciem, nec omnes copias quas trahebat instruxerit,
"sed cum veteribus illis conjurationis auctoribus, et mercenariis
"cuneis barbarorum, tanti apparatûs oblitus, irruerit.   Adeo,
"Cæsar, hoc etiam reipublicæ tribuit vestra felicitas, ut nemo
"fere Romanus occiderit, Imperio vincente Romano.   Omnes
"enim illos, ut audio, campos atque colles non nisi teterrimorum
"hostium corpora fusa texerunt.   Illa barbara, aut imitatione
"barbariæ olim cultu vestis et prolixo crine rutilantia, tunc
"vero pulvere et cruore fædata, et in diversos situs tracta, sicuti
"dolorem vulnerum fuerant secuta, jacuerunt.   Atque inter hos
"ipse Vexillarius latrocinii, cultu illo quem vivus violaverat
"sponte deposito, et vix unius velaminis repertus indicio.   Adeo
"verum, ubi dixerat, morte vicinâ, ut interfectum se nollet
"agnosci.

"Enimvero, Cæsar invicte, tanto Deorum Immortalium tibi
"est addicta consensu, omnium quidem quos adortus fueris
"hostium, sed præcipue internecio Francorum, ut illi quoque
"milites vestri, qui, per errorem nebulosi (ut paulo ante dixi)
"maris abjuncti, ad oppidum Londiniense pervenerant, quidquid
"ex mercenariâ illâ multitudine barbarorum prælio superfuerunt,
"cum direptâ civitate fugam capessere cogitarent, passim totâ
"urbe confecerint, et non solum provincialibus vestris in cæde
"hostium dederint salutem, sed etiam in spectaculo voluptatem."

The inferences to be drawn from this narrative appear to me to correspond with those which I derive from the evidence of the buried weapons and coins, and the tumuli upon the ridges surrounding the basin of Woolmer Forest. If (as is manifestly probable) Asclepiodotus landed between Portsmouth and Chichester, and if Portsmouth was the harbour near which Allectus took up the position which he so hastily abandoned, he would naturally fall back upon Clausentum (Southampton) and Venta (Winchester), by the ordinary Roman "Iter:" and, after collecting whatever treasure he found in those places, the more southerly road, corresponding with that which now goes by way of Alresford [1] and Alton [2] towards Farnham and London, would probably be that which he would take, as offering the best chance of escape, if he were closely pursued. From Alton, if he heard that Constantius was following him, by turning a few miles to the southward, to the station or settlement which (as has been seen) existed at or near Blackmoor, he would obtain the protection of a country probably then more difficult of access, in the immediate neighbourhood of the great Forest (Sylva Anderida), which certainly extended as far north-west as a part of Rogate, near the southern boundary of Selborne parish. In order to account for his meeting there with the Roman army, under Asclepiodotus, nothing more is required than that we should suppose Constantius, soon after landing, to have ordered his Prætorian præfect to cross the hills, through the country of the Meanvari, in the direction of Alton or Farnham, for the purpose of cutting off the communications between Allectus and the

---

[1] A writer on the antiquities of the neighbourhood of Bicester, Oxon., in Kennett's "Parochial Antiquities," supposes (somewhat fancifully) that the first syllable of the name of Alresford, and of some other places, was derived from Allectus.

[2] Farnham was a military station; whether identical with "Vindomis" or not is a matter of controversy. Alton was certainly a Roman town. About thirty or forty years ago some interesting remains were found there, in ground now occupied as a timber-yard by Messrs. Dyer, some of which are still in the possession of the Messrs. Dyer, and others are in the British Museum. They consisted of several sepulchral vases, set in dishes or saucers; two lachrymatories; a small wooden dice-box; a small lamp; and a signet-ring of onyx, set in gold, which was still (when found) on the calcined bone of the wearer's finger. On this seal are engraved four small figures, set upright, parellel to each other; those in the centre representing an amphora and an ear of bearded corn, between an axe with fasces on one side, and a quiver with arrows on the other. There were also some small pieces of Samian, or British Samian, ware.

military stations to the east and north-east of Winchester. The route which Asclepiodotus would follow, in the execution of such orders, would naturally take him, by Porchester and West Meon[1] (both Roman stations), either to the valley of Petersfield, up which he would move to Woolmer Forest, reversing what Mr. Sewell describes as Vespasian's march, or along the upper level of the chalk hills to Selborne or some point near it, from which he might descend suddenly upon the enemy in Woolmer Forest, unprepared for his approach. The expressions of the orator, "te fugiens," "te post terga respiciens," "incidit in tuorum manus," favour the hypothesis of such a counter-march by Asclepiodotus: and nothing can better agree with the character of the ground, on which I suppose the two armies to have met, than the words, "omnes illos campos atque colles," which "teterrimorum hostium corpora fusa texerunt." The dispersion of the bodies of the fallen, "in diversos situs tracta," agrees also with the positions of the tumuli (some in groups, and some isolated) which, if my identification of the battle-field is correct, may perhaps now cover, or formerly have covered, some of their remains.

S.

BLACKMOOR, *November,* 1874.

[1] There is an earthwork on Old Winchester Hill, at West Meon, supposed to have been the *castra æstiva* of a Roman garrison, in the country of the Meanvari, a tribe whose appellation is still preserved in the names of East and West Meon and Meonstoke. At the meeting of the Archæological Association, held at Winchester in 1845, Colonel Greenwood exhibited a Roman terra-cotta lamp found within this encampment, and some fragments of Roman pottery found in a barrow near it, together with some remains of Roman weapons found at Bramdean, a few miles further north, in the same high chalky district.

INDEX.

INDEX.

A.

Aberdavines, 108
Acclimatizing plants and animals, 203
Ænanthus (*see* Wheatear)
Ænas (*see* Woodpigeon)
Affection among animals, 126, 147, 168
Africa, migration of birds to, 107
Air, elastic at midnight. 198
Alauda pratensis, rearing young cuckoo, 104, 114
Alice Holt Forest, 1, 23, 386; fallow deer in, 19, 24; leased by the Crown, 23; soil of, 24; timber in, 25
Alton, hollow lane leading to, 11, 282; manufactures of, 13
American animals, origin of, 72; junipers, 251
Amphibious animals, 97
Anathoth, an, 200, 247
Ancient burying-ground, 441; vases found at Chapel Field, 447
Andalusia, birds of, 86, 114; stone curlew in, 108
Anguilla (*see* Eel)
Anguis fragilis (*see* Blind Worm)
Animals eating their young, 128
Anne, Queen, in Wolmer Forest, 16
Antelope, double nostril of. 42
Antipathy of birds and animals to their young, 128, 202
Antiquities, at Selborne, 447
'Αντισοργη of birds, 202
Aphides (smother flies), shower of, 235, 258
April, remarkably inclement, 98
Aquaria for fishes, 237
Aquatic plants, 205
Arrows, poisonous, of Indian, 346
Arum, the cuckoo pint, 46; thrush feeding on the roots of, 46
Arun, River, the, 2
Ash tree, ruptured, superstitions concerning, 181
Ashford, last Prior of Selborne, 422
Ashmolean Museum, Oxford, 288
Ash-shrew, 182
Aspen, shiver leaf, old, 282

Asses ploughing, 169
August, the mute month, 155, 314
Augustine Canons, 378
Auk, little, 133
Aweto, the, 848

B.

Bacon-fly, 115
Bank-swallow (*see* Sand martin)
Bank martin (*see* Sand martin)
Baptist, St. John the, little finger of, 411
Barometers, 248
Barragons, manufacture of, 18
Batfowlers, catching birds, 91, 320
Bats, 84, 146; appearance of, in warm weather, 28, 196; hybernation of, 28, 29 tame, 84; food of, 84; drink flying, 84; little, 86; breeding of, 119; anatomy of, 120
Bat, great, new species of, 68; food of, 86
Bean's pond, 20
Bears in Hampshire, 353
Beasts and birds, taming of, 64, 310
Beaufort, Bishop of Winchester, 405; register of. 405
Bees, drink flying, 138; Virgil's, 138, 199; and idiot boy, 179; swarming in hot weather, 192; injured by echoes, 199; insensible to sound, 200; injured by heat and cold; 249; eating honey dew, 257
Bee bird, 111
Beech, the, 1
Beetles, 168
Belfry of Selborne Church, 366
Bell, Professor, 280
Bells in Selborne Church, 366
Berne, Canon, Prior of Selborne, 418; provision for, 421
Bilberry, creeping or Cranberry, 205
Bin's pond, 20; parsonage, 372
Binsted parish, 25
Birdcatcher, experience of a, 288
Birdcatching, modes of, 299, 300,-302, 309, 323, 329, 388

Birds, without English names, 30, 223; influence by colour in choice of food, 31; of passage, 31; settling on ships at sea, 40; colour of, influenced by food, 45, 183, 302; turning black, 45; of summer passage, 49, 74, 81, 104, 106, 111, 141; instinct of, 73, 89, 127, 147, 239; soft-billed (non-migratory), 75; of winter passage, 75, 81; wintering in England, 75; singing after midsummer, 76, 81, 94; motions of, 77, 99, 207, 324; singing, are all Passeres, 82; in full song till midsummer, 82; that sing in the spring, 82; with slight notes, 82; which sing flying, 83; with a song, 83; some tame, others shy, 83; breeding early, 83; in Ascension Island, 83; of Andalusia, 86, 106, 114; singing during incubation, 87; fatten in frosts, 94; pairing of, 96, 339; migration of, influenced by the weather, 96, 98, 324; food of, 97; colour of, changing at breeding time, 99; thick-billed, 98; transport of, on board ship, 100; collections of, contain few soft-billed birds, 100; washing, 103; that dust do not wash, 103; which are pulveratrices, 103; migration of, to Africa, 107; of prey, 111, 155; migration of, over the sea, 111; swarms of different varieties, 128; sing in spring and autumn, 156; drinking, 159; growth of, 169; congregating, 175; dispersion of, 202; destroyed while migrating, 203; notes and language of, 209; migration of, 283; frightened at gloves, 310; arrival of, 312; seen at Zoological Gardens, London, 322; moulting, 314; soft-billed caught in April, 328; migratory, leaving the South Coast, 337

Bird's-nest ophrys, 206
Bittern, 311
Black ant, the, 17
Blackbird, 46; killed by frost, 254; nest of, ornamented with lace, 315; note of, 316; pugnacity of. 316
Blackcap, 30, 34, 87, 141, 157; arrival of, 31, 317; food of, 158, 316; note of, 158; eggs of, 317; nest of, 317
Black dolphin, 115
Black canons, 377
Black game at Selborne, 15
Blackmoor farm, 416; curious custom at, 20
Black rat, old English, 295
Blindworm, 52
Blossoming of plants, 206
Blue-bottle flies, 332
Blue rag, 9
Boars, wild, in Wolmer Forest, 25
Boars, fierce, tamed by losing their tusks, 188
Bogs in Wolmer Forest, 14, 245
Booby, the, 88
Botany, its utility, 203
Botfly, horse, 111
Bowerbird, 316
Boy bee-eater, 192

" Brace birds," 309
Brambling, greater, 84
Breathing of deer, 42; goats, 44
Brighton, fall of cliffs at, 26; bustards at, 104
Brimstone Lodge, 20
Bristowe, D., Vicar of Selborne, bequests of, 375
Brooks and springs at Selborne, 22
Buck, head of, 60
Buffalo, wild, in Wolmer Forest, 25
Bug, harvest, 115
Bullfinch, turning black, 45, 183, 302
Bullhead, 33
Bulrush caterpillar of New Zealand, 348
Buntings, 40, 105
Bunting, reed, 98
Burning the heath, 19
Burnt wood-ashes as manure, 19
Bustards, 83, 104; similar to stone curlew, 108; at Brighton, 104
Butcher bird, great ash-coloured, 132, 309; red-backed, 59, 132, 309; food of, 309; note of, 309
Buteo apivorus or *vespivorus* (see Honey buzzard)
Buzzard, honey, 142, 228
Byfields Charity, 374

C.

Caddis fly, 165
Calculus from stomach of ox, 117
Calendar, naturalists', 263
Call of birds, 209 ɩ
Canaries, 298; naturalized, 86; song of, 298; varieties of, 298
Cancer cured by toads, 56
Cane (see Weasel)
Capons, 188
Caprimulgus (see Goat-sucker)
Carniola, birds of, 98, 101
Carp, 21, 287; tame, 157; in severe weather, 157; large, 292; eggs of, 292
Castration, 187
Caterpillars, 304
Caterpillar, vegetable, of New Zealand, 348
Cats, 189; fond of fish, 157; catching swifts on the wing, 168; suckling a leveret, 189; suckling a squirrel, 190, 323; eating crickets, 225; electric, 256
Cattle frequenting the water, 22; injured by eating yew, 298, 370
Chafers destroying foliage of trees, 114; fern, 67, 120, 157
Chaffinch, 38, 46, 299; separation of sexes, 39, 108, 133; food of, 88; taming, 299; song of, 299
Chaffinches, hen, flock of, 39, 108; migration of, 39
Chalkhills, beautiful, 139
Chantry, what is a, 394
Chapelfield, 384, 432, 447; antiquities found at, 447
Charadrius himantopus (stilt plover ?), 223; *oedicnemus* (see Stone-curlew)

Chaucer, 409
Chiff-chaff, 46, 303
" Chinky-chank" (*see* Chiff-chaff)
Chimney Swallow (*see* Swallow, chimney)
Chinese dogs, 243
Chlora perfoliata (*see* Yellow-wort)
Choughs, Cornish, 104, 132, 337
Chrysomela oleracea (*see* Turnip-fly)
Church at Selborne, 281, 358, 360 ; exterior
  of, 366 ; built out of the eastward posi-
  tion, 368 ; yards, 367 ; trees in, 367 ;
  origin of, 371
Churches, scarcity of, in Sussex, 64
Churn owls (*see* Fern owls)
Churr worm (*see* Mole cricket)
Chrysosplenium oppositifolium (*see* Opposite
  Golden Saxifrage)
Claws of heron, 311
Clay's pond, fossils at, 7
Clock made by General Howe, 23
Cobwebs, shower of, 173
Coccus vitis viniferæ, 233
Coins found in Wolmer pond, 22, 353, 445,
  450
Cold injurious to vegetation, 248
Colour influencing birds' choice of food,
  31 ; of birds influenced by food, 45 ; of
  birds in paring time, 99
Columba livia (blue rock pigeon) 229
Coluber natrix (English snake), 54
Colymbus glacialis (*see* Diver, or loon)
Comarium palustræ (Marsh cinque foil), 205
Comarium (purple), 206
Comb, kept for the use of hinds, 411
Conduit wood, 431
Cornish choughs, 104, 132, 337
Corn mill at Selborne, 433
Cornua Ammonis, 7
Corrodies, meaning of, 401
Corvus monedula (*see* Jackdaw)
Country-made candles, 177
Cow's horn, structure of, 333
Cows congregating, 175
Crabs used for hunting rabbits, 292
Cranberry, 206
Cranmer lake, 21
Cressi Hall heronry, 64, 69
Cricket, eggs of, 217 ; field, 217 ; sex of,
  217 ; wings of, 217, 220, 221 ; chirping of,
  217, 219 ; fen (*see* Cricket, mole) ; mole,
  221 ; house, 219 ; tame, 219 ; food of, 220 ;
  habits of, 220 ; to destroy, 221 ; nest and
  eggs of, 223 ; chewing the cud, 222 ; cry
  of, 221
Crocus (*Sativus crocus*), spring and autumnal, 206
Crops of birds, 314
Cross bills, 33, 104, 142, 296 ; egg of, 105
Cyprinus auratus (gold fish), 237
Crow, 132 ; grey or hooded, 157
Cuckoo, 89, 317 ; choosing a nest, 88, 318 ;
  eggs of, 90, 94 ; skimming flight of, 104 ;
  food of, 104, 114 ; in nest of tit-lark, 104 ;
  reared by *Alauda pratensis*, 114 ; sings in
  different keys, 117 ; when it sings, hawks
  do not prey on other birds, 169 ; anatomy,
  185 ; why it does not hatch eggs, 185 ;
reared by sparrows, 318 ; young of, turning other birds out of nest, 318 ; notes
  of, 317
Cuckoo, pint, the, 46
Curlew, stone (*see* Stone curlew)

D.

Daker-hen (*see* Landrail)
Danewort, 206
Daphne laureola (springe laurel) *Mezereum*
  (Mezereon), 206
Davy, Mr. R., 263
Daw (*see* Jackdaw)
Daws, breeding places of, 62
Deafness of Gilbert White, 171
Decay of Selborne Priory, 412
Deeds dated on Sunday, 395
Deer, fallow (*see* Fallow deer) ; moose (*see*
  Moose deer) ; red (*see* Red deer) ; hunt-
  ing, 16 ; killing a dog, 18
Deer, breathing spiracula of, 42 ; stealers,
  17, 25
Desecration of Communion Tables, 403
Destruction of martins, 188
Destructive frosts, 42, 248, 252, 254
Dew collected by trees, 183
Dipsacus pilosus (Small teasel), 205
Disease in cattle, caused by *Œstrus bovis*,
  66
Diver or loon, 77 ; gait of, 77
Doe, brought up with cows, 175 ; tame,
  chased by dogs, 175
Dogs, killed by deer, 18 ; blinded by cob-
  webs, 173 ; Chinese, 243 ; of South
  America dumb, 243 ; ears of, 244 ; fed on
  vegetables, 244 ; refusing to eat birds
  that they hunt, 244
Dove-ring (*see* Ring-dove) ; Stock (*see*
  Stock-dove)
Dover burnt by the French, 388
Dove, stock, 228 ; house, 228 ; derived from
  blue rock pigeon, 229 ; ring, reared by
  pigeons, 230 ; and pigeons, cross be-
  tween, 230 ; house at Selborne Priory,
  433
Downs, South, 139 ; sheep on the, 140
Dragonfly, 104, 151
Dress of Canons in 1387, protest of Bishop
  Wykeham against, 402
Drinking, mode of, in deer and horses, 42
Drosera rotundifolia (round-leaved sun-
  dew), 205 ; *longifolia*, 205
Ducks, wild, 22, 34 ; King of Denmark's,
  found in England, 112
Dung of cattle, food for fish, 22

E.

Eagle, migration of, 111
Early-breeding birds, 88
Earthquakes in Sicily, 259
Earthworms, 191, 346 ; anatomy of, 347
Eastwick, 87

Echoes, 197, 200, 247; described by Ovid, 197; rules of, 198; described by Virgil, 199; injurious to bees, 199; destroyed by intervening objects, 200; a place of, 200, 247; to make, 200; described by Lucretius, 201
Edward II. in Wolmer Forest, 357
Edward III. in Wolmer Forest, 357
Eels, 21, 88; breeding of, 51, 154; two species of, 154; how to catch, 297
Eft, 52; water, 56; larva of land-eft, 52
Eggs, of carp, number of, 292; in larvæ of insects, 56
Elder, dwarf, 206
Electricity, 260
Elephant tusk, growth of, 290; injured by bullet, 291; tormented by rats. 296; tormented by flies, 332; note of, 836
Elk, European, 98
Elmer, Mr. 23
Elms, broad-leaved or wych hazel, large, 5; wych and English, 285
Emberiza miliaria (bunting), 300
Emberiza nivalis (snowflake), 301
Emshot Church, 4
Entomology, 68, 116
Ephemera (mayflies), 165
Eunuchs, 188
Euonymus Europœus (spindle tree), 156, 205
Eve-churr (*see* Mole-cricket)
Evejar (*see* Fern-owl)
Eyes and ears, large, uses of, 130

F.

Fair at Selborne, 385, 439
Falcons, 30, 32, 35, 242
Falco peregrinus (haggard falcon), 242
Fallow-deer, in Holt Forest, 24; never seen in Wolmer Forest, 25; head of, spiracula in, 42
Fattening of animals during frost, 94
Faustina, Empress, 354
February, called "sprout-cale" by the Saxons, 196
Fellwort, 205
Fens of Lincolnshire, The, 64
Fern-chafers, 66, 120, 157
Fern-owl (*see* Goatsucker)
Field-cricket (*see* Cricket, field)
Fieldfares, 27, 79, 84, 91; feeding in winter, 81, 320; not breeding in England, 84; roost on the ground, 91; breeding in England, 109
Field-mouse, 30, 35, 46; and young, 128; eating nuts, 289
Fish, shell, petrified, 7; at Selborne, 21, 33; dead, why they float, 236; gold, 236; silver. 236; food of, 236; bowls of, with birds inside, 237; ponds, 439
Flamingo, 228
Fleas, 141
Flies, plague of, 259; annoying elephants, 332
Flight of birds, 148, 207, 208; insects, 220

Floods in 1764, 148; 1784, 260
Flora of Selborne, 204
Fly, turnip, 115; depositing eggs in hairs of horses, 116; horse bot (*see* horse-fly); forest, 131; side, 131; house maggots of, 382
Flycatcher. 29, 34, 49, 127; arrival of, 31; nidification of, 159; note of, 159; spotted, 335; pellets cast up by, 335
Fogs, 183, 184; smoky, 258
Food of titlark, 31; of soft-billed birds, 28; birds guided by colour in choice of, 31; of birds, 109; of man, various, 208; of woodpecker, 401
Foot of woodpecker, 326
Forest-flies, 131
Forests, services rendered by, 18; effects of on the weather, 183; royal origin of, 857
Fossils at Selborne, 7; wood, 14, 245; oak, 245
Fowls, wild, in Wolmer Forest, 14
Foxes in Wolmer Forest, 20
Freestone, analogous to chalk, 2; grows shaky wood, 4; its uses, 8
French naturalists, 99
Fringilla (hard-billed), 161; *cœlebs* (*see* Chaffinch)
Frogs, 51; breeding of, 52; swarm of, cause of, 51, 304; migrating of, 51, 304; cultivation of, 304; croaking of, 304
Frosts, lying longer on bog oaks, 14; severe, 42, 248, 252, 254; birds fattening during, 94; effects of, on animals, 94; effect of, on birds, 94
Fruit crop, 171

G.

Gallinæ, walk of, 208
Gallows Hill, 439
Gardening among the Saxons, 196
Garlands, in churches in honour of virgins, 359
Garrulus Bohemicus (German silk-tail), 36
Gassendus, quotation from, on music, 241
Gasterosterus pungitius (*see* Stickleback); *aculeatus* (*see* Stickleback)
Gems placed in turkeys' crops, 314
Gentian, 205
Gentiana amarilla (gentian or fellwork), 205
Geology of Selborne, 2, 7, 8
German-boars, 25; silk-tail, 36
Gibraltar, migration of birds to, 106
Gill covers of *Mud Iguana*, 52
Gipsies, language of, 176
Gizzard of landrail, 78; of birds, 88, 814
Glow-worm, 78
Gnats on the snow, 81
Goats breathing through their ears, 44
Goatsucker, 64, 66, 68, 95, 120, 311; food of, 66, 811; does not injure cattle, 66; egg of, 67, 811; feeding by means of its foot, 120; anatomy of. 186; tame, 312
Gobius fluviatilis capitatus (bell-head), 33

Goldfinch, 94
Goldfish, 236
Gold-crested wren (*see* Wren)
Golden thrushes, 111
Golden maiden-hair, brush of, 179
Gossamer, a shower of, 174; origin of, 174
Gracious street, 439
Grallæ, legs of, 92; food of, 113
Graminivorus birds eating vegetables, 97
Grange, the, 432
Grass, uses of, 204
Grasshopper, 217; lark, 48, 58, 72, 153; warbler, 808
Gravel in birds' crops, 78
Graves under trees, 372
Great Britain, birds of, 159
Greatham farm, 19, 20
Green lizard, 54, 64
Gregarious habits of horses and cows, 175
Grosbeak, 33; food of, 33
Gryllus campestris (field-cricket); *domesticus* (house cricket); *Gryllus talpæ* (mole-cricket) (*see* Cricket)
Gurnsey lizard, 68
Gurdon, Sir Adam, 381; marriage of, 382; rebellion of, 387; menace against the English language, 383; death of, 389; seal of, 389

H.

Haggard falcon, 242
Hailstorm at Selborne, 261
Hampton bridge, 5
Hanger, the, 2, 12, 282; meaning of, 282
Hares, 12, 252
Harvest mouse (see Mouse, harvest); bug, 115
Hawkley hanger, 215
Hawk, sparrow, strange, 31; blue, 155; ringtail, anatomy of, 186; destroyed by poultry, 212
Hawks, 31; casting up feathers, 34; migration of, 111; do not prey while cuckoo is heard, 169
Haws, a food for birds, 36; failure of, 36
Haze, or smoky fog, 258
Hazel wych, 5
Headley Church, 18
Heat, intense, 257; spoiling fruit, 257; effects of, on hibernating animals, 198
Heathcock, formerly plentiful, 15
Heathfires, 19
Hedgehog, 91, 318; food of, 90; spines of, 90, 819; young of, 819; vertebræ of, 819; claws of, 819; resisting poison, 819; food of, 819
Hedge-sparrow and the cuckoo, 94, 318
Heliotropes, summer and winter, 213
Helleborus fœtidus (stinking hellebore), 205; *viridis* (green hellebore), 205; *niger*, 206; hellebores, order of blooming, 206; *hyemalis*, 206
Helleborine, 206
Hempseed for birds, 46, 133, 302

Hen harrier, 154
Hen and horse, friendship of, 175; and ducklings, 191
Hen, common, 211
Henry III. grants lands to Selborne Priory, 379
Heronry at Cressi Hall, 64, 69
Heron, claws of, 311
Hills and mountains, moving, 214; attracting clouds, 260
Himantopus, 223, 224
Hippoboscæ hirundinis, 131, 282
Hirundo hyberna, 105; *rupestris*, 105; *alpina*, 107; *melba*, 107; *esculenta*, 149; *riparia*, 149; (*see* also Swallow, Martin, and Swift)
Hogmer, lake, 21
Hogs, age of, 188
Hollow lane leading to Alton, 11
Holt Forest, 1, 23; ironstone in, 9; deer in, 18, 24; meaning of, 282
Holy Ghost Chapel, Basingstoke, destruction of, 437
Holy water clump, 447
Home-made candles, 177
Honey-buzzard, 142, 228
Honey-dew, 258
Hoopoe, 32, 296; egg of, 33
Hoopoes at Selborne, 32; migration of, 111
Hops, suitable soil for, 4; at Selborne, 13, 171
Horns at Lord Pembroke's, 100; of red-deer, growth of, 285; cow's, structure of, 333
Horse botfly, 116; and hen friendship, 175; should not be kept in solitude, 340
Holticulture, spread of, 196
House martins (*see* Martins, house); swallow (*see* Swallow, house)
Howe, General, machinery made by, 23
Humming in the air, 199
Hunger, power of, 109, 121
Hunter, John, birth and death of, 279
Hunting condemned by Bishop Wykeham, 406
Hybernation of swallow, 27; swift, 27
Hypericum androsæmum (Tustan, or St. John's wort), 205

I.

Icthyology, 68
Icy speculæ in the air, 256
Idiot boy and bees, 192
Incongruous companions, 121
Incubation of birds, 95
Indian grass, 68
Insectivorous birds, 31
Insect pests, 115; appearing in hot weather, 192; insensible to sound, 200; hybernation of, 219; life of, 219; diffusion of, 283, 285; appearing in frosts, 254

Instinct, 78, 127, 147, 289; of young animals, 187
Inundations rendering land poor, 191
Ireland and its natural history, 171
Ironstone in Holt Forest, 9
Italy, climate of, 95

J.

Jackdaws, 62, 310; building on the ground, 62, 68
Jamaica, birds of, 102
Jarbird (see Goatsucker)
Jealousy in birds, 121
John, King, in Wolmer Forest, 465
July, alleged decrease of birds in, 87
Juncus conglomeratus (common rush), 177
Junipers, American, 251

K.

Kestrel, 153
Kings-field, echo in, 198
Kingsley Church, 25
Kite, eating ants' eggs, 31; migration of, 111, 142
Knights' Templars, Order of, 362; property belonging to, at Selborne, 390

L.

Lacerta, 52; green, 54
Ladies' traces, 205
Lakes near Selborne, 20; in Wolmer, 21
Lampern, 83
Landrail, 12, 78; food of, 78; egg of, 78
Landslips, 215
Land-springs, 148
Land tortoise (see Tortoise)
Lanes at Selborne, 11, 282; abound in Filices, 12
Lanius minor, 80; Collurio (see Butcher-bird)
Lapwing, 15; movements of, 133
Larks, 142, 302; sky, feeding in winter, 81; white, 45; grasshopper, 48, 57, 72, 153; wood, 81, 94; dusting and washing, 114; Scotch, 303; catching, 303
Late springs, 114
Lathræa squammaria (tooth-wort), 205
Lathyrus sylvestris, 205
Laurel spurge, 206
Leaves of trees, 183
Legge, Henry Bilson, 23
Legs, length of, in small birds, 223
Lemna (duck's meat weed), 236
Leprosy, 194
Leveret and cat, friendship of, 189
Libellulæ (dragon-fly), 104, 151
Lice, of birds, 131; martins, 188; swallows, eggs of 131
Linen clothing, advantage of, 194
Linnæan system, the, 75, 77, 80, 155

Linnet, 40, 94, 100, 300; song of, 300; taming, 300
Lions following jackals, 122
Lithe, the short, 216
Liveries, meaning of, 401
Lizard, green, 54, 64; black, found in a well, 60; Guernsey, turned out at Pembroke College, Oxford, 69
Loach, 55
Loaches from Ambresbury, 55
Locusta, 48
Locustella, 72
Long-billed birds fattening during frosts, 94
Long Lythe, path by, 21
Longspee, Ela, 395
Longworth, J., Vicar of Selborne, 378
Loon, or spotted diver, 77
Lop and top, 25
Loripes, 223
Losel's wood, 5
Love in birds, 109
Loxia coccothraustes (see Grosbeak); curvirostra (see Crossbill)
Lycoperdon tuber (truffle), 206
Lyss church, 16
Lythe, the, 37

M.

Magdalen College, Oxford, land belonging to, at Selborne, 386, 440; patron of living of Selborne, 372; founded, 424; court list of, held at Selborne, 438
Maggots in cattle, 66; of house flies, 332
Magpie and missel thrush, fight between, 170
Mahommedans dusting themselves, 103
Maiden hair fern, 179
Malm, black and white, 2
Man-traps, 288
Manor house at Selborne, 383
Marcley Hill said to have moved, 214
Market at Selborne, 385, 439
Marsh cinquefoil, 205
Martins, young, appearance of, 26; late, 26, 62; house, 27, 34, 96, 102, 134, 149; sand, 28, 149; frequenting water, 28; late breeding of, 34, 38, 124, 133, 138, 157; migration of, 120; food of, 151; parasites of, 151; hybernating of, 124, 198, 232, 288; nest of, 135, 137; down on legs of, 138; colour of, 148; sand and house, feed young on the wing, 102; nest of, 28, 162; washing as they fly, 152; do not sing, 151; flight of, 152; abundance of, 152; appearance of, 192
Martlet (see House martin)
Marwick's Calendar, 265
Masses for the dead in Selborne Church, 394
May-fly, 165
Memory, comparing animals by, 106
"Meating off" birds, 317
Merops apiaster (beebird), 111
Merula torquata (see Ring ouzel)

Meteors, 258

Mazereon, 206

Migration of swallows, 27, 38, 70; of birds, 81, 38, 40, 70, 78, 75, 94, 96, 98, 108, 111; of chaffinches, 38; of birds, affected by the season, 98

Migration, a large, 69; "home," 108; at Gibraltar, 112

Mill, the old, 24

Miller's thumb, 33

Missel thrush (see Thrush, missel); bird, 132

Mist, sulphurous, 260

Moisture, effect of, on trees, 114

Moles, eaten by weasels, 158; cricket, 228, 338, 350; eating worms, 388; paw of, 838

Monasteries, effect of, 381; degeneration of, 409

Monkey, mummied, found in a tree, 831

Monogamous birds, 96

Monographs, merits of, 101, 108

Monument, to Gilbert White, 865; to Rev. W. Etty, 865

Moose deer, the, 98, 106; food of, 98; swimming in breeding time, 100

Mordaunt, Mr. 28

Mosquitoes, 131

Moss on tombstones, 282

Motacilla trochilus, 29; three kinds of, 80; 58; atricapilla (see blackcap); salicaria (see Willow wren)

Mother marking, 194

Mountains, 189;

Mouse, 42; harvest, 80; new kind, 80, 85, 46; burrowing, 42; large, 42; house, 42; red, dogs eating, 156; common, cats eating, 156; shrew, 182, 816; caught by an oyster, 297; field (see Field mouse)

Movements of animals and birds, various, 29, 207

Mud iguana, 52

Mus amphibius, 80; minimus (new kind of mouse), 80, 35, 46; domesticus medius (Ray), 85

Musca putris (see Bacon-fly) chamæleon, 116

Music, influence of, 240

Mustella weasel, 44

Mustelinum, 44

Mytilus, the, 7; fossil, at Selborne, 7

N.

Naturalist's Calendar, White and Marwick's, 263

Naturalist's summer evening walk, 78

Nautilus, fossil, 8

Nest of sand-martins, 28; mouse, 85; rooks, 44; swallow on owl's body, 147

Newt, or water-eft, 52, 304

Nidification of birds, 110,126, 150, 170, 289; house-martins, 135, 239; sand-martins, 150; chaffinch, 239; nut-hatch, 239; wren, 239

Night, birds coming forth at, 22

Nightingale, 118, 827; migration of, 113, 828; note of, 118, 153; breeding in London, 329; catching, 829

Nocturnal birds, 245

Norehill, 2, 214

Nostrils of antelope, 43

Notes of, birds, 29, 40, 43, 76, 200; willow wren, 48; grasshopper lark, 48; willow lark, 58

Noxious insects, 116

Nun, 161

Nuthatch, 47, 49, 239, 808; egg of, 48; eating nuts, 240; nest of, 808; foot of, 808;

Nuts opened differently by nuthatch, squirrel, and field-mice, 239

Nymphœa (water-lily), 98

O.

Oak, large in the Plestor, 5, 885; in Losels wood, 5; peculiar, 5, 6 : bog, 14 ; how to tell the age of, 285

Oakhanger, 18, 20

Oaks of Temple, 4; in Wolmer forest, 25 ; in Windsor forest, 285

Oedicnemus (see Stone curlew)

Oil as a remedy for snake-bites, 52

Œstrus bovis (bot-fly), causing injury to cattle, 66, 116

Ophrys spiralis (see Ladies' Traces); nidus avis (see Birds' nest ophrys)

Opposite golden saxifrage, 205

Oro pendolos, 111

Osprey, 132

Ostrich, the, 89

Otis (bustard), 83

Otter, killed near Selborne, 97; anatomy of, 828

Ouzel, ring (see Ring-ouzel); water, (see Water-ouzel)

Owl, barn (see Owl, white); brown, casting up fur and feathers, 84, 180; food of, 84; hooting of, 115; nest of swallow on an, 147; eagle, 85; fern (see Goatsucker); white, 129, 335; young of, 84; food of, 84, 129; attacking dovehouse, 96; hawking, 835; screech of, 130

Owls, pellets cast up by, 84, 130; hoot in different keys, 117, 836; ears of, 180; eyes of, 130; flight of, 180; food of, 836; to call, 836

Oxen congregating together, 175

Oxford, Guernsey lizards at Pembroke College, 69; swallows late at, 84, 70

Oyster, mouse caught by, 297

P.

Pairing of birds, 96

Palm Sunday, yew trees carried on, 372

Polumbus torquatus (see Ring dove)

Paradise Mede, Selborne, 431

Parasitic insects, 131, 218; of martins, 131, 188, 232

Paris quadrifolia, (herb Paris truelove or oneberry, 205

Partridges, 12; pairing of, 96; killed by frost, 254

Parus cœruleus (blue titmouse or wren), 161; *fringillagus* or major, (blackhead titmouse) 161; *ater*, (cole-mouse), 161; *palustris* (marsh titmouse), 161

Passer arundinaceus minor (see Reed sparrow), *torquatus (see* Reed bunting)

Passeres, note of, 210

Peacock, tails of, 116; killing vipers, 333

Peat, 14, 19

Pectines in freestone, 8

Perch, 21

Peregrine falcon, 242

Perewinkle, lesser, 206

Pettichaps (chiff-chaff), 241

Pews in Selborne Church, 360

Phalæna (gnats) 67, 86

Pheasants, 12; pursued by hen harrier, 154

Phryganea (see Caddis-fly)

Pigeon, wood (*see* Woodpigeon); drinking, 157; blue rock, 229

Pigs, eating their young, 128; length of life in, 188; eating yewberries without injury, 370

Pine plantations, near Glasgow, 172

Pitancias, 401

Planting evergreens, 251

Plants, at Selborne, 205; suffer from heat and cold, 249, 256

Plestor, the, 5, 6, 281, 884; great oak in, 281, 285

Plover, 223

Plowman, Piers, 409

Plumpton Plain, 189

Poaching at night, 17, 25

Poison-fangs of viper, 342

Poison, Wourali, 346

Poisoned arrows of Indians, 346

Poll sheep, 140

Pollard-ash, children cured of rupture by, 181; in the Plestor, 182

Ponds, on chalkhills, 184; at Selborne, dried up, 283

Pope Martin confiscates property of Selborne Priory, 408

Portugal laurels, 251

Pottery, Roman, found at Selborne, 447, 450

Poultry, 211; their notes and language, 212; destroying a hawk, 212

Prayers for the dead, 384, 394, 395, 429

Preceptores, meaning of, 393

Prior, election of a, 396, 412, 413, 414, 419

Priors of Selborne, list of, 422

Priories, alien, 380

Priory of Selborne, at Pilton, 876; in debt, 404; property of, 407; sequestrated, 408, 412; reduced to a chantry, 430

Prophecy of Piers Plowman, 409

Puckeridge (*see* Fern-owl)

Puffins, 62; breed on flat ground, 62

Pulex irritans (bed-flea), 151

Punishment of canons for misbehaviour, 403

Puritanism at Selborne, 374

Purlieus, 21

Q.

Quails, 12, 40; egg of, 43

Queen's bank, 16

Quicksilver mines, men working in, 98

R.

Rabbits, in Wolmer Forest, 18; with deformed teeth, 286; ferreted by crabs, 293

Rainfall at Selborne, 13, 68, 246; in Rutland, 110, 252; effect of trees on, 183, 340; compared with Plymouth, 246

Rana arborea (tree-frog), 52

Rats, common, 294; two kinds, 80; water, 80, 294; three varieties of, 294; tail of, 295; tormenting an elephant, 295

Rattlesnake, 306, 344; cannot rattle in wet weather, 345

Ravens, building in the Plestor Oak, 6; close sitting of, 7; driving vultures from their nests, 126

Redbreast, 87, 94, 339; tame, singing by candlelight, 87; song of, 156, 339; autumn songster, 156; food of, 156, 161; egg and nest of, 339

Red deer, 16; in Wolmer Forest, 16; never seen in Holt Forest, 18, 25; horns of, 286, 287

Redstart, 84, 49, 141; arrival of, 31; motion of tail of, 155; song of, 159

Redwing, 27, 320; feeding in winter, 31; breeding in England, 109; migration of, 118; killed by frost, 250

Reed-bunting, 98.

Reed-sparrow, 85, 94, 98; food of, 98; song of, 98

Reed-wren, 80, 314

Regulus non cristatus (see Golden-Crested wren)

Relics of Selborne priory, 410

Reptiles, stinking *se defendendo*, 80

Ring-dove, 88, 114, 228; food of, 88, 97; nidification of, 170

Ring-ouzel, 36, 42, 59, 63, 71, 84, 101; egg of, 102, 114, 142; migration of, 59, 63, 71, 79, 84, 101, 104, 121, 124; food of, 60, 71; breeding places in England, 182

Roads, at Selborne, 282; new, made by Gilbert White, 375

Roche, Peter de la, or de Rupibus, founds Selborne priory, 376; Bishop of Winchester, 376

Rocks removed by rain, 261

" Rocky Lane," leading to Alton, 11

Roman remains found at Alton, 464; Selborne, 28, 358, 445, 450; invasion of England, 460

Romulus and Remus, 190

Roofs of houses, various, 481

Rooks, 142, 302; nesting of, 44; white, 44, 302; power of smell in, 122; frightened by scarecrows, 320

Royal forests, origin of, 357

Royston crow, 114

Rupert, Prince, 23

Ruptured children placed in pollard-ashes, 181

Rush candles, 177; to make, 178

Rutland, fall of rain in, 110, 252

S.

Saffron, 206

Sallad or Sallet, 197

Salad oil as a cure for viper's sting, 52

Salamandra aquatica (water-newt, or eft), 52

Salicaria, 46, 72, 79, 85; fen (reed-wren), 314

Salmo-fario (trout), 33

Salt meat causing leprosy, 194

Salvin, Captain, his wild sow, 293

Sambucus ebulus (dwarf elder) 206

Sand-martins (see Martins, Sand) pipers, 58; pits in Wolmer forest, 149

Saxon words, meaning of, 356

Scallops, 8

Scarabœus solstitialis (see Fernchafers); *melolontha*, 67; *fullo*, 71

Scopoli, 98, 101, 103, 106

Scotland, maps of, 172

Sea-birds, 38

Sea-mouse, 347

Seal of Gurdon, 388

Sedge-bird (see Willow wren)

Sedge-warbler, 80, 98; note of, 80, 87; singing at night, 133

Selborne Parish, 1; village, 2; soil of, 2, 4; streams in, 2; fossils at, 7; extent of, 12; cottages in, salubrity of, 12; fall of rain in, 13, 68, 246; occupation of, 18; population, 18; old coach road leading into the village, 15; path by Long Lythe, 21; in Saxon times, 355; value of the living, 372; vicar of, before Domesday Book, 373; Priory, property of, 386, 407; decay of, 424, 428, 430, 436; rivulet, 432; account of, 433; ruins of, 438; importance of, 441

Serpents (see Snakes)

Sex of birds, 99

Sexes, distinguishing features of the, 99; separation of, during winter, 108

Shearing sheep, 140

Sheep, feeding before rain, 119; of Sussex, 140; congregating, 175; in Australia, 337

Shingles on roof, advantages of, 366

Short-winged birds of passage, 31, 38, 49

Shrew, water, 85, 316; ash, 182; mouse, 182, 316

Shrikes, 59, 182, 309; four kinds of, 309

Silk-wood, 179; tail, German, 36; worm, intestines of, used for fishing-tackle, 68

Silver fish, 235

Sitta Europæa (see Nuthatch)

Skunck, 80

Skylark (see lark)

Slugs injurious to wheat, 191

Smell, animals recognised by, 141

Smoky atmosphere, cause of, 247

Smother flies, 235, 258

Snails, 225, 346; shells eaten by birds, 78, 347; nutritious food, 347; French, 347

Snakes, (see also Vipers); food of, 3; feeding once a year, 54; English, 54; stink, 80; tame, 80; eating snakes, 304; eggs of, 305; nest of, 305; vertebræ of, 307

Snipes, 30, 49; in Wolmer Forest, 15, 133; make no nest, 68; stomach of, 88

Snowflake, 45, 84, 301; storms, 248, 252; bunting, 300

Sociality of animals, 175; of different natures, 189

Soft-billed birds, migration of, 41, 75; non-migratory, list of, 75

Soil, curious, 4; good for timber, 4, 5; Wolmer and Holt Forests, 24; chalky and sandy, subject to heat, 258; at Selborne, productive, 282

Solstice, summer and winter, 218

Song-birds, 29, 70, 87, 94; migration of, 75, 108; non-migratory, 75, 160; night, 76; list of, 81; loss of voice in, 95; food of, 160

Song of thrush, 155, 314; of blackbird, 155; of willow wren, 155; wood lark, 155

Sounds, association of, 218

South Sea Bubble, 279

Sow, 25; fecundity of the, 188; age of, 188; wild, 293

Spain, birds migrating to, 41

Spaniels, 244

Sparrow hawk, 153, 227; hedge, 161; flight of, 155; food of, 161; house, 96; cleaning themselves, 103; taking sand-martin's nest, 151; nidification of, 155; food of, 322; increase of, 322

Sparrows in the City, 322

Speckled diver, 77

Spiders, making gossamer webs, 174; flying, 174

Spindle trees, 153

Spiracula of fallow deer, 42

Sporting, inherent in mankind, 17, 400; dogs, training of, 244

Spring-guns, 288

Sprout-cale, February so called by Saxons, 196

Spurge laurel, 206

Squirrel, suckled by a cat, 190; eating nuts, 289

Stag, hunt a, in Wolmer Forest, 16; nostrils of, 43; beetle, larvæ of, 320

Stealing deer, 17

Stickleback, 33, 54, 307; nest of, 308

Stilt plover, 228

Stoat, 301

Stockdove (*see* Wood-pigeon)
Stonechat, 105, 133
Stone, free, 2, 4, 8
Stone curlew, 47, 108, 245, 246; food of, 2, 9; note of, 61, 245; migration of, 61; makes no nest, 68; egg of, 80; flight of, 108
Stonehenge, daws breeding at, 62
Stone, sand, 8, 10; rag, 9; yellow, 10; coffin lids in Selborne Church, 362
Stones swallowed by birds, 80
Stoparola (fly-catcher) 49
Στοργή of animals and birds, 126, 147, 168
Storm-cock, 132
Strangers elected to Selborne Priory, 414
Stratford, Bishop of Winchester, 396
Stubble burning, 19
Stype *alias* Stepe, Prior, 410, 411
Summer birds of passage, 74; short-winged, 31, 104, 106, 141; list of, 49, 74; soft-billed, 111
Sun, red, 259
Sunbury-on-Thames, 41
Sun dew, round leaved, 205
Sundial in White's garden, 281
Superstition of country people, 304
Sussex downs, 104, 139
Swallows. 94, 148, 227; young, appearance of, 27; hatchings of, 27; hybernation of, 27, 38, 111, 123, 143, 147, 227, 242; drink flying, 34; flocks of, 37; on the Thames, 36, 41; late, 37, 86, 146; migration of, 37, 70, 120, 146, 149, 169; congregation of, 70, 146; late, at Oxford, 70; house, 70, 142, 169; increase of, 87; and frosts, 96, 98; feeding young on the wing, 102, 404; and swifts, supposed rivalry between, 103; late, 122; food of, 145; lice of, 131; washing while flying, 133, 145; early, 142; nidification of, 143; eggs of, 144; song of, 145; tail of, 147, 153; and hawks, 166; appearance of, 169; appearing in hot weather, 192; chimney (*see* Swallow, house) fond of water, 242
Swans, 153; migration of, 112
Sweden, birds of, 159
Swift, hybernation of, 26; early migration of, 86, 166; great white-bellied, 107, 168; note of, 118, 167; staying late, 121; appearance of, 133, 312; or black martin, 162; nidification of, 162; propagation of, 163; food of, 164, 165, 168; and hawks, 165; young of, 165, 168; colour of, 166; fleas of, 167, 282; feet of, 167; in London, 168; similar to cuckoo in formation, 186; pairing every year in same number, 202; late breeding, 233; late departure of, 238
Sylvia loquax, lesser willow wren, 57; trochilus larger willow wren, 58; curruca lesser white throat, 241

T.

Tadpoles, 52
Tails, of woodpecker, 208, 325; rat, 294

Tameness, natural, of birds, 88, 124
Taming of animals, &c., 64, 310
Tanners' Wood, 432
Tanyard at Selborne Priory, 432
Teals, 22, 84, 129, 133
Teeth of rabbits, 288, 290
Tench, 21
Tenderness, natural, of birds, 88, 124
"Tenpenny nails in the walls," 10, 282
Thames, frozen over, 258
Thaws, 254; caused by underground vapours, 250
Thermometers, use of, 256
Thrush, the, 46, 314; food of, 46, 170; breeding of, 71; nidification of, 170; killed by frost, 254
Thrush, missel, 36, 84; fierceness of, 170 fight with a magpie, 170, food of, 185
Thunderstorms, rarity of, at Selborne, 259
Tiles first used for roofs, 431
Timber, good soil for, 4; in Holt Forest, 24
Tipula (Long-legs), 191
Titlark, or tree-pipit, 87, 105, 317; feeding in winter, 31; singing, 132; at night, 87
Titmouse, song of, 156; great, 156; food of, 161; bill of, 161; blue, 161; great blackheaded, 161; long-tailed, 161; marsh, 161; pulling straws from eaves, 161, 250
Toads, breeding of, 51; venom of, 51; tame, 51, 64; man swallowing a, 56; as a cure for cancer, 56, 63, 304
Tombs in Selborne Church, 361, 365
Tongue of woodpecker, 326
Toothwort, 205
Tortoise, land, 105, 126, 225; hybernation of, 105, 126, 142, 192, 225; food of, 105; age of, 105; feeding before rain, 126; instinct of, 225; tenacity of life in the, 226
Travelling mountains, 214
Tree beetles, 114
Trees and forests, effect of, on rainfall, 188, 340; perfect alembics, 188; killed by frost, 251, 256; in churchyards, 372
Trenches, ancient, at Selborne, 457
Tringa hypolencus (*see* Sandpiper), 58
Trotton Church, 355
Trout, 83
Truffles, 206
Tumuli at Selborne, 455
Tunbridge, 432
Turdus torquatus (*see* Ring ouzel); *pilaris* (*see* Fieldfare)
Turkey, gizzard of, power of, 314
Turnip fly, 115
Tusk of elephant, growth of, and injuries to, 291
Tustan, or St. John's wort, 205

U.

Upupa (Hoopoe), 82

V.

Vaccinium oxycoccos (cranberry); *myrtillus* (bilberry), 205
Vase found at Selborne Priory, 438 ; Chapel field, 447, 450
Verdure of trees. late, 114
Vespertilio murinus (bat), 84 ; *auritus* (long-eared bat), 84 ; *altivolans* (large-bat), 119
Vegetable caterpillar of New Zealand, 848
Vegetables as a diet, 196
Vegetation, 203
Vine, diseases of, 238 ; parasite of the, 238
Vicarage at Selborne. 868
Vicars of Selborne, list of, 873
Vinago (cow pigeon), 228
Vinca minor (lesser periwinkle), 205
Vipers, breeding, 51, 53, 187 ; oil as remedy for poison of, 52 ; eggs of, 53 ; food of, 54, 341 ; in the water, 54 ; swallowing their young, 54, 187, 341 ; young of, 187 ; peacocks kill, 333 ; skin of, 341 ; poison of, 342 ; how to catch, 344
Virgil's description of stubble burning, 19 ; bees, 133, 199 ; swallows, 143
Visitation of Bishop of Winchester, 399
Visitatio Notabilis, the, 899, *et sec.*
Vitrified stone, 8
Volcano in Norway, 259
Vultures, 111, 261 ; and dogs associating, 261

W.

Wagtails, white, 40, 301 ; 133, 160 ; motion of tail of, 155 ; food of, 160 ; pied, 301 ; four kinds, 301 ; grey, 301 ; note of, 301 ; yellow, 39, 301
Waldon lodge, 20
Waltham blacks, 16, 17, 288
Walwort, 206
War between England and France, 888
Warbler, grasshopper ; sedge (*see* Willow wren)
Wasps, 257 ; nests, 81
Water, hard and soft, 8
Water-fowl, 22 ; rat, 80, 85 ; ouzel, 104
Water at Selborne, 3
Water-ouzel, 104
Water, cattle frequenting, 80 ; efts, 52, 56 ; snake, 54 ; efts spawn in, 56 ; fowl, wings and feet of, 73 ; rat, 85 ; shrew mouse, 77, 836 ; hybernation of, 85 ; distilled from trees, 98 ; condensed by fogs, &c.. 184 ; vole, 294 ; reservoir, 501 ; pipes at Selborne, ancient, 545
Waxwing (*see* Silk-tail)
Waynflete, William of, Bishop of Winchester, 528
Weapons, ancient, found at Selborne, 562, 569
Weasel, 44, 153, 301
Weather, the, 96, 148, 171, 173, 192, 214, 248, 258 ; influencing migration of birds, 109, 118 ; at Plymouth, 246
Weavers down, 10|

Well, Ellis's farm, 71
Well-head, 2, 3
Well, lizard found in, 60
Wells, depth of. 8
Wey river, the, 3, 26
Whaddon Chapel, 546
Wheatear, 40, 41, 105, 133, 142, 301 ; food of, 164 ; does not always migrate, 40 ; migration of, 301
Wheat crops, 149 ; bread, use of, 195
Whinchat, 105, 133, 142 ; food of, 162
White malm, 4 ; rooks, 44, 302 ; larks, 45, 85 ; hares, 85
White, Gilbert, his house, 9, 281, 854 ; birth of, 279 ; prominent events in the life of, 279 ; curate of Farringdon, 282 ; tomb of, 282 ; restores Selborne Church, 374
White's Calendar, 265
Whitethroat, 84, 88, 105, 94, 96, 141, 157 ; lesser, 241 ; note of, 241, 157 ; food of, 157
Widgeon, 22, 34
Whortle, or bilberry, 205
Wild boars in Wolmer Forest, 25 ; Captain Salonis, 340 ; in England, 841 ; fowls, 34, 129 ; geese, breeding of, 85 ; ducks, 321
Willow-lark, 48, 57, 72 ; note of, 80, 87, 133
Willow-wren, 49, 79, 96, 128, 241
Willoughby, Mr., 41
Winchester Cathedral rebuilt, 858
Windhover (*see* Kestrel)
Windsor Forest, trees in, 285
Wings of birds hollow, 208 ; placed too forward, 208 ; backward, 208
Winter birds of passage, list of, 75, 76
Wishing stone, the, 65
Witches, 181
Wolmer Forest, 4, 14. 386 ; stone found in, 10 ; fossils found in, 14 ; wild-fowl in, 14 ; game in, 15 ; Queen Anne in, 16 ; limits of, 20 ; scarcity of trees in, 21 ; leased by the crown, 23 ; soil of, 24 ; boars and buffaloes in,25 ; when formed, 857 ; Sir A. Gurdon, *custos* of, 386
Wolmer Lake, 15, 21, 288, 447 ; coins found in, 23
Wolvemere (*see* Wolmer Lake)
Woodcocks, 12 ; stomach of, 88 ; carrying their young, 102 ; breeding in England, 109 ; in Austria, 110 ; migration at night, 111 ; occasional sluggishness of, 112, 119
Woodpecker, spotted, 49 ; flight of, 220 ; anatomy of, 324-326
Woodpigeon, 114, 228, 229 ; migration of, 114, 132, 280 ; wild, 228 ; food of, 230
Wood, fossil, 14 : lark, 94, song of, 155
Worldham Church (East), chancel door-way, 69
Worms, earth, 191 ; use of, 191 ; herma-phrodites, 192 ; blind (*see* Blind worm)
Wornils (maggots), 66
Wourali poison, 845
Wren, 87, 94, 820 ; golden-crested, 84, 50 ; egg of, 48 ; tameness of, 83 ; song of, 156 ; food of, 159 ; willow, 57, 808 ; egg of, 58 ; wood, 803 ; nest of, built between two stoats, 821

Wryneck, 74, 159, 339; egg and nest of, 339
Wych elms, 5, 285; hazel, 5, 285
Wykeham, Wiliam of, 150; rebuilding Winchester Cathedral, 358; Bishop of Winchester, visitation of, 397; character of, 404
Wynchester, John, elected as Prior, 405

Yellow wort, 205
Yew tree, birds feeding on, 36; ancient in Selborne Churchyard, 281, 370; berries fatal to animals, 298, 370; leaves of, very injurious to cattle, 298; difference between males and females, 370; not injurious to sheep and turkeys, 370

Y.

Yellowhammer, 87, 317; song of, 94, 317

Z.

Zig-zag, the, 282

THE END.

RICHARD CLAY AND SONS, LONDON AND BUNGAY.

Bedford Street, Strand, London, W.C.
November, 1886.

Macmillan & Co.'s Catalogue of Works in the Departments of History, Biography, Travels, Critical and Literary Essays, Politics, Political and Social Economy, Law, etc.; and Works connected with Language.

HISTORY, BIOGRAPHY, TRAVELS, &c.

ADDISON.—ESSAYS OF JOSEPH ADDISON. Chosen and edited by John Richard Green, M.A., LL.D. 18mo. 4s. 6d. (Golden Treasury Series.)

AGASSIZ (LOUIS): HIS LIFE AND CORRESPONDENCE. Edited by Elizabeth Cary Agassiz. 2 vols. Crown 8vo. 18s.

ALBEMARLE.—FIFTY YEARS OF MY LIFE. By George Thomas, Earl of Albemarle. Third and Cheaper Edition. Crown 8vo. 7s. 6d.

ALFRED THE GREAT.—By Thomas Hughes, Q.C. Crown 8vo. 6s.

AMIEL.—THE JOURNAL INTIME OF HENRI-FRÉDÉRIC AMIEL. Translated, with an Introduction and Notes, by Mrs. Humphry Ward. In 2 vols. Globe 8vo. 12s.

APPLETON.—A NILE JOURNAL. By T. G. Appleton. Illustrated by Eugene Benson. Crown 8vo. 6s.

ARNOLD (MATTHEW.)—Works by Matthew Arnold, D.C.L.
ESSAYS IN CRITICISM. New Edition, Revised. Crown 8vo. 9s.
HIGHER SCHOOLS AND UNIVERSITIES IN GERMANY. Second Edition. Crown 8vo. 6s.
DISCOURSES IN AMERICA. Crown 8vo. 4s. 6d.

ARNOLD (T.)—THE SECOND PUNIC WAR. Being Chapters of THE HISTORY OF ROME. By the late Thomas Arnold, D.D., formerly Head Master of Rugby School, and Regius Professor of Modern History in the University of Oxford. Edited, with Notes, by W. T. Arnold, M.A. With 8 Maps. Crown 8vo. 8s. 6d.

ARNOLD (W. T.)—THE ROMAN SYSTEM OF PROVINCIAL ADMINISTRATION TO THE ACCESSION OF CONSTANTINE THE GREAT. Being the Arnold Prize Essay for 1879. By W. T. Arnold, M.A., formerly Scholar of University College, Oxford. Crown 8vo. 6s.

ART.—THE YEAR'S ART: A concise Epitome of all Matters relating to the Arts of Painting, Sculpture, and Architecture, which have occurred during the Year 1880, together with Information respecting the Events of the Year 1881. Compiled by Marcus B. Huish. Crown 8vo. 2s. 6d.
THE SAME, 1879—1880. Crown 8vo. 2s. 6d.

ARTEVELDE.—JAMES AND PHILIP VAN ARTEVELDE. By W. J. Ashley, B.A., late Scholar of Balliol College, Oxford. Being the Lothian Prize Essay for 1882. Crown 8vo. 6s.

ATKINSON.—AN ART TOUR TO NORTHERN CAPITALS OF EUROPE, including Descriptions of the Towns, the Museums, and other Art Treasures of Copenhagen, Christiana, Stockholm, Abo, Helsingfors, Wiborg, St. Petersburg, Moscow, and Kief. By J. Beavington Atkinson. 8vo. 12s.

BACON (FRANCIS.)—AN ACCOUNT OF HIS LIFE AND WORKS. By EDWIN A. ABBOTT, D.D., formerly Fellow of St. John's College, Cambridge. Demy 8vo. 14s.

"BACCHANTE," 1879—1882, THE CRUISE OF H.M.S. Compiled from the Journals, Letters and Note-Books of Prince Albert Victor and Prince George of Wales. With Additions by the Rev. JOHN NEALE DALTON, Canon of Windsor. With Maps, Plans, and Illustrations. 2 vols. Medium 8vo. 52s. 6d.

BAKER (SIR SAMUEL W.)—Works by Sir SAMUEL BAKER, Pacha M.A., F.R.S., F.R.G.S.:—

CYPRUS AS I SAW IT IN 1879. With Frontispiece. 8vo. 12s. 6d.

ISMAILÏA: A Narrative of the Expedition to Central Africa for the Suppression of the Slave Trade, organised by Ismail, Khedive of Egypt. With Portraits, Map, and numerous Illustrations. New Edition. Crown 8vo. 6s.

THE ALBERT N'YANZA, Great Basin of the Nile, and Exploration of the Nile Sources. With Maps and Illustrations. Fifth Edition. Crown 8vo. 6s.

THE NILE TRIBUTARIES OF ABYSSINIA, and the Sword Hunters of the Hamran Arabs. With Maps and Illustrations. Sixth Edition. Crown 8vo. 6s.

THE EGYPTIAN QUESTION. Being Letters to the *Times* and the *Pall Mall Gazette*. With Map. Demy 8vo. 2s.

BALFOUR.—THE WORKS OF FRANCIS MAITLAND BALFOUR, M.A., LL.D., F.R.S., Fellow of Trinity College, and Professor of Animal Morphology in the University of Cambridge. Edited by M. FOSTER, F.R.S., Professor of Physiology in the University of Cambridge, and ADAM SEDGWICK, M.A., Fellow and Lecturer of Trinity College, Cambridge. In 4 vols. 8vo. £6 6s.

Vol. I. Special Memoirs, Vols. II. and III. A Treatise on Comparative Embryology. Vol. IV. Plates.

.˙. Vols. I. and IV. may be had separately. Price £3 13s. 6d.

BANCROFT.—THE HISTORY OF THE UNITED STATES OF AMERICA, FROM THE DISCOVERY OF THE CONTINENT. By GEORGE BANCROFT. New and thoroughly Revised Edition. Six Vols. Crown 8vo. 54s.

BARKER (LADY).—Works by LADY BARKER.

A YEAR'S HOUSEKEEPING IN SOUTH AFRICA. By LADY BARKER. With Illustrations. New and Cheaper Edition. Crown 8vo. 3s. 6d.

STATION LIFE IN NEW ZEALAND. New Edition. Crown 8vo. 3s. 6d.

LETTERS TO GUY. Crown 8vo. 5s.

BATH.—OBSERVATIONS ON BULGARIAN AFFAIRS. By the MAR-QUIS OF BATH. Crown 8vo. 3s. 6d.

BAZELY.—HENRY BAZELY, THE OXFORD EVANGELIST: A Memoir. By the Rev. E. L. HICKS, M.A., Rector of Fenny Compton; Hon. Canon of Worcester; sometime Fellow and Tutor of Corpus Christi College, Oxford. With a Steel Portrait engraved by STODART. Crown 8vo. 6s.

BECKER.—DISTURBED IRELAND, being the Letters Written during the Winter of 1880—1881. By BERNARD H. BECKER, Special Commissioner of *The Daily News*. With Route Maps. Crown 8vo. 6s.

BEESLY.—STORIES FROM THE HISTORY OF ROME. By Mrs. BEESLY. Extra fcap. 8vo. 2s. 6d.

BERLIOZ, HECTOR, AUTOBIOGRAPHY OF, Member of the Institute of France from 1803–1865; comprising his Travels in Italy, Germany, Russia, and England. Translated entire from the second Paris Edition by RACHEL (Scott Russell) HOLMES and ELEANOR HOLMES. 2 vols. Crown 8vo. 21s.

BERNARD (ST.)—THE LIFE AND TIMES OF ST. BERNARD, Abbot of Clairvaux. By J. C. MORISON, M.A. New Edition. Crown 8vo. 6s. (Biographical Series.)

BIOGRAPHICAL SKETCHES, 1852—1875. By HARRIET MAR-
TINEAU. With four Additional Sketches, and Autobiographical Sketch. Fifth
Edition. Crown 8vo. 6s. (Biographical Series.)

BLACKBURNE.—BIOGRAPHY OF THE RIGHT HON. FRANCIS
BLACKBURNE, Late Lord Chancellor of Ireland. Chiefly in connection with
his Public and Political Career. By his Son, EDWARD BLACKBURNE, Q.C.
With Portrait engraved by JEENS. 8vo. 12s.

BLACKIE.—WHAT DOES HISTORY TEACH? Two Edinburgh Lectures.
By JOHN STUART BLACKIE, Emeritus Professor of Greek in the University of
Edinburgh. Globe 8vo. 2s. 6d.

BLAKE.—LIFE OF WILLIAM BLAKE. With Selections from his Poems
and other Writings. Illustrated from Blake's own Works. By ALEXANDER
GILCHRIST. A new and Enlarged Edition, with additional Letters, and a
Memoir of the Author. Printed on hand-made paper, the Illustrations on India
paper, and mounted in the text. 2 vols. Cloth elegant, gilt, with Designs after
Blake by FREDERICK J. SHIELDS. Medium 8vo. £2 2s.

BLANDFORD (W. T.)—GEOLOGY AND ZOOLOGY OF ABYS-
SINIA. By W. T. BLANDFORD. 8vo. 21s.

BOLEYN, ANNE: A Chapter of English History, 1527-1536. By PAUL
FRIEDMANN. 2 vols. Demy 8vo. 28s.

BONAR.—MALTHUS AND HIS WORK. By JAMES BONAR, M.A., Balliol
College, Oxford. 8vo. 12s. 6d.

BOUGHTON—ABBEY.—SKETCHING RAMBLES IN HOLLAND.
By G. H. BOUGHTON, A.R.A., and E. A. ABBEY. With numerous Illustrationsd
Fcap. 4to. 21s.

BRIMLEY.—ESSAYS. By the late GEORGE BRIMLEY, M.A., Librarian of
Trinity College, Cambridge. Edited by W. G. CLARK, M.A., Fellow and
Tutor of Trinity College, Cambridge. New Edition. Globe 8vo. 5s.
CONTENTS.—Tennyson's Poems—Wordsworth's Poems—Poetry and Criticism—
Carlyle's Life of Sterling—" Esmond "—" Westward Ho ! "—Wilson's " Noctes
Ambrosianæ"—Comte's " Positive Philosophy," &c.

BRONTË.—CHARLOTTE BRONTË. A Monograph. By T. WEMYSS REID.
With Illustrations. Third Edition. Crown 8vo. 6s. (Biographical Series.)

BROOKE.—THE RAJA OF SARAWAK: an Account of Sir James Brooke.
K.C.B., LL.D. Given chiefly through Letters or Journals. By GERTRUDE L.
JACOB. With Portrait and Maps. Two Vols. 8vo. 25s.

BRYCE.—Works by JAMES BRYCE, M.P., D.C.L., Regius Professor of Civil
Law, Oxford :—

THE HOLY ROMAN EMPIRE. Eighth Edition, Revised and Enlarged.
Crown 8vo. 7s. 6d.

TRANSCAUCASIA AND ARARAT: being notes of a Vacation Tour in the
Autumn of 1876. With an Illustration and Map. Third Edition. Crown
8vo. 9s.

BUCKLAND.—OUR NATIONAL INSTITUTIONS. A Short Sketch for
Schools. By ANNA BUCKLAND. 18mo. 1s.

BURGOYNE.—POLITICAL AND MILITARY EPISODES DURING
THE FIRST HALF OF THE REIGN OF GEORGE III. Derived from the
Life and Correspondence of the Right Hon. J. Burgoyne, Lieut.-General in his
Majesty's Army, and M.P. for Preston. By E. B. DE FONBLANQUE. With
Portrait, Heliotype Plate, and Maps. 8vo. 16s.

BURKE.—LETTERS, TRACTS, AND SPEECHES ON IRISH
AFFAIRS. By EDMUND BURKE. Arranged and Edited by MATTHEW
ARNOLD. With a Preface. Crown 8vo. 6s.

CAMBRIDGE.—MEMORIALS OF CAMBRIDGE. Greatly Enlarged and partly Rewritten (1851—66). By Charles Henry Cooper, F.S.A. With Seventy-four Views of the Colleges, Churches, and other Public Buildings of the University and Town, engraved on steel by J. Le Keux, together with about Forty-five of those engraved on Copper by Storer, and a few Lithographs, with Twenty additional Etchings on Copper by Robert Farren. 8vo. 3 vols. £3 15s. Fifty copies of the Etchings, by R. Farren, from the "Memorials of Cambridge," proofs signed in portfolio. £3 3s.

CAMERON.—OUR FUTURE HIGHWAY. By V. Lovett Cameron, C.B., Commander, R.N. With Illustrations. 2 vols. Crown 8vo. 21s.

CAMPBELL.—LOG-LETTERS FROM THE "CHALLENGER." By Lord George Campbell. With Map. Seventh and Cheaper Edition. Crown 8vo. 6s.

CAMPBELL.—MY CIRCULAR NOTES; Extracts from Journals; Letters sent Home; Geological and other Notes, written while Travelling Westwards round the World, from July 6th, 1874, to July 6th, 1875. By J. F. Campbell, Author of "Frost and Fire." Cheaper Issue. Crown 8vo. 6s.

CARLYLE.—CARLYLE PERSONALLY AND IN HIS WRITINGS. Two Lectures by David Masson, M.A., LL.D. Extra fcap. 8vo. 2s. 6d.

EARLY LETTERS OF THOMAS CARLYLE. Edited by Charles Eliot Norton. 2 vols. With two portraits. Crown 8vo. [*Just Ready.*
LETTERS BETWEEN CARLYLE AND GOETHE. Edited by Charles Eliot Norton. Crown 8vo. [*Shortly.*
REMINISCENCES BY THOMAS CARLYLE. Edited by Charles Eliot Norton. A New Edition. 2 vols. Crown 8vo. [*Immediately.*

CARPENTER.—THE LIFE AND WORK OF MARY CARPENTER. By J. Estlin Carpenter, M.A. With Steel Portrait. Crown 8vo. 6s. (Biographical Series.)

CARR (J. COMYNS).—PAPERS ON ART. By J. Comyns Carr. Extra Crown 8vo. 8s. 6d.

CARSTARES.—WILLIAM CARSTARES: a Character and Career of the Revolutionary Epoch (1649—1715). By Robert Story, Minister of Rosneath. 8vo. 12s.

CASSEL.—MANUAL OF JEWISH HISTORY AND LITERATURE; preceded by a Brief Summary of Bible History, by Dr. D. Cassel. Translated by Mrs. Henry Lucas. Fcap. 8vo. 2s. 6d.

CAUCASUS, NOTES ON THE. By Wanderer. 8vo. 9s.

CHALLENGER.—REPORT ON THE SCIENTIFIC RESULTS OF THE VOYAGE OF H.M.S. "CHALLENGER," DURING THE YEARS 1873-76. Under the command of Captain Sir George Nares, R.N., F.R.S., and Captain Frank Tourle Thomson, R N. Prepared under the Superintendence of Sir C. Wyville Thomson, Knt., F.R.S., &c., and now of John Murray, F.R.S.E., one of the Naturalists of the Expedition. With Illustrations. *Published by order of Her Majesty's Government.*

    Volume I. Zoology. Royal, 37s. 6d. Or
Part I. Report on the Brachiopoda, 2s. 6d.
  II. Report on the Pennatulida, 4s.
  III. Report on the Ostracoda, 15s.
  IV. Report on the Bones of Cetacea, 2s.
  V. The Development of the Green Turtle, 4s. 6d.
  VI. Report on the Shore Fishes, 10s.

CHALLENGER—*continued.*

Volume II. Zoology. 50s. Or
Part VII. Report on the Corals, 15s.
VIII. Report on the Birds, 35s.

Volume III. Zoology. 50s. Or
Part IX. Report on the Echinoidea, 36s.
X. Report on the Pycnogonida, 14s.

Volume IV. Zoology. 50s. Or
Part XI. Report on the Anatomy of the Tubinares, 6s.
XII. Report on the Deep-sea Medusæ, 20s.
XIII. Report on the Holdthurioidea (Part I.), 24s.

Volume V. Zoology. 50s. Or
Part XIV. Report on the Ophiuroideæ.
XV. Some points in the Anatomy of the Thylasine, Cuscus, and Phascogale,
with an account of the Comparative Anatomy of the Intrinsic Muscles
and Nerves of the Mammalian Pes.

Volume VI. Zoology. 30s.
Part XVI. Report on the Actiniaria, 12s.
XVII. Report on the Tunicata, 30s.

Volume VII. Zoology. 30s. Or
Part XVIII. Report on the Anatomy of the Spheniscidæ, 13s. 6d.
XIX. Report on the Pelagic Hemiptera, 3s. 6d.
XX. Report on the Hydroida (first part). Plumularidæ, 9s.
XXI. Report on the Specimens of the Genus Orbitolites, 4s.

Volume VIII. Zoology. 40s. Or
Part XXIII. Report on the Copepoda, 24s.
XXIV. Reports on the Calcarea, 6s.
XXV. Report on the Cerripedia, Systematic Part, 10s.

Volume IX. Zoology. 63s. 6d. Or
Part XXII. With Vol. of 115 Plates, 63s. 6d.

Volume X. Zoology. 50s. Or
Part XXVI. Report on the Nudibranchiata, 10s.
XXVII. Report on the Myzostomida, 10s.
XXVIII. Report on the Cirripedia—Anatomical Part, 6s.
XXIX. Report on the Human Skeleton—the Crania, 6s.
XXX. Report on the Polyzoa—the Cheilostomata, 20s.

Volume XI. Zoology. 50s. Or
Part XXXI. Report on the Keratosa, 6s.
XXXII. Report on the Crinodea—the Stalked Crinoids, 38s.
XXXIII. Report on the Isopoda—the Genus Serotis, 6s.

Volume XII. Zoology. 60s.

Volume XIII. Zoology. 50s. Or
Part XXXV. Report on the Lamellibranchiata, 21s.
XXXVI. Report on the Cephyrea, 4s.
XXXVII. Report on the Schizopoda, 25s.

Volume XIV. Zoology. 42s. Or
Part XXXVIII. Report on the Tunicata. By WILLIAM A. HERDMAN, D Sc.,
F.L.S., F.R.S.E., 30s.
XXXIX. Report on the Holothurioidea. By HJALMAR THÉEL, 12s.

Volume XV. Zoology. 50s. Or
Part. XLI. Report on the Marseniadæ. By Dr. RUDOLPH BERGH, 1s. 6d.
XLII. Report on the Scaphapoda and Gasteropoda. By the Rev. ROBERT
BOOG WATSON, F.L.S., 45s.
XLIII. Report on the Polyplacophora. By ALFRED C. HADDON, M.A.,
M.R.I.A., 3s. 6d.

CHALLENGER—*continued.*

Volume XVI. Zoology.   40*.   Or
Part XLIV. Report on the Cephalopoda.   By WILLIAM EVANS HOYLE, M.A.,
(Oxon.), M.R.C.S., F.R.S.E., 18*.
XLV. Report on the Stomatopoda.   By W. K. BROOKS, 9*.
XLVI. Report on the Reef-Corals.   By JOHN J. QUELCH, B.Sc. (Lond.),
8*. 6*d*.
XLVII. Report on the Human Skeletons.   Second Part.   By Sir WILLIAM
TURNER, Knt , M.B., 1 L.D., F.R.S.S., L. and E.   4*. 6*d*.
PHYSICS AND CHEMISTRY.   Volume I.   21*.   Or
Part 1. Report on Composition of Ocean Water, 9*. 6*d*.
II. Report on Specific Gravity of Ocean Water, 3*. 6*d*.
III. Report on the Temperature of Ocean Water, 8*. 6*d*.
NARRATIVE, Volume I.   Parts I. and II.   £6 16*. 6*d*.
NARRATIVE, Volume II.   30*.   Or
Magnetical and Meteorological Observations.   25*.
Appendix A.   Report on the Pressure Errors of the " Challenger " Thermometers.
2*. 6*d*.
Appendix B.   Report on the Petrology of St. Paul's Rocks.   2*. 6*d*.
BOTANY, Volume I.   40*.   Or
Report on the Present State of Knowledge of various Insular Floras.   By W.
B. HEMSLEY, A L.S.   2*.
Part I. Report on the Botany of the Bermudas.   By W. B. HEMSLEY, A.L.S.   8*.
II. Report on the Botany of St. Paul's Rocks, Fernando-Noronha, Ascension,
St. Helena, South Trinidad, Tristan da Cunha, Prince Edward Group,
Crozets, Kerguelen, Macdonald Group, Amsterdam, and St. Paul Islands.
By W. B. HEMSLEY, A.L.S.   18*.
III. Report on the Botany of Juan Fernandez, the South-Eastern Moluccas, and
the Admiralty Islands.   By W. B. HEMSLEY, A.L.S.   12*.

CHATTERTON : A BIOGRAPHICAL STUDY.   By DANIEL WILSON,
LL.D., Professor of History and English Literature in University College,
Toronto.   Crown 8vo.   6*. 6*d*.

CHATTERTON : A STORY OF THE YEAR 1770.   By Professor MASSON,
LL.D.   Crown 8vo.   5*.

CICERO.—THE LIFE AND LETTERS OF MARCUS TULLIUS
CICERO: being a New Translation of the Letters included in Mr. Watson's
Selection.   With Historical and Critical Notes, by Rev. G. E. JEANS, M.A.,
Fellow of Hertford College, Oxford, Assistant-Master in Haileybury College,
8vo.   10*. 6*d*.

CLARK.—MEMORIALS FROM JOURNALS AND LETTERS OF
SAMUEL CLARK, M.A., formerly Principal of the National Society's Train-
ing College, Battersea.   Edited with Introduction by his WIFE.   With Portrait.
Crown 8vo.   7*. 6*d*.

CLASSICAL WRITERS.—Edited by JOHN RICHARD GREEN.   Fcap.
8vo.   Price 1*. 6*d*. each.

EURIPIDES.   By Professor MAHAFFY.
MILTON.   By the Rev. STOPFORD A. BROOKE.
LIVY.   By the Rev. W. W. CAPES, M.A.
VERGIL.   By Professor NETTLESHIP, M.A.
SOPHOCLES.   By Professor L. CAMPBELL, M.A.
DEMOSTHENES.   By Professor S. H. BUTCHER, M.A.
TACITUS.   By Rev. A. J. CHURCH, M.A., and W. J. BRODRIBB, M.A.
Other Volumes to follow.

CLIFFORD (W. K.)—LECTURES AND ESSAYS.   Edited by LESLIE
STEPHEN and FREDERICK POLLOCK, with Introduction by F. POLLOCK.   Two
Portraits.   2 vols.   8vo.   25*.
Popular Edition.   With Portrait.   Crown 8vo.   8*. 6*d*.

COMBE.—THE LIFE OF GEORGE COMBE. Author of " The Constitution of Man." By CHARLES GIBBON. With Three Portraits engraved by JEENS. Two Vols. 8vo. 37s.

CORNWALL, AN UNSENTIMENTAL JOURNEY THROUGH. By the Author of " John Halifax, Gentleman." With numerous Illustrations by C. NAPIER HEMY. Medium 4to. 12s. 6d.

COUES.—NORTH AMERICAN BIRDS, KEY TO. Containing a Concise Account of every Species of Living and Fossil Bird at present known from the Continent north of the Mexican and United States Boundary, inclusive of Greenland. Second Edition, revised to date, and entirely rewritten. With which are incorporated GENERAL ORNITHOLOGY, an Outline of the Structure and Classification of Birds; and FIELD ORNITHOLOGY, a Manual of Collecting, Preparing, and Preserving Birds. By ELLIOTT COUES, M.A., M.D., Ph.D., Member of the National Academy of Science, &c. &c. Profusely Illustrated. Demy 8vo. £2 2s.

COX (G. V.)—RECOLLECTIONS OF OXFORD. By G. V. Cox, M.A., New College, late Esquire Bedel and Coroner in the University of Oxford. Cheaper Edition. Crown 8vo. 6s.

CUNYNGHAME (SIR A. T.)—MY COMMAND IN SOUTH AFRICA, 1874—1878. Comprising Experiences of Travel in the Colonies of South Africa and the Independent States. By Sir ARTHUR THURLOW CUNYNG-HAME, G.C.B., then Lieutenant-Governor and Commander of the Forces in South Africa. Third Edition. 8vo. 12s. 6d.

"DAILY NEWS."—THE DAILY NEWS' CORRESPONDENCE of the War between Russia and Turkey, to the fall of Kars. Including the letters of Mr. Archibald Forbes, Mr. J. E. McGahan, and other Special Correspondents in Europe and Asia. Second Edition, Enlarged. Cheaper Edition. Crown 8vo. 6s.

FROM THE FALL OF KARS TO THE CONCLUSION OF PEACE. Cheaper Edition. Crown 8vo. 6s.

DARWIN.—CHARLES DARWIN: MEMORIAL NOTICES RE-PRINTED FROM "NATURE." By THOMAS H. HUXLEY, F.R.S.; G. J. ROMANES, F.R.S.; ARCHIBALD GEIKIE, F.R.S; and W. T. THISELTON DYER, F.R.S. With a Portrait engraved by C. H. JEENS. Crown 8vo. 2s. 6d. *Nature Series.*

DAVIDSON.—THE LIFE OF A SCOTTISH PROBATIONER; being a Memoir of Thomas Davidson, with his Poems and Letters. By JAMES BROWN, Minister of St. James's Street Church, Paisley. Second Edition, revised and enlarged, with Portrait. Crown 8vo. 7s. 6d.

DAWSON.—AUSTRALIAN ABORIGINES. The Language and Customs of Several Tribes of Aborigines in the Western District of Victoria, Australia. By JAMES DAWSON. Small 4to. 14s.

DEAK.—FRANCIS DEAK, HUNGARIAN STATESMAN: A Memoir With a Preface, by the Right Hon. M. E. GRANT DUFF, M.P. With Portrait. 8vo. 12s. 6d.

DEAS.—THE RIVER CLYDE. An Historical Description of the Rise and Progress of the Harbour of Glasgow, and of the Improvement of the River from Glasgow to Port Glasgow. By J. DEAS, M. Inst. C.E. 8vo. 10s. 6d.

DENISON.—A HISTORY OF CAVALRY FROM THE EARLIEST TIMES. With Lessons for the Future. By Lieut.-Colonel GEORGE DENISON, Commanding the Governor-General's Body Guard, Canada, Author of " Modern Cavalry." With Maps and Plans. 8vo. 18s.

DE WINT.—THE LIFE OF PETER DE WINT. By J. COMYNS CARR, Author of "Papers on Art," &c. Illustrated with Twenty Photogravures from the Artist's Pictures. Medium 4to.   [*In preparation.*

DICKENS'S DICTIONARY OF PARIS, 1885.—(Fourth Year.) An Unconventional Handbook. With Maps, Plans, &c. 18mo. Paper Cover, 1s. Cloth, 1s. 6d.

DICKENS'S DICTIONARY OF LONDON, 1886.—(Eight Year.) An Unconventional Handbook. With Maps, Plans, &c. 18mo. Paper Cover, 1s. Cloth, 1s. 6d.

DICKENS'S DICTIONARY OF THE THAMES, 1886.—An Unconventional Handbook. With Maps, Plans, &c. Paper Cover, 1s. Cloth, 1s. 6d.

DICKENS'S DICTIONARY OF THE UNIVERSITY OF OXFORD. 18mo. paper cover. 1s.

DICKENS'S DICTIONARY OF THE UNIVERSITY OF CAMBRIDGE. 18mo paper cover. 1s.

DICKENS'S DICTIONARY OF THE UNIVERSITIES OF OXFORD AND CAMBRIDGE. 18mo. cloth. 2s. 6d.

DICKENS'S CONTINENTAL A.B.C. RAILWAY GUIDE. Published on the 1st of each Month. 18mo. 1s.

DILKE.—GREATER BRITAIN. A Record of Travel in English-speaking Countries during 1866—67. (America, Australia, India.) By the Right Hon. Sir CHARLES WENTWORTH DILKE, M.P. Eighth Edition, with Additions. Crown 8vo. 6s.

DILETTANTI SOCIETY'S PUBLICATIONS. IONA, ANTI-QUITIES OF. Vols. I. II. and III. £2 2s. each, or £5 5s. the set.
PENROSE.—AN INVESTIGATION OF THE PRINCIPLES OF ATHE-NIAN ARCHITECTURE; or, The Results of a recent Survey conducted chiefly with reference to the Optical refinements exhibited in the construction of the Ancient Buildings at Athens. By FRANCIS CRANMER PENROSE, Archt., M.A., &c. Illustrated by numerous Engravings. £7 7s.
SPECIMENS OF ANCIENT SCULPTURE; Egyptian, Etruscan, Greek, and Roman. Selected from different Collections in Great Britain by the Society of Dilettanti. Vol. II. £5 5s.
ANTIQUITIES OF IONIA. Part IV. Folio, half-morocco. £3 13s. 6d.

DOLET.—ETIENNE DOLET: the Martyr of the Renaissance. A Biography. With a Biographical Appendix, containing a Descriptive Catalogue of the Books written, printed, or edited by Dolet. By RICHARD COPLEY CHRISTIE, Lincoln College, Oxford, Chancellor of the Diocese of Manchester. With Illustrations. 8vo. 18s.

DOYLE.—HISTORY OF AMERICA. By J. A. DOYLE. With Maps. 18mo. 4s. 6d.   [*Historical Course.*

DRUMMOND OF HAWTHORNDEN : THE STORY OF HIS LIFE AND WRITINGS. By Professor MASSON. With Portrait and Vignette engraved by C. H. JEENS. Crown 8vo. 10s. 6d.

DUFF.—Works by the Right Hon. M. E. GRANT DUFF.
NOTES OF AN INDIAN JOURNEY. With Map. 8vo. 10s. 6d.
MISCELLANIES, POLITICAL AND LITERARY. 8vo. 10s. 6d.

EADIE.—LIFE OF JOHN EADIE, D.D., LL.D. By JAMES BROWN, D.D., Author of "The Life of a Scottish Probationer." With Portrait. Second Edition. Crown 8vo. 7s. 6d.

EGYPT.—RECENSEMENT GÉNÉRAL DE L'EGYPTE. 15 Gamad Akhar 1299. 3 Mai, 1882. Direction du Recensement ministère de l'Intérieur. Tome premier. Royal 4to. £2 2s.

ELLIOTT.—LIFE OF HENRY VENN ELLIOTT, of Brighton. By JOSIAH BATEMAN, M.A. With Portrait, engraved by JEENS. Third and Cheaper Edition. Extra fcap. 8vo. 6s.

EMERSON. — THE COLLECTED WORKS OF RALPH WALDO EMERSON. (Uniform with the Eversley Edition of Charles Kingsley's Novels.) Globe 8vo. Price 5s. each volume.

1. MISCELLANIES. With an Inductory Essay by JOHN MORLEY.	4. ENGLISH TRAITS; and REPRESENTATIVE MEN.
2. ESSAYS.	5. CONDUCT OF LIFE; and SOCIETY and SOLITUDE.
3. POEMS.	6. LETTERS; AND SOCIAL AIMS, &c.

ENGLISH ILLUSTRATED MAGAZINE, THE. Profusely Illustrated. Published Monthly. Number I., October 1883. Price Sixpence.

Yearly Volume, 1883–1884, consisting of 792 closely-printed pages, and containing 428 Woodcut Illustrations of various sizes. Bound in extra cloth, coloured edges. Royal 8vo. 7s. 6d.

Yearly Volume, 1884–1885, consisting of 840 closely printed pages, and containing nearly 500 Woodcut Illustrations of various sizes. Bound in extra cloth, coloured edges. Royal 8vo. 8s.

Yearly Volume, 1885–1886, consisting of 832 closely printed pages, and containing nearly 500 Woodcut Illustrations of various sizes. Bound in extra cloth, coloured edges. Royal 8vo. 8s.
Cloth Covers for binding Volumes, 1s. 6d. each.

ENGLISH ILLUSTRATED MAGAZINE. PROOF IMPRESSIONS OF ENGRAVINGS ORIGINALLY PUBLISHED IN "THE ENGLISH ILLUSTRATED MAGAZINE," 1884. In Portfolio. 4to. 21s.

ENGLISH MEN OF LETTERS.—Edited by JOHN MORLEY. A Series of Short Books to tell people what is best worth knowing as to the Life, Character, and Works of some of the great English Writers. In Crown 8vo. price 2s. 6d. each.

I. DR. JOHNSON. By LESLIE STEPHEN.
II. SIR WALTER SCOTT. By R. H. HUTTON.
III. GIBBON. By J. COTTER MORISON.
IV. SHELLEY. By J. A. SYMONDS.
V. HUME. By THOMAS H. HUXLEY, F.R.S.
VI. GOLDSMITH. By WILLIAM BLACK.
VII. DEFOE. By W. MINTO.
VIII. BURNS. By Principal SHAIRP.
IX. SPENSER. By the Very Rev. the DEAN OF ST. PAUL'S.
X. THACKERAY. By ANTHONY TROLLOPE.
XI. BURKE. By JOHN MORLEY.
XII. MILTON. By MARK PATTISON.
XIII. HAWTHORNE. By HENRY JAMES.
XIV. SOUTHEY. By Professor DOWDEN.
XV. BUNYAN. By J. A. FROUDE.
XVI. CHAUCER. By Professor A. W. WARD.
XVII. COWPER. By GOLDWIN SMITH.
XVIII. POPE. By LESLIE STEPHEN.
XIX. BYRON. By Professor NICHOL.
XX. LOCKE. By Professor FOWLER.
XXI. WORDSWORTH. By F. W. H. MYERS.
XXII. DRYDEN. By G. SAINTSBURY.

ENGLISH MEN OF LETTERS—*continued*.

XXIII. LANDOR. By SIDNEY COLVIN.
XXIV. DE QUINCEY. By Professor MASSON.
XXV. CHARLES LAMB. By Rev. ALFRED AINGER.
XXVI. BENTLEY. By Professor R. C. JEBB.
XXVII. DICKENS. By Professor A. W. WARD.
XXVIII. GRAY. By EDMUND GOSSE.
XXIX. SWIFT. By LESLIE STEPHEN.
XXX. STERNE. By H. D. TRAILL.
XXXI. MACAULAY. By J. COTTER MORISON.
XXXII. FIELDING. By AUSTIN DOBSON.
XXXIII. SHERIDAN. By Mrs. OLIPHANT.
XXXIV. ADDISON. By W. J. COURTHOPE.
XXXV. BACON. By the Very Rev. the DEAN OF ST. PAUL'S.
XXXVI. COLERIDGE. By H. D. TRAILL.
XXXVII. SIR PHILIP SIDNEY. By J. ADDINGTON SYMONDS.
XXXVIII. KEATS. By SIDNEY COLVIN.   [*In the press.*

In Preparation :—
ADAM SMITH. By LEONARD H. COURTNEY, M.P.
BERKELEY. By THOMAS H. HUXLEY.
Other Volumes to follow.

ENGLISH POETS: SELECTIONS, with Critical Introductions by various

Writers, and a General Introduction by MATTHEW ARNOLD, Edited by T. H.
WARD, M.A., late Fellow of Brasenose College, Oxford. 4 vols. Crown 8vo.
7s. 6d. each.

Vol. I. CHAUCER to DONNE.
Vol. II. BEN JONSON to DRYDEN.
Vol. III. ADDISON to BLAKE.
Vol. IV. WORDSWORTH to ROSSETTI.

ENGLISH STATESMEN.—Under the above title Messrs. MACMILLAN

and Co. beg to announce a series of short biographies, not designed to be a
complete roll of famous statesmen, but to present in historic order the lives and
work of those leading actors in our affairs who by their direct influence have left
an abiding mark on the policy, the institutions, and the position of Great Britain
among states.
The following list of subjects is the result of careful selection. The great movements of national history are made to follow one another in a connected course,
and the series is intended to form a continuous narrative of English freedom,
order, and power.

WILLIAM THE CONQUEROR. By EDWARD A. FREEMAN, D.C.L.,
LL.D.   [*In the press.*
HENRY II. By Mrs. J. R. GREEN.
EDWARD I. By FREDERICK POLLOCK.
HENRY VII. By J. COTTER MORISON.
WOLSEY. By Prof. M. CREIGHTON.
ELIZABETH. By the DEAN OF ST. PAUL'S.
OLIVER CROMWELL. By FREDERICK HARRISON.
WILLIAM III. By H. D. TRAILL.
WALPOLE. By LESLIE STEPHEN.
CHATHAM. By J. A. FROUDE.
PITT. By JOHN MORLEY.
PEEL. By J. R. THURSFIELD.

ETON COLLEGE, HISTORY OF. By H. C. MAXWELL LYTE,

M.A. With numerous Illustrations by Professor DELAMOTTE, Coloured Plates,
and a Steel Portrait of the Founder, engraved by C. H. JEENS. New and
Cheaper Issue, with Corrections. Medium 8vo. Cloth elegant. 21s.

EUROPEAN HISTORY, Narrated in a Series of Historical Selections

from the best Authorities. Edited and arranged by E. M. SEWELL, and C. M.
YONGE. First Series, Crown 8vo. 6s. ; Second Series, 1088-1228. Third Edition.
Crown 8vo. 6s.

FAY.—MUSIC-STUDY IN GERMANY. From the Home Correspondence of AMY FAY, with a Preface by Sir GEORGE GROVE,D.C.L., Director of the Royal College of Music. Crown 8vo. 4s. 6d.

FISKE.—EXCURSIONS OF AN EVOLUTIONIST. By JOHN FISKE, M.A., LL.B., formerly Lecturer on Philosophy at Harvard University. Crown 8vo. 7s. 6d.

FISON AND HOWITT.—KAMILAROI AND KURNAI GROUP. Marriage and Relationship, and Marriage by Elopement, drawn chiefly from the usage of the Australian Aborigines. Also THE KURNAI TRIBE, their Customs in Peace and War. By LORIMER FISON, M.A., and A. W. HOWITT, F.G.S., with an Introduction by LEWIS H. MORGAN, LL.D., Author of "System of Consanguinity," "Ancient Society," &c. Demy 8vo. 15s.

FORBES (ARCHIBALD).—SOUVENIRS OF SOME CON-TINENTS. By ARCHIBALD FORBES, LL.D. Crown 8vo. 6s.

FRAMJI.—HISTORY OF THE PARSIS: Including their Manners, Customs, Religion, and Present Position. By DOSABHAI FRAMJI KARAKA, Presidency Magistrate and Chairman of Her Majesty's Bench of Justice, Bombay, Fellow of the Bombay University, Member Bombay Branch of the Royal Asiatic Society, &c. 2 vols. Medium 8vo. With Illustrations. 36s.

FRANCIS OF ASSISI. By Mrs. OLIPHANT. New Edition. Crown 8vo. 6s. (Biographical Series.)

FRASER.—THE LIFE OF JAMES FRASER, Bishop of Manchester. By THOMAS HUGHES, Q.C. 8vo. [In the press.

FREEMAN.—Works by EDWARD A. FREEMAN, D.C.L., LL.D., Regius Professor of Modern History in the University of Oxford:—

THE OFFICE OF THE HISTORICAL PROFESSOR. An Inaugural Lecture, read in the Museum at Oxford, October 15, 1884. Crown 8vo. 2s.

THE GROWTH OF THE ENGLISH CONSTITUTION FROM THE EARLIEST TIMES. Fourth Edition. Crown 8vo 5s.

HISTORICAL ESSAYS. Fourth Edition. 8vo. 10s. 6d.

CONTENTS:—I. "The Mythical and Romantic Elements in Early English History;" II. "The Continuity of English History;" III. "The Relations between the Crowns of England and Scotland;" IV. "St. Thomas of Canterbury and his Biographers;" V. "The Reign of Edward the Third;" VI. "The Holy Roman Empire;" VII. "The Franks and the Gauls;" VIII. "The Early Sieges of Paris;" IX. "Frederick the First, King of Italy;" X. "The Emperor Frederick the Second;" XI. "Charles the Bold;" XII. "Presidential Government.'

HISTORICAL ESSAYS. Second Series. Second Edition, Enlarged. 8vo, 10s. 6d.

The principal Essays are:—"Ancient Greece and Mediæval Italy:" "Mr. Gladstone's Homer and the Homeric Ages:" "The Historians of Athens:" "The Athenian Democracy:" "Alexander the Great:" "Greece during the Macedonian Period:" "Mommsen's History of Rome:" "Lucius Cornelius Sulla:" "The Flavian Cæsars."

HISTORICAL ESSAYS. Third Series. 8vo. 12s.

CONTENTS:—"First Impressions of Rome." "The Illyrian Emperors and their Land." "Augusta Treverorum." "The Goths of Ravenna." "Race and Language." "The Byzantine Empire." "First Impressions of Athens." "Mediæval and Modern Greece." "The Southern Slaves." "Sicilian Cycles." "The Normans at Palermo."

COMPARATIVE POLITICS.—Lectures at the Royal Institution. To which is added the "Unity of History," the Rede Lecture at Cambridge, 1872. 8vo. 14s.

HISTORICAL AND ARCHITECTURAL SKETCHES: chiefly Italian. With Illustrations by the Author. Crown 8vo. 10s. 6d.

FREEMAN—*continued.*

SUBJECT AND NEIGHBOUR LANDS OF VENICE. Being a Companion Volume to "Historical and Architectural Sketches." With Illustrations. Crown 8vo. 10s. 6d.

ENGLISH TOWNS AND DISTRICTS. A Series of Addresses and Essays. With Illustrations and Map. 8vo. 14s.

OLD ENGLISH HISTORY. With Five Coloured Maps. New Edition. Extra fcap. 8vo. 6s.

HISTORY OF THE CATHEDRAL CHURCH OF WELLS, as illustrating the History of the Cathedral Churches of the Old Foundation. Crown 8vo. 3s. 6d.

GENERAL SKETCH OF EUROPEAN HISTORY. Being Vol. I. of a Historical Course for Schools, edited by E. A. FREEMAN. New Edition, enlarged with Maps, Chronological Table, Index, &c. 18mo. 3s. 6d.

DISESTABLISHMENT AND DISENDOWMENT. WHAT ARE THEY? Second Edition. Crown 8vo. 1s.

GREATER GREECE AND GREATER BRITAIN: GEORGE WASHINGTON, THE EXPANDER OF ENGLAND. Two Lectures. With an Appendix on Imperial Federation. Crown 8vo. 3s. 6d.

THE METHODS OF HISTORICAL STUDY. Eight Lectures. Read in the University of Oxford in Michaelmas Term, 1884, with the Inaugural Lecture "in the Office of the Historical Professor." 8vo. 10s. 6d.

GALTON.—Works by FRANCIS GALTON, F.R.S. :

METEOROGRAPHICA ; or, Methods of Mapping the Weather. Illustrated by upwards of 600 Printed and Lithographed Diagrams. 4to. 9s.

ENGLISH MEN OF SCIENCE : Their Nature and Nurture. 8vo. 8s. 6d.

INQUIRIES INTO HUMAN FACULTY AND ITS DEVELOPMENT. With Illustrations and Coloured and Plain Plates. Demy 8vo. 16s.

RECORD OF FAMILY FACULTIES. Consisting of Tabular Forms and Directions for Entering Data, with an Explanatory Preface. 4to. 2s. 6d.

LIFE HISTORY ALBUM ; Being a Personal Note-book, combining the chief advantages of a Diary, Photograph Album, a Register of Height, Weight, and other Anthropometrical Observations, and a Record of Illnesses. Containing Tabular Forms, Charts, and Explanations especially designed for popular use. Prepared by the direction of the Collective Investigation Committee of the British Medical Association, and Edited by FRANCIS GALTON, F.R.S., Chairman of the Life History Sub-Committee. 4to. 3s. 6d. Or, with Cards of Wools for Testing Colour Vision. 4s. 6d.

GARDNER.—SAMOS AND SAMIAN COINS. By PERCY GARDNER, M.A. F.S.A. British Museum. Disnay Professor of Archæology in the University of Cambridge, and Hon. Foreign Secretary of the Numismatic Society. Demy 8vo. 7s. 6d.

GEDDES.—THE PROBLEM OF THE HOMERIC POEMS. By W. D. GEDDES, LL.D., Professor of Greek in the University of Aberdeen. 8vo. 14s.

GEIKIE.—GEOLOGICAL SKETCHES AT HOME AND ABROAD. By ARCHIBALD GEIKIE, LL.D., F.R.S., Director General of the Geological Surveys of the United Kingdom. With illustrations. 8vo. 10s. 6d.

GLADSTONE.—HOMERIC SYNCHRONISM. An inquiry into the Time and Place of Homer. By the Right Hon. W. E. GLADSTONE, M.P. Crown 8vo. 6s.

GOETHE AND MENDELSSOHN (1821—1831). Translated from the German of Dr. KARL MENDELSSOHN, Son of the Composer, by M. E. VON GLEHN. From the Private Diaries and Home Letters of Mendelssohn, with Poems and Letters of Goethe never before printed. Also with two New and Original Portraits, Fac-similes, and Appendix of Twenty Letters hitherto unpublished. Second Edition, enlarged. Crown 8vo. 5s.

GOETHE.—A LIFE OF GOETHE. By HEINRICH DÜNTZER. Translated by T. W. LYSTER, Assistant Librarian National Library of Ireland. With Illustrations. Two vols. Crown 8vo. 21s.

GOLDSMID.—TELEGRAPH AND TRAVEL. A Narrative of the Formation and Development of Telegraphic Communication between England and India, under the orders of Her Majesty's Government, with incidental Notices of the Countries traversed by the Lines. By Colonel SIR FREDERICK GOLDSMID, C.B., K.C.S.I., late Director of the Government Indo-European Telegraph. With numerous Illustrations and Maps. 8vo. 21s.

GORDON.—LAST LETTERS FROM EGYPT, to which are added Letters from the Cape. By LADY DUFF GORDON. With a Memoir by her Daughter, Mrs. Ross, and Portrait engraved by JEENS. Second Edition. Crown 8vo. 9s.

GORDON (CHARLES GEORGE). A SKETCH. By REGINALD H. BARNES, Vicar of Heavitree, and CHARLES E. BROWN, Major R.A. With Facsimile Letter. Crown 8vo. 1s.

GREAT CHRISTIANS OF FRANCE: ST. LOUIS and CALVIN. By M. GUIZOT, Member of the Institute of France. Crown 8vo. 6s. (Biographical Series.)

GREEN.—Works by JOHN RICHARD GREEN, M.A., LL.D.:—
THE MAKING OF ENGLAND. With Maps. Demy 8vo. 16s.
THE CONQUEST OF ENGLAND. With Maps. Demy 8vo. 18s.
HISTORY OF THE ENGLISH PEOPLE. Vol. I.—Early England—Foreign Kings—The Charter—The Parliament. With 8 Coloured Maps. 8vo. 16s. Vol. II.—The Monarchy, 1461—1540: The Restoration, 1540—1603. 8vo. 16s. Vol. III.—Puritan England, 1603—1660; The Revolution, 1660—1688. With 4 Maps. 8vo. 16s. Vol. IV.—The Revolution, 1683—1760: Modern England, 1760—1815. With Maps and Index. 8vo. 16s.
A SHORT HISTORY OF THE ENGLISH PEOPLE. With Coloured Maps, Genealogical Tables, and Chronological Annals. Crown 8vo. 8s. 6d. 118th Thousand.
STRAY STUDIES FROM ENGLAND AND ITALY. Crown 8vo. 8s. 6d. Containing : Lambeth and the Archbishops—The Florence of Dante—Venice and Rome—Early History of Oxford—The District Visitor—Capri—Hotels in the Clouds—Sketches in Sunshine, &c.
READINGS FROM ENGLISH HISTORY. Selected and Edited by JOHN RICHARD GREEN. In Three Parts. Fcap. 8vo. 1s. 6d. each. Part I.—From Hengest to Cressy. Part. II.—From Cressy to Cromwell. Part III.—From Cromwell to Balaklava.

GROVE.—A DICTIONARY OF MUSIC AND MUSICIANS (A.D. 1450—1886). By Eminent Writers, English and Foreign. With Illustrations and Woodcuts. Edited by Sir GEORGE GROVE, D.C.L., Director of the Royal College of Music. 8vo. Parts I. to XIV., XIX—XXI. 3s. 6d. each. Parts XV. and XVI. 7s. Parts XVII. and XVIII. 7s.
Vols. I., II., and III. 8vo. 21s. each.
Vol. I. A to Impromptu.—Vol. II. Improperia to Plain Song.—Vol. III. Planche to Sumer is Icumen In.
Cloth cases for binding Vols. I., II., and III. 1s. each.

GUEST.—LECTURES ON THE HISTORY OF ENGLAND. By M. J. GUEST. With Maps. Crown 8vo. 6s.

GUEST.—ORIGINES CELTICAE (a Fragment) and other Contributions to the History of Britain. By EDWIN GUEST, LL.D., D.C.L., F.R.S., late Master of Gonville and Caius College, Cambridge. With Maps, Plans, and a Portrait engraved on Steel by G. J. STODART. Two vols. Demy 8vo. 32s.

HAMERTON.—Works by P. G. HAMERTON:—
ETCHINGS AND ETCHERS. Third Edition, revised, with Forty-eight new Plates. Columbier 8vo.
THE INTELLECTUAL LIFE. With a Portrait of Leonardo da Vinci, etched by LEOPOLD FLAMENG. Second Edition. Crown 8vo. 10s. 6d.
THOUGHTS ABOUT ART. New Edition, revised, with an Introduction. Crown 8vo. 8s. 6d.
HUMAN INTERCOURSE. Third Thousand. Crown 8vo. 8s. 6d.

HANDEL.—THE LIFE OF GEORGE FREDERICK HANDEL. By W. S. Rockstro, Author of "A History of Music for Young Students." With an Introductory Notice by Sir George Grove, D.C.L. With a Portrait. Crown 8vo. 10s. 6d.

HARRISON.—THE CHOICE OF BOOKS; and other Literary Pieces. By Frederic Harrison. Second Edition. Globe 8vo. 6s.
A Choice Edition on large paper, 250 copies only printed. 8vo. 15s.

HARPER.—THE METAPHYSICS OF THE SCHOOL. By Thomas Harper, (S.J.) (In 5 vols.) Vols. I. and II. 8vo. 18s. each.—Vol. III., Part I. 12s.

HEINE.—A TRIP TO THE BROCKEN. By Heinrich Heine. Translated by R. McLintock. Crown 8vo. 3s. 6d.

HELLENIC STUDIES—JOURNAL OF. 8vo. Parts I. and II., constituting Vol. I. with 4to Atlas of Illustrations, 30s. Vol. II., with 4to. Atlas of Illustrations, 30s., or in Two Parts, 15s. each. Vol. III., Two Parts, with 4to Atlas of Illustrations, 15s. each. Vol. IV., Two Parts, with 4to. Atlas of Illustrations. Part I. 21s. Part II., 15s. Vol. V., Two Parts, with Illustrations, 15s. each. Vol VI., Two Parts, 15s. each. Vol. VII., Part I., 15s.
The Journal will be sold at a reduced price to Libraries wishing to subscribe, but official application must in each case be made to the Council. Information on this point, and upon the conditions of Membership, may be obtained on application to the Hon. Secretary, Mr. George Macmillan, 29, Bedford Street, Covent Garden.

HERODOTOS.—BOOKS I. TO III.—THE ANCIENT EMPIRES OF THE EAST. Edited, with Notes, Introductions, and Appendices, by A. H. Sayce, M.A. Oxford, Hon. LL.D. Dublin; Deputy-Professor of Comparative Philology. 8vo. 16s.

HERTEL.—OVERPRESSURE IN HIGH SCHOOLS IN DENMARK. By Dr. Hertel, Municipal Medical Officer, Copenhagen. Translated from the Danish by C. Godfrey Sörensen. With Introduction by Sir J. Crichton-Browne, M.D., LL.D., F.R.S. Crown 8vo. 3s. 6d.

HILL (O.)—Works by Octavia Hill.
OUR COMMON LAND. and other Essays. Extra fcap. 8vo. 3s. 6d.
HOMES OF THE LONDON POOR. Sewed. Crown 8vo. 1s.

HOBART.—ESSAYS AND MISCELLANEOUS WRITINGS OF VERE HENRY, LORD HOBART. With a Biographical Sketch. Edited by Mary, Lady Hobart. 2 vols. Demy 8vo. 25s.

HODGSON.—MEMOIR OF REV. FRANCIS HODGSON. B.D., Scholar, Poet, and Divine. By his son, the Rev. James T. Hodgson, M.A. Containing numerous Letters from Lord Byron and others. With Portrait engraved by Jeens. Two vols. Crown 8vo. 18s.

HOLE.—A GENEALOGICAL STEMMA OF THE KINGS OF ENGLAND AND FRANCE. By the Rev. C. Hole, M.A., Trinity College, Cambridge. On Sheet, 1s.
A BRIEF BIOGRAPHICAL DICTIONARY. Compiled and Arranged by the Rev. Charles Hole, M.A. Second Edition. 18mo. 4s. 6d.

HOOKER AND BALL.—MOROCCO AND THE GREAT ATLAS: Journal of a Tour in. By Sir Joseph D. Hooker, K.C.S.I., C.B., F.R.S., &c., and John Ball, F.R.S. With an Appendix, including a Sketch of the Geology of Morocco, by G. Maw, F.L.S., F.G.S. With Illustrations and Map. 8vo. 21s.

HOZIER (H. M.)—Works by Lieut.-Col. Henry M. Hozier, late Assistant Military Secretary to Lord Napier of Magdala:—
THE SEVEN WEEKS' WAR; Its Antecedents and Incidents. New and Cheaper Edition. With New Preface, Maps, and Plans. Crown 8vo. 6s.
THE INVASIONS OF ENGLAND: a History of the Past, with Lessons for the Future. Two Vols. 8vo. 28s.

HÜBNER.—A RAMBLE ROUND THE WORLD IN 1871. By M. LE BARON HÜBNER, formerly Ambassador and Minister. Translated by LADY HERBERT. New and Cheaper Edition. With numerous Illustrations. Crown 8vo. 6s.

HUGHES.—Works by THOMAS HUGHES, Q.C., Author of "Tom Brown' School Days."

MEMOIR OF A BROTHER. With Portrait of GEORGE HUGHES, after WATTS, Engraved by JEENS. Sixth Edition. Crown 8vo. 5s.

ALFRED THE GREAT. Crown 8vo. 6s.

MEMOIR OF DANIEL MACMILLAN. With Portrait after LOWES DICKINSON, Engraved by JEENS. Fifth Thousand. Crown 8vo. 4s. 6d.—POPULAR EDITION. 1s.

RUGBY, TENNESSEE. Being some account of the Settlement founded on the Cumberland Plateau by the Board of Aid to Land Ownership. With a report on the Soils of the Plateau by the Hon. F. W. KILLEBREW, A.M., Ph.D., Commissioner for Agriculture for the State of Tennessee. Crown 8vo. 4s. 6d.

GONE TO TEXAS: Letters from Our Boys. Edited by THOMAS HUGHES. Crown 8vo. 4s. 6d.

HUNT.—HISTORY OF ITALY. By the Rev. W. HUNT, M.A. Being the Fourth Volume of the Historical Course for Schools. Edited by EDWARD A. FREEMAN, D.C.L. New Edition, with Coloured Maps. 18mo. 3s. 6d.

HUTTON.—ESSAYS THEOLOGICAL AND LITERARY. By R. H. HUTTON, M.A. Cheaper issue. 2 vols. 8vo. 18s.

CONTENTS OF VOL. I. :—The moral significance of Atheism—The Atheistic Explanation of Religion—Science and Theism—Popular Pantheism—What is Revelation?—Christian Evidences, Popular and Critical—The Historical Problems of the Fourth Gospel—The Incarnation and Principles of Evidence—M. Renan's "Christ"—M. Renan's "St. Paul"—The Hard Church—Romanism, Protestantism, and Anglicanism.

CONTENTS OF VOL II. :—Goethe and his Influence—Wordsworth and his Genius—Shelley's Poetical Mysticism—Mr. Browning—The Poetry of the Old Testament—Arthur Hugh Clough—The Poetry of Matthew Arnold—Tennyson—Nathaniel Hawthorne.

IONIA.—THE ANTIQUITIES OF IONIA, see under Dilettanti Society's Publications.

IRVING.—THE ANNALS OF OUR TIME. A Diurnal of Events, Social and Political, Home and Foreign, from the Accession of Queen Victoria to the Peace of Versailles. By JOSEPH IRVING. New Edition, revised. 8vo. half-bound. 18s.

ANNALS OF OUR TIME. Supplement. From Feb. 28, 1871, to March 16, 1874. 8vo. 4s. 6d. ANNALS OF OUR TIME. Second Supplement. From March, 1874, to the Occupation of Cyprus. 8vo. 4s. 6d.

JAMES (Sir W. M.).—THE BRITISH IN INDIA. By the late Right Hon. Sir WILLIAM MILBOURNE JAMES, Lord Justice of Appeal. Edited by his Daughter, MARY J. SALIS SCHWABE. Demy 8vo. 12s. 6d.

JAMES.—Works by HENRY JAMES :

FRENCH POETS AND NOVELISTS. New Edition. Crown 8vo. 4s. 6d. CONTENTS:—Alfred de Musset; Théophile Gautier; Baudelaire; Honoré de Balzac; George Sand; The Two Ampères; Turgénieff, &c.

PORTRAITS OF PLACES. Crown 8vo. 7s. 6d.

JEBB.—MODERN GREECE. Two Lectures delivered before the Philosophical Institution of Edinburgh. With papers on "The Progress of Greece," and "Byron in Greece." By R. C. JEBB, M.A., LL.D. Edin. Professor of Greek in the University of Glasgow. Crown 8vo. 5s.

JEVONS.—LETTERS AND JOURNAL OF W. STANLEY JEVONS. Edited by his WIFE. With Portrait. Demy 8vo. 14s.

JOHNSON'S LIVES OF THE POETS.—The Six Chief Lives —Milton, Dryden, Swift, Addison, Pope, Gray. With Macaulay's "Life of Johnson." Edited, with Preface, by MATTHEW ARNOLD. New and Popular Edition. Crown 8vo. 4s. 6d.

KANT.—THE LIFE OF IMMANUEL KANT. By J. H. STUCKENBERG, D.D., late Professor in Wittenburg College, Ohio. With Portrait. 8vo. 14s.

KANT—MAX MÜLLER.—CRITIQUE OF PURE REASON BY IMMANUEL KANT. In commemoration of the Centenary of its first Publication. Translated into English by F. MAX MÜLLER. With an Historical Introduction by LUDWIG NOIRÉ. 2 vols. Demy 8vo. 16s. each.
Volume I. HISTORICAL INTRODUCTION, by LUDWIG NOIRÉ; &c. &c.
Volume II. CRITIQUE OF PURE REASON, translated by F. MAX MÜLLER. For the convenience of Students these volumes are now sold separately.

Of Professor Max Müller's translation of *The Critique of Pure Reason*, the *Times* says :—"Through this translation Kant's work has for the first time become international—the common property of the whole world."

KEARY.—ANNIE KEARY: a Memoir. By ELIZA KEARY. With a Portrait. Third Thousand. New Edition. Crown 8vo. 4s. 6d.

KELLOGG.—THE LIGHT OF ASIA AND THE LIGHT OF THE WORLD. A Comparison of the Legend, the Doctrine, and the Ethics of the Buddha with the Story, the Doctrine, and the Ethics of Christ. By S. H. KELLOGG, D.D., Professor in the Western Theological Seminary, Alleghany, Pa., U.S.A., eleven years Missionary to India, Corresponding Member of the American Oriental Society, Author of "A Grammar of the Hindi Language and Dialects," &c. Crown 8vo. 7s. 6d.

KILLEN.—ECCLESIASTICAL HISTORY OF IRELAND, from the Earliest Date to the Present Time. By W. D. KILLEN, D.D., President of Assembly's College, Belfast, and Professor of Ecclesiastical History. Two Vols. 8vo. 25s.

KINGSLEY (CHARLES).—Works by the Rev. CHARLES KINGSLEY, M.A., late Rector of Eversley and Canon of Westminster. (For other Works by the same Author, *see* THEOLOGICAL and BELLES LETTRES CATALOGUES)
AT LAST: A CHRISTMAS in the WEST INDIES. With nearly Fifty Illustrations. New Edition. Crown 8vo. 6s.
THE ROMAN AND THE TEUTON. A Series of Lectures delivered before the University of Cambridge. New and Cheaper Edition, with Preface by Professor MAX MÜLLER. Crown 8vo. 6s.
PLAYS AND PURITANS, and other Historical Essays. With Portrait of Sir WALTER RALEIGH. New Edition. Crown 8vo. 6s.
In addition to the Essay mentioned in the title, this volume contains other two— one on "Sir Walter Raleigh and his Time," and one on Froude's "History of England."
HISTORICAL LECTURES AND ESSAYS. Crown 8vo. 6s.
SANITARY AND SOCIAL LECTURES AND ESSAYS. Crown 8vo. 6s.
SCIENTIFIC LECTURES AND ESSAYS. Crown 8vo. 6s.
LITERARY AND GENERAL LECTURES. Crown 8vo. 6s.
GLAUCUS: OR THE WONDERS OF THE SHORE. With Coloured Illustrations. Crown 8vo. 6s.
Also a Presentation Edition in Ornamental Binding, gilt edges. Crown 8vo. 7s. 6d.

KINGSLEY (HENRY).—TALES OF OLD TRAVEL Re-narrated by HENRY KINGSLEY, F.R.G.S. With Eight Illustrations by HUARD. Sixth Edition. Crown 8vo. 5s.

LABBERTON.—AN HISTORICAL ATLAS. Comprising 141 Maps, to which is added, besides an Explanatory Text on the period delineated in each Map, a carefully selected Bibliography of the English Books and Magazine Articles bearing on that period. By ROBERT H. LABBERTON, Litt. Hum. Doctor. 4to. 12s. 6d.

LANFREY.—HISTORY OF NAPOLEON I. By P. LANFREY. A Translation made with the sanction of the author. New and Popular Edition. 4 vols. Crown 8vo. 30s.

LECTURES ON ART.—Delivered in support of the Society for Protection of Ancient Buildings. By REGD. STUART POOLE, Professor W. B. RICHMOND, E. J. POYNTER, R.A., J. T. MICKLETHWAITE, and WILLIAM MORRIS. Crown 8vo. 4s. 6d.

LETHBRIDGE.—A SHORT MANUAL OF THE HISTORY OF INDIA, with an account of INDIA AS IT IS. The Soil, Climate, and Productions; the People—their Races, Religions, Public Works, and Industries; the Civil Services and System of Administration. By Sir ROPER LETHBRIDGE, M.A., C.I.E., Press Commissioner with the Government of India, late Scholar of Exeter College, &c. &c. With Maps. Crown 8vo. 5s.

LIECHTENSTEIN.—HOLLAND HOUSE. By Princess MARIE LIECHTENSTEIN. With Five Steel Engravings by C. H. JEENS, after paintings by WATTS and other celebrated Artists, and numerous Illustrations drawn by Professor P. H. DELAMOTTE, and engraved on Wood by J. D. COOPER, W. PALMER, and JEWITT & Co., about 40 Illustrations by the Woodbury-type process, and India Proofs of the Steel Engravings. Two vols. Medium 4to., half morocco elegant. 4l. 4s.

LUBBOCK.—Works by Sir JOHN LUBBOCK, Bart., M.P., D.C.L., F.R.S.
ADDRESSES, POLITICAL AND EDUCATIONAL. 8vo. 8s. 6d.
FIFTY YEARS OF SCIENCE. Being the address delivered at York to the British Association, August, 1881. 8vo. 2s. 6d.

MACARTHUR.—HISTORY OF SCOTLAND. By MARGARET MACARTHUR. Being the Third Volume of the Historical Course for Schools, Edited by EDWARD A. FREEMAN, D.C.L. Second Edition. 18mo. 2s.

McLENNAN.—Works by JOHN FERGUSON McLENNAN.
THE PATRIARCHAL THEORY. Based on Papers of the late JOHN FERGUSON McLENNAN. Edited and completed by DONALD McLENNAN, of the Inner Temple, Barrister-at-Law. 8vo. 14s.
STUDIES IN ANCIENT HISTORY. Comprising a Reprint of "Primitive Marriage: an Inquiry into the Origin of the Form of Capture in Marriage Ceremonies." A New Edition. 8vo. 16s.

MACMILLAN (REV. HUGH).—For other Works by same Author, see THEOLOGICAL and SCIENTIFIC CATALOGUES.
HOLIDAYS ON HIGH LANDS; or, Rambles and Incidents in search of Alpine Plants. Second Edition, revised and enlarged. Globe 8vo. 6s.

MACMILLAN (DANIEL).—MEMOIR OF DANIEL MACMILLAN. By THOMAS HUGHES, Q.C., Author of "Tom Brown's Schooldays," etc. With Portrait engraved on Steel by C. H. JEENS, from a Painting by LOWES DICKINSON. Fifth Thousand. Crown 8vo. 4s. 6d.—POPULAR EDITION, Paper Covers. 1s.

MACREADY.—MACREADY'S REMINISCENCES AND SELECTIONS FROM HIS DIARIES AND LETTERS. Edited by Sir F. POLLOCK, Bart., one of his Executors. With Four Portraits engraved by JEENS. New and Cheaper Edition. Crown 8vo. 7s. 6d.

MAHAFFY.—Works by the Rev. J. P. MAHAFFY, M.A., Fellow of Trinity College, Dublin :—
SOCIAL LIFE IN GREECE FROM HOMER TO MENANDER. Fifth Edition, revised and enlarged, with a new chapter on Greek Art. Crown 8vo. 9s.
RAMBLES AND STUDIES IN GREECE. With Illustrations. New and enlarged Edition, with Map and Illustrations. Crown 8vo. 10s. 6d.

b

MARGARY.—THE JOURNEY OF AUGUSTUS RAYMOND MAR-GARY FROM SHANGHAE TO BHAMO AND BACK TO MANWYNE. From his Journals and Letters, with a brief Biographical Preface, a concluding chapter by Sir RUTHERFORD ALCOCK, K.C.B., and a Steel Portrait engraved by JEENS, and Map. 8vo. 10s. 6d.

MARTEL.—MILITARY ITALY. By CHARLES MARTEL. With Map. 8vo. 12s. 6d.

MARTIN.—THE HISTORY OF LLOYD'S, AND OF MARINE IN-SURANCE IN GREAT BRITAIN. With an Appendix containing Statistics relating to Marine Insurance. By FREDERICK MARTIN. 8vo. 14s.

MARTINEAU.—BIOGRAPHICAL SKETCHES, 1852-75. By HARRIET MARTINEAU. With Four Additional Sketches, and Autobiographical Sketch. Fifth Edition. Crown 8vo. 6s. (Biographical Series.)

MASSON (DAVID).—By DAVID MASSON, LL.D., Professor of Rhetoric and English Literature in the University of Edinburgh. For other Works by same Author, see PHILOSOPHICAL and BELLES LETTRES CATALOGUE.
CHATTERTON: A Story of the Year 1770. Crown 8vo. 5s.
THE THREE DEVILS: Luther's, Goethe's, and Milton's; and other Essays. Crown 8vo. 5s.
WORDSWORTH, SHELLEY, AND KEATS; and other Essays. Crown 8vo. 5s.
CARLYLE PERSONALLY AND IN HIS WRITINGS. Two Lectures. Extra fcap. 8vo. 2s. 6d.

MATHEWS.—LIFE OF CHARLES J. MATHEWS. Chiefly Autobi-ographical. With Selections from his Correspondence and Speeches. Edited by CHARLES DICKENS. Two Vols. 8vo 25s.

MAURICE.—LIFE OF FREDERICK DENISON MAURICE. Chiefly told in his own Letters. Edited by his Son, FREDERICK MAURICE. With Two Portraits. Third Edition. 2 vols. Demy 8vo. 36s.
Popular Edition. 2 vols. Crown 8vo. 16s.

MAURICE.—THE FRIENDSHIP OF BOOKS; AND OTHER LEC-TURES. By the Rev. F. D. MAURICE. Edited with Preface, by THOMAS HUGHES, Q.C. Crown 8vo. 4s. 6d.

MAURICE.—LETTERS FROM DONEGAL IN 1836. By a LADY "FELON." Edited by Colonel MAURICE, Professor of Military History, Royal Staff College. Crown 8vo. 1s.

MAXWELL.—PROFESSOR CLERK MAXWELL, A LIFE OF. With a Selection from his Correspondence and Occasional Writings, and a Sketch of his Contributions to Science. By LEWIS CAMPBELL, M.A. LL.D., Professor of Greek in the University of St. Andrews, and Professor WILLIAM GARNETT, M.A., Principal of Durham College of Science, Newcastle-upon-Tyne. New Edition, Abridged and Revised. Crown 8vo. 7s. 6d.

MAYOR (J. E. B.)—Works edited by JOHN E. B. MAYOR, M.A., Kennedy Professor of Latin at Cambridge :—
CAMBRIDGE IN THE SEVENTEENTH CENTURY. Part II. Auto-biography of Matthew Robinson. Fcap. 8vo. 5s. 6d.

MELBOURNE.—MEMOIRS OF THE RT. HON. WILLIAM, SECOND VISCOUNT MELBOURNE. By W. M. TORRENS, M.P. With Portrait after Sir T. Lawrence. Second Edition. Two Vols. 8vo. 32s.

MIALL.—LIFE OF EDWARD MIALL, formerly M.P. for Rochdale and Bradford. By his Son, ARTHUR MIALL. With a Portrait. 8vo. 10s. 6d.

MICHELET.—A SUMMARY OF MODERN HISTORY. Translated from the French of M. MICHELET, and continued to the present time by M. C. M. SIMPSON. Globe 8vo. 4s. 6d.

MILLET.—JEAN FRANÇOIS MILLET; Peasant and Painter. Trans-lated from the French of ALFRED SENSIER. With numerous Illustrations. Globe 4to. 16s.

MILTON.—LIFE OF JOHN MILTON. Narrated in connection with the Political, Ecclesiastical, and Literary History of his Time. By DAVID MASSON, M.A., LL.D., Professor of Rhetoric and English Literature in the University of Edinburgh. With Portraits. Vol. I. 1608—1639. New and Revised Edition. 8vo. 21s. Vol. II. 1638—1643. 8vo. 16s. Vol. III. 1643—1649. 8vo. 18s. Vols. IV. and V. 1649—1660. 32s. Vol. VI. 1660—1674. With Portrait. 21s.
[*Index Volume in preparation.*
This work is not only a Biography, but also a continuous Political, Ecclesiastical, and Literary History of England through Milton's whole time.

MITFORD (A. B.)—TALES OF OLD JAPAN. By A. B. MITFORD. Second Secretary to the British Legation in Japan. With upwards of 30 Illustrations, drawn and cut on Wood by Japanese Artists. New and Cheaper Edition. Crown 8vo. 6s.

MORLEY.—Works by JOHN MORLEY. New Collected Edition. In 9 vols. Globe 8vo. 5s. each.
    VOLTAIRE. 1 vol.
    ROUSSEAU. 2 vols.
    DIDEROT AND THE ENCYCLOPÆDISTS. 2 vols.
    ON COMPROMISE. 1 vol.
    MISCELLANIES. 3 vols.
    BURKE. (*English Men of Letters Series.*) Crown 8vo. 2s. 6d.

MURRAY.—ROUND ABOUT FRANCE. By E. C. GRENVILLE MURRAY. Crown 8vo. 7s. 6d.

MUSIC.—DICTIONARY OF MUSIC AND MUSICIANS (A.D. 1450—1886). By Eminent Writers, English and Foreign. Edited by SIR GEORGE GROVE, D.C.L., Director of the Royal College of Music. Three Vols. 8vo. With Illustrations and Woodcuts. Parts I. to XIV., XIX. to XXI. 3s. 6d. each. Parts XV. and XVI., 7s. Parts XVII. and XVIII., 7s. Vols. I., II., and III. 8vo. 21s. each.
Vol. I.—A to Impromptu. Vol. II.—Improperia to Plain Song. Vol. III. Planché to Sumer is Icumen in.

MYERS.—ESSAYS BY FREDERIC W. H. MYERS. 2 vols. 1. Classical II. Modern. Crown 8vo. 4s. 6d. each.

NAPOLEON.—THE HISTORY OF NAPOLEON I. By P. LANFREY. A Translation with the sanction of the Author. New and Popular Edition. Four Vols. Crown 8vo. 30s.

NEWTON.—ESSAYS ON ART AND ARCHÆOLOGY. By CHARLES THOMAS NEWTON, C.B., Ph.D., D.C.L., LL.D., Keeper of Greek and Roman Antiquities at the British Museum, &c. 8vo. 12s. 6d.

NICHOL.—TABLES OF EUROPEAN LITERATURE AND HISTORY, A.D. 200—1876. By J. NICHOL, LL.D., Professor of English Language and Literature, Glasgow. 4to. 6s. 6d.
TABLES OF ANCIENT LITERATURE AND HISTORY, B.C. 1500—A.D. 200. By the same Author. 4to. 4s. 6d.

NORDENSKIÖLD'S ARCTIC VOYAGES, 1858-79.—With Maps and numerous Illustrations. 8vo. 16s.
VOYAGE OF THE *VEGA.* By ADOLF ERIK NORDENSKIÖLD. Translated by ALEXANDER LESLIE. With numerous Illustrations, Maps, &c. Popular and Cheaper Edition. Crown 8vo. 6s.

NORGATE.—ENGLAND UNDER THE ANGEVIN KINGS. By KATE NORGATE. With Maps and Plans. 2 vols. 8vo. [*Immediately.*

OLIPHANT (MRS.).—Works by Mrs. OLIPHANT.
  THE MAKERS OF FLORENCE: Dante, Giotto, Savonarola, and their City. With numerous Illustrations from drawings by Professor DELAMOTTE, and portrait of Savonarola, engraved by JEENS. New and Cheaper Edition. Crown 8vo. 10s. 6d.
THE LITERARY HISTORY OF ENGLAND IN THE END OF THE EIGHTEENTH AND BEGINNING OF THE NINETEENTH CENTURY. New Issue, with a Preface. 3 vols. Demy 8vo. 21s.

b 2

OLIPHANT.—THE DUKE AND THE SCHOLAR; and other Essays. By T. L. KINGTON OLIPHANT. 8vo. 7s. 6d.

OLIVER.—MADAGASCAR: an Historical and Descriptive Account of the Island and its former Dependencies. Compiled by Captain S. PASFIELD OLIVER, F.S.A., F.R.G.S., late Royal Artillery. With Maps. 2 vols. Medium 8vo. £2 12s. 6d.

OTTÉ.—SCANDINAVIAN HISTORY. By E. C. OTTÉ. With Maps. Extra fcap. 8vo. 6s.

OWENS COLLEGE ESSAYS AND ADDRESSES.—By PROFESSORS AND LECTURERS OF OWENS COLLEGE, MANCHESTER. Published in Commemoration of the Opening of the New College Buildings, October 7th, 1873. 8vo. 14s.

PALGRAVE (R. F. D.)—THE HOUSE OF COMMONS: Illustrations of its History and Practice. By REGINALD F. D. PALGRAVE, Clerk Assistant of the House of Commons. New and Revised Edition. Crown 8vo. 2s. 6d.

PALGRAVE (SIR F.)—HISTORY OF NORMANDY AND OF ENGLAND. By Sir FRANCIS PALGRAVE, Deputy Keeper of Her Majesty's Public Records. Completing the History to the Death of William Rufus. 4 Vols. 8vo. 4l. 4s.

PALGRAVE (W. G.)—A NARRATIVE OF A YEAR'S JOURNEY THROUGH CENTRAL AND EASTERN ARABIA, 1862—3. By WILLIAM GIFFORD PALGRAVE, late of the Eighth Regiment Bombay N.I. Seventh Edition. With Maps, Plans, and Portrait of Author, engraved on steel by JEENS. Crown 8vo. 6s.

ESSAYS ON EASTERN QUESTIONS. By W. GIFFORD PALGRAVE. 8vo. 10s. 6d.

DUTCH GUIANA. With Maps and Plans. 8vo. 9s.

PARKMAN.—Works by FRANCIS PARKMAN.
MONTCALM AND WOLFE. Library Edition. Illustrated with Portraits and Maps. 2 vols. 8vo. 12s. 6d. each.
THE COLLECTED WORKS OF FRANCIS PARKMAN. Popular Edition. In 10 vols. Crown 8vo. 7s. 6d. each, or complete £3 13s. 6d.
PIONEERS OF FRANCE IN THE NEW WORLD. 1 vol.
THE JESUITS IN NORTH AMERICA. 1 vol.
LA SALLE AND THE DISCOVERY OF THE GREAT WEST. 1 vol.
THE OREGON TRAIL. 1 vol.
THE OLD RÉGIME IN CANADA UNDER LOUIS XIV. 1 vol.
COUNT FRONTENAC AND NEW FRANCE UNDER LOUIS XIV. 1 vol.
MONTCALM AND WOLFE. 2 vols.
THE CONSPIRACY OF PONTIAC. 2 vols.

PATTESON.—LIFE AND LETTERS OF JOHN COLERIDGE PATTESON, D.D., Missionary Bishop of the Melanesian Islands. By CHARLOTTE M. YONGE, Author of "The Heir of Redclyffe." With Portraits after RICHMOND and from Photograph, engraved by JEENS. With Map. New Edition. Two Vols. Crown 8vo. 12s.

PATTISON.—MEMOIRS. By MARK PATTISON, late Rector of Lincoln College, Oxford. Crown 8vo. 8s. 6d.

PAYNE.—A HISTORY OF EUROPEAN COLONIES. By E. J. PAYNE, M.A. With Maps. 18mo. 4s. 6d.   [*Historical Course for Schools.*

PERSIA.—EASTERN PERSIA. An Account of the Journeys of the Persian Boundary Commission, 1870-1-2.—Vol. I. The Geography, with Narratives by Majors ST. JOHN, LOVETT, and EUAN SMITH, and an Introduction by Major-General Sir FREDERIC GOLDSMID, C.B., K.C.S.I., British Commissioner and Arbitrator. With Maps and Illustrations.—Vol. II. The Zoology and Geology. By W. T. BLANDFORD, A.R.S.M., F.R.S. With Coloured Illustrations. Two Vols. 8vo. 42s.

POOLE.—A HISTORY OF THE HUGUENOTS OF THE DISPERSION AT THE RECALL OF THE EDICT OF NANTES. By REGINALD LANE POOLE. Crown 8vo. 6s.

PRICHARD.—THE ADMINISTRATION OF INDIA. From 1859 to 1868. The First Ten Years of Administration under the Crown. By I. T. PRICHARD, Barrister-at-Law. Two Vols. Demy 8vo. With Map. 21s.

REED (SIR CHAS.).—SIR CHARLES REED. A Memoir by CHARLES E. B. REED, M.A. Crown 8vo. 4s. 6d.

ROGERS (JAMES E. THOROLD).—HISTORICAL GLEAN-INGS:—A Series of Sketches. Montague, Walpole, Adam Smith, Cobbett. By Prof. ROGERS. Crown 8vo. 4s. 6d. Second Series. Wiklif, Laud, Wilkes, and Horne Tooke. Crown 8vo. 6s.

ROSSETTI.—DANTE GABRIEL ROSSETTI : a Record and a Study. By WILLIAM SHARP. With an Illustration after Dante Gabriel Rossetti. Crown 8vo. 10s. 6d.

ROUTLEDGE.—CHAPTERS IN THE HISTORY OF POPULAR PROGRESS IN ENGLAND, chiefly in Relation to the Freedom of the Press and Trial by Jury, 1660—1820. With application to later years. By J. ROUTLEDGE. 8vo. 16s.

RUMFORD.—COUNT RUMFORD'S COMPLETE WORKS, with Memoir, and Notices of his Daughter. By GEORGE ELLIS. Five Vols. 8vo. 4l. 14s. 6d.

RUSSELL.—NEW VIEWS ON IRELAND, OR IRISH LAND GRIEVANCES AND REMEDIES. By CHARLES RUSSELL, Q.C., M.P. Third Edition. Crown 8vo. 2s. 6d.

SAYCE.—THE ANCIENT EMPIRES OF THE EAST. By A. H. SAYCE, Deputy-Professor of Comparative Philology, Oxford ; Hon. LL.D. Dublin. Crown 8vo. 6s.

SCHILLER.—THE LIFE OF SCHILLER. By HEINRICH DÜNTZER. Translated by PERCY E. PINKERTON. With Illustrations. Crown 8vo. 10s. 6d.

SEELEY.—Works by J. R. SEELEY, M.A., Regius Professor of Modern History in the University of Cambridge, Fellow of Gonville and Caius College, Fellow of the Royal Historical Society, and Honorary Member of the Historical Society of Massachusetts :—
THE EXPANSION OF ENGLAND. Two Courses of Lectures. Crown 8vo. 4s. 6d.
LECTURES AND ESSAYS. 8vo. 10s. 6d.
CONTENTS :—Roman Imperialism : 1. The Great Roman Revolution ; 2. The Proximate Cause of the Fall of the Roman Empire ; The Later Empire.—Milton's Political Opinions—Milton's Poetry—Elementary Principles in Art—Liberal Education in Universities—English in Schools—The Church as a Teacher of Morality—The Teaching of Politics : an Inaugural Lecture delivered at Cambridge.

SHELBURNE.—LIFE OF WILLIAM, EARL OF SHELBURNE, AFTERWARDS FIRST MARQUIS OF LANDSDOWNE. With Extracts from his Papers and Correspondence. By Lord EDMOND FITZMAURICE. In Three Vols. 8vo. Vol. I. 1737—1766, 12s. ; Vol. II. 1766—1776, 12s. ; Vol. III. 1776—1805. 16s.

SIBSON.—COLLECTED WORKS OF FRANCIS SIBSON, M.D., Lond., Fellow of the Royal Society, Honorary M.D. Trinity College, Dublin, and D.C.L. Durham, Fellow of the Royal College of Physicians, &c. Edited by WILLIAM M. ORD, M.D. With Illustrations. Four Volumes. 8vo. 3l. 3s.

SIME.—HISTORY OF GERMANY. By JAMES SIME, M.A. 18mo. 3s. Being Vol. V. of the Historical Course for Schools. Edited by EDWARD A. FREEMAN, D.C.L.

SMITH (GOLDWIN).—THREE ENGLISH STATESMEN. A Course of Lectures on the Political History of England. By GOLDWIN SMITH, M.A., D.C.L. New Edition. Crown 8vo. 5s.

SPINOZA.—SPINOZA: a Study of. By James Martineau, LL.D., D.D., Fellow of Manchester New College, London. With Portrait. Second Edition. Crown 8vo. 6s.

ST. ANSELM.—By the Very Rev. R. W. Church, M.A., Dean of St. Paul's. New Edition. Crown 8vo. 6s. (Biographical Series.)

STATESMAN'S YEAR-BOOK, THE.—A Statistical and Historical Annual of the States of the Civilised World for the Year 1886. Twenty-third Annual Publication. Revised after Official Returns. Edited by J. Scott Keltie. Crown 8vo. 10s. 6d.

STATHAM.—BLACKS, BOERS, AND BRITISH: A Three-Cornered Problem. By F. R. Statham. Crown 8vo. 6s.

STEPHEN.—THE STORY OF NUNCOMAR AND THE IMPEACHMENT OF SIR ELIJAH IMPEY. By Sir James Fitzjames Stephen, K.C.S.I., D.C.L., a Judge of High Court of Justice, Queen's Bench Division. 2 vols. Crown 8vo. 15s.

STEVENSON.—HOUSE ARCHITECTURE. By J. J. Stevenson, Fellow of the Royal Institution of British Architects. With numerous Illustrations. Royal 8vo. 2 Vols. 18s. each. Vol. I. Architecture. Vol. II. House Planning.

ST. JOHNSTON.—CAMPING AMONG CANNIBALS. By Alfred St. Johnston. Crown 8vo. 4s. 6d.

STRANGFORD.—EGYPTIAN SHRINES AND SYRIAN SEPULCHRES, including a Visit to Palmyra. By Emily A. Beaufort (Viscountess Strangford), Author of "The Eastern Shores of the Adriatic." New Edition. Crown 8vo. 7s. 6d.

TAIT.—AN ANALYSIS OF ENGLISH HISTORY, based upon Green's "Short History of the English People." By C. W. A. Tait, M.A., Assistant Master, Clifton College. Crown 8vo. 3s. 6d.

TAIT.—CATHARINE AND CRAUFURD TAIT, WIFE AND SON OF ARCHIBALD CAMPBELL, ARCHBISHOP OF CANTERBURY: a Memoir, Edited, at the request of the Archbishop, by the Rev. W. Benham, B.D., Rector of St. Edmund-the-King and St. Nicholas Acons, One of the Six Preachers of Canterbury Cathedral. With Two Portraits engraved by Jeens. New and Cheaper Edition. Crown 8vo. 6s. (Biographical Series.) Abridged Edition. Crown 8vo. 2s. 6d.

TERESA.—THE LIFE OF ST. TERESA. By Maria Trench. With Portrait engraved by Jeens. Crown 8vo, cloth extra. 8s. 6d.

THOMPSON.—HISTORY OF ENGLAND. By Edith Thompson. Being Vol. II. of the Historical Course for Schools, Edited by Edward A. Freeman, D.C.L. New Edition, revised and enlarged, with Coloured Maps. 18mo. 2s. 6d.

THOMPSON.—PUBLIC OPINION AND LORD BEACONSFIELD, 1875-1880. By Geo. Carslake Thompson, LL.M., of the Inner Temple, Barrister-at-Law. 2 vols. Demy 8vo. 36s.

THROUGH THE RANKS TO A COMMISSION.—New and Popular Edition. Crown 8vo. 2s. 6d.

TODHUNTER.—THE CONFLICT OF STUDIES; AND OTHER ESSAYS ON SUBJECTS CONNECTED WITH EDUCATION. By Isaac Todhunter, M.A., F.R.S., late Fellow and Principal Mathematical Lecturer of St. John's College, Cambridge. 8vo. 10s. 6d.

TROLLOPE. — A HISTORY OF THE COMMONWEALTH OF FLORENCE FROM THE EARLIEST INDEPENDENCE OF THE COMMUNE TO THE FALL OF THE REPUBLIC IN 1831. By T. Adolphus Trollope. 4 Vols. 8vo. Cloth, 21s.

TURNER.—SAMOA. A Hundred Years ago and long before, together with Notes on the Cults and Customs of Twenty-three other Islands in the Pacific. By GEORGE TURNER. LL.D., of the London Missionary Society. With a Preface by E. B. TYLOR, F.R.S. With Maps. Crown 8vo. 9s.

TYLOR.—ANTHROPOLOGY : an Introduction to the Study of Man and Civilisation. By E. B. TYLOR, D.C.L., F.R.S. With Illustrations. Crown 8vo. 7s. 6d.

UPPINGHAM BY THE SEA.—A NARRATIVE OF THE YEAR AT BORTH. By J. H. S. Crown 8vo. 3s. 6d.

VICTOR EMMANUEL II., FIRST KING OF ITALY. By G. S. GODKIN. New Edition. Crown 8vo. 6s. (Biographical Series.)

WALLACE.—THE MALAY ARCHIPELAGO : the Land of the Orang Utan and the Bird of Paradise. By ALFRED RUSSEL WALLACE. A Narrative of Travel with Studies of Man and Nature. With Maps and numerous Illustrations. Eighth Edition. Crown 8vo. 7s. 6d.

WALLACE (D. M.)—EGYPT : and the Egyptian Question. By D. MACKENZIE WALLACE, M.A., Author of "Russia: a Six Years' Residence," &c. 8vo. 14s.

WARD.—A HISTORY OF ENGLISH DRAMATIC LITERATURE TO THE DEATH OF QUEEN ANNE. By A. W. WARD, M.A., Professor of History and English Literature in Owens College, Manchester. Two Vols. 8vo. 32s.

WARD (J.)—EXPERIENCES OF A DIPLOMATIST. Being recollections of Germany founded on Diaries kept during the years 1840—1870. By JOHN WARD, C.B., late H.M. Minister-Resident to the Hanse Towns. 8vo. 10s. 6d.

WARD.—ENGLISH POETS. Selections, with Critical Introductions by various writers, and a General Introduction by MATTHEW ARNOLD. Edited by T. H. WARD, M.A. 4 vols. New Edition. Crown 8vo. 7s. 6d. each.

Vol. I. CHAUCER to DONNE.
Vol. II. BEN JONSON to DRYDEN.
Vol. III. ADDISON to BLAKE.
Vol. IV. WORDSWORTH to ROSSETTI.

WATERTON (C.)—WANDERINGS IN SOUTH AMERICA, THE NORTH-WEST OF THE UNITED STATES, AND THE ANTILLES IN 1812, 1816, 1820, and 1824. With Original Instructions for the perfect Preservation of Birds, etc., for Cabinets of Natural History. By CHARLES WATERTON. New Edition, edited with Biographical Introduction and Explanatory Index by the Rev. J. G. WOOD. M.A. With 100 Illustrations. Cheaper Edition. Crown 8vo. 6s.

PEOPLE'S ILLUSTRATED EDITION. Demy 4to. 6d.

WATSON.—A VISIT TO WAZAN, THE SACRED CITY OF MOROCCO. By ROBERT SPENCE WATSON. With Illustrations. 8vo. 10s. 6d.

WATSON (ELLEN.)—A RECORD OF ELLEN WATSON. Arranged and Edited by ANNA BUCKLAND. With Portrait. Third Edition. Crown 8vo. 6s.

WESLEY.—JOHN WESLEY AND THE EVANGELICAL REACTION of the Eighteenth Century. By JULIA WEDGWOOD. Crown 8vo. 8s. 6d.

WHEELER.—Works by J. TALBOYS WHEELER, late Assistant-Secretary to the Government of India, Foreign Department, and late Secretary to the Government of British Burma.
A SHORT HISTORY OF INDIA, AND OF THE FRONTIER STATES OF AFGHANISTAN, NEPAUL, AND BURMA. With Maps and Tables. Crown 8vo. 12s.
INDIA UNDER BRITISH RULE FROM THE FOUNDATION OF THE EAST INDIA COMPANY. Demy 8vo. 12s. 6d.

WHEWELL.—WILLIAM WHEWELL, D.D., late Master of Trinity College, Cambridge. An account of his Writings, with Selections from his Literary and Scientific correspondence. By I. TODHUNTER, M.A., F.R.S. Two Vols. 8vo. 25s.

WHITE.—THE NATURAL HISTORY AND ANTIQUITIES OF SEL-BORNE. By GILBERT WHITE. Edited, with Memoir and Notes, by FRANK BUCKLAND. A Chapter on Antiquities by LORD SELBORNE, and numerous Illustrations by P. H. DELAMOTTE. New and Cheaper Edition. Crown 8vo. 6s.

Also a Large Paper Edition, containing, in addition to the above, upwards of Thirty Woodburytype Illustrations from Drawings by Prof. DELAMOTTE. Two Vols. 4to. Half morocco, elegant. 4l. 4s.

WILSON.—A MEMOIR OF GEORGE WILSON, M.D., F.R.S.E., Regius Professor of Technology in the University of Edinburgh. By his SISTER. New Edition. Crown 8vo. 6s.

WILSON (DANIEL, LL.D.)—Works by DANIEL WILSON, LL.D., Professor of History and English Literature in University College, Toronto :—
PREHISTORIC ANNALS OF SCOTLAND. New Edition, with numerous Illustrations. Two Vols. Demy 8vo. 36s.
PREHISTORIC MAN : Researches into the Origin of Civilization in the Old and New World. New Edition, revised and enlarged throughout, with numerous Illustrations and Two Coloured Plates. Two Vols. 8vo. 36s.
CHATTERTON : A Biographical Study. Crown 8vo. 6s. 6d.

YONGE (CHARLOTTE M.)—Works by CHARLOTTE M. YONGE, Author of the "Heir of Redclyffe," &c. &c. :—
CAMEOS FROM ENGLISH HISTORY. From Rollo to Edward II. Extra Fcap. 8vo. Third Edition. 5s.
SECOND SERIES, THE WARS IN FRANCE. Extra fcap. 8vo. Third Edition. 5s.
THIRD SERIES, THE WARS OF THE ROSES. Extra fcap. 8vo. 5s.
FOURTH SERIES, REFORMATION TIMES. Extra fcap. 8vo. 5s.
FIFTH SERIES, ENGLAND AND SPAIN. Extra fcap. 8vo. 5s.
HISTORY OF FRANCE. Maps. 18mo. 3s. 6d.
[*Historical Course for Schools.*
HISTORY OF CHRISTIAN NAMES. New Edition, Revised. Crown 8vo. 7s. 6d.
THE VICTORIAN HALF CENTURY. Crown 8vo. 1s.

POLITICS, POLITICAL AND SOCIAL ECONOMY, LAW, AND KINDRED SUBJECTS.

ANGLO-SAXON LAW.—ESSAYS IN. Contents: Law Courts—Land and Family Laws and Legal Procedure generally. With Select Cases. Medium 8vo. 18s.

ARNOLD.—THE ROMAN SYSTEM OF PROVINCIAL ADMINIS-TRATION TO THE ACCESSION OF CONSTANTINE THE GREAT. Being the Arnold Prize Essay for 1879. By W. T. ARNOLD, M.A. Crown 8vo. 6s.

BERNARD.—FOUR LECTURES ON SUBJECTS CONNECTED WITH DIPLOMACY. By MONTAGUE BERNARD, M. A., Chichele Professor of International Law and Diplomacy, Oxford. 8vo. 9s.

BIGELOW.—HISTORY OF PROCEDURE IN ENGLAND, FROM THE NORMAN CONQUEST. The Norman Period, 1066-1204. By MELVILLE MADISON BIGELOW, Ph.D., Harvard University. 8vo. 16s.

BIRKBECK.—HISTORICAL SKETCH OF THE DISTRIBUTION OF LAND IN ENGLAND. With Suggestions for some Improvement in the Law. By WILLIAM LLOYD BIRKBECK, M.A., Master of Downing College, and Downing Professor of the Laws of England in the University of Cambridge. Crown 8vo. 4s. 6d.

BRIGHT (JOHN, M.P.).—Works by the Right Hon. JOHN BRIGHT, M.P.
SPEECHES ON QUESTIONS OF PUBLIC POLICY. Edited by Professor THOROLD ROGERS. Author's Popular Edition. Globe 8vo. 3s. 6d.
LIBRARY EDITION. Two Vols. 8vo. With Portrait. 25s.
PUBLIC ADDRESSES. Edited by J. THOROLD ROGERS, 8vo. 14s.

BUCKNILL.—THE CARE OF THE INSANE, AND THEIR LEGAL CONTROL. By J. C. BUCKNILL, M.D., F.R.S., late Lord Chancellor's Visitor of Lunatics. Crown 8vo. 3s. 6d.

CAIRNES.—Works by J. E. CAIRNES, M.A., sometime Professor of Political Economy in University College, London.
POLITICAL ESSAYS. 8vo. 10s. 6d.
THE CHARACTER AND LOGICAL METHOD OF POLITICAL ECONOMY. New Edition, enlarged. 8vo. 7s. 6d.

CLARKE.—SPECULATIONS FROM POLITICAL ECONOMY. By C. B. CLARKE, F.R.S. Crown 8vo. 3s. 6d.

COBDEN (RICHARD).—SPEECHES ON QUESTIONS OF PUBLIC POLICY. By RICHARD COBDEN. Edited by the Right Hon. John Bright, M.P., and J. E. Thorold Rogers, Popular Edition. 8vo. 3s. 6d.

COSSA.—GUIDE TO THE STUDY OF POLITICAL ECONOMY. By Dr. LUIGI COSSA, Professor of Political Economy in the University of Pavia. Translated from the Second Italian Edition. With a Preface by W. STANLEY JEVONS, F.R.S. Crown 8vo. 4s. 6d.

DICEY.—Works by A. V. DICEY, B.C.L., of the Inner Temple; Barrister-at-Law; Vinerian Professor of English Law in the University of Oxford; Fellow of All Souls' College; Hon. LL.D., Glasgow.
LECTURES INTRODUCTORY TO THE STUDY OF THE LAW OF THE CONSTITUTION. Second Edition. Demy 8vo. 12s. 6d.
THE PRIVY COUNCIL. 8vo. [*In the Press.*

FAWCETT.—Works by Right Hon. HENRY FAWCETT M.A., F.R.S., late Fellow of Trinity Hall, and sometime Professor of Political Economy in the University of Cambridge.
MANUAL OF POLITICAL ECONOMY. Sixth Edition, revised, with a Chapter on State Socialism and the Nationalisation of the Land, and an Index, etc. Crown 8vo. 12s.
SPEECHES ON SOME CURRENT POLITICAL QUESTIONS. 8vo. 10s. 6d.
FREE TRADE AND PROTECTION: an Inquiry into the Causes which have retarded the general adoption of Free Trade since its introduction into England. Sixth and Cheaper Edition. Crown 8vo. 3s. 6d.
INDIAN FINANCE. Three Essays, with Introduction and Appendix. 8vo. 7s. 6d.

FAWCETT (MRS.)—Works by MILLICENT GARRETT FAWCETT.
POLITICAL ECONOMY FOR BEGINNERS. WITH QUESTIONS. New Edition. 18mo. 2s. 6d.
TALES IN POLITICAL ECONOMY. Crown 8vo. 3s.

FISKE.—AMERICAN POLITICAL IDEAS VIEWED FROM THE STANDPOINT OF UNIVERSAL HISTORY. Three Lectures delivered at the Royal Institution of Great Britain. By JOHN FISKE, Author of "Darwinism: and other Essays," "Excursions of an Evolutionist," &c. Crown 8vo. 4s.

GOSCHEN.—REPORTS AND SPEECHES ON LOCAL TAXATION. By GEORGE J. GOSCHEN, M.P. Royal 8vo. 5s.

GUIDE TO THE UNPROTECTED, in Every Day Matters Relating to Property and Income. By a BANKER'S DAUGHTER. Fifth Edition, Revised. Extra fcap. 8vo. 3s. 6d.

HARWOOD.—Works by GEORGE HARWOOD, M.A. DISESTABLISHMENT : a Defence of the Principle of a National Church. 8vo. 12s. THE COMING DEMOCRACY. Crown 8vo. 6s.

HILL.—Works by OCTAVIA HILL:— OUR COMMON LAND; and other Short Essays. Extra fcap. 8vo. 3s. 6d. CONTENTS:—Our Common Land. District Visiting. A more Excellent Way of Charity. A Word on Good Citizenship. Open Spaces. Effectual Charity. The Future of our Commons. HOMES OF THE LONDON POOR. Popular Edition. Cr. 8vo. Sewed. 1s.

HOLLAND.—THE TREATY RELATIONS OF RUSSIA AND TURKEY FROM 1774 TO 1853. A Lecture delivered at Oxford, April 1877. By T. E. HOLLAND, D.C.L., Professor of International Law and Diplomacy, Oxford. Crown 8vo. 2s.

JEVONS.—Works by W. STANLEY JEVONS, LL.D., M.A., F.R.S. (For other Works by the same Author, see EDUCATIONAL and PHILOSOPHICAL CATALOGUES.) THE THEORY OF POLITICAL ECONOMY. Second Edition, revised, with new Preface and Appendices. 8vo. 10s. 6d. PRIMER OF POLITICAL ECONOMY. 18mo. 1s. METHODS OF SOCIAL REFORM, and other Papers. Demy 8vo. 10s. 6d. INVESTIGATIONS IN CURRENCY AND FINANCE. Edited, with an Introduction, by H. S. FOXWELL, M.A., Fellow and Lecturer of St. John's College, Cambridge, and Professor of Political Economy at University College, London. Illustrated by 20 Diagrams. Demy 8vo. 21s.

LIGHTWOOD.—THE NATURE OF POSITIVE LAW. By JOHN M. LIGHTWOOD, M.A., of Lincoln's Inn, Barrister-at-Law, Fellow of Trinity Hall, Cambridge. Demy 8vo. 12s. 6d.

LUBBOCK.—ADDRESSES, POLITICAL AND EDUCATIONAL. By Sir JOHN LUBBOCK, Bart., M.P., &c., &c. 8vo. 8s. 6d.

MACDONELL.—THE LAND QUESTION, WITH SPECIAL REFERENCE TO ENGLAND AND SCOTLAND. By JOHN MACDONELL, Barrister-at-Law. 8vo. 10s. 6d.

MAITLAND.—PLEAS OF THE CROWN FOR THE COUNTY OF GLOUCESTER, BEFORE THE ABBOT OF READING AND HIS FELLOW JUSTICES ITINERANT, IN THE FIFTH YEAR OF THE REIGN OF KING HENRY THE THIRD AND THE YEAR OF GRACE, 1221. Edited by F. W. MAITLAND. 8vo. 7s. 6d.

MARSHALL.—THE ECONOMICS OF INDUSTRY. By A. MARSHALL, M.A., Professor of Political Economy in the University of Cambridge, late Principal of University College Bristol, and MARY PALEY MARSHALL, late Lecturer at Newnham Hall, Cambridge. Extra fcap. 8vo. 2s. 6d.

MONAHAN.—THE METHOD OF LAW: an Essay on the Statement and Arrangement of the Legal Standard of Conduct. By J. H. MONAHAN, Q.C. Crown 8vo. 6s.

PATERSON.—Works by JAMES PATERSON, M.A., Barrister-at-Law, sometime Commissioner for English and Irish Fisheries, &c. THE LIBERTY OF THE SUBJECT AND THE LAWS OF ENGLAND RELATING TO THE SECURITY OF THE PERSON. Commentaries on. Cheaper issue. Crown 8vo. 21s. THE LIBERTY OF THE PRESS, OF SPEECH, AND OF PUBLIC WORSHIP. Being Commentaries on the Liberty of the Subject and the Laws of England. Crown 8vo. 12s.

PHILLIMORE.—PRIVATE LAW AMONG THE ROMANS, from the Pandects. By John George Phillimore, Q.C. 8vo. 16s.

POLLOCK (F.).—ESSAYS IN JURISPRUDENCE AND ETHICS. By Frederick Pollock, M.A., LL.D., Corpus Christi Professor of Jurisprudence in the University of Oxford; late Fellow of Trinity College, Camb. 8vo. 10s. 6d.

PRACTICAL POLITICS.—ISSUED BY THE NATIONAL LIBERAL FEDERATION. Complete in one volume. 8vo. 6s. Or:—
L. THE TENANT FARMER: Land Laws and Landlords. By James Howard. 8vo. 1s.
II. FOREIGN POLICY. By Right Hon. M. E. Grant Duff, M.P. 8vo. 1s.
III. FREEDOM OF LAND. By G. Shaw Lefevre, M.P. 8vo. 2s. 6d.
IV. BRITISH COLONIAL POLICY. By Sir David Wedderburn, Bart., M.P. 8vo. 1s.

RICHEY.—THE IRISH LAND LAWS. By Alexander G. Richey, Q.C., LL.D., Deputy Regius Professor of Feudal and English Law in the University of Dublin. Crown 8vo. 3s. 6d.

SIDGWICK.—Works by Henry Sidgwick, M.A., LL.D., Knightbridge Professor of Moral Philosophy in the University of Cambridge, &c.:
THE PRINCIPLES OF POLITICAL ECONOMY. Demy 8vo. 16s.
THE METHODS OF ETHICS. Third Edition, Revised and Enlarged. Demy 8vo. 14s.
A SUPPLEMENT TO THE SECOND EDITION. Containing all the Important Additions and Alterations in the Third Edition. Demy 8vo. 6s.
THE SCOPE AND METHOD OF ECONOMIC SCIENCE. An Address delivered to the Economic Science and Statistics Section of the British Association at Aberdeen, 1885. Crown 8vo. 2s.
OUTLINES OF THE HISTORY OF ETHICS FOR ENGLISH READERS. Crown 8vo. 3s. 6d.

STATESMAN'S YEAR BOOK, THE: A STATISTICAL AND HISTORICAL ANNUAL OF THE STATES OF THE CIVILIZED WORLD, FOR THE YEAR 1886. Twenty-third Annual Publication. Revised after Official Returns. Edited by J. Scott Keltie. Crown 8vo. 10s. 6d.

STEPHEN (C. E.)—THE SERVICE OF THE POOR; Being an Inquiry into the Reasons for and against the Establishment of Religious Sisterhoods for Charitable Purposes. By Caroline Emilia Stephen. Crown 8vo. 6s. 6d.

STEPHEN.—Works by Sir James Fitzjames Stephen, K.C.S.I., D.C.L, A Judge of the High Court of Justice, Queen's Bench Division.
A DIGEST OF THE LAW OF EVIDENCE. Fourth Edition, with new Preface Crown 8vo. 6s.
A HISTORY OF THE CRIMINAL LAW OF ENGLAND. Three Vols. Demy 8vo. 48s.
A DIGEST OF THE CRIMINAL LAW. (Crimes and Punishments.) 8vo. 16s.
A DIGEST OF THE LAW OF CRIMINAL PROCEDURE IN INDICT-ABLE OFFENCES. By Sir James F. Stephen, K.C.S.I., a Judge of the High Court of Justice, Queen's Bench Division, and Herbert Stephen. L.L.M, of the Middle Temple. Barrister-at-Law. 8vo. 12s. 6d.
LETTERS ON THE ILBERT BILL. Reprinted from *The Times*. 8vo. 2s.

STEPHEN (J. K.).—INTERNATIONAL LAW AND INTERNATIONAL RELATIONS: an Attempt to Ascertain the Best Method of Discussing the Topics of International Law. By J. K. Stephen, B.A., of the Inner Temple, Barrister-at-Law. Crown 8vo. 6s.

STUBBS.—VILLAGE POLITICS. Addresses and Sermons on the Labour Question. By C. W. Stubbs, M.A., Vicar of Granborough, Bucks. Extra fcap. 8vo. 3s. 6d.

THOMPSON.—PUBLIC OPINION AND LORD BEACONSFIELD, 1875-1880. By Geo. Carslake Thompson, LL.M., of the Inner Temple, Barrister-at-Law. 2 vols. Demy 8vo. 36s.

THORNTON.—Works by W. T. THORNTON, C.B., Secretary for Public Works in the India Office :—

A PLEA FOR PEASANT PROPRIETORS: With the Outlines of a Plan for their Establishment in Ireland. New Edition, revised. Crown 8vo. 7s. 6d.
INDIAN PUBLIC WORKS AND COGNATE INDIAN TOPICS. With Map of Indian Railways. Crown 8vo. 8s. 6d.

TREVELYAN.—CAWNPORE. By the Right Honourable Sir GEORGE O. TREVELYAN, Bart., M.P., Author of "The Competition Wallah." New Edition. Crown 8vo. 6s.

WALLACE.—BAD TIMES. An Essay on the present Depression of Trade tracing it to its Sources in enormous Foreign Loans, excessive War Expenditure the increase of Speculation and of Millionaires, and the Depopulation of th Rural Districts. With suggested Remedies. By ALFRED RUSSEL WALLACE Crown 8vo. 2s. 6d.

WALKER.—Works by F. A. WALKER, M.A., Ph.D., Professor of Political Economy and History, Yale College.
THE WAGES QUESTION. A Treatise on Wages and the Wages Class. 8vo. 14s.
MONEY. 8vo. 16s.
MONEY IN ITS RELATIONS TO TRADE AND INDUSTRY. Crown 8vo. 7s. 6d.
POLITICAL ECONOMY. 8vo. 10s. 6d.
LAND AND ITS RENT. Fcap. 8vo. 3s. 6d.
A BRIEF TEXT-BOOK OF POLITICAL ECONOMY. Crown 8vo. 6s. 6d.

WILLIAMS.—FORENSIC FACTS AND FALLACIES. A Popular Consideration of some Legal Points and Principles. By SYDNEY E. WILLIAMS, Barrister-at-Law. Globe 8vo. 4s. 6d.

WORKS CONNECTED WITH THE SCIENCE OR THE HISTORY OF LANGUAGE.

ABBOTT.—A SHAKESPERIAN GRAMMAR: An Attempt to illustrate some of the Differences between Elizabethan and Modern English. By the Rev. E. A. ABBOTT, D.D., Head Master of the City of London School. New and Enlarged Edition. Extra fcap. 8vo. 6s.

BREYMANN.—A FRENCH GRAMMAR BASED ON PHILOLOGICAL PRINCIPLES. By HERMANN BREYMANN, Ph.D., Professor of Philology in the University of Munich, Lecturer on French Language and Literature in Owens College, Manchester. Extra fcap. 8vo. 4s. 6d.

ELLIS.—PRACTICAL HINTS ON THE QUANTITATIVE PRO-NUNCIATION OF LATIN, FOR THE USE OF CLASSICAL TEACHERS AND LINGUISTS. By A. J. ELLIS, B.A., F.R.S., &c. Extra fcap. 8vo. 4s. 6d.

FASNACHT.—Works by G. EUGÈNE FASNACHT, Author of "Macmillan's Progressive French Course," Editor of "Macmillan's Foreign School Classics," &c.
THE ORGANIC METHOD OF STUDYING LANGUAGES. I. French. Crown 8vo. 3s. 6d.
A SYNTHETIC FRENCH GRAMMAR FOR SCHOOLS. Crown 8vo. 3s. 6d.

FLEAY.—A SHAKESPEARE MANUAL. By the Rev. F. G. FLEAY, M.A., Head Master of Skipton Grammar School. Extra fcap. 8vo. 4s. 6d.

GOODWIN.—Works by W. W. GOODWIN, Professor of Greek Literature in Harvard University.

SYNTAX OF THE GREEK MOODS AND TENSES. New Edition. Crown 8vo. 6s. 6d.

A SCHOOL GREEK GRAMMAR. Crown 8vo. 3s. 6d.

A GREEK GRAMMAR. Crown 8vo. 6s.

GREEK TESTAMENT.—THE NEW TESTAMENT IN THE ORIGINAL GREEK. The Text revised by B. F. WESTCOTT, D.D., Regius Professor of Divinity, and F. J. A. HORT, D.D., Hulsean Professor of Divinity, Fellow of Emmanuel College, Cambridge; late Fellows of Trinity College, Cambridge. Two Vols. Crown 8vo. 10s. 6d.

Vol. I. Text.—Vol. II. Introduction and Appendix.

THE NEW TESTAMENT IN THE ORIGINAL GREEK, FOR SCHOOLS. The Text Revised by BROOKE FOSS WESTCOTT, D.D., and FENTON JOHN ANTHONY HORT, D.D. 12mo. cloth. 4s. 6d.; 18mo. roan, red edges, 5s. 6d.

HADLEY.—ESSAYS PHILOLOGICAL AND CRITICAL. Selected from the Papers of JAMES HADLEY, LL.D., Professor of Greek in Yale College, &c. 8vo. 16s.

HALES.—LONGER ENGLISH POEMS. With Notes, Philological and Explanatory, and an Introduction on the Teaching of English. Chiefly for use in Schools. Edited by J. W. HALES, M.A., Professor of English Literature at King's College, London, &c. &c. Eleventh Edition. Extra fcap. 8vo. 4s. 6d.

HELFENSTEIN (JAMES).—A COMPARATIVE GRAMMAR OF THE TEUTONIC LANGUAGES: Being at the same time a Historical Grammar of the English Language, and comprising Gothic, Anglo-Saxon, Early English, Modern English, Icelandic (Old Norse), Danish, Swedish, Old High German, Middle High German, Modern German, Old Saxon, Old Frisian, and Dutch. By JAMES HELFENSTEIN, Ph.D. 8vo. 18s.

MASSON (GUSTAVE).—A COMPENDIOUS DICTIONARY OF THE FRENCH LANGUAGE (French-English and English-French). Adapted from the Dictionaries of Professor ALFRED ELWALL. Followed by a List of the Principal Diverging Derivations, and preceded by Chronological and Historical Tables. By GUSTAVE MASSON, Assistant-Master and Librarian, Harrow School. Fourth Edition. Crown 8vo. 6s.

MAYOR.—A BIBLIOGRAPHICAL CLUE TO LATIN LITERATURE. Edited after Dr. E. HUBNER. With large Additions by JOHN E. B. MAYOR. M.A., Professor of Latin in the University of Cambridge. Crown 8vo. 10s. 6d.

MORRIS.—Works by the Rev. RICHARD MORRIS, LL.D., President of the Philological Society. Editor of "Specimens of Early English," &c., &c.

HISTORICAL OUTLINES OF ENGLISH ACCIDENCE, comprising Chapters on the History and Development of the Language, and on Word-formation. New Edition. Fcap. 8vo. 6s.

ELEMENTARY LESSONS IN HISTORICAL ENGLISH GRAMMAR, containing Accidence and Word-formation. New Edition. 18mo. 2s. 6d.

OLIPHANT.—Works by T. L. KINGTON OLIPHANT, M.A., of Balliol College, Oxford.

THE OLD AND MIDDLE ENGLISH. A New Edition, revised and greatly enlarged, of "The Sources of Standard English." Extra fcap. 8vo. 9s.

THE NEW ENGLISH. 2 vols. Crown 8vo. [Immediately.]

PHILOLOGY.—THE JOURNAL OF SACRED AND CLASSICAL PHILOLOGY. Four Vols. 8vo. 12s. 6d. each.

THE JOURNAL OF PHILOLOGY. New Series. Edited by JOHN E. B. MAYOR, M.A., and W. ALDIS WRIGHT, M.A. 4s. 6d. (Half-yearly.)

THE AMERICAN JOURNAL OF PHILOLOGY. Edited by BASIL L. GILDERSLEEVE, Professor of Greek in the Johns Hopkins University. 8vo. 4s. 6d. (Quarterly.)

PHRYNICHUS.—THE NEW PHRYNICHUS. Being a Revised Text of The Ecloga of the Grammarian Phrynichus. With Introductions and Commentary. By W. GUNION RUTHERFORD, M.A., LL.D. of Balliol College Head-Master of Westminster School. 8vo. 18s.

ROBY (H. J.)—Works by HENRY JOHN ROBY, M.A., late Fellow of St. John's College, Cambridge.
A GRAMMAR OF THE LATIN LANGUAGE, FROM PLAUTUS TO SUETONIUS. In Two Parts. Second Edition. Part I. containing:—Book I. Sounds. Book II. Inflexions. Book III. Word Formation. Appendices. Crown 8vo. 8s. 6d. Part II.—Syntax. Prepositions, &c. Crown 8vo. 10s. 6d.
A LATIN GRAMMAR FOR SCHOOLS. Crown 8vo. 5s.

SCHAFF.—THE GREEK TESTAMENT AND THE ENGLISH VERSION, A COMPANION TO. By PHILIP SCHAFF, D D., President of the American Committee of Revision. With Facsimile Illustrations of MSS. and Standard Editions of the New Testament. Crown 8vo. 12s.

SCHMIDT.—THE RHYTHMIC AND METRIC OF THE CLASSICAL LANGUAGES. To which are added, the Lyric Parts of the "Medea" of Euripides and the "Antigone" of Sophocles; with Rhythmical Scheme and Commentary. By Dr. J. H. SCHMIDT. Translated from the German by J. W. WHITE, D.D. 8vo. 10s. 6d.

TAYLOR.—Works by the Rev. ISAAC TAYLOR, M.A.
ETRUSCAN RESEARCHES. With Woodcuts. 8vo. 14s.
WORDS AND PLACES; or, Etymological Illustrations of History, Ethnology, and Geography. By the Rev. ISAAC TAYLOR. Third Edition, revised and compressed. With Maps. Globe 8vo. 6s.
GREEKS AND GOTHS: a Study of the Runes. 8vo. 9s

VINCENT AND DICKSON.—A HANDBOOK TO MODERN GREEK. By EDGAR VINCENT, and T. G. DICKSON. Second Edition, revised and enlarged. With an Appendix on the Relation of Modern Greek to Classical Greek. By Professor R. C. JEBB. Crown 8vo. 6s.

WHITNEY.—A COMPENDIOUS GERMAN GRAMMAR. By W. D. WHITNEY, Professor of Sanskrit and Instructor in Modern Languages in Yale College. Crown 8vo. 6s.

WHITNEY AND EDGREN.—A COMPENDIOUS GERMAN AND ENGLISH DICTIONARY, with Notation of Correspondences and Brief Etymologies. By Professor W. D. WHITNEY. assisted by A. H. EDGREN. Crown 8vo. 7s. 6d.
The GERMAN-ENGLISH Part may be had separately. Price 5s.

WRIGHT (ALDIS).—THE BIBLE WORD-BOOK: a Glossary of Archaic Words and Phrases in the Authorised Version of the Bible and the Book of Common Prayer. By W. ALDIS WRIGHT, M.A., Fellow and Bursar of Trinity College, Cambridge. Second Edition, revised and enlarged. Crown 8vo. 7s. 6d.

ZECHARIAH.—THE HEBREW STUDENT'S COMMENTARY ON HEBREW AND LXX. With Excursus on Several Grammatical Subjects. By W. H. LOWE, M.A., Hebrew Lecturer at Christ's College, Cambridge. Demy 8vo. 10s. 6d.

THE GOLDEN TREASURY SERIES.

UNIFORMLY printed in 18mo, with Vignette Titles by Sir J. E. MILLAIS, T. WOOLNER, W. HOLMAN HUNT, Sir NOEL PATON, ARTHUR HUGHES, &c. Engraved on Steel by JEENS. Bound in extra cloth, 4s. 6d. each volume.
   "Messrs. Macmillan have, in their Golden Treasury Series, especially provided editions of standard works, volumes of selected poetry, and original compositions, which entitle this series to be called classical. Nothing can be better than the literary execution, nothing more elegant than the material workmanship."—BRITISH QUARTERLY REVIEW.

THE GOLDEN TREASURY OF THE BEST SONGS AND LYRICAL POEMS IN THE ENGLISH LANGUAGE. Selected and arranged, with Notes, by FRANCIS TURNER PALGRAVE.

THE CHILDREN'S GARLAND FROM THE BEST POETS. Selected and arranged by COVENTRY PATMORE.

THE BOOK OF PRAISE. From the best English Hymn Writers. Selected and arranged by the Right Hon. the EARL OF SELBORNE. *A New and Enlarged Edition.*

THE FAIRY BOOK; the Best Popular Fairy Stories. Selected and rendered anew by the Author of "JOHN HALIFAX, GENTLEMAN."

THE BALLAD BOOK. A Selection of the Choicest British Ballads. Edited by WILLIAM ALLINGHAM.

THE JEST BOOK. The Choicest Anecdotes and Sayings. Selected and arranged by MARK LEMON.

BACON'S ESSAYS AND COLOURS OF GOOD AND EVIL. With Notes and Glossarial Index. By W. ALDIS WRIGHT, M.A.

THE PILGRIM'S PROGRESS from this World to that which is to come. By JOHN BUNYAN.

THE SUNDAY BOOK OF POETRY FOR THE YOUNG. Selected and arranged by C. F. ALEXANDER.

A BOOK OF GOLDEN DEEDS of All Times and All Countries. Gathered and Narrated Anew. By the Author of "THE HEIR OF REDCLYFFE."

THE ADVENTURES OF ROBINSON CRUSOE. Edited, from the Original Edition, by J. W. CLARK, M.A., Fellow of Trinity College, Cambridge.

THE REPUBLIC OF PLATO, TRANSLATED INTO ENGLISH, with Notes by J. LL. DAVIES, M.A., and D. J. VAUGHAN, M.A.

THE SONG BOOK. Words and Tunes from the best Poets and Musicians. Selected and arranged by JOHN HULLAH, late Professor of Vocal Music in King's College, London.

LA LYRE FRANÇAISE. Selected and arranged, with Notes, by GUSTAVE MASSON, French Master in Harrow School.

TOM BROWN'S SCHOOL DAYS. By AN OLD BOY.

A BOOK OF WORTHIES. Gathered from the Old Histories and written anew by the Author of "THE HEIR OF REDCLYFFE."

GUESSES AT TRUTH. By Two BROTHERS. *New Edition.*

THE CAVALIER AND HIS LADY. Selections from the Works of the First Duke and Duchess of Newcastle. With an Introductory Essay by EWDARD JENKINS, Author of "Ginx's Baby," &c

SCOTCH SONG. A Selection of the Choicest Lyrics of Scotland. Compiled and arranged, with brief Notes, by MARY CARLYLE AITKIN.

DEUTSCHE LYRIK : The Golden Treasury of the best German Lyrical Poems. Selected and arranged, with Notes and Literary Introduction, by Dr. BUCHHEIM.

HERRICK : Selections from the Lyrical Poems. Arranged, with Notes, by F. T. PALGRAVE.

POEMS OF PLACES. Edited by H. W. LONGFELLOW. England and Wales. Two Vols.

MATTHEW ARNOLD'S SELECTED POEMS.

THE STORY OF THE CHRISTIANS AND MOORS IN SPAIN. By C. M. YONGE, Author of the "Heir of Redclyffe." With Vignette by HOLMAN HUNT.

POEMS OF WORDSWORTH. Chosen and Edited, with Preface by MATTHEW ARNOLD. (Also a Large Paper Edition. Crown 8vo. 9s.)

SHAKESPEARE'S SONNETS. Edited by F. T. PALGRAVE.

POEMS FROM SHELLEY. Selected and arranged by STOPFORD A. BROOKE, M.A. (Also a Large Paper Edition. Crown 8vo. 12s. 6d.)

ESSAYS OF JOSEPH ADDISON. Chosen and Edited by JOHN RICHARD GREEN, M.A., LL.D.

POETRY OF BYRON. Chosen and arranged by MATTHEW ARNOLD, (Also a Large Paper Edition, Crown 8vo. 9s.)

SELECTIONS FROM THE WRITINGS OF WALTER SAVAGE LANDOR.—Arranged and Edited by SIDNEY COLVIN.

SIR THOMAS BROWNE'S RELIGIO MEDICI; Letter to a Friend. &c., and Christian Morals. Edited by W. A GREENHILL, M.D.

THE SPEECHES AND TABLE-TALK OF THE PROPHET MOHAMMAD.—Chosen and Translated, with an Introduction and Notes, by STANLEY LANE-POOLE.

SELECTIONS FROM COWPER'S POEMS.—With an Introduction by Mrs. OLIPHANT.

LETTERS OF WILLIAM COWPER.—Edited, with Introduction. By the Rev. W. BENHAM, B.D., Editor of the "Globe Edition" of Cowper's Poetical Works.

THE POETICAL WORKS OF JOHN KEATS.—Reprinted from the Original Editions, with Notes. By FRANCIS TURNER PALGRAVE.

LYRICAL POEMS. By LORD TENNYSON. Selected and Annotated by FRANCIS TURNER PALGRAVE.

IN MEMORIAM. By LORD TENNYSON, Poet Laureate.
*** Large Paper Edition. 8vo. 9s.

THE TRIAL AND DEATH OF SOCRATES. Being the Euthyphron, Apology, Crito, and Phaedo of Plato. Translated into English by F. J. CHURCH. *** *Other Volumes to follow.*

Now ready, in Crown 8vo. Price 3s. 6d. each.

The English Citizen.

A SERIES OF SHORT BOOKS ON HIS RIGHTS AND RESPONSIBILITIES.

This series is intended to meet the demand for accessible information on the ordinary conditions, and the current terms, of our political life. The series will deal with the details of the machinery whereby our Constitution works, and the broad lines upon which it has been constructed.

EDITED BY **HENRY CRAIK, M.A. (OXON.); LL.D. (GLASGOW).**

The following are the titles to the Volumes:—

CENTRAL GOVERNMENT. H. D. TRAILL, D.C.L., late Fellow of St. John's College, Oxford.

THE ELECTORATE and THE LEGISLATURE. SPENCER WALPOLE, Author of "The History of England from 1815."

LOCAL GOVERNMENT. M. D. CHALMERS, M.A.

THE STATE IN ITS RELATION TO EDUCATION. By HENRY CRAIK, M.A., LL.D.

THE NATIONAL BUDGET: THE NATIONAL DEBT, TAXES, AND RATES. A. J. WILSON.

THE POOR LAW. Rev. T. W. FOWLE, M.A.

THE STATE IN ITS RELATION TO TRADE. Sir T. H. FARRER, Bt.

THE STATE AND THE CHURCH. Hon. A. ELLIOT, M.P.

THE STATE IN RELATION TO LABOUR. W. STANLEY JEVONS, LL.D., M.A., F.R.S.

THE LAND LAWS. Professor F. POLLOCK, M.A. late Fellow of Trinity College, Cambridge, &c.

FOREIGN RELATIONS. SPENCER WALPOLE, Author of "The History of England from 1815."

COLONIES & DEPENDENCIES:— Part I. INDIA. By J. S. COTTON, M.A. Part II. THE COLONIES. By E. J. PAYNE, M.A.

THE PUNISHMENT AND PREVENTION OF CRIME. By Colonel Sir EDMUND DU CANE, K.C.B.

JUSTICE AND POLICE. By F. W. MAITLAND.

THE NATIONAL DEFENCES. By Lieut-Colonel MAURICE, R.A.
[In Preparation.

MACMILLAN & CO., LONDON.

RICHARD CLAY AND SONS, LONDON AND BUNGAY.